POCKET CRIMINAL CODE

Incorporating R.S.C. *1985 and subsequent amendments*

EDITOR
Gary P. Rodrigues, B.A., LL.B.
of the Ontario Bar
INDEX EDITOR
Jean Ouellet

CARSWELL
Thomson Professional Publishing

ISBN 0-459-55157-4

Typesetting: Video Text Inc., Barrie, Ontario, Canada

CARSWELL
Thomson Professional Publishing

One Corporate Plaza, 2075 Kennedy Road, Scarborough,
Ontario M1T 3V4
Customer Service:
Toronto 1-416-609-3800
Elsewhere in Canada/U.S. 1-800-387-5164
Fax 1-416-298-5094

PREFACE

The 1993 Pocket Criminal Code is being published earlier in the year than usual. In recent years, Parliament has adopted a practice of enacting a series of amendments to the *Criminal Code* in the spring and our change in the publishing date reflects this new reality.

This spring's amendments included:

- the "rape shield provisions" contained in s. 276 of the Code and the related sections which define consent for purposes of sexual offences and set out circumstances where consent is not deemed to be obtained.
- the re-enactment of ss. 632 to 637 and ss. 641 to 644 in regard to jury selection provide for the maximum number of pre-emptory challenges for the prosecutor and for the accused for different charges.
- a new part (Part XX.1) has been added whereby the defence of insanity has been replaced by the defence of "mental disorder".

Along with these crucial developments, the 1993 Pocket Criminal Code continues to provide the full text of the Canadian *Criminal Code* together with the following federal statutes that form the basis of the criminal law of Canada:

- *Canada Evidence Act*
- *Canadian Bill of Rights*
- *Canadian Charter of Rights and Freedoms*
- *Criminal Records Act*
- *Extradition Act*
- *Food and Drugs Act*
- *Identification of Criminals Act*
- *Interpretation Act*
- *Motor Vehicle Transport Act*
- *Narcotic Control Act*
- *Young Offenders Act*

Amendments that have been enacted but not yet proclaimed appear as shaded text.

As is customary, the 1993 Pocket Criminal Code includes a detailed Table of Contents, a comprehensive Index, and Tables of Concordance linking the R.S.C. 1985 and the R.S.C. 1970.

Finally, a French language edition is now being published simultaneously with this edition.

August 1992 Gary P. Rodrigues

SUMMARY OF CONTENTS

(As amended to 23 June 1992)

TABLE OF CONTENTS

CRIMINAL CODE

SHORT TITLE

INTERPRETATION

PART I

PART II
OFFENCES AGAINST PUBLIC ORDER

PART III
FIREARMS AND OTHER OFFENSIVE WEAPONS

PART IV
OFFENCES AGAINST THE ADMINISTRATION OF LAW AND JUSTICE

PART V
SEXUAL OFFENCES, PUBLIC MORALS AND DISORDERLY CONDUCT

PART VI
INVASION OF PRIVACY

PART VII
DISORDERLY HOUSES, GAMING AND BETTING

PART VIII
OFFENCES AGAINST THE PERSON AND REPUTATION

PART X
FRAUDULENT TRANSACTIONS RELATING TO CONTRACTS AND TRADE

PART XI
WILFUL AND FORBIDDEN ACTS IN RESPECT OF CERTAIN PROPERTY

PART XII
OFFENCES RELATING TO CURRENCY

PART XII.1
INSTRUMENTS AND LITERATURE FOR ILLICIT DRUG USE

PART XII.2
PROCEEDS OF CRIME

PART XIII
ATTEMPTS — CONSPIRACIES — ACCESSORIES

PART XIV
JURISDICTION

PART XV
SPECIAL PROCEDURE AND POWERS

PART XVI
COMPELLING APPEARANCE OF ACCUSED BEFORE A JUSTICE AND INTERIM RELEASE

PART XVII
LANGUAGE OF ACCUSED

PART XVIII
PROCEDURE ON PRELIMINARY INQUIRY

PART XIX
INDICTABLE OFFENCES — TRIAL WITHOUT JURY

PART XX
PROCEDURE IN JURY TRIALS AND GENERAL PROVISIONS

PART XX.1
MENTAL DISORDER

PART XXI

APPEALS — INDICTABLE OFFENCES

PART XXII
PROCURING ATTENDANCE

PART XXIII
PUNISHMENTS, FINES, FORFEITURES, COSTS AND RESTITUTION OF PROPERTY

PART XXIV
DANGEROUS OFFENDERS

PART XXV
EFFECT AND ENFORCEMENT OF RECOGNIZANCES

PART XXVI
EXTRAORDINARY REMEDIES

PART XXVII
SUMMARY CONVICTIONS

PART XXVIII

CANADA EVIDENCE ACT
SHORT TITLE

PART I
APPLICATION

PART II
APPLICATION

CRIMINAL RECORDS ACT

EXTRADITION ACT

PART I

EXTRADITION UNDER TREATY

PART II
ADMINISTRATION AND ENFORCEMENT

PART III
CONTROLLED DRUGS

PART IV
RESTRICTED DRUGS

IDENTIFICATION OF CRIMINALS ACT

INTERPRETATION ACT

MOTOR VEHICLE TRANSPORT ACT, 1987

PART I
BUS TRANSPORT

PART II
TRUCKING

PART III
INTRA-PROVINCIAL TRUCKING

PART IV
EXEMPTIONS AND ENFORCEMENT

PART V
CONSEQUENTIAL AMENDMENTS AND COMING INTO FORCE

NARCOTIC CONTROL ACT

PART I
OFFENCES AND ENFORCEMENT

PART II
[To be proclaimed in Force]
PREVENTIVE DETENTION AND CUSTODY FOR TREATMENT

YOUNG OFFENDERS ACT

TABLE OF CONCORDANCE

R.S.C. 1970, c. C-34	R.S.C. 1985, c. C-46
1	1
2	2
2 “court of criminal jurisdiction”	2 “court of criminal jurisdiction”
2 “magistrate”	2 “magistrate”
2 “motor vehicle”	2 “motor vehicle”
2 “peace officer”	2 “peace officer”
(d.1)	(e)
(e)	(f)
(f)	(g)
2 “railway equipment”	2 “railway equipment”
2 “superior court of criminal jurisdiction”	2 “superior court of criminal jurisdiction”
(c)	(c)
(d)	(e)
(e)	(d)
(f)	(f)
(g)	(g)
2.1	3
Part I	Part I
3(1)	4
3(2)	4(1)
3(3)	4(2)
3(4)	4(3)
3(5)	4(4)
3(6)	4(5)
3(7)	4(6)
3(8)	4(7)
4	5
5	6
6	7
6(1.1)	7(2)
6(1.2)	7(3)
6(1.3)	7(3.1)
6(1.4)	7(3.2)

R.S.C. 1970, c. C-34	R.S.C. 1985, c. C-46
6(1.5)	7(3.3)
6(1.6)	7(3.4)
6(1.7)	7(3.5)
6(1.8)	7(3.6)
6(1.9)	7(3.7)
6(1.91)	7(3.71)
6(1.92)	7(3.72)
6(1.93)	7(3.73)
6(1.94)	7(3.74)
6(1.95)	7(3.75)
6(1.96)	7(3.76)
6(1.97)	7(3.77)
6(2)	7(4)
6(3)	7(5)
6(3.1)	7(5.1)
6(4)	7(6)
6(5)	7(7)
6(6)	7(8)
6(7)	7(9)
6(8)	7(10)
6(9)	7(11)
7	8
7(1)(a)	8(1)(b)
7(1)(b)	8(1)(a)
8	9
9	10
10	11
11	12
12	13
13	—
14	14
15	15
16	16
17	17
18	18
19	19
20	20
21	21
22	22
23	23

R.S.C. 1970, c. C-34	R.S.C. 1985, c. C-46
23.1	23.1
24	24
25	25
26	26
27	27
28	28
29	29
30	30
31	31
32	32
33	33
34	34
35	35
36	36
37	37
38	38
39	39
40	40
41	41
42	42
43	43
44	44
45	45
Part II	Part II
46	46
47	47
48	48
49	49
50	50
51	51
52	52
53	53
54	54
55	55
56	—
57	56
58	57
59	58
60	59
61	60
62	61
63	62
64	63
65	64
66	65
67	66
68	67
69	68
70	69
71	70
72	71
73	72
74	73
75	74
76	75
76.1	76
76.2	77
76.3	78
77	79
78	80
79	81
80	82
81	83
Part II.1	Part III
82	84
83	85
84	86
85	87
86	88
87	89
88	90
89	91
90	92
91	93
92	94
93	95
94	96
95	97
96	98
97	99
98	100
98(11) "appeal	100(11) "appeal

R.S.C. 1970, c. C-34	R.S.C. 1985, c. C-46	R.S.C. 1970, c. C-34	R.S.C. 1985, c. C-46
178.22(2)(j)	195(2)(k)	198	216
178.22(2)(k)	195(2)(l)	199	217
178.22(2)(l)	195(2)(m)	200	218
178.22(2)(m)	195(2)(n)	201	—
178.23	196	202	219
178.23(2)	—	203	220
178.23(3)	196(2)	204	221
178.23(4)	196(3)	205	222
178.23(5)	196(4)	206	223
		207	224
Part V	Part VII	208	225
179	197	209	226
180	198	210	227
181	199	211	228
182-183	—	212	229
184	200	213	230
185	201	214	231
186	202	214(6)	231(6)
187	203	215	232
188	204	216	233
188(6.1)	204(7)	217	234
188(6.2)	204(8)	218	235
188(6.3)	204(8.1)	219	236
188(7)	204(9)	220	237
188(7.1)	204(9.1)	221	238
188(8)	204(10)	222	239
188(9)	204(11)	223	240
188.1	205	224	241
189	206	225	—
190	207	226	242
191	208	227	243
192	209	228	244
193	210	229	245
194	211	230	246
195	212	231	247
195(2)-(4)	212	232	248
195.1	213	233	249
		233(1)(d)	249(1)(d)
Part VI	Part VIII	234	250
196	214	235	251
196 "operate"	214 "operate"	235(1)(c)	251(1)(c)
197	215	235(2)(c)	251(2)(c)

R.S.C. 1970, c. C-34	R.S.C. 1985, c. C-46	R.S.C. 1970, c. C-34	R.S.C. 1985, c. C-46
235(3)	251(3)	249	280
236	252	250	281
237	253	250.1	282
238	254	250.2	283
238(2)	254(2)	250.3	284
238(6)	254(6)	250.4	285
239	255	250.5	286
240	256	251	287
240.1	257	251(6) "Minister of Health"	287(6) "Minister of Health"
241	258	(a)	(a)
241(1)(a)	258(1)(a)	(a.1)	(d)
242	259	(b)	(c)
242(1)	259(1)	(c)	(b)
242(2)	259(2)	(d)	(e)
242(4)	259(4)	252	288
242(5)(a)	259(5)(a)	253	289
243	260	254	290
243.1	261	255	291
243.2	262	256	292
243.3	263	257	293
—	264	258	294
243.4	264.1	259	295
244	265	260	296
245	266	261	297
245.1	267	262	298
245.2	268	263	299
245.3	269	264	300
245.4	269.1	265	301
246	270	266	302
246.1	271	267	303
246.1(2)	—	268	304
246.2	272	269	305
246.3	273	270	306
246.4	274	271	307
246.5	275	272	308
246.6	276	273	309
246.6(1)	276(1)	274	310
246.7	277	275	311
246.8	278	276	312
247	279	277	313
247.1	279.1	278	314
248	—		

R.S.C. 1970, c. C-34	R.S.C. 1985, c. C-46	R.S.C. 1970, c. C-34	R.S.C. 1985, c. C-46
279	315	302	343
280	316	303	344
281	317	304	345
281.1	318	305	346
281.2	319	305.1	347
281.3	320	306	348
281.3(8) "court"	320(8) "court"	306(3)	—
(a)	(a)	306(4)	348(3)
(a.1)	(b)	307	349
(b)	(c)	308	350
(c)	(d)	309	351
281.3(8) "judge"	320(8) "judge"	310	352
		311	353
Part VII	Part IX	312	354
282	321	313	355
283	322	314	356
284	323	315	357
285	324	316	358
286	325	317	359
287	326	318	360
287.1	327	319	361
288	328	320	362
289	329	321	363
290	330	322	364
291	331	323	365
292	332	324	366
293	333	325	367
294	334	326	368
295	335	327	369
295(1)	335(1)	328	370
295(2)	335(2)	329	371
296	336	330	372
297	337	331	373
298	338	332	374
298(1.1)	338(2)	333	375
298(2)	338(3)	334	376
298(3)	338(4)	335	377
299	339	336	378
300	340		
301	341	Part VIII	Part X
301.1	342	337	379
301.2	342.1	338	380

R.S.C. 1970, c. C-34	R.S.C. 1985, c. C-46	R.S.C. 1970, c. C-34	R.S.C. 1985, c. C-46
339	381	381	423
340	382	381.1	424
341	383	382	425
342	384	383	426
343	385	384	427
344	386		
345	387	Part IX	Part XI
346	388	385	428
347	389	386	429
348	390	387	430
349	391	387.1	431
350	392	388	432
351	393	389	433
352	394	390	434
353	395	391	435
354	396	392	436
355	397	393	437
356	398	394	438
357	399	395	439
358	400	396	440
359	401	397	441
360	402	398	442
361	403	399	443
362	404	400	444
363	405	401	445
364	406	402	446
365	407	403	447
366	408	404-405	—
367	409		
368	410	Part X	Part XII
369	411	406	448
370	412	407	449
371	413	408	450
372	414	409	451
373	415	410	452
374	416	411	453
375	417	412	454
376	418	413	455
377	419	414	456
378	420	415	457
379	421	416	458
380	422	417	459

R.S.C. 1970, c. C-34	R.S.C. 1985, c. C-46
418	460
419	461
420	462
Part X.1	Part XII.1
420.1	462.1
420.2	462.2
Part X.1	Part XII.2
420.1	462.3
420.11	462.31
420.12	462.32
420.13	462.33
420.14	462.34
420.15	462.35
420.16	462.36
420.17	462.37
420.18	462.38
420.19	462.39
420.2	462.4
420.21	462.41
420.22	462.42
420.23	462.43
420.24	462.44
420.25	462.45
420.26	462.46
420.27	462.47
420.28	462.48
420.29	462.49
420.3	462.5
Part XI	Part XIII
421	463
422	464
423	465
423(1)(c)	—
423(1)(d)	465(1)(c)
423(1)(e)	465(1)(d)
423(2)	465(2)
424	466
425	467

R.S.C. 1970, c. C-34	R.S.C. 1985, c. C-46
Part XII	Part XIV
426	468
427	469
428	470
429	471
429.1	472
430	473
431	474
431.1	475
432	476
433	477
434	478
435	479
436	480
437	481
438	482
438(1.1)	482(2)
438(2)	482(3)
438(3)	—
438(4)	482(4)
438(5)	482(5)
Part XIII	Part XV
439	483
440	484
440.1	485
440.2	485.1
441	—
442	486
442(2.1)	486(2.1)
442(2.2)	486(2.2)
442(3)	486(3)
442(3.1)	486(4)
442(4)	486(5)
442(5)	—
443	487
443.1	487.1
443.2	487.2
444	488
444.1	488.1
445	489
445.1	489.1

R.S.C. 1970, c. C-34	R.S.C. 1985, c. C-46	R.S.C. 1970, c. C-34	R.S.C. 1985, c. C-46
446	490	457(2.1)	515(2.1)
446.1	491	457(3)	515(3)
446.2	491.1	457(4)	515(4)
446.3	491.2	457(5)	515(5)
447	492	457(5.1)	515(6)
		457(5.2)	515(7)
Part XIV	Part XVI	457(5.3)	515(8)
448	493	457(6)	515(9)
448 "judge"	493 "judge"	457(7)	515(10)
(b)	(b)	457(8)	515(11)
(c)	(c)	457.1	516
(d)	(d)	457.2	517
(e)	(e)	457.3	518
449	494	457.4	519
450	495	457.5	520
451	496	457.6	521
452	497	457.7	522
453	498	457.7(2.1)	522(3)
453.1	499	457.7(2.2)	522(4)
453.2	500	457.7(3)	522(5)
453.3	501	457.7(4)	522(6)
453.4	502	457.8	523
454	503	458	524
454(1.1)	503(2)	458(4.1)	524(5)
454(2)	503(3)	458(4.2)	524(6)
454(2.1)	503(3.1)	458(4.3)	524(7)
454(3)	503(4)	458(5)	524(8)
454(4)	503(5)	458(5.1)	524(9)
455	504	458(6)	524(10)
455.1	505	458(7)	524(11)
455.2	506	458(8)	524(12)
455.3	507	458(9)	524(13)
455.4	508	459	525
455.5	509	459.1	526
455.6	510	460	527
456	511	461	528
456.1	512	462	529
456.2	513		
456.3	514	Part XIV.1	Part XVII
457	515	462.1	530
457(2)(c.1)	515(2)(d)		530.1
457(2)(d)	515(2)(e)	462.2	531

R.S.C. 1970, c. C-34	R.S.C. 1985, c. C-46	R.S.C. 1970, c. C-34	R.S.C. 1985, c. C-46
462.3	532	(f)	(h)
462.4	533	(g)	(f)
—	534	(h)	(i)
		"magistrate"	"magistrate"
Part XV	Part XVIII	483	553
463	535	484	554
464	536	484(2)-(4)	—
465	537	485	555
465(1)(a)	—	486	556
465(1)(b)	537(1)(a)	487	557
465(1)(c)	537(1)(b)	488	558
465(1)(d)	537(1)(c)	489	559
465(1)(e)	537(1)(d)	490	560
465(1)(f)	537(1)(e)	490(5)	—
465(1)(g)	—	491	561
465(1)(h)	537(1)(f)	492	562
465(1)(i)	537(1)(g)	493	563
465(1)(j)	537(1)(h)	494	564
465(1)(k)	537(1)(i)	495	565
466	538	496	566
467	539	497	567
468	540	498	568
469	541	499	569
470	542	500	570
471	543	501	571
471.1	544	502	572
472	545	503	573
473	546		
474	547	Part XVII	Part XX
474.1	547.1	504	574
475	548	505	575
476	549	506	576
477	550	507	577
478	551	507.1	578
479-481	—	508	579
		509	580
Part XVI	Part XIX	510	581
482	552	511	582
482 "judge"	552 "judge"	512	583
(c.1)	(d)	513	584
(d)	(g)	514	585
(e)	(e)	515	586

R.S.C. 1970, c. C-34	R.S.C. 1985, c. C-46	R.S.C. 1970, c. C-34	R.S.C. 1985, c. C-46
516	587	547	619
517	588	548	620
518	589	549	621
519	590	550	622
520	591	551	623
521	592	552	624
522	593	553	625
523-525	594-596		625.1
526	597	554	626
526.1	598	555	627
527	599	556	—
527(1.1)	599(2)	557	628
527(2)	599(3)	558	629
527(3)	599(4)	559	630
527(4)	599(5)	560	631
528	600	561	632
529	601	562	633
530	602	563	634
531	603	564	635
532	604	565	636
533	605	566	637
534	606	567	638
535	607	568	639
	607(6)	569	640
536	608	570	641
537	609	571	642
538	610	572	643
539	611	573	644
540	612	574	645
541	613	575	646
542	614	576	647
543	615	576.1	648
543(2.1)	615(3)	576.2	649
543(3)	615(4)	577	650
543(4)	615(5)	578	651
543(5)	615(6)	579	652
543(6)	615(7)	580	653
543(7)	615(8)	581	654
543(8)	615(9)	582	655
544	616	583	656
545	617	584	657
546	618	584.1	657.1

R.S.C. 1970, c. C-34	R.S.C. 1985, c. C-46	R.S.C. 1970, c. C-34	R.S.C. 1985, c. C-46
585	658	612	685
586	659	613	686
587	660	614	687
588	661	615	688
589	662	616	689
590	663	616(1)	689(1)
591	664	617	690
592	665	618	691
593	666	618(1)(b)	691(1)(b)
594	667	619	—
594(3.1)	667(4)	620	692
594(4)	667(5)	620(3)(b)	692(3)(b)
595	668	621	693
596	669	621(1)	693(1)
597	669.1	622	694
597.1	669.2	622.1	694.1
598	670	622.2	694.2
599	671	623	695
600	672	624	696
		Part XIX	Part XXII
Part XVIII	Part XXI	625	697
601	673	626	698
601 "sentence"	673	627	699
	"sentence"	628	700
602	674	629	701
603	675	630	702
603(1.1)	675(2)	631	703
603(2)	675(3)	631.1	703.1
603(3)	675(4)	631.2	703.2
604	—	632	704
605	676	633	705
606	677	634	706
607	678	635	707
607.1	678.1	636	708
608	679	637	709
608.1	680	638	710
608.2	681	639	711
609	682	640	712
610	683	640(3)	
610(5)	683(5)	641	713
611	684	642	714

R.S.C. 1970, c. C-34	R.S.C. 1985, c. C-46	R.S.C. 1970, c. C-34	R.S.C. 1985, c. C-46
643	715	663	737
	715.1	664	738
		665	739
Part XX	Part XXIII	666	740
644	716	667	741
645	717	668	741.1
646	718	669	742
	718.1	670	743
647	719	671	744
648	720	672	745
649	721	672(6)(a)	745(6)
650	722	672(6)(a)(i)	745(6)(e)
651	723	672(6)(a)(ii)	745(6)(c)
652	724	672(6)(a)(iii)	745(6)(d)
653	725	672(6)(a)(iv)	—
654	726	672(6)(a)(v)	745(6)(a)
655	727	672(6)(a)(vi)	745(6)(b)
655.1	727.1	672(6)(b)	745(6)(f) part
655.2	727.2	672(6)(c)	745(6)(f) part
655.3	727.3	673	746
655.4	727.4	674	747
655.5	727.5	675-681	—
655.6	727.6	682	748
655.7	727.7	682(3.1)	748(4)
655.8	727.8	682(3.2)	748(5)
655.9	727.9	682(4)	748(6)
656	728	683	749
657	729	684	—
658	730	685	750
659	731	686	751
659(6.1)	731(7)		
659(7)	731(8)	Part XXI	Part XXIV
660	732	687	752
660.1	733	688	753
661	734	689	754
662	735	690	755
662(1.1)	735(1.1)	691	756
662(1.2)	735(1.2)	692	757
662(1.3)	735(1.3)	693	758
662(1.4)	735(1.4)	694	759
662(2)	735(2)	695	760
662.1	736	695.1	761

R.S.C. 1970, c. C-34	R.S.C. 1985, c. C-46	R.S.C. 1970, c. C-34	R.S.C. 1985, c. C-46
Part XXII	Part XXV	731	795
696	762	732	796
697	763	732.1	797
698	764	733	798
699	765	734	799
700	766	735	800
701	767	736	801
701.1	767.1	736(4)-(5)	
702	768	737	802
703	769	738	803
704	770	738(2)	—
705	771	738(3)	803(2)
706	772	738(3.1)	803(3)
707	773	739	804
		740	805
Part XXIII	Part XXVI	741	806
708	774	742	807
709	775	743	808
710	776	744	809
711	777	745	810
712	778	746	811
713	779	747	812
714	780	747 "appeal court"	812 "appeal court"
715	781	747(a)	812(f)
716	782	747(b)	812(g)
717	783	747(c)	812(c)
718	—	747(d)	812(b)
719	784	747(e)	812(a)
		747(f)	812(d)
Part XXIV	Part XXVII	747(g)	—
720	785	747(h)	812(e)
721	786	747(i)	812(h)
722	787	748	813
723	788	749	814
724	789	750	815
725	790	751	—
725(3)-(5)	—	752	816
726	791	752.1	817
727	—	752.2	818
728	792	752.3	819
729	793	753	820
730	794	754	821

R.S.C. 1970, c. C-34	R.S.C. 1985, c. C-46
755	822
755.1	823
756	824
757	825
758	826
759	827
760	828
761	829
762	830
763	831
764	832
765	833
766	834
767	835
768	836
769	837
770	838
771	839
772	840
Part XXV	Part XXVIII
773	841
	841(3)
Forms 1-2	Forms 1-2
Form 3	Form 3
Form 4	Form 4
Form 5	Form 5
Form 5.1	Form 5.1
Form 5.2	Form 5.2
	Form 5.3
Form 6	Form 6
Form 7	Form 7
Form 8	Form 8
Form 8.1	Form 9
Form 8.2	Form 10
Form 8.3	Form 11
Form 9	Form 12
Form 9.1	Form 13
Form 9.2	Form 14
Form 10	Form 15
Form 11	Form 16
Form 12	Form 17

R.S.C. 1970, c. C-34	R.S.C. 1985, c. C-46
Form 13	Form 18
Form 14	Form 19
Form 15	—
Form 16	Form 20
Form 17	—
Form 18	Form 21
Form 19	Form 22
Form 20	Form 23
Form 21	Form 24
Form 22	Form 25
Form 23	Form 26
Form 24	Form 27
Form 25	Form 28
Form 25.1	Form 29
Form 26	Form 30
Form 27	Form 31
Form 28	Form 32
Form 29	Form 33
Form 30	Form 34
Form 31	Form 35
Form 32	Form 36
Form 33	Form 37
Form 34	Form 38
Form 35	Form 39
Form 36	Form 40
Form 37	Form 41
Form 38	Form 42
Form 39	Form 43
Forms 40-41	—
Form 42	Form 44
Form 43	Form 45
Form 44	Form 46
Form 45	Form 47
774	—

CRIMINAL CODE

AN ACT RESPECTING THE CRIMINAL LAW

REVISED STATUTES OF CANADA, 1985

CHAPTER C-46

and Amendments

SHORT TITLE

Short title.

1. This Act may be cited as the *Criminal Code.*

INTERPRETATION

Definitions — "Act" — "Attorney General" — "Bank-note" — "Canadian Forces" — "Cattle" — "Clerk of the court" — "Complainant" — "Counsel" — "Count" — "Court of appeal" — "Court of criminal jurisdiction" — "Day" — "Document of title to goods" — "Document of title to lands" — "Dwelling-house" — "Every one" — "Person" — "Owner" — "Explosive substance" — "Her Majesty's Forces" — "Highway" — "Indictment" — "Internationally protected person" — "Justice" — "Mental disorder" — "Military" — "Military law" — "Motor vehicle" — "Municipality" — "Newly-born child" — "Night" — "Offender" — "Offensive weapon" — "Peace officer" — "Prison" — "Property" — "Prosecutor" — "Provincial court judge" — "Public department" — "Public officer" — "Public stores" — "Railway equipment" — "Steal" — "Superior court of criminal jurisdiction" — "Territorial division" — "Testamentary instrument" — "Trustee" — "Unfit to stand trial" — "Valuable security" — "Weapon" — "Wreck" — "Writing".

2. In this Act,

"Act" includes

(*a*) an Act of Parliament,

(*b*) an Act of the legislature of the former Province of Canada,

(*c*) an Act of the legislature of a province, and

(*d*) an Act or ordinance of the legislature of a province, territory or place in force at the time that province, territory or place became a province of Canada;

"Attorney General"

(*a*) with respect to proceedings to which this Act applies, means the Attorney

General or Solicitor General of the province in which those proceedings are taken and includes his lawful deputy, and

(*b*) with respect to

(i) the Northwest Territories and the Yukon Territory, or

(ii) proceedings commenced at the instance of the Government of Canada and conducted by or on behalf of that Government in respect of a contravention of or conspiracy to contravene any Act of Parliament other than this Act or any regulation made thereunder,

means the Attorney General of Canada and includes his lawful deputy;

"bank-note" includes any negotiable instrument

(*a*) issued by or on behalf of a person carrying on the business of banking in or out of Canada, and

(*b*) issued under the authority of Parliament or under the lawful authority of the government of a state other than Canada,

intended to be used as money or as the equivalent of money, immediately on issue or at some time subsequent thereto, and includes bank bills and bank post bills;

"Canadian Forces" means the armed forces of Her Majesty raised by Canada;

"cattle" means neat cattle or an animal of the bovine species by whatever technical or familiar name it is known, and includes any horse, mule, ass, pig, sheep or goat;

"clerk of the court" includes a person, by whatever name or title he may be designated, who from time to time performs the duties of a clerk of the court;

"complainant" means the victim of an alleged offence;

"counsel" means a barrister or solicitor, in respect of the matters or things that barristers and solicitors, respectively, are authorized by the law of a province to do or perform in relation to legal proceedings;

"count" means a charge in an information or indictment;

"court of appeal" means

(*a*) in the Province of Ontario, the Court of Appeal,

(*b*) in the Province of Quebec, the Court of Appeal,

(*c*) in the Province of Nova Scotia, the Appeal Division of the Supreme Court,

(*d*) in the Province of New Brunswick, the Court of Appeal,

(*e*) in the Province of British Columbia, the Court of Appeal,

(*f*) in the Province of Prince Edward Island, the Appeal Division of the Supreme Court,

(*g*) in the Province of Manitoba, the Court of Appeal,

(*h*) in the Province of Saskatchewan, the Court of Appeal,

(*i*) in the Province of Alberta, the Court of Appeal,

(*j*) in the Province of Newfoundland, the Court of Appeal,

(*k*) in the Yukon Territory, the Court of Appeal, and

(*l*) in the Northwest Territories, the Court of Appeal;

"court of criminal jurisdiction" means

(*a*) a court of general or quarter sessions of the peace, when presided over by a superior, county or district court judge,

(*a*.1) in the Province of Quebec, the Court of Quebec, the municipal court of Montreal and the municipal court of Quebec,

(*b*) a provincial court judge or judge acting under Part XIX, and

(*c*) in the Province of Ontario, the Ontario Court of Justice;

"day" means the period between six o'clock in the forenoon and nine o'clock in the afternoon of the same day;

"document of title to goods" includes a bought and sold note, bill of lading, warrant, certificate or order for the delivery or transfer of goods or any other valuable thing, and any other document used in the ordinary course of business as evidence of the possession or control of goods, authorizing or purporting to authorize, by endorsement or by delivery, the person in possession of the document to transfer or receive any goods thereby represented or therein mentioned or referred to;

"document of title to lands" includes any writing that is or contains evidence of the title, or any part of the title, to real property or to any interest in real property, and any notarial or registrar's copy thereof and any duplicate instrument, memorial, certificate or document authorized or required by any law in force in any part of Canada with respect to registration of titles that relates to title to real property or to any interest in real property;

"dwelling-house" means the whole or any part of a building or structure that is kept or occupied as a permanent or temporary residence, and includes

(*a*) a building within the curtilage of a dwelling-house that is connected to it by a doorway or by a covered and enclosed passage-way, and

(*b*) a unit that is designed to be mobile and to be used as a permanent or temporary residence and that is being used as such a residence;

"every one", "person", "owner", and similar expressions include Her Majesty and public bodies, bodies corporate, societies, companies and inhabitants of counties, parishes, municipalities or other districts in relation to the acts and things that they are capable of doing and owning respectively;

"explosive substance" includes

(*a*) anything intended to be used to make an explosive substance,

(*b*) anything, or any part thereof, used or intended to be used, or adapted to cause, or to aid in causing an explosion in or with an explosive substance, and

(*c*) an incendiary grenade, fire bomb, molotov cocktail or other similar incendiary substance or device and a delaying mechanism or other thing intended for use in connection with such a substance or device;

"feeble-minded person" [Repealed R.S. 1991, c. 43 s. 9, Sch., item 1.]

"Her Majesty's Forces" means the naval, army and air forces of Her Majesty wherever raised, and includes the Canadian Forces;

"highway" means a road to which the public has the right of access, and includes bridges over which or tunnels through which a road passes;

"indictment" includes

(*a*) information or a count therein,

(*b*) a plea, replication or other pleading, and

(*c*) any record;

"internationally protected person" means

(*a*) a head of state, including any member of a collegial body that performs the functions of a head of state under the constitution of the state concerned, a head of a government or a minister of foreign affairs, whenever that person is in a state other than the state in which he holds that position or office,

(*b*) a member of the family of a person described in paragraph (*a*) who accompanies that person in a state other than the state in which that person holds that position or office,

(*c*) a representative or an official of a state or an official or agent of an international organization of an intergovernmental character who, at the time when and at the place where an offence referred to in subsection 7(3) is committed against his person or any property referred to in section 431 that is used by him, is entitled, pursuant to international law, to special protection from any attack on his person, freedom or dignity, or

(*d*) a member of the family of a representative, official or agent described in paragraph (*c*) who forms part of his household, if the representative, official or agent, at the time when and at the place where any offence referred to in subsection 7(3) is committed against the member of his family or any property referred to in section 431 that is used by that member, is entitled, pursuant to international law, to special protection from any attack on his person, freedom or dignity;

"justice" means a justice of the peace or a provincial court judge, and includes two or more justices where two or more justices are, by law, required to act or, by law, act or have jurisdiction;

"magistrate" [Repealed R.S. 1985, c. 27 (1st Supp.), s. 2(4).]

"mental disorder" means a disease of the mind;

"military" shall be construed as relating to all or any of the Canadian Forces;

"military law" includes all laws, regulations or orders relating to the Canadian Forces;

"motor vehicle" means a vehicle that is drawn, propelled or driven by any means other than muscular power, but does not include railway equipment;

"municipality" includes the corporation of a city, town, village, county, township, parish or other territorial or local division of a province, the inhabitants of which are incorporated or are entitled to hold property collectively for a public purpose;

"newly-born child" means a person under the age of one year;

"night" means the period between nine o'clock in the afternoon and six o'clock in the forenoon of the following day;

"offender" means a person who has been determined by a court to be guilty of an offence, whether on acceptance of a plea of guilty or on a finding of guilt;

"offensive weapon" has the same meaning as "weapon";

"peace officer" includes

(*a*) a mayor, warden, reeve, sheriff, deputy sheriff, sheriff's officer and justice of the peace,

(*b*) a member of the Correctional Service of Canada who is designated as a peace officer pursuant to the *Penitentiary Act*, and a warden, deputy warden, instructor, keeper, jailer, guard and any other officer or permanent employee of a prison other than a penitentiary as defined in the *Penitentiary Act*,

(*c*) a police officer, police constable, bailiff, constable, or other person employed for the preservation and maintenance of the public peace or for the service or execution of civil process,

(*d*) an officer or a person having the powers of a customs or excise officer when performing any duty in the administration of the *Customs Act* or the *Excise Act*,

(*e*) a person designated as a fishery guardian under the *Fisheries Act* when performing any duties or functions under that Act and a person designated as a fishery officer under the *Fisheries Act* when performing any duties or functions under that Act, the *Coastal Fisheries Protection Act*, the *North Pacific Fisheries Convention Act*, the *Northern Pacific Halibut Fisheries Convention Act* or the *Pacific Fur Seals Convention Act*,

(*f*) the pilot in command of an aircraft

(i) registered in Canada under regulations made under the *Aeronautics Act*, or

(ii) leased without crew and operated by a person who is qualified under regulations made under the *Aeronautics Act* to be registered as owner of an aircraft registered in Canada under those regulations,

while the aircraft is in flight, and

(*g*) officers and non-commissioned members of the Canadian Forces who are

(i) appointed for the purposes of section 156 of the *National Defence Act*, or

(ii) employed on duties that the Governor in Council, in regulations made under the *National Defence Act* for the purposes of this paragraph, has prescribed to be of such a kind as to necessitate that the officers and non-commissioned members performing them have the powers of peace officers;

"prison" includes a penitentiary, common jail, public or reformatory prison, lock-up, guard-room or other place in which persons who are charged with or convicted of offences are usually kept in custody;

"property" includes

(*a*) real and personal property of every description and deeds and instruments relating to or evidencing the title or right to property, or giving a right to recover or receive money or goods,

(*b*) property originally in the possession or under the control of any person, and any property into or for which it has been converted or exchanged and anything acquired at any time by the conversion or exchange, and

(*c*) any postal card, postage stamp or other stamp issued or prepared for issue under the authority of Parliament or the legislature of a province for the payment to the Crown or a corporate body of any fee, rate or duty, whether or not it is in the possession of the Crown or of any person;

"prosecutor" means the Attorney General or, where the Attorney General does not intervene, means the person who institutes proceedings to which this Act applies, and includes counsel acting on behalf of either of them;

"provincial court judge" means a person appointed or authorized to act by or pursuant to an Act of the legislature of a province, by whatever title that person may be designated, who has the power and authority of two or more justices of the peace and includes the lawful deputy of that person;

"public department" means a department of the Government of Canada or a branch thereof or a board, commission, corporation or other body that is an agent of Her Majesty in right of Canada;

"public officer" includes

(*a*) an officer of customs or excise,

(*b*) an officer of the Canadian Forces,

(*c*) an officer of the Royal Canadian Mounted Police, and

(*d*) any officer while the officer is engaged in enforcing the laws of Canada relating to revenue, customs, excise, trade or navigation;

"public stores" includes any personal property that is under the care, supervision, administration or control of a public department or of any person in the service of a public department;

"railway equipment" means

(*a*) any machine that is constructed for movement exclusively on lines of railway, whether or not the machine is capable of independent motion, or

(*b*) any vehicle that is constructed for movement both on and off lines of railway while the adaptations of that vehicle for movement on lines of railway are in use;

"steal" means to commit theft;

"superior court of criminal jurisdiction" means

(*a*) in the Province of Ontario, the Court of Appeal or the Ontario Court (General Division),

(*b*) in the Province of Quebec, the Superior Court,

(*c*) in the Provinces of Nova Scotia and Prince Edward Island, the Supreme Court,

(*d*) in the Provinces of New Brunswick, Manitoba, Saskatchewan and Alberta, the Court of Appeal or the Court of Queen's Bench,

(*e*) in the Provinces of British Columbia and Newfoundland, the Supreme Court or the Court of Appeal,

(*f*) in the Yukon Territory, the Supreme Court, and

(*g*) in the Northwest Territories, the Supreme Court;

"territorial division" includes any province, county, union of counties, township, city, town, parish or other judicial division or place to which the context applies;

"testamentary instrument" includes any will, codicil or other testamentary writing or appointment, during the life of the testator whose testamentary disposition it purports to be and after his death, whether it relates to real or personal property or to both;

"trustee" means a person who is declared by any Act to be a trustee or is, by the law of a province, a trustee, and, without restricting the generality of the foregoing, includes a trustee on an express trust created by deed, will or instrument in writing, or by parol;

"unfit to stand trial" means unable on account of mental disorder to conduct a defence at any stage of the proceedings before a verdict is rendered or to instruct counsel to do so, and, in particular, unable on account of mental disorder to

(*a*) understand the nature or object of the proceedings,

(*b*) understand the possible consequences of the proceedings, or

(*c*) communicate with counsel;

"valuable security" includes

(*a*) an order, exchequer acquittance or other security that entitles or evidences the title of any person

(i) to a share or interest in a public stock or fund or in any fund of a body corporate, company or society, or

(ii) to a deposit in a savings bank or other bank,

(*b*) any debenture, deed, bond, bill, note, warrant, order or other security for money or for payment of money,

(*c*) a document of title to lands or goods wherever situated,

(*d*) a stamp or writing that secures or evidences title to or an interest in a chattel personal, or that evidences delivery of a chattel personal, and

(*e*) a release, receipt, discharge or other instrument evidencing payment of money;

"weapon" means

(*a*) anything used or intended for use in causing death or injury to persons whether designed for that purpose or not, or

(*b*) anything used or intended for use for the purpose of threatening or intimidating any person,

and, without restricting the generality of the foregoing, includes any firearm as defined in section 84;

[1991, c. 40, s. 1 will repeal the definition "weapon" and substitute the following.]

"weapon" means

(*a*) anything used, designed to be used or intended for use in causing death or injury to any person, or

(*b*) anything used, designed to be used or intended for use for the purpose of threatening or intimidating any person,

and, without restricting the generality of the foregoing, includes any firearm as defined in subsection 84(1);

"wreck" includes the cargo, stores and tackle of a vessel and all parts of a vessel separated from the vessel, and the property of persons who belong to, are on board or have quitted a vessel that is wrecked, stranded or in distress at any place in Canada;

"writing" includes a document of any kind and any mode in which, and any material on which, words or figures, whether at length or abridged, are written, printed or otherwise expressed, or a map or plan is inscribed. R.S. 1985, c. 11 (1st Supp.), s. 2; c. 27 (1st Supp.), ss. 2, 203; c. 31 (1st Supp.), s. 61; c. 1 (2d Supp.), Sched. IV; c. 27 (2d Supp.), Sched.; c. 35 (2d Supp.), s. 34; c. 28 (4th Supp.), s. 34; c. 32 (4th Supp.), s. 55; c. 40 (4th Supp.), Schedule, item 1; 1990, c. 17, s. 7; 1991, c. 40, s. 1; c. 43 s. 1; c. 43, s. 9, Sch., item 1.

[1992, c. 20, s. 216(1)(*a*) will repeal the expression "*Penitentiary Act*" wherever it occurs in section 2 and substitute the expression "Part I of the *Corrections and Conditional Release Act*".]

Descriptive cross references.

3. Where, in any provision of this Act, a reference to another provision of this Act or a provision of any other Act is followed by words in parenthesis that are or purport to be descriptive of the subject-matter of the provision referred to, the words in parenthesis form no part of the provision in which they occur but shall be deemed to have been inserted for convenience of reference only.

PART I

General

Postcard a chattel, value — Value of valuable security — Possession — Expressions taken from other Acts — Sexual intercourse — Service — Proof of service by affidavit — Attendance for examination.

4. (1) For the purposes of this Act, a postal card or stamp referred to in paragraph (*c*) of the definition "property" in section 2 shall be deemed to be a chattel and to be equal in value to the amount of the postage, rate or duty expressed on its face.

(2) For the purposes of this Act, the following rules apply for the purpose of determining the value of a valuable security where value is material:

(*a*) where the valuable security is one mentioned in paragraph (*a*) or (*b*) of the definition "valuable security" in section 2, the value is the value of the share, interest, deposit or unpaid money, as the case may be, that is secured by the valuable security;

(*b*) where the valuable security is one mentioned in paragraph (*c*) or (*d*) of the definition "valuable security" in section 2, the value is the value of the lands, goods, chattel personal or interest in the chattel personal, as the case may be; and

(*c*) where the valuable security is one mentioned in paragraph (*e*) of the definition "valuable security" in section 2, the value is the amount of money that has been paid.

(3) For the purposes of this Act,

(*a*) a person has anything in possession when he has it in his personal possession or knowingly

(i) has it in the actual possession or custody of another person, or

(ii) has it in any place, whether or not that place belongs to or is occupied by him, for the use or benefit of himself or of another person; and

(*b*) where one of two or more persons, with the knowledge and consent of the rest, has anything in his custody or possession, it shall be deemed to be in the custody and possession of each and all of them.

(4) Where an offence that is dealt with in this Act relates to a subject that is dealt with in another Act, the words and expressions used in this Act with respect to that offence have, subject to this Act, the meaning assigned to them in that other Act.

(5) For the purposes of this Act, sexual intercourse is complete on penetration to even the slightest degree, notwithstanding that seed is not emitted.

(6) For the purposes of this Act, service of any document may be proved by oral evidence given under oath by, or by the affidavit or solemn declaration of, the person claiming to have served it.

(7) Notwithstanding subsection (6), the court may require the person who

appears to have signed an affidavit or solemn declaration referred to in that subsection to appear before it for examination or cross-examination in respect of the issue of proof of service. R.S. 1985, c. 27 (1st Supp.,), s. 3.

Canadian Forces not affected.

5. Nothing in this Act affects any law relating to the government of the Canadian Forces.

Presumption of innocence — Offences outside Canada — Definition of "enactment".

6. (1) Where an enactment creates an offence and authorizes a punishment to be imposed in respect of that offence,

(*a*) a person shall be deemed not to be guilty of the offence until he is convicted or discharged under section 736 of the offence; and

(*b*) a person who is convicted or discharged under section 736 of the offence is not liable to any punishment in respect thereof other than the punishment prescribed by this Act or by the enactment that creates the offence.

(2) Subject to this Act or any other Act of Parliament, no person shall be convicted or discharged under section 736 of an offence committed outside Canada.

(3) In this section "enactment" means

(*a*) an Act of Parliament, or

(*b*) an Act of the legislature of a province that creates an offence to which Part XXVII applies,

or any regulation made thereunder. R.S. 1985, c. 27 (1st Supp.), s. 4.

Offences committed on aircraft — Idem — Offence against internationally protected person — Offence of hostage taking — Offences involving nuclear material — Idem — Idem — Idem — Definition of "nuclear material" — Jurisdiction — Jurisdiction: war crimes and crimes against humanity — Procedure and evidence — Defences — Conflict with internal law — Attorney General of Canada — Definitions — "Conventional international law" — "Crime against humanity" — "War crime" — Meaning of "act or omission" — Offences by Public Service employees — Jurisdiction — Appearance of accused at trial — Where previously tried outside Canada — Consent — Definition of "flight" and "in flight" — Definition of "in service" — Certificate as evidence — Idem.

7. (1) Notwithstanding anything in this Act or any other Act, every one who

(*a*) on or in respect of an aircraft

(i) registered in Canada under regulations made under the *Aeronautics Act*, or

(ii) leased without crew and operated by a person who is qualified under regulations made under the *Aeronautics Act* to be registered as owner of an aircraft registered in Canada under those regulations, while the aircraft is in flight, or

(*b*) on any aircraft, while the aircraft is in flight if the flight terminated in Canada,

commits an act or omission in or outside Canada that if committed in Canada would be an offence punishable by indictment shall be deemed to have committed that act or omission in Canada.

(2) Notwithstanding this Act or any other Act, every one who

(*a*) on an aircraft, while the aircraft is in flight, commits an act or omission outside Canada that if committed in Canada or on an aircraft registered in Canada under regulations made under the *Aeronautics Act* would be an offence against section 76 or paragraph 77(*a*),

(*b*) in relation to an aircraft in service, commits an act or omission outside Canada that if committed in Canada would be an offence against any of paragraphs 77(*b*), (*c*) or (*e*), or

(*c*) in relation to an air navigation facility used in international air navigation, commits an act or omission outside Canada that if committed in Canada would be an offence against paragraph 77(*d*)

shall, if he is found anywhere in Canada, be deemed to have committed that act or omission in Canada.

(3) Notwithstanding anything in this Act or any other Act, every one who, outside Canada, commits an act or omission against the person of an internationally protected person or against any property referred to in section 431 used by that person that if committed in Canada would be an offence against section 235, 236, 266, 267, 268, 269, 271, 272, 273, 279, 279.1, 280 to 283, 424 or 431 shall be deemed to commit that act or omission in Canada if

(*a*) the act or omission is committed on a ship that is registered or licensed, or for which an identification number has been issued, pursuant to any Act of Parliament;

(*b*) the act or omission is committed on an aircraft

(i) registered in Canada under regulations made under the *Aeronautics Act*, or

(ii) leased without crew and operated by a person who is qualified under regulations made under the *Aeronautics Act* to be registered as owner of an aircraft in Canada under those regulations;

(*c*) the person who commits the act or omission is a Canadian citizen or is, after the act or omission has been committed, present in Canada; or

(*d*) the act or omission is against

(i) a person who enjoys the status of an internationally protected person by virtue of the functions that person performs on behalf of Canada, or

(ii) a member of the family of a person described in subparagraph (i) who qualifies under paragraph (*b*) or (*d*) of the definition "internationally protected person" in section 2.

(3.1) Notwithstanding anything in this Act or any other Act, every one who, outside Canada, commits an act or omission that if committed in Canada would be an offence against section 279.1 shall be deemed to commit that act or omission in Canada if

(*a*) the act or omission is committed on a ship that is registered or licensed, or for which an identification number has been issued, pursuant to any Act of Parliament;

(*b*) the act or omission is committed on an aircraft

(i) registered in Canada under regulations made under the *Aeronautics Act,* or

(ii) leased without crew and operated by a person who is qualified under regulations made under the *Aeronautics Act* to be registered as owner of an aircraft in Canada under such regulations;

(*c*) the person who commits the act or omission

(i) is a Canadian citizen, or

(ii) is not a citizen of any state and ordinarily resides in Canada;

(*d*) the act or omission is committed with intent to induce Her Majesty in right of Canada or of a province to commit or cause to be committed any act or omission;

(*e*) a person taken hostage by the act or omission is a Canadian citizen; or

(*f*) the person who commits the act or omission is, after the commission thereof, present in Canada.

(3.2) Notwithstanding anything in this Act or any other Act, where

(*a*) a person, outside Canada, receives, has in his possession, uses, transfers the possession of, sends or delivers to any person, transports, alters, disposes of, disperses or abandons nuclear material and thereby

(i) causes or is likely to cause the death of, or serious bodily harm to, any person, or

(ii) causes or is likely to cause serious damage to, or destruction of, property, and

(*b*) the act or omission described in paragraph (*a*) would, if committed in Canada, be an offence against this Act,

that person shall be deemed to commit that act or omission in Canada if paragraph (3.5)(*a*), (*b*) or (*c*) applies in respect of the act or omission.

(3.3) Notwithstanding anything in this Act or any other Act, every one who, outside Canada, commits an act or omission that if committed in Canada would constitute

(*a*) a conspiracy or an attempt to commit,

(*b*) being an accessory after the fact in relation to, or

(*c*) counselling in relation to,

an act or omission that is an offence by virtue of subsection (3.2) shall be deemed to commit the act or omission in Canada if paragraph (3.5)(*a*), (*b*) or (*c*) applies in respect of the act or omission.

(3.4) Notwithstanding anything in this Act or any other Act, every one who, outside Canada, commits an act or omission that if committed in Canada would constitute an offence against, a conspiracy or an attempt to commit or being an accessory after the fact in relation to an offence against, or any counselling in relation to an offence against,

(*a*) section 334, 341, 344 or 380 or paragraph 362(1)(*a*) in relation to nuclear material,

(*b*) section 346 in respect of a threat to commit an offence against section 334 or 344 in relation to nuclear material,

(*c*) section 423 in relation to a demand for nuclear material, or

(*d*) paragraph 264.1(1)(*a*) or (*b*) in respect of a threat to use nuclear material

shall be deemed to commit that act or omission in Canada if paragraph (3.5)(*a*), (*b*) or (*c*) applies in respect of the act or omission.

(3.5) For the purposes of subsections (3.2) to (3.4), a person shall be deemed to commit an act or omission in Canada if

(*a*) the act or omission is committed on a ship that is registered or licensed, or for which an identification number has been issued, pursuant to any Act of Parliament;

(*b*) the act or omission is committed on an aircraft

(i) registered in Canada under regulations made under the *Aeronautics Act*, or

(ii) leased without crew and operated by a person who is qualified under regulations made under the *Aeronautics Act* to be registered as owner of an aircraft in Canada under such regulations; or

(*c*) the person who commits the act or omission is a Canadian citizen or is, after the act or omission has been committed, present in Canada.

(3.6) For the purposes of this section, "nuclear material" means

(*a*) plutonium, except plutonium with an isotopic concentration of plutonium-238 exceeding eighty per cent,

(*b*) uranium-233.

(*c*) uranium containing uranium-233 or uranium-235 or both in such an amount that the abundance ratio of the sum of those isotopes to the isotope uranium-238 is greater than 0.72 per cent,

(*d*) uranium with an isotopic concentration equal to that occurring in nature, and

(*e*) any substance containing anything described in paragraphs (*a*) to (*d*),

but does not include uranium in the form of ore or ore-residue.

(3.7) Notwithstanding anything in this Act or any other Act, every one who, outside Canada, commits an act or omission that, if committed in Canada, would constitute an offence against, a conspiracy or an attempt to commit an offence against, being an accessory after the fact in relation to an offence against, or any counselling in relation to an offence against, section 269.1 shall be deemed to commit that act or omission in Canada if

(*a*) the act or omission is committed on a ship that is registered or licensed, or for which an identification number has been issued, pursuant to any Act of Parliament;

(*b*) the act or omission is committed on an aircraft

(i) registered in Canada under regulations made under the *Aeronautics Act,* or

(ii) leased without crew and operated by a person who is qualified under regulations made under the *Aeronautics Act* to be registered as owner of an aircraft in Canada under those regulations;

(*c*) the person who commits the act or omission is a Canadian citizen;

(*d*) the complainant is a Canadian citizen; or

(*e*) the person who commits the act or omission is, after the commission thereof, present in Canada.

(3.71) Notwithstanding anything in this Act or any other Act, every person who, either before or after the coming into force of this subsection, commits an act or omission outside Canada that constitutes a war crime or a crime against humanity and that, if committed in Canada, would constitute an offence against the laws of Canada in force at the time of the act or omission shall be deemed to commit that act or omission in Canada at that time if,

(*a*) at the time of the act or omission,

(i) that person is a Canadian citizen or is employed by Canada in a civilian or military capacity,

(ii) that person is a citizen of, or is employed in a civilian or military capacity by, a state that is engaged in an armed conflict against Canada, or

(iii) the victim of the act or omission is a Canadian citizen or a citizen of a state that is allied with Canada in an armed conflict; or

(*b*) at the time of the act or omission, Canada could, in conformity with international law, exercise jurisdiction over the person with respect to the act or omission on the basis of the person's presence in Canada and subsequent to the time of the act or omission, the person is present in Canada.

(3.72) Any proceedings with respect to an act or omission referred to in subsection (3.71) shall be conducted in accordance with the laws of evidence and procedure in force at the time of the proceedings.

(3.73) In any proceedings with respect to an act or omission referred to in subsection (3.71), notwithstanding that the act or omission is an offence under the laws of Canada in force at the time of the act or omission, the accused may, subject to subsection 607(6), rely on any justification, excuse or defence available under the laws of Canada or under international law at that time or at the time of the proceedings.

(3.74) Notwithstanding subsection (3.73) and section 15, a person may be convicted of an offence in respect of an act or omission referred to in subsection (3.71) even if the act or omission is committed in obedience to or in conformity with the law in force at the time and in the place of its commission.

(3.75) Notwithstanding any other provision of this Act, no proceedings may be commenced with respect to an act or omission referred to in subsection (3.71) without the personal consent in writing of the Attorney General or Deputy Attorney General of Canada, and such proceedings may only be conducted by the Attorney General of Canada or counsel acting on his behalf.

(3.76) For the purposes of this section,

"conventional international law" means

(*a*) any convention, treaty or other international agreement that is in force and to which Canada is a party, or

(*b*) any convention, treaty or other international agreement that is in force and the provisions of which Canada has agreed to accept and apply in an armed conflict in which it is involved;

"crime against humanity" means murder, extermination, enslavement, deportation, persecution or any other inhumane act or omission that is committed against any civilian population or any identifiable group of persons, whether or not it constitutes a contravention of the law in force at the time and in the place of its commission, and that, at that time and in that place, constitutes a contravention of customary international law or conventional international law or is criminal according to the general principles of law recognized by the community of nations;

"war crime" means an act or omission that is committed during an international armed conflict, whether or not it constitutes a contravention of the law in force at the time and in the place of its commission, and that, at that time and in that place, constitutes a contravention of the customary international law or conventional international law applicable in international armed conflicts.

(3.77) In the definitions "crime against humanity" and "war crime" in subsection (3.76), "act or omission" includes, for greater certainty, attempting or conspiring to commit, counselling any person to commit, aiding or abetting any person in the commission of, or being an accessory after the fact in relation to, an act or omission.

(4) Every one who, while employed as an employee within the meaning of the *Public Service Employment Act* in a place outside Canada, commits an act or omission in that place that is an offence under the laws of that place and that, if committed in Canada, would be an offence punishable by indictment shall be deemed to have committed that act or omission in Canada.

(5) Where a person is alleged to have committed an act or omission that is an offence by virtue of this section, proceedings in respect of that offence may, whether or not that person is in Canada, be commenced in any territorial division in Canada and the accused may be tried and punished in respect of

that offence in the same manner as if the offence had been committed in that territorial division.

(5.1) For greater certainty, the provisions of this Act relating to

(*a*) requirements that an accused appear at and be present during proceedings, and

(*b*) the exceptions to those requirements,

apply to proceedings commenced in any territorial division pursuant to subsection (5).

(6) Where a person is alleged to have committed an act or omission that is an offence by virtue of this section and that person has been tried and dealt with outside Canada in respect of the offence in such a manner that, if that person had been tried and dealt with in Canada, he would be able to plead *autrefois acquit, autrefois convict* or pardon, that person shall be deemed to have been so tried and dealt with in Canada.

(7) No proceedings shall be instituted under this section without the consent of the Attorney General of Canada if the accused is not a Canadian citizen.

(8) For the purposes of this section, of the definition "peace officer" in section 2 and of sections 76 and 77, "flight" means the act of flying or moving through the air and an aircraft shall be deemed to be in flight from the time when all external doors are closed following embarkation until the later of

(*a*) the time at which any such door is opened for the purpose of disembarkation, and

(*b*) where the aircraft makes a forced landing in circumstances in which the owner or operator thereof or a person acting on behalf of either of them is not in control of the aircraft, the time at which control of the aircraft is restored to the owner or operator thereof or a person acting on behalf of either of them.

(9) For the purposes of this section and section 77, an aircraft shall be deemed to be in service from the time when pre-flight preparation of the aircraft by ground personnel or the crew thereof begins for a specific flight until

(*a*) the flight is cancelled before the aircraft is in flight,

(*b*) twenty-four hours after the aircraft, having commenced the flight, lands, or

(*c*) the aircraft, having commenced the flight, ceases to be in flight,

whichever is the latest.

(10) If in any proceedings under this Act a question arises as to whether any person is a person who is entitled, pursuant to international law, to special protection from any attack on his person, freedom or dignity, a certificate purporting to have been issued by or under the authority of the Secretary of State for External Affairs stating any fact relevant to that question is admissible in evidence in such proceedings without proof of the signature or authority of the person appearing to have signed it, and in the absence of evidence to the contrary is proof of the facts so stated.

(11) A certificate purporting to have been issued by or under the authority of the Secretary of State for External Affairs stating

(*a*) that at a certain time any state was engaged in an armed conflict against Canada or was allied with Canada in an armed conflict,

(*b*) that at a certain time any convention, treaty or other international agreement was or was not in force and that Canada was or was not a party thereto, or

(*c*) that Canada agreed or did not agree to accept and apply the provisions of any convention, treaty or other international agreement in an armed conflict in which Canada was involved,

is admissible in evidence in any proceedings without proof of the signature or authority of the person appearing to have issued it, and is proof of facts so stated. R.S. 1985, c. 27 (1st Supp.), s. 5; c. 10 (3rd Supp.), s. 1; c. 30 (3rd Supp.), s. 1(1), (3); 1992, c. 1, s. 58(1), Sch. I, items 1(1), (2).

Application to territories — Application of criminal law of England — Common law principles continued.

8. (1) The provisions of this Act apply throughout Canada except

(*a*) in the Yukon Territory, in so far as they are inconsistent with the *Yukon Act*; and

(*b*) in the Northwest Territories, in so far as they are inconsistent with the *Northwest Territories Act*.

(2) The criminal law of England that was in force in a province immediately before April 1, 1955 continues in force in the province except as altered, varied, modified or affected by this Act or any other Act of the Parliament of Canada.

(3) Every rule and principle of the common law that renders any circumstance a justification or excuse for an act or a defence to a charge continues in force and applies in respect of proceedings for an offence under this Act or any other Act of Parliament except in so far as they are altered by or are inconsistent with this Act or any other Act of Parliament.

Criminal offences to be under law of Canada.

9. Notwithstanding anything in this Act or any other Act, no person shall be convicted or discharged under section 736

(*a*) of an offence at common law,

(*b*) of an offence under an Act of the Parliament of England, or of Great Britain, or of the United Kingdom of Great Britain and Ireland, or

(*c*) of an offence under an Act or ordinance in force in any province, territory or place before that province, territory or place became a province of Canada,

but nothing in this section affects the power, jurisdiction or authority that a court, judge, justice or provincial court judge had, immediately before April 1, 1955, to impose punishment for contempt of court. R.S. 1985, c. 27 (1st Supp.), s. 6.

Appeal — Idem — Part XXI applies.

10. (1) Where a court, judge, justice or provincial court judge summarily convicts a person for a contempt of court committed in the face of the court and imposes punishment in respect thereof, that person may appeal

(*a*) from the conviction; or

(*b*) against the punishment imposed.

(2) Where a court or judge summarily convicts a person for a contempt of court not committed in the face of the court and punishment is imposed in respect thereof, that person may appeal

(*a*) from the conviction; or

(*b*) against the punishment imposed.

(3) An appeal under this section lies to the court of appeal of the province in which the proceedings take place, and, for the purposes of this section, the provisions of Part XXI apply, with such modifications as the circumstances require. R.S. 1985, c. 27 (1st Supp.), s. 203.

Civil remedy not suspended.

11. No civil remedy for an act or omission is suspended or affected by reason that the act or omission is a criminal offence.

Offence punishable under more than one Act.

12. Where an act or omission is an offence under more than one Act of Parliament, whether punishable by indictment or on summary conviction, a person who does the act or makes the omission is, unless a contrary intention appears, subject to proceedings under any of those Acts, but is not liable to be punished more than once for the same offence.

Child under twelve.

13. No person shall be convicted of an offence in respect of an act or omission on his part while that person was under the age of twelve years.

Consent to death.

14. No person is entitled to consent to have death inflicted on him, and such consent does not affect the criminal responsibility of any person by whom death may be inflicted on the person by whom consent is given.

Obedience to de facto law.

15. No person shall be convicted of an offence in respect of an act or omission in obedience to the laws for the time being made and enforced by persons in *de facto* possession of the sovereign power in and over the place where the act or omission occurs.

Defences of Mental Disorder — Presumption — Burden of proof.

16. (1) No person is criminally responsible for an act committed or an omission made while suffering from a mental disorder that rendered the person incapable of appreciating the nature and quality of the act or omission or of knowing that it was wrong.

(2) Every person is presumed not to suffer from a mental disorder so as to be exempt from criminal responsibility by virtue of subsection (1), until the contrary is proved on the balance of probabilities.

(3) The burden of proof that an accused was suffering from a mental disorder so as to be exempt from criminal responsibility is on the party that raises the issue. 1991, c. 43, s. 2.

Compulsion by threats.

17. A person who commits an offence under compulsion by threats of immediate death or bodily harm from a person who is present when the offence is committed is excused for committing the offence if the person believes that the threats will be carried out and if the person is not a party to a conspiracy or association whereby the person is subject to compulsion, but this section does not apply where the offence that is committed is high treason or treason, murder, piracy, attempted murder, sexual assault, sexual assault with a weapon, threats to a third party or causing bodily harm, aggravated sexual assault, forcible abduction, hostage taking, robbery, assault with a weapon or causing bodily harm, aggravated assault, unlawfully causing bodily harm, arson or an offence under sections 280 to 283 (abduction and detention of young persons). R.S. 1985, c. 27 (1st Supp.), s. 40(2).

Compulsion of spouse.

18. No presumption arises that a married person who commits an offence does so under compulsion by reason only that the offence is committed in the presence of the spouse of that married person.

Ignorance of the law.

19. Ignorance of the law by a person who commits an offence is not an excuse for committing that offence.

Certain acts on holidays valid.

20. A warrant or summons that is authorized by this Act or an appearance notice, promise to appear, undertaking or recognizance issued, given or entered into in accordance with Part XVI, XXI or XXVII may be issued, executed, given or entered into, as the case may be, on a holiday.

Parties to Offences

Parties to offence — Common intention.

21. (1) Every one is a party to an offence who

(*a*) actually commits it;

(*b*) does or omits to do anything for the purpose of aiding any person to commit it; or

(*c*) abets any person in committing it.

(2) Where two or more persons form an intention in common to carry out an unlawful purpose and to assist each other therein and any one of them, in carrying out the common purpose, commits an offence, each of them who knew or ought to have known that the commission of the offence would be a probable consequence of carrying out the common purpose is a party to that offence.

Person counselling offence — Idem — Definition of "Counsel".

22. (1) Where a person counsels another person to be a party to an offence and that other person is afterwards a party to that offence, the person who counselled is a party to that offence, notwithstanding that the offence was committed in a way different from that which was counselled.

(2) Every one who counsels another person to be a party to an offence is a party to every offence that the other commits in consequence of the counselling that the person who counselled knew or ought to have known was likely to be committed in consequence of the counselling.

(3) For the purposes of this Act, "counsel" includes procure, solicit or incite. R.S. 1985, c. 27 (1st Supp.), s. 7(1).

Accessory after the fact — Husband or wife, when not accessory.

23. (1) An accessory after the fact to an offence is one who, knowing that a person has been a party to the offence, receives, comforts or assists that person for the purpose of enabling that person to escape.

(2) No married person whose spouse has been a party to an offence is an accessory after the fact to that offence by receiving, comforting or assisting the spouse for the purpose of enabling the spouse to escape.

Where one party cannot be convicted.

23.1 For greater certainty, sections 21 to 23 apply in respect of an accused notwithstanding the fact that the person whom the accused aids or abets, counsels or procures or receives, comforts or assists cannot be convicted of the offence. R.S. 1985, c. 24 (2d Supp.), s. 45.

Attempts — Question of law.

24. (1) Every one who, having an intent to commit an offence, does or omits to do anything for the purpose of carrying out the intention is guilty of an attempt to commit the offence whether or not it was possible under the circumstances to commit the offence.

(2) The question whether an act or omission by a person who has an intent to commit an offence is or is not mere preparation to commit the offence, and too remote to constitute an attempt to commit the offence, is a question of law.

Protection of Persons Administering and Enforcing the Law

Protection of persons acting under authority — Idem — When not protected — When protected.

25. (1) Every one who is required or authorized by law to do anything in the administration or enforcement of the law

(*a*) as a private person,

(*b*) as a peace officer or public officer,

(*c*) in aid of a peace officer or public officer, or

(*d*) by virtue of his office,

is, if he acts on reasonable grounds, justified in doing what he is required or authorized to do and in using as much force as is necessary for that purpose.

(2) Where a person is required or authorized by law to execute a process or to carry out a sentence, that person or any person who assists him is, if that person acts in good faith, justified in executing the process or in carrying out the sentence notwithstanding that the process or sentence is defective or that it was issued or imposed without jurisdiction or in excess of jurisdiction.

(3) Subject to subsection (4), a person is not justified for the purposes of subsection (1) in using force that is intended or is likely to cause death or grievous bodily harm unless he believes on reasonable grounds that it is necessary for the purpose of preserving himself or any one under his protection from death or grievous bodily harm.

(4) A peace officer who is proceeding lawfully to arrest, with or without warrant, any person for an offence for which that person may be arrested without warrant, and every one lawfully assisting the peace officer, is justified, if the person to be arrested takes flight to avoid arrest, in using as much force as is necessary to prevent the escape by flight, unless the escape can be prevented by reasonable means in a less violent manner.

Excessive force.

26. Every one who is authorized by law to use force is criminally responsible for any excess thereof according to the nature and quality of the act that constitutes the excess.

Use of force to prevent commission of offence.

27. Every one is justified in using as much force as is reasonably necessary

(*a*) to prevent the commission of an offence

(i) for which, if it were committed, the person who committed it might be arrested without warrant, and

(ii) that would be likely to cause immediate and serious injury to the person or property of anyone, or (*b*) to prevent anything being done that, on reasonable grounds, he believes would, if it were done, be an offence mentioned in paragraph (*a*).

Arrest of wrong person — Person assisting.

28. (1) Where a person who is authorized to execute a warrant to arrest believes, in good faith and on reasonable grounds, that the person whom he arrests is the person named in the warrant, he is protected from criminal responsibility in respect thereof to the same extent as if that person were the person named in the warrant.

(2) Where a person is authorized to execute a warrant to arrest,

(*a*) every one who, being called on to assist him, believes that the person in whose arrest he is called on to assist is the person named in the warrant, and

(*b*) every keeper of a prison who is required to receive and detain a person who he believes has been arrested under the warrant,

is protected from criminal responsibility in respect thereof to the same extent as if that person were the person named in the warrant.

Duty of person arresting — Notice — Failure to comply.

29. (1) It is the duty of every one who executes a process or warrant to have it with him, where it is feasible to do so, and to produce it when requested to do so.

(2) It is the duty of every one who arrests a person, whether with or without a warrant, to give notice to that person, where it is feasible to do so, of

(*a*) the process or warrant under which he makes the arrest; or

(*b*) the reason for the arrest.

(3) Failure to comply with subsection (1) or (2) does not of itself deprive a person who executes a process or warrant, or a person who makes an arrest, or those who assist them, of protection from criminal responsibility.

Preventing breach of peace.

30. Every one who witnesses a breach of the peace is justified in interfering to prevent the continuance or renewal thereof and may detain any person who commits or is about to join in or to renew the breach of the peace, for the purpose of giving him into the custody of a peace officer, if he uses no more force than is reasonably necessary to prevent the continuance or renewal of the breach of the peace or than is reasonably proportioned to the danger to be apprehended from the continuance or renewal of the breach of the peace.

Arrest for breach of peace — Giving person in charge.

31. (1) Every peace officer who witnesses a breach of the peace and every one who lawfully assists the peace officer is justified in arresting any person whom he finds committing the breach of the peace or who, on reasonable grounds, the peace officer believes is about to join in or renew the breach of the peace.

(2) Every peace officer is justified in receiving into custody any person who is given into his charge as having been a party to a breach of the peace by one who has, or who on reasonable grounds the peace officer believes has, witnessed the breach of the peace.

Suppression of Riots

Use of force to suppress riot — Person bound by military law — Obeying order of peace officer — Apprehension of serious mischief — Question of law.

32. (1) Every peace officer is justified in using or in ordering the use of as much force as the peace officer believes, in good faith and on reasonable grounds,

(*a*) is necessary to suppress a riot; and

(*b*) is not excessive, having regard to the danger to be apprehended from the continuance of the riot.

(2) Every one who is bound by military law to obey the command of his superior officer is justified in obeying any command given by his superior officer for the suppression of a riot unless the order is manifestly unlawful.

(3) Every one is justified in obeying an order of a peace officer to use force to suppress a riot if

(*a*) he acts in good faith; and

(*b*) the order is not manifestly unlawful.

(4) Every one who, in good faith and on reasonable grounds, believes that serious mischief will result from a riot before it is possible to secure the attendance of a peace officer is justified in using as much force as he believes in good faith and on reasonable grounds,

(*a*) is necessary to suppress the riot; and

(*b*) is not excessive, having regard to the danger to be apprehended from the continuance of the riot.

(5) For the purposes of this section, the question whether an order is manifestly unlawful or not is a question of law.

Duty of officers if rioters do not disperse — Protection of officers — Section not restrictive.

33. (1) Where the proclamation referred to in section 67 has been made or an offence against paragraph 68(*a*) or (*b*) has been committed, it is the duty of a peace officer and of a person who is lawfully required by him to assist, to disperse or to arrest persons who do not comply with the proclamation.

(2) No civil or criminal proceedings lie against a peace officer or a person

who is lawfully required by a peace officer to assist him in respect of any death or injury that by reason of resistance is caused as a result of the performance by the peace officer or that person of a duty that is imposed by subsection (1).

(3) Nothing in this section limits or affects any powers, duties or functions that are conferred or imposed by this Act with respect to the suppression of riots.

Defence of Person

Self-defence against unprovoked assault — Extent of justification.

34. (1) Every one who is unlawfully assaulted without having provoked the assault is justified in repelling force by force if the force he uses is not intended to cause death or grievous bodily harm and is no more than is necessary to enable him to defend himself.

(2) Every one who is unlawfully assaulted and who causes death or grievous bodily harm in repelling the assault is justified if

(*a*) he causes it under reasonable apprehension of death or grievous bodily harm from the violence with which the assault was originally made or with which the assailant pursues his purposes; and

(*b*) he believes, on reasonable grounds, that he cannot otherwise preserve himself from death or grievous bodily harm.

Self-defence in case of aggression.

35. Every one who has without justification assaulted another but did not commence the assault with intent to cause death or grievous bodily harm, or has without justification provoked an assault on himself by another, may justify the use of force subsequent to the assault if

(*a*) he uses the force

(i) under reasonable apprehension of death or grievous bodily harm from the violence of the person whom he has assaulted or provoked, and

(ii) in the belief, on reasonable grounds, that it is necessary in order to preserve himself from death or grievous bodily harm;

(*b*) he did not, at any time before the necessity of preserving himself from death or grievous bodily harm arose, endeavour to cause death or grievous bodily harm; and

(*c*) he declined further conflict and quitted or retreated from it as far as it was feasible to do so before the necessity of preserving himself from death or grievous bodily harm arose.

Provocation

36. Provocation includes, for the purposes of sections 34 and 35, provocation by blows, words or gestures.

Preventing assault — Extent of justification.

37. (1) Every one is justified in using force to defend himself or any one under his protection from assault, if he uses no more force than is necessary to prevent the assault or the repetition of it.

(2) Nothing in this section shall be deemed to justify the wilful infliction of any hurt or mischief that is excessive, having regard to the nature of the assault that the force used was intended to prevent.

Defence of Property

Defence of personal property — Assault by trespasser.

38. (1) Every one who is in peaceable possession of personal property, and every one lawfully assisting him, is justified

(*a*) in preventing a trespasser from taking it, or

(*b*) in taking it from a trespasser who has taken it,

if he does not strike or cause bodily harm to the trespasser.

(2) Where a person who is in peaceable possession of personal property lays hands on it, a trespasser who persists in attempting to keep it or take it from him or from any one lawfully assisting him shall be deemed to commit an assault without justification or provocation.

Defence with claim of right — Defence without claim of right.

39. (1) Every one who is in peaceable possession of personal property under a claim of right, and every one acting under his authority, is protected from criminal responsibility for defending that possession, even against a person entitled by law to possession of it, if he uses no more force than is necessary.

(2) Every one who is in peaceable possession of personal property, but does not claim it as of right or does not act under the authority of a person who claims it as of right, is not justified or protected from criminal responsibility for defending his possession against a person who is entitled by law to possession of it.

Defence of dwelling.

40. Every one who is in peaceable possession of a dwelling-house, and every one lawfully assisting him or acting under his authority, is justified in using as much force as is necessary to prevent any person from forcibly breaking into or forcibly entering the dwelling-house without lawful authority.

Defence of house or real property — Assault by trespasser.

41. (1) Every one who is in peaceable possession of a dwelling-house or real property, and every one lawfully assisting him or acting under his authority, is justified in using force to prevent any person from trespassing on the dwelling-house or real property, or to remove a trespasser therefrom, if he uses no more force than is necessary.

(2) A trespasser who resists an attempt by a person who is in peaceable possession of a dwelling-house or real property, or a person lawfully assisting him or acting under his authority to prevent his entry or to remove him, shall be deemed to commit an assault without justification or provocation.

Assertion of right to house or real property — Assault in case of lawful entry — Trespasser provoking assault.

42. (1) Every one is justified in peaceably entering a dwelling-house or real property by day to take possession of it if he, or a person under whose authority he acts, is lawfully entitled to possession of it.

(2) Where a person

(*a*) not having peaceable possession of a dwelling-house or real property under a claim of right, or

(*b*) not acting under the authority of a person who has peaceable possession of a dwelling-house or real property under a claim of right,

assaults a person who is lawfully entitled to possession of it and who is entering it peaceably by day to take possession of it, for the purpose of preventing him from entering, the assault shall be deemed to be without justification or provocation.

(3) Where a person

(*a*) having peaceable possession of a dwelling-house or real property under a claim of right, or

(*b*) acting under the authority of a person who has peaceable possession of a dwelling-house or real property under a claim of right,

assaults any person who is lawfully entitled to possession of it and who is entering it peaceably by day to take possession of it, for the purpose of preventing him from entering, the assault shall be deemed to be provoked by the person who is entering.

Protection of Persons in Authority

Correction of child by force.

43. Every schoolteacher, parent or person standing in the place of a parent is justified in using force by way of correction toward a pupil or child, as the case may be, who is under his care, if the force does not exceed what is reasonable under the circumstances.

Master of ship maintaining discipline.

44. The master or officer in command of a vessel on a voyage is justified in using as much force as he believes, on reasonable grounds, is necessary for the purpose of maintaining good order and discipline on the vessel.

Surgical operations.

45. Every one is protected from criminal responsibility for performing a surgical operation on any person for the benefit of that person if

(*a*) the operation is performed with reasonable care and skill; and

(*b*) it is reasonable to perform the operation, having regard to the state of health of the person at the time the operation is performed and to all the circumstances of the case.

PART II

OFFENCES AGAINST PUBLIC ORDER

Treason and other Offences against the Queen's Authority and Person

High treason — Treason — Canadian citizen — Overt act.

46. (1) Every one commits high treason who, in Canada,

(*a*) kills or attempts to kill Her Majesty, or does her any bodily harm tending to death or destruction, maims or wounds her, or imprisons or restrains her;

(*b*) levies war against Canada or does any act preparatory thereto; or

(*c*) assists an enemy at war with Canada, or any armed forces against whom Canadian Forces are engaged in hostilities, whether or not a state of war exists between Canada and the country whose forces they are.

(2) Every one commits treason who, in Canada,

(*a*) uses force or violence for the purpose of overthrowing the government of Canada or a province;

(*b*) without lawful authority, communicates or makes available to an agent of a state other than Canada, military or scientific information or any sketch, plan, model, article, note or document of a military or scientific character that he knows or ought to know may be used by that state for a purpose prejudicial to the safety or defence of Canada;

(*c*) conspires with any person to commit high treason or to do anything mentioned in paragraph (*a*);

(*d*) forms an intention to do anything that is high treason or that is mentioned in paragraph (*a*) and manifests that intention by an overt act; or

(*e*) conspires with any person to do anything mentioned in paragraph (*b*) or forms an intention to do anything mentioned in paragraph (*b*) and manifests that intention by an overt act.

(3) Notwithstanding subsection (1) or (2), a Canadian citizen or a person who owes allegiance to Her Majesty in right of Canada,

(*a*) commits high treason if, while in or out of Canada, he does anything mentioned in subsection (1); or

(*b*) commits treason if, while in or out of Canada, he does anything mentioned in subsection (2).

(4) Where it is treason to conspire with any person, the act of conspiring is an overt act of treason.

Punishment for high treason — Punishment for treason — Corroboration — Minimum punishment.

47. (1) Every one who commits high treason is guilty of an indictable offence and shall be sentenced to imprisonment for life.

(2) Every one who commits treason is guilty of an indictable offence and liable

(*a*) to be sentenced to imprisonment for life if he is guilty of an offence under paragraph 46(2)(*a*), (*c*) or (*d*);

(*b*) to be sentenced to imprisonment for life if he is guilty of an offence under paragraph 46(2)(*b*) or (*e*) committed while a state of war exists between Canada and another country; or

(*c*) to be sentenced to imprisonment for a term not exceeding fourteen years if he is guilty of an offence under paragraph 46(2)(*b*) or (*e*) committed while no state of war exists between Canada and another country.

(3) No person shall be convicted of high treason or treason on the evidence of only one witness, unless the evidence of that witness is corroborated in a material particular by evidence that implicates the accused.

(4) For the purposes of Part XXIII, the sentence of imprisonment for life prescribed by subsection (1) is a minimum punishment.

Limitation — Information for treasonable words.

48. (1) No proceedings for an offence of treason as defined by paragraph 46(2)(*a*) shall be commenced more than three years after the time when the offence is alleged to have been committed.

(2) No proceedings shall be commenced under section 47 in respect of an overt act of treason expressed or declared by open and considered speech unless

(*a*) an information setting out the overt act and the words by which it was expressed or declared is laid under oath before a justice within six days after the time when the words are alleged to have been spoken; and

(*b*) a warrant for the arrest of the accused is issued within ten days after the time when the information is laid.

Prohibited Acts

Acts intended to alarm Her Majesty or break public peace.

49. Every one who wilfully, in the presence of Her Majesty,

(*a*) does an act with intent to alarm Her Majesty or to break the public peace, or

(*b*) does an act that is intended or is likely to cause bodily harm to her Majesty,

is guilty of an indictable offence and liable to imprisonment for a term not exceeding fourteen years.

Assisting alien enemy to leave Canada, or omitting to prevent treason — Punishment.

50. (1) Every one commits an offence who

(*a*) incites or wilfully assists a subject of

(i) a state that is at war with Canada, or

(ii) a state against whose forces Canadian Forces are engaged in hostilities, whether or not a state of war exists between Canada and the state whose forces they are,

to leave Canada without the consent of the Crown, unless the accused establishes that assistance to the state referred to in subparagraph (i) or the forces of the state referred to in subparagraph (ii), as the case may be, was not intended thereby; or

(*b*) knowing that a person is about to commit high treason or treason does not, with all reasonable dispatch, inform a justice of the peace or other peace officer thereof or make other reasonable efforts to prevent that person from committing high treason or treason.

(2) Every one who commits an offence under subsection (1) is guilty of an indictable offence and liable to imprisonment for a term not exceeding fourteen years.

Intimidating Parliament or legislature.

51. Every one who does an act of violence in order to intimidate Parliament or the legislature of a province is guilty of an indictable offence and liable to imprisonment for a term not exceeding fourteen years.

Sabotage — "Prohibited act" — Saving — Idem.

52. (1) Every one who does a prohibited act for a purpose prejudicial to

(*a*) the safety, security or defence of Canada, or

(*b*) the safety or security of the naval, army or air forces of any state other than Canada that are lawfully present in Canada,

is guilty of an indictable offence and liable to imprisonment for a term not exceeding ten years.

(2) In this section, "prohibited act" means an act or omission that

(*a*) impairs the efficiency or impedes the working of any vessel, vehicle, aircraft, machinery, apparatus or other thing; or

(*b*) causes property, by whomever it may be owned, to be lost, damaged or destroyed.

(3) No person does a prohibited act within the meaning of this section by reason only that

(*a*) he stops work as a result of the failure of his employer and himself to agree on any matter relating to his employment;

(*b*) he stops work as a result of the failure of his employer and a bargaining agent acting on his behalf to agree on any matter relating to his employment; or

(*c*) he stops work as a result of his taking part in a combination of workmen or employees for their own reasonable protection as workmen or employees.

(4) No person does a prohibited act within the meaning of this section by

reason only that he attends at or near or approaches a dwelling-house or place for the purpose only of obtaining or communicating information.

Inciting to mutiny.

53. Every one who

(*a*) attempts, for a traitorous or mutinous purpose, to seduce a member of the Canadian Forces from his duty and allegiance to Her Majesty, or

(*b*) attempts to incite or to induce a member of the Canadian Forces to commit a traitorous or mutinous act,

is guilty of an indictable offence and liable to imprisonment for a term not exceeding fourteen years.

Assisting deserter.

54. Every one who aids, assists, harbours or conceals a person who he knows is a deserter or absentee without leave from the Canadian Forces is guilty of an offence punishable on summary conviction, but no proceedings shall be instituted under this section without the consent of the Attorney General of Canada.

Evidence of overt acts.

55. In proceedings for an offence against any provision in section 47 or sections 49 to 53, no evidence is admissible of an overt act unless that overt act is set out in the indictment or unless the evidence is otherwise relevant as tending to prove an overt act that is set out therein.

Offences in relation to members of R.C.M.P.

56. Every one who wilfully

(*a*) persuades or counsels a member of the Royal Canadian Mounted Police to desert or absent himself without leave,

(*b*) aids, assists, harbours or conceals a member of the Royal Canadian Mounted Police who he knows is a deserter or absentee without leave, or

(*c*) aids or assists a member of the Royal Canadian Mounted Police to desert or absent himself without leave, knowing that the member is about to desert or absent himself without leave,

is guilty of an offence punishable on summary conviction. R.S. 1985, c. 27 (1st Supp.), s. 8.

Passports

Forgery of or uttering forged passport — False statement in relation to passport — Possession of forged, etc., passport — Special provisions applicable — "Passport" — Jurisdiction — Appearance of accused at trial.

57. (1) Every one who, while in or out of Canada,

(*a*) forges a passport, or

(*b*) knowing that a passport is forged

(i) uses, deals with or acts on it, or

(ii) causes or attempts to cause any person to use, deal with, or act on it, as if the passport were genuine,

is guilty of an indictable offence and liable to imprisonment for a term not exceeding fourteen years.

(2) Every one who, while in or out of Canada, for the purpose of procuring a passport for himself or any other person or for the purpose of procuring any material alteration or addition to any such passport, makes a written or an oral statement that he knows is false or misleading

(*a*) is guilty of an indictable offence and liable to imprisonment for a term not exceeding two years; or

(*b*) is guilty of an offence punishable on summary conviction.

(3) Every one who without lawful excuse, the proof of which lies on him, has in his possession a forged passport or a passport in respect of which an offence under subsection (2) has been committed is guilty of an indictable offence and liable to imprisonment for a term not exceeding five years.

(4) For the purposes of proceedings under this section,

(*a*) the place where a passport was forged is not material; and

(*b*) the definition "false document" in section 321, section 366 and subsection 367(2) are applicable with such modifications as the circumstances require.

(5) In this section, "passport" means a document issued by or under the authority of the Secretary of State for External Affairs for the purpose of identifying the holder thereof.

(6) Where a person is alleged to have committed, while out of Canada, an offence under this section, proceedings in respect of that offence may, whether or not that person is in Canada, be commenced in any territorial division in Canada and the accused may be tried and punished in respect of that offence in the same manner as if the offence had been committed in that territorial division.

(7) For greater certainty, the provisions of this Act relating to

(*a*) requirements that an accused appear at and be present during proceedings, and

(*b*) the exceptions to those requirements,

apply to proceedings commenced in any territorial division pursuant to subsection (6). R.S. 1985, c. 27 (1st Supp.), s. 9.

Fraudulent use of certificate of citizenship — "Certificate of citizenship", "certificate of naturalization".

58. (1) Every one who, while in or out of Canada,

(*a*) uses a certificate of citizenship or a certificate of naturalization for a fraudulent purpose, or

(*b*) being a person to whom a certificate of citizenship or a certificate of naturalization has been granted, knowingly parts with the possession of that certificate with intent that it should be used for a fraudulent purpose,

is guilty of an indictable offence and liable to imprisonment for a term not exceeding two years.

(2) In this section, "certificate of citizenship" and "certificate of naturalization", respectively, mean a certificate of citizenship and a certificate of naturalization as defined by the *Citizenship Act*.

Sedition

Seditious words — Seditious libel — Seditious conspiracy — Seditious intention.

59. (1) Seditious words are words that express a seditious intention.

(2) A seditious libel is a libel that expresses a seditious intention.

(3) A seditious conspiracy is an agreement between two or more persons to carry out a seditious intention.

(4) Without limiting the generality of the meaning of the expression "seditious intention", every one shall be presumed to have a seditious intention who

(*a*) teaches or advocates, or

(*b*) publishes or circulates any writing that advocates,

the use, without the authority of law, of force as a means of accomplishing a governmental change within Canada.

Exception.

60. Notwithstanding subsection 59(4), no person shall be deemed to have a seditious intention by reason only that he intends, in good faith,

(*a*) to show that Her Majesty has been misled or mistaken in her measures;

(*b*) to point out errors or defects in

(i) the government or constitution of Canada or a province,

(ii) Parliament or the legislature of a province, or

(iii) the administration of justice in Canada;

(*c*) to procure, by lawful means, the alteration of any matter of government in Canada; or

(*d*) to point out, for the purpose of removal, matters that produce or tend to produce feelings of hostility and ill-will between different classes of persons in Canada.

Punishment of seditious offences.

61. Every one who

(*a*) speaks seditious words,

(*b*) publishes a seditious libel, or

(*c*) is a party to a seditious conspiracy,

is guilty of an indictable offence and liable to imprisonment for a term not exceeding fourteen years.

Offences in relation to military forces — "Member of a force".

62. (1) Every one who wilfully

(*a*) interferes with, impairs or influences the loyalty or discipline of a member of a force,

(*b*) publishes, edits, issues, circulates or distributes a writing that advises, counsels or urges insubordination, disloyalty, mutiny or refusal of duty by a member of a force, or

(*c*) advises, counsels, urges or in any manner causes insubordination, disloyalty, mutiny or refusal of duty by a member of a force,

is guilty of an indictable offence and liable to imprisonment for a term not exceeding five years.

(2) In this section, "member of a force" means a member of

(*a*) the Canadian Forces; or

(*b*) the naval, army or air forces of a state other than Canada that are lawfully present in Canada.

Unlawful Assemblies and Riots

Unlawful assembly — Lawful assembly becoming unlawful — Exception.

63. (1) An unlawful assembly is an assembly of three or more persons who, with intent to carry out any common purpose, assemble in such a manner or so conduct themselves when they are assembled as to cause persons in the neighbourhood of the assembly to fear, on reasonable grounds, that they

(*a*) will disturb the peace tumultuously; or

(*b*) will by that assembly needlessly and without reasonable cause provoke other persons to disturb the peace tumultuously.

(2) Persons who are lawfully assembled may become an unlawful assembly if they conduct themselves with a common purpose in a manner that would have made the assembly unlawful if they had assembled in that manner for that purpose.

(3) Persons are not unlawfully assembled by reason only that they are assembled to protect the dwelling-house of any one of them against persons who are threatening to break and enter it for the purpose of committing an indictable offence therein.

Riot.

64. A riot is an unlawful assembly that has begun to disturb the peace tumultuously.

Punishment of rioter.

65. Every one who takes part in a riot is guilty of an indictable offence and liable to imprisonment for a term not exceeding two years.

Punishment for unlawful assembly

66. Every one who is a member of an unlawful assembly is guilty of an offence punishable on summary conviction.

Reading proclamation.

67. A justice, mayor or sheriff, or the lawful deputy of a mayor or sheriff, who receives notice that, at any place within his jurisdiction, twelve or more persons are unlawfully and riotously assembled together shall go to that place and, after approaching as near as safely he may do, if he is satisfied that a riot is in progress, shall command silence and thereupon make or cause to be made in a loud voice a proclamation in the following words or to the like effect:

Her Majesty the Queen charges and commands all persons being assembled immediately to disperse and peaceably to depart to their habitations or to their lawful business on the pain of being guilty of an offence for which, on conviction, they may be sentenced to imprisonment for life. GOD SAVE THE QUEEN.

Offences related to proclamation.

68. Every one is guilty of an indictable offence and liable to imprisonment for life who

(*a*) opposes, hinders or assaults, wilfully and with force, a person who begins to make or is about to begin to make or is making the proclamation referred to in section 67 so that it is not made;

(*b*) does not peaceably disperse and depart from a place where the proclamation referred to in section 67 is made within thirty minutes after it is made; or

(*c*) does not depart from a place within thirty minutes when he has reasonable grounds to believe that the proclamation referred to in section 67 would have been made in that place if some person had not opposed, hindered or assaulted, wilfully and with force, a person who would have made it.

Neglect by peace officer.

69. A peace officer who receives notice that there is a riot within his jurisdiction and, without reasonable excuse, fails to take all reasonable steps to suppress the riot is guilty of an indictable offence and liable to imprisonment for a term not exceeding two years.

Unlawful Drilling

Orders by Governor in Council — General or special order — Punishment.

70. (1) The Governor in Council may by proclamation, make orders

(*a*) to prohibit assemblies, without lawful authority, of persons for the purpose

(i) of training or drilling themselves,

(ii) of being trained or drilled to the use of arms, or

(iii) of practising military exercises; or

(*b*) to prohibit persons when assembled for any purpose from training or drilling themselves or from being trained or drilled.

(2) An order that is made under subsection (1) may be general or may be made applicable to particular places, districts or assemblies to be specified in the order.

(3) Every one who contravenes an order made under this section is guilty of an indictable offence and liable to imprisonment for a term not exceeding five years.

Duels

Duelling.

71. Every one who

(*a*) challenges or attempts by any means to provoke another person to fight a duel,

(*b*) attempts to provoke a person to challenge another person to fight a duel, or

(*c*) accepts a challenge to fight a duel,

is guilty of an indictable offence and liable to imprisonment for a term not exceeding two years.

Forcible Entry and Detainer

Forcible entry — Matters not material — Forcible detainer — Questions of law.

72. (1) A person commits forcible entry when that person enters real property that is in the actual and peaceable possession of another in a manner that is likely to cause a breach of the peace or reasonable apprehension of a breach of the peace.

(1.1) For the purposes of subsection (1), it is immaterial whether or not a person is entitled to enter the real property or whether or not that person has any intention of taking possession of the real property.

(2) A person commits forcible detainer when, being in actual possession

of real property without colour of right, he detains it in a manner that is likely to cause a breach of the peace or reasonable apprehension of a breach of the peace, against a person who is entitled by law to possession of it.

(3) The questions whether a person is in actual and peaceable possession or is in actual possession without colour of right are questions of law. R.S. 1985, c. 27 (1st Supp.), s. 10.

Punishment.

73. Every person who commits forcible entry or forcible detainer is guilty of

(*a*) an offence punishable on summary conviction; or

(*b*) an indictable offence and liable to imprisonment for a term not exceeding two years. R.S. 1985, c. 27 (1st Supp.), s. 11; 1992, c. 1, s. 58(1), Sch. I, item 2.

Piracy

Piracy by law of nations — Punishment.

74. (1) Every one commits piracy who does any act that, by the law of nations, is piracy.

(2) Every one who commits piracy while in or out of Canada is guilty of an indictable offence and liable to imprisonment for life.

Piratical acts.

75. Every one who, while in or out of Canada,

(*a*) steals a Canadian ship,

(*b*) steals or without lawful authority throws overboard, damages or destroys anything that is part of the cargo, supplies or fittings in a Canadian ship,

(*c*) does or attempts to do a mutinous act on a Canadian ship, or

(*d*) counsels a person to do anything mentioned in paragraph (*a*), (*b*) or (*c*),

is guilty of an indictable offence and liable to imprisonment for a term not exceeding fourteen years. R.S. 1985, c. 27 (1st Supp.) s. 7(3).

Offences Relating to Aircraft

Hijacking.

76. Every one who, unlawfully, by force or threat thereof, or by any other form of intimidation, seizes or exercises control of an aircraft with intent

(*a*) to cause any person on board the aircraft to be confined or imprisoned against his will,

(*b*) to cause any person on board the aircraft to be transported against his will to any place other than the next scheduled place of landing of the aircraft, (*c*) to hold any person on board the aircraft for ransom or to service against his will, or

(*d*) to cause the aircraft to deviate in a material respect from its flight plan,

is guilty of an indictable offence and liable to imprisonment for life.

Endangering safety of aircraft in flight and rendering aircraft incapable of flight.

77. Every one who,

(*a*) on board an aircraft in flight, commits an assault that is likely to endanger the safety of the aircraft,

(*b*) causes damage to an aircraft in service that renders the aircraft incapable of flight or that is likely to endanger the safety of the aircraft in flight,

(*c*) places or causes to be placed on board an aircraft in service anything that is likely to cause damage to the aircraft that will render it incapable of flight or that is likely to endanger the safety of the aircraft in flight,

(*d*) causes damages to or interferes with the operation of any air navigation facility where the damage or interference is likely to endanger the safety of an aircraft in flight, or

(*e*) endangers the safety of an aircraft in flight by communicating to any other person any information that he knows to be false,

is guilty of an indictable offence and liable to imprisonment for life.

Offensive weapons and explosive substances — Definition of "civil aircraft".

78. (1) Every one, other than a peace officer engaged in the execution of his duty, who takes on board a civil aircraft an offensive weapon or any explosive substance

(*a*) without the consent of the owner or operator of the aircraft or of a person duly authorized by either of them to consent thereto, or

(*b*) with the consent referred to in paragraph (*a*) but without complying with all terms and conditions on which the consent was given,

is guilty of an indictable offence and liable to imprisonment for a term not exceeding fourteen years.

(2) For the purposes of this section, "civil aircraft" means all aircraft other than aircraft operated by the Canadian Forces, a police force in Canada or persons engaged in the administration or enforcement of the *Customs Act* or the *Excise Act*. R.S. 1985, c. 1 (2d Supp.), Sched. III.

Dangerous Substances

Duty of care re explosive.

79. Every one who has an explosive substance in his possession or under his care or control is under a legal duty to use reasonable care to prevent bodily harm or death to persons or damage to property by that explosive substance.

Breach of duty.

80. Every one who, being under a legal duty within the meaning of section 79, fails without lawful excuse to perform that duty, is guilty of an indictable offence and, if as a result an explosion of an explosive substance occurs that

(*a*) causes death or is likely to cause death to any person, is liable to imprisonment for life; or

(*b*) causes bodily harm or damage to property or is likely to cause bodily harm or damage to property, is liable to imprisonment for a term not exceeding fourteen years.

Using Explosives — Punishment.

81. (1) Every one commits an offence who

(*a*) does anything with intent to cause an explosion of an explosive substance that is likely to cause serious bodily harm or death to persons or is likely to cause serious damage to property;

(*b*) with intent to do bodily harm to any person

(i) causes an explosive substance to explode,

(ii) sends or delivers to a person or causes a person to take or receive an explosive substance or any other dangerous substance or thing, or

(iii) places or throws anywhere or at or on a person a corrosive fluid, explosive substance or any other dangerous substance or thing;

(*c*) with intent to destroy or damage property without lawful excuse, places or throws an explosive substance anywhere; or

(*d*) makes or has in his possession or has under his care or control any explosive substance with intent thereby

(i) to endanger life or to cause serious damage to property, or

(ii) to enable another person to endanger life or to cause serious damage to property.

(2) Every one who commits an offence under subsection (1) is guilty of an indictable offence and liable

(*a*) for an offence under paragraph (1)(*a*) or (*b*) , to imprisonment for life, or

(*b*) for an offence under paragraph (1)(*c*) or (*d*), to imprisonment for a term not exceeding fourteen years.

Possession without lawful excuse.

82. Every one who, without lawful excuse, the proof of which lies on him, makes or has in his possession or under his care or control any explosive substance is guilty of an indictable offence and liable to imprisonment for a term not exceeding five years. R.S. 1985, c. 27 (1st Supp.), s. 12.

Prize Fights

Engaging in prize fight — Definition of "prize fight".

83. (1) Every one who

(*a*) engages as a principal in a prize fight,

(*b*) advises, encourages or promotes a prize fight, or

(*c*) is present at a prize fight as an aid, second, surgeon, umpire, backer or reporter,

is guilty of an offence punishable on summary conviction.

(2) In this section, "prize fight" means an encounter or fight with fists or hands between two persons who have met for that purpose by previous arrangement made by or for them, but a boxing contest between amateur sportsmen, where the contestants wear boxing gloves of not less than one hundred and forty grams each in mass, or any boxing contest held with the permission or under the authority of an athletic board or commission or similar body established by or under the authority of the legislature of a province for the control of sport within the province, shall be deemed not to be a prize fight. R.S. 1985, c. 27 (1st Supp.), s. 186.

PART III

FIREARMS AND OTHER OFFENSIVE WEAPONS

Interpretation

Definitions — "Antique firearm" — "Chief provincial firearms officer" — "Commissioner" — "Firearm" — "Firearms acquisition certificate" — "Firearms officer" — "Local registrar of firearms" — "Permit" — "Prohibited weapon" — "Registration certificate" — "Regulations" — "Restricted weapon" — Certain weapons deemed not to be firearms — Designated officer or constable.

84. (1) For the purposes of this Part,

"antique firearm" means any firearm manufactured before 1898 that was not designed to use rim-fire or centre-fire ammunition and that has not been redesigned to use such ammunition or, if so designed or redesigned, is capable only of using rim-fire or centre-fire ammunition that is no longer commercially manufactured;

[1991, c. 40, s. 2(1) will repeal the definition "antique firearm" and substitute the following.]

"antique firearm" means any firearm manufactured before 1898 that was not designed to use rim-fire or centre-fire ammunition and that has not been redesigned to use such ammunition, or, if so designed or redesigned, is capable only of using rim-fire or centre-fire ammunition that is not commonly available in Canada;

"chief provincial firearms officer" means a person who has been designated in writing by the Attorney General of a province as the chief provincial firearms officer for that province;

"Commissioner" means the Commissioner of the Royal Canadian Mounted Police;

"firearm" means any barrelled weapon from which any shot, bullet or other missile can be discharged and that is capable of causing serious bodily injury or death to a person, and includes any frame or receiver of such a barrelled weapon and anything that can be adapted for use as a firearm;

[1991, c. 40, s. 2(1) will repeal the definition "firearm" and substitute the following.]

"firearm" means any barrelled weapon from which any shot, bullet or other projectile can be discharged and that is capable of causing serious bodily injury or death to a person, and includes any frame or receiver of such a barrelled weapon and anything that can be adapted for use as a firearm;

"firearms acquisition certificate" means a firearms acquisition certificate issued by a firearms officer under section 106 or a hunting licence, certificate, permit or other document issued under the authority of a law of a province that, by virtue of an order issued under section 107, is deemed to be a firearms acquisition certificate;

[1991, c. 40, s. 2(1) will repeal the definition "firearms acquisition certificate" and substitute the following.]

"firearms acquisition certificate" means a firearms acquisition certificate issued by a firearms officer under section 106 or 107;

"firearms officer" means any person who has been designated in writing as a firearms officer by the Commissioner or the Attorney General of a province or who is a member of a class of persons that has been so designated;

[1991, c. 40, s. 2(5) will further amend s. 84(1) by adding the following.]

"Genuine gun collector" — "Large-capacity cartridge magainze".

"genuine gun collector" means an individual who possesses or seeks to acquire one or more restricted weapons that are related or distinguished by historical, technological or scientific characteristics, has knowledge of those characteristics, has consented to the periodic inspection, conducted in a reasonable manner and in accordance with the regulations, of the premises in which the restricted weapons are to be kept and has complied with such other requirements as are prescribed by regulation respecting knowledge, secure storage and the keeping of records in respect of the restricted weapons;

"large-capacity cartridge magazine" means any device or container from which ammunition may be fed into the firing chamber of a firearm;

"local registrar of firearms" means any person who has been designated in writing as a local registrar of firearms by the Commissioner or the Attorney General of a province or who is a member of a class of police officers or police constables that has been so designated;

"permit" means a permit issued under section 110;

"prohibited weapon" means

(*a*) any device or contrivance designed or intended to muffle or stop the sound or report of a firearm,

(*b*) any knife that has a blade that opens automatically by gravity or centrifugal force or by hand pressure applied to a button, spring or other device in or attached to the handle of the knife,

(*c*) any firearm, not being a restricted weapon described in paragraph (*c*) of the definition of that expression in this subsection, that is capable of firing bullets in rapid succession during one pressure of the trigger,

[1991, c. 40, s. 2(2) will repeal paragraph (*c*) of the definition "prohibited weapon" and substitute the following.]

(*c*) any firearm, not being a restricted weapon described in paragraph (*c*) or (*c.1*) of the definition of that expression in this subsection, that is capable of, or assembled or designed and manufactured with the capability of, firing projectiles in rapid succession during one pressure of the trigger, whether or not it has been altered to fire only one projectile with one such pressure,

(*d*) any firearm adapted from a rifle or shotgun, whether by sawing, cutting or other alteration or modification, that, as so adapted, has a barrel that is less than 457 mm in length or that is less than 660 mm in overall length, or

(*e*) a weapon of any kind, not being an antique firearm or a firearm of a kind commonly used in Canada for hunting or sporting purposes, that is declared by order of the Governor in Council to be a prohibited weapon;

[1991, c. 40, s. 2(3) will strike out the word "or" at the end of paragraph (*d*) and repeal paragraph (*e*) and substitute the following.]

(*e*) a weapon of any kind, not being an antique firearm or a firearm of a kind commonly used in Canada for hunting or sporting purposes, or a part, component or accessory of such a weapon, or any ammunition, that is declared by order of the Governor in Counci to be a prohibited weapon, or

(*f*) a large-capacity cartridge magazine prescribed by regulation;

"registration certificate" means a restricted weapon registration certificate issued under section 109;

"regulations" means regulations made by the Governor in Council pursuant to section 116;

"restricted weapon" means

(*a*) any firearm, not being a prohibited weapon, designed, altered or intended to be aimed and fired by the action of one hand,

(*b*) any firearm that

(i) is not a prohibited weapon, has a barrel that is less than 470 mm in length and is capable of discharging centre-fire ammunition in a semi-automatic manner, or

(ii) is designed or adapted to be fired when reduced to a length of less than 660 mm by folding, telescoping or otherwise, or

(*c*) any firearm that is designed, altered or intended to fire bullets in rapid succession during one pressure of the trigger and that, on January 1, 1978, was registered as a restricted weapon and formed part of a gun collection in Canada of a genuine gun collector, or

[1991, c. 40, s. 2(4) will amend the definition "restricted weapon" by striking out the word "or" at the end of paragraph (*c*) and adding the following.]

(*c.1*) any firearm that is assembled or designed and manufactured with the capability of firing projectiles in rapid succession with one pressure of the trigger, to the extent that

(i) the firearm is altered to fire only one projectile with one such pressure,

(ii) on October 1, 1992, the firearm was registered as a restricted weapon, or an application for a registration certificate was made to a local regstrar of firearms in respect of the firearm, and the firearm formed part of a gun collection in Canada of a genuine gun collector, and

(iii) subsections 109(4.1) and (4.2) were complied with in respect of that firearm, or

(*d*) a weapon of any kind, not being a prohibited weapon or a shotgun or rifle of a kind that, in the opinion of the Governor in Council, is reasonable for use in Canada for hunting or sporting purposes, that is declared by order of the Governor in Council to be a restricted weapon.

[1991, c. 40, s. 2(6) will amend s. 84 by adding the following immediately after subsection (1).]

Barrel length — Weapon to be a restricted weapon.

(1.1) For the purposes of paragraph (*d*) of the definition "prohibited weapon" and of subparagraph (*b*)(i) of the definition "restricted weapon" in subsection (1), the length of a barrel of a firearm means

(*a*) in the case of a revolver, the distance from the muzzle of the barrel to the breach end immediately in front of the cylinder; and

(*b*) in any other case, the distance from the muzzle of the barrel to and including the chamber, but not including the length of any part or accessory including parts or accessories designed or intended to suppress the muzzle flash or reduce recoil.

(1.2) Where the Governor in Council makes an order referred to in paragraph (*e*) of the definition "prohibited weapon" in subsection (1), the Governor in Council may also, by order, declare that a person who possesses a weapon referred to in that paragraph prior to the coming into force of the order referred to in that paragraph shall only retain the ownership and possession of the weapon if the person obtains a registration certificate in respect of the weapon in accordance with section 109 and, where the Governor in Council makes such an order, the weapon is deemed to be a restricted weapon for that person for the purposes of this Act.

(2) Notwithstanding the definition "firearm" in subsection (1), for the purposes of the definitions "prohibited weapon" and "restricted weapon" in that subsection and for the purpose of section 93, subsections 97(1) and (3) and sections 102, 104, 105 and 116, the following weapons shall be deemed not to be firearms:

(*a*) an antique firearm unless

(i) but for this subsection, it would be a restricted weapon, and

(ii) the person in possession thereof intends to discharge it;

(*b*) any device designed, and intended by the person in possession thereof, for use exclusively for

(i) signalling, notifying of distress or firing stud cartridges, explosive-driven rivets or similar industrial ammunition, or

(ii) firing blank cartridges;

(*c*) any shooting device designed, and intended by the person in possession thereof, for use exclusively for

(i) slaughtering of domestic animals,

(ii) tranquilizing animals, or

(iii) discharging projectiles with lines attached thereto; and

(*d*) any other barrelled weapon where it is proved that that weapon is not designed or adapted to discharge a shot, bullet or other missile at a muzzle velocity exceeding 152.4 m per second or to discharge a shot, bullet or other missile that is designed or adapted to attain a velocity exceeding 152.4 m per second.

[1991, c. 40, s. 2(7) will repeal paragraph 84(2)(d) and substitute the following.]

(*d*) any other barrelled weapon where it is proved that that weapon is not designed or adapted to discharge a shot, bullet or other projectile at a muzzle velocity exceeding 152.4 m per second or to discharge a shot, bullet or other projectile that is designed or adapted to attain a velocity exceeding 152.4 m per second.

(3) A police officer or police constable designated in writing by the Commissioner or the Attorney General of a province for the purposes of this subsection or who is a member of a class of police officers or police constables that has been so designated may perform such functions and duties of a local registrar of firearms under subsections 109(1) to (6) and subsections 110(3) and (4) as are specified in the designation. R.S. 1985, c. 27 (1st Supp.), s. 186.

Offences Related to the Use of Firearms and other Offensive Weapons

Use of firearm during commission of offence, etc. — Sentences to be served consecutively.

85. (1) Every one who uses a firearm

(*a*) while committing or attempting to commit an indictable offence, or

(*b*) during his flight after committing or attempting to commit an indictable offence,

whether or not he causes or means to cause bodily harm to any person as a result thereof, is guilty of an indictable offence and liable to imprisonment

(*c*) in the case of a first offence, except as provided in paragraph (*d*), for not more than fourteen years and not less than one year, and

(*d*) in the case of a second or subsequent offence, or in the case of a first offence committed by a person who, prior to January 1, 1978, was convicted of an indictable offence or an attempt to commit an indictable offence, in the course of which or during his flight after the commission or attempted commission of which he used a firearm, for not more than fourteen years and not less than three years.

(2) A sentence imposed on a person for an offence under subsection (1) shall be served consecutively to any other punishment imposed on him for an offence arising out of the same event or series of events and to any other sentence to which he is subject at the time the sentence is imposed on him for an offence under subsection (1).

Pointing a firearm — Careless use, etc., of firearm.

86. (1) Every one who, without lawful excuse, points a firearm at another person, whether the firearm is loaded or unloaded,

(*a*) is guilty of an indictable offence and liable to imprisonment for a term not exceeding five years; or

(*b*) is guilty of an offence punishable on summary conviction.

(2) Every one who, without lawful excuse, uses, carries, handles, ships or stores any firearm or ammunition in a careless manner or without reasonable precautions for the safety of other persons

(*a*) is guilty of an indictable offence and liable to imprisonment

(i) in the case of a first offence, for a term not exceeding two years, and

(ii) in the case of a second or subsequent offence, for a term not exceeding five years; or

(*b*) is guilty of an offence punishable on summary conviction.

[1991, c. 40, s. 3 will repeal subsection 86(2) and substitute the following.]

Careless handling of firearm — Storage, etc. of firearms.

(2) Every person who uses, carries, handles, ships or stores any firearm or ammunition in a manner that shows wanton or reckless disregard for the lives or safety of other persons

(*a*) is guilty of an indictable offence and liable to imprisonment for a term not exceeding five years; or

(*b*) is guilty of an offence punishable on summary conviction.

(3) Every person who stores, displays, handles or transports any firearm in a manner contrary to a regulation made under paragraph 116(1)(g)

(*a*) is guilty of an indictable offence and liable to imprisonment for a term not exceeding two years; or

(*b*) is guilty of an offence punishable on summary conviction.

Offences Related to Possession of Firearms and other Offensive Weapons

Possession of weapon or imitation.

87. Every one who carries or has in his possession a weapon or imitation thereof, for a purpose dangerous to the public peace or for the purpose of committing an offence, is guilty of an indictable offence and liable to imprisonment for a term not exceeding ten years.

While attending public meeting.

88. Every one who, without lawful excuse, has a weapon in his possession while he is attending or is on his way to attend a public meeting is guilty of an offence punishable on summary conviction.

Carrying concealed weapon.

89. Every one who carries a weapon concealed, unless he is the holder of a permit under which he may lawfully so carry it,

(*a*) is guilty of an indictable offence and liable to imprisonment for a term not exceeding five years; or

(*b*) is guilty of an offence punishable on summary conviction.

Possession of prohibited weapon — Prohibited weapon in motor vehicle — Saving provision — Classes of persons — Idem.

90. (1) Every one who has in his possession a prohibited weapon

(*a*) is guilty of an indictable offence and liable to imprisonment for a term not exceeding five years; or

[1991, c. 40, s. 4(1) will repeal paragraph 90(1)(*a*) and substitute the following.]

(*a*) is guilty of an indictable offence and liable to imprisonment for a term not exceeding ten years; or

(*b*) is guilty of an offence punishable on summary conviction.

(2) Every one who is an occupant of a motor vehicle in which he knows there is a prohibited weapon

(*a*) is guilty of an indictable offence and liable to imprisonment for a term not exceeding five years; or

(*b*) is guilty of an offence punishable on summary conviction.

(3) Subsection (1) does not apply to a person who comes into possession of a prohibited weapon by operation of law and thereafter, with reasonable despatch, lawfully disposes thereof.

(3.1) Subsection (1) does not apply in a province with respect to any person designated by the Attorney General of the province if the person belongs to a class of persons who require a prohibited weapon described in paragraph (*c*) or (*e*) of the definition "prohibited weapon" in subsection 84(1) or components or parts thereof for a purpose that the Governor in Council prescribes by regulation to be an industrial purpose.

[1991, c. 40, s. 4(2) will amend section 90 by adding the following immediately after subsection (3).]

Classes of persons — Large-capacity cartridge magazines.

(3.1) Subsection (1) does not apply in a province with respect to any person designated by the Attorney General of the province as a person who belongs to a class of persons who require a prohibited weapon described in paragraph (*c*), (*e*) or (*f*) of the definition "prohibited weapon" in subsection 84(1) or any component or part thereof for a purpose that the Governor in Council prescribes by regulation to be an industrial purpose, or to any person who is under the direct and immediate supervision of such a person.

(3.2) Notwithstanding anything in this Act, no person is guilty of an offence under subsection (1) by reason only that the person possesses a prohibited weapon described in paragraph (*f*) of the definition of that expression in subsection 84(1), where

(*a*) that person has been authorized in writing by the local registrar of firearms to be a person who may possess such a weapon for use in conjunction with a firearm that is suitable for use in shooting competitions designated by the Attorney General and is lawfully possessed by the person and where that person has complied with all conditions for the possession of that weapon that are prescribed by regulations or that are required by the local registrar of firearms in the particular circumstances and in the interests of the safety of the person or of any other person; or

(*b*) that person is a person who is designated for the purposes of paragraph 95(2)(*b*).

(4) Subsection (2) does not apply to an occupant of a motor vehicle in which there is a prohibited weapon where, by virtue of subsection (3) or section 92, subsection (1) does not apply to the person who is in possession of that weapon. S.C. 1991, c. 28, s. 6.

[1991, c. 40, s. 4(3) will add after section 90 the following.]

Refusal and notification — Request for reference to judge — Hearing — Burden of proof — Order — Appeal — Definition of "appeal court".

90.1 (1) Where, pursuant to paragraph 90(3.2)(*a*), a local registrar of firearms refuses to authorize in writing that a person is a person who may possess a prohibited weapon referred to in that paragraph for use in conjunction with a firearm that is suitable for use in shooting competitions designated by the Attorney General, the local registrar of firearms shall notify the person in writing of the refusal and the reasons for it and include in the notification a copy of this section.

(2) A person who has received a notification referred to in subsection (1) may, within 30 days after receiving the notification or within such time as is, before or after the expiration of that period, allowed by a provincial court judge, request in writing the local registrar of firearms to refer the matter to a provincial court judge having jurisdiction in the territorial division in which the person resides.

(3) On a reference by the local registrar of firearms pursuant to subsection (2), the provincial court judge shall fix a date for the hearing of the reference and direct that notice of the hearing be given to the person and to the local registrar of firearms, in such manner as the provincial court judge may specify.

(4) In a hearing under subsection (3) the burden of proof is on the person to satisfy the provincial court judge that the refusal was not justified.

(5) Where at the conclusion of the hearing under subsection (3), the person has satisfied the provincial court judge that the refusal was not justified, the provincial court judge shall, by order, direct the local registrar of firearms to authorize in writing that the person may possess a prohibited weapon referred to in paragraph 90(3.2)(*a*) for use in conjunction with a firearm that is suitable for use in shooting competitions designated by the Attorney General and the local registrar of firearms shall immediately comply with the order.

(6) Where a provincial court judge makes an order pursuant to subsection (5), the local registrar of firearms may appeal to the appeal court against the order and the provisions of Part XXVII except sections 816 to 819 and 829 to 836 apply, with such modifications as the circumstances require, in respect of the appeal.

(7) In this section, "appeal court" has the meaning given that expression in subsection 100(11).

Possession of unregistered restricted weapon — Possession elsewhere than at place authorized — Restricted weapon in motor vehicle — Saving provision — Idem — Idem.

91. (1) Every one who has in his possession a restricted weapon for which he does not have a registration certificate

(*a*) is guilty of an indictable offence and liable to imprisonment for a term not exceeding five years; or

(*b*) is guilty of an offence punishable on summary conviction.

(2) Every one who has in his possession a restricted weapon elsewhere than at the place at which he is entitled to possess it, as indicated on the registration certificate issued therefor, is, unless he is the holder of a permit under which he may lawfully so possess it,

(*a*) guilty of an indictable offence and liable to imprisonment for a term not exceeding five years; or

(*b*) guilty of an offence punishable on summary conviction.

(3) Every one who is an occupant of a motor vehicle in which he knows there is a restricted weapon is, unless some occupant of the motor vehicle is the holder of a permit under which he may lawfully have that weapon in his possession in the vehicle, or he establishes that he had reason to believe that some occupant of the motor vehicle was the holder of such permit,

(*a*) guilty of an indictable offence and liable to imprisonment for a term not exceeding five years; or

(*b*) guilty of an offence punishable on summary conviction.

(4) Subsection (1) does not apply to a person

(*a*) to whom a permit relating to a restricted weapon has been issued under subsection 110(3) or (4) and who has the weapon in his possession for the purpose for which that permit was issued;

[1991, c. 40, s. 5(1) will repeal paragraph 91(4)(*a*) and substitute the following.]

(*a*) in respect of a restricted weapon, where a permit relating to the restricted weapon has been issued under subsection 110(1), (2.1) or (3.1) and the person is not the person mentioned in the registration certificate issued in respect of that restricted weapon;

(*a.1*) to whom a permit relating to a restricted weapon has been issued under subsection 110(3) or (4) and who possesses the weapon for the purpose for which that permit was issued;

(*b*) who has a restricted weapon in his possession while he is under the immediate supervision of a person who may lawfully possess the weapon for the purpose of using the weapon in a manner in which the supervising person may lawfully use it; or

(*c*) who comes into possession of a restricted weapon by operation of law and thereafter, with reasonable despatch, lawfully disposes of it or obtains a registration certificate or permit under which he may lawfully possess it.

[1991, c. 40, s. 5(2) will amend section 91 by adding the following immediately after subsection (4).]

Idem.

(4.1) Subsection (2) does not apply to a person to whom a permit to possess a particular restricted weapon has been issued under subsection 110(1) where the person is not the person mentioned in the registration certificate issued in respect of the restricted weapon, when the person to whom the permit has been issued possesses the restricted weapon at the place authorized by the permit.

(5) Subsection (3) does not apply to an occupant of a motor vehicle in which there is a restricted weapon where, by virtue of subsection (4) or section 92, subsections (1) and (2) do not apply to the person who is in possession of that weapon.

(6) Subject to sections 100 and 103, subsection 105(4) and to a condition of a probation order referred to in paragraph 737(2)(*d*), nothing in this Act makes it unlawful for a person to be in possession of a restricted weapon in the ordinary course of a business described in paragraph 105(1)(*a*) or subparagraph 105(2)(*b*)(ii). S.C. 1991, c. 28, s. 7.

[1991, c. 40, s. 36 will repeal subsection 91(6) and substitute the following.]

Idem.

(6) Subject to sections 100 and 103, subsection 105(4) and to a condition of a probation order referred to in paragraph 737(2)(*d*), nothing in this Act makes it unlawful for a person to be in possession of a restricted weapon, other than a restricted weapon described in paragraph (*c.1*) of the definition

of that expression in subsection 84(1), in the ordinary course of a business described in paragraph 105(1)(*a*) or (*b*) or subparagraph 105(2)(*b*)(ii).

[1991, c. 40, s. 6 will add the following immediately after section 91.]

Amnesty periods — Idem.

91.1(1) The Governor in Council may make orders specifying periods of time as amnesty periods with respect to weapons or classes of weapons, or explosive substances, and where the Governor in Council makes such an order, no person who, during that period, delivers such a weapon or explosive substance that is unlawfully in the person's possession to a peace officer, local registrar of firearms or firearms officer for registration or destruction or other disposition as provided in the order is, by reason only of the fact that the person was in possession of the weapon or explosive substance prior to the delivery or by reason only of the fact that the person transported the weapon or explosive substance for purposes of the delivery, guilty of an offence under section 82, 90 or 91, as the case may be.

(2) Any proceedings taken under section 82, 90 or 91 against any person for any action taken by the person in reliance on subsection (1) following an order referred to therein are a nullity.

Members of forces, peace officers, etc. — Museums.

92. (1) Notwithstanding anything in this Act,

(*a*) a member of the Canadian Forces or of the armed forces of a state other than Canada that are lawfully present in Canada,

(*b*) a peace officer or public officer of a class prescribed by the regulations for the purposes of this Part,

(*c*) an officer under the *Immigration Act*, the *Customs Act* or the *Excise Act*, or

(*d*) a person who, under the authority of the Canadian Armed Forces or a police force that includes peace officers or public officers of a class referred to in paragraph (*b*), imports, manufactures, repairs, alters, modifies or sells weapons for or on behalf of the Canadian Armed Forces or that police force,

is not guilty of an offence under this Act by reason only that, in the case of a person described in any of paragraphs (*a*) to (*c*), he has in his possession a restricted or prohibited weapon for the purpose of his duties or employment and, in the case of a person described in paragraph (*d*), he has in his possession a restricted or prohibited weapon in the course of his business on behalf of the Canadian Armed Forces or a police force referred to in that paragraph.

(2) Notwithstanding anything in this Act, no operator of or person employed in a museum approved for the purposes of this Part by the Commissioner or the Attorney General of the province in which it is situated is guilty of an offence under this Act by reason only that he has in his possession a restricted or prohibited weapon for the purpose of exhibiting that weapon or of storing,

repairing, restoring, maintaining or transporting that weapon for the purpose of exhibiting it. R.S.C. 1985, c. 1 (2d Supp.), Sched. III.

[1991, c. 40, s. 7 will repeal s. 92 and substitute the following.]

Members of forces, peace officers, etc. — Museums.

92. (1) Notwithstanding anyting in this Act,

(*a*) a member of the Canadian Forces or of the armed forces of a state other than Canada who is authorized under paragraph 14(*a*) of the *Visiting Forces Act* or who is attached or seconded to any of the Canadian Forces,

(*b*) a peace officer or a person in the public service of Canada or employed by the government of a province,

(*c*) an officer under the *Immigration Act*, the *Customs Act* or the *Excise Act*, or

(*d*) a person who, under the authority of the Canadian Forces or a police force that includes peace officers or public officers, imports, manufactures, repairs, alters, modifies or sells weapons for or on behalf of the Canadian Forces or that police force is not guilty of an offence under this Act by reason only that, in the case of a person described in any of paragraphs (*a*) to (*c*), the person is required to possess and possesses a restricted or prohibited weapon for the purpose of the person's duties or employment and, in the case of a person described in paragraph (*d*), the person possesses a restricted or prohibited weapon in the course of business on behalf of the Canadian Forces or a police force referred to in that paragraph.

(2) Notwithstanding anything in this Act, no operator of or person employed in a museum established by the Chief of the Defence Staff or a museum approved for the purposes of this Part by the Commissioner or the Attorney General of the province in which it is situated is guilty of an offence under this Act by reason only that the person possesses a restricted or prohibited weapon for the purpose of exhibiting that weapon or of storing, repairing, restoring, maintaining or transporting that weapon for the purpose of exhibiting it.

Offences Related to Sale, Delivery or Acquisition of Firearms and other Offensive Weapons

Transfer of firearm to person under 16 — Saving provision.

93. (1) Every one who gives, lends, transfers or delivers any firearm to a person under the age of sixteen years who is not the holder of a permit under which he may lawfully possess the firearm

[1991, c. 40, s. 8(1) will repeal all that portion of subsection 93(1) preceding paragraph (a) and substitute the following.]

Transfer of firearm to person under 18.

93. (1) Every one who gives, lends, transfers or delivers any firearm to a person under the age of eighteen years who is not the holder of a permit under which the person may lawfully possess the firearm

(*a*) is guilty of an indictable offence and liable to imprisonment for a term not exceeding two years; or

(*b*) is guilty of an offence punishable on summary conviction.

(2) Subsection (1) does not apply to a person lawfully in possession of a firearm who permits a person under the age of sixteen years to use the firearm under his immediate supervision in the same manner in which he may lawfully use it.

[1991, c. 40, s. 8(2) will repeal subsection 93(2) and substitute the following.]

Saving provision.

(2) Subsection (1) does not apply to a person lawfully in possession of a firearm who permits a person under the age of eighteen years to use the firearm under the direct and immediate supervision of the person lawfully in possession of the firearm in the same manner in which that person may lawfully use it.

Wrongful delivery of firearms, etc.

94. Every one who sells, barters, gives, lends, transfers or delivers any firearm or other offensive weapon or any ammunition or explosive substance to a person who he knows or has good reason to believe is of unsound mind, is impaired by alcohol or drugs, or is a person who is prohibited by an order made pursuant to section 100 or 103 or by a condition of a probation order referred to in paragraph 737(2)(*d*) from possessing the firearm or other offensive weapon, ammunition or explosive substance so sold, bartered, given, lent, transferred or delivered,

(*a*) is guilty of an indictable offence and liable to imprisonment for a term not exceeding five years; or

(*b*) is guilty of an offence punishable on summary conviction.

Importing or exporting prohibited weapon — Saving provision — Idem.

95. (1) Every one who imports, exports, buys, sells, barters, gives, lends, transfers or delivers a prohibited weapon or any component or part designed exclusively for assembly into a prohibited weapon is guilty of

(*a*) an indictable offence and liable to imprisonment for a term not exceeding ten years; or

(*b*) an offence punishable on summary conviction.

(2) Notwithstanding subsection (1), a person who carries on a business described in paragraph 105(1)(*b*) may export or import for a purpose that the Governor in Council prescribes by regulation to be an industrial purpose a prohibited weapon described in paragraph (*c*) or (*e*) of the definition "prohibited weapon" in subsection 84(1) or components or parts thereof, if that person does so under and in accordance with an export permit or an import permit, as the case may be, issued under the Export and Import Permits Act.

(3) Notwithstanding subsection (1), a person who carries on a business described in paragraph 105(1)(*b*) may transfer to a person designated by the Attorney General of a province pursuant to subsection 90(3.1) a prohibited weapon described in paragraph (*c*) or (*e*) of the definition "prohibited weapon" in subsection 84(1) or components or parts thereof. S.C. 1991, c. 28, s. 8.

[1991, c. 40, s. 37 will repeal section 95 and substitute the following.]

Importing or delivering prohibited weapon — Saving Provision — Exception — Saving Provision.

95.(1) Every person who imports, exports, buys, sells, barters, gives, lends, transfers or delivers a prohibited weapon or any component or part designed exclusively for use in the manufacture or assembly into a prohibited weapon

(*a*) is guilty of an indictable offence and liable to imprisonment for a term not exceeding ten years; or

(*b*) is guilty of an offence punishable on summary conviction.

(2) Notwithstanding subsection (1), a person who carries on a business described in paragraph 105(1)(*b*) may export or import for a purpose that the Governor in Council prescribes by regulation, for the purposes of subsection 90(3.1), to be an industrial purpose a prohibited weapon described in paragraph (*c*), (*e*) or (*f*) of the definition "prohibited weapon" in subsection 84(1) or components or parts thereof, if that person does so under and in accordance with an export permit or an import permit, as the case may be, issued under the *Export and Import Permits Act.*

(3) Subsection (1) does not apply to a person who

(*a*) carries on a business referred to in paragraph 105(1)(*a*) and who, on behalf of a person described in subsection 90(3.2), imports, buys, sells, barters, gives, lends, transfers or delivers a prohibited weapon described in paragraph (*f*) of the definition of that expression in subsection 84(1); or

(*b*) manufactures a prohibited weapon described in paragraph (*f*) of the definition of that expression in subsection 84(1) for the purpose of exporting the prohibited weapon or of selling it in Canada to a person who may lawfully possess such a prohibited weapon, where the person who manufactures the prohibited weapon is designated for the purposes of this subsection by the Attorney General of the province in which the prohibited weapon is manufactured.

(4) Notwithstanding subsection (1), a person who carries on a business described in paragraph 105(1)(*b*) may transfer to a person designated by the Attorney General of a province pursuant to subsection 90(3.1) a prohibited weapon described in paragraph (*c*), (*e*) or (*f*) of the definition "prohibited weapon" in subsection 84(1) or components or parts thereof.

[1991, c. 40, s. 9 will add the following immediately after section 95.]

Making automatic firearm.

95.1 Every person who, without lawful justification or excuse, alters a firearm so that it is capable of, or manufactures or assembles any firearm with intent to produce a firearm that is capable of, firing projectiles in rapid succession during one pressure of the trigger is guilty of

(*a*) an indictable offence and liable to imprisonment for a term not exceeding five years; or

(*b*) an offence punishable on summary conviction.

Delivery of restricted weapon to person without permit — Saving provision — Importation.

96. (1) Every one who sells, barters, gives, lends, transfers or delivers any restricted weapon to a person who is not the holder of a permit authorizing him to possess that weapon

(*a*) is guilty of an indictable offence and liable to imprisonment for a term not exceeding five years; or

(*b*) is guilty of an offence punishable on summary conviction.

(2) Subsection (1) does not apply to a person lawfully in possession of a restricted weapon who permits a person who is not the holder of a permit authorizing him to possess that weapon to use the weapon under his immediate supervision in the same manner in which he may lawfully use it.

(3) Every one who imports any restricted weapon when he is not the holder of a permit authorizing him to possess that weapon

(*a*) is guilty of an indictable offence and liable to imprisonment for a term not exceeding five years; or

(*b*) is guilty of an offence punishable on summary conviction.

Delivery of firearm to person without firearms acquisition certificate — Saving provision — Acquisition of firearm without firearms acquisition certificate — Saving provision.

97. (1) Every one who sells, barters, gives, lends, transfers or delivers any firearm to a person who does not, at the time of the sale, barter, giving, lending, transfer or delivery or, in the case of a mail-order sale, within a reasonable time prior thereto, produce a firearms acquisition certificate for inspection by the person selling, bartering, giving, lending, transferring or delivering the firearm, that that person has no reason to believe is invalid or was issued to a person other than the person so producing it,

(*a*) is guilty of an indictable offence and liable to imprisonment for a term not exceeding two years; or

(*b*) is guilty of an offence punishable on summary conviction.

(2) Subsection (1) does not apply to a person

(*a*) lawfully in possession of a firearm who lends the firearm

(i) to a person for use by that person in his company and under his guidance or supervision in the same manner in which he may lawfully use it,

(ii) to a person who requires the firearm to hunt or trap in order to sustain himself or his family, or

(iii) to a person who is the holder of a permit under which he may lawfully possess the firearm;

[1991, c. 40, s. 10(1) will repeal subparagraph 97(2)(*a*)(iii) and substitute the following.]

(iii) to a person who is the holder of a permit issued under subsection 110(1), (6) or (7) permitting the lawful possession of the firearm;

(*b*) who returns a firearm to a person who lent it to him in circumstances described in paragraph (*a*); or

(*c*) who comes into possession of a firearm in the ordinary course of a business described in subsection 105(1) and who returns that firearm to the person from whom he received it.

[1991, c. 40, s. 38(*a*) will repeal paragraph 97(2)(*c*) and substitute the following.]

(*c*) who comes into possession of a firearm in the ordinary course of a business described in paragraph 105(1)(*a*) and who returns the firearm to the person from whom it is received; or

[1991, c. 40, s. 10(2) will amend subsection 97(2) by striking out the word "or" at the end of paragraph (*b*), by adding the word "or" at the end of paragraph (*c*) and by adding the following.]

(*d*) who is a peace officer, local registrar of firearms or firearms officer who returns a firearm to a person who had lawfully possessed the firearm and subsequently lost it or from whom it had been stolen.

(3) Every one who imports or otherwise acquires possession in any manner whatever of a firearm while he is not the holder of a firearms acquisition certificate

(*a*) is guilty of an indictable offence and liable to imprisonment for a term not exceeding two years; or

(*b*) is guilty of an offence punishable on summary conviction.

(4) Subsection (3) does not apply to a person who

(*a*) acquires a firearm in circumstances such that, by virtue of subsection (2), subsection (1) does not apply to the person from whom he acquires the firearm;

(*b*) reacquires a firearm from a person to whom he lent the firearm;

(*c*) imports a firearm at a time when he is not a resident of Canada;

(*d*) comes into possession of a firearm by operation of law and thereafter, with reasonable despatch, lawfully disposes thereof or obtains a firearms acquisition certificate under which he could have lawfully acquired the firearm; or (*e*) comes into possession of a firearm in the ordinary course of a business described in subsection 105(1) or (2).

[1991, c. 40, s. 39(*b*) will repeal paragraph 97(4)(*e*) and substitute the following.]

(*e*) comes into possession of a firearm in the ordinary course of a business described in paragraph 105(1)(*a*) or (*b*) or 105(2)(*a*) or (*b*); or

[1991, c. 40, s. 10(3) will amend subsection 97(4) by striking out the word "or" at the end of paragraph (*d*) by adding the word "or" at the end of paragraph (*e*) and by adding the following.]

(*f*) has lawfully possessed a firearm and has subsequently lost it, or from whom it had been stolen, and who then reacquires it from a peace officer, local registrar of firearms or firearms officer or finds it and so reports to a peace officer, local registrar of firearms or firearms officer.

Members of forces, peace officers, etc. — Importation, etc., on behalf of armed forces and police forces — Importation, etc., on behalf of museums.

98. (1) Notwithstanding sections 95 to 97,

(*a*) a member of the Canadian Forces or of the armed forces of a state other than Canada that are lawfully present in Canada,

(*b*) a peace officer or public officer of a class prescribed by the regulations for the purposes of this Part, or

(*c*) an operator of or a person employed in a museum approved for the purposes of this Part by the Commissioner or the Attorney General of the province in which it is situated,

is not guilty of an offence under this Act by reason only that he imports or otherwise acquires possession in any manner whatever of any weapon or component or part of a weapon in the course of his duties or employment.

[1991, c. 40, s. 11(1) will repeal subsection 98(1) and substitute the following.]

Members of forces, peace officers, etc.

98.(1) Notwithstanding sections 95 to 97,

(*a*) a member of the Canadian Forces, or of the armed forces of a state other than Canada, referred to in paragraph 92(1)(*a*),

(*b*) a peace officer or a person in the public service of Canada or employed by the government of a province, or

(*c*) an operator of or a person employed in a museum established by the Chief of the Defence Staff or a museum approved for the purposes of this Part by the Commissioner or the Attorney General of the province in which it is situated is not guilty of an offence under this Act by reason only that the person imports or otherwise acquires possession in any manner of any weapon or component or part of a weapon in the course of the duties or employment of that person.

(2) Notwithstanding sections 95 to 97, a person who, under the authority of the Canadian Armed Forces or a police force that includes peace officers

or public officers of a class referred to in paragraph (1)(*b*), imports, manufactures, repairs, alters, modifies or sells weapons or components or parts of weapons for or on behalf of the Canadian Armed Forces or such a police force, is not guilty of an offence under this Act by reason only that that person imports or manufactures weapons or components or parts thereof or sells, barters, gives, lends, transfers or delivers weapons or components or parts thereof to the Canadian Armed Forces or such a police force.

(3) Notwithstanding sections 95 to 97, a person who, under the supervision of an operator or of a person employed in a museum approved for the purposes of this Part by the Commissioner or the Attorney General of the province in which it is situated, imports, buys, repairs, restores or maintains weapons or components or parts of weapons for or on behalf of the museum is not guilty of an offence under this Act by reason only that he so imports, repairs, restores or maintains weapons or components or parts thereof or sells, barters, gives, lends, transfers or delivers weapons or components or parts thereof to the museum. R.S. 1985, c. 27 (1st Supp.), s. 13.

[1991, c. 40, s. 11(2) will repeal subsection 98(3) and substitute the following.]

Importation, etc., on behalf of museum.

(3) Notwithstanding sections 95 to 97, a person who, under the supervision of an operator of or a person employed in a museum established by the Chief of the Defence Staff or a museum approved for the purposes of this Part by the Commissioner or the Attorney General of the province in which it is situated, imports, buys, repairs, restores or maintains weapons or components or parts of weapons for or on behalf of the museum is not guilty of an offence under this Act by reason only that that person so imports, buys, repairs, restores or maintains weapons or components or parts thereof or sells, barters, gives, lends, transfers or delivers weapons or components or parts thereof to the museum.

Exception.

99. Notwithstanding sections 96 and 97, a person is not guilty of an offence under this Act by reason only that he transfers or delivers

(*a*) any restricted weapon to a person who carries on a business described in subparagraph 105(2)(*b*)(ii), or

(*b*) any firearm, other than a restricted weapon, to a person who carries on a business described in subsection 105(1) or subparagraph 105(2)(*b*)(ii)

for use in the course of that business.

Prohibition Orders, Seizure and Forfeiture

Order prohibiting possession of firearms, etc. — Discretionary order prohibiting possession of firearms, etc. — Definition of "release from imprisonment" — Application for order of prohibition — Fixing date for hearing and notice — Hearing of application and disposition — Hearing of reference and disposition — Idem — Where hearing may proceed ex parte — Appeal to appeal court in certain cases — Definitions — "Appeal court" — "Provincial court judge" — Possession of firearm, ammunition, etc., while prohibited by order — Defence.

100. (1) Where an offender is convicted or discharged under section 736 of an indictable offence in the commission of which violence against a person is used, threatened or attempted and for which the offender may be sentenced to imprisonment for ten years or more or of an offence under section 85, the court that sentences the offender shall, in addition to any other punishment that may be imposed for that offence, make an order prohibiting the offender from having in his possession any firearm or any ammunition or explosive substance for any period of time specified in the order that commences on the day the order is made and expires not earlier than

(*a*) in the case of a first conviction for such an offence, five years, and

(*b*) in any other case, ten years,

after the time of the offender's release from imprisonment after conviction for the offence or, if the offender is not then imprisoned or subject to imprisonment, after the time of the offender's conviction or discharge for that offence.

(2) Where an offender is convicted or discharged under section 736 of an offence involving the use, carriage, possession, handling, shipping or storage of any firearm or ammunition or any offence, other than an offence referred to in subsection (1), in the commission of which violence against a person was used, threatened or attempted, the court that sentences the offender may, in addition to any other punishment that may be imposed for that offence, make an order prohibiting the offender from having in his possession any firearm or any ammunition or explosive substance for any period of time specified in the order that commences on the day the order is made and expires not later than five years after the time of the offender's release from imprisonment after conviction for the offence or, if the offender is not then imprisoned or subject to imprisonment, after the time of the offender's conviction or discharge for that offence.

[1991, c. 40, s. 12(1) will repeal subsections 100(1) and (2) and substitute the following.]

Order prohibiting possession of firearms, etc. — Where order not to be made — Criteria — Reasons — Discretionary order prohibiting possession of firearms, etc. — Duration of order.

100.(1) Where an offender is convicted or discharged under section 736 of an indictable offence in the commission of which violence against a person is used, threatened or attempted and for which the offender may be sentenced to imprisonment for ten years or more or of an offence under section 85, the court that sentences the offender shall, subject to subsections (1.1) to (1.3), in addition to any other punishment that may be imposed for that offence, make an order prohibiting the offender from possessing any firearm or any ammunition or explosive substance for any period of time specified in the order that commences on the day on which the order is made and expires not earlier than

(*a*) in the case of a first conviction for such an offence, ten years, and

(*b*) in any other case, life,

after the time of the offender's release from imprisonment after conviction for the offence or, if the offender is not then imprisoned or subject to imprisonment, after the time of the offender's conviction or discharge for that offence.

(1.1) The court is not required to make an order under subsection (1) where the court is satisfied that the offender has established that

(*a*) it is not desirable in the interests of the safety of the offender or of any other person that the order be made; and

(*b*) the circumstances are such that it would not be appropriate to make the order.

(1.2) In considering whether the circumstances are such that it would not be appropriate to make an order under subsection (1), the court shall consider

(*a*) the criminal record of the offender, the nature of the offence and the circumstances surrounding its commission;

(*b*) whether the offender needs a firearm for the sustenance of the offender or the offender's family; and

(*c*) whether the order would constitute a virtual prohibition against employment in the only vocation open to the offender.

(1.3) Where the court does not make an order under subsection (1), the court shall give reasons why the order is not being made.

(2) When an offender is convicted or discharged under section 736 of

(*a*) an offence involving the use, carriage, possession, handling or storage of any firearm or ammunition,

(*b*) an offence, other than an offence referred to in subsection (1), in the commission of which violence against a person was used, threatened or attempted, or (*c*) an offence described in subsection 39(1) or (2) or 48(1) or (2) of the *Food and Drugs Act* or in subsection 4(1) or (2) or 5(1) of the *Narcotic Control Act*,

the court that sentences the offender, in addition to any other punishment that may be imposed for the offence, shall consider whether it is desirable, in the interests of the safety of the offender or of any other person, to make an order prohibiting the offender from possessing any firearm or any ammunition or explosive substance and ordering the offender to surrender any firearms acquisition certificate that the offender possesses, and where the court decides that it is not desirable, in the interests of the safety of the offender or of any other person, for the offender to possess any of those things, the court shall so order.

(2.1) An order referred to in subsection (2) may be for any period of time specified in the order but shall not expire later than ten years after the time of the offender's release from imprisonment after conviction for the offence to which the order relates, or, if the offender is not then imprisoned or subject to imprisonment, after the time of the offender's conviction or discharge from that offence.

(3) For the purposes of subsections (1) and (2), "release from imprisonment" means release from confinement by reason of expiration of sentence, commencement of mandatory supervision or grant of parole other than day parole.

(4) Where a peace officer believes on reasonable grounds that it is not desirable in the interests of the safety of any person that a particular person should possess any firearm or any ammunition or explosive substance, he may apply to a provincial court judge for an order prohibiting that particular person from having in his possession any firearm or any ammunition or explosive substance.

(5) On receipt of an application made pursuant to subsection (4) or on a reference by a firearms officer, pursuant to subsection 106(7), of his opinion that it is not desirable in the interests of the safety of an applicant for a firearms acquisition certificate or of any other person that the applicant for a firearms acquisition certificate acquire a firearm, the provincial court judge to whom the application or reference is made shall fix a date for the hearing of the application or reference and direct that notice of the hearing be given to the person against whom the order of prohibition is sought or the applicant for the firearms acquisition certificate and the firearms officer, as the case may be, in such manner as the provincial court judge may specify.

(6) At the hearing of an application made pursuant to subsection (4), the provincial court judge shall hear all relevant evidence presented by or on behalf of the applicant and the person against whom the order of prohibition is sought and where, at the conclusion of the hearing, the provincial court judge is satisfied that there are reasonable grounds to believe that it is not desirable in the interests of the safety of the person against whom the order of prohibition is sought

or of any other person that the person against whom the order is sought should possess any firearm or any ammunition or explosive substance, the provincial court judge shall make an order prohibiting him from having in his possession any firearm or any ammunition or explosive substance for any period of time, not exceeding five years, specified in the order and computed from the day the order is made.

(7) At the hearing of a reference referred to in subsection (5), the provincial court judge shall hear all relevant evidence presented by or on behalf of the firearms officer and the applicant for a firearms acquisition certificate and where, at the conclusion of the hearing, the firearms officer has satisfied the provincial court judge that his opinion that it is not desirable in the interests of the safety of the applicant for a firearms acquisition certificate or of any other person that the applicant for a firearms acquisition certificate acquire a firearm is justified, the provincial court judge shall, by order, confirm that opinion and prohibit the applicant for a firearms acquisition certificate from having in his possession any firearm, ammunition or explosive substance for any period of time, not exceeding five years, specified in the order and computed from the day the order is made.

[1991, c. 40, s. 12(2) will repeal subsection 100(7) and substitute the following.]

Hearing of reference and disposition — Revocation on order.

(7) At the hearing of a reference referred to in subsection (5), the provincial court judge shall hear all relevant evidence presented by or on behalf of the firearms officer and the applicant for a firearms acquisition certificate and where, at the conclusion of the hearing, the firearms officer has satisfied the provincial court judge that the opinion of the firearms officer that it is not desirable in the interests of the safety of the applicant or of any other person that the applicant acquire a firearm is justified, the provincial court judge shall, by order, confirm that opinion and the refusal to issue the firearms acquisition certificate and may prohibit the applicant from possessing any firearm, ammunition or explosive substance for any period, not exceeding five years, specified in the order and computed from the day the order is made.

(7.1) Where an order is made under subsection (1), (2) or (7), any firearms acquisition certificate that is held by the person who is the subject of the order is automatically revoked.

(8) Where, at the conclusion of a hearing referred to in subsection (7), the firearms officer has not satisfied the provincial court judge that his opinion that it is not desirable in the interests of the safety of the applicant for a firearms acquisition certificate or of any other person that the applicant for a firearms acquisition certificate acquire a firearm is justified, the provincial court judge shall, by order, direct the firearms officer to issue to that person a firearms acquisition certificate and, on payment of the fee, if any, fixed for such a certificate, the firearms officer shall forthwith comply with the direction.

(9) A provincial court judge may proceed *ex parte* to hear and determine an application made pursuant to subsection (4) or a reference referred to in subsection (5) in the absence of the person against whom the order of prohibition is sought or the applicant for a firearms acquisition certificate, as the case may be, in circumstances in which a summary conviction court may, pursuant to Part XXVII, proceed with a trial in the absence of the defendant as fully and effectually as if the defendant had appeared.

(10) Where a provincial court judge

(*a*) makes an order pursuant to subsection (6) or (7), the prohibited person,

(*b*) refuses to make an order pursuant to subsection (6), the person who made the application pursuant to subsection (4), or

(*c*) makes an order pursuant to subsection (8), the firearms officer by whom the application for a firearms acquisition certificate that is the subject of the order was referred to the provincial court judge,

[1991, c. 40, s. 12(3) will repeal paragraphs 100(10)(*a*) to (*c*) and substitute the following.]

(*a*) makes an order pursuant to subsection (6) or (7), the prohibited person, or

(*b*) refuses to make an order pursuant to subsection (6), or makes an order pursuant to subsection (8), the Attorney General

may appeal to the appeal court against the order or refusal to make an order, as the case may be, and the provisions of Part XXVII except sections 816 to 819 and sections 829 to 838 apply, with such modifications as the circumstances require in respect of the appeal.

(11) In this section,

"appeal court" means

(*a*) in the Province of Ontario, the Ontario Court (General Division) sitting in the region, district or county or group of counties where the adjudication was made,

(*b*) in the Province of Quebec, the Superior Court,

(*b*.1) in the Province of Nova Scotia, the district or county court of the district or county where the adjudication was made,

(*c*) in the Provinces of New Brunswick, Manitoba, Saskatchewan and Alberta, the Court of Queen's Bench,

(*d*) in the Provinces of Prince Edward Island and Newfoundland, the Trial Division of the Supreme Court, and

(*e*) in the Province of British Columbia, the Yukon Territory and Northwest Territories, the Supreme Court;

"provincial court judge" means a provincial court judge having jurisdiction in the territorial division where the person against whom the relevant application for an order of prohibition was brought or in respect of whom the reference was made, as the case may be, resides.

(12) Every one who has in his possession any firearm or any ammunition or explosive substance while he is prohibited from doing so by any order made pursuant to this section

(*a*) is guilty of an indictable offence and liable to imprisonment for a term not exceeding five years; or

[1991, c. 40, s. 12(4) will repeal paragraph 100(12)(*a*) and substitute the following.]

(*a*) is guilty of an indictable offence and liable to imprisonment for a term not exceeding ten years; or

(*b*) is guilty of an offence punishable on summary conviction.

(13) An order made pursuant to subsection (1), (2), (6) or (7) shall specify therein a reasonable period of time within which the person against whom the order is made may surrender to a police officer or firearms officer or otherwise lawfully dispose of any firearm or any ammunition or explosive substance lawfully possessed by him prior to the making of the order, and subsection (12) does not apply to him during that period of time. R.S. 1985, c. 27 (1st Supp.), s. 14; 203; R.S. 1985, c. 27 (2d Supp.), Schedule; 1990, c. 16, s. 2; 1990, c. 17, s. 8.

[1991, c. 40, s. 12(5) will repeal subsection 100(13) and substitute the following.]

Defence.

(13) An order made pursuant to subsection (1), (2), (6) or (7) shall

(*a*) specify a reasonable period within which the person against whom the order is made may surrender to a police officer or firearms officer, to be disposed of as the Attorney General directs, or otherwise lawfully dispose of any firearm or any ammunition or explosive substance lawfully possessed by that person prior to the making of the order, and during which subsection (12) does not apply to that person; and

(*b*) state that if that person fails to dispose of the firearm, ammunition or explosive substance within the period specified in the order, the firearm, ammunition or explosive substance is forfeited to Her Majesty and must be surrendered to a police officer or firearms officer to be disposed of as the Attorney General directs.

Search and seizure — Disposition — "Dwelling-house".

101. (1) Whenever a peace officer believes on reasonable grounds that an offence is being committed or has been committed against any of the provisions of this Act relating to prohibited weapons, restricted weapons, firearms or ammunition, he may search, without warrant, a person or vehicle, or place or premises other than a dwelling-house, and may seize anything by means of or in relation to which he believes on reasonable grounds the offence is being committed or has been committed.

[1991, c. 40, s. 13 will repeal subsection 101(1) and substitute the following.]

Search and seizure.

101. (1) Whenever a peace officer believes on reasonable grounds that an offence is being committed or has been committed against any of the provisions of this Act relating to prohibited weapons, restricted weapons, firearms or ammunition and that evidence of the offence is likely to be found on a person, in a vehicle or in any place or premises other than a dwelling-house, the peace officer may, where the conditions for obtaining a warrant exist but, by reason of exigent circumstances, it would not be practicable to obtain a warrant, search, without warrant, the person, vehicle, place or premises, and may seize anything by means of or in relation to which that officer believes on reasonable grounds the offence is being committed or has been committed.

(2) Anything seized pursuant to subsection (1) shall be dealt with in accordance with sections 490 and 491.

(3) For the purposes of this section, "dwelling-house" does not include a unit that is designed to be mobile other than such a unit that is being used as a permanent residence.

Seizure — Return — Forfeiture.

102. (1) Notwithstanding section 101, a peace officer who finds

(*a*) a person in possession of any restricted weapon who fails then and there to produce, for inspection by the peace officer, a registration certificate or permit under which he may lawfully possess the weapon,

(*b*) a person under the age of sixteen years in possession of any firearm who fails then and there to produce, for inspection by the peace officer, a permit under which he may lawfully possess the firearm, or

(*c*) any person in possession of a prohibited weapon,

may, unless possession of the restricted weapon, firearm or prohibited weapon by the person in the circumstances in which it is so found is authorized by any provision of this Part, seize the restricted weapon, firearm or prohibited weapon.

[1991, c. 40, s. 14 will add the following immediately after subsection 102(1).]

Exception — Immediate supervision.

(1.1) A person under the age of eighteen years is authorized to be in possession of a firearm where

(*a*) the person is under the direct and immediate supervision of another person who may lawfully possess the firearm; or

(*b*) the person possesses a permit under which the person may lawfully possess the firearm.

(2) Where a person from whom a restricted weapon, firearm or prohibited weapon was seized under subsection (1), within fourteen days after the seizure, claims it and produces for inspection by the peace officer by whom it was seized, or any other peace officer having custody thereof, a registration certificate or permit under which the person from whom the seizure was made

is lawfully entitled to possess the restricted weapon, firearm or prohibited weapon, the restricted weapon, firearm or prohibited weapon shall forthwith be returned to that person.

(3) Where any restricted weapon, firearm or prohibited weapon that was seized pursuant to subsection (1) is not returned as and when provided by subsection (2), a peace officer shall forthwith take it before a provincial court judge who may, after affording the person from whom it was seized or the owner thereof, if known, an opportunity to establish that he is lawfully entitled to the possession thereof, declare it to be forfeited to Her Majesty, whereupon it shall be disposed of as the Attorney General directs. S.C. 1991, c. 28, s. 9.

Application for warrant to seize — Seizure without warrant — Return to provincial court judge — Application for disposition — Hearing of application — Finding and order of court — Where no finding or application — Appeal — Definitions — "Appeal court" — "Provincial court judge" — Possession of firearm or ammunition while prohibited by order.

103. (1) Where, on application to a provincial court judge made by or on behalf of the Attorney General with respect to any person, the provincial court judge is satisfied that there are reasonable grounds for believing that it is not desirable in the interests of the safety of that person, or of any other person, that that person should have in his possession, custody or control any firearm or other offensive weapon or any ammunition or explosive substance, the provincial court judge may issue a warrant authorizing the search for and seizure of any firearm or other offensive weapon or any ammunition or explosive substance in the possession, custody or control of that person.

(2) Where, with respect to any person, a peace officer is satisfied that there are reasonable grounds for believing that it is not desirable in the interests of the safety of that person, or of any other person, that that person should have in his possession, custody or control any firearm or other offensive weapon or any ammunition or explosive substance and that the danger to the safety of that person or other persons is such that to proceed by way of an application under subsection (1) would be impracticable, the peace officer may without warrant search for and seize any firearm or other offensive weapon or any ammunition or explosive substance in the possession, custody or control of that person.

(3) On execution of a warrant referred to in subsection (1) or following a search without warrant under subsection (2), the Attorney General shall forthwith make a return to the provincial court judge by whom the warrant was issued or, if no warrant was issued, to a provincial court judge by whom a warrant might have issued showing,

(*a*) in the case of an execution of a warrant referred to in subsection (1), the articles, if any, seized and the date of execution of the warrant; and

(*b*) in the case of a search without warrant under subsection (2), the grounds on which it was concluded that the peace officer who conducted the search without warrant was entitled to do so and the articles, if any, seized.

(4) Where any articles have been seized pursuant to subsection (1) or (2), the provincial court judge by whom a warrant was issued or, if no warrant was issued, a provincial court judge by whom a warrant might have issued shall, on application to him for an order for the disposition of the articles so seized made by or on behalf of the Attorney General within thirty days from the date of execution of the warrant or of the seizure without warrant, as the case may be, fix a date for the hearing of the application and direct that notice of the hearing be given to such persons or in such manner as the provincial court judge may specify.

(5) At the hearing of an application described in subsection (4), the provincial court judge shall hear any relevant evidence, including evidence as to the value of the articles in respect of which the application was made.

(6) If, following the hearing of an application described in subsection (4) made with respect to any person, the provincial court judge finds that it is not desirable, in the interests of the safety of that person or of any other person, that that person should have in his possession, custody or control any firearm or other offensive weapon or any ammunition or explosive substance, the provincial court judge may

(*a*) order that any or all of the articles seized be disposed of on such terms as the provincial court judge deems fair and reasonable, and give such directions concerning the payment or application of the proceeds, if any, of the disposition as the provincial court judge sees fit; and

(*b*) where the provincial court judge is satisfied that the circumstances warrant such action, order that the possession by that person of any firearm or other offensive weapon or any ammunition or explosive substance specified in the order, or of all such articles be prohibited during any period of time, not exceeding five years, specified in the order and computed from the day the order is made.

(7) Any articles seized under subsection (1) or (2) in respect of which,

(*a*) no application under subsection (4) is made within thirty days from the date of execution of the warrant or of the seizure without warrant, as the case may be, or

(*b*) where an application under subsection (4) is made within the period referred to in paragraph (*a*), the provincial court judge does not make a finding as described in subsection (6),

shall be returned to the person from whom they were seized.

(8) Where a provincial court judge

(*a*) makes an order under subsection (6) with respect to any person, that person, or

(*b*) does not make a finding as described in subsection (6) following the hearing of an application under subsection (4), or makes the finding but does not make an order to the effect described in paragraph (6)(*a*) and to the effect described in paragraph (6)(*b*), the Attorney General or counsel instructed by him for that purpose

may appeal to the appeal court against the making of the order, or against the failure to make the finding or to make an order to the effects so described, as the case may be, and the provisions of Part XXVII except sections 816 to 819 and sections 829 to 838 apply, with such modifications as the circumstances require in respect of the appeal.

(9) In this section,

"appeal court" has the meaning given that expression in subsection 100(11).

"provincial court judge" means a provincial court judge having jurisdiction in the territorial division where the person with respect to whom an application is made under subsection (1) or the person with respect to whom a search without warrant is made under subsection (2) resides.

(10) Every one who has in his possession any firearm or other offensive weapon or any ammunition or explosive substance while he is prohibited from doing so by any order made pursuant to paragraph (6)(*b*)

(*a*) is guilty of an indictable offence and liable to imprisonment for a term not exceeding five years; or

(*b*) is guilty of an offence punishable on summary conviction. R.S., c. C-34, s. 101; R.S. 1985, c. 27 (1st Supp.), s. 203.

[1991, c. 40, s. 15 will repeal section 103 and substitute the following.]

Application for warrant to seize — Seizure without warrant — Return to justice — Where certificate not seized — Application for disposition — Ex parte hearing — Hearing of application — Finding and order of court — Where no finding or application — Restriction of authorization, etc. — Appeal — Definitions — "Appeal court" — "Justice" — Possession while prohibited by order.

103. (1) Where, on application to a justice made by a peace officer with respect to any person, the justice is satisfied that there are reasonable grounds for believing that it is not desirable in the interests of the safety of that person, or of any other person, that that person possess, or have custody or control of, any firearm or other offensive weapon or any ammunition or explosive substance, the justice may issue a warrant authorizing the search for and seizure of any firearm or other offensive weapon or any ammunition, explosive substance, authorization referred to in subsection 90(3.2), firearms acquisition certificate, registration certificate issued under section 109 or permit issued under section 110, in the possession, custody or control of that person.

(2) Where, with respect to any person, a peace officer is satisfied that there are reasonable grounds for believing that it is not desirable in the interests of the safety of that person, or of any other person, that that person possess, or have custody or control of, any firearm or other offensive weapon or any

ammunition or explosive substance, the peace officer may, where the conditions for obtaining a warrant under subsection (1) exist but by reason of a possible danger to the safety of that person or any other person, it would not be practicable to obtain a warrant, search for and seize any firearm or other offensive weapon or any ammunition, explosive substance, authorization referred to in subsection 90(3.2), firearms acquisition certificate, registration certificate issued under section 109 or permit issued under section 110, in the possession, custody or control of that person.

(3) A peace officer who executes a warrant referred to in subsection (1) or who conducts a search without warrant under subsection (2) shall forthwith make a return to the justice by whom the warrant was issued or, if no warrant was issued, to a justice by whom a warrant might have been issued showing

(*a*) in the case of an execution of a warrant, the articles, if any, seized and the date of execution of the warrant; and

(*b*) in the case of a search without warrant, the grounds on which it was concluded that the peace officer was entitled to conduct the search and the articles, if any, seized.

(3.1) Where a peace officer who performs a seizure under subsection (1) or (2) is unable to seize an authorization referred to in subsection 90(3.2), a firearms acquisition certificate, a registration certificate issued under section 109 or a permit issued under section 110, the authorization, firearms acquisition certificate, registration certificate or permit is automatically revoked.

(4) Where any articles have been seized pursuant to subsection (1) or (2), the justice by whom a warrant was issued or, if no warrant was issued, a justice by whom a warrant might have been issued shall, on application for an order for the disposition of the articles so seized made by the peace officer within thirty days after the date of execution of the warrant or of the seizure without warrant, as the case may be, fix a date for the hearing of the application and direct that notice of the hearing be given to such persons or in such manner as the justice may specify.

(4.1) A justice may proceed to hear and determine an application under subsection (4) in the absence of the person against whom the order is sought in circumstances in which a summary conviction court may, pursuant to Part XXVII, proceed with a trial in the absence of the defendant as fully and effectually as if the defendant had appeared.

(5) At the hearing of an application under subsection (4), the justice shall hear all relevant evidence, including evidence respecting the value of the articles in respect of which the application was made.

(6) If, following the hearing of an application under subsection (4) made with respect to any person, the justice finds that it is not desirable in the interests of the safety of that person or of any other person that that person should possess, or have custody or control of, any firearm or other offensive weapon or any ammunition or explosive substance, the justice may

(*a*) order that any or all of the articles seized be disposed of on such terms as the justice deems fair and reasonable, and give such directions concerning the payment or application of the proceeds, if any, of the disposition as the justice sees fit; and

(*b*) where the justice is satisfied that the circumstances warrant such action,

(i) order that the possession by that person of any firearm or other offensive weapon or any ammunition or explosive substance specified in the order, or of all such articles, be prohibited during any period, not exceeding five years, specified in the order and computed from the day on which the order is made, and

(ii) order that any firearms acquisition certificate issued to the person be revoked and prohibit the person from applying for a firearms acquisition certificate for any period referred to in subparagraph (i).

(7) Any articles seized pursuant to subsection (1) or (2) in respect of which

(*a*) no application under subsection (4) is made within thirty days after the date of execution of the warrant or of the seizure without warrant, as the case may be, or

(*b*) where an application under subsection (4) is made within the period referred to in paragraph (*a*), the justice does not make a finding as described in subsection (6)

shall be returned to the person from whom they were seized.

(7.1) Where, pursuant to subsection (7), articles are returned to a person from whom they were seized and an authorization, a firearms acquisition certificate, a registration certificate or a permit has been revoked pursuant to subsection (3.1), the justice referred to in paragraph (7)(*b*) may order that the revocation be reversed and that the authorization, firearms acquisition certificate, registration certificate or permit be restored.

(8) Where a justice

(*a*) makes an order under subsection (6) with respect to any person, that person, or

(*b*) does not make a finding as described in subsection (6) following the hearing of an application under subsection (4), or makes the finding but does not make an order to the effect described in paragraph (6)(*a*) or to the effect described in paragraph (6)(*b*), the Attorney General

may appeal to the appeal court against the making of the order, or against the failure to make the finding or to make an order to the effects so described, as the case may be, and the provisions of Part XXVII except sections 816 to 819 and 829 to 838 apply, with such modifications as the circumstances require, in respect of the appeal.

(9) In this section,

"appeal court" has the meaning given that expression in subsection 100(11);

"justice" means a justice having jurisdiction in the territorial division where the person with respect to whom an application is made under subsection (1) or the person with respect to whom a search without warrant is made under subsection (2) resides.

(10) Every person who possesses any firearm or other offensive weapon or any ammunition, explosive substance or firearms acquisition certificate while prohibited from doing so by any order made pursuant to paragraph (6)(*b*)

(*a*) is guilty of an indictable offence and liable to imprisonment for a term not exceeding ten years; or

(*b*) is guilty of an offence punishable on summary conviction.

Found, Lost, Mislaid, Stolen and Defaced Firearms and other Weapons

Finding weapon — Lost weapon, etc. — Tampering with serial number — Evidence — Punishment.

104. (1) Every one commits an offence who, on finding a prohibited weapon, restricted weapon or firearm that he has reasonable grounds to believe has been lost or abandoned, does not with reasonable despatch

(*a*) deliver it to a peace officer, a local registrar of firearms or a firearms officer; or

(*b*) report to a peace officer, a local registrar of firearms or a firearms officer that he has found it.

(2) Every one commits an offence who, having lost or mislaid a restricted weapon for which he has a registration certificate or permit or having had the weapon stolen from his possession, does not with reasonable despatch report to a peace officer or a local registrar of firearms that he has lost or mislaid the weapon or that the weapon has been stolen from him.

(3) Every one commits an offence who, without lawful excuse, the proof of which lies on him,

(*a*) alters, defaces or removes a serial number on a firearm; or

(*b*) has in his possession a firearm knowing that the serial number thereon has been altered, defaced or removed.

[1991, c. 40, s. 16(1) will repeal subsection 104(3) and substitute the following.]

Tampering with serial number.

(3) Every one commits an offence who, without lawful excuse, the proof of which lies on that person,

(*a*) alters, defaces or removes a serial number on a firearm; or

(*b*) possesses a firearm knowing that the serial number thereon has been altered, defaced or removed.

(4) In proceedings under subsection (3), evidence that a person has in his possession a firearm the serial number of which has been wholly or partially obliterated is, in the absence of any evidence to the contrary, proof that such

person has the firearm in his possession knowing that the serial number thereon has been altered, defaced or removed.

[1991, c. 40, s. 16(2) will repeal subsection 104(4) and substitute the following.]

Exception — Evidence.

(3.1) No person is guilty of an offence under paragraph (3)(*b*) by reason only of possessing a restricted weapon the serial number on which has been altered, defaced or removed, where that serial number has been replaced and a registration certificate has been issued in respect of the restricted weapon that mentions the new serial number.

(4) In proceedings under subsection (3), evidence that a person possess a firearm the serial number of which has been wholly or partially abliterated otherwise than through normal use over time is, in the absence of evidence to the contrary, proof that the person possesses the firearm knowing that the serial number thereon has been altered, defaced or removed.

(5) Every one who contravenes this section

(*a*) is guilty of an indictable offence and liable to imprisonment for a term not exceeding five years; or

(*b*) is guilty of an offence punishable on summary conviction.

Firearms and other Businesses

[1991, c. 40, s. 17 will repeal the heading preceding section 105 and substitute the following.]

Museums and Weapons Businesses

Record of transaction in firearms, etc. — Requirements — Report of loss, destruction or theft — Form of report — Permit to carry on business — Each location a separate business — Handling, secure storage, etc. — Idem — Handling and transportation — Punishment.

105. (1) Every person who carries on a business that includes

(*a*) the manufacturing, buying or selling at wholesale or retail, importing, repairing, modifying or taking in pawn of restricted weapons or firearms, or

(*b*) the manufacturing, importing or exporting, for a purpose that the Governor in Council prescribes by regulation to be an industrial purpose, of prohibited weapons described in paragraph (*c*) or (*e*) of the definition "prohibited weapon" in subsection 84(1) or components or parts thereof

shall meet the requirements set out in subsection (1.1).

[1991, c. 40, s. 39(1) will repeal subsection 105(1) and substitute the following.]

Record of transaction in weapons or firearms, etc.

105. (1) Every person who operates a museum approved for the purposes of this Part by the Commissioner or the Attorney General of the province in which it is situated, or who carries on a business that includes

(*a*) the manufacturing, buying or selling at wholesale or retail, storing, importing, repairing, modifying or taking in pawn of restricted weapons or firearms, or, in the case referred to in subsection 95(2), the importing, buying, selling, transferring or delivering, at wholesale or retail, of prohibited weapons described in paragraph (f) of the definition "prohibited weapon" in subsection 84(1), or

(*b*) the manufacturing, importing or exporting, for a purpose that the Governor in Council prescribes by regulation, for the purposes of subsection 90(3.1), to be an industrial purpose, of prohibited weapons described in paragraph (*c*), (*e*) or (*f*) of the definition "prohibted weapon" in subsection 84(1) or components or parts thereof,

shall meet the requirements set out in subsection (1.1).

(1.1) Every person who carries on a business described in paragraph (1)(*a*) or (*b*) shall

(*a*) keep records of transactions entered into by that person with respect to the restricted weapons or firearms or the prohibited weapons or the components or parts thereof referred to in paragraph (1)(*b*), as the case may be, in a form prescribed by the Commissioner and containing such information as is prescribed by the Commissioner;

(*b*) keep an inventory of all the restricted weapons or firearms, or the prohibited weapons or the components or parts thereof referred to in paragraph (1)(*b*), as the case may be, on hand at that person's place of business;

(*c*) produce the records and inventory for inspection at the request of any police officer or police constable or any other person authorized by regulations made by the Governor in Council pursuant to paragraph 116(*a*) or (*a*.1), as the case may be, to enter any place where the business described in paragraph (1)(*a*) or (*b*), as the case may be, is carried on; and

(*d*) mail a copy of the records and inventory to the Commissioner or to any person authorized by subsection 110(5) to issue a permit to carry on the business in accordance with any request in writing made by the Commissioner or person so authorized.

[1991, c. 40, s. 39(2) will repeal subsection 105(1.1) and substitute the following.]

Requirements.

(1.1) Every person who operates a museum referred to in subsection 105(1), or who carries on a business described in paragraph (1)(*a*) or (*b*) shall

(*a*) keep records of transactions entered into by that person with respect to the prohibited or restricted weapons or firearms or the prohibited weapons or the components or parts thereof referred to in paragraph (1)(*b*), as the case may be, in a form prescribed by the Commissioner and containing such information as is prescribed by the Commissioner;

(*b*) keep an inventory of all the prohibited weapons or firearms, or the prohibited weapons or the components or parts thereof referred to in paragraph (1)(*b*), as the case may be, on hand at the location of the museum or at that person's place of business;

(*c*) produce the records and inventory for inspection at the request of any police officer or police constable or any other person authorized by regulations made by the Governor in Council pursuant to paragraph 116(1)(*a*) or (*b*), as the case may be, to enter any place where the museum is located or any place where the business described in paragraph (1)(*a*) or (*b*), as the case may be, is carred on; and

(*d*) mail a copy of the records and inventory to the Commissioner or to any person authorized by subsection 110(5) to issue a permit to carry on the business in accordance with any request in writing made by the Commissioner or person so authorized.

(2) A person who carries on

(*a*) a business described in subsection (1), or

(*b*) a business that includes

(i) the manufacturing, buying or selling at wholesale or retail or importing of ammunition, or

(ii) the transportation or shipping of restricted weapons, firearms or ammunition,

shall immediately report to a local registrar of firearms or a peace officer any loss, destruction or theft of any restricted weapon, firearm or ammunition, or any loss, destruction, theft or transfer of any prohibited weapon or a component or part thereof, that occurs in the course of the business.

[1991, c. 40, s. 39(3) will repeal subsection 105(2) and substitute the following.]

Firearms acquisition certificate — Exception — Report of loss, destruction or theft.

(1.2) A person who operates a museum referred to in subsection (1) or who carries on a business described in paragraph (1)(*a*) or (*b*) shall ensure that any person employed in or in connection with the museum or business whose duties include the handling of firearms or restricted or prohibited weapons holds a firearms acquisition certificate.

(1.3) Notwithstanding subsection (1.2), the Attorney General of the province in which a manufacturing business referred to in that subsection is located may designate, for the purposes of this subsection, any person or class of persons employed in or in connection with the business, as a person who need not hold a firearms acquisition certificate for the purposes of employment.

(2) A person who

(*a*) operates a museum referred to in subsection (1) or carries on a business referred to in paragraph (1)(*a*) or (*b*), or (*b*) carries on a business that includes

(i) the manufacturing, buying or selling at wholesale or retail or importing of ammunition, or

(ii) the transportation or shipping of prohibited or restricted weapons, firearms or ammunition

shall immediately report to a local registrar of firearms or a peace officer any loss, destruction or theft of any restricted weapon, firearm or ammunition, or any loss, destruction, theft or transfer of any prohibited weapon or component or part thereof, that occurs in the operation of the museum or in the course of business.

(3) A report made pursuant to subsection (2) shall be in a form prescribed by the Commissioner and shall be made forthwith after the loss, destruction or theft occurs or is discovered.

(4) No person shall carry on a business described in subsection (1) or subparagraph (2)(*b*)(i) unless he is the holder of a permit to carry on that business.

[1991, c. 40, s. 39(4)(*a*) will repeal subsection 105(4) and substitute the following.]

Permit to carry on business.

(4) No person shall carry on a business described in paragraph (1)(*a*) or (*b*) unless the person holds a permit to carry on that busness.

[1991, c. 40, s. 39(4)(*b*) will add the following immediately after subsection 105(4).]

Application.

(4.1) A permit referred to in subsection (4) may be issued by the chief provincial firearms officer to

(*a*) any person who wishes to carry on a business described in paragraph (1)(*a*) or subparagraph (2)(*b*)(i); or

(*b*) a person designated by the Attorney General of the province in which the business is or is to be carried on, and who is a member of a class of persons who require a prohibited weapon described in paragraph (*c*), (*e*) or (*f*) of the definition "prohibited weapon" in subsection 84(1) or parts thereof for a purpose that the Governor in Council prescribed by regulation to be an industrial purpose,

and who applies for such a permit using the form prescribed by the Commissioner.

(5) Where a person carries on a business described in subsection (1) or subparagraph (2)(*b*)(i) at more than one location, each location shall be deemed for the purposes of this section and regulations made pursuant to paragraphs 116(*a*) to (*c*) to be a separate business.

[1991, c. 40, s. 39(4)(*c*) will repeal subsection 105(5) and substitute the following.]

Each location separate.

(5) Where a person operates a museum referred to in subsection (1), or carries on a business described in paragraph (1)(*a*) or (*b*) or in subparagraph (2)(*b*)(i), at more than one location, each location shall be deemed for the purposes of this section and regulations made pursuant to paragraphs 116(1)(*a*) to (*c*) to be a separate museum or business.

(6) No person shall, in the course of a business described in paragraph (1)(*a*) or subparagraph (2)(*b*)(i),

(*a*) handle, store, display or advertise any restricted weapon, firearm or ammunition in a manner that contravenes any regulation made by the Governor in Council pursuant to paragraph 116(*a*); or

(*b*) sell by mail-order any restricted weapon, firearm or ammunition in a manner that contravenes any regulation made by the Governor in Council pursuant to paragraph 116(*c*).

[1991, c. 40, s. 39(4)(*d*) will repeal subsection 105(6) and substitute the following.]

Handling, secure storage, etc.

(6) No person shall, in the course of operating a museum referred to in subsection (1) or of carrying on a business described in paragraph (1)(*a*) or (*b*) or in subparagraph (2)(*b*)(i),

(*a*) handle, store, display or advertise any restricted weapon, firearm or ammunition in a manner that contravenes any regulation made pursuant to paragraph 116(1)(*a*); or

(*b*) sell by mail-order any restricted weapon, firearm or ammunition in a manner that contravenes any regulation made pursuant to paragraph 116(1)(*c*).

(6.1) No person shall, in the course of a business described in paragraph (1)(*b*), handle or store any prohibited weapon referred to in that paragraph or any component or part thereof in a manner that contravenes any regulation made by the Governor in Council pursuant to paragraph 116(*a*.1).

[1991, c. 40, s. 39(*a*) will repeal subsection 105(6.1) and substitute the following.]

Idem.

(6.1) No person shall, in the course of carrying on a business described in paragraph (1)(*b*), handle or store any prohibited weapon referred to in that paragraph or any component or part thereof in a manner that contravenes any regulation made by the Governor in Council pursuant to paragraph 116(1)(*a*.1).

(7) No person shall, in the course of a business described in subsection (1) or (2), knowingly handle, ship, store or transport any firearm or ammunition, or any prohibited weapon referred to in paragraph (1)(*b*) or any component

or part thereof, in a manner that contravenes any regulation made by the Governor in Council pursuant to paragraph 116(*d*).

[1991, c. 40, s. 39(*c*) will repeal subsection 105(7) and substitute the following.]

Handling and transportation.

(7) No person shall, in the course of operating a museum referred to in subsection (1) or of carrying on a business described in paragraph (1)(*a*) or (*b*) or paragraph (2)(*a*) or (*b*), knowingly handle, ship, store or transport any firearm or ammunition, or any prohibited weapon referred to in paragraph (1)(b) or any component or part thereof, in a manner that contravenes any regulation made by the Governor in Council pursuant to paragraph 116(1)(*d*).

(8) Every one who contravenes subsection (1), (2), (4), (6) or (7)

[1991, c. 40, s. 39(*d*) will repeal all that portion of subsection 105(8) preceding paragraph (*a*) and substitute the following.]

Punishment.

(8) Every one who contravenes subsection (1), (2), (4), (6), (6.1) or (7)

(*a*) is guilty of an indictable offence and liable to imprisonment for a term not exceeding five years; or

(*b*) is guilty of an offence punishable on summary conviction.

Firearms Acquisition Certificates

Consideration of application and issuance of firearms acquisition certificate — Where no certificate may be issued — Coming in force of para. (2)(*c*) — Deemed notice — Notice to be given — Material to accompany notice — Reference to provincial court judge — Application for firearms acquisition certificate — Further information — Limitation — Term for which certificate valid and fee — Exception — Validity of certificate.

106. (1) Where a firearms officer to whom an application for a firearms acquisition certificate is made, after considering the information contained in the application, any further information that is submitted to him pursuant to a requirement made under subsection (9) and such other information as may reasonably be regarded as relevant to the application, does not have notice of any matter that may render it desirable in the interests of the safety of the applicant or any other person that the applicant should not acquire a firearm, he shall, subject to subsection (2) and on receipt by him of the appropriate fee, if any, issue a firearms acquisition certificate to the applicant.

[1991, c. 40, s. 19(1) will repeal subsection 106(1) and substitute the following.]

Consideration of application and issuance of firearms acquisition certificate — Appearance and photograph — Exception for renewals.

106.(1) Where a firearms officer who has received an application for a firearms acquisition certificate and the fee prescribed by regulation does not, after considering the information contained in the application, any further information that is submitted to the firearms officer pursuant to a requirement under subsection (9) and such other information as may reasonably be regarded as relevant to the application, have notice of any matter that may render it desirable in the interests of the safety of the applicant or of any other person that the applicant should not acquire a firearm, the firearms officer shall, subject to subsection (2), and after at least twenty-eight days have elapsed since the application was received, issue a firearms acquisition certificate to the applicant.

(1.1) For greater certainty, an application for a firearms acquisition certificate need not be submitted in person, but the firearms officer who receives the application may require that the applicant appear in person before the firearms acquisition certificate is issued and the firearms officer must be satisfied that any photograph of the applicant that is to be attached to the firearms acquisition certificate is a current photograph of the applicant sufficient to accurately identify the applicant.

(1.2) Notwithstanding subsection (1), where an applicant for a firearms acquisition certificate holds a valid firearms acquisition certificate at the time of applying for a new firearms acquisition certificate.

(*a*) the firearms officer may issue the new firearms acquisition certificate before the twenty-eight days referred to in subsection (1) have elapsed; and

(*b*) the fee prescribed by regulation for the new firearms acquisition certificate shall be reduced by one-half.

(2) No firearms acquisition certificate may be issued to a person who

(*a*) is under the age of sixteen years;

[1991, c. 40, s. 19(2) will repeal paragraph 106(2)(*a*) and substitute the following.]

(*a*) is under the age of eighteen years;

(*b*) is prohibited by an order made pursuant to section 100 or 103 or by a condition of a probation order referred to in paragraph 737(2)(*d*) from having a firearm in his possession; or

(*c*) fails to produce evidence in conjunction with his application for a firearms acquisition certificate that he has

(i) completed a course in the safe handling and use of firearms, or

(ii) successfully completed a test relating to the safe handling and use of firearms

that, at the time he completed the course or test, was approved for the purposes of this section by the Attorney General of the province in which he took the course or test.

[1991, c. 40, s. 19(3) will repeal paragraph 106(2)(*c*) and substitute the following.]

(*c*) subject to subsection (2.2), fails to produce evidence in conjunction with an application for a firearms acquisition certificate that the person has, at any time prior to the application,

(i) successfully completed a course in, or a test relating to, the safe handling and use of and the laws relating to firearms, that was approved for the purposes of this section by the Attorney General of the province in which the course or test is administered, or

(ii) been certified by a firearms officer, in circumstances prescribed by regulation, as meeting the criteria of competence in the safe handling and use of firearms and the laws relating to firearms prescribed by regulation.

[1991, c. 40, s. 19(4) will amend section 106 by adding the following immediately after subsection 106(2).]

Notice — Where prohibition order.

(2.1) Where a firearms officer certifies that an applicant is competent for the purposes of subparagraph 106(2)(*c*)(ii), the firearms officer shall immediately so inform the chief provincial firearms officer in writing and shall give reasons for the certification.

(2.2) In the case of an applicant who has been the subject of an order under subsection 100(1), (2) or (7), the applicant shall produce evidence that the applicant successfully completed both the course and the test referred to in subparagraph (2)(*c*)(i) after the expiration of the order.

(3) Paragraph (2)(*c*) shall come into force in any province only on a day fixed in a proclamation declaring that paragraph to be in force in that province.

(4) A firearms officer shall be deemed to have notice of a matter that may render it desirable in the interests of the safety of an applicant for a firearms acquisition certificate or of any other person that the applicant should not acquire a firearm and a provincial court judge, on a reference pursuant to subsection (7), is entitled to confirm the opinion of a firearms officer that it is not desirable in the interests of the safety of the applicant or of any other person that the applicant should acquire a firearm, where it is made to appear to him that the applicant

(*a*) has been convicted within five years immediately preceding the date of his application, in proceedings on indictment, of

(i) an offence in the commission of which violence against another person was used, threatened or attempted, or

(ii) an offence under this Part;

(*b*) within five years immediately preceding the date of his application, has been treated for a mental disorder, whether in a hospital, mental institute or psychiatric clinic or otherwise and whether or not he was, during that period, confined to such a hospital, institute or clinic, where the disorder for which he was so treated was associated with violence or threatened or attempted violence on the part of the applicant against himself or any other person; or (*c*) has a history of behaviour occurring within five years immediately preceding the date of his application, that included violence or threatened or attempted violence on the part of the applicant against himself or any other person.

[1991, c. 40, s. 19(5) will repeal subsection 106(4) and substitute the following.]

Deemed notice.

(4) A firearms officer shall be deemed to have notice of a matter that may render it desirable in the interests of the safety of an applicant for a firearms acquisition certificate or of any other person that the applicant should not acquire a firearm and a provincial court judge, on a reference pursuant to subsection (7), is entitled to confirm the opinion of a firearms officer that it is not desirable in the interests of the safety of the applicant or of any other person that the applicant should acquire a firearm, where it is made to appear to the judge that

(*a*) the applicant has been convicted within five years immediately preceding the date of the application, in proceedings on indictment, of

(i) an offence in the commission of which violence against another person was used, threatened or attempted, or

(ii) an offence under this Part;

(*b*) the applicant, within five years immediately preceding the date of the application, has been treated for a mental disorder, whether in a hospital, mental institute or psychiatric clinic or otherwise and whether or not the applicant was, during that period, confined to such a hospital, institute or clinic, where the disorder was associated with violence or threatened or attempted violence on the part of the applicant against any person;

(*c*) the applicant has a history of behaviour occurring within five years immediately preceding the date of the application, that included violence or threatened or attempted violence on the part of the applicant against any person; or

(*d*) there is another good and sufficient reason for confirming the opinion.

(5) Where a firearms officer to whom an application for a firearms acquisition certificate is made has notice of any matter that may render it desirable in the interests of the safety of the applicant or of any other person that the applicant should not acquire a firearm, he shall notify the applicant in writing that in his opinion it is not desirable in the interests of the safety of the applicant or of any other person or description of persons specified in the notice that the applicant acquire a firearm, and of his reasons therefor, and that, unless within thirty days from the day on which the notice is received by the applicant or within such further time as is, before or after the expiration of that period, allowed by a provincial court judge, the applicant, in writing, requests the firearms officer to refer his opinion to a provincial court judge for confirmation or variation thereof, the application for the firearms acquisition certificate will be refused by him.

[1991, c. 40, s. 19(5) will repeal subsection 106(5) and substitute the following.]

Notice to be given.

(5) Where a firearms officer who has received an application for a firearms acquisition certificate has notice of any matter that may render it desirable in the interests of the safety of the applicant or of any other person that the applicant should not acquire a firearm, the firearms officer shall notify the applicant in writing that, in the opinion of the firearms officer, it is not desirable in the interests of the safety of the applicant or of any other person that the applicant acquire a firearm and of the reasons therefor, and that, unless within thirty days after the day on which the notice is received by the applicant or within such further time as is, before or after the expiration of that period, allowed by a provincial court judge, the applicant, in writing, requests the firearms officer to refer the opinion to a provincial court judge for confirmation or variation thereof, the applicant for the firearms acquisition certificate will be refused.

(6) A notice given by a firearms officer under this section shall be accompanied by a copy or an extract of the provisions of this section and of subsections 100(5) to (13).

(7) On receipt by a firearms officer, within the time provided in subsection (5) of a request in writing to refer his opinion referred to in that subsection to a provincial court judge for confirmation or variation thereof, the firearms officer shall forthwith comply with that request.

(8) An application for a firearms acquisition certificate shall be in a form prescribed by the Commissioner and shall be made to a firearms officer.

[1991, c. 40, s. 19(6) will repeal subsection 106(8) and substitute the following.]

Application for firearms acquisition certificate — No civil liability.

(8) An application for a firearms acquisition certifcate shall be made to a firearms officer in a form prescribed by the Commissioner and shall be accompanied by the names of two persons who belong to a class of persons prescribed by regulation who have known the applicant for at least three years and who can confirm that the information on the application, and any further information submitted pursuant to subsection (9), is true.

(8.1) No person who is referred to in subsection (8) incurs any civil liability by reason of any action taken by that person in connection with the person's name having accompanied an appliation for a firearms acquisition certificate.

(9) A firearms officer to whom an application for a firearms acquisition certificate is made may require the applicant to submit such further information in addition to that included in the application as may reasonably be regarded as relevant for the purpose of determining whether there is any matter that might render it dangerous for the safety of the applicant or of any other person if the applicant acquired a firearm.

[1991, c. 40, s. 19(6) will repeal subsection 106(9) and substitute the following.]

Further information — Investigation.

(9) A firearms officer who has received an application for a firearms acquisition certificate may require the applicant to submit such further information in addition to that included in the application as may reasonably be regarded as relevant for the purpose of determining whether there is any matter that might render it dangerous for the safety of the applicant or of any other person if the applicant acquired a firearm.

(9.1) Without restricting the scope of the inquiries a firearms officer may make under subsection (1), a firearms officer who has received an application for a firearms acquisition certificate may conduct an investigation which may consist of interviews with the applicant's neighbours, community/social workers, spouse, dependents, or whomever in the opinion of the firearms officer may provide information pertaining to whether the applicant has a history of violent behaviour, including violence in the home.

(10) No local registrar of firearms, firearms officer or other person shall require as information, to be submitted by an applicant for a firearms acquisition certificate or permit, details concerning the makes or serial numbers of shotguns or rifles of a type, kind or design commonly used in Canada for hunting or sporting purposes.

(11) A firearms acquisition certificate is valid for five years from the day on which it is issued, and the fee payable for the issue thereof is ten dollars.

[1991, c. 40, s. 19(7) will repeal subsection 106(11) and substitute the following.]

Form of and term for certificate.

(11) The firearms acquisition certificate shall be in a form prescribed by the Commissioner, shall, except where the Commissioner deems that to do so would be inappropriate, have a photograph of the holder attached to it, and shall be valid for five years after the day on which it is issued, unless it is revoked before that time.

(12) Notwithstanding subsection (11), no fee is payable in respect of a firearms acquisition certificate that is issued to a person who requires a firearm to hunt or trap in order to sustain himself or his family.

(13) A firearms acquisition certificate is valid throughout Canada. R.S. 1985, c. 27 (1st Supp.), s. 203.

[1991, c. 40, s. 19(8) will amend section 106 by adding the following immediately after subsection 106(13).]

Refusal to issue — Reference to provincial court judge — Fixing date for hearing and notice — Burden of proof — Hearing of reference and disposition — Appeal to appeal court in certain cases — Definition of "appeal court".

(14) Where a firearms officer refuses to issue a firearms acquisition

certificate, the firearms officer shall notify the applicant in writing of the refusal and the reasons for it and include in the notification a copy of this subsection and subsections (15) to (20).

(15) Where a firearms officer refuses to issue a firearms acquisition certificate, the applicant may, within thirty days after being notified of the refusal or within such further time as is, before or after the expiration of that period, allowed by a provincial court judge, request, in writing, the firearms officer to refer the matter to a provincial court judge having jurisdiction in the territorial division in which the applicant resides.

(16) On a reference by a firearms officer pursuant to subsection (15), the provincial court judge shall fix a date for the hearing of the reference and direct that notice of the hearing be given to the applicant and to the firearms officer, in such manner as the provincial court judge may specify.

(17) In a hearing under subsection (16), the burden of proof is on the applicant for the firearms acquisition certificate to satisfy the provincial court judge that the refusal to issue the firearms acquisition certificate was not justified.

(18) Where, at the conclusion of a hearing under subsection (16), the applicant has satisfied the provincial court judge that the refusal to issue the firearms acquisition certificate was not justified, the provincial court judge shall, by order, direct the firearms officer to issue to the applicant a firearms acquisition certificate and the firearms officer shall immediately comply with the order.

(19) Where a provincial court judge makes an order pursuant to subsection (18), the firearms officer may appeal to the appeal court against the order, and the provisions of Part XXVII except sections 816 and 819 and 829 to 838 apply, with such modifications as the circumstances require, in respect of the appeal.

(20) In this section, "appeal court" has the meaning given that expression in subsection 100(11).

Alternative firearms acquisition certificate.

107. The Governor in Council may, on application by the Attorney General of a province, by order, declare any hunting licence, certificate, permit, or other document described in the order that is issued under the authority of a law of a province to be a valid firearms acquisition certificate where, in the opinion of the Governor in Council, the licence, certificate, permit or other document may only be issued to persons to whom and in circumstances in which a firearms acquisition certificate could validly be issued if an application were made for the certificate, and where an order is made under this section, a licence, certificate, permit or other document to which the order relates shall, on and after a day specified in the order, be deemed for all purposes of this Part to be a firearms acquisition certificate, whether or not the licence, certificate, permit or other document was issued before, on or after the day specified in the order.

[1991, c. 40, s. 20 will repeal section 107 and substitute the following.]

Firearms acquisition certificate for other persons — Application — Agreements with provinces.

107. (1) Notwithstanding subsection 106(2), the Governor in Council may make regulations prescribing the persons, other than individuals, or classes of such persons to which firearms acquisition certificates may be issued, and subsections 106(1), (5) to (7), (9) to (11) and (13) to (20) apply, with such modifications as the circumstances require, in respect of firearms acquisition certificates issued to such persons.

(2) An application for a firearms acquisition certificate by a person or a member of a class of persons prescribed pursuant to subsection (1) shall be made to a firearms officer in a form prescribed by the Commissioner.

Agreements with provinces.

108. The Solicitor General of Canada, with the approval of the Governor in Council, may enter into agreements with the governments of the provinces for the coordination, to the maximum extent possible, of the administration of sections 106, 109 and 110 with the administration by provinces of provincial laws and programs relating to game hunting, firearms competency testing and firearms safety training.

[1991, c. 40, s. 20 will repeal section 108 and substitute the following.]

Agreements with provinces.

108. The Minister of Justice of Canada, with the approval of the Governor in Council, may enter into agreements with the governments of the provinces for the coordination, to the maximum extent possible, of the administration of sections 106, 107, 109, 109.1 and 110 with the administration by provinces of provincial laws and programs relating to game hunting, firearms competency testing and firearms safety training.

Restricted Weapon Registration Certificates

Application for registration certificate — Permit to convey — Limitation — Idem — Distribution of copies of application — Matters to be reported to Commissioner — Registration certificate — Limitation.

109. (1) An application for a registration certificate in respect of a restricted weapon shall be in a form prescribed by the Commissioner and shall be made to a local registrar of firearms.

(2) On receiving an application for a registration certificate, a local registrar

of firearms may issue a permit under subsection 110(4) authorizing the applicant to convey the weapon to him for examination.

(3) A registration certificate may be issued only where a local registrar of firearms indicates on the copy of the application for the certificate that is sent to the Commissioner pursuant to subsection (5) that

(*a*) the applicant for the certificate is the holder of a firearms acquisition certificate and is eighteen or more years of age, and

(*b*) the restricted weapon to which the application relates bears a serial number sufficient to distinguish it from other restricted weapons or, in the case of an antique firearm that does not bear such a serial number, it is accurately described in the application,

and further that the restricted weapon to which the application relates

(*c*) is required by the applicant

(i) to protect life,

(ii) for use in connection with his lawful profession or occupation,

(iii) for use in target practice under the auspices of a shooting club approved for the purposes of this section by the Attorney General of the province in which the premises of the shooting club are located, or

(iv) for use in target practice in accordance with conditions proposed to be attached to the permit to be issued in respect of the restricted weapon under subsection 110(1),

[1991, c. 40, s. 21(2) will repeal subparagraph 109(3)(*c*)(iii) and substitute the following.]

(iii) for use in target practice under the auspices of a shooting club approved for the purposes of this section by the Attorney General of the province in which the premises of the shooting club are located or by an agent specially designated by that Attorney General in writing for the purpose of this subsection, or

(*d*) will form part of a gun collection of the applicant who is a genuine gun collector, or

[1991, c. 40, s. 21(3) will repeal paragraph 109(3)(*d*) and substitute the following.]

(*d*) will form part of a gun collection of the applicant who is a genuine gun collector and who has complied with any regulations relating to the secure storage of, and the keeping of records respecting, restricted weapons made pursuant to subsection 116(1), or

(*e*) is or is deemed pursuant to paragraph 116(*f*) to be a relic for the purposes of this Part.

(4) A registration certificate may only be issued in respect of a restricted weapon described in paragraph (*c*) of the definition "restricted weapon" in subsection 84(1) where a local registrar of firearms, in addition to the matters referred to in subsection (3), indicates on the copy of the application that is sent to the Commissioner pursuant to subsection (5) that the restricted weapon

will form part of a gun collection of the applicant who is a genuine gun collector whose collection includes one or more restricted weapons described in that paragraph.

[1991, c. 40, s. 21(4) will amend section 109 by adding the following immediately after subsection 109(4).]

Idem — Changes — Time of ownership.

(4.1) A registration certificate may only be issued in respect of a restricted weapon described in paragraph (*c*.1) of the definition "restricted weapon" in subsection 84(1) where a local registrar of firearms, in addition to the matters referred to in subsection (3),

(*a*) indicates on the copy of the application that is sent to the Commissioner pursuant to subsection (5) that the restricted weapon will form part of a gun collection of the applicant who is a genuine gun collector whose collection includes one or more restricted weapons described in that paragraph; and

(*b*) describes on the copy referred to in paragraph (*a*) all alterations that have been made to the restricted weapon to enable it to fire only one projectile with one pressure of the trigger.

(4.2) Where the description of the alterations referred to in paragraph (4.1)(*b*) changes in respect of a restricted weapon, the restricted weapon registration certificate issued in respect of the weapon is automatically revoked and the holder of that certificate shall immediately apply for a new registration certificate in respect of the weapon.

(4.3) Notwithstanding anything in this Act, no registration certificate may be issued in respect of a restricted weapon described in paragraph (*c*.1) of the definition "restricted weapon" in subsection 84(1) to a person who did not lawfully possess such a restricted weapon at the time of the coming into force of this subsection.

(5) The local registrar of firearms by whom an application for a registration certificate is received shall

(*a*) send one copy thereof to the Commissioner;

(*b*) deliver one copy thereof to the applicant for the certificate; and

(*c*) retain one copy thereof.

(6) Where a local registrar of firearms to whom an application for a registration certificate is made has notice of any matter that may render it desirable in the interests of the safety of the applicant or any other person that the applicant should not possess a restricted weapon, he shall report that matter to the Commissioner and he may, if the restricted weapon is conveyed to him for examination, hold the weapon pending the final disposition of the application for a registration certificate in respect thereof.

(7) On receiving an endorsed copy of an application for a registration certificate, the Commissioner shall, subject to subsections (3) and (4) and

section 112, register the restricted weapon described in the application and issue a restricted weapon registration certificate therefor to the applicant, in such form as the Commissioner may prescribe, indicating thereon the place at which the holder of the certificate is thereby entitled to possess the restricted weapon.

(8) No place other than the usual dwelling-house of the applicant for a registration certificate or his ordinary place of business may be indicated on the registration certificate as the place at which the holder of the certificate is thereby entitled to possess the restricted weapon to which the certificate relates.

[1991, c. 40, s. 22 will amend the act by adding section 109.1 immediately after section 109.]

Registration certificate for other persons.

109.1 Notwithstanding paragraphs 109(3)(*a*) and (*d*), the Governor in Council may make regulations prescribing the persons, other than individuals, or classes of such persons, to which restricted weapon registration certificates may be issued, and subsections 109(1) to (3) and (5) to (8) apply, with such modifications as the circumstances require, in respect of registration certificates issued to such persons.

Carriage Permits, Business Permits and Minors Permits

Permit to carry restricted weapon — Limitation — Permit to transport restricted weapon — Permit to convey restricted weapon — Permit to carry on business — Permits for persons hunting as a way of life — Permit to person between 12 and 16 years of age — Idem — Where no fee payable and fee for business permits — Validity of permit — Form and conditions of permit.

110. (1) A permit authorizing a person to have in his possession a restricted weapon elsewhere than at the place at which he is otherwise entitled to possess it, as indicated on the registration certificate issued in respect thereof, may be issued by the Commissioner, the Attorney General of a province, a chief provincial firearms officer or a member of a class of persons that has been designated in writing for that purpose by the Commissioner or the Attorney General of a province and shall remain in force until the expiration of the period for which it is expressed to be issued, unless it is sooner revoked.

[1991, c. 40, s. 23(1) will repeal subsection 110(1) and substitute the following.]

Permit to carry restricted weapon.

(1) A permit that authorizes a person to possess a particular restricted weapon, whether or not that person is the person mentioned in the registration certificate issued in respect of the weapon, elsewhere than at the place at which the person is otherwise entitled to possess it, as indicated on the registration

certificate issued in respect thereof, may be issued by the Commissioner, the Attorney General of a province, a chief provincial firearms officer or a member of a class of persons that has been designated in writing for that purpose by the Commissioner or the Attorney General of a province, and remains in force until the expiration of the period for which it is expressed to be issued, unless it is revoked before that expiration.

(2) A permit described in subsection (1) may be issued only where the person authorized to issue it is satisfied that the applicant therefor requires the restricted weapon to which the application relates

(*a*) to protect life;

(*b*) for use in connection with his lawful profession or occupation;

(*c*) for use in target practice under the auspices of a shooting club approved for the purposes of this section by the Attorney General of the province in which the premises of the shooting club are located; or

(*d*) for use in target practice in accordance with the conditions attached to the permit.

[1991, c. 40, s. 23(2) will add the following immediately after subsection 110(2).]

Temporary permit to carry.

(2.1) A permit may be issued by a person authorized to issue a permit under subsection (1) that authorizes a person who does not reside in Canada to possess and carry between the places specified in the permit a restricted weapon described in the permnit for use in a target shooting competition that is held under the auspices of a shooting club referred to in subparagraph 109(3)(*c*)(iii), and remains in force until the expiration of the period for which it is expressed to be issued, unless it is revoked before that expiration.

(3) A permit to transport a restricted weapon from one place to another place specified therein may be issued by a local registrar of firearms to any person who is required to transport that weapon by reason of a change of residence or for any other *bona fide* reason, and shall remain in force until the expiration of the period for which it is expressed to be issued, unless it is sooner revoked.

[1991, c. 40, s. 23(3) will add the following immediately after subsection 110(3).]

Temporary storage permit — Contents of permit — Validity of permit.

(3.1) A permit that authorizes a holder of a registration certificate in respect of a restricted weapon to temporarily store the restricted weapon elsewhere than at the place at which that holder is otherwise entitled to possess it may be issued by a local registrar of firearms jointly to the holder and an individual under whose control the restricted weapon is to be stored.

(3.2) A permit described in subsection (3.1) shall describe the restricted weapon in respect of which it is issued, shall specify the place at which that restricted weapon is to be stored and shall authorize, in addition to the storage of the weapon, either person named in the permit to transport the restricted weapon, prior to the beginning of the period of storage, to the place where it is to be stored and, after the end of the period of storage, to the place at which the holder of the restricted weapon registration certificate in respect of the restricted weapon is entitled to possess that restricted weapon.

(3.3) A permit described in subsection (3.1) shall remain in force until the expiration of the period, not exceeding one year, for which it is expressed to be issued, unless it is revoked before that expiration, but either the holder of the registration certificate in respect of the restricted weapon in respect of which the permit is issued or the individual under whose control the restricted weapon is stored may apply to the local registrar of firearms for renewal of the permit.

(4) A permit authorizing an applicant for a registration certificate to convey the weapon to which the application relates to a local registrar of firearms may be issued by a local registrar of firearms and shall remain in force until the expiration of the period for which it is expressed to be issued, unless it is sooner revoked.

(5) A permit to carry on a business described in subsection 105(1) or subparagraph 105(2)(*b*)(i) may be issued by the Commissioner, the Attorney General or chief provincial firearms officer of the province where the business is or is to be carried on or by any person whom the Commissioner or the Attorney General designates in writing for that purpose and shall remain in force until the expiration of the period, not exceeding one year, for which it is expressed to be issued, unless it is sooner revoked.

(6) A permit to possess a firearm, other than a restricted weapon, may be issued by a firearms officer to a person under the age of sixteen years who hunts or traps as a way of life if the firearms officer is satisfied that the person needs to hunt or trap in order to sustain himself or his family and the application for the permit includes a consent to the issuance of the permit signed by a parent of the applicant or, if a consent by a parent cannot be obtained because of the death of both parents or for any other reason it is not practicable or desirable in the opinion of the firearms officer to whom the application is made to obtain a parent's consent, a person having custody or control of the applicant.

(7) A permit authorizing a person who is twelve or more years of age but under the age of sixteen years to possess a firearm, other than a restricted weapon, may be issued by a firearms officer if he is satisfied that the applicant therefor requires such a permit in order to enable him to possess a firearm for the purpose of target practice, game hunting or instruction in the use of firearms in accordance with conditions for supervision attached to the permit and the application for the permit includes a consent to the issuance of the permit signed by a parent of the applicant or, if a consent by a parent cannot

be obtained because of the death of both parents or for any other reason it is not practicable or desirable in the opinion of the firearms officer to whom the application is made to obtain a parent's consent, a person having custody or control of the applicant.

(8) A permit mentioned in subsection (6) or (7) shall remain in force until

(*a*) the expiration of the period for which it is expressed to be issued, or

(*b*) the person to whom it is issued attains the age of sixteen years,

whichever first occurs, unless it is sooner revoked.

(9) Permits mentioned in subsections (1), (3), (4), (6) and (7) shall be issued without payment of a fee but no permit mentioned in subsection (5) may be issued unless the application therefor is accompanied by the prescribed fee.

[1991, c. 40, s. 23(4) will repeal subsections 110(5) to (9) and substitute the following.]

Permit to carry on business — Permits to persons hunting as a way of life — Permit to person between 12 and 18 years of age — Idem — Where no fee payable and fee for business permits.

(5) A permit to carry on a business described in paragraph 105(1)(*a*) or (*b*) or subparagrapn 105(2)(*b*)(i) may be issued by the Commissioner, the Attorney General or the chief provincial firearms officer of the province where the business is or is to be carried on or by any person whom the Commissioner or the Attorney General designates in writing for that purpose, the fee payable on application for such a permit is the fee prescribed by regulation, and the permit remains in force until the expiration of the period, not exceeding one year, for which it is expressed to be issued, unless it is revoked before that expiration.

(6) A permit to possess a firearm, other than a restricted weapon, may be issued by a firearms officer to a person under the age of eighteen years who hunts or traps as a way of life if the firearms officer is satisfied that the person needs to hunt or trap in order to sustain the person or the person's family and the application for the permit includes a consent to the issuance of the permit signed by a parent of the applicant or, if a consent by a parent cannot be obtained because of the death of both parents or for any other reason it is not practicable or desirable in the opinion of the firearms officer to whom the application is made to obtain a parent's consent, a person having custody or control of the applicant.

(7) A permit authorizing a person who is twelve or more years of age but under the age of eighteen years to possess a firearm, other than a restricted weapon, may be issued by a firearms officer if the firearms officer is satisfied that the applicant therefor requires such a permit in order to enable the applicant to possess a firearm for the purpose of target practice, game hunting or instruction in the use of firearms in accordance with conditions for supervision attached to the permit signed by a parent of the applicant or, if a consent

by a parent cannot be obtained because of the death of both parents or for any other reason it is not practicable or desirable in the opinion of the firearms officer to whom the application is made to obtain a parent's consent, a person having custody or control of the applicant.

(8) A permit mentioned in subsection (6) or (7) shall remain in force until

(*a*) the expiration of the period for which it is expressed to be issued, or

(*b*) the person to whom it is issued attains the age of eighteen years,

whichever first occurs, unless it is sooner revoked.

(9) Permits mentioned in subsections (1), (2.1), (3), (3.1), (4), (6) and (7) shall be issued without payment of a fee, but no permit mentioned in subsection (5) may be issued unless the application therefor is accompanied by the fee prescribed by regulation.

(10) No permit, other than

(*a*) a permit for the possession of a restricted weapon for use as described in paragraph (2)(*c*),

(*b*) a permit to transport a restricted weapon from one place to another place specified therein as mentioned in subsection (3), or

[1991, c. 40, s. 23(5) will amend subsection 110(10) by striking out the word "or" at the end of paragraph (*b*) and adding the following immediately after paragraph 110(10)(*b*).]

(*b*.1) a permit that authorizes a person who does not reside in Canada to possess and carry a restricted weapon for use in a target shooting competition as mentioned in subsection (2.1),

(*b*.2) a permit that authorizes a holder of a registration certificate in respect of a restricted weapon to temporarily store the restricted weapon elsewhere than at the place at which that holder is otherwise entitled to possess it, as mentioned in subsection (3.1), or

(*c*) a permit authorizing an applicant for a registration certificate to convey the weapon to which the application relates to a local registrar of firearms as mentioned in subsection (4),

is valid outside the province in which it is issued unless it is issued by the Commissioner or a person designated in writing by him and authorized in writing by him to issue permits valid outside the province and is endorsed for the purposes of this subsection by the person who issued it as being valid within the provinces indicated therein.

(11) Every permit shall be in a form prescribed by the Commissioner, but any person who is authorized to issue a permit relating to any restricted weapon, firearm or ammunition may attach to the permit any reasonable condition relating to the use, carriage, possession, handling or storage of weapons or ammunition that he deems desirable in the particular circumstances and in the interests of the safety of the applicant therefor or any other person.

Agreements with provinces.

111. The Solicitor General of Canada, with the approval of the Governor in Council, may enter into agreements with the governments of the provinces providing for payments by Canada to the provinces in respect of costs actually incurred by the provinces in the administration of sections 105, 106 and subsection 110(5).

[1991, c. 40, s. 24 will repeal section 111 and substitute the following.]

Agreements with provinces.

111. The Minister of Justice of Canada, with the approval of the Governor in Council, may enter into agreements with the governments of the provinces providing for payments by Canada to the provinces in respect of costs actually incurred by the provinces in the administration of sections 105, 106 and 107 and subsection 110(5).

Refusal to Issue and Revocation of Registration Certificates and Permits and Appeals

[1991, c. 40, s. 25 will repeal the heading preceding section 112 and substitute the following.]

Refusal to Issue and Revocation of Registration Certificates and Permits Revocation of Authorizations, Revocation of Firearms Acquisition Certificates and Appeals

Revocation of certificate — Revocation of permit — Refusal to issue a certificate — Refusal to issue a permit — Notice to be given — Disposal of restricted weapons, etc. — Idem — Appeal — Service of notice of appeal — Appellant as witness — Disposition of appeal — Burden on applicant — Appeal to appeal court — Definitions — "Appeal court" — "Provincial court judge".

112. (1) A Registration certificate may be revoked by the Commissioner.

(2) A permit may be revoked by any person who is authorized to issue such a permit.

[1991, c. 40, s. 26(1) will add the following immediately after subsection 112(2).]

Revocation of authorization.

(2.1) An authorization referred to in subsection 90(3.2) may be revoked by a local registrar of firearms.

(3) The Commissioner may refuse to issue a registration certificate where he has notice of any matter that may render it desirable in the interests of the safety of the applicant therefor or any other person that the applicant should not possess a restricted weapon.

(4) Any person who is authorized to issue a permit under any of subsections

110(3) to (7) may refuse to issue such a permit where he has notice of any matter that may render it desirable in the interests of the safety of the applicant therefor or any other person that such a permit should not be issued to the applicant.

(5) Where a registration certificate or permit is revoked or the issue of any registration certificate or permit is refused under this section, the person by whom it is revoked or by whom its issue is refused shall notify the holder of the registration certificate or permit or the applicant therefor, as the case may be, in writing of the revocation or refusal and of his reasons therefor and shall include in such notification a copy or an extract of the provisions of this section.

(6) A notice under subsection (5) shall specify therein a reasonable period of time within which the person affected by the revocation or refusal may surrender to a police officer or otherwise lawfully dispose of any restricted weapon, firearm or ammunition lawfully possessed by him prior to the revocation or refusal the possession of which by him has thereby become unlawful, and that person is not liable to prosecution by reason only of his having the restricted weapon, firearm or ammunition in his possession during that period of time.

[1991, c. 40, s. 26(2) will repeal subsections 112(4) to 112(6) and substitute the following.]

Refusal to issue a permit — Notice to be given — Disposal of restricted weapons, etc.

(4) Any person who is authorized to issue a permit under any of subsections 110(2.1) to (7) may refuse to issue such a permit where that person has notice of any matter that may render it desirable in the interests of the safety of the applicant therefore or any other person that such a permit should not be issued to the applicant.

(5) Where a registration certificate or a permit is revoked or a firearms acquisition certificate is revoked pursuant to subsection 100(7.1) or 103(3.1) or subparagraph 103(6)(*b*)(ii) or the issue of any registration certificate or permit is refused under this section, the person by whom it is revoked or by whom its issue is refused shall give notice to the holder of the registration certificate, permit or firearms acquisition certificate or the applicant therefor, as the case may be, in writing, of the revocation or refusal and of the reasons therefor and shall include in the notification a copy or an extract of the provisions of this section.

(6) A notice under subsection (5) shall

(*a*) specify a reasonable period within which the person affected by the revocation or refusal may surrender to a police officer or otherwise lawfully dispose of any restricted weapon, firearm or ammunition in respect of which the notice applies, and during which that person is not liable to prosecution by reason only that the person posssesses the restricted weapon, firearm or ammunition during that period of time; and

(*b*) state that if that person fails to dispose of the restricted weapon, firearm or ammunition within the period specified in the notice, the restricted weapon, firearm or ammunition is forfeited to Her Majesty and must be surrendered to a police officer or firearms officer to be disposed of as the Attorney General directs.

(7) Where an appeal is taken under subsection (8), the period of time referred to in subsection (6) does not commence until that appeal is finally disposed of.

(8) A person who feels himself aggrieved by

(*a*) any action or decision taken under this section, or

(*b*) the failure of a local registrar of firearms to indicate on the copy of an application for a registration certificate that is sent by him to the Commissioner pursuant to subsection 109(5), any of the matters referred to in subsections 109(3) and (4) that is applicable in respect of the application,

may, within thirty days from the day on which he was notified of the action or decision or became aware of the failure, unless before or after the expiration of that period further time is allowed by a provincial court judge, appeal to a provincial court judge from the action, decision or failure by filing with the provincial court judge a notice of appeal, setting out with reasonable certainty the action, decision or failure complained of and the grounds of appeal, together with such further material as the provincial court judge may require.

(9) A copy of any notice of appeal filed with a provincial court judge under subsection (8) and of any further material required to be filed therewith shall be served within fourteen days of the filing of the notice, unless before or after the expiration of that period further time is allowed by a provincial court judge, on the person who took the action or decision or who was responsible for the failure being appealed from or on such other person as the provincial court judge may direct.

(10) For the purposes of an appeal under subsection (8), the appellant is a competent and compellable witness.

(11) On the hearing of an appeal under subsection (8), the provincial court judge may

(*a*) dismiss the appeal; or

(*b*) allow the appeal and

(i) cancel the revocation of the registration certificate or permit or direct that a registration certificate or permit be issued to the applicant therefor, as the case may be, or

[1991, c. 40, s. 32 will repeal subparagraph 112(11)(*b*)(i) and substitute the following.]

(i) cancel the revocation of the registration certificate, permit or firearms acquisition certificate or direct that a registration certificate or permit be issued to the applicant therefore, as the case may be, or

(ii) direct that a registration certificate be issued notwithstanding the failure referred to in paragraph (8)(*b*).

(12) A provincial court judge shall dispose of an appeal under subsection (8) heard by him by dismissing it unless the applicant establishes to the satisfaction of the provincial court judge that a disposition referred to in paragraph (11)(*b*) is warranted.

(13) Where the provincial court judge

(*a*) dismisses an appeal under subsection (11), the appellant, or

(*b*) allows an appeal under subsection (11),

(i) the Attorney General of Canada or counsel instructed by him for the purpose, if the person who took the action or decision or who was responsible for the failure referred to in paragraph (8)(*b*) that was appealed from to the provincial court judge was the Commissioner or a local registrar of firearms appointed by him, or

(ii) the Attorney General or counsel instructed by him for the purpose, in any other case,

may appeal to the appeal court against the dismissal or against the allowing of the appeal, as the case may be, and the provisions of Part XXVII except sections 816 to 819 and sections 829 to 838 apply, with such modifications as the circumstances require, in respect of that appeal.

(14) In this section,

"appeal court" has the meaning given that expression in subsection 100(11);

"provincial court judge" means a judge having jurisdiction in the territorial division where the person who feels himself aggrieved as described in subsection (8) resides. R.S. 1985, c. 27 (1st Supp.), s. 203.

Offences Relating to Certificate and Permits

False statements to procure firearms acquisition certificate, etc. — Tampering with firearms acquisition certificate, registration certificate or permit — Failure to comply with conditions of permit — Failure to deliver up firearms acquisition certificate, etc.

113. (1) Every one who, for the purpose of procuring a firearms acquisition certificate, registration certificate or permit for himself or any other person, knowingly makes a statement orally or in writing that is false or misleading or knowingly fails to disclose any information that is relevant to the application for the firearms acquisition certificate, registration certificate or permit

(*a*) is guilty of an indictable offence and liable to imprisonment for a term not exceeding two years; or

(*b*) is guilty of an offence punishable on summary conviction.

(2) Every one who, without lawful excuse the proof of which lies on him, alters, defaces or falsifies a firearms acquisition certificate, registration certificate or permit

(*a*) is guilty of an indictable offence and liable to imprisonment for a term not exceeding two years; or

(*b*) is guilty of an offence punishable on summary conviction.

(3) Every one who, without lawful excuse, fails to comply with any condition of a permit held by him

(*a*) is guilty of an indictable offence and liable to imprisonment for a term not exceeding two years; or

(*b*) is guilty of an offence punishable on summary conviction.

(4) Every one who,

(*a*) being a holder of a registration certificate or permit that is revoked in accordance with this Part, or

[1991, c. 40, s. 27 will repeal paragraph 113(4)(*a*) and substitute the following.]

(*a*) being a holder of a registration certificate, permit or firearms acquisition certificate that is revoked in accordance with this Part, or

(*b*) being a person against whom an order prohibiting possession of any firearm or ammunition is made under section 100 or paragraph 103(6)(*b*), or being prohibited by a condition of a probation order referred to in paragraph 737(2)(*d*) from having a firearm in his possession,

fails to deliver up the registration certificate or permit or, in a case described in paragraph (*b*), any firearms acquisition certificate, registration certificate or permit held by him, to a peace officer, a local registrar of firearms or a firearms officer forthwith after the revocation or the making of the order or probation order is guilty of an offence punishable on summary conviction.

Registry

Registry to be maintained — Information to be submitted to Commissioner — Idem.

114. (1) The Commissioner shall cause a registry to be maintained in which shall be kept a record of

(*a*) every registration certificate that is issued under section 109;

(*b*) every registration certificate that is revoked under subsection 112(1);

(*c*) every application for a registration certificate that is refused under subsection 112(3);

(*d*) every permit issued under subsection 110(5) that is revoked under subsection 112(2);

(*e*) every application for a permit under subsection 110(5) that is refused under subsection 112(4);

(*f*) every application for a firearms acquisition certificate that is refused;

(*g*) every prohibition order made under section 100 or paragraph 103(6)(*b*); and

(*h*) every probation order to which a condition referred to in paragraph 737(2)(*d*) is attached.

(2) Each person by whom

(*a*) a firearms acquisition certificate or permit is issued,

(*b*) a permit is revoked, or

(*c*) an application for a permit is refused,

shall submit such information in relation thereto at such time and in such form as is prescribed by the regulations for the purpose of enabling the Commissioner to compile the reports referred to in section 117.

(3) Every firearms officer by whom an application for a firearms acquisition certificate is refused, every person by whom an application for a permit under subsection 110(5) is refused or by whom a permit issued under that subsection is revoked, every court, judge, justice or provincial court judge that makes a prohibition order under section 100 or paragraph 103(6)(*b*) and every court that prescribes as a condition of a probation order a condition referred to in paragraph 737(2)(*d*) shall forthwith cause the Commissioner to be notified thereof. R.S 1985, c. 27 (1st Supp.), s. 203.

General

Onus on the accused — Firearms acquisition certificate, etc., as evidence.

115. (1) Where, in any proceedings under any of sections 85 to 113, any question arises as to whether a person is or was the holder of a firearms acquisition certificate, registration certificate or permit, the onus is on the accused to prove that that person is or was the holder of the firearms acquisition certificate, registration certificate or permit.

(2) In any proceedings under any of sections 85 to 113, a document purporting to be a firearms acquisition certificate, registration certificate or permit is evidence of the statements contained therein.

Regulations — Tabling of regulatins — Definition of "sitting day".

116. (1) The Governor in Council may make regulations

(*a*) regulating the handling, secure storage, display and advertising of restricted weapons, firearms and ammunition by persons carrying on businesses described in paragraph 105(1)(*a*) or subparagraph 105(2)(*b*)(i), and providing authority for police officers and police constables and members of any other class of persons designated for a province by the Attorney General of that province to enter any place where any such business is carried on, at any time during ordinary business hours, for the purpose of inspecting the secure storage facilities therein and the manner in which restricted weapons, firearms and ammunition are handled and displayed in the course of the business;

[1991, c. 40, s. 41 will repeal paragraph 116(1)(*a*) and substitute the following.]

(a) regulating the handling, secure storage, display and advertising of restricted weapons, firearms and ammunition by persons operating museums described in subsection 105(1) or carrying on businesses described in paragraph 105(1)(*a*) o subparagraph 105(2)(*b*)(i) and providing authority for police officers and police constables and members of any other class of persons designated for the purposes of a province by the Attorney General of that province to enter any place at which the museum is located or where any such business is carried on, at any time during ordinary business hours, for the purpose of inspecting the secure storage facilities therein and the manner in which restricted weapons, firearms and ammunition are handled and displayed in the course of the business;

(*a*.1) regulating the handling and secure storage or prohibited weapons or components or parts thereof referred to in paragraph 105(1)(*b*) by persons carrying on businesses described in that paragraph, and providing authority for police officers and police constables and members of any other class of persons designated for a province by the Attorney General of that province to enter any place where any such business is carried on, at any time during ordinary business hours, for the purpose of inspecting the secure storage facilities therein and the manner in which such prohibited weapons and components or parts thereof are handled in the course of the business;

(*b*) regulating the handling, secure storage and display of weapons by operators of and persons employed in museums approved for the purposes of this Part by the Commissioner or the Attorney General of the province in which they are situated;

(*c*) regulating the mail-order sale of restricted weapons, firearms and ammunition by persons carrying on businesses described in paragraph 105(1)(*a*) or subparagraph 105(2)(*b*)(i);

(*d*) providing for the secure handling, shipping, storage and transportation of firearms and ammunition, and prohibited weapons and components or parts thereof referred to in paragraph 105(1)(*b*), by persons engaged in businesses that include the transportation of goods;

(*e*) prescribing the fees to be paid to Her Majesty in right of Canada on application for certificates mentioned in section 106 or 107 or for permits mentioned in subsection 110(5);

(*f*) prescribing classes of firearms that shall be deemed to be relics for the purposes of this Part;

(*g*) respecting the storage, display, handling and transportation of firearms;

(*h*) authorizing the destruction, at such times as are specified in the regulations, of such records and inventories that are required by the provisions of this Part to be maintained as are designated in the regulations; and (*i*) prescribing anything that is, by any provision of this Part, required to be prescribed by the regulations.

(2) The Minister of Justice shall lay or cause to be laid before each House of Parliament, at least thirty sitting days before its effective date, every regulation that is proposed to be made under subsection (1) and every appropriate committee as determined by the rules of each House of Parliament may conduct enquiries or public hearings with respect to the proposed regulation and report its findings to the appropriate House.

(3) For the purposes of this section, "sitting day" means, in respect of either House of Parliament, a day on which that House sits. S.C. 1991, c. 28, s. 11(1), (2); 1991, c. 40, s. 28(1)-(4).

Report to Parliament.

117. The Commissioner shall, within three months after the end of each year and at such other times as the Solicitor General of Canada may, in writing, request, submit to the Solicitor General a report, in such form and setting forth such information as the Solicitor General may direct, with regard to the administration of the provisions of this Part respecting firearms acquisition certificates, registration certificates and permits and the information contained in the registry maintained pursuant to section 114, and the Solicitor General shall cause each report to be laid before Parliament within fifteen days after the receipt thereof by him, or, if Parliament is not then sitting, on any of the first fifteen days next thereafter that Parliament is sitting.

[1991, c. 40, s. 29 will repeal section 117 and substitute the following.]

Report to Parliament.

117. The Commissioner shall, within five months after the end of each year and at such other times as the Solicitor General of Canada may, in writing, request, submit to the Solicitor General a report, in such form and setting forth such information as the Solicitor General may direct, with regard to the administration of the provisions of this Part respecting firearms acquisition certificates, registration certificates and permits and the information contained in the registry maintained pursuant to section 114, and the Solicitor General shall cause each report to be laid before Parliament on any of the first fifteen days on which Parliament is sitting after the Solicitor General receives it.

PART IV

OFFENCES AGAINST THE ADMINISTRATION OF LAW AND JUSTICE

Interpretation

Definitions — "Evidence" or "Statement" — "Government" — "Judicial proceeding" — "Office" — "Official" — "Witness".

118. In this Part

"evidence" or "statement" means an assertion of fact, opinion, belief or knowledge whether material or not and whether admissible or not;

"government" means

(*a*) the Government of Canada,

(*b*) the government of a province, or

(*c*) Her Majesty in right of Canada or a province;

"judicial proceeding" means a proceeding

(*a*) in or under the authority of a court of justice

(*b*) before the Senate or House of Commons or a committee of the Senate or House of Commons, or before a legislative council, legislative assembly or house of assembly or a committee thereof that is authorized by law to administer an oath,

(*c*) before a court, judge, justice, provincial court judge or coroner,

(*d*) before an arbitrator or umpire, or a person or body of persons authorized by law to make an inquiry and take evidence therein under oath, or

(*e*) before a tribunal by which a legal right or legal liability may be established,

whether or not the proceeding is invalid for want of jurisdiction or for any other reason;

"office" includes

(*a*) an office or appointment under the government,

(*b*) a civil or military commission, and

(*c*) a position or an employment in a public department;

"official" means a person who

(*a*) holds an office, or

(*b*) is appointed to discharge a public duty;

"witness" means a person who gives evidence orally under oath or by affidavit in a judicial proceeding, whether or not he is competent to be a witness, and includes a child of tender years who gives evidence but does not give it under oath, because, in the opinion of the person presiding, the child does not understand the nature of an oath. R.S. 1985, c. 27 (1st Supp.), ss. 15, 203.

Corruption and Disobedience

Bribery of judicial officers, etc. — Consent of Attorney General.

119. (1) Every one who

(*a*) being the holder of a judicial office, or being a member of Parliament or of the legislature of a province, corruptly

(i) accepts or obtains,

(ii) agrees to accept, or

(iii) attempts to obtain,

any money, valuable consideration, office, place or employment for himself or another person in respect of anything done or omitted or to be done or omitted by him in his official capacity, or

(*b*) gives or offers, corruptly, to a person mentioned in paragraph (*a*) any money, valuable consideration, office, place or employment in respect of anything done or omitted or to be done or omitted by him in his official capacity for himself or another person,

is guilty of an indictable offence and liable to imprisonment for a term not exceeding fourteen years.

(2) No proceedings against a person who holds a judicial office shall be instituted under this section without the consent in writing of the Attorney General of Canada.

Bribery of officers.

120. Every one who

(*a*) being a justice, police commissioner, peace officer, public officer or officer of a juvenile court, or being employed in the administration of criminal law, corruptly

(i) accepts or obtains,

(ii) agrees to accept, or

(iii) attempts to obtain,

for himself or any other person any money, valuable consideration, office, place or employment with intent

(iv) to interfere with the administration of justice,

(v) to procure or facilitate the commission of an offence, or

(vi) to protect from detection or punishment a person who has committed or who intends to commit an offence, or

(*b*) gives or offers, corruptly, to a person mentioned in paragraph (*a*) any money, valuable consideration, office, place or employment with intent that the person should do anything mentioned in subparagraph (*a*)(iv), (v) or (vi),

is guilty of an indictable offence and liable to imprisonment for a term not exceeding fourteen years.

Frauds on the government — Contractor subscribing to election fund — Punishment.

121. (1) Every one commits an offence who

(*a*) directly or indirectly

(i) gives, offers, or agrees to give or offer to an official or to any member of his family, or to any one for the benefit of an official, or

(ii) being an official, demands, accepts or offers or agrees to accept from any person for himself or another person,

a loan, reward, advantage or benefit of any kind as consideration for cooperation, assistance, exercise of influence or an act or omission in connection with

(iii) the transaction of business with or any matter of business relating to the government, or

(iv) a claim against Her Majesty or any benefit that Her Majesty is authorized or is entitled to bestow,

whether or not, in fact, the official is able to cooperate, render assistance, exercise influence or do or omit to do what is proposed, as the case may be;

(*b*) having dealings of any kind with the government, pays a commission or reward to or confers an advantage or benefit of any kind on an employee or official of the government with which he deals, or to any member of his family, or to any one for the benefit of the employee or official, with respect to those dealings, unless he has the consent in writing of the head of the branch of government with which he deals, the proof of which lies on him;

(*c*) being an official or employee of the government, demands, accepts or offers or agrees to accept from a person who has dealings with the government a commission, reward, advantage or benefit of any kind directly or indirectly, by himself or through a member of his family or through any one for his benefit, unless he has the consent in writing of the head of the branch of government that employs him or of which he is an official, the proof of which lies on him;

(*d*) having or pretending to have influence with the government or with a minister of the government or an official, demands, accepts or offers or agrees to accept for himself or another person a reward, advantage or benefit of any kind as consideration for cooperation, assistance, exercise of influence or an act or omission in connection with

(i) anything mentioned in subparagraph (*a*)(iii) or (iv), or

(ii) the appointment of any person, including himself, to an office;

(*e*) gives, offers, or agrees to give or offer to a minister of the government or an official a reward, advantage or benefit of any kind as consideration for cooperation, assistance, exercise of influence or an act or omission in connection with

(i) anything mentioned in subparagraph (*a*)(iii) or (iv), or

(ii) the appointment of any person, including himself, to an office; or

(*f*) having made a tender to obtain a contract with the government

(i) gives, offers or agrees to give or offer to another person who has made a tender or to a member of his family, or to another person for the benefit of that person, a reward, advantage or benefit of any kind as consideration for the withdrawal of the tender of that person, or

(ii) demands, accepts or offers or agrees to accept from another person who has made a tender a reward, advantage or benefit of any kind as consideration for the withdrawal of his tender.

(2) Every one commits an offence who, in order to obtain or retain a contract with the government, or as a term of any such contract, whether express or implied, directly or indirectly subscribes or gives, or agrees to subscribe or give, to any person any valuable consideration

(*a*) for the purpose of promoting the election of a candidate or a class or party of candidates to Parliament or the legislature of a province; or

(*b*) with intent to influence or affect in any way the result of an election conducted for the purpose of electing persons to serve in Parliament or the legislature of a province.

(3) Every one who commits an offence under this section is guilty of an indictable offence and liable to imprisonment for a term not exceeding five years.

Breach of trust by public officer.

122. Every official who, in connection with the duties of his office, commits fraud or a breach of trust is guilty of an indictable offence and liable to imprisonment for a term not exceeding five years, whether or not the fraud or breach of trust would be an offence if it were committed in relation to a private person.

Municipal corruption — Influencing municipal official — "Municipal official".

123. (1) Every one who

(*a*) gives, offers or agrees to give or offer to a municipal official, or

(*b*) being a municipal official, demands, accepts or offers or agrees to accept from any person,

a loan, reward, advantage or benefit of any kind as consideration for the official

(*c*) to abstain from voting at a meeting of the municipal council or a committee thereof,

(*d*) to vote in favour of or against a measure, motion or resolution,

(*e*) to aid in procuring or preventing the adoption of a measure, motion or resolution, or

(*f*) to perform or fail to perform an official act,

is guilty of an indictable offence and liable to imprisonment for a term not exceeding five years.

(2) Every one who

(*a*) by suppression of the truth, in the case of a person who is under a duty to disclose the truth,

(*b*) by threats or deceit, or

(*c*) by any unlawful means,

influences or attempts to influence a municipal official to do anything mentioned in paragraphs (1)(*c*) to (*f*) is guilty of an indictable offence and liable to imprisonment for a term not exceeding five years.

(3) In this section "municipal official" means a member of a municipal council or a person who holds an office under a municipal government. R.S. 1985, c. 27 (1st Supp.), s. 16.

Selling or purchasing office.

124. Every one who

(*a*) purports to sell or agrees to sell an appointment to or resignation from an office, or a consent to any such appointment or resignation, or receives or agrees to receive a reward or profit from the purported sale thereof, or

(*b*) purports to purchase or gives a reward or profit for the purported purchase of any such appointment, resignation or consent, or agrees or promises to do so,

is guilty of an indictable offence and liable to imprisonment for a term not exceeding five years.

Influencing or negotiating appointments or dealing in offices.

125. Every one who

(*a*) receives, agrees to receive, gives or procures to be given, directly or indirectly, a reward, advantage or benefit of any kind as consideration for cooperation, assistance or exercise of influence to secure the appointment of any person to an office,

(*b*) solicits, recommends or negotiates in any manner with respect to an appointment to or resignation from an office, in expectation of a direct or indirect reward, advantage or benefit, or

(*c*) keeps without lawful authority, the proof of which lies on him, a place for transacting or negotiating any business relating to

(i) the filling of vacancies in offices,

(ii) the sale or purchase of offices, or

(iii) appointments to or resignations from offices,

is guilty of an indictable offence and liable to imprisonment for a term not exceeding five years.

Disobeying a statute — Attorney General of Canada may act.

126. (1) Every one who, without lawful excuse, contravenes an Act of

Parliament by wilfully doing anything that it forbids or by wilfully omitting to do anything that it requires to be done is, unless a punishment is expressly provided by law, guilty of an indictable offence and liable to imprisonment for a term not exceeding two years.

(2) Any proceedings in respect of a contravention of or conspiracy to contravene an Act mentioned in subsection (1), other than this Act, may be instituted at the instance of the Government of Canada and conducted by or on behalf of that Government.

Disobeying order of court — Attorney General of Canada may act.

127. (1) Every one who, without lawful excuse, disobeys a lawful order made by a court of justice or by a person or body of persons authorized by any Act to make or give the order, other than an order for the payment of money, is, unless a punishment or other mode of proceeding is expressly provided by law, guilty of an indictable offence and liable to imprisonment for a term not exceeding two years.

(2) Where the order referred to in subsection (1) was made in proceedings instituted at the instance of the Government of Canada and conducted by or on behalf of that Government, any proceedings in respect of a contravention of or conspiracy to contravene that order may be instituted and conducted in like manner.

Misconduct of officers executing process.

128. Every peace officer or coroner who, being entrusted with the execution of a process, wilfully

(*a*) misconducts himself in the execution of the process, or

(*b*) makes a false return to the process,

is guilty of an indictable offence and liable to imprisonment for a term not exceeding two years.

Offences relating to public or peace officer.

129. Every one who

(*a*) resists or wilfully obstructs a public officer or peace officer in the execution of his duty or any person lawfully acting in aid of such an officer,

(*b*) omits, without reasonable excuse, to assist a public officer or peace officer in the execution of his duty in arresting a person or in preserving the peace, after having reasonable notice that he is required to do so, or

(*c*) resists or wilfully obstructs any person in the lawful execution of a process against lands or goods or in making a lawful distress or seizure,

is guilty of

(*d*) an indictable offence and liable to imprisonment for a term not exceeding two years, or

(*e*) an offence punishable on summary conviction.

Personating peace officer.

130. Every one who

(*a*) falsely represents himself to be a peace officer or a public officer, or

(*b*) not being a peace officer or public officer, uses a badge or article of uniform or equipment in a manner that is likely to cause persons to believe that he is a peace officer or a public officer, as the case may be,

is guilty of an offence punishable on summary conviction.

Misleading Justice

Perjury — Idem — Application.

131. (1) Subject to subsection (3), every one commits perjury who, with intent to mislead, makes before a person who is authorized by law to permit it to be made before him, a false statement under oath or solemn affirmation, by affidavit, solemn declaration or deposition or orally, knowing that the statement is false.

(2) Subsection (1) applies whether or not a statement referred to in that subsection is made in a judicial proceeding.

(3) Subsection (1) does not apply to a statement referred to in that subsection that is made by a person who is not specially permitted, authorized or required by law to make that statement. R.S. 1985, c. 27 (1st Supp.), s. 17.

Punishment.

132. Every one who commits perjury is guilty of an indictable offence and liable to imprisonment for a term not exceeding fourteen years, but if a person commits perjury to procure the conviction of another person for an offence punishable by death, the person who commits perjury is liable to a maximum term of imprisonment for life. R.S. 1985, c. 27 (1st Supp.), s. 17.

Corroboration.

133. No person shall be convicted of an offence under section 132 on the evidence of only one witness unless the evidence of that witness is corroborated in a material particular by evidence that implicates the accused. R.S. 1985, c. 27 (1st Supp.), s. 17.

Idem — Application.

134. (1) Subject to subsection (2), every one who, not being specially permitted, authorized or required by law to make a statement under oath or solemn affirmation, makes such a statement, by affidavit, solemn declaration or deposition or orally before a person who is authorized by law to permit it to be made before him, knowing that the statement is false, is guilty of an offence punishable on summary conviction.

(2) Subsection (1) does not apply to a statement referred to in that subsection

that is made in the course of a criminal investigation. R.S. 1985, c. 27 (1st Supp.), s. 17.

135. [Repealed, R.S. 1985, c. 27 (1st Supp.), s. 17.]

Witness giving contradictory evidence — "Evidence" — Proof of former trial — Consent required.

136. (1) Every one who, being a witness in a judicial proceeding, gives evidence with respect to any matter of fact or knowledge and who subsequently, in a judicial proceeding, gives evidence that is contrary to his previous evidence is guilty of an indictable offence and liable to imprisonment for a term not exceeding fourteen years, whether or not the prior or later evidence or either is true, but no person shall be convicted under this section unless the court, judge or provincial court judge, as the case may be, is satisfied beyond a reasonable doubt that the accused, in giving evidence in either of the judicial proceedings, intended to mislead.

(2) Notwithstanding the definition "evidence" in section 118, "evidence", for the purposes of this section, does not include evidence that is not material.

(2.1) Where a person is charged with an offence under this section, a certificate specifying with reasonable particularity the proceeding in which that person is alleged to have given the evidence in respect of which the offence is charged, is evidence that it was given in a judicial proceeding, without proof of the signature or official character of the person by whom the certificate purports to be signed if it purports to be signed by the clerk of the court or other official having the custody of the record of that proceeding or by his lawful deputy.

(3) No proceedings shall be instituted under this section without the consent of the Attorney General. R.S. 1985, c. 27 (1st Supp.), ss. 18, 203.

Fabricating evidence.

137. Every one who, with intent to mislead, fabricates anything with intent that it shall be used as evidence in a judicial proceeding, existing or proposed, by any means other than perjury or incitement to perjury is guilty of an indictable offence and liable to imprisonment for a term not exceeding fourteen years.

Offences relating to affidavits.

138. Every one who

(*a*) signs a writing that purports to be an affidavit or statutory declaration and to have been sworn or declared before him when the writing was not so sworn or declared or when he knows that he has no authority to administer the oath or declaration,

(*b*) uses or offers for use any writing purporting to be an affidavit or statutory declaration that he knows was not sworn or declared, as the case may be, by the affiant or declarant or before a person authorized in that behalf, or

(*c*) signs as affiant or declarant a writing that purports to be an affidavit or statutory declaration and to have been sworn or declared by him, as the case may be, when the writing was not so sworn or declared,

is guilty of an indictable offence and liable to imprisonment for a term not exceeding two years.

Obstructing justice — Idem — Idem.

139. (1) Every one who wilfully attempts in any manner to obstruct, pervert or defeat the course of justice in a judicial proceeding,

(*a*) by indemnifying or agreeing to indemnify a surety, in any way and either in whole or in part, or

(*b*) where he is a surety, by accepting or agreeing to accept a fee or any form of indemnity whether in whole or in part from or in respect of a person who is released or is to be released from custody,

is guilty of

(*c*) an indictable offence and is liable to imprisonment for a term not exceeding two years, or

(*d*) an offence punishable on summary conviction.

(2) Every one who wilfully attempts in any manner other than a manner described in subsection (1) to obstruct, pervert or defeat the course of justice is guilty of an indictable offence and liable to imprisonment for a term not exceeding ten years.

(3) Without restricting the generality of subsection (2), every one shall be deemed wilfully to attempt to obstruct, pervert or defeat the course of justice who in a judicial proceeding, existing or proposed,

(*a*) dissuades or attempts to dissuade a person by threats, bribes or other corrupt means from giving evidence;

(*b*) influences or attempts to influence by threats, bribes or other corrupt means a person in his conduct as a juror; or

(*c*) accepts or obtains, agrees to accept or attempts to obtain a bribe or other corrupt consideration to abstain from giving evidence, or to do or to refrain from doing anything as a juror.

Public mischief — Punishment.

140. (1) Every one commits public mischief who, with intent to mislead, causes a peace officer to enter on or continue an investigation by

(*a*) making a false statement that accuses some other person of having committed an offence;

(*b*) doing anything that is intended to cause some other person to be suspected of having committed an offence that the other person has not committed, or to divert suspicion from himself;

(*c*) reporting that an offence has been committed when it has not been committed; or

(*d*) reporting or in any other way making it known or causing it to be made known that he or some other person has died when he or that other person has not died.

(2) Every one who commits public mischief

(*a*) is guilty of an indictable offence and liable to imprisonment for a term not exceeding five years; or

(*b*) is guilty of an offence punishable on summary conviction. R.S. 1985, c. 27 (1st Supp.), s. 19.

Compounding indictable offence — Exception for diversion agreements.

141. (1) Every one who asks for or obtains or agrees to receive or obtain any valuable consideration for himself or any other person by agreeing to compound or conceal an indictable offence is guilty of an indictable offence and liable to imprisonment for a term not exceeding two years.

(2) No offence is committed under subsection (1) where valuable consideration is received or obtained or is to be received or obtained under an agreement for compensation or restitution or personal services that is

(*a*) entered into with the consent of the Attorney General; or

(*b*) made as part of a program, approved by the Attorney General, to divert persons charged with indictable offences from criminal proceedings. R.S. 1985, c. 27 (1st Supp.), s. 19.

Corruptly taking reward for recovery of goods.

142. Every one who corruptly accepts any valuable consideration, directly or indirectly, under pretence or on account of helping any person to recover anything obtained by the commission of an indictable offence is guilty of an indictable offence and liable to imprisonment for a term not exceeding five years.

Advertising reward and immunity.

143. Every one who

(*a*) publicly advertises a reward for the return of anything that has been stolen or lost, and in the advertisement uses words to indicate that no questions will be asked if it is returned,

(*b*) uses words in a public advertisement to indicate that a reward will be given or paid for anything that has been stolen or lost, without interference with or inquiry about the person who produces it,

(*c*) promises or offers in a public advertisement to return to a person who has advanced money by way of loan on, or has bought, anything that has been stolen or lost, the money so advanced or paid, or any other sum of money for the return of that thing, or

(*d*) prints or publishes any advertisement referred to in paragraph (*a*), (*b*) or (*c*),

is guilty of an offence punishable on summary conviction.

Escapes and Rescues

Prison breach.

144. Every one who

(*a*) by force or violence breaks a prison with intent to set at liberty himself or any other person confined therein, or

(*b*) with intent to escape forcibly breaks out of, or makes any breach in, a cell or other place within a prison in which he is confined,

is guilty of an indictable offence and liable to imprisonment for a term not exceeding ten years.

Escape and being at large without excuse — Failure to attend court — Failure to comply with condition of undertaking or recognizance — Failure to appear or to comply with summons — Failure to appear or to comply with appearance notice or promise to appear — Idem — Where person charged with summary conviction offence — Proof of certain facts by certificate — Attendance and right to cross-examination — Notice of intention to produce.

145. (1) Every one who

(*a*) escapes from lawful custody, or

(*b*) is, before the expiration of a term of imprisonment to which he was sentenced, at large in or out of Canada without lawful excuse, the proof of which lies on him,

is guilty of an indictable offence and liable to imprisonment for a term not exceeding two years or is guilty of an offence punishable on summary conviction.

(2) Every one who,

(*a*) being at large on his undertaking or recognizance given to or entered into before a justice or judge, fails, without lawful excuse, the proof of which lies on him, to attend court in accordance with the undertaking or recognizance, or

(*b*) having appeared before a court, justice or judge, fails, without lawful excuse, the proof of which lies on him, to attend court as thereafter required by the court, justice or judge,

or to surrender himself in accordance with an order of the court, justice or judge, as the case may be, is guilty of an indictable offence and liable to imprisonment for a term not exceeding two years or is guilty of an offence punishable on summary conviction.

(3) Every one who, being at large on his undertaking or recognizance given to or entered into before a justice or a judge and being bound to comply with a condition of that undertaking or recognizance directed by a justice or a judge, fails, without lawful excuse, the proof of which lies on him, to comply with that condition, is guilty of

(*a*) an indictable offence and is liable to imprisonment for a term not exceeding two years; or
(*b*) an offence punishable on summary conviction.

(4) Every one who is served with a summons and who fails, without lawful excuse, the proof of which lies on him, to appear at a time and place stated therein, if any, for the purposes of the *Identification of Criminals Act* or to attend court in accordance therewith, is guilty of
(*a*) an indictable offence and is liable to imprisonment for a term not exceeding two years; or
(*b*) an offence punishable on summary conviction.

(5) Every one who is named in an appearance notice or promise to appear, or in a recognizance entered into before an officer in charge, that has been confirmed by a justice under section 508 and who fails, without lawful excuse, the proof of which lies on him, to appear at a time and place stated therein, if any, for the purposes of the *Identification of Criminals Act* or to attend court in accordance therewith, is guilty of
(*a*) an indictable offence and is liable to imprisonment for a term not exceeding two years; or
(*b*) an offence punishable on summary conviction.

(6) For the purposes of subsection (5), it is not a lawful excuse that an appearance notice, promise to appear or recognizance states defectively the substance of the alleged offence.

(7) [Repealed, R.S. 1985, c. 27 (1st Supp.), s. 20(2).]

(8) For the purposes only of the *Identification of Criminals Act*, a person charged with or convicted of an offence under this section punishable on summary conviction shall be deemed to be charged with or to have been convicted of an indictable offence.

(9) In any proceedings under subsection (2), (4) or (5), a certificate of the clerk of the court or a judge of the court before which the accused is alleged to have failed to attend or of the person in charge of the place at which it is alleged the accused failed to attend for the purposes of the *Identification of Criminals Act* stating that,
(*a*) in the case of proceedings under subsection (2), the accused gave or entered into an undertaking or recognizance before a justice or judge and failed to attend court in accordance therewith,
(*b*) in the case of proceedings under subsection (4), a summons was issued to and served on the accused and the accused failed to attend court in accordance therewith or failed to appear at the time and place stated therein for the purposes of the *Identification of Criminals Act*, as the case may be, and
(*c*) in the case of proceedings under subsection (5), the accused was named in an appearance notice, a promise to appear or a recognizance entered into before an officer in charge, that was confirmed by a justice under section

508, and the accused failed to attend court in accordance therewith or failed to appear at the time and place stated therein for the purposes of the *Identification of Criminals Act*, as the case may be,

is evidence of the statements contained in the certificate without proof of the signature or the official character of the person appearing to have signed the certificate.

(10) An accused against whom a certificate described in subsection (9) is produced may, with leave of the court, require the attendance of the person making the certificate for the purposes of cross-examination.

(11) No certificate shall be received in evidence pursuant to subsection (9) unless the party intending to produce it has, before the trial, given to the accused reasonable notice of his intention together with a copy of the certificate. R.S. 1985, c. 27 (1st Supp.), s. 20.

Permitting or assisting escape.

146. Every one who

(*a*) permits a person whom he has in lawful custody to escape, by failing to perform a legal duty,

(*b*) conveys or causes to be conveyed into a prison anything, with intent to facilitate the escape of a person imprisoned therein, or

(*c*) directs or procures, under colour of pretended authority, the discharge of a prisoner who is not entitled to be discharged,

is guilty of an indictable offence and liable to imprisonment for a term not exceeding two years.

Rescue or permitting escape.

147. Every one who

(*a*) rescues any person from lawful custody or assists any person in escaping or attempting to escape from lawful custody,

(*b*) being a peace officer, wilfully permits a person in his lawful custody to escape, or

(*c*) being an officer of or an employee in a prison, wilfully permits a person to escape from lawful custody therein,

is guilty of an indictable offence and liable to imprisonment for a term not exceeding five years.

Assisting prisoner of war to escape.

148. Every one who knowingly and wilfully

(*a*) assists a prisoner of war in Canada to escape from a place where he is detained, or

(*b*) assists a prisoner of war, who is permitted to be at large on parole in Canada, to escape from the place where he is at large on parole,

is guilty of an indictable offence and liable to imprisonment for a term not exceeding five years.

Service of term for escape — Determination of term of imprisonment — Definition of "escape".

149. (1) A person convicted for an escape committed while undergoing imprisonment shall be sentenced to serve the term of imprisonment to which he is sentenced for the escape either concurrently with the portion of the term of imprisonment that he was serving at the time of his escape that he had not served or, if the court, judge, justice or provincial court judge by whom he is sentenced for the escape so orders, consecutively, and such imprisonment shall be served

(*a*) in a penitentiary if the time to be served is two years or more; or

(*b*) if the time to be served is less than two years,

(i) in a prison, or

(ii) notwithstanding the *Parole Act* and section 731, in a penitentiary if the court, judge, justice or provincial court judge by whom he is sentenced for the escape so orders.

[1992, c. 20, s. 199(1) will repeal subparagraph 149(1)(*b*)(ii) and substitute the following.]

(ii) notwithstanding section 731, in a penitentiary if the court, judge, justice or provincial court judge by whom he is sentenced for the escape so orders.

(2) For the purpose of subsection (1), section 20 of the *Parole Act* applies in determining the term of imprisonment that a person who escapes while undergoing imprisonment was serving at the time of his escape.

[1992, c. 20, s. 199(2) will repeal subsection 149(2) and substitute the following.]

Determination of term of imprisonment.

(2) For the purposes of subsection (1), section 139 of the *Corrections and Condtional Release Act* applies in determining the term of imprisonment that a person who escapes while undergoing imprisonment was serving at the time of his escape.

(3) For the purposes of subsection (1), "escape" means breaking prison, escaping from lawful custody or, without lawful excuse, being at large before the expiration of a term of imprisonment to which a person has been sentenced. R.S. 1985, c. 27 (1st Supp.), s. 203.

PART V

SEXUAL OFFENCES, PUBLIC MORALS AND DISORDERLY CONDUCT

Interpretation

Definitions — "Guardian" — "Public place" — "Theatre".

150. In this Part,

"guardian" includes any person who has in law or in fact the custody or control of another person;

"public place" includes any place to which the public have access as of right or by invitation, express or implied;

"theatre" includes any place that is open to the public where entertainments are given, whether or not any charge is made for admission.

Sexual Offences

Consent no defence — Exception — Exemption for accused aged twelve or thirteen — Mistake of age — Idem.

150.1. (1) Where an accused is charged with an offence under section 151 or 152 or subsection 153(1), 160(3) or 173(2) or is charged with an offence under section 271, 272 or 273 in respect of a complainant under the age of fourteen years, it is not a defence that the complainant consented to the activity that forms the subject-matter of the charge.

(2) Notwithstanding subsection (1), where an accused is charged with an offence under section 151 or 152, subsection 173(2) or section 271 in respect of a complainant who is twelve years of age or more but under the age of fourteen years, it is not a defence that the complainant consented to the activity that forms the subject-matter of the charge unless the accused

(*a*) is twelve years of age or more but under the age of sixteen years;

(*b*) is less than two years older than the complainant; and

(*c*) is neither in a position of trust or authority towards the complainant nor is a person with whom the complainant is in a relationship of dependency.

(3) No person aged twelve or thirteen years shall be tried for an offence under section 151 or 152 or subsection 173(2) unless the person is in a position of trust or authority towards the complainant or is a person with whom the complainant is in a relationship of dependency.

(4) It is not a defence to a charge under section 151 or 152, subsection 160(3) or 173(2), or section 271, 272 or 273 that the accused believed that the complainant was fourteen years of age or more at the time the offence

is alleged to have been committed unless the accused took all reasonable steps to ascertain the age of the complainant.

(5) It is not a defence to a charge under section 153, 159, 170, 171 or 172 or subsection 212(2) or (4) that the accused believed that the complainant was eighteen years of age or more at the time the offence is alleged to have been committed unless the accused took all reasonable steps to ascertain the age of the complainant. R.S. 1985, c. 19 (3rd Supp.), s. 1.

Sexual interference.

151. Every person who, for a sexual purpose, touches, directly or indirectly, with a part of the body or with an object, any part of the body of a person under the age of fourteen years is guilty of an indictable offence and is liable to imprisonment for a term not exceeding ten years or is guilty of an offence punishable on summary conviction. R.S. 1985, c. 19 (3rd Supp.), s. 1.

Invitation to sexual touching.

152. Every person who, for a sexual purpose, invites, counsels or incites a person under the age of fourteen years to touch, directly or indirectly, with a part of the body or with an object, the body of any person, including the body of the person who so invites, counsels or incites and the body of the person under the age of fourteen years, is guilty of an indictable offence and is liable to imprisonment for a term not exceeding ten years or is guilty of an offence punishable on summary conviction. R.S. 1985, c. 19 (3rd Supp.), s. 1.

Sexual exploitation — Definition of "young person".

153. (1) Every person who is in a position of trust or authority towards a young person or is a person with whom the young person is in a relationship of dependency and who

(*a*) for a sexual purpose, touches, directly or indirectly, with a part of the body or with an object, any part of the body of the young person, or

(*b*) for a sexual purpose, invites, counsels or incites a young person to touch, directly or indirectly, with a part of the body or with an object, the body of any person, including the body of the person who so invites, counsels or incites and the body of the young person,

is guilty of an indictable offence and liable to imprisonment for a term not exceeding five years or is guilty of an offence punishable on summary conviction.

(2) In this section, "young person" means a person fourteen years of age or more but under the age of eighteen years. R.S. 1985, c. 19 (3rd Supp.), s. 1.

154. [Repealed R.S. 1985, c. 19 (3rd Supp.), s. 1.]

Incest — Punishment — Defence — "Brother", "sister".

155. (1) Every one commits incest who, knowing that another person is by blood relationship his or her parent, child, brother, sister, grandparent or grandchild, as the case may be, has sexual intercourse with that person.

(2) Every one who commits incest is guilty of an indictable offence and liable to imprisonment for a term not exceeding fourteen years.

(3) No accused shall be determined by a court to be guilty of an offence under this section if the accused was under restraint, duress or fear of the person with whom the accused had the sexual intercourse at the time the sexual intercourse occurred.

(4) In this section, "brother" and "sister", respectively, include half-brother and half-sister. R.S. 1985, c. 27 (1st Supp.), s. 21.

156. [Repealed R.S. 1985, c. 19 (3rd Supp.), s. 2.]

157. [Repealed R.S. 1985, c. 19 (3rd Supp.), s. 2.]

158. [Repealed, R.S. 1985, c. 19 (3rd Supp.), s. 2.]

Anal intercourse — Exception — Idem.

159. (1) Every person who engages in an act of anal intercourse is guilty of an indictable offence and liable to imprisonment for a term not exceeding ten years or is guilty of an offence punishable on summary conviction.

(2) Subsection (1) does not apply to any act engaged in, in private, between

(*a*) husband and wife, or

(*b*) any two persons, each of whom is eighteen years of age or more,

both of whom consent to the act.

(3) For the purposes of subsection (2),

(*a*) an act shall be deemed not to have been engaged in in private if it is engaged in in a public place or if more than two persons take part or are present; and

(*b*) a person shall be deemed not to consent to an act

(i) if the consent is extorted by force, threats or fear of bodily harm or is obtained by false and fraudulent misrepresentations respecting the nature and quality of the act, or

(ii) if the court is satisfied beyond a reasonable doubt that the person could not have consented to the act by reason of mental disability. R.S. 1985, c. 19 (3rd Supp.), s. 3.

Bestiality — Compelling the commission of bestiality — Bestiality in presence of or by child.

160. (1) Every person who commits bestiality is guilty of an indictable offence and liable to imprisonment for a term not exceeding ten years or is guilty of an offence punishable on summary conviction.

(2) Every person who compels another to commit bestiality is guilty of an

indictable offence and liable to imprisonment for a term not exceeding ten years or is guilty of an offence punishable on summary conviction.

(3) Notwithstanding subsection (1), every person who commits bestiality in the presence of a person who is under the age of fourteen years or who incites a person under the age of fourteen years to commit bestiality is guilty of an indictable offence and is liable to imprisonment for a term not exceeding ten years or is guilty of an offence punishable on summary conviction. R.S. 1985, c. 19 (3rd Supp.), s. 3.

161. [Repealed R.S. 1985, c. 19 (3rd Supp.), s. 4.]

162. [Repealed R.S. 1985, c. 19 (3rd Supp.), s. 4.]

Offences Tending to Corrupt Morals

Corrupting morals — Idem — Defence of public good — Question of law and question of fact — Motives irrelevant — Ignorance of nature no defence — "Crime comic" — Obscene publication.

163. (1) Every one commits an offence who

(*a*) makes, prints, publishes, distributes, circulates, or has in his possession for the purpose of publication, distribution or circulation any obscene written matter, picture, model, phonograph record or other thing whatever; or

(*b*) makes, prints, publishes, distributes, sells or has in his possession for the purpose of publication, distribution or circulation a crime comic.

(2) Every one commits an offence who knowingly, without lawful justification or excuse,

(*a*) sells, exposes to public view or has in his possession for such a purpose any obscene written matter, picture, model, phonograph record or other thing whatever;

(*b*) publicly exhibits a disgusting object or an indecent show;

(*c*) offers to sell, advertises or publishes an advertisement of, or has for sale or disposal any means, instructions, medicine, drug or article intended or represented as a method of causing abortion or miscarriage; or

(*d*) advertises or publishes an advertisement of any means, instructions, medicine, drug or article intended or represented as a method for restoring sexual virility or curing venereal diseases or diseases of the generative organs.

(3) No person shall be convicted of an offence under this section if he establishes that the public good was served by the acts that are alleged to constitute the offence and that the acts alleged did not extend beyond what served the public good.

(4) For the purposes of this section, it is a question of law whether an act served the public good and whether there is evidence that the act alleged went beyond what served the public good, but it is a question of fact whether the acts did or did not extend beyond what served the public good.

(5) For the purposes of this section, the motives of an accused are irrelevant.

(6) Where an accused is charged with an offence under subsection (1), the fact that the accused was ignorant of the nature or presence of the matter, picture, model, phonograph record, crime comic or other thing by means of or in relation to which the offence was committed is not a defence to the charge.

(7) In this section, "crime comic" means a magazine, periodical or book that exclusively or substantially comprises matter depicting pictorially

(*a*) the commission of crimes, real or fictitious; or

(*b*) events connected with the commission of crimes, real or fictitious, whether occurring before or after the commission of the crime.

(8) For the purposes of this Act, any publication a dominant characteristic of which is the undue exploitation of sex, or of sex and any one or more of the following subjects, namely, crime, horror, cruelty and violence, shall be deemed to be obscene.

Warrant of seizure — Summons to occupier — Owner and author may appear — Order of forfeiture — Disposal of matter — Appeal — Consent — Definitions — "Court" — "Crime comic" — "Judge".

164. (1) A judge who is satisfied by information on oath that there are reasonable grounds for believing that any publication, copies of which are kept for sale or distribution in premises within the jurisdiction of the court, is obscene or a crime comic shall issue a warrant under his hand authorizing seizure of the copies.

(2) Within seven days of the issue of a warrant under subsection (1), the judge shall issue a summons to the occupier of the premises requiring him to appear before the court and show cause why the matter seized should not be forfeited to Her Majesty.

(3) The owner and the author of the matter seized under subsection (1), and alleged to be obscene or a crime comic, may appear and be represented in the proceedings in order to oppose the making of an order for the forfeiture of the said matter.

(4) If the court is satisfied that the publication referred to in subsection (1) is obscene or a crime comic, it shall make an order declaring the matter forfeited to Her Majesty in right of the province in which the proceedings take place, for disposal as the Attorney General may direct.

(5) If the court is not satisfied that the publication referred to in subsection (1) is obscene or a crime comic, it shall order that the matter be restored to the person from whom it was seized forthwith after the time for final appeal has expired.

(6) An appeal lies from an order made under subsection (4) or (5) by any person who appeared in the proceedings

(*a*) on any ground of appeal that involves a question of law alone,

(*b*) on any ground of appeal that involves a question of fact alone, or

(*c*) on any ground of appeal that involves a question of mixed law and fact,

as if it were an appeal against conviction or against a judgment or verdict of acquittal, as the case may be, on a question of law alone under Part XXI and sections 673 to 696 apply with such modifications as the circumstances require.

(7) Where an order has been made under this section by a judge in a province with respect to one or more copies of a publication, no proceedings shall be instituted or continued in that province under section 163 with respect to those or other copies of the same publication without the consent of the Attorney General.

(8) In this section

"court" means

(*a*) in the Province of Quebec, the Court of Quebec, the municipal court of Montreal and the municipal court of Quebec;

(*a*.1) in the Province of Ontario, the Ontario Court (General Division),

(*b*) in the Provinces of New Brunswick, Manitoba, Saskatchewan and Alberta, the Court of Queen's Bench;

(*c*) in the Provinces of Prince Edward Island and Newfoundland, the Trial Division of the Supreme Court;

(*c*.1) in the Province of British Columbia, the Yukon Territory and the Northwest Territories, the Supreme Court, and

(*d*) in the Province of Nova Scotia, a county or district court;

"crime comic" has the same meaning as in section 163;

"judge" means a judge of a court. R.S. 1985, c. 27 (2d Supp.), Sched.; c. 40 (4th Supp.), Schedule, item 1; 1990, c. 16, s. 3; 1990, c. 17, s. 9(1), (2); 1992, c. 1, s. 58(1), Sch. I, item 3.

Tied sale.

165. Every one commits an offence who refuses to sell or supply to any other person copies of any publication for the reason only that the other person refuses to purchase or acquire from him copies of any other publication that the other person is apprehensive may be obscene or a crime comic.

Restriction on publication of reports of judicial proceedings — Saving — Consent of Attorney General — Exceptions.

166. (1) A proprietor, an editor, a master printer or a publisher commits an offence who prints or publishes

(*a*) in relation to any judicial proceedings, any indecent matter or indecent medical, surgical or physiological details, being matter or details that, if published, are calculated to injure public morals;

(*b*) in relation to any judicial proceedings for dissolution of marriage, nullity of marriage, judicial separation or restitution of conjugal rights, any particulars other than

(i) the names, addresses and occupations of the parties and witnesses,

(ii) a concise statement of the charges, defences and countercharges in support of which evidence has been given,

(iii) submissions on a point of law arising in the course of the proceedings, and the decision of the court in connection therewith, and

(iv) the summing up of the judge, the finding of the jury, the judgment of the court and the observations that are made by the judge in giving judgment.

(2) Nothing in paragraph (1)(*b*) affects the operation of paragraph (1)(*a*).

(3) No proceedings for an offence under this section shall be commenced without the consent of the Attorney General.

(4) This section does not apply to a person who

(*a*) prints or publishes any matter for use in connection with any judicial proceedings or communicates it to persons who are concerned in the proceedings;

(*b*) prints or publishes a notice or report pursuant to the directions of a court; or

(*c*) prints or publishes any matter

(i) in a volume or part of a genuine series of law reports that does not form part of any other publication and consists solely of reports of proceedings in courts of law, or

(ii) in a publication of a technical character that is *bona fide* intended for circulation among members of the legal or medical professions.

Immoral theatrical performance — Person taking part.

167. (1) Every one commits an offence who, being the lessee, manager, agent or person in charge of a theatre, presents or gives or allows to be presented or given therein an immoral, indecent or obscene performance, entertainment or representation.

(2) Every one commits an offence who takes part or appears as an actor, a performer or an assistant in any capacity, in an immoral, indecent or obscene performance, entertainment or representation in a theatre.

Mailing obscene matter.

168. Every one commits an offence who makes use of the mails for the purpose of transmitting or delivering anything that is obscene, indecent, immoral or scurrilous, but this section does not apply to a person who makes use of the mails for the purpose of transmitting or delivering anything mentioned in subsection 166(4).

Punishment.

169. Every one who commits an offence under section 163, 165, 166, 167 or 168 is guilty of

(*a*) an indictable offence and is liable to imprisonment for a term not exceeding two years; or

(*b*) an offence punishable on summary conviction.

Parent or guardian procuring sexual activity.

170. Every parent or guardian of a person under the age of eighteen years who procures that person for the purpose of engaging in any sexual activity prohibited by this Act with a person other than the parent or guardian is guilty of an indictable offence and liable to imprisonment for a term not exceeding five years, if the person procured for that purpose is under the age of fourteen years, or to imprisonment for a term not exceeding two years if the person so procured is fourteen years of age or more but under the age of eighteen years. R.S. 1985, c. 19 (3rd Supp.), s. 5.

Householder permitting sexual activity.

171. Every owner, occupier or manager of premises or other person who has control of premises or assists in the management or control of premises who knowingly permits a person under the age of eighteen years to resort to or to be in or on the premises for the purpose of engaging in any sexual activity prohibited by this Act is guilty of an indictable offence and is liable to imprisonment for a term not exceeding five years if the person in question is under the age of fourteen years or to imprisonment for a term not exceeding two years if the person in question is fourteen years of age or more but under the age of eighteen years. R.S. 1985, c. 19 (3rd Supp.), s. 5.

Corrupting children — Definition of "Child" — Who may institute prosecutions.

172. (1) Every one who, in the home of a child, participates in adultery or sexual immorality or indulges in habitual drunkenness or any other form of vice, and thereby endangers the morals of the child or renders the home an unfit place for the child to be in, is guilty of an indictable offence and liable to imprisonment for a term not exceeding two years.

(2) [Repealed R.S. 1985, c. 19 (3rd Supp.), s. 6.]

(3) For the purposes of this section, "child" means a person who is or appears to be under the age of eighteen years.

(4) No proceedings shall be commenced under subsection (1) without the consent of the Attorney General, unless they are instituted by or at the instance of a recognized society for the protection of children or by an officer of a juvenile court. R.S. 1985, c. 19 (3rd Supp.), s. 6.

Disorderly Conduct

Indecent acts — Exposure.

173. (1) Every one who wilfully does an indecent act

(*a*) in a public place in the presence of one or more persons, or

(*b*) in any place, with intent thereby to insult or offend any person,

is guilty of an offence punishable on summary conviction.

(2) Every person who, in any place, for a sexual purpose, exposes his or her genital organs to a person who is under the age of fourteen years is guilty of an offence punishable on summary conviction. R.S. 1985, c. 19 (3rd Supp.), s. 7.

Nudity — Nude — Consent of Attorney General.

174. (1) Every one who, without lawful excuse,

(*a*) is nude in a public place, or

(*b*) is nude and exposed to public view while on private property, whether or not the property is his own,

is guilty of an offence punishable on summary conviction.

(2) For the purposes of this section, a person is nude who is so clad as to offend against public decency or order.

(3) No proceedings shall be commenced under this section without the consent of the Attorney General.

Causing disturbance, indecent exhibition, loitering, etc. — Evidence of peace officer.

175. (1) Every one who

(*a*) not being in a dwelling-house, causes a disturbance in or near a public place,

(i) by fighting, screaming, shouting, swearing, singing or using insulting or obscene language,

(ii) by being drunk, or

(iii) by impeding or molesting other persons,

(*b*) openly exposes or exhibits an indecent exhibition in a public place,

(*c*) loiters in a public place and in any way obstructs persons who are in that place, or

(*d*) disturbs the peace and quiet of the occupants of a dwelling-house by discharging firearms or by other disorderly conduct in a public place or who, not being an occupant of a dwelling-house comprised in a particular building or structure, disturbs the peace and quiet of the occupants of a dwelling-house comprised in the building or structure by discharging firearms or by other disorderly conduct in any part of a building or structure to which, at the time of such conduct, the occupants of two or more dwelling-houses comprised in the building or structure have access as of right or by invitation, express or implied, is guilty of an offence punishable on summary conviction.

(2) In the absence of other evidence, or by way of corroboration of other evidence, a summary conviction court may infer from the evidence of a peace officer relating to the conduct of a person or persons, whether ascertained or not, that a disturbance described in paragraph (1)(*a*) or (*d*) was caused or occurred.

Obstructing or violence to or arrest of officiating clergyman — Disturbing religious worship or certain meetings — Idem.

176. (1) Every one who

(*a*) by threats or force, unlawfully obstructs or prevents or endeavours to obstruct or prevent a clergyman or minister from celebrating divine service or performing any other function in connection with his calling, or

(*b*) knowing that a clergyman or minister is about to perform, is on his way to perform or is returning from the performance of any of the duties or functions mentioned in paragraph (*a*)

(i) assaults or offers any violence to him, or

(ii) arrests him on a civil process, or under the pretence of executing a civil process,

is guilty of an indictable offence and liable to imprisonment for a term not exceeding two years.

(2) Every one who wilfully disturbs or interrupts an assemblage of persons met for religious worship or for a moral, social or benevolent purpose is guilty of an offence punishable on summary conviction.

(3) Every one who, at or near a meeting referred to in subsection (2), wilfully does anything that disturbs the order or solemnity of the meeting is guilty of an offence punishable on summary conviction.

Trespassing at night.

177. Every one who, without lawful excuse, the proof of which lies on him, loiters or prowls at night on the property of another person near a dwelling-house situated on that property is guilty of an offence punishable on summary conviction.

Offensive volatile substance.

178. Every one other than a peace officer engaged in the discharge of his duty who has in his possession in a public place or who deposits, throws or injects or causes to be deposited, thrown or injected in, into or near any place,

(*a*) an offensive volatile substance that is likely to alarm, inconvenience, discommode or cause discomfort to any person or to cause damage to property, or

(*b*) a stink or stench bomb or device from which any substance mentioned in paragraph (*a*) is or is capable of being liberated,

is guilty of an offence punishable on summary conviction.

Vagrancy — Punishment.

179. (1) Every one commits vagrancy who

(*a*) supports himself in whole or in part by gaming or crime and has no lawful profession or calling by which to maintain himself; or

(*b*) having at any time been convicted of an offence under section 151, 152 or 153, subsection 160(3) or 173(2) or section 271, 272 or 273, or of an offence under a provision referred to in paragraph (*b*) of the definition "serious personal injury offence" in section 687 of the *Criminal Code*, chapter C-34 of the Revised Statutes of Canada, 1970 as it read before January 4, 1983, is found loitering in or near a school ground, playground, public park or bathing area.

(2) Every one who commits vagrancy is guilty of an offence punishable on summary conviction. R.S. 1985, c. 27 (1st Supp.), s. 22; c. 19 (3rd Supp.), s. 8.

Nuisances

Common nuisance — Definition.

180. (1) Every one who commits a common nuisance and thereby

(*a*) endangers the lives, safety or health of the public, or

(*b*) causes physical injury to any person,

is guilty of an indictable offence and liable to imprisonment for a term not exceeding two years.

(2) For the purposes of this section, every one commits a common nuisance who does an unlawful act or fails to discharge a legal duty and thereby

(*a*) endangers the lives, safety, health, property or comfort of the public; or

(*b*) obstructs the public in the exercise or enjoyment of any right that is common to all the subjects of Her Majesty in Canada.

Spreading false news.

181. Every one who wilfully publishes a statement, tale or news that he knows is false and that causes or is likely to cause injury or mischief to a public interest is guilty of an indictable offence and liable to imprisonment for a term not exceeding two years.

Dead body.

182. Every one who

(*a*) neglects, without lawful excuse, to perform any duty that is imposed on him by law or that he undertakes with reference to the burial of a dead human body or human remains, or

(*b*) improperly or indecently interferes with or offers any indignity to a dead human body or human remains, whether buried or not,

is guilty of an indictable offence and liable to imprisonment for a term not exceeding five years.

PART VI

INVASION OF PRIVACY

Definitions

Definitions — "Authorization" — "Electro-magnetic, acoustic, mechanical or other device" — "Intercept" — "Offence" — "Private communication" — "Sell" — "Solicitor".

183. In this Part,

"authorization" means an authorization to intercept a private communication given under section 186 or subsection 188(2);

"electro-magnetic, acoustic, mechanical or other device" means any device or apparatus that is used or is capable of being used to intercept a private communication, but does not include a hearing aid used to correct subnormal hearing of the user to not better than normal hearing;

"intercept" includes listen to, record or acquire a communication or acquire the substance, meaning or purport thereof;

"offence" means an offence contrary to, any conspiracy or attempt to commit or being an accessory after the fact in relation to an offence contrary to, or any counselling in relation to an offence contrary to section 47 (high treason), 51 (intimidating Parliament or a legislature), 52 (sabotage), 57 (forgery, etc.), 61 (sedition), 76 (hijacking), 77 (endangering aircraft, etc.), 78 (offensive weapons, etc., on aircraft), 80 (breach of duty), 81 (using explosives), 82 (possessing explosive), 90 (possession of prohibited weapon), 95 (importing or exporting of prohibited weapon), 119 (bribery, etc.), 120 (bribery, etc.), 121 (fraud on government), 122 (breach of trust), 123 (municipal corruption), 132 (perjury), 139 (obstructing justice), 144 (prison breach), 184 (unlawful interception), 191 (possession of intercepting device), 235 (murder), 264.1 (uttering threats), 267 (assault with a weapon or causing bodily harm), 268 (aggravated assault), 269 (unlawfully causing bodily harm), 271 (sexual assault), 272 (sexual assault with a weapon, threats to a third party or causing bodily harm), 273 (aggravated sexual assault), 279 (kidnapping), 279.1 (hostage taking), 318 (advocating genocide), 344 (robbery), 346 (extortion), 347 (criminal interest rate), 348 (breaking and entering), 354 (possession of property obtained by crime), 356 (theft from mail), 367 (forgery), 368 (uttering forged document), 380 (fraud), 381 (using mail to defraud), 382 (fraudulent manipulation of stock exchange transactions), 424 (threat to commit offences against internationally protected person), 426 (secret commissions), 433 (arson), 449 (making counterfeit money), 450 (possession, etc., of counterfeit money), 452 (uttering, etc., counterfeit money), or 462.31 (laundering proceeds of crime), subsection 145(1) (escape, etc.), 201(1) (keeping gaming or betting house), 212(1) (procuring) or 462.33(11) (acting in contravention of restraint order) or paragraph 163(1)(*a*) (obscene materials), 202(1)(*e*) (pool-selling, etc.), or 334(*a*) (theft in excess of $1,000, etc.), section 4 (trafficking), 5 (importing or exporting), 19.1 (possession of property obtained by certain offences) or 19.2 (laundering proceeds of certain offences) of the *Narcotic Control Act*, section 39 (trafficking), 44.2 (possession of property obtained by trafficking in controlled drugs), 44.3 (laundering proceeds of trafficking in controlled drugs), 48 (trafficking), 50.2 (possession of property obtained by trafficking in restricted drugs) or 50.3 (laundering proceeds of trafficking in restricted drugs) of the *Food and Drugs Act*, section 153 or 159 (smuggling, etc.) of the *Customs Act*, sections 94.1 and 94.2 (organizing entry into Canada), 94.3 (disembarking persons at sea) and 94.4 (counselling false statements) of the *Immigration Act* section 158 or 163 (unlawful distillation or selling of spirits) of the *Excise Act*, section 198 (fraudulent bankruptcy) of the *Bankruptcy Act*, section 3 (spying) of the *Official Secrets Act*, section 13 (export or attempt to export), 14 (import or attempt to import), 15 (diversion, etc.), 16 (no transfer of permits), 17 (false information) or 18 (aiding and abetting) of the *Export and Import Permits Act*, or any other offence created by this Act for which an offender may be sentenced to imprisonment for five years or more or that is an offence mentioned in section 20 of the *Small Loans Act*, chapter S-11 of the Revised Statutes of Canada, 1970, that there are reasonable grounds to believe is part of a pattern of criminal activity planned and organized by a number of persons acting in concert;

"private communication" means any oral communication or any telecommunication made under circumstances in which it is reasonable for the originator thereof to expect that it will not be intercepted by any person other than the person intended by the originator thereof to receive it;

"sell" includes offer for sale, expose for sale, have in possession for sale or distribute or advertise for sale;

"solicitor" means, in the Province of Quebec, an advocate or a notary and, in any other province, a barrister or solicitor. R.S. 1985, c. 27 (1st Supp.), ss. 7(2), 23; c. 1 (2d Supp.), s. 213(1), Schedule I, item 2; c. 1 (4th) Supp.), s. 13; c. 29 (4th Supp.), s. 17; c. 42 (4th Supp.), s. 1; 1991, c. 28, s. 12.

Interception of Communications

Interception — Saving provision — Consent to interception.

184. (1) Every one who, by means of any electro-magnetic, acoustic, mechanical or other device, wilfully intercepts a private communication is guilty of an indictable offence and liable to imprisonment for a term not exceeding five years.

(2) Subsection (1) does not apply to

(*a*) a person who has the consent to intercept, express or implied, of the originator of the private communication or of the person intended by the originator thereof to receive it;

(*b*) a person who intercepts a private communication in accordance with an authorization or any person who in good faith aids in any way a person who he believes on reasonable grounds is acting with an authorization;

(*c*) a person engaged in providing a telephone, telegraph or other communication service to the public who intercepts a private communication,

(i) if the interception is necessary for the purpose of providing the service,

(ii) in the course of service observing or random monitoring necessary for the purpose of mechanical or service quality control checks, or

(iii) if the interception is necessary to protect the person's rights or property directly related to providing the service; or

(*d*) an officer or servant of Her Majesty in right of Canada in respect of a private communication intercepted by him in the course of random monitoring that is necessarily incidental to radio frequency spectrum management in Canada.

(3) Where a private communication is originated by more than one person or is intended by the originator thereof to be received by more than one person, a consent to the interception thereof by any one of those persons is sufficient for the purposes of paragraph (2)(*a*) and subsections 189(1) and 193(1).

Application for authorization — Extension of period for notification — Where extension to be granted — Where extension not granted.

185. (1) An application for an authorization shall be made *ex parte* and in writing to a judge of a superior court of criminal jurisdiction or a judge as defined in section 552 and shall be signed by the Attorney General of the province in which the application is made or the Solicitor General of Canada or an agent specially designated in writing for the purposes of this section by

(*a*) the Solicitor General of Canada personally, if the offence under investigation is one in respect of which proceedings, if any, may be instituted at the instance of the Government of Canada and conducted by or on behalf of the Attorney General of Canada, or

(*b*) the Attorney General of a province personally, in respect of any other offence in that province,

and shall be accompanied by an affidavit, which may be sworn on the information and belief of a peace officer or public officer deposing to the following matters:

(*c*) the facts relied on to justify the belief that the authorization should be given together with particulars of the offence,

(*d*) the type of private communication proposed to be intercepted,

(*e*) the names, addresses and occupations, if known, of all persons, the interception of whose private communications there are reasonable grounds to believe may assist the investigation of the offence, a general description of the nature and location of the place, if known, at which private communications are proposed to be intercepted and a general description of the manner of interception proposed to be used,

(*f*) the number of instances, if any, on which an application has been made under this section in relation to the offence and a person named in the affidavit pursuant to paragraph (*e*) and on which the application was withdrawn or no authorization was given, the date on which each application was made and the name of the judge to whom each application was made,

(*g*) the period for which the authorization is requested, and

(*h*) whether other investigative procedures have been tried and have failed or why it appears they are unlikely to succeed or that the urgency of the matter is such that it would be impractical to carry out the investigation of the offence using only other investigative procedures.

(2) An application for an authorization may be accompanied by an application, personally signed by the Attorney General of the province in which the application for the authorization is made or the Solicitor General of Canada if the application for the authorization is made by him or on his behalf, to substitute for the period mentioned in subsection 196(1) such longer period not exceeding three years as is set out in the application.

(3) Where an application for an authorization is accompanied by an application referred to in subsection (2), the judge to whom the applications are made shall first consider the application referred to in subsection (2) and where, on the basis of the affidavit in support of the application for the authorization and any other affidavit evidence submitted in support of the application referred to in subsection (2), the judge is of the opinion that the interests of justice warrant the granting of the application, he shall fix a period, not exceeding three years, in substitution for the period mentioned in subsection 196(1).

(4) Where the judge to whom an application for an authorization and an application referred to in subsection (2) are made refuses to fix a period in substitution for the period mentioned in subsection 196(1) or where the judge fixes a period in substitution therefor that is less than the period set out in the application referred to in subsection (2), the person appearing before the judge on the application for the authorization may withdraw the application for the authorization and thereupon the judge shall not proceed to consider the application for the authorization or to give the authorization and shall return to the person appearing before him on the application for the authorization both applications and all other material pertaining thereto.

Judge to be satisfied — Where authorization not to be given — Terms and conditions — Content and limitation of authorization — Persons designated — Renewal of authorization — Renewal.

186. (1) An authorization may be given if the judge to whom the application is made is satisfied (*a*) that it would be in the best interests of the administration of justice to do so; and

(*b*) that other investigative procedures have been tried and have failed, other investigative procedures are unlikely to succeed or the urgency of the matter is such that it would be impractical to carry out the investigation of the offence using only other investigative procedures.

(2) No authorization may be given to intercept a private communication at the office or residence of a solicitor, or at any other place ordinarily used by a solicitor and by other solicitors for the purpose of consultation with clients, unless the judge to whom the application is made is satisfied that there are reasonable grounds to believe that the solicitor, any other solicitor practising with him, any person employed by him or any other such solicitor or a member of the solicitor's household has been or is about to become a party to an offence.

(3) Where an authorization is given in relation to the interception of private communications at a place described in subsection (2), the judge by whom the authorization is given shall include therein such terms and conditions as he considers advisable to protect privileged communications between solicitors and clients.

(4) An authorization shall

(*a*) state the offence in respect of which private communications may be intercepted;

(*b*) state the type of private communication that may be intercepted;

(*c*) state the identity of the persons, if known, whose private communications are to be intercepted, generally describe the place at which private communications may be intercepted, if a general description of that place can be given, and generally describe the manner of interception that may be used;

(*d*) contain such terms and conditions as the judge considers advisable in the public interest; and

(*e*) be valid for the period, not exceeding sixty days, set out therein.

(5) The Solicitor General of Canada or the Attorney General, as the case may be, may designate a person or persons who may intercept private communications under authorizations.

(6) Renewals of an authorization may be given by a judge of a superior court of criminal jurisdiction or a judge as defined in section 552 on receipt by him of an *ex parte* application in writing signed by the Attorney General of the province in which the application is made or the Solicitor General of Canada or an agent specially designated in writing for the purposes of section 185 by the Solicitor General of Canada or the Attorney General, as the case may be, accompanied by an affidavit of a peace officer or public officer deposing to the following matters:

(*a*) the reason and period for which the renewal is required,

(*b*) full particulars, together with times and dates, when interceptions, if any, were made or attempted under the authorization, and any information that has been obtained by any interception, and

(*c*) the number of instances, if any, on which, to the knowledge and belief of the deponent, an application has been made under this subsection in relation to the same authorization and on which the application was withdrawn or no renewal was given, the date on which each application was made and the name of the judge to whom each application was made,

and supported by such other information as the judge may require.

(7) A renewal of an authorization may be given if the judge to whom the application is made is satisfied that any of the circumstances described in subsection (1) still obtain, but no renewal shall be for a period exceeding sixty days.

Manner in which application to be kept secret — Order of judge.

187. (1) All documents relating to an application made pursuant to section 185 or subsection 186(6) or 196(2) are confidential and, with the exception of the authorization, shall be placed in a packet and sealed by the judge to whom the application is made immediately on determination of the application, and that packet shall be kept in the custody of the court in a place to which the public has no access or in such other place as the judge may authorize and shall not be

(*a*) opened or the contents thereof removed except

(i) for the purpose of dealing with an application for renewal of the authorization, or

(ii) pursuant to an order of a judge of a superior court of criminal jurisdiction or a judge as defined in section 552; and

(*b*) destroyed except pursuant to an order of a judge referred to in subparagraph (*a*)(ii).

(2) An order under subsection (1) may only be made after the Attorney General or the Solicitor General by whom or on whose authority the application was made for the authorization to which the order relates has been given an opportunity to be heard. R.S. 1985, c. 27 (1st Supp.), s. 24.

Applications to specially appointed judges — Authorizations in emergency — Certain interceptions deemed not lawful — Definition of "Chief Justice" — Inadmissibility of evidence.

188. (1) Notwithstanding section 185, an application for an authorization may be made *ex parte* to a judge of a superior court of criminal jurisdiction, or a judge as defined in section 552, designated from time to time by the Chief Justice, by a peace officer specially designated in writing for the purposes of this section by

(*a*) the Solicitor General of Canada, if the offence is one in respect of which proceedings, if any, may be instituted by the Government of Canada and conducted by or on behalf of the Attorney General of Canada, or (*b*) the Attorney General of a province, in respect of any other offence in the province,

if the urgency of the situation requires interception of private communications to commence before an authorization could, with reasonable diligence, be obtained under section 186.

(2) Where the judge to whom an application is made pursuant to subsection (1) is satisfied that the urgency of the situation requires that interception of private communications commence before an authorization could, with reasonable diligence, be obtained under section 186, he may, on such terms and conditions, if any, as he considers advisable, give an authorization in writing for a period of up to thirty-six hours.

(3) For the purposes of section 189 only, an interception of a private communication in accordance with an authorization given pursuant to this section shall be deemed not to have been lawfully made unless the judge who gave the authorization or, if that judge is unable to act, a judge of the same jurisdiction, certifies that if the application for the authorization had been made to him pursuant to section 185 he would have given the authorization.

(4) In this section, "Chief Justice" means

(*a*) in the Province of Ontario, the Chief Justice of the Ontario Court;

(*b*) in the Province of Quebec, the Chief Justice of the Superior Court;

(*c*) in the Provinces of Nova Scotia, Prince Edward Island and Newfoundland, the Chief Justice of the Supreme Court, Trial Division;

(*d*) in the Provinces of New Brunswick, Manitoba, Saskatchewan and Alberta, the Chief Justice of the Court of Queen's Bench;

(*e*) in the Province of British Columbia, the Chief Justice of the Supreme Court; and

(*f*) in the Yukon Territory and the Northwest Territories, the judge of the Supreme Court with the earliest date of appointment to the court in question.

(5) The trial judge may deem inadmissible the evidence obtained by means of an interception of a private communication pursuant to a subsequent authorization given under this section, where he finds that the application for the subsequent authorization was based on the same facts, and involved the interception of the private communications of the same person or persons, or related to the same offence, on which the application for the original authorization was based. R.S. 1985, c. 27 (1st Supp.), s. 25; R.S. 1985, c. 27 (2d Supp.), Schedule, item 6; 1990, c. 17, s. 10; 1992, c. 1, s. 58(1), Sch. I, item 4.

Intercepted private communication admissibility — Idem — Idem — Idem —Notice of intention to produce evidence — Privileged evidence.

189. (1) A private communication that has been intercepted is inadmissible as evidence against the originator of the communication or the person intended by the originator to receive it unless (*a*) the interception was lawfully made, or

(*b*) the originator thereof or the person intended by the originator to receive it has expressly consented to the admission thereof,

but evidence obtained directly or indirectly as a result of information acquired by interception of a private communication is not inadmissible by reason only that the private communication is itself inadmissible as evidence.

(2) Notwithstanding subsection (1), the judge or provincial court judge presiding at any proceedings may refuse to admit evidence obtained directly or indirectly as a result of information acquired by interception of a private communication that is itself inadmissible as evidence where he is of the opinion that the admission thereof would bring the administration of justice into disrepute.

(3) Where the judge or provincial court judge presiding at any proceedings is of the opinion that a private communication that, by virtue of subsection (1), is inadmissible as evidence in the proceedings

(*a*) is relevant to a matter at issue in the proceedings, and

(*b*) is inadmissible as evidence therein by reason only of a defect of form or an irregularity in procedure, not being a substantive defect or irregularity, in the application for or the giving of the authorization under which the private communication was intercepted,

he may, notwithstanding subsection (1), admit the private communication as evidence in the proceedings.

(4) A private communication that has been intercepted and that is admissible as evidence may be admitted in any criminal proceeding or in any civil proceeding or other matter whatever respecting which Parliament has jurisdiction, whether or not the criminal proceeding or the civil proceeding or other matter relates to the offence specified in the authorization pursuant to which the communication was intercepted.

(5) A private communication that has been lawfully intercepted shall not be received in evidence unless the party intending to adduce it has given to the accused reasonable notice of his intention together with

(*a*) a transcript of the private communication, where it will be adduced in the form of a recording, or a statement setting out full particulars of the private communication, where evidence of the private communication will be given *viva voce*; and

(*b*) a statement respecting the time, place and date of the private communication and the parties thereto, if known.

(6) Any information obtained by an interception that, but for the interception, would have been privileged remains privileged and inadmissible as evidence without the consent of the person enjoying the privilege. R.S. 1985, c. 27 (1st Supp.), s. 203.

Further particulars.

190. Where an accused has been given notice pursuant to subsection 189(5), any judge of the court in which the trial of the accused is being or is to be held may at any time order that further particulars be given of the private communication that is intended to be adduced in evidence.

Possession, etc. — Exemptions — Terms and conditions of licence.

191. (1) Every one who possesses, sells or purchases any electro-magnetic, acoustic, mechanical or other device or any component thereof knowing that the design thereof renders it primarily useful for surreptitious interception of private communications is guilty of an indictable offence and liable to imprisonment for a term not exceeding two years.

(2) Subsection (1) does not apply to

(*a*) a police officer or police constable in possession of a device or component described in subsection (1) in the course of his employment;

(*b*) a person in possession of such a device or component for the purpose of using it in an interception made or to be made in accordance with an authorization;

(*b*.1) a person in possession of such a device or component under the direction of a police officer or police constable in order to assist that officer or constable in the course of his duties as a police officer or police constable;

(*c*) an officer or a servant of Her Majesty in right of Canada or a member of the Canadian Forces in possession of such a device or component in the course of his duties as such an officer, servant or member, as the case may be; and

(*d*) any other person in possession of such a device or component under the authority of a licence issued by the Solicitor General of Canada.

(3) A licence issued for the purpose of paragraph (2)(*d*) may contain such terms and conditions relating to the possession, sale or purchase of a device or component described in subsection (1) as the Solicitor General of Canada may prescribe. R.S. 1985, c. 27 (1st Supp.), s. 26.

Forfeiture — Limitation.

192. (1) Where a person is convicted of an offence under section 184 or 191, any electro-magnetic, acoustic, mechanical or other device by means of which the offence was committed or the possession of which constituted the offence, on the conviction, in addition to any punishment that is imposed, may be ordered forfeited to Her Majesty whereupon it may be disposed of as the Attorney General directs.

(2) No order for forfeiture shall be made under subsection (1) in respect of telephone, telegraph or other communication facilities or equipment owned by a person engaged in providing telephone, telegraph or other communication service to the public or forming part of the telephone, telegraph or other

communication service or system of that person by means of which an offence under section 184 has been committed if that person was not a party to the offence.

Disclosure of information — Exemptions — Publishing of prior lawful disclosure.

193. (1) Where a private communication has been intercepted by means of an electro-magnetic, acoustic, mechanical or other device without the consent, express or implied, of the originator thereof or of the person intended by the originator thereof to receive it, every one who, without the express consent of the originator thereof or of the person intended by the originator thereof to receive it, wilfully

(*a*) uses or discloses the private communication or any part thereof or the substance, meaning or purport thereof or of any part thereof, or

(*b*) discloses the existence thereof,

is guilty of an indictable offence and liable to imprisonment for a term not exceeding two years.

(2) Subsection (1) does not apply to a person who discloses a private communication or any part thereof or the substance, meaning or purport thereof or of any part thereof or who discloses the existence of a private communication

(*a*) in the course of or for the purpose of giving evidence in any civil or criminal proceedings or in any other proceedings in which he may be required to give evidence on oath where the private communication is admissible as evidence under section 189 or would be admissible under that section if it applied in respect of the proceedings;

(*b*) in the course of or for the purpose of any criminal investigation if the private communication was lawfully intercepted;

(*c*) in giving notice under section 189 or furnishing further particulars pursuant to an order under section 190;

(*d*) in the course of the operation of

(i) a telephone, telegraph or other communication service to the public, or

(ii) a department or an agency of the Government of Canada,

if the disclosure is necessarily incidental to an interception described in paragraph 184(2)(*c*) or (*d*); or

(*e*) where disclosure is made to a peace officer or prosecutor in Canada or to a person or authority with responsibility in a foreign state for the investigation or prosecution of offences and is intended to be in the interests of the administration of justice in Canada or elsewhere; or

(*f*) where the disclosure is made to the Director of the Canadian Security Intelligence Service or to an employee of the Service for the purpose of enabling the Service to perform its duties and functions under section 12 of the *Canadian Security Intelligence Service Act.*

(3) Subsection (1) does not apply to a person who discloses a private

communication or any part thereof or the substance, meaning or purport thereof or of any part thereof or who discloses the existence of a private communication where that which is disclosed by him was, prior to the disclosure, lawfully disclosed in the course of or for the purpose of giving evidence in proceedings referred to in paragraph (2)(*a*). R.S. 1985, c. 30 (4th Supp.), s. 45.

Damages — No damages where civil proceedings commenced — Judgment may be registered — Moneys in possession of accused may be taken.

194. (1) Subject to subsection (2), a court that convicts an accused of an offence under section 184 or 193 may, on the application of a person aggrieved, at the time sentence is imposed, order the accused to pay to that person an amount not exceeding five thousand dollars as punitive damages.

(2) No amount shall be ordered to be paid under subsection (1) to a person who has commenced an action under Part II of the *Crown Liability Act.*

(3) Where an amount that is ordered to be paid under subsection (1) is not paid forthwith, the applicant may, by filing the order, enter as a judgment, in the superior court of the province in which the trial was held, the amount ordered to be paid, and that judgment is enforceable against the accused in the same manner as if it were a judgment rendered against the accused in that court in civil proceedings.

(4) All or any part of an amount that is ordered to be paid under subsection (1) may be taken out of moneys found in the possession of the accused at the time of his arrest, except where there is a dispute respecting ownership of or right of possession to those moneys by claimants other than the accused.

Annual report — Information respecting authorizations — Other information — Report to be laid before Parliament — Report by Attorneys General.

195. (1) The Solicitor General of Canada shall, as soon as possible after the end of each year, prepare a report relating to

(*a*) authorizations for which he and agents to be named in the report who were specially designated in writing by him for the purposes of section 185 made application, and

(*b*) authorizations given under section 188 for which peace officers to be named in the report who were specially designated by him for the purposes of that section made application,

and interceptions made thereunder in the immediately preceding year.

(2) The report referred to in subsection (1) shall, in relation to authorizations and interceptions made thereunder, set out

(*a*) the number of applications made for authorizations;

(*b*) the number of applications made for renewal of authorizations;

(*c*) the number of applications referred to in paragraphs (*a*) and (*b*) that were granted, the number of those applications that were refused and the number of applications referred to in paragraph (*a*) that were granted subject to terms and conditions;

(*d*) the number of persons identified in an authorization against whom proceedings were commenced at the instance of the Attorney General of Canada in respect of

(i) an offence specified in the authorization,

(ii) an offence other than an offence specified in the authorization but in respect of which an authorization may be given, and

(iii) an offence in respect of which an authorization may not be given;

(*e*) the number of persons not identified in an authorization against whom proceedings were commenced at the instance of the Attorney General of Canada in respect of

(i) an offence specified in such an authorization,

(ii) an offence other than an offence specified in such an authorization but in respect of which an authorization may be given, and

(iii) an offence other than an offence specified in such an authorization and for which no such authorization may be given,

and whose commission or alleged commission of the offence became known to a peace officer as a result of an interception of a private communication under an authorization;

(*f*) the average period for which authorizations were given and for which renewals thereof were granted;

(*g*) the number of authorizations that, by virtue of one or more renewals thereof, were valid for more than sixty days, for more than one hundred and twenty days, for more than one hundred and eighty days and for more than two hundred and forty days;

(*h*) the number of notifications given pursuant to section 196;

(*i*) the offences in respect of which authorizations were given, specifying the number of authorizations given in respect of each of those offences;

(*j*) a description of all classes of places specified in authorizations and the number of authorizations in which each of those classes of places was specified;

(*k*) a general description of the methods of interception involved in each interception under an authorization;

(*l*) the number of persons arrested whose identity became known to a peace officer as a result of an interception under an authorization;

(*m*) the number of criminal proceedings commenced at the instance of the Attorney General of Canada in which private communications obtained by interception under an authorization were adduced in evidence and the number of those proceedings that resulted in a conviction; and

(*n*) the number of criminal investigations in which information obtained as a result of the interception of a private communication under an authorization was used although the private communication was not adduced in evidence in criminal proceedings commenced at the instance of the Attorney General of Canada as a result of the investigations.

(3) The report referred to in subsection (1) shall, in addition to the information referred to in subsection (2), set out

(*a*) the number of prosecutions commenced against officers or servants of Her Majesty in right of Canada or members of the Canadian Forces for offences under section 184 or 193; and

(*b*) a general assessment of the importance of interception of private communications for the investigation, detection, prevention and prosecution of offences in Canada.

(4) The Solicitor General of Canada shall cause a copy of each report prepared by him under subsection (1) to be laid before Parliament forthwith on completion thereof, or if Parliament is not then sitting, on any of the first fifteen days next thereafter that Parliament is sitting.

(5) The Attorney General of each province shall, as soon as possible after the end of each year, prepare and publish or otherwise make available to the public a report relating to

(*a*) authorizations for which he and agents specially designated in writing by him for the purposes of section 185 made application, and

(*b*) authorizations given under section 188 for which peace officers specially designated by him for the purposes of that section made application,

and interceptions made thereunder in the immediately preceding year setting out, with such modifications as the circumstances require, the information described in subsections (2) and (3). R.S. 1985, c. 27 (1st Supp.), s. 27.

Written notification to be given — Extension of period for notification — Where extension to be granted — Application to be accompanied by affidavit.

196. (1) The Attorney General of the province in which an application for an authorization was made or the Solicitor General of Canada if the application was made by him or on his behalf shall, within ninety days next following the period for which the authorization was given or renewed or within such other period as is fixed pursuant to subsection 185(3) or subsection (3) of this section, notify in writing the person who was the object of the interception pursuant to the authorization and shall, in a manner prescribed by regulations made by the Governor in Council, certify to the court that issued the authorization that the person has been so notified.

(2) At any time within the ninety day period mentioned in subsection (1) or any other period that is less than three years that was fixed by a judge pursuant to subsection 185(3) or substituted pursuant to this subsection in relation to a particular authorization, the Attorney General by or on whose behalf the application for the authorization was made or the Solicitor General of Canada, if the application was made by him or on his behalf, may apply

to a judge of a superior court of criminal jurisdiction or a judge as defined in section 552 to substitute for the ninety day period mentioned in subsection (1), or the other period so fixed or substituted, such longer period not exceeding three years as is set out in the application.

(3) Where the judge to whom an application referred to in subsection (2) is made, on the basis of an affidavit submitted in support of the application, is satisfied that

(*a*) the investigation of the offence to which the authorization relates, or

(*b*) a subsequent investigation of an offence listed in section 183 commenced as a result of information obtained from the investigation referred to in paragraph (*a*),

is continuing and is of the opinion that the interests of justice warrant the granting of the application, that judge shall fix a period, not exceeding three years, in substitution for the ninety day period mentioned in subsection (1) or the period fixed pursuant to subsection 185(3).

(4) An application pursuant to subsection (2) shall be accompanied by an affidavit, which may be sworn on the information and belief of a peace officer or public officer, deposing to

(*a*) the facts relied on to justify the belief that an extension of the ninety day period mentioned in subsection (1) or any other period fixed or substituted therefor should be granted; and

(*b*) the number of instances, if any, on which an appliction has been made under that subsection in relation to the particular authorization and on which the application was withdrawn or the application was not granted, the date on which each application was made and the name of the judge to whom each application was made. R.S. 1985, c. 27 (1st Supp.), s. 28.

PART VII

DISORDERLY HOUSES, GAMING AND BETTING

Interpretation

Definitions — "Bet" — "Common bawdy-house" — "Common betting house" — "Common gaming house" — "Disorderly house" — "Game" — "Gaming equipment" — "Keeper" — "Place" — "Prostitute" — "Public place" — Exception — Onus — Effect when game partly played on premises.

197. (1) In this Part

"bet" means a bet that is placed on any contingency or event that is to take place in or out of Canada, and without restricting the generality of the foregoing, includes a bet that is placed on any contingency relating to a horse-race, fight, match or sporting event that is to take place in or out of Canada;

"common bawdy-house" means a place that is

(*a*) kept or occupied, or

(*b*) resorted to by one or more persons

for the purpose of prostitution or the practice of acts of indecency;

"common betting house" means a place that is opened, kept or used for the purpose of

(*a*) enabling, encouraging or assisting persons who resort thereto to bet between themselves or with the keeper, or

(*b*) enabling any person to receive, record, register, transmit or pay bets or to announce the results of betting;

"common gaming house" means a place that is

(*a*) kept for gain to which persons resort for the purpose of playing games, or

(*b*) kept or used for the purpose of playing games

(i) in which a bank is kept by one or more but not all of the players,

(ii) in which all or any portion of the bets on or proceeds from a game is paid, directly or indirectly, to the keeper of the place,

(iii) in which, directly or indirectly, a fee is charged to or paid by the players for the privilege of playing or participating in a game or using gaming equipment, or

(iv) in which the chances of winning are not equally favourable to all persons who play the game, including the person, if any, who conducts the game;

"disorderly house" means a common bawdy-house, a common betting house or a common gaming house;

"game" means a game of chance or mixed chance and skill;

"gaming equipment" means anything that is or may be used for the purpose of playing games or for betting;

"keeper" includes a person who

(*a*) is an owner or occupier of a place,

(*b*) assists or acts on behalf of an owner or occupier of a place,

(*c*) appears to be, or to assist or act on behalf of an owner or occupier of a place,

(*d*) has the care or management of a place, or

(*e*) uses a place permanently or temporarily, with or without the consent of the owner or occupier;

"place" includes any place, whether or not

(*a*) it is covered or enclosed,

(*b*) it is used permanently or temporarily, or

(*c*) any person has an exclusive right of user with respect to it;

"prostitute" means a person of either sex who engages in prostitution;

"public place" includes any place to which the public have access as of right or by invitation, express or implied.

(2) A place is not a common gaming house within the meaning of paragraph (*a*) or subparagraph (*b*)(ii) or (iii) of the definition "common gaming house" in subsection (1) while it is occupied and used by an incorporated genuine social club or branch thereof, if

(*a*) the whole or any portion of the bets on or proceeds from games played therein is not directly or indirectly paid to the keeper thereof; and

(*b*) no fee is charged to persons for the right or privilege of participating in the games played therein other than under the authority of and in accordance with the terms of a licence issued by the Attorney General of the province in which the place is situated or by such other person or authority in the province as may be specified by the Attorney General thereof.

(3) The onus of proving that, by virtue of subsection (2), a place is not a common gaming house is on the accused.

(4) A place may be a common gaming house notwithstanding that

(*a*) it is used for the purpose of playing part of a game and another part of the game is played elsewhere;

(*b*) the stake that is played for is in some other place, or

(*c*) it is used on only one occasion in the manner described in paragraph (*b*) of the definition "common gaming house" in subsection (1), if the keeper or any person acting on behalf or in concert with the keeper has used another place on another occasion in the manner described in that paragraph. R.S. 1985, c. 27 (1st Supp.), s. 29.

Presumptions

Presumptions — Conclusive presumption from slot machine — "Slot machine" defined.

198. (1) In proceedings under this Part,

(*a*) evidence that a peace officer who was authorized to enter a place was wilfully prevented from entering or was wilfully obstructed or delayed in entering is, in the absence of any evidence to the contrary, proof that the place is a disorderly house;

(*b*) evidence that a place was found to be equipped with gaming equipment or any device for concealing, removing or destroying gaming equipment is, in the absence of any evidence to the contrary, proof that the place is a common gaming house or a common betting house, as the case may be;

(*c*) evidence that gaming equipment was found in a place entered under a warrant issued pursuant to this Part, or on or about the person of anyone found therein, is, in the absence of any evidence to the contrary, proof that the place is a common gaming house and that the persons found therein were playing games, whether or not any person acting under the warrant observed any persons playing games therein; and

(*d*) evidence that a person was convicted of keeping a disorderly house is, for the purpose of proceedings against any one who is alleged to have been an inmate or to have been found in that house at the time the person committed the offence of which he was convicted, in the absence of any evidence to the contrary, proof that the house was, at that time, a disorderly house.

(2) For the purpose of proceedings under this Part, a place that is found to be equipped with a slot machine shall be conclusively presumed to be a common gaming house.

(3) In subsection (2), "slot machine" means any automatic machine or slot machine

(*a*) that is used or intended to be used for any purpose other than vending merchandise or services, or

(*b*) that is used or intended to be used for the purpose of vending merchandise or services if

(i) the result of one of any number of operations of the machine is a matter of chance or uncertainty to the operator,

(ii) as a result of a given number of successive operations by the operator the machine produces different results, or

(iii) on any operation of the machine it discharges or emits a slug or token

but does not include an automatic machine or slot machine that dispenses as prizes only one or more free games on that machine.

Search

Warrant to search — Search without warrant, seizure and arrest — Disposal of property seized — When declaration or direction may be made — Conversion into money — Telephones exempt from seizure — Exception.

199. (1) A justice who receives from a peace officer a report in writing that he believes on reasonable grounds that an offence under section 201, 202, 203, 206, 207 or 210 is being committed at any place within the jurisdiction of the justice may issue a warrant under his hand authorizing a peace officer to enter and search the place by day or night and seize anything found therein that may be evidence that an offence under section 201, 202, 203, 206, 207 or 210, as the case may be, is being committed at that place, and to take into custody all persons who are found in or at that place and requiring those persons and things to be brought before him or before another justice having jurisdiction, to be dealt with according to law.

(2) A peace officer may, whether or not he is acting under a warrant issued pursuant to this section, take into custody any person whom he finds keeping a common gaming house and any person whom he finds therein, and may seize anything that may be evidence that such an offence is being committed and shall bring those persons and things before a justice having jurisdiction, to be dealt with according to law.

(3) Except where otherwise expressly provided by law, a court, judge, justice or provincial court judge before whom anything that is seized under this section is brought may declare that the thing is forfeited, in which case it shall be disposed of or dealt with as the Attorney General may direct if no person shows sufficient cause why it should not be forfeited.

(4) No declaration or direction shall be made pursuant to subsection (3) in respect of anything seized under this section until

(*a*) it is no longer required as evidence in any proceedings that are instituted pursuant to the seizure; or

(*b*) the expiration of thirty days from the time of seizure where it is not required as evidence in any proceedings.

(5) The Attorney General may, for the purpose of converting anything forfeited under this section into money, deal with it in all respects as if he were the owner thereof.

(6) Nothing in this section or in section 489 authorizes the seizure, forfeiture or destruction of telephone, telegraph or other communication facilities or equipment that may be evidence of or that may have been used in the commission of an offence under section 201, 202, 203, 206, 207 or 210 and that is owned by a person engaged in providing telephone, telegraph or other communication service to the public or forming part of the telephone, telegraph or other communication service or system of that person.

(7) Subsection (6) does not apply to prohibit the seizure, for use as evidence, of any facility or equipment described in that subsection that is designed or adapted to record a communication. R.S. 1985, c. 27 (1st Supp.), s. 203.

200. [Repealed R.S. 1985, c. 27 (1st Supp.), s. 30.]

Gaming and Betting

Keeping gaming or betting house — Person found in or owner permitting use.

201. (1) Every one who keeps a common gaming house or common betting house is guilty of an indictable offence and liable to imprisonment for a term not exceeding two years.

(2) Every one who

(*a*) is found, without lawful excuse, in a common gaming house or common betting house, or

(*b*) as owner, landlord, lessor, tenant, occupier or agent, knowingly permits a place to be let or used for the purposes of a common gaming house or common betting house,

is guilty of an offence punishable on summary conviction.

Betting, pool-selling, book-making, etc. — Punishment.

202. (1) Every one commits an offence who

(*a*) uses or knowingly allows a place under his control to be used for the purposes of recording or registering bets or selling a pool;

(*b*) imports, makes, buys, sells, rents, leases, hires or keeps, exhibits, employs or knowingly allows to be kept, exhibited or employed in any place under his control any device or apparatus for the purpose of recording or registering bets or selling a pool, or any machine or device for gambling or betting;

(*c*) has under his control any money or other property relating to a transaction that is an offence under this section;

(*d*) records or registers bets or sells a pool;

(*e*) engages in book-making or pool-selling, or in the business or occupation of betting, or makes any agreement for the purchase or sale of betting or gaming privileges, or for the purchase or sale of information that is intended to assist in book-making, pool-selling or betting;

(*f*) prints, provides or offers to print or provide information intended for use in connection with book-making, pool-selling or betting on any horse-race, fight, game or sport, whether or not it takes place in or outside Canada or has or has not taken place;

(*g*) imports or brings into Canada any information or writing that is intended or is likely to promote or be of use in gambling, book-making, pool-selling or betting on a horse-race, fight, game or sport, and where this paragraph applies it is immaterial

(i) whether the information is published before, during or after the race, fight, game or sport, or

(ii) whether the race, fight, game or sport takes place in Canada or elsewhere,

but this paragraph does not apply to a newspaper, magazine or other periodical published in good faith primarily for a purpose other than the publication of such information;

(*h*) advertises, prints, publishes, exhibits, posts up, or otherwise gives notice of any offer, invitation or inducement to bet on, to guess or to foretell the results of a contest, or a result of or contingency relating to any contest;

(*i*) wilfully and knowingly sends, transmits, delivers or receives any message by radio, telegraph, telephone, mail or express that conveys any information relating to book-making, pool-selling, betting or wagering, or that is intended to assist in book-making, pool-selling, betting or wagering; or

(*j*) aids or assists in any manner in anything that is an offence under this section.

(2) Every one who commits an offence under this section is guilty of an indictable offence and liable

(*a*) for a first offence, to imprisonment for not more than two years;

(*b*) for a second offence, to imprisonment for not more than two years and not less than fourteen days; and

(*c*) for each subsequent offence, to imprisonment for not more than two years and not less than three months.

Placing bets on behalf of others.

203. Every one who

(*a*) places or offers or agrees to place a bet on behalf of another person for a consideration paid or to be paid by or on behalf of that other person,

(*b*) engages in the business or practice of placing or agreeing to place bets on behalf of other persons, whether for a consideration or otherwise, or

(*c*) holds himself out or allows himself to be held out as engaging in the business or practice of placing or agreeing to place bets on behalf of other persons, whether for a consideration or otherwise,

is guilty of an indictable offence and liable

(*d*) for a first offence, to imprisonment for not more than two years,

(*e*) for a second offence, to imprisonment for not more than two years and not less than fourteen days, and

(*f*) for each subsequent offence, to imprisonment for not more than two years and not less than three months.

Exemption — Exception — Presumption — Operation of pari-mutuel system — Supervision of pari-mutuel system — Percentage that may be deducted and retained — Idem — Stopping of betting — Regulations — Approvals — Regulations — 900 metre zone — Contravention — Definition of "Association".

204. (1) Sections 201 and 202 do not apply to

(*a*) any person or association by reason of his or their becoming the custodian or depository of any money, property or valuable thing staked, to be paid to

(i) the winner of a lawful race, sport, game or exercise,

(ii) the owner of a horse engaged in a lawful race, or

(iii) the winner of any bets between not more than ten individuals;

(*b*) a private bet between individuals not engaged in any way in the business of betting;

(*c*) bets made or records of bets made through the agency of a pari-mutuel system on running, trotting or pacing horse-races if

(i) the bets or records of bets are made on the race-course of an association in respect of races conducted at that race-course or another race-course in or out of Canada, and, in the case of a race conducted on a race-course situated outside Canada, the governing body that regulates the race has been certified as acceptable by the Minister of Agriculture or a person designated by that Minister pursuant to subsection (8.1) and that Minister or person has permitted pari-mutuel betting in Canada on the race pursuant to that subsection, and

(ii) the provisions of this section and the regulations are complied with.

(1.1) For greater certainty, a person may, in accordance with the regulations, do anything described in section 201 or 202, if the person does it for the purposes of legal pari-mutuel betting.

(2) For the purposes of paragraph (1)(*c*), bets made, in accordance with the regulations, in a betting theatre referred to in paragraph (8)(*e*), or by telephone calls to the race-course of an association or to such a betting theatre, are deemed to be made on the race-course of the association.

(3) No person or association shall use a pari-mutuel system of betting in respect of a horse race unless the system has been approved by and its operation is carried on under the supervision of an officer appointed by the Minister of Agriculture.

(4) Every person or association operating a pari-mutuel system of betting in accordance with this section in respect of a horse race, whether or not the person or association is conducting the race-meeting at which the race is run, shall pay to the Receiver General in respect of each individual pool of the race and each individual feature pool one-half of one per cent, or such greater fraction not exceeding one per cent as may be fixed by the Governor in Council, of the total amount of money that is bet through the agency of the pari-mutuel system of betting.

(5) Where any person or association becomes a custodian or depository of any money, bet or stakes under a pari-mutuel system in respect of a horse-race, that person or association shall not deduct or retain any amount from the total amount of money, bets or stakes unless it does so pursuant to subsection (6).

(6) An association operating a pari-mutuel system of betting in accordance with this section in respect of a horse-race, or any other association or person acting on its behalf, may deduct and retain from the total amount of money that is bet through the agency of the pari-mutuel system, in respect of each individual pool of each race or each individual feature pool, a percentage not exceeding the percentage prescribed by the regulations plus any odd cents over any multiple of five cents in the amount calculated in accordance with the regulations to be payable in respect of each dollar bet.

(7) Where an officer appointed by the Minister of Agriculture is not satisfied that the provisions of this section and the regulations are being carried out in good faith by any person or association in relation to a race meeting, he may, at any time, order any betting in relation to the race meeting to be stopped for any period that he considers proper.

(8) The Minister of Agriculture may make regulations

(*a*) prescribing the maximum number of races for each race-course on which a race meeting is conducted, in respect of which a pari-mutuel system of betting may be used for the race meeting or on any one calendar day during the race meeting, and the circumstances in which the Minister of Agriculture or a person designated by him for that purpose may approve of the use of that system in respect of additional races on any race-course for a particular race meeting or on a particular day during the race meeting;

(*b*) prohibiting any person or association from using a pari-mutuel system of betting for any race-course on which a race meeting is conducted in respect of more than the maximum number of races prescribed pursuant to paragraph (*a*) and the additional races, if any, in respect of which the use of a pari-mutuel system of betting has been approved pursuant to that paragraph;

(*c*) prescribing the maximum percentage that may be deducted and retained pursuant to subsection (6) by or on behalf of a person or association operating a pari-mutuel system of betting in respect of a horse-race in accordance with this section and providing for the determination of the percentage that each such person or association may deduct and retain;

(*d*) respecting pari-mutuel betting in Canada on horse-races conducted on a race-course situated outside Canada; and

(*e*) authorizing pari-mutuel betting and governing the conditions for pari-mutuel betting, including the granting of licences therefor, that is conducted by an association in a betting theatre owned or leased by the association in a province in which the Lieutenant Governor in Council, or such other person or authority in the province as may be specified by the Lieutenant Governor in Council thereof, has issued a licence to that association for the betting theatre.

(8.1) The Minister of Agriculture or a person designated by that Minister may, with respect to a horse-race conducted on a race-course situated outside Canada,

(*a*) certify as acceptable, for the purposes of this section, the governing body that regulates the race; and

(*b*) permit pari-mutuel betting in Canada on the race.

(9) The Minister of Agriculture may make regulations respecting

(*a*) the supervision and operation of pari-mutuel systems related to race meetings, and the fixing of the dates on which and the places at which an association may conduct such meetings;

(*b*) the method of calculating the amount payable in respect of each dollar bet;

(*c*) the conduct of race-meetings in relation to the supervision and operation of pari-mutuel systems, including photo-finishes, video patrol and the testing of bodily substances taken from horses entered in a race at such meetings, including, in the case of a horse that dies while engaged in racing or immediately before or after the race, the testing of any tissue taken from its body;

(*d*) the prohibition, restriction or regulation of

(i) the possession of drugs or medicaments or of equipment used in the administering of drugs or medicaments at or near race-courses, or

(ii) the administering of drugs or medicaments to horses participating in races run at a race meeting during which a pari-mutuel system of betting is used; and

(*e*) the provision, equipment and maintenance of accommodation, services or other facilities for the proper supervision and operation of pari-mutuel systems related to race meetings, by associations conducting those meetings or by other associations.

(9.1) For the purposes of this section, the Minister of Agriculture may designate, with respect to any race-course, a zone that shall be deemed to be part of the race-course, if

(*a*) the zone is immediately adjacent to the race-course;

(*b*) the farthest point of that zone is not more than 900 metres from the nearest point on the race track of the race-course; and

(*c*) all real property situated in that zone is owned or leased by the person or association that owns or leases the race-course.

(10) Every person who contravenes or fails to comply with any of the provisions of this section or of any regulations made under this section is guilty of

(*a*) an indictable offence and is liable to imprisonment for a term not exceeding two years, or

(*b*) an offence punishable on summary conviction.

(11) For the purposes of this section, "association" means an association incorporated by or pursuant to an Act of the Parliament or of the legislature

of a province that owns or leases a race-course and conducts horse-races in the ordinary course of its business and, to the extent that the applicable legislation requires that the purposes of the association be expressly stated in its constating instrument, having as one of its purposes the conduct of horse-races. R.S. 1985, c. 47 (1st Supp.), s. 1; 1989, c. 2, s. 1.

205. [Repealed R.S. 1985, c. 52 (1st Supp.), s. 1.]

Offence in relation to lotteries and games of chance — "Three-card monte" — Exemption for fairs — Definition of "fair or exhibition" — Offence — Lottery sale void — Bona fide exception — Foreign lottery included — Saving.

206. (1) Every one is guilty of an indictable offence and liable to imprisonment for a term not exceeding two years who

(*a*) makes, prints, advertises or publishes, or causes or procures to be made, printed, advertised or published, any proposal, scheme or plan for advancing, lending, giving, selling or in any way disposing of any property by lots, cards, tickets or any mode of chance whatever;

(*b*) sells, barters, exchanges or otherwise disposes of, or causes or procures, or aids or assists in, the sale, barter, exchange or other disposal of, or offers for sale, barter or exchange, any lot, card, ticket or other means or device for advancing, lending, giving, selling or otherwise disposing of any property by lots, tickets or any mode of chance whatever;

(*c*) knowingly sends, transmits, mails, ships, delivers or allows to be sent, transmitted, mailed, shipped or delivered, or knowingly accepts for carriage or transport or conveys any article that is used or intended for use in carrying out any device, proposal, scheme or plan for advancing, lending, giving, selling or otherwise disposing of any property by any mode of chance whatever;

(*d*) conducts or manages any scheme, contrivance or operation of any kind for the purpose of determining who, or the holders of what lots, tickets, numbers or chances, are the winners of any property so proposed to be advanced, lent, given, sold or disposed of;

(*e*) conducts, manages or is a party to any scheme, contrivance or operation of any kind by which any person, on payment of any sum of money, or the giving of any valuable security, or by obligating himself to pay any sum of money or give any valuable security, shall become entitled under the scheme, contrivance or operation to receive from the person conducting or managing the scheme, contrivance or operation, or any other person, a larger sum of money or amount of valuable security than the sum or amount paid or given, or to be paid or given, by reason of the fact that other persons have paid or given, or obligated themselves to pay or give any sum of money or valuable security under the scheme, contrivance or operation;

(*f*) disposes of any goods, wares or merchandise by any game of chance or any game of mixed chance and skill in which the contestant or competitor pays money or other valuable consideration;

(*g*) induces any person to stake or hazard any money or other valuable property or thing on the result of any dice game, three-card monte, punch board, coin table or on the operation of a wheel of fortune;

(*h*) for valuable consideration carries on or plays or offers to carry on or to play, or employs any person to carry on or play in a public place or a place to which the public have access, the game of three-card monte;

(*i*) receives bets of any kind on the outcome of a game of three-card monte; or

(*j*) being the owner of a place, permits any person to play the game of three-card monte therein.

(2) In this section "three-card monte" means the game commonly known as three-card monte and includes any other game that is similar to it, whether or not the game is played with cards and notwithstanding the number of cards or other things that are used for the purpose of playing.

(3) Paragraphs (1)(*f*) and (*g*), in so far as they do not relate to a dice game, three-card monte, punch board or coin table, do not apply to the board of an annual fair or exhibition, or to any operator of a concession leased by that board within its own grounds and operated during the fair or exhibition on those grounds.

(3.1) For the purposes of this section, "fair or exhibition" means an event where agricultural or fishing products are presented or where activities relating to agriculture or fishing take place.

(4) Every one who buys, takes or receives a lot, ticket or other device mentioned in subsection (1) is guilty of an offence punishable on summary conviction.

(5) Every sale, loan, gift, barter or exchange of any property, by any lottery, ticket, card or other mode of chance depending on or to be determined by chance or lot, is void, and all property sold, lent, given, bartered or exchanged is forfeited to Her Majesty.

(6) Subsection (5) does not affect any right or title to property acquired by any *bona fide* purchaser for valuable consideration without notice.

(7) This section applies to the printing or publishing, or causing to be printed or published, of any advertisement, scheme, proposal or plan of any foreign lottery, and the sale or offer for sale of any ticket, chance or share, in any such lottery, or the advertisement for sale of such ticket, chance or share, and the conducting or managing of any such scheme, contrivance or operation for determining the winners in any such lottery.

(8) This section does not apply to

(*a*) the division by lot or chance of any property by joint tenants or tenants in common, or persons having joint interests in any such property;

(*b*) the distribution by lot of premiums given as rewards to promote thrift by punctuality in making periodical deposits of weekly savings in any chartered savings bank; or

(*c*) bonds, debentures, debenture stock or other securities recallable by drawing of lots and redeemable with interest and providing for payment of premiums on redemption or otherwise. R.S. 1985, c. 52 (1st Supp.), s. 2.

Permitted lotteries — Terms and conditions of licence — Offence — Definition of "lottery scheme" — Exception re: pari-mutuel betting.

207. (1) Notwithstanding any of the provisions of this Part relating to gaming and betting, it is lawful

(*a*) for the government of a province, either alone or in conjunction with the government of another province, to conduct and manage a lottery scheme in that province, or in that and the other province, in accordance with any law enacted by the legislature of that province;

(*b*) for a charitable or religious organization, pursuant to a licence issued by the Lieutenant Governor in Council of a province or by such other person or authority in the province as may be specified by the Lieutenant Governor in Council thereof, to conduct and manage a lottery scheme in that province if the proceeds from the lottery scheme are used for a charitable or religious object or purpose.

(*c*) for the board of a fair or of an exhibition or an operator of a concession leased by that board, to conduct and manage a lottery scheme in a province where the Lieutenant Governor in Council of the province or such other person or authority in the province as may be specified by the Lieutenant Governor in Council thereof has

(i) designated that fair or exhibition as a fair or exhibition where a lottery scheme may be conducted and managed, and

(ii) issued a licence for the conduct and management of a lottery scheme to that board or operator;

(*d*) for any person, pursuant to a licence issued by the Lieutenant Governor in Council of a province or by such other person or authority in the province as may be specified by the Lieutenant Governor in Council thereof, to conduct and manage a lottery scheme at a public place of amusement in that province if

(i) the amount or value of each prize awarded does not exceed five hundred dollars, and

(ii) the money or other valuable consideration paid to secure a chance to win a prize does not exceed two dollars;

(*e*) for the government of a province to agree with the government of another province that lots, cards or tickets in relation to a lottery scheme that is by any of paragraphs (*a*) to (*d*) authorized to be conducted and managed in that other province may be sold in the province;

(*f*) for any person, pursuant to a licence issued by the Lieutenant Governor in Council of a province or such other person or authority in the province as may be designated by the Lieutenant Governor in Council thereof, to conduct and manage in the province a lottery scheme that is authorized to be conducted and managed in one or more other provinces where the authority by which the lottery scheme was first authorized to be conducted and managed consents thereto;

(*g*) for any person, for the purpose of a lottery scheme that is lawful in a province under any of paragraphs (*a*) to (*f*), to do anything in the province, in accordance with the applicable law or licence, that is required for the conduct, management or operation of the lottery scheme or for the person to participate in the scheme; and

(*h*) for any person to make or print anywhere in Canada or to cause to be made or printed anywhere in Canada anything relating to gaming and betting that is to be used in a place where it is or would, if certain conditions provided by law are met, be lawful to use such a thing, or to send, transmit, mail, ship, deliver or allow to be sent, transmitted, mailed, shipped or delivered or to accept for carriage or transport or convey any such thing where the destination thereof is such a place.

(2) Subject to this Act, a licence issued by or under the authority of the Lieutenant Governor in Council of a province as described in paragraph (1)(b), (c), (d) or (f) may contain such terms and conditions relating to the conduct, management and operation of or participation in the lottery scheme to which the licence relates as the Lieutenant Governor in Council of that province, the person or authority in the province designated by the Lieutenant Governor in Council thereof or any law enacted by the legislature of that province may prescribe.

(3) Every one who, for the purposes of a lottery scheme, does anything that is not authorized by or pursuant to a provision of this section

(*a*) in the case of the conduct, management or operation of that lottery scheme

(i) is guilty of an indictable offence and liable to imprisonment for a term not exceeding two years, or

(ii) is guilty of an offence punishable on summary conviction; or

(*b*) in the case of participating in that lottery scheme, is guilty of an offence punishable on summary conviction.

(4) In this section, "lottery scheme" means a game or any proposal, scheme, plan, means, device, contrivance or operation described in any of paragraphs 206(1)(*a*) to (*g*), whether or not it involves betting, pool selling or a pool system of betting other than

(*a*) a dice game, three-card monte, punch board or coin table;

(*b*) bookmaking, pool selling or the making or recording of bets, including bets made through the agency of a pool or pari-mutuel system, on any race or fight, or on a single sport event or athletic contest; or

(*c*) for the purposes of paragraphs (1)(*b*) to (*f*), a game or proposal, scheme, plan, means, device, contrivance or operation described in any of paragraphs 206(1)(*a*) to (*g*) that is operated on or through a computer, video device or slot machine, within the meaning of subsection 198(3).

(5) For greater certainty, nothing in this section shall be construed as authorizing the making or recording of bets on horse-races through the agency of a pari-mutuel system other than in accordance with section 204. R.S. 1985, c. 27 (1st Supp.), s. 31, c. 52 (1st Supp.), s. 3.

208. [Repealed R.S. 1985, c. 27 (1st Supp.), s. 32.]

Cheating at play.

209. Every one who, with intent to defraud any person, cheats while playing a game or in holding the stakes for a game or in betting is guilty of an indictable offence and liable to imprisonment for a term not exceeding two years.

Bawdy-houses

Keeping common bawdy-house — Landlord, inmate, etc. — Notice of conviction to be served on owner — Duty of landlord on notice.

210. (1) Every one who keeps a common bawdy-house is guilty of an indictable offence and liable to imprisonment for a term not exceeding two years.

(2) Every one who

(*a*) is an inmate of a common bawdy-house,

(*b*) is found, without lawful excuse, in a common bawdy-house, or

(*c*) as owner, landlord, lessor, tenant, occupier, agent or otherwise having charge or control of any place, knowingly permits the place or any part thereof to be let or used for the purposes of a common bawdy-house,

is guilty of an offence punishable on summary conviction.

(3) Where a person is convicted of an offence under subsection (1), the court shall cause a notice of the conviction to be served on the owner, landlord or lessor of the place in respect of which the person is convicted or his agent, and the notice shall contain a statement to the effect that it is being served pursuant to this section.

(4) Where a person on whom a notice is served under subsection (3) fails forthwith to exercise any right he may have to determine the tenancy or right of occupation of the person so convicted, and thereafter any person is convicted of an offence under subsection (1) in respect of the same premises, the person on whom the notice was served shall be deemed to have committed an offence

under subsection (1) unless he proves that he has taken all reasonable steps to prevent the recurrence of the offence.

Transporting person to bawdy-house.

211. Every one who knowingly takes, transports, directs, or offers to take, transport, or direct any other person to a common bawdy-house is guilty of an offence punishable on summary conviction.

Procuring

Procuring — Idem — Presumptions — Offence in relation to juvenile prostitution.

212. (1) Every one who

(*a*) procures, attempts to procure or solicits a person to have illicit sexual intercourse with another person, whether in or out of Canada,

(*b*) inveigles or entices a person who is not a prostitute or a person of known immoral character to a common bawdy-house or house of assignation for the purpose of illicit sexual intercourse or prostitution,

(*c*) knowingly conceals a person in a common bawdy-house or house of assignation,

(*d*) procures or attempts to procure a person to become, whether in or out of Canada, a prostitute,

(*e*) procures or attempts to procure a person to leave the usual place of abode of that person in Canada, if that place is not a common bawdy-house, with intent that the person may become an inmate or frequenter of a common bawdy-house, whether in or out of Canada,

(*f*) on the arrival of a person in Canada, directs or causes that person to be directed or takes or causes that person to be taken, to a common bawdy-house or house of assignation,

(*g*) procures a person to enter or leave Canada, for the purpose of prostitution,

(*h*) for the purposes of gain, exercises control, direction or influence over the movements of a person in such manner as to show that he is aiding, abetting or compelling that person to engage in or carry on prostitution with any person or generally,

(*i*) applies or administers to a person or causes that person to take any drug, intoxicating liquor, matter or thing with intent to stupefy or overpower that person in order thereby to enable any person to have illicit sexual intercourse with that person, or

(*j*) lives wholly or in part on the avails of prostitution of another person,

is guilty of an indictable offence and liable to imprisonment for a term not exceeding ten years.

(2) Notwithstanding paragraph (1)(*j*), every person who lives wholly or in part on the avails of prostitution of another person who is under the age of

eighteen years is guilty of an indictable offence and is liable to imprisonment for a term not exceeding fourteen years.

(3) Evidence that a person lives with or is habitually in the company of a prostitute or lives in a common bawdy-house or in a house of assignation is, in the absence of evidence to the contrary, proof that the person lives on the avails of prostitution, for the purposes of paragraph (1)(*j*) and subsection (2).

(4) Every person who, in any place, obtains or attempts to obtain, for consideration, the sexual services of a person who is under the age of eighteen years is guilty of an indictable offence and is liable to imprisonment for a term not exceeding five years. R.S. 1985, c. 19 (3rd Supp.), s. 9.

Offence in Relation to Prostitution

Offence in relation to prostitution — Definition of "public place".

213. (1) Every person who in a public place or in any place open to public view

(*a*) stops or attempts to stop any motor vehicle,

(*b*) impedes the free flow of pedestrian or vehicular traffic or ingress to or egress from premises adjacent to that place, or

(*c*) stops or attempts to stop any person or in any manner communicates or attempts to communicate with any person

for the purpose of engaging in prostitution or of obtaining the sexual services of a prostitute is guilty of an offence punishable on summary conviction.

(2) In this section, "public place" includes any place to which the public have access as of right or by invitation, express or implied, and any motor vehicle located in a public place or in any place open to public view. R.S. 1985, c. 51 (1st Supp.), s. 1.

[NOTE: R.S. 1985, c. 51 (1st Supp.), s. 2 provides that:

***2.** (1) Three years after the coming into force of this Act, a comprehensive review of the provisions of section 213 of the Criminal Code as enacted by this Act, shall be undertaken by such committee of the House of Commons as may be designated or established by the House for that purpose.*

(2) The committee referred to in subsection (1) shall, within a year after the review is undertaken or within such further time as the House of Commons may authorize, submit a report on the review to the House including a statement of any changes the committee recommends.]

PART VIII

OFFENCES AGAINST THE PERSON AND REPUTATION

Interpretation

Definitions — "Abandon" or "Expose" — "Aircraft" — "Child" — "Form of marriage" — "Guardian" — "Operate" — "Vessel".

214. In this Part,

"abandon" or "expose" includes

(*a*) a wilful omission to take charge of a child by a person who is under a legal duty to do so, and

(*b*) dealing with a child in a manner that is likely to leave that child exposed to risk without protection;

"aircraft" does not include a machine designed to derive support in the atmosphere primarily from reactions against the earth's surface of air expelled from the machine;

"child" includes an adopted child and an illegitimate child;

"form of marriage" includes a ceremony of marriage that is recognized as valid

(*a*) by the law of the place where it was celebrated, or

(*b*) by the law of the place where an accused is tried, notwithstanding that it is not recognized as valid by the law of the place where it was celebrated;

"guardian" includes a person who has in law or in fact the custody or control of a child.

"operate"

(*a*) means, in respect of a motor vehicle, to drive the vehicle,

(*b*) means, in respect of railway equipment, to participate in the direct control of its motion, whether

(i) as a member of the crew of the equipment,

(ii) as a person who, by remote control, acts in lieu of such crew, or

(iii) as other than a member or person described in subparagraphs (i) and (ii), and

(*c*) includes, in respect of a vessel or an aircraft, to navigate the vessel or aircraft;

"vessel" includes a machine designed to derive support in the atmosphere primarily from reactions against the earth's surface of air expelled from the machine. R.S. 1985, c. 27 (1st Supp.), s. 33; c. 32 (4th Supp.), s. 56.

Duties Tending to Preservation of Life

Duty of persons to provide necessaries — Offence — Punishment — Presumptions.

215. (1) Every one is under a legal duty

(*a*) as a parent, foster parent, guardian or head of a family, to provide necessaries of life for a child under the age of sixteen years;

(*b*) as a married person, to provide necessaries of life to his spouse; and

(*c*) to provide necessaries of life to a person under his charge if that person

(i) is unable, by reason of detention, age, illness, mental disorder or other cause, to withdraw himself from that charge, and

(ii) is unable to provide himself with necessaries of life.

(2) Every one commits an offence who, being under a legal duty within the meaning of subsection (1), fails without lawful excuse, the proof of which lies on him, to perform that duty, if

(*a*) with respect to a duty imposed by paragraph (1)(*a*) or (*b*),

(i) the person to whom the duty is owed is in destitute or necessitous circumstances, or

(ii) the failure to perform the duty endangers the life of the person to whom the duty is owed, or causes or is likely to cause the health of that person to be endangered permanently; or

(*b*) with respect to a duty imposed by paragraph (1)(*c*), the failure to perform the duty endangers the life of the person to whom the duty is owed or causes or is likely to cause the health of that person to be injured permanently.

(3) Every one who commits an offence under subsection (2) is guilty of

(*a*) an indictable offence and is liable to imprisonment for a term not exceeding two years; or

(*b*) an offence punishable on summary conviction.

(4) For the purpose of proceedings under this section,

(*a*) evidence that a person has cohabited with a person of the opposite sex or has in any way recognized that person as being his spouse is, in the absence of any evidence to the contrary, proof that they are lawfully married;

(*b*) evidence that a person has in any way recognized a child as being his child is, in the absence of any evidence to the contrary, proof that the child is his child;

(*c*) evidence that a person has left his spouse and has failed, for a period of any one month subsequent to the time of his so leaving, to make provision for the maintenance of his spouse or for the maintenance of any child of his under the age of sixteen years is, in the absence of any evidence to the contrary, proof that he has failed without lawful excuse to provide necessaries of life for them; and

(*d*) the fact that a spouse or child is receiving or has received necessaries of life from another person who is not under a legal duty to provide them is not a defence. S.C. 1991, c. 43, s. 9, Sch., item 2.

Duty of persons undertaking acts dangerous to life.

216. Every one who undertakes to administer surgical or medical treatment to another person or to do any other lawful act that may endanger the life of another person is, except in cases of necessity, under a legal duty to have and to use reasonable knowledge, skill and care in so doing.

Duty of persons undertaking acts.

217. Every one who undertakes to do an act is under a legal duty to do it if an omission to do the act is or may be dangerous to life.

Abandoning child.

218. Every one who unlawfully abandons or exposes a child who is under the age of ten years, so that its life is or is likely to be endangered or its health is or is likely to be permanently injured, is guilty of an indictable offence and liable to imprisonment for a term not exceeding two years.

Criminal Negligence

Criminal negligence — "Duty".

219. (1) Every one is criminally negligent who

(*a*) in doing anything, or

(*b*) in omitting to do anything that it is his duty to do,

shows wanton or reckless disregard for the lives or safety of other persons.

(2) For the purposes of this section, "duty" means a duty imposed by law.

Causing death by criminal negligence.

220. Every one who by criminal negligence causes death to another person is guilty of an indictable offence and liable to imprisonment for life.

Causing bodily harm by criminal negligence.

221. Every one who by criminal negligence causes bodily harm to another person is guilty of an indictable offence and liable to imprisonment for a term not exceeding ten years.

Homicide

Homicide — Kinds of homicide — Non culpable homicide — Culpable homicide — Idem — Exception.

222. (1) A person commits homicide when, directly or indirectly, by any means, he causes the death of a human being.

(2) Homicide is culpable or not culpable.

(3) Homicide that is not culpable is not an offence.

(4) Culpable homicide is murder or manslaughter or infanticide.

(5) A person commits culpable homicide when he causes the death of a human being,

(*a*) by means of an unlawful act,

(*b*) by criminal negligence,

(*c*) by causing that human being, by threats or fear of violence or by deception, to do anything that causes his death, or

(*d*) by wilfully frightening that human being, in the case of a child or sick person.

(6) Notwithstanding anything in this section, a person does not commit homicide within the meaning of this Act by reason only that he causes the death of a human being by procuring, by false evidence, the conviction and death of that human being by sentence of the law.

When child becomes human being — Killing child.

223. (1) A child becomes a human being within the meaning of this Act when it has completely proceeded, in a living state, from the body of its mother whether or not

(*a*) it has breathed,

(*b*) it has an independent circulation, or

(*c*) the navel string is severed.

(2) A person commits homicide when he causes injury to a child before or during its birth as a result of which the child dies after becoming a human being.

Death which might have been prevented.

224. Where a person, by an act or omission, does any thing that results in the death of a human being, he causes the death of that human being notwithstanding that death from that cause might have been prevented by resorting to proper means.

Death from treatment of injury.

225. Where a person causes to a human being a bodily injury that is of itself of a dangerous nature and from which death results, he causes the death of that human being notwithstanding that the immediate cause of death is proper or improper treatment that is applied in good faith.

Acceleration of death.

226. Where a person causes to a human being a bodily injury that results in death, he causes the death of that human being notwithstanding that the effect of the bodily injury is only to accelerate his death from a disease or disorder arising from some other cause.

Death within year and a day.

227. No person commits culpable homicide or the offence of causing the death of a person by criminal negligence or by means of the commission of an offence under subsection 249(4) or subsection 255(3) unless the death occurs within one year and one day from the time of the occurrence of the last event by means of which the person caused or contributed to the cause of death. R.S. 1985, c. 27 (1st Supp.), s. 34.

Killing by influence on the mind.

228. No person commits culpable homicide where he causes the death of a human being

(*a*) by any influence on the mind alone, or

(*b*) by any disorder or disease resulting from influence on the mind alone,

but this section does not apply where a person causes the death of a child or sick person by wilfully frightening him.

Murder, Manslaughter and Infanticide

Murder.

229. Culpable homicide is murder

(*a*) where the person who causes the death of a human being

(i) means to cause his death, or

(ii) means to cause him bodily harm that he knows is likely to cause his death, and is reckless whether death ensues or not;

(*b*) where a person, meaning to cause death to a human being or meaning to cause him bodily harm that he knows is likely to cause his death, and being reckless whether death ensues or not, by accident or mistake causes death to another human being, notwithstanding that he does not mean to cause death or bodily harm to that human being; or

(*c*) where a person, for an unlawful object, does anything that he knows or ought to know is likely to cause death, and thereby causes death to a human being, notwithstanding that he desires to effect his object without causing death or bodily harm to any human being.

Murder in commission of offences.

230. Culpable homicide is murder where a person causes the death of a human being while committing or attempting to commit high treason or treason or an offence mentioned in section 52 (sabotage), 75 (piratical acts), 76 (hijacking an aircraft), 144 or subsection 145(1) or sections 146 to 148 (escape or rescue from prison or lawful custody), section 270 (assaulting a peace officer), section 271 (sexual assault), 272 (sexual assault with a weapon, threats to a third party or causing bodily harm), 273 (aggravated sexual assault), 279 (kidnapping and forcible confinement), 279.1 (hostage taking), 343 (robbery), 348 (breaking and entering) or 433 or 434 (arson), whether or not the person means to cause death to any human being and whether or not he knows that death is likely to be caused to any human being, if

(*a*) he means to cause bodily harm for the purpose of

(i) facilitating the commission of the offence, or

(ii) facilitating his flight after committing or attempting to commit the offence,

and the death ensues from the bodily harm;

(*b*) he administers a stupefying or overpowering thing for a purpose mentioned in paragraph (*a*), and the death ensues therefrom; or

(*c*) he wilfully stops, by any means, the breath of a human being for a purpose mentioned in paragraph (*a*), and the death ensues therefrom. R.S. 1985, c. 27 (1st Supp.), s. 40(2); 1991, c. 4, s. 1.

Classification of murder — Planned and deliberate murder — Contracted murder — Murder of peace officer, etc. — Hijacking, sexual assault or kidnapping — Second degree murder.

231. (1) Murder is first degree murder or second degree murder.

(2) Murder is first degree murder when it is planned and deliberate.

(3) Without limiting the generality of subsection (2), murder is planned and deliberate when it is committed pursuant to an arrangement under which money or anything of value passes or is intended to pass from one person to another, or is promised by one person to another, as consideration for that other's causing or assisting in causing the death of anyone or counselling another person to do any act causing or assisting in causing that death.

(4) Irrespective of whether a murder is planned and deliberate on the part of any person, murder is first degree murder when the victim is

(*a*) a police officer, police constable, constable, sheriff, deputy sheriff, sheriff's officer or other person employed for the preservation and maintenance of the public peace, acting in the course of his duties;

(*b*) a warden, deputy warden, instructor, keeper, jailer, guard or other officer or a permanent employee of a prison, acting in the course of his duties; or

(*c*) a person working in a prison with the permission of the prison authorities and acting in the course of his work therein.

(5) Irrespective of whether a murder is planned and deliberate on the part of any person, murder is first degree murder in respect of a person when the death is caused by that person while committing or attempting to commit an offence under one of the following sections:

(*a*) section 76 (hijacking an aircraft);

(*b*) section 271 (sexual assault);

(*c*) section 272 (sexual assault with a weapon, threats to a third party or causing bodily harm);

(*d*) section 273 (aggravated sexual assault);

(*e*) section 279 (kidnapping and forcible confinement); or

(*f*) section 279.1 (hostage taking).

(6) [Repealed R.S. 1985, c. 27 (1st Supp.), s. 35.]

(7) All murder that is not first degree murder is second degree murder. R.S. 1985, c. 27 (1st Supp.), ss. 7(2), 35, 40(2).

Murder reduced to manslaughter — What is provocation — Questions of fact — Death during illegal arrest.

232. (1) Culpable homicide that otherwise would be murder may be reduced to manslaughter if the person who committed it did so in the heat of passion caused by sudden provocation.

(2) A wrongful act or insult that is of such a nature as to be sufficient to deprive an ordinary person of the power of self-control is provocation for the purposes of this section if the accused acted on it on the sudden and before there was time for his passion to cool.

(3) For the purposes of this section, the questions

(*a*) whether a particular wrongful act or insult amounted to provocation, and

(*b*) whether the accused was deprived of the power of self-control by the provocation that he alleges he received,

are questions of fact, but no one shall be deemed to have given provocation to another by doing anything that he had a legal right to do, or by doing anything that the accused incited him to do in order to provide the accused with an excuse for causing death or bodily harm to any human being.

(4) Culpable homicide that otherwise would be murder is not necessarily manslaughter by reason only that it was committed by a person who was being arrested illegally, but the fact that the illegality of the arrest was known to the accused may be evidence of provocation for the purpose of this section.

Infanticide.

233. A female person commits infanticide when by a wilful act or omission she causes the death of her newly-born child, if at the time of the act or omission she is not fully recovered from the effects of giving birth to the child and by reason thereof or of the effect of lactation consequent on the birth of the child her mind is then disturbed.

Manslaughter.

234. Culpable homicide that is not murder or infanticide is manslaughter.

Punishment for murder — Minimum punishment.

235. (1) Every one who commits first degree murder or second degree murder is guilty of an indictable offence and shall be sentenced to imprisonment for life.

(2) For the purposes of Part XXIII, the sentence of imprisonment for life prescribed by this section is a minimum punishment.

Punishment for manslaughter.

236. Every one who commits manslaughter is guilty of an indictable offence and liable to imprisonment for life.

Punishment for infanticide.

237. Every female person who commits infanticide is guilty of an indictable offence and liable to imprisonment for a term not exceeding five years.

Killing unborn child in act of birth — Saving.

238. (1) Every one who causes the death, in the act of birth, of any child that has not become a human being, in such a manner that, if the child were a human being, he would be guilty of murder, is guilty of an indictable offence and liable to imprisonment for life.

(2) This section does not apply to a person who, by means that, in good faith, he considers necessary to preserve the life of the mother of a child, causes the death of that child.

Attempt to commit murder.

239. Every one who attempts by any means to commit murder is guilty of an indictable offence and liable to imprisonment for life.

Accessory after fact to murder.

240. Every one who is an accessory after the fact to murder is guilty of an indictable offence and liable to imprisonment for life.

Suicide

Counselling or aiding suicide.

241. Every one who

(*a*) counsels a person to commit suicide, or

(*b*) aids or abets a person to commit suicide,

whether suicide ensues or not, is guilty of an indictable offence and liable to imprisonment for a term not exceeding fourteen years. R.S. 1985, c. 27 (1st Supp.), s. 7(3).

Neglect in Child-birth and Concealing Dead Body

Neglect to obtain assistance in child-birth.

242. A female person who, being pregnant and about to be delivered, with intent that the child shall not live or with intent to conceal the birth of the child, fails to make provision for reasonable assistance in respect of her delivery is, if the child is permanently injured as a result thereof or dies immediately before, during or in a short time after birth, as a result thereof, guilty of an indictable offence and is liable to imprisonment for a term not exceeding five years.

Concealing body of child.

243. Every one who in any manner disposes of the dead body of a child, with intent to conceal the fact that its mother has been delivered of it, whether the child died before, during or after birth, is guilty of an indictable offence and liable to imprisonment for a term not exceeding two years.

Bodily Harm and Acts and Omissions Causing Danger to the Person

Causing bodily harm with intent.

244. Every one who, with intent

(*a*) to wound, maim or disfigure any person,

(*b*) to endanger the life of any person, or

(*c*) to prevent the arrest or detention of any person,

discharges a firearm, air gun or air pistol at any person, whether or not that person is the one mentioned in paragraph (*a*), (*b*) or (*c*), is guilty of an indictable offence and liable to imprisonment for a term not exceeding fourteen years.

Administering noxious thing.

245. Every one who administers or causes to be administered to any person or causes any person to take poison or any other destructive or noxious thing is guilty of an indictable offence and liable

(*a*) to imprisonment for a term not exceeding fourteen years, if he intends thereby to endanger the life of or to cause bodily harm to that person; or

(*b*) to imprisonment for a term not exceeding two years, if he intends thereby to aggrieve or annoy that person.

Overcoming resistance to commission of offence.

246. Every one who, with intent to enable or assist himself or another person to commit an indictable offence,

(*a*) attempts, by any means, to choke, suffocate or strangle another person, or by any means calculated to choke, suffocate or strangle, attempts to render another person insensible, unconscious or incapable of resistance, or

(*b*) administers, or causes to be administered to any person, or attempts to administer to any person, or causes or attempts to cause any person to take a stupefying or overpowering drug, matter or thing,

is guilty of an indictable offence and liable to imprisonment for life.

Traps likely to cause bodily harm — Permitting traps on premises.

247. (1) Every one who, with intent to cause death or bodily harm to persons, whether ascertained or not, sets or places or causes to be set or placed a trap, device or other thing whatever that is likely to cause death or bodily harm to persons is guilty of an indictable offence and liable to imprisonment for a term not exceeding five years.

(2) A person who, being in occupation or possession of a place where anything mentioned in subsection (1) has been set or placed, knowingly and wilfully permits it to remain at that place, shall be deemed, for the purposes of that subsection, to have set or placed it with the intent mentioned therein.

Interfering with transportation facilities.

248. Every one who, with intent to endanger the safety of any person, places anything on or does anything to any property that is used for or in connection with the transportation of persons or goods by land, water or air that is likely to cause death or bodily harm to persons is guilty of an indictable offence and liable to imprisonment for life.

Motor Vehicles, Vessels and Aircraft

Dangerous operation of motor vehicles, vessels and aircraft — Punishment — Dangerous operation causing bodily harm — Dangerous operation causing death.

249. (1) Every one commits an offence who operates

(*a*) a motor vehicle on a street, road, highway or other public place in a manner that is dangerous to the public, having regard to all the circumstances, including the nature, condition and use of that place and the amount of traffic that at the time is or might reasonably be expected to be on that place;

(*b*) a vessel or any water skis, surf-board, water sled or other towed object on or over any of the internal waters of Canada or the territorial sea of Canada, in a manner that is dangerous to the public, having regard to all the circumstances, including the nature and condition of those waters or sea and the use that at the time is or might reasonably be expected to be made of those waters or sea;

(*c*) an aircraft in a manner that is dangerous to the public, having regard to all the circumstances, including the nature and condition of that aircraft or the place or air space in or through which the aircraft is operated; or

(*d*) railway equipment in a manner that is dangerous to the public, having regard to all the circumstances, including the nature and condition of the equipment or the place in or through which the equipment is operated.

(2) Every one who commits an offence under subsection (1)

(*a*) is guilty of an indictable offence and liable to imprisonment for a term not exceeding five years; or

(*b*) is guilty of an offence punishable on summary conviction.

(3) Every one who commits an offence under subsection (1) and thereby causes bodily harm to any other person is guilty of an indictable offence and liable to imprisonment for a term not exceeding ten years.

(4) Every one who commits an offence under subsection (1) and thereby causes the death of any other person is guilty of an indictable offence and liable to imprisonment for a term not exceeding fourteen years. R.S., 1985, c. 27 (1st Supp.), s. 36; c. 32 (4th Supp.), s. 57.

Failure to keep watch on person towed — Towing of person after dark.

250. (1) Every one who operates a vessel while towing a person on any water skis, surf-board, water sled or other object, when there is not on board such vessel another responsible person keeping watch on the person being towed, is guilty of an offence punishable on summary conviction.

(2) Every one who operates a vessel while towing a person on any water skis, surf-board, water sled or other object during the period from one hour after sunset to sunrise is guilty of an offence punishable on summary conviction. R.S. 1985, c. 27 (1st Supp.), s. 36.

Unseaworthy vessel and unsafe aircraft — Defences — Consent of Attorney General.

251. (1) Every one who knowingly

(*a*) sends or being the master takes a vessel that is registered or licensed, or for which an identification number has been issued, pursuant to any Act of Parliament and that is unseaworthy

(i) on a voyage from a place in Canada to any other place in or out of Canada, or

(ii) on a voyage from a place on the inland waters of the United States to a place in Canada,

(*b*) sends an aircraft on a flight or operates an aircraft that is not fit and safe for flight, or

(*c*) sends for operation or operates railway equipment that is not fit and safe for operation.

and thereby endangers the life of any person, is guilty of an indictable offence and liable to imprisonment for a term not exceeding five years.

(2) An accused shall not be convicted of an offence under this section where the accused establishes that,

(*a*) in the case of an offence under paragraph (1)(*a*),

(i) the accused used all reasonable means to ensure that the vessel was seaworthy, or

(ii) to send or take the vessel while it was unseaworthy was, under the circumstances, reasonable and justifiable;

(*b*) in the case of an offence under paragraph (1)(*b*),

(i) the accused used all reasonable means to ensure that the aircraft was fit and safe for flight, or

(ii) to send or operate the aircraft while it was not fit and safe for flight was, under the circumstances, reasonable and justifiable; and

(*c*) in the case of an offence under paragraph (1)(*c*),

(i) the accused used all reasonable means to ensure that the railway equipment was fit and safe for operation, or

(ii) to send the railway equipment for operation or to operate it while it was not fit and safe for operation was, under the circumstances, reasonable and justifiable.

(3) No proceedings shall be instituted under this section in respect of a vessel or aircraft, or in respect of railway equipment sent for operation or operated on a line of railway that is within the legislative authority of Parliament, without the consent in writing of the Attorney General of Canada. R.S. 1985, c. 27 (1st Supp.), s. 36; c. 32 (4th Supp.), s. 58.

Failure to stop at scene of accident — Evidence.

252. (1) Every one who has the care, charge or control of a vehicle, vessel or aircraft that is involved in an accident with

(*a*) another person,

(*b*) a vehicle, vessel or aircraft, or

(*c*) in the case of a vehicle, cattle in the charge of another person,

and with intent to escape civil or criminal liability fails to stop his vehicle, vessel or, where possible, his aircraft, give his name and address and, where any person has been injured or appears to require assistance, offer assistance, is guilty of an indictable offence and liable to imprisonment for a term not exceeding two years or is guilty of an offence punishable on summary conviction.

(2) In proceedings under subsection (1), evidence that an accused failed to stop his vehicle, vessel or, where possible, his aircraft, as the case may be, offer assistance where any person has been injured or appears to require assistance and give his name and address is, in the absence of evidence to the contrary, proof of an intent to escape civil or criminal liability. R.S. 1985, c. 27 (1st Supp.), s. 36.

Operation while impaired.

253. Every one commits an offence who operates a motor vehicle or vessel or operates or assists in the operation of an aircraft or of railway equipment or has the care or control of a motor vehicle, vessel, aircraft or railway equipment, whether it is in motion or not,

(*a*) while the person's ability to operate the vehicle, vessel, aircraft or railway equipment is impaired by alcohol or a drug; or

(*b*) having consumed alcohol in such a quantity that the concentration in the person's blood exceeds eighty milligrams of alcohol in one hundred millilitres of blood. R.S. 1985, c. 27 (1st Supp.), s. 36; c. 32 (4th Supp.), s. 59.

Definitions — "analyst" — "approved container" — "approved instrument" — "approved screening device" — "qualified medical practitioner" — "qualified technician" — Testing for presence of alcohol in the blood — Samples of breath or blood where reasonable belief of commission of offence — Exception — Failure or refusal to provide sample — Only one determination of guilt for failure to comply with demand.

254. (1) In this section and sections 255 to 258,

"analyst" means a person designated by the Attorney General as an analyst for the purposes of section 258;

"approved container" means

(*a*) in respect of breath samples, a container of a kind that is designed to receive a sample of the breath of a person for analysis and is approved as suitable for the purposes of section 258 by order of the Attorney General of Canada, and

(*b*) in respect of blood samples, a container of a kind that is designed to receive a sample of the blood of a person for analysis and is approved as suitable for the purposes of section 258 by order of the Attorney General of Canada;

"approved instrument" means an instrument of a kind that is designed to receive and make an analysis of a sample of the breath of a person in order to measure the concentration of alcohol in the blood of that person and is approved as suitable for the purposes of section 258 by order of the Attorney General of Canada;

"approved screening device" means a device of a kind that is designed to ascertain the presence of alcohol in the blood of a person and that is approved for the purposes of this section by order of the Attorney General of Canada;

"qualified medical practitioner" means a person duly qualified by provincial law to practise medicine.

"qualified technician" means,

(*a*) in respect of breath samples, a person designated by the Attorney General as being qualified to operate an approved instrument, and

(*b*) in respect of blood samples, any person or person of a class of persons designated by the Attorney General as being qualified to take samples of blood for the purposes of this section and sections 256 and 258.

(2) Where a peace officer reasonably suspects that a person who is operating a motor vehicle or vessel or operating or assisting in the operation of an aircraft or of railway equipment or who has the care or control of a motor vehicle, vessel, aircraft or railway equipment, whether it is in motion or not, has alcohol in the person's body, the peace officer may, by demand made to that person, require the person to provide forthwith such a sample of breath as in the opinion

of the peace officer is necessary to enable a proper analysis of the breath to be made by means of an approved screening device and, where necessary, to accompany the peace officer for the purpose of enabling such a sample of breath to be taken.

(3) Where a peace officer believes on reasonable and probable grounds that a person is committing, or at any time within the preceding two hours has committed, as a result of the consumption of alcohol, an offence under section 253, the peace officer may, by demand made to that person forthwith or as soon as practicable, require that person to provide then or as soon thereafter as is practicable

(*a*) such samples of the person's breath as in the opinion of a qualified technician, or

(*b*) where the peace officer has reasonable and probable grounds to believe that, by reason of any physical condition of the person,

(i) the person may be incapable of providing a sample of his breath, or

(ii) it would be impracticable to obtain a sample of his breath,

such samples of the person's blood, under the conditions referred to in subsection (4), as in the opinion of the qualified medical practitioner or qualified technician taking the samples

are necessary to enable proper analysis to be made in order to determine the concentration, if any, of alcohol in the person's blood, and to accompany the peace officer for the purpose of enabling such samples to be taken.

(4) Samples of blood may only be taken from a person pursuant to a demand made by a peace officer under subsection (3) if the samples are taken by or under the direction of a qualified medical practitioner and the qualified medical practitioner is satisfied that the taking of those samples would not endanger the life or health of the person.

(5) Every one commits an offence who, without reasonable excuse, fails or refuses to comply with a demand made to him by a peace officer under this section.

(6) A person who is convicted of an offence committed under subsection (5) for a failure or refusal to comply with a demand made under subsection (2) or paragraph (3)(*a*) or (*b*) in respect of any transaction may not be convicted of another offence committed under subsection (5) in respect of the same transaction. R.S. 1985, c. 27 (1st Supp.), s. 36; c. 1, s. 14; c. 32 (4th Supp.), s. 60.

Punishment — Impaired driving causing bodily harm — Impaired driving causing death — Previous convictions — Conditional discharge.

255. (1) Every one who commits an offence under section 253 or 254 is guilty of an indictable offence or an offence punishable on summary conviction and is liable, (*a*) whether the offence is prosecuted by indictment or punishable on summary conviction, to the following minimum punishment, namely,

(i) for a first offence, to a fine of not less than three hundred dollars,

(ii) for a second offence, to imprisonment for not less than fourteen days, and

(iii) for each subsequent offence, to imprisonment for not less than ninety days;

(*b*) where the offence is prosecuted by indictment, to imprisonment for a term not exceeding five years; and

(*c*) where the offence is punishable on summary conviction, to imprisonment for a term not exceeding six months.

(2) Every one who commits an offence under paragraph 253(*a*) and thereby causes bodily harm to any other person is guilty of an indictable offence and liable to imprisonment for a term not exceeding ten years.

(3) Every one who commits an offence under paragraph 253(*a*) and thereby causes the death of any other person is guilty of an indictable offence and liable to imprisonment for a term not exceeding fourteen years.

(4) Where a person is convicted of an offence committed under paragraph 253(*a*) or (*b*) or subsection 254(5), that person shall, for the purposes of this Act, be deemed to be convicted for a second or subsequent offence, as the case may be, if the person has previously been convicted of

(*a*) an offence committed under any of those provisions;

(*b*) an offence under subsection (2) or (3); or

(*c*) an offence under section 250, 251, 252, 253, 259 or 260 or subsection 258(4) of this Act as this Act read immediately before the coming into force of this subsection.

(5) Notwithstanding subsection 736(1), a court may, instead of convicting a person of an offence committed under section 253, after hearing medical or other evidence, if it considers that the person is in need of curative treatment in relation to his consumption of alcohol or drugs and that it would not be contrary to the public interest, by order direct that the person be discharged under section 736 on the conditions prescribed in a probation order, including a condition respecting the person's attendance for curative treatment in relation to his consumption of alcohol or drugs. R.S. 1985, c. 27 (1st Supp.), s. 36.

[NOTE: S. 255(5) has been proclaimed in force in the provinces of Alberta, Manitoba, New Brunswick, Nova Scotia, Prince Edward Island, Saskatchewan and in Yukon Territory and Northwest Territories.]

Warrants to obtain blood samples — Form — Information on oath — Duration of warrant — Facsimile to person.

256. (1) Subject to subsection (2), where a justice is satisfied, on an information on oath in Form 1 or on an information on oath submitted to the justice pursuant to section 487.1 by telephone or other means of telecommunication, that there are reasonable grounds to believe that

(*a*) a person has, within the preceding two hours, committed, as a result of the consumption of alcohol, an offence under section 253 and the person was involved in an accident resulting in the death of another person or in bodily harm to himself or herself or to any other preson, and

(*b*) a qualified medical practitioner is of the opinion that

(i) by reason of any physical or mental condition of the person that resulted from the consumption of alcohol, the accident or any other occurrence related to or resulting from the accident, the person is unable to consent to the taking of samples of his blood, and

(ii) the taking of samples of blood from the person would not endanger the life or health of the person,

the justice may issue a warrant authorizing a peace officer to require a qualified medical practitioner to take, or to cause to be taken by a qualified technician under the direction of the qualified medical practitioner, such samples of the blood of the person as in the opinion of the person taking the samples are necessary to enable a proper analysis to be made in order to determine the concentration, if any, of alcohol in his blood.

(2) A warrant issued pursuant to subsection (1) may be in Form 5 or 5.1 varied to suit the case.

(3) Notwithstanding paragraphs 487.1(4)(*b*) and (*c*), an information on oath submitted by telephone or other means of telecommunication for the purposes of this section shall include, instead of the statements referred to in those paragraphs, a statement setting out the offence alleged to have been committed and identifying the person from whom blood samples are to be taken.

(4) Samples of blood may be taken from a person pursuant to a warrant issued pursuant to subsection (1) only during such time as a qualified medical practitioner is satisfied that the conditions referred to in subparagraphs (1)(*b*)(i) and (ii) continue to exist in respect of that person.

(5) Where a warrant issued pursuant to subsection (1) is executed, the peace officer shall, as soon as practicable thereafter, give a copy or, in the case of a warrant issued by telephone or other means of telecommunication, a facsimile of the warrant to the person from whom the blood samples were taken. R.S. 1985, c. 27 (1st Supp.), s. 36; 1992, c. 1, s. 58(1), Sch. I, item 5.

No offence committed — No criminal or civil liability.

257. (1) No qualified medical practitioner or qualified technician is guilty of an offence only by reason of his refusal to take a sample of blood from a person for the purposes of section 254 or 256 and no qualified medical practitioner is guilty of an offence only by reason of his refusal to cause to be taken by a qualified technician under his direction a sample of blood from a person for such purposes.

(2) No qualified medical practitioner by whom or under whose direction a sample of blood is taken from a person pursuant to a demand made under subsection 254(3) or a warrant issued under section 256 and no qualified technician acting under the direction of a qualified medical practitioner incurs any criminal or civil liability for anything necessarily done with reasonable care and skill in the taking of such a sample of blood. R.S. 1985, c. 27 (1st Supp.), s. 36.

Proceedings under section 255 — No obligation to give sample except as required under s. 254 — Evidence of failure to comply with demand — Release of specimen for testing — Testing blood for presence of drugs — Attendance and right to cross-examine — Notice of intention to produce certificate.

258. (1) In any proceedings under subsection 255(1) in respect of an offence committed under section 253 or in any proceedings under subsection 255(2) or (3),

(*a*) where it is proved that the accused occupied the seat or position ordinarily occupied by a person who operates a motor vehicle, vessel, aircraft or railway equipment or who assists in the operation of an aircraft or of railway equipment, the accused shall be deemed to have had the care or control of the vehicle, vessel, aircraft or railway equipment, as the case may be, unless the accused establishes that the accused did not occupy that seat or position for the purpose of setting the vehicle, vessel, aircraft or railway equipment in motion or assisting in the operation of the aircraft or railway equipment, as the case may be;

(*b*) the result of an analysis of a sample of the breath or blood of the accused (other than a sample taken pursuant to a demand made under subsection 254(3)) or of the urine or other bodily substance of the accused may be admitted in evidence notwithstanding that, before the accused gave the sample, he was not warned that he need not give the sample or that the result of the analysis of the sample might be used in evidence;

(*c*) where samples of the breath of the accused have been taken pursuant to a demand made under subsection 254(3), if

(i) at the time each sample was taken, the person taking the sample offered to provide to the accused a specimen of the breath of the accused in an approved container for his own use, and, at the request of the accused made at that time, such a specimen was thereupon provided to the accused,

(ii) each sample was taken as soon as practicable after the time when the offence was alleged to have been committed and, in the case of the first sample, not later than two hours after that time, with an interval of at least fifteen minutes between the times when the samples were taken,

(iii) each sample was received from the accused directly into an approved container or into an approved instrument operated by a qualified technician, and

(iv) an analysis of each sample was made by means of an approved instrument operated by a qualified technician,

evidence of the results of the analyses so made is, in the absence of evidence to the contrary, proof that the concentrations of alcohol in the blood of the accused at the time when the offence was alleged to have been committed was, where the results of the analyses are the same, the concentration determined by the analyses and, where the results of the analyses are different, the lowest of the concentrations determined by the analyses;

(*d*) where a sample of the blood of the accused has been taken pursuant to a demand made under subsection 254(3) or otherwise with the consent of the accused or pursuant to a warrant issued under section 256, if

(i) at the time the sample was taken, the person taking the sample took an additional sample of the blood of the accused and one of the samples was retained, to permit an analysis thereof to be made by or on behalf of the accused and, at the request of the accused made within three months from the taking of the samples, one of the samples was ordered to be released pursuant to subsection (4),

(ii) both samples referred to in subparagraph (i) were taken as soon as practicable after the time when the offence was alleged to have been committed and in any event not later than two hours after that time,

(iii) both samples referred to in subparagraph (i) were taken by a qualified medical practitioner or a qualified technician under the direction of a qualified medical practitioner,

(iv) both samples referred to in subparagraph (i) were received from the accused directly into, or placed directly into, approved containers that were subsequently sealed, and

(v) an analysis was made by an analyst of at least one of the samples that was contained in a sealed approved container,

evidence of the result of the analysis is, in the absence of evidence to the contrary, proof that the concentration of alcohol in the blood of the accused at the time when the offence was alleged to have been committed was the concentration determined by the analysis or, where more than one sample was analyzed and the results of the analyses are the same, the concentration determined by the analyses and, where the results of the analyses are different, the lowest of the concentrations determined by such analyses;

(*e*) a certificate of an analyst stating that the analyst has made an analysis of a sample of the blood, urine, breath or other bodily substance of the accused and stating the result of his analysis is evidence of the facts alleged in the certificate without proof of the signature or the official character of the person appearing to have signed the certificate;

(*f*) a certificate of an analyst stating that the analyst has made an analysis of a sample of an alcohol standard that is identified in the certificate and intended for use with an approved instrument and that the sample of the standard analyzed by the analyst was found to be suitable for use with an approved instrument, is evidence that the alcohol standard so identified is suitable for use with an approved instrument without proof of the signature or the official character of the person appearing to have signed the certificate;

(*g*) where samples of the breath of the accused have been taken pursuant to a demand made under subsection 254(3), a certificate of a qualified technician stating

(i) that the analysis of each of the samples has been made by means of an approved instrument operated by the technician and ascertained by the technician to be in proper working order by means of an alcohol standard, identified in the certificate, that is suitable for use with an approved instrument,

(ii) the results of the analyses so made, and

(iii) if the samples were taken by the technician,

(A) that at the time each sample was taken the technician, offered to provide the accused with a specimen of the breath of the accused in an approved container for his own use and, at the request of the accused made at that time, the accused was thereupon provided with such a specimen,

(B) the time when and place where each sample and any specimen described in clause (A) was taken, and

(C) that each sample was received from the accused directly into an approved container or into an approved instrument operated by the technician,

is evidence of the facts alleged in the certificate without proof of the signature or the official character of the person appearing to have signed the certificate;

(*h*) where a sample of the blood of the accused has been taken pursuant to a demand made under subsection 254(3) or otherwise with the consent of the accused or pursuant to a warrant issued under section 256,

(i) a certificate of a qualified medical practitioner stating that

(A) the medical practitioner took the sample and that before the sample was taken he was of the opinion that the taking of blood samples from the accused would not endanger the life or health of the accused and, in the case of a demand made pursuant to a warrant issued pursuant to section 256, that by reason of any physical or mental condition of the accused that resulted from the consumption of alcohol, the accident or any other occurrence related to or resulting from the accident, the accused was unable to consent to the taking of his blood,

(B) at the time the sample was taken, the medical practitioner took an additional sample of the blood of the accused to permit an analysis of one of the samples to be made by or on behalf of the accused,

(C) the time when and place where both samples referred to in clause (B) were taken, and

(D) both samples referred to in clause (B) were received from the accused directly into, or placed directly into, approved containers that were subsequently sealed and that are identified in the certificate,

(ii) a certificate of a qualified medical practitioner stating that the medical practitioner caused the sample to be taken by a qualified technician under his direction and that before the sample was taken the qualified medical practitioner was of the opinion referred to in clause (i)(A), or

(iii) a certificate of a qualified technician stating that the technician took the sample and the facts referred to in clauses (i)(B) to (D)

is evidence of the facts alleged in the certificate without proof of the signature or official character of the person appearing to have signed the certificate; and

(*i*) a certificate of an analyst stating that the analyst has made an analysis of a sample of the blood of the accused that was contained in a sealed approved container identified in the certificate, the date on which and place where the sample was analyzed and the result of that analysis is evidence of the facts alleged in the certificate without proof of the signature or official character of the person appearing to have signed it.

(2) No person is required to give a sample of urine or other bodily substance for analysis for the purposes of this section except breath or blood as required under section 254, and evidence that a person failed or refused to give such a sample or that such a sample was not taken is not admissible nor shall such a failure or refusal or the fact that a sample was not taken be the subject of comment by any person in the proceedings.

(3) In any proceedings under subsection 255(1) in respect of an offence committed under paragraph 253(*a*) or in any proceedings under subsection 255(2) or (3), evidence that the accused, without reasonable excuse, failed or refused to comply with a demand made to him by a peace officer under section 254 is admissible and the court may draw an inference therefrom adverse to the accused.

(4) A judge of a superior court of criminal jurisdiction or a court of criminal jurisdiction shall, on the summary application of the accused made within three months from the day on which samples of the blood of the accused were taken, order the release of one of the samples for the purpose of an examination or analysis thereof, subject to such terms as appear to be necessary or desirable to ensure the safeguarding of the sample and its preservation for use in any proceedings in respect of which it was retained.

(5) Where a sample of blood of an accused has been taken pursuant to a demand made under subsection 254(3) or otherwise with the consent of the accused or pursuant to a warrant issued under section 256, the sample may be tested for the presence of drugs in the blood of the accused.

(6) A party against whom a certificate described in paragraph (1)(*e*), (*f*), (*g*), (*h*) or (*i*) is produced may, with leave of the court, require the attendance

of the qualified medical practitioner, analyst or qualified technician, as the case may be, for the purposes of cross-examination.

(7) No certificate shall be received in evidence pursuant to paragraph (1)(*e*), (*f*), (*g*), (*h*) or (*i*) unless the party intending to produce it has, before the trial, given to the other party reasonable notice of his intention and a copy of the certificate. R.S. 1985, c. 27 (1st Supp.), s. 36.

[NOTE: S. 258(1)(*c*)(i) and (*g*)(iii)(A) is to come into force on proclamation.]

Mandatory order of prohibition — Discretionary order of prohibition — Saving — Operation while disqualified — Definition of "disqualification".

259. (1) Where an offender is convicted of an offence committed under section 253 or 254 or discharged under section 736 of an offence committed under section 253 and, at the time the offence was committed or, in the case of an offence committed under section 254, within the two hours preceding that time, was operating or had the care or control of a motor vehicle, vessel, aircraft or railway equipment or was assisting in the operation of an aircraft or of railway equipment, the court that sentences the offender shall, in addition to any other punishment that may be imposed for that offence, make an order prohibiting the offender from operating a motor vehicle on any street, road, highway or other public place, or from operating a vessel, aircraft or railway equipment, as the case may be,

(*a*) for a first offence, during a period of not more than three years and not less than three months;

(*b*) for a second offence, during a period of not more than three years and not less than six months; and

(*c*) for each subsequent offence, during a period of not more than three years and not less than one year.

(2) Where an offender is convicted or discharged under section 736 of an offence under section 220, 221, 236, 249, 250, 251 or 252, subsection 255(2) or (3) or this section committed by means of a motor vehicle, vessel, aircraft or railway equipment, the court that sentences the offender may, in addition to any other punishment that may be imposed for that offence, make an order prohibiting the offender from operating a motor vehicle on any street, road, highway or other public place, or from operating a vessel, aircraft or railway equipment, as the case may be,

(*a*) during any period that the court considers proper, if the offender is liable to imprisonment for life in respect of that offence;

(*b*) during any period not exceeding ten years, if the offender is liable to imprisonment for more than five years but less than life in respect of that offence; and

(*c*) during any period not exceeding three years, in any other case.

(3) No order made under subsection (1) or (2) shall operate to prevent any

person from acting as master, mate or engineer of a vessel that is required to carry officers holding certificates as master, mate or engineer.

(4) Every one who operates a motor vehicle, vessel, aircraft or railway equipment in Canada while disqualified from doing so

(*a*) is guilty of an indictable offence and liable to imprisonment for a term not exceeding two years; or

(*b*) is guilty of an offence punishable on summary conviction.

(5) For the purposes of this section, "disqualification" means

(*a*) a prohibition from operating a motor vehicle, vessel, aircraft or railway equipment ordered pursuant to subsection (1) or (2); or

(*b*) a disqualification or any other form of legal restriction of the right or privilege to operate a motor vehicle, vessel or aircraft imposed

(i) in the case of a motor vehicle, under the law of a province, or

(ii) in the case of a vessel or an aircraft, under an Act of Parliament,

in respect of a conviction or discharge under section 736 of any offence referred to in subsection (1) or (2). R.S. 1985, c. 27 (1st Supp.), s. 36; c. 32 (4th Supp.), s. 62.

Proceedings on making of prohibition order — Endorsement by offender — Validity of order not affected — Onus — Certificate admissible in evidence — Notice to accused — Definition of "registrar of motor vehicles".

260. (1) Where a court makes a prohibition order under subsection 259(1) or (2) in relation to an offender, it shall cause

(*a*) the order to be read by or to the offender;

(*b*) a copy of the order to be given to the offender; and

(*c*) the offender to be informed of subsection 259(4).

(2) After subsection (1) has been complied with in relation to an offender who is bound by an order referred to in that subsection, the offender shall endorse the order, acknowledging receipt of a copy thereof and that the order has been explained to him.

(3) The failure of an offender to endorse an order pursuant to subsection (2) does not affect the validity of the order.

(4) In the absence of evidence to the contrary, where it is proved that a disqualification referred to in paragraph 259(5)(*b*) has been imposed on a person and that notice of the disqualification has been mailed by registered or certified mail to that person, that person shall, after five days following the mailing of the notice, be deemed to have received the notice and to have knowledge of the disqualification, of the date of its commencement and of its duration.

(5) In proceedings under section 259, a certificate setting out with reasonable particularity that a person is disqualified from

(*a*) driving a motor vehicle in a province, purporting to be signed by the registrar of motor vehicles for that province, or (*b*) operating a vessel or aircraft, purporting to be signed by the Minister of Transport or any person authorized by the Minister of Transport for that purpose

is evidence of the facts alleged therein without proof of the signature or official character of the person by whom it purports to be signed.

(6) Subsection (5) does not apply in any proceedings unless at least seven days notice in writing is given to the accused that it is intended to tender the certificate in evidence.

(7) In subsection (5), "registrar of motor vehicles" includes the deputy of that registrar and any other person or body, by whatever name or title designated, that from time to time performs the duties of superintending the registration of motor vehicles in the province. R.S. 1985, c. 27 (1st Supp.), s. 36.

Stay of order pending appeal.

261. Where an appeal is taken against a conviction or discharge under section 736 for an offence committed under any of sections 220, 221, 236 or 249 to 255 or 259, the court being appealed to may direct that any order under subsection 259(1) or (2) arising out of the conviction or discharge shall be stayed, pending the final disposition of the appeal or until otherwise ordered by that court. R.S. 1985, c. 27 (1st Supp.), s. 36.

Impeding attempt to save life.

262. Every one who

(*a*) prevents or impedes or attempts to prevent or impede any person who is attempting to save his own life, or

(*b*) without reasonable cause prevents or impedes or attempts to prevent or impede any person who is attempting to save the life of another person,

is guilty of an indictable offence and liable to imprisonment for a term not exceeding ten years.

Duty to safeguard opening in ice — Excavation on land — Offences.

263. (1) Every one who makes or causes to be made an opening in ice that is open to or frequented by the public is under a legal duty to guard it in a manner that is adequate to prevent persons from falling in by accident and is adequate to warn them that the opening exists.

(2) Every one who leaves an excavation on land that he owns or of which he has charge or supervision is under a legal duty to guard it in a manner that is adequate to prevent persons from falling in by accident and is adequate to warn them that the excavation exists.

(3) Every one who fails to perform a duty imposed by subsection (1) or (2) is guilty of

(*a*) manslaughter, if the death of any person results therefrom;

(*b*) an offence under section 269, if bodily harm to any person results therefrom; or (*c*) an offence punishable on summary conviction.

264. [Repealed R.S. 1985, c. 27 (1st Supp.), s. 37.]

Uttering threats — Punishment — Idem.

264.1 (1) Every one commits an offence who, in any manner, knowingly utters, conveys or causes any person to receive a threat

(*a*) to cause death or serious bodily harm to any person;

(*b*) to burn, destroy or damage real or personal property; or

(*c*) to kill, poison or injure an animal or bird that is the property of any person.

(2) Every one who commits an offence under paragraph (1)(*a*) is guilty of an indictable offence and liable to imprisonment for a term not exceeding five years.

(3) Every one who commits an offence under paragraph (1)(*b*) or (*c*)

(*a*) is guilty of an indictable offence and liable to imprisonment for a term not exceeding two years; or

(*b*) is guilty of an offence punishable on summary conviction. R.S. 1985, c. 27 (1st Supp.), s. 38.

Assaults

Assault — Application — Consent — Accused's belief as to consent.

265. (1) A person commits an assault when

(*a*) without the consent of another person, he applies force intentionally to that other person, directly or indirectly;

(*b*) he attempts or threatens, by an act or a gesture, to apply force to another person, if he has, or causes that other person to believe on reasonable grounds that he has, present ability to effect his purpose; or

(*c*) while openly wearing or carrying a weapon or an imitation thereof, he accosts or impedes another person or begs.

(2) This section applies to all forms of assault, including sexual assault, sexual assault with a weapon, threats to a third party or causing bodily harm and aggravated sexual assault.

(3) For the purposes of this section, no consent is obtained where the complainant submits or does not resist by reason of

(*a*) the application of force to the complainant or to a person other than the complainant;

(*b*) threats or fear of the application of force to the complainant or to a person other than the complainant;

(*c*) fraud; or

(*d*) the exercise of authority.

(4) Where an accused alleges that he believed that the complainant

consented to the conduct that is the subject-matter of the charge, a judge, if satisfied that there is sufficient evidence and that, if believed by the jury, the evidence would constitute a defence, shall instruct the jury, when reviewing all the evidence relating to the determination of the honesty of the accused's belief, to consider the presence or absence of reasonable grounds for that belief.

Assault.

266. Every one who commits an assault is guilty of

(*a*) an indictable offence and is liable to imprisonment for a term not exceeding five years; or

(*b*) an offence punishable on summary conviction.

Assault with a weapon or causing bodily harm — Definition of "bodily harm".

267. (1) Every one who, in committing an assault,

(*a*) carries, uses or threatens to use a weapon or an imitation thereof, or

(*b*) causes bodily harm to the complainant,

is guilty of an indictable offence and liable to imprisonment for a term not exceeding ten years.

(2) For the purposes of this section and sections 269 and 272, "bodily harm" means any hurt or injury to the complainant that interferes with the health or comfort of the complainant and that is more than merely transient or trifling in nature.

Aggravated assault — Punishment.

268. (1) Every one commits an aggravated assault who wounds, maims, disfigures or endangers the life of the complainant.

(2) Every one who commits an aggravated assault is guilty of an indictable offence and liable to imprisonment for a term not exceeding fourteen years.

Unlawfully causing bodily harm.

269. Every one who unlawfully causes bodily harm to any person is guilty of an indictable offence and liable to imprisonment for a term not exceeding ten years.

Torture — Definitions — "Official" — "Torture" — No defence — Evidence.

269.1 (1) Every official, or every person acting at the instigation of or with the consent or acquiescence of an official, who inflicts torture on any other person is guilty of an indictable offence and is liable to imprisonment for a term not exceeding fourteen years.

(2) For the purposes of this section,

"official" means

(*a*) a peace officer,

(*b*) a public officer,

(*c*) a member of the Canadian Forces, or

(*d*) any person who may exercise powers, pursuant to a law in force in a foreign state, that would, in Canada be exercised by a person referred to in paragraph (*a*), (*b*), or (*c*),

whether the person exercises powers in Canada or outside Canada;

"torture" means any act or omission by which severe pain or suffering, whether physical or mental, is intentionally inflicted on a person

(*a*) for a purpose including

(i) obtaining from the person or from a third person information or a statement,

(ii) punishing the person for an act that the person or a third person has committed or is suspected of having committed, and

(iii) intimidating or coercing the person or a third person, or

(*b*) for any reason based on discrimination of any kind,

but does not include any act or omission arising only from, inherent in or incidental to lawful sanctions.

(3) It is no defence to a charge under this section that the accused was ordered by a superior or a public authority to perform the act or omission that forms the subject-matter of the charge nor that the act or omission is alleged to have been justified by exceptional circumstances, including a state of war, a threat of war, internal political instability or any other public emergency.

(4) In any proceedings over which Parliament has jurisdiction, any statement obtained as a result of the commission of an offence under this section is inadmissible in evidence except as evidence that the statement was so obtained. R.S. 1985, c. 10 (3rd Supp.), s. 2.

Assaulting a peace officer — Punishment.

270. (1) Every one commits an offence who

(*a*) assaults a public officer or peace officer engaged in the execution of his duty or a person acting in aid of such an officer;

(*b*) assaults a person with intent to resist or prevent the lawful arrest or detention of himself or another person; or

(*c*) assaults a person

(i) who is engaged in the lawful execution of a process against lands or goods or in making a lawful distress or seizure, or

(ii) with intent to rescue anything taken under lawful process, distress or seizure.

(2) Every one who commits an offence under subsection (1) is guilty of

(*a*) an indictable offence and is liable to imprisonment for a term not exceeding five years; or

(*b*) an offence punishable on summary conviction.

Sexual assault.

271. (1) Every one who commits a sexual assault is guilty of

(*a*) an indictable offence and is liable to imprisonment for a term not exceeding ten years; or

(*b*) an offence punishable on summary conviction. R.S. 1985, c. 19 (3rd Supp.), s. 10.

(2) [Repealed R.S. 1985, c. 19 (3rd Supp.), s. 10.]

Sexual assault with a weapon, threats to a third party or causing bodily harm.

272. Every one who, in committing a sexual assault,

(*a*) carries, uses or threatens to use a weapon or an imitation thereof,

(*b*) threatens to cause bodily harm to a person other than the complainant,

(*c*) causes bodily harm to the complainant, or

(*d*) is a party to the offence with any other person,

is guilty of an indictable offence and liable to imprisonment for a term not exceeding fourteen years.

Aggravated sexual assault — Punishment.

273. (1) Every one commits an aggravated sexual assault who, in committing a sexual assault, wounds, maims, disfigures or endangers the life of the complainant.

(2) Every one who commits an aggravated sexual assault is guilty of an indictable offence and liable to imprisonment for life.

[1992, c. 38, s. 1 will add the following sections immediately after section 273.]

Meaning of "consent" — Where no consent obtained — Subsection (2) not limiting.

273.1 (1) Subject to subsection (2) and subsection 265(3), "consent" means, for the purposes of sections 271, 272 and 273, the voluntary agreement of the complainant to engage in the sexual activity in question.

(2) No consent is obtained, for the purposes of sections 271, 272 and 273, where

(*a*) the agreement is expressed by the words or conduct of a person other than the complainant;

(*b*) the complainant is incapable of consenting to the activity;

(*c*) the accused induces the complainant to engage in the activity by abusing a position of trust, power or authority;

(*d*) the complainant expresses, by words or conduct, a lack of agreement to engage in the activity; or

(*e*) the complainant, having consented to engage in sexual activity, expresses, by words or conduct, a lack of agreement to continue to engage in the activity.

(3) Nothing in subsection (2) shall be construed as limiting the circumstances in which no consent is obtained.

Where belief in consent not a defence.

273.2 It is not a defence to a charge under section 271, 272 or 273 that the accused believed that the complainant consented to the activity that forms the subject-matter of the charge, where

(*a*) the accused's belief arose from the accused's

(i) self-induced intoxication, or

(ii) recklessness or wilful blindness; or

(*b*) the accused did not take reasonable steps, in the circumstances known to the accused at the time, to ascertain that the complainant was consenting.

Corroboration not required.

274. Where an accused is charged with an offence under section 151, 152, 153, 155, 159, 160, 170, 171, 172, 173, 212, 271, 272 or 273, no corroboration is required for a conviction and the judge shall not instruct the jury that it is unsafe to find the accused guilty in the absence of corroboration. 1987, c. 24, s. 11.

Rules respecting recent complaint abrogated.

275. The rules relating to evidence of recent complaint are hereby abrogated with respect to offences under sections 151, 152, 153, 155 and 159, subsections 160(2) and (3), and sections 170, 171, 172, 173, 271, 272 and 273. R.S. 1985, c. 19 (3rd Supp.), s. 11.

No evidence concerning sexual activity — Notice — Hearing — Publication prohibited — Offence — Definition of "newspaper".

276. (1) In proceedings in respect of an offence under section 151, 152, 153, 155 or 159, subsections 160(2) or (3), or section 170, 171, 172, 173, 271, 272 or 273, no evidence shall be adduced by or on behalf of the accused concerning the sexual activity of the complainant with any person other than the accused unless

(*a*) it is evidence that rebuts evidence of the complainant's sexual activity or absence thereof that was previously adduced by the prosecution;

(*b*) it is evidence of specific instances of the complainant's sexual activity tending to establish the identity of the person who had sexual contact with the complainant on the occasion set out in the charge; or

(*c*) it is evidence of sexual activity that took place on the same occasion as the sexual activity that forms the subject-matter of the charge, where that evidence relates to the consent that the accused alleges he believed was given by the complainant.

(2) No evidence is admissible under paragraph (1)(*c*) unless

(*a*) reasonable notice in writing has been given to the prosecutor by or on behalf of the accused of his intention to adduce the evidence together with particulars of the evidence sought to be adduced; and

(*b*) a copy of the notice has been filed with the clerk of the court.

(3) No evidence is admissible under subsection (1) unless the judge, magistrate or justice, after holding a hearing in which the jury and the members of the public are excluded and in which the complainant is not a compellable witness, is satisfied that the requirements of this section are met.

(4) The notice given under subsection (2) and the evidence taken, the information given or the representations made at a hearing referred to in subsection (3) shall not be published in any newspaper or broadcast.

(5) Every one who, without lawful excuse the proof of which lies on him, contravenes subsection (4) is guilty of an offence punishable on summary conviction.

(6) In this section, "newspaper" has the same meaning as in section 297. R.S. 1985, c. 19 (3rd Supp.), s. 12.

[1992, c. 38, s. 2 will repeal section 276 and substitute the following.]

Evidence of complainant's sexual activity — Idem — Factors that judge must consider.

276. (1) In proceedings in respect of an offence under section 151, 152, 153, 155 or 159, subsection 160(2) or (3) or section 170, 171, 172, 173, 271, 272 or 273, evidence that the complainant has engaged in sexual activity, whether with the accused or with any other person, is not admissible to support an inference that, by reason of the sexual nature of that activity, the complainant

(*a*) is more likely to have consented to the sexual activity that forms the subject-matter of the charge; or

(*b*) is less worthy of belief.

(2) In proceedings in respect of an offence referred to in subsection (1), no evidence shall be adduced by or on behalf of the accused that the complainant has engaged in sexual activity other than the sexual activity that forms the subject-matter of the charge, whether with the accused or with any other person, unless the judge, provincial court judge or justice determines, in accordance with the procedures set out in sections 276.1 and 276.2, that the evidence

(*a*) is of specific instances of sexual activity;

(*b*) is relevant to an issue at trial; and

(*c*) has significant probative value that is not substantially outweighed by the danger of prejudice to the proper administration of justice.

(3) In determining whether evidence is admissible under subsection (2), the judge, provincial court judge or justice shall take into account

(*a*) the interests of justice, including the right of the accused to make a full answer and defence;

(*b*) society's interest in encouraging the reporting of sexual assault offences;

(*c*) whether there is a reasonable prospect that the evidence will assist in arriving at a just determination in the case;

(*d*) the need to remove from the fact-finding process any discriminatory belief or bias;

(*e*) the risk that the evidence may unduly arouse sentiments of prejudice, sympathy or hostility in the jury;

(*f*) the potential prejudice to the complainant's personal dignity and right of privacy;

(*g*) the right of the complainant and of every individual to personal security and to the full protection and benefit of the law; and

(*h*) any other factor that the judge, provincial court judge or justice considers relevant.

Application for hearing — Form and content of application — Jury and public excluded — Judge may decide to hold hearing.

276.1 (1) Application may be made to the judge, provincial court judge or justice by or on behalf of the accused for a hearing under section 276.2 to determine whether evidence is admissible under subsection 276(2).

(2) An application referred to in subsection (1) must be made in writing and set out

(*a*) detailed particulars of the evidence that the accused seeks to adduce, and

(*b*) the relevance of that evidence to an issue at trial,

and a copy of the application must be given to the prosecutor and to the clerk of the court.

(3) The judge, provincial court judge or justice shall consider the application with the jury and the public excluded.

(4) Where the judge, provincial court judge or justice is satisfied

(*a*) that the application was made in accordance with subsection (2),

(*b*) that a copy of the application was given to the prosecutor and to the clerk of the court at least seven days previously, or such shorter interval as the judge, provincial court judge or justice may allow where the interests of justice so require, and

(*c*) that the evidence sought to be adduced is capable of being admissible under subsection 276(2),

the judge, provincial court judge or justice shall grant the application and hold a hearing under section 276.2 to determine whether the evidence is admissible under subsection 276(2).

Jury and public excluded — Complainant not compellable — Judge's determination and reasons — Record of reasons.

276.2 (1) At a hearing to determine whether evidence is admissible under subsection 276(2), the jury and the public shall be excluded.

(2) The complainant is not a compellable witness at the hearing.

(3) At the conclusion of the hearing, the judge, provincial court judge or justice shall determine whether the evidence, or any part thereof, is admissible under subsection 276(2) and shall provide reasons for that determination, and

(*a*) where not all of the evidence is to be admitted, the reasons must state the part of the evidence that is to be admitted;

(*b*) the reasons must state the factors referred to in subsection 276(3) that affected the determination; and

(*c*) where all or any part of the evidence is to be admitted, the reasons must state the manner in which that evidence is expected to be relevant to an issue at trial.

(4) The reasons provided under subsection (3) shall be entered in the record of the proceedings or, where the proceedings are not recorded, shall be provided in writing.

Publication prohibited — Offence.

276.3 (1) No person shall publish in a newspaper, as defined in section 297, or in a broadcast, any of the following:

(*a*) the contents of an application made under section 276.1;

(*b*) any evidence taken, the information given and the representations made at an application under section 276.1 or at a hearing under section 276.2;

(*c*) the decision of a judge, provincial court judge or justice under subsection 276.1(4), unless the judge, provincial court judge or justice, after taking into account the complainant's right of privacy and the interests of justice, orders that the decision may be published; and

(*d*) the determination made and the reasons provided under section 276.2, unless

(i) that determination is that evidence is admissible, or

(ii) the judge, provincial court judge or justice, after taking into account the complainant's right of privacy and the interests of justice, orders that the determination and reasons may be published.

(2) Every person who contravenes subsection (1) is guilty of an offence punishable on summary conviction.

Judge to instruct jury re use of evidence.

276.4 Where evidence is admitted at trial pursuant to a determination made under section 276.2, the judge shall instruct the jury as to the uses that the jury may and may not make of that evidence.

Appeal.

276.5 For the purposes of sections 675 and 676, a determination made under section 276.2 shall be deemed to be a question of law.

Reputation evidence.

277. In proceedings in respect of an offence under section 151, 152, 153, 155 or 159, subsection 160(2) or (3), or section 170, 171, 172, 173, 271, 272 or 273, evidence of sexual reputation, whether general or specific, is not admissible for the purpose of challenging or supporting the credibility of the complainant. R.S. 1985, c. 19 (3rd Supp.), s. 13.

Spouse may be charged.

278. A husband or wife may be charged with an offence under section 271, 272 or 273 in respect of his or her spouse, whether or not the spouses were living together at the time the activity that forms the subject-matter of the charge occurred.

Kidnapping, Hostage Taking and Abduction

Kidnapping — Forcible confinement — Non-resistance.

279. (1) Every one who kidnaps a person with intent

(*a*) to cause him to be confined or imprisoned against his will,

(*b*) to cause him to be unlawfully sent or transported out of Canada against his will, or

(*c*) to hold him for ransom or to service against his will,

is guilty of an indictable offence and liable to imprisonment for life.

(2) Every one who, without lawful authority, confines, imprisons or forcibly seizes another person is guilty of an indictable offence and liable to imprisonment for a term not exceeding ten years.

(3) In proceedings under this section, the fact that the person in relation to whom the offence is alleged to have been committed did not resist is not a defence unless the accused proves that the failure to resist was not caused by threats, duress, force or exhibition or force. R.S. 1985, c. 27 (1st Supp.), s. 39.

Hostage taking — Punishment — Non-resistance.

279.1 (1) Every one takes a person hostage who

(*a*) confines, imprisons, forcibly seizes or detains that person, and

(*b*) in any manner utters, conveys or causes any person to receive a threat that the death of, or bodily harm to, the hostage will be caused or that the confinement, imprisonment or detention of the hostage will be continued

with intent to induce any person, other than the hostage, or any group of persons or any state or international or intergovernmental organization to commit or cause to be committed any act or omission as a condition, whether express or implied, of the release of the hostage.

(2) Every one who takes a person hostage is guilty of an indictable offence and liable to a maximum term of imprisonment for life.

(3) Subsection 279(3) applies to proceedings under this section as if the offence under this section were an offence under section 279. R.S. 1985, c. 27 (1st Supp.), s. 40(1).

Abduction of person under sixteen — Definition of "guardian".

280. (1) Every one who, without lawful authority, takes or causes to be taken an unmarried person under the age of sixteen years out of the possession of and against the will of the parent or guardian of that person or of any other person who has the lawful care or charge of that person is guilty of an indictable offence and liable to imprisonment for a term not exceeding five years.

(2) In this section and sections 281 to 283, "guardian" includes any person who has in law or in fact the custody or control of another person.

Abduction of person under fourteen.

281. Every one who, not being the parent, guardian or person having the lawful care or charge of a person under the age of fourteen years, unlawfully takes, entices away, conceals, detains, receives or harbours that person with intent to deprive a parent or guardian, or any other person who has the lawful care or charge of that person, of the possession of that person is guilty of an indictable offence and liable to imprisonment for a term not exceeding ten years.

Abduction in contravention of custody order.

282. Every one who, being the parent, guardian or person having the lawful care or charge of a person under the age of fourteen years, takes, entices away, conceals, detains, receives or harbours that person, in contravention of the custody provisions of a custody order in relation to that person made by a court anywhere in Canada, with intent to deprive a parent or guardian or any other person who has the lawful care or charge of that person, of the possession of that person is guilty of

(*a*) an indictable offence and is liable to imprisonment for a term not exceeding ten years; or

(*b*) an offence punishable on summary conviction.

Abduction where no custody order — Consent required.

283. (1) Every one who, being the parent, guardian or person having the lawful care or charge of a person under the age of fourteen years, takes, entices away, conceals, detains, receives or harbours that person, in relation to whom no custody order has been made by a court anywhere in Canada, with intent to deprive a parent or guardian, or any other person who has the lawful care or charge of that person, of the possession of that person, is guilty of

(*a*) an indictable offence and is liable to imprisonment for a term not exceeding ten years; or

(*b*) an offence punishable on summary conviction.

(2) No proceedings may be commenced under subsection (1) without the consent of the Attorney General or counsel instructed by him for that purpose.

Defence.

284. No one shall be found guilty of an offence under sections 281 to 283 if he establishes that the taking, enticing away, concealing, detaining, receiving or harbouring of any young person was done with the consent of the parent, guardian or other person having the lawful possession, care or charge of that young person.

Defence.

285. No one shall be found guilty of an offence under sections 280 to 283 if the court is satisfied that the taking, enticing away, concealing, detaining, receiving or harbouring of any young person was necessary to protect the young person from danger of imminent harm.

No defence.

286. In proceedings in respect of an offence under sections 280 to 283, it is not a defence to any charge that a young person consented to or suggested any conduct of the accused.

Abortion

Procuring miscarriage — Woman procuring her own miscarriage — "Means" — Exceptions — Information requirement — Definitions — "Accredited hospital" — "Approved hospital" — "Board" — "Minister of Health" — "Qualified medical practitioner" — "Therapeutic abortion committee" — Requirement of consent not affected.

287. (1) Every one who, with intent to procure the miscarriage of a female person, whether or not she is pregnant, uses any means for the purpose of carrying out his intention is guilty of an indictable offence and liable to imprisonment for life.

(2) Every female person who, being pregnant, with intent to procure her own miscarriage, uses any means or permits any means to be used for the purpose of carrying out her intention is guilty of an indictable offence and liable to imprisonment for a term not exceeding two years.

(3) In this section, "means" includes

(*a*) the administration of a drug or other noxious thing;

(*b*) the use of an instrument; and

(*c*) manipulation of any kind.

(4) Subsections (1) and (2) do not apply to

(*a*) a qualified medical practitioner, other than a member of a therapeutic abortion committee for any hospital, who in good faith uses in an accredited or approved hospital any means for the purpose of carrying out his intention to procure the miscarriage of a female person, or

(*b*) a female person who, being pregnant, permits a qualified medical practitioner to use in an accredited or approved hospital any means for the purpose of carrying out her intention to procure her own miscarriage,

if, before the use of those means, the therapeutic abortion committee for that accredited or approved hospital, by a majority of the members of the committee and at a meeting of the committee at which the case of the female person has been reviewed,

(*c*) has by certificate in writing stated that in its opinion the continuation of the pregnancy of the female person would or would be likely to endanger her life or health, and

(*d*) has caused a copy of that certificate to be given to the qualified medical practitioner.

(5) The Minister of Health of a province may by order

(*a*) require a therapeutic abortion committee for any hospital in that province, or any member thereof, to furnish him with a copy of any certificate described in paragraph (4)(*c*) issued by that committee, together with such other information relating to the circumstances surrounding the issue of that certificate as he may require, or

(*b*) require a medical practitioner who, in that province, has procured the miscarriage of any female person named in a certificate described in paragraph (4)(*c*), to furnish him with a copy of that certificate, together with such other information relating to the procuring of the miscarriage as he may require.

(6) For the purposes of subsections (4) and (5) and this subsection

"accredited hospital" means a hospital accredited by the Canadian Council on Hospital Accreditation in which diagnostic services and medical, surgical and obstetrical treatment are provided;

"approved hospital" means a hospital in a province approved for the purposes of this section by the Minister of Health of that province;

"board" means the board of governors, management or directors, or the trustees, commission or other person or group of persons having the control and management of an accredited or approved hospital;

"Minister of Health" means

(*a*) in the Provinces of Ontario, Quebec, New Brunswick, Prince Edward Island, Manitoba, and Newfoundland, the Minister of Health,

(*b*) in the Provinces of Nova Scotia and Saskatchewan, the Minister of Public Health, and

(*c*) in the Province of British Columbia, the Minister of Health Services and Hospital Insurance,

(*d*) in the Province of Alberta, the Minister of Hospitals and Medical Care, (*e*) in the Yukon Territory and the Northwest Territories, the Minister of National Health and Welfare;

"qualified medical practitioner" means a person entitled to engage in the practice of medicine under the laws of the province in which the hospital referred to in subsection (4) is situated;

"therapeutic abortion committee" for any hospital means a committee, comprised of not less than three members each of whom is a qualified medical practitioner, appointed by the board of that hospital for the purpose of considering and determining questions relating to terminations of pregnancy within that hospital.

(7) Nothing in subsection (4) shall be construed as making unnecessary the obtaining of any authorization or consent that is or may be required, otherwise than under this Act, before any means are used for the purpose of carrying out an intention to procure the miscarriage of a female person.

Supplying noxious things.

288. Every one who unlawfully supplies or procures a drug or other noxious thing or an instrument or thing, knowing that it is intended to be used or employed to procure the miscarriage of a female person, whether or not she is pregnant, is guilty of an indictable offence and liable to imprisonment for a term not exceeding two years.

289. [Repealed R.S. 1985, c. 27 (1st Supp.), s. 41.]

Offences Against Conjugal Rights

Bigamy — Matters of defence — Incompetency no defence — Validity presumed — Act or omission by accused.

290. (1) Every one commits bigamy who

(*a*) in Canada,

(i) being married, goes through a form of marriage with another person,

(ii) knowing that another person is married, goes through a form of marriage with that person, or

(iii) on the same day or simultaneously, goes through a form of marriage with more than one person; or

(*b*) being a Canadian citizen resident in Canada leaves Canada with intent to do anything mentioned in subparagraphs (*a*)(i) to (iii) and, pursuant thereto, does outside Canada anything mentioned in those subparagraphs in circumstances mentioned therein.

(2) No person commits bigamy by going through a form of marriage if

(*a*) that person in good faith and on reasonable grounds believes that his spouse is dead,

(*b*) the spouse of that person has been continuously absent from him for seven years immediately preceding the time when he goes through the form of marriage, unless he knew that his spouse was alive at any time during those seven years,

(*c*) that person has been divorced from the bond of the first marriage, or

(*d*) the former marriage has been declared void by a court of competent jurisdiction.

(3) Where a person is alleged to have committed bigamy, it is not a defence that the parties would, if unmarried, have been incompetent to contract marriage under the law of the place where the offence is alleged to have been committed.

(4) Every marriage or form of marriage shall, for the purpose of this section, be deemed to be valid unless the accused establishes that it was invalid.

(5) No act or omission on the part of an accused who is charged with bigamy invalidates a marriage or form of marriage that is otherwise valid.

Punishment — Certificate of marriage.

291. (1) Every one who commits bigamy is guilty of an indictable offence and liable to imprisonment for a term not exceeding five years.

(2) For the purposes of this section, a certificate of marriage issued under the authority of law is evidence of the marriage or form of marriage to which it relates without proof of the signature or official character of the person by whom it purports to be signed.

Procuring feigned marriage — Corroboration.

292. (1) Every person who procures or knowingly aids in procuring a feigned marriage between himself and another person is guilty of an indictable offence and liable to imprisonment for a term not exceeding five years.

(2) No person shall be convicted of an offence under this section on the evidence of only one witness unless the evidence of that witness is corroborated in a material particular by evidence that implicates the accused.

Polygamy — Evidence in case of polygamy.

293. (1) Every one who

(*a*) practises or enters into or in any manner agrees or consents to practise or enter into

(i) any form of polygamy, or

(ii) any kind of conjugal union with more than one person at the same time,

whether or not it is by law recognized as a binding form of marriage; or

(*b*) celebrates, assists or is a party to a rite, ceremony, contract or consent that purports to sanction a relationship mentioned in subparagraph (*a*)(i) or (ii),

is guilty of an indictable offence and liable to imprisonment for a term not exceeding five years.

(2) Where an accused is charged with an offence under this section, no

averment or proof of the method by which the alleged relationship was entered into, agreed to or consented to is necessary in the indictment or on the trial of the accused, nor is it necessary on the trial to prove that the persons who are alleged to have entered into the relationship had or intended to have sexual intercourse.

Unlawful Solemnization of Marriage

Pretending to solemnize marriage.

294. Every one who

(*a*) solemnizes or pretends to solemnize a marriage without lawful authority, the proof of which lies upon him, or

(*b*) procures a person to solemnize a marriage knowing that he is not lawfully authorized to solemnize the marriage,

is guilty of an indictable offence and liable to imprisonment for a term not exceeding two years.

Marriage contrary to law.

295. Every one who, being lawfully authorized to solemnize marriage, knowingly and wilfully solemnizes a marriage in contravention of the laws of the province in which the marriage is solemnized is guilty of an indictable offence and liable to imprisonment for a term not exceeding two years.

Blasphemous Libel

Offence — Question of fact — Saving.

296. (1) Every one who publishes a blasphemous libel is guilty of an indictable offence and liable to imprisonment for a term not exceeding two years.

(2) It is a question of fact whether or not any matter that is published is a blasphemous libel.

(3) No person shall be convicted of an offence under this section for expressing in good faith and in decent language, or attempting to establish by argument used in good faith and conveyed in decent language, an opinion on a religious subject.

Defamatory Libel

"Newspaper".

297. In sections 303, 304 and 308, "newspaper" means any paper, magazine or periodical containing public news, intelligence or reports of events, or any remarks or observations thereon, printed for sale and published periodically or in parts or numbers, at intervals not exceeding thirty-one days between the publication of any two such papers, parts or numbers, and any paper, magazine or periodical printed in order to be dispersed and made public, weekly or more often, or at intervals not exceeding thirty-one days, that contains advertisements, exclusively or principally.

Definition — Mode of expression.

298. (1) A defamatory libel is matter published, without lawful justification or excuse, that is likely to injure the reputation of any person by exposing him to hatred, contempt or ridicule, or that is designed to insult the person of or concerning whom it is published.

(2) A defamatory libel may be expressed directly or by insinuation or irony

(*a*) in words legibly marked upon any substance, or

(*b*) by any object signifying a defamatory libel otherwise than by words.

Publishing.

299. A person publishes a libel when he

(*a*) exhibits it in public,

(*b*) causes it to be read or seen, or

(*c*) shows or delivers it, or causes it to be shown or delivered, with intent that it should be read or seen by the person whom it defames or by any other person.

Punishment of libel known to be false.

300. Every one who publishes a defamatory libel that he knows is false is guilty of an indictable offence and liable to imprisonment for a term not exceeding five years.

Punishment for defamatory libel.

301. Every one who publishes a defamatory libel is guilty of an indictable offence and liable to imprisonment for a term not exceeding two years.

Extortion by libel — Idem — Punishment.

302. (1) Every one commits an offence who, with intent

(*a*) to extort money from any person, or

(*b*) to induce a person to confer on or procure for another person an appointment or office of profit or trust,

publishes or threatens to publish or offers to abstain from publishing or to prevent the publication of a defamatory libel.

(2) Every one commits an offence who, as the result of the refusal of any person to permit money to be extorted or to confer or procure an appointment or office of profit or trust, publishes or threatens to publish a defamatory libel.

(3) Every one who commits an offence under this section is guilty of an

indictable offence and liable to imprisonment for a term not exceeding five years.

Proprietor of newspaper presumed responsible — General authority to manager when negligence — Selling newspapers.

303. (1) The proprietor of a newspaper shall be deemed to publish defamatory matter that is inserted and published therein, unless he proves that the defamatory matter was inserted in the newspaper without his knowledge and without negligence on his part.

(2) Where the proprietor of a newspaper gives to a person general authority to manage or conduct the newspaper as editor or otherwise, the insertion by that person of defamatory matter in the newspaper shall, for the purposes of subsection (1), be deemed not to be negligence on the part of the proprietor unless it is proved that

(*a*) he intended the general authority to include authority to insert defamatory matter in the newspaper; or

(*b*) he continued to confer general authority after he knew that it had been exercised by the insertion of defamatory matter in the newspaper.

(3) No person shall be deemed to publish a defamatory libel by reason only that he sells a number or part of a newspaper that contains a defamatory libel, unless he knows that the number or part contains defamatory matter or that defamatory matter is habitually contained in the newspaper.

Selling book containing defamatory libel — Sale by servant.

304. (1) No person shall be deemed to publish a defamatory libel by reason only that he sells a book, magazine, pamphlet or other thing, other than a newspaper that contains defamatory matter if, at the time of the sale, he does not know that it contains the defamatory matter.

(2) Where a servant, in the course of his employment, sells a book, magazine, pamphlet or other thing, other than a newspaper, the employer shall be deemed not to publish any defamatory matter contained therein unless it is proved that the employer authorized the sale knowing that

(*a*) defamatory matter was contained therein; or

(*b*) defamatory matter was habitually contained therein, in the case of a periodical.

Publishing proceedings of courts of justice.

305. No person shall be deemed to publish a defamatory libel by reason only that he publishes defamatory matter

(*a*) in a proceeding held before or under the authority of a court exercising judicial authority; or

(*b*) in an inquiry made under the authority of an Act or by order of Her Majesty, or under the authority of a public department or a department of the government of a province.

Parliamentary papers.

306. No person shall be deemed to publish a defamatory libel by reason only that he

(*a*) publishes to the Senate or House of Commons or to a legislature of a province defamatory matter contained in a petition to the Senate or House of Commons or to the legislature of a province, as the case may be;

(*b*) publishes by order or under the authority of the Senate or House of Commons or of the legislature of a province a paper containing defamatory matter; or

(*c*) publishes, in good faith and without ill-will to the person defamed, an extract from or abstract of a petition or paper mentioned in paragraph (*a*) or (*b*).

Fair reports of parliamentary or judicial proceedings — Divorce proceedings an exception.

307. (1) No person shall be deemed to publish a defamatory libel by reason only that he publishes in good faith, for the information of the public, a fair report of the proceedings of the Senate or House of Commons or the legislature of a province, or a committee thereof, or of the public proceedings before a court exercising judicial authority, or publishes, in good faith, any fair comment on any such proceedings.

(2) This section does not apply to a person who publishes a report of evidence taken or offered in any proceeding before the Senate or House of Commons or any committee thereof, on a petition or bill relating to any matter of marriage or divorce, if the report is published without authority from or leave of the House in which the proceeding is held or is contrary to any rule, order or practice of that House.

Fair report of public meeting.

308. No person shall be deemed to publish a defamatory libel by reason only that he publishes in good faith, in a newspaper, a fair report of the proceedings of any public meeting if

(*a*) the meeting is lawfully convened for a lawful purpose and is open to the public;

(*b*) the report is fair and accurate;

(*c*) the publication of the matter complained of is for the public benefit; and

(*d*) he does not refuse to publish in a conspicuous place in the newspaper a reasonable explanation or contradiction by the person defamed in respect of the defamatory matter.

Public benefit.

309. No person shall be deemed to publish a defamatory libel by reason only that he publishes defamatory matter that, on reasonable grounds, he believes is true, and that is relevant to any subject of public interest, the public discussion of which is for the public benefit.

Fair comment on public person or work of art.

310. No person shall be deemed to publish a defamatory libel by reason only that he publishes fair comments

(*a*) upon the public conduct of a person who takes part in public affairs; or

(*b*) upon a published book or other literary production, or on any composition or work of art or performance publicly exhibited, or on any other communicaition made to the public on any subject, if the comments are confined to criticism thereof.

When truth a defence.

311. No person shall be deemed to publish a defamatory libel where he proves that the publication of the defamatory matter in the manner in which it was published was for the public benefit at the time when it was published and that the matter itself was true.

Publication invited or necessary.

312. No person shall be deemed to publish a defamatory libel by reason only that he publishes defamatory matter

(*a*) on the invitation or challenge of the person in respect of whom it is published, or

(*b*) that it is necessary to publish in order to refute defamatory matter published in respect of him by another person,

if he believes that the defamatory matter is true and it is relevant to the invitation, challenge or necessary refutation, as the case may be, and does not in any respect exceed what is reasonably sufficient in the circumstances.

Answer to inquiries.

313. No person shall be deemed to publish a defamatory libel by reason only that he publishes, in answer to inquiries made to him, defamatory matter relating to a subject-matter in respect of which the person by whom or on whose behalf the inquiries are made has an interest in knowing the truth or who, on reasonable grounds, the person who publishes the defamatory matter believes has such an interest, if

(*a*) the matter is published, in good faith, for the purpose of giving information in answer to the inquiries;

(*b*) the person who publishes the defamatory matter believes that it is true;

(*c*) the defamatory matter is relevant to the inquiries; and

(*d*) the defamatory matter does not in any respect exceed what is reasonably sufficient in the circumstances.

Giving information to person interested.

314. No person shall be deemed to publish a defamatory libel by reason only that he publishes to another person defamatory matter for the purpose of giving information to that person with respect to a subject-matter in which the person to whom the information is given has, or is believed on reasonable grounds by the person who gives it to have, an interest in knowing the truth with respect to that subject-matter if

(*a*) the conduct of the person who gives the information is reasonable in the circumstances;

(*b*) the defamatory matter is relevant to the subject-matter; and

(*c*) the defamatory matter is true, or if it is not true, is made without ill-will toward the person who is defamed and is made in the belief, on reasonable grounds, that it is true.

Publication in good faith for redress of wrong.

315. No person shall be deemed to publish a defamatory libel by reason only that he publishes defamatory matter in good faith for the purpose of seeking remedy or redress for a private or public wrong or grievance from a person who has, or who on reasonable grounds he believes has, the right or is under an obligation to remedy or redress the wrong or grievance, if

(*a*) he believes that the defamatory matter is true;

(*b*) the defamatory matter is relevant to the remedy or redress that is sought; and

(*c*) the defamatory matter does not in any respect exceed what is reasonably sufficient in the circumstances.

Proving publication by order of legislature — Directing verdict — Certificate of order.

316. (1) An accused who is alleged to have published a defamatory libel may, at any stage of the proceedings, adduce evidence to prove that the matter that is alleged to be defamatory was contained in a paper published by order or under the authority of the Senate or House of Commons or the legislature of a province.

(2) Where at any stage in proceedings referred to in subsection (1) the court, judge, justice or provincial court judge is satisfied that the matter alleged to be defamatory was contained in a paper published by order or under the authority of the Senate or House of Commons or the legislature of a province, he shall direct a verdict of not guilty to be entered and shall discharge the accused.

(3) For the purposes of this section, a certificate under the hand of the Speaker or clerk of the Senate or House of Commons or the legislature of a province to the effect that the matter that is alleged to be defamatory was contained in a paper published by order or under the authority of the Senate,

House of Commons or the legislature of a province, as the case may be, is conclusive evidence thereof. R.S. 1985, c. 27 (1st Supp.), s. 203.

Verdicts

Verdicts in cases of defamatory libel.

317. Where, on the trial of an indictment for publishing a defamatory libel, a plea of not guilty is pleaded, the jury that is sworn to try the issue may give a general verdict of guilty or not guilty on the whole matter put in issue on the indictment, and shall not be required or directed by the judge to find the defendant guilty merely on proof of publication by the defendant of the alleged defamatory libel, and of the sense ascribed thereto in the indictment, but the judge may, in his discretion, give a direction or opinion to the jury on the matter in issue as in other criminal proceedings, and the jury may, on the issue, find a special verdict.

Hate Propaganda

Advocating genocide — Definition of "genocide" — Consent — Definition of "identifiable group".

318. (1) Every one who advocates or promotes genocide is guilty of an indictable offence and liable to imprisonment for a term not exceeding five years.

(2) In this section "genocide" means any of the following acts committed with intent to destroy in whole or in part any identifiable group, namely,

(*a*) killing members of the group; or

(*b*) deliberately inflicting on the group conditions of life calculated to bring about its physical destruction.

(3) No proceeding for an offence under this section shall be instituted without the consent of the Attorney General.

(4) In this section "identifiable group" means any section of the public distinguished by colour, race, religion or ethnic origin.

Public incitement of hatred — Wilful promotion of hatred — Defences — Forfeiture — Exemption from seizure of communication facilities — Consent — Definitions — "Communicating" — "Identifiable group" — "Public place" — Statements.

319. (1) Every one who, by communicating statements in any public place, incites hatred against any identifiable group where such incitement is likely to lead to a breach of the peace is guilty of

(*a*) an indictable offence and is liable to imprisonment for a term not exceeding two years; or

(*b*) an offence punishable on summary conviction.

(2) Every one who, by communicating statements, other than in private conversation, wilfully promotes hatred against any identifiable group is guilty of

(*a*) an indictable offence and is liable to imprisonment for a term not exceeding two years; or

(*b*) an offence punishable on summary conviction.

(3) No person shall be convicted of an offence under subsection (2)

(*a*) if he establishes that the statements communicated were true;

(*b*) if, in good faith, he expressed or attempted to establish by argument an opinion upon a religious subject;

(*c*) if the statements were relevant to any subject of public interest, the discussion of which was for the public benefit, and if on reasonable grounds he believed them to be true; or

(*d*) if, in good faith, he intended to point out, for the purpose of removal, matters producing or tending to produce feelings of hatred towards an identifiable group in Canada.

(4) Where a person is convicted of an offence under section 318 or subsection (1) or (2) of this section, anything by means of or in relation to which the offence was committed, on such conviction, may, in addition to any other punishment imposed, be ordered by the presiding provincial court judge or judge to be forfeited to Her Majesty in right of the province in which that person is convicted, for disposal as the Attorney General may direct.

(5) Subsections 199(6) and (7) apply with such modifications as the circumstances require to section 318 or subsection (1) or (2) of this section.

(6) No proceeding for an offence under subsection (2) shall be instituted without the consent of the Attorney General.

(7) In this section,

"communicating" includes communicating by telephone, broadcasting or other audible or visible means;

"identifiable group" has the same meaning as in section 318;

"public place" includes any place to which the public have access as of right or by invitation, express or implied;

"statements" includes words spoken or written or recorded electronically or electro-magnetically or otherwise, and gestures, signs or other visible representations.

Warrant of seizure — Summons to occupier — Owner and author may appear — Order of forfeiture — Disposal of matter — Appeal — Consent — Definitions — "Court" — "Genocide" — "Hate propaganda" — "Judge".

320. (1) A judge who is satisfied by information on oath that there are reasonable grounds for believing that any publication, copies of which are kept for sale or distribution in premises within the jurisdiction of the court, is hate propaganda shall issue a warrant under his hand authorizing seizure of the copies.

(2) Within seven days of the issue of a warrant under subsection (1), the judge shall issue a summons to the occupier of the premises requiring him to appear before the court and show cause why the matter seized should not be forfeited to Her Majesty.

(3) The owner and the author of the matter seized under subsection (1) and alleged to be hate propaganda may appear and be represented in the proceedings in order to oppose the making of an order for the forfeiture of the matter.

(4) If the court is satisfied that the publication referred to in subsection (1) is hate propaganda, it shall make an order declaring the matter forfeited to Her Majesty in right of the province in which the proceedings take place, for disposal as the Attorney General may direct.

(5) If the court is not satisfied that the publication referred to in subsection (1) is hate propaganda, it shall order that the matter be restored to the person from whom it was seized forthwith after the time for final appeal has expired.

(6) An appeal lies from an order made under subsection (4) or (5) by any person who appeared in the proceedings

(*a*) on any ground of appeal that involves a question of law alone,

(*b*) on any ground of appeal that involves a question of fact alone, or

(*c*) on any ground of appeal that involves a question of mixed law and fact,

as if it were an appeal against conviction or against a judgment or verdict of acquittal, as the case may be, on a question of law alone under Part XXI, and sections 673 to 696 apply with such modifications as the circumstances require.

(7) No proceeding under this section shall be instituted without the consent of the Attorney General.

(8) In this section

"court" means

(*a*) in the Province of Quebec, the Court of Quebec;

(*a*.1) in the Province of Ontario, the Court (General Division),

(*b*) in the Provinces of New Brunswick, Manitoba, Saskatchewan and Alberta, the Court of Queen's Bench;

(*c*) in the Provinces of Prince Edward Island and Newfoundland, the Supreme Court, Trial Division;

(*c*.1) in the Province of British Columbia, the Yukon Territory and the Northwest Territories, the Supreme Court, or

(*d*) the Province of Nova Scotia, a county or district court;

"genocide" has the same meaning as it has in section 318;

"hate propaganda" means any writing, sign or visible representation that advocates or promotes genocide or the communication of which by any person would constitute an offence under section 319;

"judge" means a judge of a court. R.S. 1985, c. 27 (2d Supp.), Sched., item 6; c. 40 (4th Supp.), s. 2; 1990, c. 16, s. 4; 1990, c. 17, s. 11(1), (2); 1991, c. 1, s. 58(1), Sch. I, item 6.

PART IX

OFFENCES AGAINST RIGHTS OF PROPERTY

Interpretation

Definitions — "Break" — "Credit card" — "Document" — "Exchequer bill" — "Exchequer bill paper" — "False document" — "Revenue paper".

321. In this Part,

"break" means

(*a*) to break any part, internal or external, or

(*b*) to open any thing that is used or intended to be used to close or to cover an internal or external opening;

"credit card" means any card, plate, coupon book or other device issued or otherwise distributed for the purpose of being used

(*a*) on presentation to obtain, on credit, money, goods, services or any other thing of value, or

(*b*) in an automated teller machine, a remote service unit or a similar automated banking device to obtain any of the services offered through the machine, unit or device;

"document" means any paper, parchment or other material on which is recorded or marked anything that is capable of being read or understood by a person, computer system or other device, and includes a credit card, but does not include trade marks on articles of commerce or inscriptions on stone or metal or other like material;

"exchequer bill" means a bank note, bond, note, debenture or security that is issued or guaranteed by Her Majesty under the authority of Parliament or the legislature of a province;

"exchequer bill paper" means paper that is used to manufacture exchequer bills;

"false document" means a document

(*a*) the whole or a material part of which purports to be made by or on behalf of a person

(i) who did not make it or authorize it to be made, or

(ii) who did not in fact exist,

(*b*) that is made by or on behalf of the person who purports to make it but is false in some material particular,

(*c*) that is made in the name of an existing person, by him or under his authority, with a fraudulent intention that it should pass as being made by a person, real or fictitious, other than the person who makes it or under whose authority it is made;

"revenue paper" means paper that is used to make stamps, licences or permits or for any purpose connected with the public revenue. R.S. 1985, c. 27 (1st Supp.), s. 42.

Theft

Theft — Time when theft completed — Secrecy — Purpose of taking — Wild living creature.

322. (1) Every one commits theft who fraudulently and without colour of right takes, or fraudulently and without colour of right converts to his use or to the use of another person, anything, whether animate or inanimate, with intent,

(*a*) to deprive, temporarily or absolutely, the owner of it, or a person who has a special property or interest in it, of the thing or of his property or interest in it;

(*b*) to pledge it or deposit it as security;

(*c*) to part with it under a condition with respect to its return that the person who parts with it may be unable to perform; or

(*d*) to deal with it in such a manner that it cannot be restored in the condition in which it was at the time it was taken or converted.

(2) A person commits theft when, with intent to steal anything, he moves it or causes it to move or to be moved, or begins to cause it to become movable.

(3) A taking or conversion of anything may be fraudulent notwithstanding that it is effected without secrecy or attempt at concealment.

(4) For the purposes of this Act, the question whether anything that is converted is taken for the purpose of conversion, or whether it is, at the time it is converted, in the lawful possession of the person who converts it is not material.

(5) For the purposes of this section, a person who has a wild living creature in captivity shall be deemed to have a special property or interest in it while it is in captivity and after it has escaped from captivity.

Oysters — Oyster bed.

323. (1) Where oysters and oyster brood are in oyster beds, layings or fisheries that are the property of any person and are sufficiently marked out or known as the property of that person, that person shall be deemed to have a special property or interest in them.

(2) An indictment is sufficient if it describes an oyster bed, laying or fishery by name or in some other way, without stating that it is situated in a particular territorial division.

Theft by bailee of things under seizure.

324. Every one who is a bailee of anything that is under lawful seizure by a peace officer or public officer in the execution of the duties of his office, and who is obliged by law or agreement to produce and deliver it to that officer or to another person entitled thereto at a certain time and place, or on demand, steals it if he does not produce and deliver it in accordance with his obligation, but he does not steal it if his failure to produce and deliver it is not the result of a wilful act or omission by him.

Agent pledging goods, when not theft.

325. A factor or agent does not commit theft by pledging or giving a lien on goods or documents of title to goods that are entrusted to him for the purpose of sale or for any other purpose, if the pledge or lien is for an amount that does not exceed the sum of

(*a*) the amount due to him from his principal at the time the goods or documents are pledged or the lien is given; and

(*b*) the amount of any bill of exchange that he has accepted for or on account of his principal.

Theft of telecommunication service — "Telecommunication" defined.

326. (1) Every one commits theft who fraudulently, maliciously, or without colour of right,

(*a*) abstracts, consumes or uses electricity or gas or causes it to be wasted or diverted; or

(*b*) uses any telecommunication facility or obtains any telecommunication service.

(2) In this section and section 327, "telecommunication" means any transmission, emission or reception of signs, signals, writing, images or sounds or intelligence of any nature by wire, radio, visual, or other electro-magnetic system.

Possession of device to obtain telecommunication facility or service — Forfeiture — Limitation.

327. (1) Every one who, without lawful excuse, the proof of which lies on him, manufactures, possesses, sells or offers for sale or distributes any instrument or device or any component thereof, the design of which renders it primarily useful for obtaining the use of any telecommunication facility or service, under circumstances that give rise to a reasonable inference that the device has been used or is or was intended to be used to obtain the use of any telecommunication facility or service without payment of a lawful charge therefor, is guilty of an indictable offence and liable to imprisonment for a term not exceeding two years.

(2) Where a person is convicted of an offence under subsection (1) or paragraph 326(1)(*b*), any instrument or device in relation to which the offence was committed or the possession of which constituted the offence, upon such conviction, in addition to any punishment that is imposed, may be ordered forfeited to Her Majesty, whereupon it may be disposed of as the Attorney General directs.

(3) No order for forfeiture shall be made under subsection (2) in respect of telephone, telegraph or other communication facilities or equipment owned by a person engaged in providing telephone, telegraph or other communication service to the public or forming part of the telephone, telegraph or other communication service or system of such a person by means of which an offence under subsection (1) has been committed if such person was not a party to the offence.

Theft by or from person having special property or interest.

328. A person may be convicted of theft notwithstanding that anything that is alleged to have been stolen was stolen

(*a*) by the owner of it from a person who has a special property or interest in it;

(*b*) by a person who has a special property or interest in it from the owner of it;

(*c*) by a lessee of it from his reversioner;

(*d*) by one of several joint owners, tenants in common or partners of or in it from the other persons who have an interest in it; or

(*e*) by the directors, officers or members of a company, body corporate, unincorporated body or of a society associated together for a lawful purpose from the company, body corporate, unincorporated body or society, as the case may be.

Husband or wife — Theft by spouse while living apart — Assisting or receiving.

329. (1) Subject to subsection (2), no husband or wife, during cohabitation, commits theft of anything that is by law the property of the other.

(2) A husband or wife commits theft who, intending to desert or on deserting the other or while living apart from the other, fraudulently takes or converts anything that is by law the property of the other in a manner that, if it were done by another person, would be theft.

(3) Every one commits theft who, during cohabitation of a husband and wife, knowingly,

(*a*) assists either of them in dealing with anything that is by law the property of the other in a manner that would be theft if they were not married; or

(*b*) receives from either of them anything that is by law the property of the other and has been obtained from the other by dealing with it in a manner that would be theft if they were not married.

Theft by person required to account — Effect of entry in account.

330. (1) Every one commits theft who, having received anything from any person on terms that require him to account for or pay it or the proceeds of it or a part of the proceeds to that person or another person, fraudulently fails to account for or pay it or the proceeds of it or the part of the proceeds of it accordingly.

(2) Where subsection (1) otherwise applies, but one of the terms is that the thing received or the proceeds or part of the proceeds of it shall be an item in a debtor and creditor account between the person who receives the thing and the person to whom he is to account for or to pay it, and that the latter shall rely only on the liability of the other as his debtor in respect thereof, a proper entry in that account of the thing received or the proceeds or part of the proceeds of it, as the case may be, is a sufficient accounting therefor, and no fraudulent conversion of the thing or the proceeds or part of the proceeds of it thereby accounted for shall be deemed to have taken place.

Theft by person holding power of attorney.

331. Every one commits theft who, being entrusted, whether solely or jointly with another person, with a power of attorney for the sale, mortgage, pledge or other disposition of real or personal property, fraudulently sells, mortgages, pledges or otherwise disposes of the property or any part of it, or fraudulently converts the proceeds of a sale, mortgage, pledge or other disposition of the property, or any part of the proceeds, to a purpose other than that for which he was entrusted by the power of attorney.

Misappropriation of money held under direction — Effect of entry in account.

332. (1) Every one commits theft who, having received, either solely or jointly with another person, money or valuable security or a power of attorney for the sale of real or personal property, with a direction that the money or a part of it, or the proceeds or a part of the proceeds of the security or the property shall be applied to a purpose or paid to a person specified in the direction, fraudulently and contrary to the direction applies to any other purpose or pays to any other person the money or proceeds or any part of it.

(2) This section does not apply where a person who receives anything mentioned in subsection (1) and the person from whom he receives it deal with each other on such terms that all money paid to the former would, in the absence of any such direction, be properly treated as an item in a debtor and creditor account between them, unless the direction is in writing.

Taking ore for scientific purpose.

333. No person commits theft by reason only that he takes, for the purpose of exploration or scientific investigation, a specimen of ore or mineral from land that is not enclosed and is not occupied or worked as a mine, quarry or digging.

Punishment for theft.

334. Except where otherwise provided by law, every one who commits theft

(*a*) is guilty of an indictable offence and liable to imprisonment for a term not exceeding ten years, where the property stolen is a testamentary instrument or where the value of what is stolen exceeds one thousand dollars;

(*b*) is guilty

(i) of an indictable offence and liable to imprisonment for a term not exceeding two years, or

(ii) of an offence punishable on summary conviction,

where the value of what is stolen does not exceed one thousand dollars. R.S. 1985, c. 27 (1st Supp.), s. 43.

Offences Resembling Theft

Taking motor vehicle or vessel without consent — Definition of "vessel".

335. (1) Every one who, without the consent of the owner, takes a motor vehicle or vessel with intent to drive, use, navigate or operate it or cause it to be driven, used, navigated or operated is guilty of an offence punishable on summary conviction.

(2) For the purposes of subsection (1), "vessel" has the meaning assigned by section 214. R.S. 1985, c. 1 (4th Supp.), s. 15.

Criminal breach of trust.

336. Every one who, being a trustee of anything for the use or benefit, whether in whole or in part, of another person, or for a public or charitable purpose, converts, with intent to defraud and in contravention of his trust, that thing or any part of it to a use that is not authorized by the trust is guilty of an indictable offence and liable to imprisonment for a term not exceeding fourteen years.

Public servant refusing to deliver property.

337. Every one who, being or having been employed in the service of Her Majesty in right of Canada or in right of a province, or in the service of a municipality, and entrusted by virtue of that employment with the receipt, custody, management or control of anything, refuses or fails to deliver it to a person who is authorized to demand it and does demand it is guilty of an indictable offence and liable to imprisonment for a term not exceeding fourteen years.

Fraudulently taking cattle or defacing brand — Punishment for theft of cattle — Evidence of property in cattle — Presumption from possession.

338. (1) Every one who, without the consent of the owner,

(*a*) fraudulently takes, holds, keeps in his possession, conceals, receives, appropriates, purchases or sells cattle that are found astray, or

(*b*) fraudulently, in whole or in part,

(i) obliterates, alters or defaces a brand or mark on cattle, or

(ii) makes a false or counterfeit brand or mark on cattle,

is guilty of an indictable offence and liable to imprisonment for a term not exceeding five years.

(2) Every one who commits theft of cattle is guilty of an indictable offence and liable to imprisonment for a term not exceeding ten years.

(3) In any proceedings under this Act, evidence that cattle are marked with a brand or mark that is recorded or registered in accordance with any Act is, in the absence of any evidence to the contrary, proof that the cattle are owned by the registered owner of that brand or mark.

(4) Where an accused is charged with an offence under subsection (1) or (2), the burden of proving that the cattle came lawfully into the possession of the accused or his employee or into the possession of another person on behalf of the accused is on the accused, if the accused is not the registered owner of the brand or mark with which the cattle are marked, unless it appears that possession of the cattle by an employee of the accused or by another person on behalf of the accused was without the knowledge and authority, sanction or approval of the accused.

Taking possession etc., of drift timber — Dealer in second-hand goods — Search for timber unlawfully detained — Evidence of property in timber — Presumption from possession — Definitions — "Coastal waters of Canada" — "Lumber" — "Lumbering equipment".

339. (1) Every one is guilty of an indictable offence and liable to imprisonment for a term not exceeding five years who, without the consent of the owner,

(*a*) fraudulently takes, holds, keeps in his possession, conceals, receives, appropriates, purchases or sells,

(*b*) removes, alters, obliterates or defaces a mark or number on, or

(*c*) refuses to deliver up to the owner or to the person in charge thereof on behalf of the owner or to a person authorized by the owner to receive it,

any lumber or lumbering equipment that is found adrift, cast ashore or lying on or embedded in the bed or bottom, or on the bank or beach of a river, stream or lake in Canada, or in the harbours or any of the coastal waters of Canada.

(2) Every one who, being a dealer in second-hand goods of any kind, trades or traffics in or has in his possession for sale or traffic any lumbering equipment that is marked with the mark, brand, registered timber mark, name or initials of a person, without the written consent of that person, is guilty of an offence punishable on summary conviction.

(3) A peace officer who suspects, on reasonable grounds, that any lumber owned by any person and bearing the registered timber mark of that person is kept or detained in or on any place without the knowledge or consent of that person, may enter into or on that place to ascertain whether or not it is detained there without the knowledge or consent of that person.

(4) Where any lumber or lumbering equipment is marked with a timber

mark or a boom chain brand registered under any Act, the mark or brand is, in proceedings under subsection (1), and, in the absence of any evidence to the contrary, proof that it is the property of the registered owner of the mark or brand.

(5) Where an accused or his servants or agents are in possession of lumber or lumbering equipment marked with the mark, brand, registered timber mark, name or initials of another person, the burden of proving that it came lawfully into his possession or into possession of his servants or agents is, in proceedings under subsection (1), on the accused.

(6) In this section

"coastal waters of Canada" includes all of Queen Charlotte Sound, all the Strait of Georgia and the Canadian waters of the Strait of Juan de Fuca;

"lumber" means timber, mast, spar, shingle bolt, sawlog or lumber of any description;

"lumbering equipment" includes a boom chain, chain, line and shackle.

Destroying documents of title.

340. Every one who, for a fraudulent purpose, destroys, cancels, conceals or obliterates

(*a*) a document of title to goods or lands,

(*b*) a valuable security or testamentary instrument, or

(*c*) a judicial or official document,

is guilty of an indictable offence and liable to imprisonment for a term not exceeding ten years.

Fraudulent concealment.

341. Every one who, for a fraudulent purpose, takes, obtains, removes or conceals anything is guilty of an indictable offence and liable to imprisonment for a term not exceeding two years.

Theft, forgery, etc., of credit card — Jurisdiction.

342. (1) Every one who

(*a*) steals a credit card,

(*b*) forges or falsifies a credit card,

(*c*) has in his possession, uses or deals in any other way with a credit card that he knows was obtained

(i) by the commission in Canada of an offence, or

(ii) by an act or omission anywhere that, if it had occurred in Canada, would have constituted an offence, or

(*d*) uses a credit card that he knows has been revoked or cancelled

is guilty of

(*e*) an indictable offence and is liable to imprisonment for a term not exceeding ten years, or (*f*) an offence punishable on summary conviction.

(2) An accused who is charged with an offence under subsection (1) may be tried and punished by any court having jurisdiction to try that offence in the place where the offence is alleged to have been committed or in the place where the accused is found, is arrested or is in custody, but where the place where the accused is found, is arrested or is in custody is outside the province in which the offence is alleged to have been committed, no proceedings in respect of that offence shall be commenced in that place without the consent of the Attorney General of that province. R.S. 1985, c. 27 (1st Supp.), s. 44.

(3) [Repealed R.S. 1985, c. 27 (1st Supp.), s. 44.]

Unauthorized use of computer — Definitions — "computer program" — "computer service" — "computer system" — "data" — "electro-magnetic, acoustic, mechanical or other device" — "function" — "intercept".

342.1 (1) Every one who, fraudulently and without color of right,

(*a*) obtains, directly or indirectly, any computer service,

(*b*) by means of an electro-magnetic, acoustic, mechanical or other device, intercepts or causes to be intercepted, directly or indirectly, any function of a computer system, or

(*c*) uses or causes to be used, directly or indirectly, a computer system with intent to commit an offence under paragraph (*a*) or (*b*) or an offence under section 430 in relation to data or a computer system

is guilty of an indictable offence and liable to imprisonment for a term not exceeding ten years, or is guilty of an offence punishable on summary conviction.

(2) In this section,

"computer program" means data representing instructions or statements that, when executed in a computer system, causes the computer system to perform a function;

"computer service" includes data processing and the storage or retrieval of data;

"computer system" means a device that, or a group of interconnected or related devices one or more of which,

(*a*) contains computer programs or other data, and

(*b*) pursuant to computer programs,

(i) performs logic and control, and

(ii) may perform any other function;

"data" means representations of information or of concepts that are being prepared or have been prepared in a form suitable for use in a computer system;

"electro-magnetic, acoustic, mechanical or other device" means any device or apparatus that is used or is capable of being used to intercept any function of a computer system, but does not include a hearing aid used to correct subnormal hearing of the user to not better than normal hearing;

"function" includes logic, control, arithmetic, deletion, storage and retrieval and communication or telecommunication to, from or within a computer system;

"intercept" includes listen to or record a function of a computer system, or acquire the substance, meaning or purport thereof. R.S. 1985, c. 27 (1st Supp.), s. 45.

Robbery and Extortion

Robbery.

343. Every one commits robbery who

(*a*) steals, and for the purpose of extorting whatever is stolen or to prevent or overcome resistance to the stealing, uses violence or threats of violence to a person or property;

(*b*) steals from any person and, at the time he steals or immediately before or immediately thereafter, wounds, beats, strikes or uses any personal violence to that person;

(*c*) assaults any person with intent to steal from him; or

(*d*) steals from any person while armed with an offensive weapon or imitation thereof.

Punishment for robbery.

344. Every one who commits robbery is guilty of an indictable offence and liable to imprisonment for life.

Stopping mail with intent.

345. Every one who stops a mail conveyance with intent to rob or search it is guilty of an indictable offence and liable to imprisonment for life.

Extortion — Punishment — Saving.

346. (1) Every one commits extortion who, without reasonable justification or excuse and with intent to obtain anything, by threats, accusations, menaces or violence induces or attempts to induce any person, whether or not he is the person threatened, accused or menaced or to whom violence is shown, to do anything or cause anything to be done.

(1.1) Every one who commits extortion is guilty of an indictable offence and liable to a maximum term of imprisonment for life.

(2) A threat to institute civil proceedings is not a threat for the purposes of this section. R.S. 1985, c. 27 (1st Supp.), s. 46.

Criminal Interest Rate

Criminal interest rate — Definitions — "credit advanced" — "criminal rate" — "insurance charge" — "interest" — "official fee" — "overdraft charge" — "required deposit balance" — Presumption — Proof of effective annual rate — Notice — Cross examination with leave — Consent required for proceedings — Application.

347. (1) Notwithstanding any Act of the Parliament of Canada, every one who

(*a*) enters into an agreement or arrangement to receive interest at a criminal rate, or

(*b*) receives a payment or partial payment of interest at a criminal rate,

is guilty of

(*c*) an indictable offence and is liable to imprisonment for a term not exceeding five years, or

(*d*) an offence punishable on summary conviction and is liable to a fine not exceeding twenty-five thousand dollars or to imprisonment for a term not exceeding six months or to both.

(2) In this section,

"credit advanced" means the aggregate of the money and the monetary value of any goods, services or benefits actually advanced or to be advanced under an agreement or arrangement minus the aggregate of any required deposit balance and any fee, fine, penalty, commission and other similar charge or expense directly or indirectly incurred under the original or any collateral agreement or arrangement;

"criminal rate" means an effective annual rate of interest calculated in accordance with generally accepted actuarial practices and principles that exceeds sixty per cent on the credit advanced under an agreement or arrangement;

"insurance charge" means the cost of insuring the risk assumed by the person who advances or is to advance credit under an agreement or arrangement, where the face amount of the insurance does not exceed the credit advanced;

"interest" means the aggregate of all charges and expenses, whether in the form of a fee, fine, penalty, commission or other similar charge or expense or in any other form, paid or payable for the advancing of credit under an agreement or arrangement, by or on behalf of the person to whom the credit is or is to be advanced, irrespective of the person to whom any such charges and expenses are or are to be paid or payable, but does not include any repayment of credit advanced or any insurance charge, official fee, overdraft charge, required deposit balance or, in the case of a mortgage transaction, any amount required to be paid on account of property taxes.

"official fee" means a fee required by law to be paid to any governmental authority in connection with perfecting any security under an agreement or arrangement for the advancing of credit;

"overdraft charge" means a charge not exceeding five dollars for the creation of or increase in an overdraft, imposed by a credit union or caisse populaire the membership of which is wholly or substantially comprised of natural persons or a deposit taking institution the deposits in which are insured, in whole or in part, by the Canada Deposit Insurance Corporation or guaranteed, in whole or in part, by the Quebec Deposit Insurance Board;

"required deposit balance" means a fixed or an ascertainable amount of the money actually advanced or to be advanced under an agreement or arrangement that is required, as a condition of the agreement or arrangement, to be deposited or invested by or on behalf of the person to whom the advance is or is to be made and that may be available, in the event of his defaulting in any payment, to or for the benefit of the person who advances or is to advance the money.

(3) Where a person receives a payment or partial payment of interest at a criminal rate, he shall, in the absence of evidence to the contrary, be deemed to have knowledge of the nature of the payment and that it was received at a criminal rate.

(4) In any proceedings under this section, a certificate of a Fellow of the Canadian Institute of Actuaries stating that he has calculated the effective annual rate of interest on any credit advanced under an agreement or arrangement and setting out the calculations and the information on which they are based is, in the absence of evidence to the contrary, proof of the effective annual rate without proof of the signature or official character of the person appearing to have signed the certificate.

(5) A certificate referred to in subsection (4) shall not be received in evidence unless the party intending to produce it has given to the accused or defendant reasonable notice of that intention together with a copy of the certificate.

(6) An accused or a defendant against whom a certificate referred to in subsection (4) is produced may, with leave of the court, require the attendance of the actuary for the purposes of cross-examination.

(7) No proceedings shall be commenced under this section without the consent of the Attorney General.

(8) This section does not apply to any transaction to which the *Tax Rebate Discounting Act* applies.

Breaking and Entering

Breaking and entering with intent, committing offence or breaking out — Presumptions — Definition of "place".

348. (1) Every one who

(*a*) breaks and enters a place with intent to commit an indictable offence therein,

(*b*) breaks and enters a place and commits an indictable offence therein, or

(*c*) breaks out of a place after

(i) committing an indictable offence therein, or

(ii) entering the place with intent to commit an indictable offence therein,

is guilty of an indictable offence and liable

(*d*) to imprisonment for life, if the offence is committed in relation to a dwelling-house, or

(*e*) to imprisonment for a term not exceeding fourteen years, if the offence is committed in relation to a place other than a dwelling-house.

(2) For the purposes of proceedings under this section, evidence that an accused

(*a*) broke and entered a place or attempted to break and enter a place is, in the absence of any evidence to the contrary, proof that he broke and entered the place or attempted to do so, as the case may be, with intent to commit an indictable offence therein; or

(*b*) broke out of a place is, in the absence of any evidence to the contrary, proof that he broke out after

(i) committing an indictable offence therein, or

(ii) entering with intent to commit an indictable offence therein.

(3) For the purposes of this section, and section 351, "place" means

(*a*) a dwelling-house;

(*b*) a building or structure or any part thereof, other than a dwelling-house;

(*c*) a railway vehicle, a vessel, an aircraft or a trailer; or

(*d*) a pen or an enclosure in which fur-bearing animals are kept in captivity for breeding or commercial purposes. R.S. 1985, c. 27 (1st Supp.), s. 47.

Being unlawfully in dwelling-house — Presumption.

349. (1) Every one who without lawful excuse, the proof of which lies on him, enters or is in a dwelling-house with intent to commit an indictable offence therein is guilty of an indictable offence and liable to imprisonment for a term not exceeding ten years.

(2) For the purposes of proceedings under this section, evidence that an accused, without lawful excuse, entered or was in a dwelling-house is, in the absence of any evidence to the contrary, proof that he entered or was in the dwelling-house with intent to commit an indictable offence therein.

Entrance.

350. For the purposes of sections 348 and 349,

(*a*) a person enters as soon as any part of his body or any part of an instrument that he uses is within any thing that is being entered; and

(*b*) a person shall be deemed to have broken and entered if

(i) he obtained entrance by a threat or artifice or by collusion with a person within, or

(ii) he entered without lawful justification or excuse, the proof of which lies on him, by a permanent or temporary opening.

Possession of break-in instrument — Disguise with intent.

351. (1) Every one who, without lawful excuse, the proof of which lies on him, has in his possession any instrument suitable for the purpose of breaking into any place, motor vehicle, vault or safe under circumstances that give rise to a reasonable inference that the instrument has been used or is or was intended to be used for any such purpose, is guilty of an indictable offence and liable to imprisonment for a term not exceeding ten years.

(2) Every one who, with intent to commit an indictable offence, has his face masked or coloured or is otherwise disguised is guilty of an indictable offence and liable to imprisonment for a term not exceeding ten years. R.S. 1985, c. 27 (1st Supp.), s. 48.

Possession of instruments for breaking into coin-operated or currency exchange devices.

352. Every one who, without lawful excuse, the proof of which lies on him, has in his possession any instrument suitable for breaking into a coin-operated device or a currency exchange device, under circumstances that give rise to a reasonable inference that the instrument has been used or is or was intended to be used for breaking into a coin-operated device or a currency exchange device, is guilty of an indictable offence and liable to imprisonment for a term not exceeding two years.

Selling, etc., automobile master key — Terms and conditions of licence — Record to be kept — Failure to comply with subsection (3) — "Automobile master key".

353. (1) Every one who

(*a*) sells, offers for sale or advertises in a province an automobile master key otherwise than under the authority of a licence issued by the Attorney General of that province, or

(*b*) purchases or has in his possession in a province an automobile master key otherwise than under the authority of a licence issued by the Attorney General of that province,

is guilty of an indictable offence and liable to imprisonment for a term not exceeding two years.

(2) A licence issued by the Attorney General of a province as described in paragraph (1)(*a*) or (*b*) may contain such terms and conditions relating to the sale, offering for sale, advertising, purchasing or having in possession of an automobile master key as the Attorney General of that province may prescribe.

(3) Every one who sells an automobile master key

(*a*) shall keep a record of the transaction showing the name and address of the purchaser and particulars of the licence issued to the purchaser as described in paragraph (1)(*b*); and

(*b*) shall produce the record for inspection at the request of a peace officer.

(4) Every one who fails to comply with subsection (3) is guilty of an offence punishable on summary conviction.

(5) For the purposes of this section, "automobile master key" includes a key, pick, rocker key or other instrument designed or adapted to operate the ignition or other switches or locks of a series of motor vehicles.

Having in Possession

Possession of property obtained by crime — Obliterated vehicle identification number — "Vehicle identification number" defined.

354. (1) Every one commits an offence who has in his possession any property or thing or any proceeds of any property or thing knowing that all or part of the property or thing or of the proceeds was obtained by or derived directly or indirectly from

(*a*) the commission in Canada of an offence punishable by indictment; or

(*b*) an act or omission anywhere that, if it had occurred in Canada, would have constituted an offence punishable by indictment.

(2) In proceedings in respect of an offence under subsection (1), evidence that a person has in his possession a motor vehicle the vehicle identification number of which has been wholly or partially removed or obliterated or a part of a motor vehicle being a part bearing a vehicle identification number that has been wholly or partially removed or obliterated is, in the absence of any evidence to the contrary, proof that the motor vehicle or part, as the case may be, was obtained, and that such person had the motor vehicle or part, as the case may be, in his possession knowing that it was obtained,

(*a*) by the commission in Canada of an offence punishable by indictment; or

(*b*) by an act or omission anywhere that, if it had occurred in Canada, would have constituted an offence punishable by indictment.

(3) For the purposes of subsection (2), "vehicle identification number" means any number or other mark placed on a motor vehicle for the purpose of distinguishing the motor vehicle from other similar motor vehicles.

Punishment.

355. Every one who commits an offence under section 354

(*a*) is guilty of an indictable offence and is liable to imprisonment for a term not exceeding ten years, where the subject-matter of the offence is a testamentary instrument or the value of the subject-matter of the offence exceeds one thousand dollars; or

(*b*) is guilty

(i) of an indictable offence and is liable to imprisonment for a term not exceeding two years, or

(ii) of an offence punishable on summary conviction,

where the value of the subject-matter of the offence does not exceed one thousand dollars. R.S. 1985, c. 27 (1st Supp.), s. 49.

Theft from mail — Allegation of value not necessary.

356. (1) Every one who

(*a*) steals

(i) any thing sent by post, after it is deposited at a post office and before it is delivered,

(ii) a bag, sack or other container or covering in which mail is conveyed, whether or not it contains mail, or

(iii) a key suited to a lock adopted for use in the Canada Post Corporation, or

(*b*) has in his possession anything in respect of which he knows that an offence has been committed under paragraph (*a*),

is guilty of an indictable offence and liable to imprisonment for a term not exceeding ten years.

(2) In proceedings for an offence under this section it is not necessary to allege in the indictment or to prove on the trial that anything in respect of which the offence was committed had any value.

Bringing into Canada property obtained by crime

357. Every one who brings into or has in Canada anything that he has obtained outside Canada by an act that, if it had been committed in Canada, would have been the offence of theft or an offence under section 342 or 354, is guilty of an indictable offence and liable to a term of imprisonment not exceeding ten years. R.S. 1985, c. 27 (1st Supp.), s. 50.

Having in possession when complete.

358. For the purposes of sections 342 and 354 and paragraph 356(1)(*b*), the offence of having in possession is complete when a person has, alone or jointly with another person, possession of or control over anything mentioned in those sections or when he aids in concealing or disposing of it, as the case may be. R.S. 1985, c. 27 (1st Supp.), s. 50.

Evidence — Notice to accused.

359. (1) Where an accused is charged with an offence under section 342 or 354 or paragraph 356(1)(*b*), evidence is admissible at any stage of the proceedings to show that property other than the property that is the subject-matter of the proceedings (*a*) was found in the possession of the accused, and

(*b*) was stolen within twelve months before the proceedings were commenced,

and that evidence may be considered for the purpose of proving that the accused knew that the property that forms the subject-matter of the proceedings was stolen property.

(2) Subsection (1) does not apply unless

(*a*) at least three days notice in writing is given to the accused that in the proceedings it is intended to prove that property other than the property that is the subject-matter of the proceedings was found in his possession; and

(*b*) the notice sets out the nature or description of the property and describes the person from whom it is alleged to have been stolen. R.S. 1985, c. 27 (1st Supp.), s. 51.

Evidence of previous conviction — Notice to accused.

360. (1) Where an accused is charged with an offence under section 354 or paragraph 356(1)(*b*) and evidence is adduced that the subject-matter of the proceedings was found in his possession, evidence that the accused was, within five years before the proceedings were commenced, convicted of an offence involving theft or an offence under section 354 is admissible at any stage of the proceedings and may be taken into consideration for the purpose of proving that the accused knew that the property that forms the subject-matter of the proceedings was unlawfully obtained.

(2) Subsection (1) does not apply unless at least three days notice in writing is given to the accused that in the proceedings it is intended to prove the previous conviction.

False Pretences

False pretence — Exaggeration — Question of fact.

361. (1) A false pretence is a representation of a matter of fact either present or past, made by words or otherwise, that is known by the person who makes it to be false and that is made with a fraudulent intent to induce the person to whom it is made to act on it.

(2) Exaggerated commendation or depreciation of the quality of anything is not a false pretence unless it is carried to such an extent that it amounts to a fraudulent misrepresentation of fact.

(3) For the purposes of subsection (2), it is a question of fact whether commendation or depreciation amounts to a fraudulent misrepresentation of fact.

False pretence or false statement — Punishment — Idem — Presumption from cheque issued without funds — "Cheque".

362. (1) Every one commits an offence who

(*a*) by a false pretence, whether directly or through the medium of a contract obtained by a false pretence, obtains anything in respect of which the offence of theft may be committed or causes it to be delivered to another person;

(*b*) obtains credit by a false pretence or by fraud;

(*c*) knowingly makes or causes to be made, directly or indirectly, a false statement in writing with intent that it should be relied on, with respect to the financial condition or means or ability to pay of himself or any person, firm or corporation that he is interested in or that he acts for, for the purpose of procuring, in any form whatever, whether for his benefit or the benefit of that person, firm or corporation,

(i) the delivery of personal property,

(ii) the payment of money,

(iii) the making of a loan,

(iv) the grant or extension of credit,

(v) the discount of an account receivable, or

(vi) the making, accepting, discounting or endorsing of a bill of exchange, cheque, draft or promissory note; or

(*d*) knowing that a false statement in writing has been made with respect to the financial condition or means or ability to pay of himself or another person, firm or corporation that he is interested in or that he acts for, procures on the faith of that statement, whether for his benefit or for the benefit of that person, firm or corporation, anything mentioned in subparagraphs (*c*)(i) to (vi).

(2) Every one who commits an offence under paragraph (1)(*a*)

(*a*) is guilty of an indictable offence and liable to a term of imprisonment not exceeding ten years, where the property obtained is a testamentary instrument or where the value of what is obtained exceeds one thousand dollars; or

(*b*) is guilty

(i) of an indictable offence and is liable to imprisonment for a term not exceeding two years, or

(ii) of an offence punishable on summary conviction,

where the value of what is obtained does not exceed one thousand dollars.

(3) Every one who commits an offence under paragraph (1)(*b*), (*c*) or (*d*) is guilty of an indictable offence and liable to imprisonment for a term not exceeding ten years.

(4) Where, in proceedings under paragraph (1)(*a*), it is shown that anything was obtained by the accused by means of a cheque that, when presented for payment within a reasonable time, was dishonoured on the ground that no funds or insufficient funds were on deposit to the credit of the accused in the

bank or other institution on which the cheque was drawn, it shall be presumed to have been obtained by a false pretence, unless the court is satisfied by evidence that when the accused issued the cheque he believed on reasonable grounds that it would be honoured if presented for payment within a reasonable time after it was issued.

(5) In this section, "cheque" includes, in addition to its ordinary meaning, a bill of exchange drawn on any institution that makes it a business practice to honour bills of exchange or any particular kind thereof drawn on it by depositors. R.S. 1985, c. 27 (1st Supp.), s. 52.

Obtaining execution of valuable security by fraud.

363. Every one who, with intent to defraud or injure another person, by a false pretence causes or induces any person

(*a*) to execute, make, accept, endorse or destroy the whole or any part of a valuable security, or

(*b*) to write, impress or affix a name or seal on any paper or parchment in order that it may afterwards be made or converted into or used or dealt with as a valuable security,

is guilty of an indictable offence and liable to imprisonment for a term not exceeding five years.

Fraudulently obtaining food and lodging — Presumption — "Cheque".

364. (1) Every one who fraudulently obtains food, lodging or other accommodation at a hotel or an inn or at a lodging, boarding or eating house is guilty of an offence punishable on summary conviction.

(2) In proceedings under this section, evidence that an accused obtained food, lodging or other accommodation at a hotel or an inn or at a lodging, boarding or eating house, and did not pay for it and

(*a*) made a false or fictitious show or pretence of having baggage,

(*b*) had any false or pretended baggage,

(*c*) surreptitiously removed or attempted to remove his baggage or any material part of it,

(*d*) absconded or surreptitiously left the premises,

(*e*) knowingly made a false statement to obtain credit or time for payment, or

(*f*) offered a worthless cheque, draft or security in payment for his food, lodging or other accommodation,

is, in the absence of any evidence to the contrary, proof of fraud.

(3) In this section "cheque" includes, in addition to its ordinary meaning, a bill of exchange drawn on any institution that makes it a business practice to honour bills of exchange or any particular kind thereof drawn upon it by depositors.

Pretending to practise witchcraft, etc.

365. Every one who fraudulently

(*a*) pretends to exercise or to use any kind of witchcraft, sorcery, enchantment or conjuration,

(*b*) undertakes, for a consideration, to tell fortunes, or

(*c*) pretends from his skill in or knowledge of an occult or crafty science to discover where or in what manner anything that is supposed to have been stolen or lost may be found,

is guilty of an offence punishable on summary conviction.

Forgery and Offences Resembling Forgery

Forgery — Making false document — When forgery complete — Forgery complete though document incomplete.

366. (1) Every one commits forgery who makes a false document, knowing it to be false, with intent

(*a*) that it should in any way be used or acted upon as genuine, to the prejudice of any one whether within Canada or not, or

(*b*) that a person should be induced, by the belief that it is genuine, to do or to refrain from doing anything, whether within Canada or not.

(2) Making a false document includes

(*a*) altering a genuine document in any material part;

(*b*) making a material addition to a genuine document or adding to it a false date, attestation, seal or other thing that is material; or

(*c*) making a material alteration in a genuine document by erasure, obliteration, removal or in any other way.

(3) Forgery is complete as soon as a document is made with the knowledge and intent referred to in subsection (1), notwithstanding that the person who makes it does not intend that any particular person should use or act on it as genuine or be induced, by the belief that it is genuine, to do or refrain from doing anything.

(4) Forgery is complete notwithstanding that the false document is incomplete or does not purport to be a document that is binding in law, if it is such as to indicate that it was intended to be acted on as genuine.

Punishment for forgery — Corroboration.

367. (1) Every one who commits forgery is guilty of an indictable offence and liable to imprisonment for a term not exceeding fourteen years.

(2) No person shall be convicted of an offence under this section upon the evidence of only one witness unless the evidence of that witness is corroborated in a material particular by evidence that implicates the accused.

Uttering forged document — Wherever forged.

368. (1) Every one who, knowing that a document is forged,

(*a*) uses, deals with or acts upon it, or

(*b*) causes or attempts to cause any person to use, deal with or act upon it,

as if the document were genuine, is guilty of an indictable offence and liable to imprisonment for a term not exceeding fourteen years.

(2) For the purposes of proceedings under this section, the place where a document was forged is not material.

Exchequer bill paper, public seals, etc.

369. Every one who, without lawful authority or excuse, the proof of which lies on him,

(*a*) makes, uses or knowingly has in his possession

(i) any exchequer bill paper, revenue paper or paper that is used to make bank notes, or

(ii) any paper that is intended to resemble paper mentioned in subparagraph (i),

(*b*) makes, offers or disposes of or knowingly has in his possession any plate, die, machinery, instrument or other writing or material that is adapted and intended to be used to commit forgery, or

(*c*) makes, reproduces or uses a public seal of Canada or of a province, or the seal of a public body or authority in Canada, or of a court of law,

is guilty of an indictable offence and liable to imprisonment for a term not exceeding fourteen years.

Counterfeit proclamation, etc.

370. Every one who knowingly

(*a*) prints a proclamation, order, regulation or appointment, or notice thereof, and causes it falsely to purport to have been printed by the Queen's Printer for Canada, or the Queen's Printer for a province, or

(*b*) tenders in evidence a copy of a proclamation, order, regulation or appointment that falsely purports to have been printed by the Queen's Printer for Canada or the Queen's Printer for a province,

is guilty of an indictable offence and liable to imprisonment for a term not exceeding five years.

Telegram, etc., in false name.

371. Every one who, with intent to defraud, causes or procures a telegram, cablegram or radio message to be sent or delivered as being sent by the authority of another person, knowing that it is not sent by his authority and with intent that the message should be acted on as being sent by his authority, is guilty of an indictable offence and liable to imprisonment for a term not exceeding five years.

False messages — Indecent telephone calls — Harassing telephone calls.

372. (1) Every one who, with intent to injure or alarm any person, conveys or causes or procures to be conveyed by letter, telegram, telephone, cable, radio or otherwise information that he knows is false is guilty of an indictable offence and liable to imprisonment for a term not exceeding two years.

(2) Every one who, with intent to alarm or annoy any person, makes any indecent telephone call to that person is guilty of an offence punishable on summary conviction.

(3) Every one who, without lawful excuse and with intent to harass any person, makes or causes to be made repeated telephone calls to that person is guilty of an offence punishable on summary conviction.

373. [Repealed R.S. 1985, c. 27 (1st Supp.), s. 53.]

Drawing document without authority, etc.

374. Every one who

(*a*) with intent to defraud and without lawful authority makes, executes, draws, signs, accepts or endorses a document in the name or on the account of another person by procuration or otherwise, or

(*b*) makes use of or utters a document knowing that it has been made, executed, signed, accepted or endorsed with intent to defraud and without lawful authority, in the name or on the account of another person, by procuration or otherwise,

is guilty of an indictable offence and liable to imprisonment for a term not exceeding fourteen years.

Obtaining, etc., by instrument based on forged document.

375. Every one who demands, receives or obtains anything, or causes or procures anything to be delivered or paid to any person under, on or by virtue of any instrument issued under the authority of law, knowing that it is based on a forged document, is guilty of an indictable offence and liable to imprisonment for a term not exceeding fourteen years.

Counterfeiting stamp, etc. — Counterfeiting mark — Definitions — "Mark" — "Stamp".

376. (1) Every one who

(*a*) fraudulently uses, mutilates, affixes, removes or counterfeits a stamp or part thereof,

(*b*) knowingly and without lawful excuse, the proof of which lies on him, has in his possession

(i) a counterfeit stamp or a stamp that has been fraudulently mutilated, or

(ii) anything bearing a stamp of which a part has been fraudulently erased, removed or concealed, or

(*c*) without lawful excuse, the proof of which lies on him, makes or knowingly has in his possession a die or instrument that is capable of making the impression of a stamp or part thereof,

is guilty of an indictable offence and liable to imprisonment for a term not exceeding fourteen years.

(2) Every one who, without lawful authority,

(*a*) makes a mark,

(*b*) sells, or exposes for sale, or has in his possession a counterfeit mark,

(*c*) affixes a mark to anything that is required by law to be marked, branded, sealed or wrapped other than the thing to which the mark was originally affixed or was intended to be affixed, or

(*d*) affixes a counterfeit mark to anything that is required by law to be marked, branded, sealed or wrapped,

is guilty of an indictable offence and liable to imprisonment for a term not exceeding fourteen years.

(3) In this section

"mark" means a mark, brand, seal, wrapper or design used by or on behalf of

(*a*) the Government of Canada or a province,

(*b*) the government of a state other than Canada, or

(*c*) any department, board, commission or agent established by a government mentioned in paragraph (*a*) or (*b*) in connection with the service or business of that government;

"stamp" means an impressed or adhesive stamp used for the purpose of revenue by the Government of Canada or of a province or by the government of a state other than Canada.

Damaging documents — Definition of "election document".

377. (1) Every one who unlawfully

(*a*) destroys, defaces or injures a register, or any part of a register of births, baptisms, marriages, deaths or burials that is required or authorized by law to be kept in Canada, or a copy or any part of a copy of such a register that is required by law to be transmitted to a registrar or other officer,

(*b*) inserts or causes to be inserted in a register or copy referred to in paragraph (*a*) an entry, that he knows is false, of any matter relating to a birth, baptism, marriage, death or burial, or erases any material part from that register or copy,

(*c*) destroys, damages or obliterates an election document or causes an election document to be destroyed, damaged or obliterated, or

(*d*) makes or causes to be made an erasure, alteration or interlineation in or on an election document,

is guilty of an indictable offence and liable to imprisonment for a term not exceeding five years.

(2) In this section, "election document" means any document or writing

issued under the authority of an Act of Parliament or the legislature of a province with respect to an election held pursuant to the authority of that Act.

Offences in relation to registers.

378. Every one who

(*a*) being authorized or required by law to make or issue a certified copy of, extract from or certificate in respect of a register, record or document, knowingly makes or issues a false certified copy, extract or certificate,

(*b*) not being authorized or required by law to make or issue a certified copy of, extract from or certificate in respect of a register, record or document, fraudulently makes or issues a copy, extract or certificate that purports to be certified as authorized or required by law, or

(*c*) being authorized or required by law to make a certificate or declaration concerning any particular required for the purpose of making entries in a register, record or document, knowingly and falsely makes the certificate or declaration,

is guilty of an indictable offence and liable to imprisonment for a term not exceeding five years.

PART X

FRAUDULENT TRANSACTIONS RELATING TO CONTRACTS AND TRADE

Interpretation

Definitions — "Goods" — "Trading stamps".

379. In this Part,

"goods" means anything that is the subject of trade or commerce;

"trading stamps" includes any form of cash receipt, receipt, coupon, premium ticket or other device, designed or intended to be given to the purchaser of goods by the vendor thereof or on his behalf, and to represent a discount on the price of the goods or a premium to the purchaser thereof

(*a*) that may be redeemed

(i) by any person other than the vendor, the person from whom the vendor purchased the goods or the manufacturer of the goods,

(ii) by the vendor, the person from whom the vendor purchased the goods or the manufacturer of the goods in cash or in goods that are not his property in whole or in part, or

(iii) by the vendor elsewhere than in the premises where the goods are purchased, or

(*b*) that does not show upon its face the place where it is delivered and the merchantable value thereof, or

(*c*) that may not be redeemed on demand at any time,

but an offer, endorsed by the manufacturer on a wrapper or container in which goods are sold, of a premium or reward for the return of that wrapper or container to the manufacturer is not a trading stamp.

Fraud

Fraud — Affecting public market.

380. (1) Every one who, by deceit, falsehood or other fraudulent means, whether or not it is a false pretence within the meaning of this Act, defrauds the public or any person, whether ascertained or not, of any property, money or valuable security,

(*a*) is guilty of an indictable offence and liable to a term of imprisonment not exceeding ten years, where the subject-matter of the offence is a testamentary instrument or where the value of the subject-matter of the offence exceeds one thousand dollars; or

(*b*) is guilty

(i) of an indictable offence and is liable to imprisonment for a term not exceeding two years, or

(ii) of an offence punishable on summary conviction,

where the value of the subject-matter of the offence does not exceed one thousand dollars.

(2) Every one who, by deceit, falsehood or other fraudulent means, whether or not it is a false pretence within the meaning of this Act, with intent to defraud, affects the public market price of stocks, shares, merchandise or anything that is offered for sale to the public, is guilty of an indictable offence and liable to imprisonment for a term not exceeding ten years. R.S. 1985, c. 27 (1st Supp.), s. 54.

Using mails to defraud.

381. Every one who makes use of the mails for the purpose of transmitting or delivering letters or circulars concerning schemes devised or intended to deceive or defraud the public, or for the purpose of obtaining money under false pretences, is guilty of an indictable offence and liable to imprisonment for a term not exceeding two years.

Fraudulent manipulation of stock exchange transactions.

382. Every one who, through the facility of a stock exchange, curb market or other market, with intent to create a false or misleading appearance of active public trading in a security or with intent to create a false or misleading appearance with respect to the market price of a security,

(*a*) effects a transaction in the security that involves no change in the beneficial ownership thereof,

(*b*) enters an order for the purchase of the security, knowing that an order of substantially the same size at substantially the same time and at substantially the same price for the sale of the security has been or will be entered by or for the same or different persons, or

(*c*) enters an order for the sale of the security, knowing that an order of substantially the same size at substantially the same time and at substantially the same price for the purchase of the security has been or will be entered by or for the same or different persons,

is guilty of an indictable offence and liable to imprisonment for a term not exceeding five years.

Gaming in stocks or merchandise — Onus.

383. (1) Every one is guilty of an indictable offence and liable to imprisonment for a term not exceeding five years who, with intent to make gain or profit by the rise or fall in price of the stock of an incorporated or unincorporated company or undertaking, whether in or outside Canada, or of any goods, wares or merchandise,

(*a*) makes or signs, or authorizes to be made or signed, any contract or agreement, oral or written, purporting to be for the purchase or sale of shares of stock or goods, wares or merchandise, without the *bona fide* intention of acquiring the shares, goods, wares or merchandise or of selling them, as the case may be, or

(*b*) makes or signs, or authorizes to be made or signed, any contract or agreement, oral or written, purporting to be for the sale or purchase of shares of stock or goods, wares or merchandise in respect of which no delivery of the thing sold or purchased is made or received, and without the *bona fide* intention of making or receiving delivery thereof, as the case may be,

but this section does not apply where a broker, on behalf of a purchaser, receives delivery, notwithstanding that the broker retains or pledges what is delivered as security for the advance of the purchase money or any part thereof.

(2) Where, in proceedings under this section, it is established that the accused made or signed a contract or an agreement for the sale or purchase of shares of stock or goods, wares or merchandise, or acted, aided or abetted in the making or signing thereof, the burden of proof of a *bona fide* intention to acquire or to sell the shares, goods, wares or merchandise or to deliver or to receive delivery thereof, as the case may be, lies on the accused.

Broker reducing stock by selling for his own account.

384. Every one is guilty of an indictable offence and liable to imprisonment for a term not exceeding five years who, being an individual, or a member or an employee of a partnership, or a director, officer or an employee of a corporation, where he or the partnership or corporation is employed as a broker by any customer to buy and carry on margin any shares of an incorporated or unincorporated company or undertaking, whether in or out of Canada, thereafter sells or causes to be sold shares of the company or undertaking for any account in which

(*a*) he or his firm or a partner thereof, or

(*b*) the corporation or a director thereof,

has a direct or indirect interest, if the effect of the sale is, otherwise than unintentionally, to reduce the amount of those shares in the hands of the broker or under his control in the ordinary course of business below the amount of those shares that the broker should be carrying for all customers.

Fraudulent concealment of title documents — Consent required.

385. (1) Every one who, being a vendor or mortgagor of property or of a chose in action or being a solicitor for or agent of a vendor or mortgagor of property or a chose in action, is served with a written demand for an abstract of title by or on behalf of the purchaser or mortgagee before the completion of the purchase or mortgage, and who

(*a*) with intent to defraud and for the purpose of inducing the purchaser or mortgagee to accept the title offered or produced to him, conceals from him any settlement, deed, will or other instrument material to the title, or any encumbrance on the title, or

(*b*) falsifies any pedigree on which the title depends,

is guilty of an indictable offence and liable to imprisonment for a term not exceeding two years.

(2) No proceedings shall be instituted under this section without the consent of the Attorney General.

Fraudulent registration of title.

386. Every one who, as principal or agent, in a proceeding to register title to real property, or in a transaction relating to real property that is or is proposed to be registered, knowingly and with intent to deceive,

(*a*) makes a material false statement or representation,

(*b*) suppresses or conceals from a judge or registrar, or any person employed by or assisting the registrar, any material document, fact, matter or information, or

(*c*) is privy to anything mentioned in paragraph (*a*) or (*b*),

is guilty of an indictable offence and liable to imprisonment for a term not exceeding five years.

Fraudulent sale of real property.

387. Every one who, knowing of an unregistered prior sale or of an existing unregistered grant, mortgage, hypothec, privilege or encumbrance of or on real property, fraudulently sells the property or any part thereof is guilty of an indictable offence and liable to imprisonment for a term not exceeding two years.

Misleading receipt.

388. Every one who wilfully

(*a*) with intent to mislead, injure or defraud any person, whether or not that person is known to him, gives to a person anything in writing that purports to be a receipt for or an acknowledgment of property that has been delivered to or received by him, before the property referred to in the purported receipt or acknowledgment has been delivered to or received by him, or

(*b*) accepts, transmits or uses a purported receipt or acknowledgment to which paragraph (*a*) applies,

is guilty of an indictable offence and liable to imprisonment for a term not exceeding two years.

Fraudulent disposal of goods on which money advanced — Saving.

389. (1) Every one who

(*a*) having shipped or delivered to the keeper of a warehouse or to a factor, an agent or a carrier anything on which the consignee thereof has advanced money or has given valuable security, thereafter, with intent to deceive, defraud or injure the consignee, disposes of it in a manner that is different from and inconsistent with any agreement that has been made in that behalf between him and the consignee, or (*b*) knowingly and wilfully aids or assists any person to make a disposition of anything to which paragraph (*a*) applies for the purpose of deceiving, defrauding or injuring the consignee,

is guilty of an indictable offence and liable to imprisonment for a term not exceeding two years.

(2) No person is guilty of an offence under this section where, before disposing of anything in a manner that is different from and inconsistent with any agreement that has been made in that behalf between him and the consignee, he pays or tenders to the consignee the full amount of money or valuable security that the consignee has advanced.

Fraudulent receipts under *Bank Act*.

390. Every one is guilty of an indictable offence and liable to imprisonment for a term not exceeding two years who

(*a*) wilfully makes a false statement in a receipt, certificate or acknowledgment for anything that may be used for a purpose mentioned in the *Bank Act*; or

(*b*) wilfully,

(i) after giving to another person,

(ii) after a person employed by him has, to his knowledge, given to another person, or

(iii) after obtaining and endorsing or assigning to another person,

a receipt, certificate or acknowledgment for anything that may be used for a purpose mentioned in the *Bank Act*, without the consent in writing of the holder or endorsee or the production and delivery of the receipt, certificate or acknowledgment, alienates or parts with, or does not deliver to the holder or owner the property mentioned in the receipt, certificate or acknowledgment.

Saving.

391. Where an offence is committed under section 388, 389 or 390 by a person who acts in the name of a corporation, firm or partnership, no person other than the person who does the act by means of which the offence is committed or who is secretly privy to the doing of that act is guilty of the offence.

Disposal of property to defraud creditors.

392. Every one who,

(*a*) with intent to defraud his creditors,

(i) makes or causes to be made any gift, conveyance, assignment, sale, transfer or delivery of his property, or

(ii) removes, conceals or disposes of any of his property, or

(*b*) with intent that any one should defraud his creditors, receives any property by means of or in relation to which an offence has been committed under paragraph (*a*),

is guilty of an indictable offence and liable to imprisonment for a term not exceeding two years.

Fraud in relation to fares, etc. — Idem — Fraudulently obtaining transportation.

393. (1) Every one whose duty it is to collect a fare, toll, ticket or admission who wilfully

(*a*) fails to collect it,

(*b*) collects less than the proper amount payable in respect thereof, or

(*c*) accepts any valuable consideration for failing to collect it or for collecting less than the proper amount payable in respect thereof,

is guilty of an indictable offence and liable to imprisonment for a term not exceeding two years.

(2) Every one who gives or offers to a person whose duty it is to collect a fare, toll, ticket or admission fee, any valuable consideration

(*a*) for failing to collect it, or

(*b*) for collecting an amount less than the amount payable in respect thereof,

is guilty of an indictable offence and liable to imprisonment for a term not exceeding two years.

(3) Every one who, by any false pretence or fraud, unlawfully obtains transportation by land, water or air is guilty of an offence punishable on summary conviction.

Fraud in relation to minerals — Seizure and forfeiture.

394. (1) Every one is guilty of an indictable offence and liable to imprisonment for a term not exceeding five years who

(*a*) being the holder of a lease or licence issued

(i) under an Act relating to the mining of precious metals, or

(ii) by the owner of land that is supposed to contain precious metals,

by a fraudulent device or contrivance defrauds or attempts to defraud any person of any precious metals or money payable or reserved by the lease or licence, or fraudulently conceals or makes a false statement with respect to the amount of precious metals procured by him;

(*b*) sells or purchases any rock, mineral, or other substance that contains precious metals or unsmelted, untreated, unmanufactured, or partly smelted, partly treated or partly manufactured precious metals, unless he establishes that he is the owner or agent of the owner or is acting under lawful authority; or

(*c*) has in his possession or knowingly has upon his premises

(i) any rock or mineral of a value of fifty-five cents per kilogram or more,

(ii) any mica of a value of fifteen cents per kilogram or more, or

(iii) any precious metals,

that there are reasonable grounds to believe have been stolen or have been dealt with contrary to this section, unless he establishes that he is lawfully in possession thereof.

(2) Where a person is convicted of an offence under this section, the court may order anything by means of or in relation to which the offence was committed, on such conviction, to be forfeited to Her Majesty in right of the province in which the proceedings take place. R.S. 1985, c. 27 (1st Supp.), s. 186.

Search for precious metals — Power to seize — Appeal.

395. (1) Where an information in writing is laid under oath before a justice by any person having an interest in a mining claim, that any precious metals or rock, mineral or other substance containing precious metals is unlawfully deposited in any place or held by any person contrary to law, the justice may issue a warrant to search any of the places or persons mentioned in the information.

(2) Where, on search, anything mentioned in subsection (1) is found, it shall be seized and carried before the justice who shall order

(*a*) that it be detained for the purposes of an inquiry or a trial; or

(*b*) if it is not detained for the purposes of an inquiry or a trial,

(i) that it be restored to the owner, or

(ii) that it be forfeited to Her Majesty in right of the province in which the proceedings take place if the owner cannot be ascertained.

(3) An appeal lies from an order made under paragraph (2)(*b*) in the manner in which an appeal lies in summary conviction proceedings under Part XXVII and the provisions of that Part relating to appeals apply to appeals under this subsection.

Offences in relation to mines — Presumption.

396. (1) Every one who

(*a*) adds anything to or removes anything from any existing or prospective mine, mining claim or oil well with a fraudulent intent to affect the result of an assay, a test or a valuation that has been made or is to be made with respect to the mine, mining claim or oil well, or

(*b*) adds anything to, removes anything from or tampers with a sample or material that has been taken or is being or is about to be taken from any existing or prospective mine, mining claim or oil well for the purpose of being assayed, tested or otherwise valued, with a fraudulent intent to affect the result of the assay, test or valuation,

is guilty of an indictable offence and liable to imprisonment for a term not exceeding ten years.

(2) For the purposes of proceedings under subsection (1), evidence that

(*a*) something has been added to or removed from anything to which subsection (1) applies, or

(*b*) anything to which subsection (1) applies has been tampered with,

is, in the absence of any evidence to the contrary, proof of a fraudulent intent to affect the result of an assay, test or a valuation.

Falsification of Books and Documents

Books and documents — Privy.

397. (1) Every one who, with intent to defraud,

(*a*) destroys, mutilates, alters, falsifies, or makes a false entry in, or

(*b*) omits a material particular from, or alters a material particular in,

a book, paper, writing, valuable security or document is guilty of an indictable offence and liable to imprisonment for a term not exceeding five years.

(2) Every one who, with intent to defraud his creditors, is privy to the commission of an offence under subsection (1) is guilty of an indictable offence and liable to imprisonment for a term not exceeding five years.

Falsifying employment record.

398. Every one who, with intent to deceive, falsifies an employment record by any means, including the punching of a time clock, is guilty of an offence punishable on summary conviction.

False return by public officer.

399. Every one who, being entrusted with the receipt, custody or management of any part of the public revenues, knowingly furnishes a false statement or return of

(*a*) any sum of money collected by him or entrusted to his care, or

(*b*) any balance of money in his hands or under his control,

is guilty of an indictable offence and liable to imprisonment for a term not exceeding five years.

False prospectus, etc. — "Company".

400. (1) Every one who makes, circulates or publishes a prospectus, statement or an account, whether written or oral, that he knows is false in a material particular, with intent

(*a*) to induce persons, whether ascertained or not, to become shareholders or partners in a company,

(*b*) to deceive or defraud the members, shareholders or creditors, whether ascertained or not, of a company,

(*c*) to induce any person to entrust or advance anything to a company, or

(*d*) to enter into any security for the benefit of a company,

is guilty of an indictable offence and liable to imprisonment for a term not exceeding ten years.

(2) In this section, "company" means a syndicate, body corporate or company, whether existing or proposed to be created.

Obtaining carriage by false billing — Forfeiture.

401. (1) Every one who, by means of a false or misleading representation, knowingly obtains or attempts to obtain the carriage of anything by any person into a country, province, district or other place, whether or not within Canada, where the importation or transportation of it is, in the circumstances of the case, unlawful is guilty of an offence punishable on summary conviction.

(2) Where a person is convicted of an offence under subsection (1), anything by means of or in relation to which the offence was committed, on such conviction, in addition to any punishment that is imposed, is forfeited to Her Majesty and shall be disposed of as the court may direct.

Trader failing to keep accounts — Saving.

402. (1) Every one who, being a trader or in business,

(*a*) is indebted in an amount exceeding one thousand dollars,

(*b*) is unable to pay his creditors in full, and

(*c*) has not kept books of account that, in the ordinary course of the trade or business in which he is engaged, are necessary to exhibit or explain his transactions,

is guilty of an indictable offence and liable to imprisonment for a term not exceeding two years.

(2) No person shall be convicted of an offence under this section

(*a*) where, to the satisfaction of the court or judge, he

(i) accounts for his losses, and

(ii) shows that his failure to keep books was not intended to defraud his creditors; or

(*b*) where his failure to keep books occurred at a time more than five years prior to the day on which he was unable to pay his creditors in full.

Personation

Personation with intent.

403. Every one who fraudulently personates any person, living or dead,

(*a*) with intent to gain advantage for himself or another person,

(*b*) with intent to obtain any property or an interest in any property, or

(*c*) with intent to cause disadvantage to the person whom he personates or another person,

is guilty of an indictable offence and liable to imprisonment for a term not exceeding fourteen years.

Personation at examination.

404. Every one who falsely, with intent to gain advantage for himself or some other person, personates a candidate at a competitive or qualifying examination held under the authority of law or in connection with a university, college or school or who knowingly avails himself of the results of such personation is guilty of an offence punishable on summary conviction.

Acknowledging instrument in false name.

405. Every one who, without lawful authority or excuse, the proof of which lies on him, acknowledges, in the name of another person before a court or a judge or other person authorized to receive the acknowledgment, a recognizance of bail, a confession of judgment, a consent to judgment or a judgment, deed or other instrument is guilty of an indictable offence and liable to imprisonment for a term not exceeding five years.

Forgery of Trade-marks and Trade Descriptions

Forging trade-mark.

406. For the purposes of this Part, every one forges a trade-mark who

(*a*) without the consent of the proprietor of the trade mark, makes or reproduces in any manner that trade-mark or a mark so nearly resembling it as to be calculated to deceive; or

(*b*) falsifies, in any manner, a genuine trade-mark.

Offence.

407. Every one commits an offence who, with intent to deceive or defraud the public or any person, whether ascertained or not, forges a trade-mark.

Passing off.

408. Every one commits an offence who, with intent to deceive or defraud the public or any person, whether ascertained or not,

(*a*) passes off other wares or services as and for those ordered or required; or

(*b*) makes use, in association with wares or services, of any description that is false in a material respect regarding

(i) the kind, quality, quantity or composition,

(ii) the geographical origin, or

(iii) the mode of the manufacture, production or performance

of those wares or services.

Instruments for forging trade-mark — Saving.

409. (1) Every one commits an offence who makes, has in his possession or disposes of a die, block, machine or other instrument designed or intended to be used in forging a trade-mark.

(2) No person shall be convicted of an offence under this section where

he proves that he acted in good faith in the ordinary course of his business or employment.

Other offences in relation to trade-marks.

410. Every one commits an offence who, with intent to deceive or defraud,

(*a*) defaces, conceals or removes a trade-mark or the name of another person from anything without the consent of that other person; or

(*b*) being a manufacturer, dealer, trader or bottler, fills any bottle or siphon that bears the trade-mark or name of another person, without the consent of that other person, with a beverage, milk, by-product of milk or other liquid commodity for the purpose of sale or traffic.

Used goods sold without disclosure.

411. Every one commits an offence who sells, exposes or has in his possession for sale, or advertises for sale, goods that have been used, reconditioned or remade and that bear the trade-mark or the trade-name of another person, without making full disclosure that the goods have been reconditioned, rebuilt or remade for sale and that they are not then in the condition in which they were originally made or produced.

Punishment — Forfeiture.

412. (1) Every one who commits an offence under section 407, 408, 409, 410 or 411 is guilty of

(*a*) an indictable offence and is liable to imprisonment for a term not exceeding two years; or

(*b*) an offence punishable on summary conviction.

(2) Anything by means of or in relation to which a person commits an offence under section 407, 408, 409, 410 or 411 is, unless the court otherwise orders, forfeited on the conviction of that person for that offence.

Falsely claiming royal warrant.

413. Every one who falsely represents that goods are made by a person holding a royal warrant, or for the service of Her Majesty, a member of the Royal Family or a public department is guilty of an offence punishable on summary conviction.

Presumption from port of shipment.

414. Where, in proceedings under this Part, the alleged offence relates to imported goods, evidence that the goods were shipped to Canada from a place outside Canada is, in the absence of any evidence to the contrary, proof that the goods were made or produced in the country from which they were shipped.

Wreck

Offences in relation to wreck.

415. Every one who

(*a*) secretes wreck, defaces or obliterates the marks on wreck, or uses any means to disguise or conceal the fact that anything is wreck, or in any manner conceals the character of wreck, from a person who is entitled to inquire into the wreck,

(*b*) receives wreck, knowing that it is wreck, from a person other than the owner thereof or a receiver of wreck, and does not within forty-eight hours thereafter inform the receiver of wreck thereof,

(*c*) offers wreck for sale or otherwise deals with it, knowing that it is wreck, and not having a lawful authority to sell or deal with it,

(*d*) keeps wreck in his possession knowing that it is wreck, without lawful authority to keep it, for any time longer than the time reasonably necessary to deliver it to the receiver of wreck, or

(*e*) boards, against the will of the master, a vessel that is wrecked, stranded or in distress unless he is a receiver of wreck or a person acting under orders of a receiver of wreck,

is guilty of

(*f*) an indictable offence and is liable to imprisonment for a term not exceeding two years, or

(*g*) an offence punishable on summary conviction.

Public Stores

Distinguishing mark on public stores.

416. The Governor in Council may, by notice to be published in the *Canada Gazette*, prescribe distinguishing marks that are appropriate for use on public stores to denote the property of Her Majesty therein, whether the stores belong to Her Majesty in right of Canada or to Her Majesty in any other right.

Applying or removing marks without authority — Unlawful transactions in public stores — Definition of "distinguishing mark".

417. (1) Every one who,

(*a*) without lawful authority, the proof of which lies on him, applies a distinguishing mark to anything, or

(*b*) with intent to conceal the property of Her Majesty in public stores, removes, destroys or obliterates, in whole or in part, a distinguishing mark,

is guilty of an indictable offence and liable to imprisonment for a term not exceeding two years.

(2) Every one who, without lawful authority, the proof of which lies on him,

receives, possesses, keeps, sells or delivers public stores that he knows bear a distinguishing mark is guilty of

(*a*) an indictable offence and is liable to imprisonment for a term not exceeding two years; or

(*b*) an offence punishable on summary conviction.

(3) For the purposes of this section, "distinguishing mark" means a distinguishing mark that is appropriated for use on public stores pursuant to section 416.

Selling defective stores to Her Majesty — Offences by officers and employees of corporations.

418. (1) Every one who knowingly sells or delivers defective stores to Her Majesty or commits fraud in connection with the sale, lease or delivery of stores to Her Majesty or the manufacture of stores for Her Majesty is guilty of an indictable offence and liable to imprisonment for a term not exceeding fourteen years.

(2) Every one who, being a director, an officer, an agent or an employee of a corporation that commits, by fraud, an offence under subsection (1),

(*a*) knowingly takes part in the fraud, or

(*b*) knows or has reason to suspect that the fraud is being committed or has been or is about to be committed and does not inform the responsible government, or a department thereof, of Her Majesty,

is guilty of an indictable offence and liable to imprisonment for a term not exceeding fourteen years.

Unlawful use of military uniforms or certificates.

419. Every one who without lawful authority, the proof of which lies on him,

(*a*) wears a uniform of the Canadian Forces or any other naval, army or air force or a uniform that is so similar to the uniform of any of those forces that it is likely to be mistaken therefor,

(*b*) wears a distinctive mark relating to wounds received or service performed in war, or a military medal, ribbon, badge, chevron or any decoration or order that is awarded for war services, or any imitation thereof, or any mark or device or thing that is likely to be mistaken for any such mark, medal, ribbon, badge, chevron, decoration or order,

(*c*) has in his possession a certificate of discharge, certificate of release, statement of service or identity card from the Canadian Forces or any other naval, army or air force that has not been issued to and does not belong to him, or

(*d*) has in his possession a commission or warrant or a certificate of discharge, certificate of release, statement of service or identity card issued to an officer or a person in or who has been in the Canadian Forces or any other naval, army or air force, that contains any alteration that is not verified by the initials of the officer who issued it, or by the initials of an officer thereto lawfully authorized,

is guilty of an offence punishable on summary conviction.

Military stores — Exception.

420. (1) Every one who buys, receives or details from a member of the Canadian Forces or a deserter or an absentee without leave therefrom any military stores that are owned by Her Majesty or for which the member, deserter or absentee without leave is accountable to Her Majesty is guilty of

(*a*) an indictable offence and is liable to imprisonment for a term not exceeding five years; or

(*b*) an offence punishable on summary conviction.

(2) No person shall be convicted of an offence under this section where he establishes that he did not know and had no reason to suspect that the military stores in respect of which the offence was committed were owned by Her Majesty or were military stores for which the member, deserter or absentee without leave was accountable to Her Majesty.

Evidence of enlistment — Presumption when accused a dealer in stores.

421. (1) In proceedings under sections 417 to 420, evidence that a person was at any time performing duties in the Canadian Forces is, in the absence of any evidence to the contrary, proof that his enrolment in the Canadian Forces prior to that time was regular.

(2) An accused who is charged with an offence under subsection 417(2) shall be presumed to have known that the stores in respect of which the offence is alleged to have been committed bore a distinguishing mark within the meaning of that subsection at the time the offence is alleged to have been committed if he was, at that time, in the service or employment of Her Majesty or was a dealer in marine stores or in old metals.

Breach of Contract, Intimidation and Discrimination Against Trade Unionists

Criminal breach of contract — Saving — Consent required.

422. (1) Every one who wilfully breaks a contract, knowing or having reasonable cause to believe that the probable consequences of doing so, whether alone or in combination with others, will be

(*a*) to endanger human life,

(*b*) to cause serious bodily injury,

(*c*) to expose valuable property, real or personal, to destruction or serious injury,

(*d*) to deprive the inhabitants of a city or place, or part thereof, wholly or to a great extent, of their supply of light, power, gas or water, or

(*e*) to delay or prevent the running of a locomotive engine, tender, freight or passenger train or car, on a railway that is a common carrier, is guilty of

(*f*) an indictable offence and is liable to imprisonment for a term not exceeding five years, or

(*g*) an offence punishable on summary conviction.

(2) No person wilfully breaks a contract within the meaning of subsection (1) by reason only that

(*a*) being the employee of an employer, he stops work as a result of the failure of his employer and himself to agree upon any matter relating to his employment, or,

(*b*) being a member of an organization of employees formed for the purpose of regulating relations between employers and employees, he stops work as a result of the failure of the employer and a bargaining agent acting on behalf of the organization to agree on any matter relating to the employment of members of the organization,

if, before the stoppage of work occurs, all steps provided by law with respect to the settlement of industrial disputes are taken and any provision for the final settlement of differences, without stoppage of work, contained in or by law deemed to be contained in a collective agreement is complied with and effect given thereto.

(3) No proceedings shall be instituted under this section without the consent of the Attorney General.

Intimidation — Exception.

423. (1) Every one who, wrongfully and without lawful authority, for the purpose of compelling another person to abstain from doing anything that he has a lawful right to do, or to do anything that he has a lawful right to abstain from doing,

(*a*) uses violence or threats of violence to that person or his spouse or children, or injures his property,

(*b*) intimidates or attempts to intimidate that person or a relative of that person by threats that, in Canada or elsewhere, violence or other injury will be done to or punishment inflicted upon him or a relative of his, or that the property of any of them will be damaged,

(*c*) persistently follows that person about from place to place,

(*d*) hides any tools, clothes or other property owned or used by that person, or deprives him of them or hinders him in the use of them,

(*e*) with one or more other persons, follows that person, in a disorderly manner, on a highway,

(*f*) besets or watches the dwelling-house or place where that person resides, works, carries on business or happens to be, or

(*g*) blocks or obstructs a highway,

is guilty of an offence punishable on summary conviction.

(2) A person who attends at or near or approaches a dwelling-house or place,

for the purpose only of obtaining or communicating information, does not watch or beset within the meaning of this section.

Threat to commit offence against internationally protected person.

424. Every one who threatens to commit an offence under section 235, 266, 279 or 279.1 against an internationally protected person or who threatens to commit an offence under section 431 is guilty of an indictable offence and liable to imprisonment for a term not exceeding five years. R.S. 1985, c. 27 (1st Supp.), s. 55.

Offences by employers.

425. Every one who, being an employer or the agent of an employer, wrongfully and without lawful authority

(*a*) refuses to employ or dismisses from his employment any person for the reason only that the person is a member of a lawful trade union or of a lawful association or combination of workmen or employees formed for the purpose of advancing, in a lawful manner, their interests and organized for their protection in the regulation of wages and conditions of work,

(*b*) seeks by intimidation, threat of loss of position or employment, or by causing actual loss of position or employment, or by threatening or imposing any pecuniary penalty, to compel workmen or employees to abstain from belonging to a trade union, association or combination to which they have a lawful right to belong, or

(*c*) conspires, combines, agrees or arranges with any other employer or his agent to do anything mentioned in paragraph (*a*) or (*b*),

is guilty of an offence punishable on summary conviction.

Secret Commissions

Secret commissions — Privity to offence — Punishment — Definitions of "agent" and "principal".

426. (1) Every one commits an offence who

(*a*) corruptly

(i) gives, offers or agrees to give or offer to an agent, or

(ii) being an agent, demands, accepts or offers or agrees to accept from any person,

any reward, advantage or benefit of any kind as consideration for doing or forbearing to do, or for having done or forborne to do, any act relating to the affairs or business of his principal or for showing or forbearing to show favour or disfavour to any person with relation to the affairs or business of his principal; or

(*b*) with intent to deceive a principal, gives to an agent of that principal, or, being an agent, uses with intent to deceive his principal, a receipt, account or other writing

(i) in which the principal has an interest,

(ii) that contains any statement that is false or erroneous or defective in any material particular, and

(iii) that is intended to mislead the principal.

(2) Every one commits an offence who is knowingly privy to the commission of an offence under subsection (1).

(3) A person who commits an offence under this section is guilty of an indictable offence and liable to imprisonment for a term not exceeding five years.

(4) In this section "agent" includes an employee, and "principal" includes an employer. R.S. 1985, c. 27 (1st Supp.), s. 56.

Trading Stamps

Issuing trading stamps — Giving to purchaser of goods.

427. (1) Every one who, by himself or his employee or agent, directly or indirectly issues, gives, sells or otherwise disposes of, or offers to issue, give, sell or otherwise dispose of trading stamps to a merchant or dealer in goods for use in his business is guilty of an offence punishable on summary conviction.

(2) Every one who, being a merchant or dealer in goods, by himself or his employee or agent, directly or indirectly gives or in any way disposes of, or offers to give or in any way dispose of, trading stamps to a person who purchases goods from him is guilty of an offence punishable on summary conviction.

PART XI

WILFUL AND FORBIDDEN ACTS IN RESPECT OF CERTAIN PROPERTY

Interpretation

"Property".

428. In this Part, "property" means real or personal corporeal property.

Wilfully causing event to occur — Colour of right — Interest.

429. (1) Every one who causes the occurrence of an event by doing an act or by omitting to do an act that it is his duty to do, knowing that the act or omission will probably cause the occurrence of the event and being reckless whether the event occurs or not, shall be deemed, for the purposes of this Part, wilfully to have caused the occurrence of the event.

(2) No person shall be convicted of an offence under sections 430 to 446 where he proves that he acted with legal justification or excuse and with colour of right.

(3) Where it is an offence to destroy or to damage anything,

(*a*) the fact that a person has a partial interest in what is destroyed or damaged does not prevent him from being guilty of the offence if he caused the destruction or damage; and

(*b*) the fact that a person has a total interest in what is destroyed or damaged does not prevent him from being guilty of the offence if he caused the destruction or damage with intent to defraud.

Mischief

Mischief — Mischief in relation to data — Punishment — Idem — Idem — Idem — Offence — Saving — Idem — Definition of "data".

430. (1) Every one commits mischief who wilfully

(*a*) destroys or damages property;

(*b*) renders property dangerous, useless, inoperative or ineffective;

(*c*) obstructs, interrupts or interferes with the lawful use, enjoyment or operation of property; or

(*d*) obstructs, interrupts or interferes with any person in the lawful use, enjoyment or operation of property.

(1.1) Every one commits mischief who wilfully

(*a*) destroys or alters data;

(*b*) renders data meaningless, useless or ineffective;

(*c*) obstructs, interrupts or interferes with the lawful use of data; or (*d*) obstructs, interrupts or interferes with any person in the lawful use of data or denies access to data to any person who is entitled to access thereto.

(2) Every one who commits mischief that causes actual danger to life is guilty of an indictable offence and liable to imprisonment for life.

(3) Every one who commits mischief in relation to property that is a testamentary instrument or the value of which exceeds one thousand dollars

(*a*) is guilty of an indictable offence and liable to imprisonment for a term not exceeding ten years; or

(*b*) is guilty of an offence punishable on summary conviction.

(4) Every one who commits mischief in relation to property, other than property described in subsection (3),

(*a*) is guilty of an indictable offence and liable to imprisonment for a term not exceeding two years; or

(*b*) is guilty of an offence punishable on summary conviction.

(5) Every one who commits mischief in relation to data

(*a*) is guilty of an indictable offence and liable to imprisonment for a term not exceeding ten years; or

(*b*) is guilty of an offence punishable on summary conviction.

(5.1) Every one who wilfully does an act or wilfully omits to do an act that it is his duty to do, if that act or omission is likely to constitute mischief causing actual danger to life, or to constitute mischief in relation to property or data,

(*a*) is guilty of an indictable offence and liable to imprisonment for a term not exceeding five years; or

(*b*) is guilty of an offence punishable on summary conviction.

(6) No person commits mischief within the meaning of this section by reason only that

(*a*) he stops work as a result of the failure of his employer and himself to agree on any matter relating to his employment;

(*b*) he stops work as a result of the failure of his employer and a bargaining agent acting on his behalf to agree on any matter relating to his employment; or

(*c*) he stops work as a result of his taking part in a combination of workmen or employees for their own reasonable protection as workmen or employees.

(7) No person commits mischief within the meaning of this section by reason only that he attends at or near or approaches a dwelling-house or place for the purpose only of obtaining or communicating information.

(8) In this section, "data" has the same meaning as in section 342.1. R.S. 1985, c. 27 (1st Supp.), s. 57.

Attack on premises, residence or transport of internationally protected person.

431. Every one who commits an attack on the official premises, private accommodation or means of transport of an internationally protected person that is likely to endanger the life or liberty of such person is guilty of an indictable offence and liable to imprisonment for a term not exceeding fourteen years. R.S. 1985, c. 27 (1st Supp.), s. 58.

432. [Repealed R.S. 1985, c. 27 (1st Supp.), s. 58.]

Arson and Other Fires

Arson — Disregard for human life.

433. Every person who intentionally or recklessly causes damage by fire or explosion to property, whether or not that person owns the property, is guilty of an indictable offence and liable to imprisonment for life where

(*a*) the person that is reckless with respect to whether the property is inhabited or occupied

(*b*) the fire or explosion causes bodily harm to another person. 1990, c. 15, s. 1.

Arson — Damage to property.

434. Every person who intentionally or recklessly causes damage by fire or explosion to property that is not wholly owned by that person is guilty of an indictable offence and liable to imprisonment for a term not exceeding fourteen years. 1990, c. 15, s. 1.

Arson — Own property

434.1 Every person who intentionally or recklessly causes damage by fire or explosion to property that is owned, in whole or in part, by that person is guilty of an indicatable offence and liable to imprisonment for a term not exceeding fourteen years, where the fire or explosion seriously threatens the health, safety or property of another person. 1990, c. 15, s. 1.

Arson for fraudulent purpose — Holder or beneficiary of fire insurance policy.

435. (1) Every person who, with intent to defraud any other person, causes damage by fire or explosion to property, whether or not that person owns, in whole or in part, the property, is guilty of an indicatable offence and is liable to imprisonment for a term not exceeding ten years.

(2) Where a person is charged with an offence under subsection (1), the fact that the person was the holder of or was named as a beneficiary under a policy of fire insurance relating to the property in respect of which the offence is alleged to have been committed is a fact from which intent to defraud may be inferred by the court. 1990, c. 15, s. 1.

Arson by negligence — Non-compliance with prevention laws.

436. (1) Every person who owns, in whole or in part, or controls property is guilty of an indictable offence and liable to imprisonment for a term not exceeding five years where as a result of a marked departure from the standard of care that a reasonably prudent person would use to prevent or control the spread of fires or to prevent explosions, that person is a cause of a fire or explosion in that property that causes bodily harm to another person or damage to property.

(2) Where a person is charged with an offence under subsection (1), the fact that the person has failed to comply with any law respecting the prevention or control of fires or explosions in the property is a fact from which a marked departure from the standard of care referred to in that subsection may be inferred by the court. 1990, c. 15, s. 1.

Possession of incendiary material.

436.1 Every person who possesses any incendiary material, incendiary device or explosive substance for the purpose of committing an offence under any of sections 433 to 436 is guilty of an indictable offence and liable to imprisonment for a term not exceeding five years. 1990, c. 15, s. 1.

Other Interference with Property

False alarm of fire.

437. Every one who wilfully, without reasonable cause, by outcry, ringing bells, using a fire alarm, telephone or telegraph, or in any other manner, makes or circulates or causes to be made or circulated an alarm of fire is guilty of

(*a*) an indictable offence and is liable to imprisonment for a term not exceeding two years; or

(*b*) an offence punishable on summary conviction.

Interfering with saving of wrecked vessel — Interfering with saving of wreck.

438. (1) Every one who wilfully prevents or impedes, or who wilfully endeavours to prevent or impede,

(*a*) the saving of a vessel that is wrecked, stranded, abandoned or in distress, or

(*b*) a person who attempts to save a vessel that is wrecked, stranded, abandoned or in distress,

is guilty of an indictable offence and liable to imprisonment for a term not exceeding five years.

(2) Every one who wilfully prevents or impedes or wilfully endeavours to prevent or impede the saving of wreck is guilty of an offence punishable on summary conviction.

Interfering with marine signal, etc. — Idem.

439. (1) Every one who makes fast a vessel or boat to a signal, buoy or other sea-mark that is used for purposes of navigation is guilty of an offence punishable on summary conviction.

(2) Every one who wilfully alters, removes or conceals a signal, buoy or other sea-mark that is used for purposes of navigation is guilty of an indictable offence and liable to imprisonment for a term not exceeding ten years.

Removing natural bar without permission.

440. Every one who wilfully and without the written permission of the Minister of Transport, the burden of proof of which lies on the accused, removes any stone, wood, earth or other material that forms a natural bar necessary to the existence of a public harbour, or that forms a natural protection to such a bar, is guilty of an indictable offence and liable to imprisonment for a term not exceeding two years.

Occupant injuring building.

441. Every one who, wilfully and to the prejudice of a mortgagee or an owner, pulls down, demolishes or removes, all or any part of a dwelling-house or other building of which he is in possession or occupation, or severs from the freehold any fixture fixed therein or thereto is guilty of an indictable offence and liable to imprisonment for a term not exceeding five years.

Interfering with boundary lines.

442. Every one who wilfully pulls down, defaces, alters or removes anything planted or set up as the boundary line or part of the boundary line of land is guilty of an offence punishable on summary conviction.

Interfering with international boundary marks, etc. — Saving provision.

443. (1) Every one who wilfully pulls down, defaces, alters or removes

(*a*) a boundary mark lawfully placed to mark an international, provincial, county or municipal boundary, or

(*b*) a boundary mark lawfully placed by a land surveyor to mark any limit, boundary or angle of a concession, range, lot or parcel of land,

is guilty of an indictable offence and liable to imprisonment for a term not exceeding five years.

(2) A land surveyor does not commit an offence under subsection (1) where, in his operations as a land surveyor,

(*a*) he takes up, when necessary, a boundary mark mentioned in paragraph (1)(*b*) and carefully replaces it as it was before he took it up, or

(*b*) he takes up a boundary mark mentioned in paragraph (1)(*b*) in the course of surveying for a highway or other work that, when completed, will make it impossible or impracticable for that boundary mark to occupy its original position, and he establishes a permanent record of the original position sufficient to permit that position to be ascertained.

Cattle and Other Animals

Injuring or endangering cattle.

444. Every one who wilfully

(*a*) kills, maims, wounds, poisons or injures cattle, or

(*b*) places poison in such a position that it may easily be consumed by cattle,

is guilty of an indictable offence and liable to imprisonment for a term not exceeding five years.

Injuring or endangering other animals.

445. Every one who wilfully and without lawful excuse

(*a*) kills, maims, wounds, poisons or injures dogs, birds or animals that are not cattle and are kept for a lawful purpose, or

(*b*) places poison in such a position that it may easily be consumed by dogs, birds or animals that are not cattle and are kept for a lawful purpose,

is guilty of an offence punishable on summary conviction.

Cruelty to Animals

Causing unnecessary suffering — Punishment — Failure to exercise reasonable care as evidence — Presence at baiting as evidence — Order of prohibition — Breach of order.

446. (1) Every one commits an offence who

(*a*) wilfully causes or, being the owner, wilfully permits to be caused unnecessary pain, suffering or injury to an animal or bird;

(*b*) by wilful neglect causes damage or injury to animals or birds while they are being driven or conveyed;

(*c*) being the owner or the person having the custody or control of a domestic animal or a bird or an animal or a bird wild by nature that is in captivity, abandons it in distress or wilfully neglects or fails to provide suitable and adequate food, water, shelter and care for it;

(*d*) in any manner encourages, aids or assists at the fighting or baiting of animals or birds;

(*e*) wilfully, without reasonable excuse, administers a poisonous or an injurious drug or substance to a domestic animal or bird or an animal or a bird wild by nature that is kept in captivity or, being the owner of such an animal or a bird, wilfully permits a poisonous or an injurious drug or substance to be administered to it;

(*f*) promotes, arranges, conducts, assists in, receives money for or takes part in any meeting, competition, exhibition, pastime, practice, display, or event at or in the course of which captive birds are liberated by hand, trap, contrivance or any other means for the purpose of being shot when they are liberated; or

(*g*) being the owner, occupier, or person in charge of any premises, permits the premises or any part thereof to be used for a purpose mentioned in paragraph (*f*).

(2) Every one who commits an offence under subsection (1) is guilty of an offence punishable on summary conviction.

(3) For the purposes of proceedings under paragraph (1)(*a*) or (*b*), evidence that a person failed to exercise reasonable care or supervision of an animal or a bird thereby causing it pain, suffering, damage or injury is, in the absence of any evidence to the contrary, proof that the pain, suffering, damage or injury was caused or was permitted to be caused wilfully or was caused by wilful neglect, as the case may be.

(4) For the purpose of proceedings under paragraph (1)(*d*), evidence that an accused was present at the fighting or baiting of animals or birds is, in the absence of any evidence to the contrary, proof that he encouraged, aided or assisted at the fighting or baiting.

(5) Where an accused is convicted of an offence under subsection (1), the court may, in addition to any other sentence that may be imposed for the offence, make an order prohibiting the accused from owning or having the custody or control of an animal or bird during any period not exceeding two years.

(6) Every one who owns or has the custody or control of an animal or a bird while he is prohibited from doing so by reason of an order made under subsection (5) is guilty of an offence punishable on summary conviction.

Keeping cockpit — Confiscation.

447. (1) Every one who builds, makes, maintains or keeps a cockpit on premises that he owns or occupies, or allows a cockpit to be built, made, maintained or kept on such premises is guilty of an offence punishable on summary conviction.

(2) A peace officer who finds cocks in a cockpit or on premises where a cockpit is located shall seize them and take them before a justice who shall order them to be destroyed.

PART XII

OFFENCES RELATING TO CURRENCY

Interpretation

Definitions — "Counterfeit money" — "Counterfeit token of value" — "Current" — "Utter".

448. In this Part,

"counterfeit money" includes

(*a*) a false coin or false paper money that resembles or is apparently intended to resemble or pass for a current coin or current paper money,

(*b*) a forged bank note or forged blank bank note, whether complete or incomplete,

(*c*) a genuine coin or genuine paper money that is prepared or altered to resemble or pass for a current coin or current paper money of a higher denomination,

(*d*) a current coin from which the milling is removed by filing or cutting the edges and on which new milling is made to restore its appearance,

(*e*) a coin cased with gold, silver or nickel, as the case may be, that is intended to resemble or pass for a current gold, silver or nickel coin, and

(*f*) a coin or a piece of metal or mixed metals washed or coloured by any means with a wash or material capable of producing the appearance of gold, silver or nickel and that is intended to resemble or pass for a current gold, silver or nickel coin;

"counterfeit token of value" means a counterfeit excise stamp, postage stamp or other evidence of value, by whatever technical, trivial or deceptive designation it may be described, and includes genuine coin or paper money that has no value as money;

"current" means lawfully current in Canada or elsewhere by virtue of a law, proclamation or regulation in force in Canada or elsewhere as the case may be;

"utter" includes sell, pay, tender and put off.

Making

Making.

449. Every one who makes or begins to make counterfeit money is guilty of an indictable offence and liable to imprisonment for a term not exceeding fourteen years.

Possession

Possession, etc., of counterfeit money.

450. Every one who, without lawful justification or excuse, the proof of which lies on him,

(*a*) buys, receives or offers to buy or receive,

(*b*) has in his custody or possession, or

(*c*) introduces into Canada,

counterfeit money is guilty of an indictable offence and liable to imprisonment for a term not exceeding fourteen years.

Having clippings, etc.

451. Every one who, without lawful justification or excuse, the proof of which lies on him, has in his custody or possession

(*a*) gold or silver filings or clippings,

(*b*) gold or silver bullion, or

(*c*) gold or silver in dust, solution or otherwise,

produced or obtained by impairing, diminishing or lightening a current gold or silver coin, knowing that it has been so produced or obtained, is guilty of an indictable offence and liable to imprisonment for a term not exceeding five years.

Uttering

Uttering, etc., counterfeit money.

452. Every one who, without lawful justification or excuse, the proof of which lies on him,

(*a*) utters or offers to utter counterfeit money or uses counterfeit money as if it were genuine, or

(*b*) exports, sends or takes counterfeit money out of Canada,

is guilty of an indictable offence and liable to imprisonment for a term not exceeding fourteen years.

Uttering coin.

453. Every one who, with intent to defraud, knowingly utters

(*a*) a coin that is not current, or

(*b*) a piece of metal or mixed metals that resembles in size, figure or colour a current coin for which it is uttered,

is guilty of an indictable offence and liable to imprisonment for a term not exceeding two years.

Slugs and tokens.

454. Every one who without lawful excuse, the proof of which lies on him,

(*a*) manufactures, produces or sells, or

(*b*) has in his possession

anything that is intended to be fraudulently used in substitution for a coin or token of value that any coin or token-operated device is designed to receive is guilty of an offence punishable on summary conviction.

Defacing or Impairing

Clipping and uttering clipped coin.

455. Every one who

(*a*) impairs, diminishes or lightens a current gold or silver coin with intent that it should pass for a current gold or silver coin, or

(*b*) utters a coin, knowing that it has been impaired, diminished or lightened contrary to paragraph (*a*),

is guilty of an indictable offence and liable to imprisonment for a term not exceeding fourteen years.

Defacing current coins.

456. Every one who

(*a*) defaces a current coin, or

(*b*) utters a current coin that has been defaced,

is guilty of an offence punishable on summary conviction.

Printing circulars, etc., in likeness of notes — Printing anything in likeness of bank-note, etc. — When no conviction under subsection (2).

457. (1) Every one who designs, engraves, prints or in any manner makes, executes, issues, distributes, circulates or uses any business or professional card, notice, placard, circular, handbill or advertisement in the likeness or appearance of

(*a*) a current bank-note or current paper money, or

(*b*) any obligation or security of a government or a bank,

is guilty of an offence punishable on summary conviction.

(2) Every one who publishes or prints anything in the likeness or appearance of

(*a*) all or part of a current bank-note or current paper money, or

(*b*) all or part of any obligation or security of a government or a bank,

is guilty of an offence punishable on summary conviction.

(3) No person shall be convicted of an offence under subsection (2) where it is established that, in publishing or printing anything to which that subsection applies,

(*a*) no photography was used at any stage for the purpose of publishing or printing it, except in connection with processes necessarily involved in transferring a finished drawing or sketch to a printed surface;

(*b*) except for the word "Canada", nothing having the appearance of a word, letter or numeral was a complete word, letter or numeral;
(*c*) no representation of a human face or figure was more than a general indication of features, without detail;
(*d*) no more than one colour was used; and
(*e*) nothing in the likeness or appearance of the back of a current bank note or current paper money was published or printed in any form.

Instruments or Materials

Making, having or dealing in instruments for counterfeiting.

458. Every one who, without lawful justification or excuse, the proof of which lies on him,
(*a*) makes or repairs,
(*b*) begins or proceeds to make or repair,
(*c*) buys or sells, or
(*d*) has in his custody or possession,
any machine, engine, tool, instrument, material or thing that he knows has been used or that he knows is adapted and intended for use in making counterfeit money or counterfeit tokens of value is guilty of an indictable offence and liable to imprisonment for a term not exceeding fourteen years.

Conveying instruments for coining out of mint.

459. Every one who, without lawful justification or excuse, the proof of which lies on him, knowingly conveys out of any of Her Majesty's mints in Canada,
(*a*) any machine, engine, tool, instrument, material or thing used or employed in connection with the manufacture of coins,
(*b*) a useful part of anything mentioned in paragraph (*a*), or
(*c*) coin, bullion, metal or a mixture of metals,
is guilty of an indictable offence and liable to imprisonment for a term not exceeding fourteen years.

Advertising and Trafficking in Counterfeit Money or Counterfeit Tokens of Value

Advertising and dealing in counterfeit money, etc. — Fraudulent use of money genuine but valueless.

460. (1) Every one who
(*a*) by an advertisement or any other writing, offers to sell, procure or dispose of counterfeit money or counterfeit tokens of value or to give information with respect to the manner in which or the means by which counterfeit money or counterfeit tokens of value may be sold, procured or disposed of, or
(*b*) purchases, obtains, negotiates or otherwise deals with counterfeit tokens of value, or offers to negotiate with a view to purchasing or obtaining them,

is guilty of an indictable offence and liable to imprisonment for a term not exceeding five years.

(2) No person shall be convicted of an offence under subsection (1) in respect of genuine coin or genuine paper money that has no value as money unless, at the time when the offence is alleged to have been committed, he knew that the coin or paper money had no value as money and he had a fraudulent intent in his dealings with or with respect to the coin or paper money.

Special Provisions as to Proof

When counterfeit complete — Certificate of examiner of counterfeit — Cross-examination and notice.

461. (1) Every offence relating to counterfeit money or counterfeit tokens of value shall be deemed to be complete notwithstanding that the money or tokens of value in respect of which the proceedings are taken are not finished or perfected or do not copy exactly the money or tokens of value that they are apparently intended to resemble or for which they are apparently intended to pass.

(2) In any proceedings under this Part, a certificate signed by a person designated as an examiner of counterfeit by the Solicitor General of Canada, stating that any coin, paper money or bank note described therein is counterfeit money or that any coin, paper money or bank note described therein is genuine and is or is not, as the case may be, current in Canada or elsewhere, is evidence of the statements contained in the certificate without proof of the signature or official character of the person appearing to have signed the certificate.

(3) Subsections 258(6) and (7) apply, with such modification as the circumstances require, in respect of a certificate described in subsection (2). 1992, c. 1, s. 58(1), Sch. I, item 7.

Forfeiture

Ownership — Seizure.

462. (1) Counterfeit money, counterfeit tokens of value and anything that is used or is intended to be used to make counterfeit money or counterfeit tokens of value belong to Her Majesty.

(2) A peace officer may seize and detain

(*a*) counterfeit money,

(*b*) counterfeit tokens of value, and

(*c*) machines, engines, tools, instruments, materials or things that have been used or that have been adapted and are intended for use in making counterfeit money or counterfeit tokens of value,

and anything seized shall be sent to the Minister of Finance to be disposed of or dealt with as he may direct, but anything that is required as evidence in any proceedings shall not be sent to the Minister until it is no longer required in those proceedings.

PART XII.1

INSTRUMENTS AND LITERATURE FOR ILLICIT DRUG USE

Interpretation

"Consume" — "Consumption" — "Illicit drug" — "Illicit drug use" — "Instrument for illicit drug use" — "Literature for illicit drug use" — "Sell".

462.1 In this Part,

"consume", "consumption" includes smoking, inhaling, masticating and injecting into the human body;

"illicit drug" means a narcotic, drug or other substance whose import, export, cultivation, sale or possession is prohibited pursuant to the *Narcotic Control Act* controlled pursuant to Part III of the *Food and Drugs Act* or restricted pursuant to Part IV of the *Food and Drugs Act*;

"illicit drug use" means the importation, exportation, cultivation, sale or possession of a narcotic, drug or other substance contrary to the *Narcotic Control Act* or Part III or IV of the *Food and Drugs Act* or a regulation made thereunder;

"instrument for illicit drug use" means anything designed primarily or intended under the circumstances for consuming or to facilitate the consumption of an illicit drug, but does not include a "device" as that term is defined in section 2 of the *Food and Drugs Act*;

"literature for illicit drug use" means any printed matter or video describing or depicting, and designed primarily or intended under the circumstances to promote, encourage or advocate the production, preparation or consumption of illicit drugs;

"sell" includes offer for sale, expose for sale, have in possession for sale and distribute, whether or not the distribution is made for consideration. R.S. 1985, c. 50 (4th Supp.), s. 1.

Offence

Offence.

462.2 Every one who knowingly imports into Canada, exports from Canada, manufactures, promotes or sells instruments or literature for illicit drug use is guilty of an offence and is liable on summary conviction

(*a*) for a first offence, to a fine not exceeding one hundred thousand dollars or to imprisonment for a term not exceeding six months or to both; or

(*b*) for a second or subsequent offence, to a fine not exceeding three hundred thousand dollars or to imprisonment for a term not exceeding one year or to both. R.S. 1985, c. 50 (4th Supp.), s. 1.

PART XII.2

PROCEEDS OF CRIME

Interpretation

Definitions — "Designated drug offence" — "Enterprise crime offence" — "Judge" — "Proceeds of crime".

462.3 In this Part,

"designated drug offence" means

(*a*) an offence against section 39, 44.2, 44.3, 48, 50.2 or 50.3 of the *Food and Drugs Act*,

(*b*) an offence against section 4, 5, 6, 19.1 or 19.2 of the *Narcotic Control Act*, or

(*c*) a conspiracy or an attempt to commit, being an accessory after the fact in relation to or any counselling in relation to, an offence referred to in paragraph (*a*) or (*b*);

"enterprise crime offence" means

(*a*) an offence against any of the following provisions, namely,

(i) section 119 (bribery of judicial officers, etc.).

(ii) section 120 (bribery of officers),

(iii) section 121 (frauds upon the government),

(iv) section 122 (breach of trust by public officer),

(v) section 163 (corrupting morals),

(vi) subsection 201(1) (keeping gaming or betting house),

(vii) section 202 (betting, pool-selling, book-making, etc),

(viii) section 210 (keeping common bawdy-house),

(ix) section 212 (procuring),

(x) section 235 (punishment for murder),

(xi) section 334 (punishment for theft),

(xii) section 344 (punishment for robbery),

(xiii) section 346 (extortion),

(xiv) section 367 (punishment for forgery),

(xv) section 368 (uttering forged document),

(xvi) section 380 (fraud),

(xvii) section 382 (fraudulent manipulation of stock exchange transactions),

(xviii) section 426 (secret commissions),

(xix) section 433 (arson)

(xx) section 449 (making counterfeit money),

(xxi) section 450 (possession, etc., of counterfeit money),

(xxii) section 452 (uttering, etc., counterfeit money), or

(xxiii) section 462.31 (laundering proceeds of crime),

(*b*) an offence against section 354 (possession of property obtained by crime), committed in relation to any property, thing or proceeds obtained or derived directly or indirectly as a result of

(i) the commission in Canada of an offence referred to in paragraph (*a*) or a designated drug offence, or

(ii) an act or omission anywhere that, if it had occurred in Canada, would have constituted an offence referred to in paragraph (*a*) or a designated drug offence, or

(*c*) a conspiracy or an attempt to commit, being an accessory after the fact in relation to, or any counselling in relation to, an offence referred to in paragraph (*a*) or (*b*);

"judge" means a judge as defined in section 552 or a judge of a superior court of criminal jurisdiction;

"proceeds of crime" means an property, benefit or advantage, within or outside Canada, obtained or derived directly or indirectly as a result of

(*a*) the commission in Canada of an enterprise crime offence or a designated drug offence, or

(*b*) an act or omission anywhere that, if it had occurred in Canada, would have constituted an enterprise crime offence or a designated drug offence. R.S. 1985, c. 42 (4th Supp.), s. 2.

Offence

Laundering proceeds of crime — Punishment.

462.31 (1) Every one commits an offence who uses, transfers the possession of, sends or delivers to any person or place, transports, transmits, alters, disposes of or otherwise deals with, in any manner and by any means, any property or any proceeds of any property with intent to conceal or convert that property or those proceeds and knowing that all or a part of that property or of those proceeds was obtained or derived directly or indirectly as a result of

(*a*) the commission in Canada of an enterprise crime offence or a designated drug offence; or

(*b*) an act or omission anywhere that, if it had occurred in Canada, would have constituted an enterprise crime offence or a designated drug offence.

(2) Every one who commits an offence under subsection (1)

(*a*) is guilty of an indictable offence and is liable to imprisonment for a term not exceeding ten years; or

(*b*) is guilty of an offence punishable on summary conviction. R.S. 1985, c. 42 (4th Supp.), s. 2.

Search, Seizure and Detention of Proceeds of Crime

Special search warrant — Procedure — Execution of warrant in other territorial jurisdictions — Records of property seized — Notice — Undertaking by Attorney General.

462.32 (1) Subject to subsection (3), where a judge, on application of the Attorney General, is satisfied by information on oath in Form 1 that there are reasonable grounds to believe that there is in any building, receptacle or place any property in respect of which an order of forfeiture may be made under subsection 462.37(1) or 462.38(2), the judge may issue a warrant authorizing a person named therein or a peace officer to search the building, receptacle or place for that property and to seize that property and any other property in respect of which that person or peace officer believes, on reasonable grounds, that an order of forfeiture may be made under that subsection.

(2) An application for a warrant under subsection (1) may be made ex parte and shall be made in writing.

(3) Subsections 487(2) to (4) and section 488 apply, with such modifications as the circumstances require, to a warrant issued under this section.

(4) Every person who executes a warrant issued by a judge under this section shall

(*a*) detain or cause to be detained the property seized, taking reasonable care to ensure that the property is preserved so that it may be dealt with in accordance with the law;

(*b*) as soon as practicable after the execution of the warrant but within a period not exceeding seven days thereafter, prepare a report in Form 5.3, identifying the property seized and the location where the property is being detained and cause the report to be filed with the clerk of the court; and

(*c*) cause a copy of the report to be provided, on request, to the person from whom the property was seized and to any other person who, in the opinion of the judge, appears to have a valid interest in the property.

(5) Before issuing a warrant under this section in relation to any property, a judge ,may require notice to be given to and may hear any person who, in the opinion of the judge, appears to have a valid interest the property unless the judge is of the opinion that giving such notice before the issuance of the warrant would result in the disappearance, dissipation or reduction in value of the property or otherwise affect the property so that all or a part thereof could not be seized pursuant to the warrant.

(6) Before issuing a warrant under this section, a judge shall require the Attorney General to give such undertakings as the judge considers appropriate with respect to the payment of damages or costs, or both, in relation to the issuance and execution of the warrant. R.S. 1985, c. 42 (4th Supp.), s. 2.

Application for restraint order — Procedure — Restraint order — Idem — Notice — Order in writing — Undertakings by Attorney General — Service of order — Registration of order — Continues in force — Offence.

462.33 (1) The Attorney General may make an application in accordance with subsection (2) for a restraint order under subsection (3) in respect of any property.

(2) An application made under subsection (1) for a restraint order under subsection (3) in respect of any property may be made ex parte and shall be made in writing to a judge and be accompanied by an affidavit sworn on the information and belief of the Attorney General or any other person deposing to the following matters, namely,

(*a*) the offence or matter under investigation;

(*b*) the person who is believed to be in possession of the property;

(*c*) the grounds for the belief that an order of forfeiture may be made under subsection 462.37(1) or 462.38(2) in respect of the property; and

(*d*) a description of the property.

(3) Where an application for a restraint order is made to a judge under subsection (1), the judge may, if satisfied that there are reasonable grounds to believe that there exists any property in respect of which an order of forfeiture may be made under subsection 462.37(1) or 462.38(2), make an order

(*a*) prohibiting any person from disposing of, or otherwise dealing with any interest in, the property specified in the order otherwise than in such manner as may be specified in the order; and

(*b*) at the request of the Attorney General, where the judge is of the opinion that the circumstances so require,

(i) appointing a person to take control of and to manage or otherwise deal with all or part of that property in accordance with the directions of the judge, and

(ii) requiring any person having possession of that property to give possession of the property to the person appointed under subparagraph (i).

(4) An order made by a judge under subsection (3) may be subject to such reasonable conditions as the judge thinks fit.

(5) Before making an order subsection (3) in relation to any property, a judge may require notice to be given to and may hear any person who, in the opinion of the judge, appears to have a valid interest in the property unless the judge is of the opinion that giving such notice before making the order would result in the disappearance, dissipation or reduction in value of the property or otherwise affect the property so that all or a part thereof could not be subject to an order of forfeiture under subsection 462.37(1) or 462.38(2).

(6) An order made under subsection (3) shall be made in writing.

(7) Before making an order under subsection (3), a judge shall require the

Attorney General to give such undertakings as the judge considers appropriate with respect to the payment of damages or costs, or both, in relation to the making and execution of the order.

(8) A copy of an order made by a judge under subsection (3) shall be served on the person to whom the order is addressed in such manner as the judge directs or as may be prescribed by rules of court.

(9) A copy of an order made under subsection (3), shall be registered against any property in accordance with the laws of the province in which the property is situated.

(10) An order made under subsection (3) remains in effect until

(*a*) it is revoked or varied under subsection 462.34(4) or revoked under paragraph 462.43 (*a*);

(*b*) it ceases to be in force under section 462.35; or

(*c*) an order of forfeiture or restoration of the property is made under subsection 462.37(1), 462.38(2) or 462.41(3) or any other provision of this or any other Act of Parliament.

(11) Any person on whom an order made under subsection (3) is served in accordance with this section and who, while the order is in force, acts in contravention of or fails to comply with the order is guilty of an indictable offence or an offence punishable on summary conviction. R.S. 1985, c. 42 (4th Supp.), s. 2.

Application for review of special warrants and restraint orders — Notice to Attorney General — Conditions for examinations order — Order of restoration of property or revocation or variation of order — Hearing — Conditions to be satisfied — Saving provision — Form of recognizance.

462.34 (1) Any person who has an interest in property that was seized under a warrant issued pursuant to section 462.32 or in respect of which a restraint order was made under subsection 462.33(3) may, at any time, apply to a judge

(*a*) for an order under subsection (4);or

(*b*) for permission to examine the property.

(2) Where an application is made under paragraph (1)(*a*),

(*a*) the application shall not, without the consent of the Attorney General, be heard by a judge unless the applicant has given to the Attorney General at least two clear days notice in writing of the application; and

(*b*) the judge may require notice of the application to be given to and may hear any person who, in the opinion of the judge, appears to have a valid interest in the property.

(3) A judge may, on an application made to the judge under paragraph (1)(*b*), order that the applicant be permitted to examine property subject to such terms as appear to the judge to be necessary or desirable to ensure that the property is safeguarded and preserved for any purpose for which it may subsequently be required.

(4) On an application made to a judge under paragraph (1)(*a*) in respect

of any property and after hearing the applicant and the Attorney General and any other person to whom notice was given pursuant to paragraph (2)(*b*), the judge may order that the property or a part thereof be returned to the applicant or, in the case of a restraint order made under subsection 462.33(3), revoke the order, vary the order to exclude the property or any interest in the property or part thereof from the application of the order or make the order subject to such reasonable conditions as the judge thinks fit,

(*a*) if the applicant enters into a recognizance before the judge, with or without sureties, in such amount and with such conditions, if any, as the judge directs and, where the judge considers it appropriate, deposits with the judge such sum of money or other valuable security as the judge directs;

(*b*) if the conditions referred to in subsection (6) are satisfied; or

(*c*) for the purpose of

(i) meeting the reasonable living expenses of the person who was in possession of the property at the time the warrant was executed or the order was made or any person who, in the opinion of the judge, has a valid interest in the property and of the dependants of that person,

(ii) meeting the reasonable business and legal expenses of a person referred to in subparagraph (i), or

(iii) permitting the use of the property in order to enter into a recognizance under Part XVI.

(5) For the purpose of determining the reasonableness of legal expenses, referred to in subparagraph (4)(*c*)(ii), a judge shall hold an in camera hearing and without the presence of the Attorney General.

(6) An order under paragraph (4)(*b*) in respect of property may be made by a judge if the judge is satisfied

(*a*) where the application is made by

(i) a person charged with an enterprise crime offence or a designated drug offence, or

(ii) any person who acquired title to or a right of possession of that property from a person referred to in subparagraph (i) under circumstances that give rise to a reasonable inference that the title or right was transferred from that person for the purpose of avoiding the forfeiture of the property,

that a warrant should not have been issued pursuant to section 462.32 or a restraint order under subsection 462.33(3) should not have been made in respect of that property, or

(*b*) in any other case, that the applicant is the lawful owner of or lawfully entitled to possession of the property and appears innocent of any complicity in an enterprise crime offence or designated drug offence or of any collusion in relation to such an offence,

and that the property will no longer be required for the purpose of any investigation or as evidence in any proceeding.

(7) Section 354 of this Act, sections 44.2 and 50.2 of the *Food and Drugs*

Act and section 17.1 of the *Narcotic Control Act* do not apply to a person who comes into possession of any property or thing that, pursuant to an order made under paragraph (4)(*c*), was returned to any person after having been seized or was excluded from the application of a restraint order made under subsection 462.33(3).

(8) A recognizance entered into pursuant to paragraph (4)(*a*) may be in Form 32. R.S. 2985, c. 42 (4th Supp.), s. 2.

Automatic expiry of special warrants and restraint orders.

462.35 Where property has been seized under a warrant issued pursuant to section 462.32 or a restraint order has been made under section 462.33 in relation to property, the property shall not be detained under the authority of this section or the order shall not continue in force, as the case may be, for a period of more than six months after the time of the seizure or the making of the order, as the case may be, unless, before the expiration of that period, the Attorney General establishes to the satisfaction of a judge that the property may be required after the expiration of that period for the purpose of section 462.37 or 462.38 or any other provision of this or any other Act of Parliament respecting forfeiture or for the purpose of any investigation or as evidence in any proceeding. R.S. 1985, c. 42 (4th Supp.), s. 2.

When accused ordered to stand trial.

462.36 Where a judge issues a warrant under section 462.32 or makes a restraint order under section 462.33 in respect of any property, the clerk of the court shall, when an accused is ordered to stand trial for an enterprise crime offence, cause to be forwarded to the clerk of the court to which the accused has been ordered to stand trail a copy of the report filed pursuant to paragraph 462.32(4)(*b*) or of the restraint order in respect of the property. R.S. 1985, c. 42 (4th Supp.), s. 2.

Forfeiture of Proceeds of Crime

Order of forfeiture of property on conviction — Proceeds of crime derived from other offences — Fine instead of forfeiture — Imprisonment in default of payment of fine — Fine option not available to offender

462.37 (1) Subject to this section and sections 462.39 to 462.41, where an offender is convicted or discharged under section 736 of an enterprise crime offence and the court imposing sentence on the offender, on application of the Attorney General, is satisfied, on a balance of probabilities, that any property is proceeds of crime and that the enterprise crime offence was committed in relation to that property, the court shall order that the property be forfeited to Her Majesty to be disposed of as the Attorney General directs or otherwise dealt with in accordance with the law.

(2) Where the evidence does not establish to the satisfaction of the court

that the enterprise crime offence of which the offender is convicted or discharged under section 736 was committed in relation to property in respect of which an order of forfeiture would otherwise be made under subsection (1) but the court is satisfied, beyond a reasonable doubt, that that property is proceeds of crime, the court may make an order of forfeiture under subsection (1) in relation to that property.

(3) Where a court is satisfied that an order of forfeiture under subsection (1) should be made in respect of any property of an offender, but that that property or any part thereof or interest therein cannot be made subject to such an order and, in particular,

(*a*) cannot, on the exercise of due diligence, be located,

(*b*) has been transferred to a third party,

(*c*) is located outside Canada,

(*d*) has been substantially diminished in value or rendered worthless, or

(*e*) has been commingled with other property that cannot be divided without difficulty,

the court may, instead of ordering that property or part thereof or interest therein to be forfeited pursuant to subsection (1), order the offender to pay a fine in an amount equal to the value of that property, part or interest.

(4) Where a court orders an offender to pay a fine pursuant to subsection (3), the court shall

(*a*) impose, in default of payment of that fine, a term of imprisonment

(i) not exceeding six months, where the amount of the fine does not exceed ten thousand dollars,

(ii) of not less than six months and not exceeding twelve months, where the amount of the fine exceeds ten thousand dollars but does not exceed twenty thousand dollars,

(iii) of not less than twelve months and not exceeding eighteen months, where the amount of the fine exceeds twenty thousand dollars but does not exceed fifty thousand dollars,

(iv) of not less than eighteen months and not exceeding two years, where the amount of the fine exceeds fifty thousand dollars but does not exceed one hundred thousand dollars,

(v) of not less than two years and not exceeding three years, where the amount of the fine exceeds one hundred thousand dollars but does not exceed two hundred and fifty thousand dollars,

(vi) of not less than three years and not exceeding five years, where the amount of the fine exceeds two hundred and fifty thousand dollars but does not exceed one million dollars, or

(vii) of not less than five years and not exceeding ten years, where the amount of the fine exceeds one million dollars; and

(*b*) direct that the term of imprisonment imposed pursuant to paragraph (*a*) be served consecutively to any other term of imprisonment imposed on the offender or that the offender is then serving.

(5) Section 718.1 does not apply to an offender against whom a fine is imposed pursuant to subsection (3). R.S. 1985, c. 42 (4th Supp.), s. 2.

Application for *in rem* forfeiture hearing — Order of forfeiture of property — Person deemed absconded.

462.38 (1) Where an information has been laid in respect of an enterprise crime offence, the Attorney General may make an application to a judge for an order of forfeiture under subsection (2) in respect of any property.

(2) Subject to sections 462.39 to 462.41, where an application is made to a judge under subsection (1), the judge shall, if the judge is satisfied that

(*a*) any property is, beyond a reasonable doubt, proceeds of crime,

(*b*) proceedings in respect of an enterprise crime offence committed in relation to that property were commenced, and

(*c*) the accused charged with the offence referred to in paragraph (*b*) has died or absconded,

order that the property be forfeited to Her Majesty to be disposed of as the Attorney General directs or otherwise dealt with in accordance with the law.

(3) For the purposes of this section a person shall be deemed to have absconded in connection with an enterprise crime offence if

(*a*) an information has been laid alleging the commission of the offence by the person,

(*b*) a warrant for the arrest of the person has been issued in relation to that information, and

(*c*) reasonable attempts to arrest the person pursuant to the warrant have been unsuccessful during the period of six months commencing on the day the warrant was issued,

and the person shall be deemed to have so absconded on the last day of that period of six months. R.S. 1985, c. 42 (4th Supp.), s. 2.

Inference.

462.39 For the purpose of subsection 462.37(1) or 462.38(2), the court may infer that property was obtained or derived as a result of the commission of an enterprise crime offence where evidence establishes that the value, after the commission of that of offence, of all property of the person alleged to have committed the offence exceeds the value of all the property of that person before the commission of that offence and the court is satisfied that the income of that person from sources unrelated to enterprise crime offences or designated drug offences committed by that person cannot reasonably account for such an increase in value. R.S. 1985, c. 42 (4th Supp.), s. 2.

Voidable transfers.

462.4 A court may,

(*a*) prior to ordering property to be forfeited under subsection 462.37(1) or 462.38(2), and (*b*) in the case of property in respect of which a restraint order was made under section 462.33, where the order was served in accordance with subsection 462.33(8),

set aside any conveyance or transfer of the property that occurred after the seizure of the property or the service of the order under section 462.33, unless the conveyance or transfer was for valuable consideration to a person acting in good faith and without notice. R.S. 1985, c. 42 (4th Supp.), s. 2.

Notice — Manner of giving notice — Order of restoration of property.

462.41 (1) Before making an order under subsection 462.37(1) or 462.38(2) in relation to any property, a court shall require notice in accordance with subsection (2) to be given to and may hear any person who, in the opinion of the court, appears to have a valid interest in the property.

(2) A notice given under subsection (1) shall

(*a*) be given or served in such manner as the court directs or as may be prescribed by the rules of the court;

(*b*) be of such duration as the court considers reasonable or as may be prescribed by the rules of the court; and

(*c*) set out the enterprise crime offence charged and a description of the property.

(3) Where a court is satisfied that any person, other than

(*a*) a person who was charged with an enterprise crime offence or a designated drug offence, or

(*b*) a person who acquired title to or a right of possession of that property from a person referred to in paragraph (*a*) under circumstances that give rise to a reasonable inference that the title or right was transferred for the purpose of avoiding the forfeiture of the property,

is the lawful owner or is lawfully entitled to possession of any property or any part thereof that would otherwise be forfeited pursuant to subsection 462.37(1) or 462.38(2) and that the person appears innocent of any complicity in an offence referred to in paragraph (*a*) or of any collusion in relation to such an offence, the court may order that the property or part thereof be returned to that person. R.S. 1985, c. 42 (4th Supp.), s. 2.

Application by person claiming interest for relief from forfeiture — Fixing day for hearing — Notice — Order declaring interest not subject to forfeiture — Appeal from order under subsection (4) — Return of property.

462.42 (1) Where any property is forfeited to Her Majesty under subsection 462.37(1) or 462.38(2), any person who claims an interest in the property, other than

(*a*) a person who was charged with an enterprise crime offence or a designated drug offence that was committed in relation to the property forfeited, or

(*b*) a person who acquired title to or a right of possession of that property from a person referred to in paragraph (*a*) under circumstances that give rise to a reasonable inference that the title or right was transferred from that person for the purpose of avoiding the forfeiture of the property,

may, within thirty days after that forfeiture, apply by notice in writing to a judge for an order under subsection (4).

(2) The judge to whom an application is made under subsection (1) shall fix a day not less than thirty days after the date of filing of the application for the hearing thereof.

(3) An applicant shall serve a notice of the application made under subsection (1) and of the hearing thereof on the Attorney General at least fifteen days before the day fixed for the hearing.

(4) Where, on the hearing of an application made under subsection (1), the judge is satisfied that the applicant is not a person referred to in paragraph (1)(*a*) or (*b*) and appears innocent of any complicity in any enterprise crime offence or designated drug offence that resulted in the forfeiture or of any collusion in relation to any such offence, the judge may make an order declaring that the interest of the applicant is not affected by the forfeiture and declaring the nature and extent of the interest.

(5) An applicant or the Attorney General may appeal to the court of appeal from an order under subsection (4) and the provisions of Part XXI with respect to procedure on appeals apply, with such modifications as the circumstances require, to appeals under this subsection.

(6) The Attorney General shall, on application made to the Attorney General by any person who has obtained an order under subsection (4) and where the periods with respect to the taking of appeals from that order taken under subsection (5) has been determined,

(*a*) direct that the property or the part thereof to which the interest of the applicant relates be returned to the applicant; or

(*b*) direct that an amount equal to the value of the interest of the applicant, as declared in the order, be paid to the applicant. R.S. 1985, c. 42 (4th Supp.), s. 2.

Residual disposal of property seized or dealt with pursuant to special warrants or restraint orders.

462.43 Where property has been seized under a warrant issued pursuant to section 462.32, a restraint order has been made under section 462.33 in relation to any property or a recognizance has been entered into pursuant to paragraph 462.34(4)(*a*) in relation to any property and a judge, on application made to the judge by the Attorney General or any person having an interest in the property or on the judge's own motion, after notice given to the Attorney General and any other person having an interest in the property, is satisfied that the property will no longer be required for the purposes of section 462.37, 462.38 or any other provision of this or any other Act of Parliament respecting forfeiture or for the purpose of any investigation or as evidence in any proceeding, the judge

(*a*) in the case of a restraint order, shall revoke the order;

(*b*) in the case of a recognizance, shall cancel the recognizance; and

(*c*) in the case of property seized under a warrant issued pursuant to section 462.32 or property under the control of a person appointed pursuant to subparagraph 462.33(3)(*b*)(i),

(i) if possession of it by the person from whom it was taken is lawful, shall order that it be returned to that person,

(ii) if possession of it by the person from whom it was taken is unlawful and the lawful owner or person who is lawfully entitled to its possession is known, shall order that it be returned to the lawful owner or the person who is lawfully entitled to its possession, or

(iii) if possession of it by the person from whom it was taken is unlawful and the lawful owner or person who is lawfully entitled to its possession is not known, may order that it be forfeited to Her Majesty, to be disposed of as the Attorney General directs, or otherwise dealt with in accordance with the law. R.S. 1985, c. 42 (4th Supp.), s. 2.

Appeals from orders under subsection 462.38(2) or section 462.43

462.44 Any person who considers himself aggrieved by an order made under subsection 462.38(2) or section 462.43 may appeal from the order as if the order were an appeal against conviction or against a judgment or verdict of acquittal, as the case may be, under Part XXI and that Part applies, with such modifications as the circumstances require, to such an appeal. R.S. 1985, c. 42 (4th Supp.), s. 2.

Suspension of forfeiture pending appeal.

462.45 Notwithstanding anything in this Part, the operation of an order of forfeiture or restoration of property under subsection 462.34(4), 462.37(1), 462.38(2) or 462.41(3) or section 462.43 is suspended pending

(*a*) any application made in respect of the property under any of those provisions or any other provision of this or any other Act of Parliament that provides for the restoration or forfeiture of such property,

(*b*) any appeal taken from an order of forfeiture or restoration in respect of the property, or

(*c*) any other proceeding in which the right of seizure of the property is questioned,

and property shall not be disposed of within thirty days after an order of forfeiture is made under any of those provisions. R.S. 1985, c. 42 (4th Supp.), s. 2.

Copies of documents returned or forfeited — Probative force.

462.46 (1) Where any document is returned or ordered to be returned, forfeited or otherwise dealt with under subsection 462.34(3) or (4), 462.37(1), 462.38(2) or 462.41(3) or section 462.43, the Attorney General may, before returning the document or complying with the order, cause a copy of the document to be made and retained.

(2) Every copy made under subsection (1) shall, if certified as a true copy by the Attorney General, be admissible in evidence and, in the absence of evidence to the contrary, shall have the same probative force as the original document would have had if it had been proved in the ordinary way. R.S. 1985, c. 42 (4th Supp.), s. 2.

Disclosure Provisions

No civil or criminal liability incurred by informants.

462.47 For greater certainty but subject to section 241 of the Income Tax Act, a person is justified in disclosing to a peace officer or the Attorney General any facts on the basis of which that person reasonably suspects that any property is proceeds of crime or that any person has committed or is about to commit an enterprise crime offence or a designated drug offence. R.S. 1985, c. 42 (4th Supp.), s. 2.

Disclosure of income tax information — Application — Order for disclosure of information — Service of order — Extension of period for compliance with order — Objection to disclosure of information — Determination of objection — Judge may examine information — Limitation period — Appeal to Federal Court of Appeal — Limitation period for appeal — Special rules for hearings — *Ex parte* representation — Copies — Further disclosure — Form — Definition of "police officer".

462.48 (1) The Attorney General may, for the purposes of an investigation in relation to

(*a*) a designated drug offence, or

(*b*) an offence against section 354 or 462.31 where the offence is alleged to have been committed in relation to any property, thing or proceeds obtained or derived directly or indirectly as a result of

(i) the commission in Canada of a designated drug offence, or

(ii) an act or omission anywhere that, if it had occurred in Canada, would have constituted a designated drug offence,

make an application in accordance with subsection (2) for an order for disclosure of information under subsection (3).

(2) An application under subsection (1) shall be made ex parte in writing to a judge and be accompanied by an affidavit sworn on the information and belief of the Attorney General or a person specially designated by the Attorney General for that purpose deposing to the following matters, namely,

(*a*) the offence or matter under investigation;

(*b*) the person in relation to whom the information or documents referred to in paragraph (*c*) are required;

(*c*) the type of information or book, record, writing, return or other document obtained by or on behalf of the Minister of Nation Revenue for the purposes of the Income Tax Act to which access is sought or that is proposed to be examined or communicated; and

(*d*) the facts relied on to justify the belief, on reasonable grounds, that the person referred to in paragraph (*b*) has committed or benefited from the commission of an offence referred to in paragraph (1)(*a*) or (*b*) and that the information or documents referred to in paragraph (*c*) are likely to be of substantial value, whether alone or together with other material, to the investigation for the purposes of which the application is made.

(3) Where the judge to whom an application under subsection (1) is made is satisfied

(*a*) of the matters referred to in paragraph (2)(*d*), and

(*b*) that there are reasonable grounds for believing that it is in the public interest to allow access to the information or documents to which the application relates, having regard to the benefit likely to accrue to the investigation if the access is obtained,

the judge may, subject to such conditions as the judge considers advisable in the public interest, order the Deputy Minister of National Revenue for Taxation or any person specially designated in writing by that Deputy Minister for the purposes of this section

(*c*) to allow a police officer named in the order access to all such information and documents and to examine them, or

(*d*) where the judge considers it necessary in the circumstances, to produce all such information and documents to the police officer and allow the police officer to remove the information and documents from the possession of that person,

within such period as the judge may specify after the expiration of seven clear days following the service of the order pursuant to subsection (4).

(4) A copy of an order made by a judge under subsection (3) shall be served on the person to whom the order is addressed in such manner as the judge directs or as may be prescribed by rules of court.

(5) A judge who makes an order under subsection (3) may, on application of the Minister of National Revenue, extend the period within which the order is to be complied with.

(6) The Minister of National Revenue or any person specially designated in writing by that Minister for the purposes of this section may object to the disclosure of any information or document in respect of which an order under subsection (3) has been made by certifying orally or in writing that the information or document should not be disclosed on the ground that

(*a*) the Minister of National Revenue is prohibited from disclosing the information or document by any bilateral or international treaty, convention or other agreement respecting taxation to which the Government of Canada is signatory;

(*b*) a privilege is attached by law to the information or document;

(*c*) the information or document has been placed in a sealed package pursuant to law or an order of a court of competent jurisdiction; or

(*d*) disclosure of the information or document would not, for any other reason, be in the public interest.

(7) Where an objection to the disclosure of information or a document is made under subsection (6), the objection may be determined, on application, in accordance with subsection (8), by the Chief Justice of the Federal Court, or by such other judge of that court as the Chief Justice may designate to hear such applications.

(8) A judge who is to determine an objection pursuant to subsection (7) may, if the judge considers it necessary to determine the objection, examine the information or document in relation to which the objection is made and shall grant the objection and order that disclosure of the information or document be refused where the judge is satisfied of any of the grounds mentioned in subsection (6).

(9) An application under subsection (7) shall be made within ten days after the objection is made or within such greater or lesser period as the Chief Justice of the Federal Court, or such other judge of that court as the Chief Justice may designate to hear such applications, considers appropriate.

(10) An appeal lies from a determination under subsection (7) to the Federal Court of Appeal.

(11) An appeal under subsection (10) shall be brought within ten days from the date of the determination appealed from or within such further time as the Federal Court of Appeal considers appropriate in the circumstances.

(12) An application under subsection (7) or an appeal brought in respect of that application shall

(*a*) be heard in camera; and

(*b*) on the request of the person objecting to the disclosure of information, be heard and determined in the National Capital Region described in the schedule to the National Capital Act.

(13) During the hearing of an application under subsection (7) or an appeal brought in respect of that application, the person who made the objection in respect of which the application was made or the appeal was brought shall, on the request of that person, be given the opportunity to make representations ex parte.

(14) Where any information or document is examined or provided under subsection (3), the person by whom it is examined or to whom it is provided or any officer of the Department of National Revenue may make, or cause to be made, one or more copies thereof and any copy purporting to be certified

by the Minister of National Revenue or an authorized person to be a copy made pursuant to this subsection is evidence of the nature and content of the original information or document and has the same probative force as the original information or document would have had if it had been proved in the ordinary way.

(15) No person to whom information or documents have been disclosed or provided pursuant to this subsection or pursuant to an order made under subsection (3) shall further disclose the information or documents except for the purposes of the investigation in relation to which the order was made.

(16) An order made under subsection (3) may be in Form 47.

(17) In this section, "police officer" means any officer, constable or other person employed for the preservation and maintenance of the public peace. R.S. 1985, c. 42 (4th Supp.), s. 2.

Specific Rules of Forfeiture

Specific forfeiture provisions unaffected by this Part — Priority for restitution of victims of crime.

462.49 (1) This Part does not affect the operation of any other provision of this or any other Act of Parliament respecting the forfeiture of property.

(2) The property of an offender may be used to satisfy the operation of a provision of this or any other Act of Parliament respecting the forfeiture of property only to the extent that it is not required to satisfy the operation of any other provision of this or any other Act of Parliament respecting the restitution or compensation of persons affected by the commission of offences. R.S. 1985, c. 42 (4th Supp.), s. 2.

Regulations

Regulations.

462.5 The Attorney General may make regulations governing the manner of disposing of or otherwise dealing with, in accordance with the law, property, forfeited under this Part. R.S. 1985, c. 42 (4th Supp.), s. 2.

PART XIII

ATTEMPTS — CONSPIRACIES — ACCESSORIES

Attempts, accessories.

463. Except where otherwise expressly provided by law, the following provisions apply in respect of persons who attempt to commit or are accessories after the fact to the commission of offences:

(*a*) every one who attempts to commit or is an accessory after the fact to the commission of an indictable offence for which, on conviction, an accused is liable to be sentenced to death or to imprisonment for life is guilty of an indictable offence and liable to imprisonment for a term not exceeding fourteen years;

(*b*) every one who attempts to commit or is an accessory after the fact to the commission of an indictable offence for which, on conviction, an accused is liable to imprisonment for fourteen years or less is guilty of an indictable offence and liable to imprisonment for a term that is one-half of the longest term to which a person who is guilty of that offence is liable;

(*c*) every one who attempts to commit or is an accessory after the fact to the commission of an offence punishable on summary conviction is guilty of an offence punishable on summary conviction; and

(*d*) every one who attempts to commit or is an accessory after the fact to the commission of an offence for which the offender may be prosecuted by indictment or for which he is punishable on summary conviction

(i) is guilty of an indictable offence and liable to imprisonment for a term not exceeding a term that is one-half of the longest term to which a person who is guilty of that offence is liable, or

(ii) is guilty of an offence punishable on summary conviction. R.S. 1985, c. 27 (1st Supp.), s. 59.

Counselling offence that is not committed.

464. Except where otherwise expressly provided by law, the following provisions apply in respect of persons who counsel other persons to commit offences, namely,

(*a*) every one who counsels another person to commit an indictable offence is, if the offence is not committed, guilty of an indictable offence and liable to the same punishment to which a person who attempts to commit that offence is liable; and

(*b*) every one who counsels another person to commit an offence punishable on summary conviction is, if the offence is not committed, guilty of an offence punishable on summary conviction. R.S. 1985, c. 27 (1st Supp.), s. 60.

Conspiracy — Conspiracy to commit offences — Idem — Jurisdiction — Appearance of accused at trial — Where previously tried outside Canada.

465. (1) Except where otherwise expressly provided by law, the following provisions apply in respect of conspiracy:

(*a*) every one who conspires with any one to commit murder or to cause another person to be murdered, whether in Canada or not, is guilty of an indictable offence and liable to a maximum term of imprisonment for life;

(*b*) every one who conspires with any one to prosecute a person for an alleged offence, knowing that he did not commit that offence, is guilty of an indictable offence and liable

(i) to imprisonment for a term not exceeding ten years, if the alleged offence is one for which, on conviction, the person would be liable to be sentenced to death or to imprisonment for life or for a term not exceeding fourteen years, or

(ii) to imprisonment for a term not exceeding five years, if the alleged offence is one for which, on conviction, that person would be liable to imprisonment for less than fourteen years; and

(*c*) every one who conspires with any one to commit an indictable offence not provided for in paragraph (*a*) or (*b*) is guilty of an indictable offence and liable to the same punishment as that to which an accused who is guilty of that offence would, on conviction, be liable; and

(*d*) every one who conspires with any one to commit an offence punishable on summary conviction is guilty of an offence punishable on summary conviction.

(2) [Repealed, R.S. 1985, c. 27 (1st Supp.), s. 61(3).]

(3) Every one who, while in Canada, conspires with any one to do anything referred to in subsection (1) in a place outside Canada that is an offence under the laws of that place shall be deemed to have conspired to do that thing in Canada.

(4) Every one who, while in a place outside Canada, conspires with any one to do anything referred to in subsection (1) in Canada shall be deemed to have conspired in Canada to do that thing.

(5) Where a person is alleged to have conspired to do anything that is an offence by virtue of subsection (3) or (4), proceedings in respect of that offence may, whether or not that person is in Canada, be commenced in any territorial division in Canada, and the accused may be tried and punished in respect of that offence in the same manner as if the offence had been committed in that territorial division.

(6) For greater certainty, the provisions of this Act relating to

(*a*) requirements that an accused appear at and be present during proceedings, and

(*b*) the exceptions to those requirements,

apply to proceedings commenced in any territorial division pursuant to subsection (5).

(7) Where a person is alleged to have conspired to do anything that is an offence by virtue of subsection (3) or (4) and that person has been tried and dealt with outside Canada in respect of the offence in such a manner that, if the person had been tried and dealt with in Canada, he would be able to plead *autrefois acquit*, *autrefois convict* or pardon, the person shall be deemed to have been so tried and dealt with in Canada. R.S. 1985, c. 27 (1st Supp.), s. 61.

Conspiracy in restraint of trade — Trade union, exception.

466. (1) A conspiracy in restraint of trade is an agreement between two or more persons to do or to procure to be done any unlawful act in restraint of trade.

(2) The purposes of a trade union are not, by reason only that they are in restraint of trade, unlawful within the meaning of subsection (1).

Saving — "Trade combination".

467. (1) No person shall be convicted of the offence of conspiracy by reason only that he

(*a*) refuses to work with a workman or for an employer; or

(*b*) does any act or causes any act to be done for the purpose of a trade combination, unless such act is an offence expressly punishable by law.

(2) In this section, "trade combination" means any combination between masters or workmen or other persons for the purpose of regulating or altering the relations between masters or workmen, or the conduct of a master or workman in or in respect of his business, employment or contract of employment or service.

PART XIV

JURISDICTION

General

Superior court of criminal jurisdiction.

468. Every superior court of criminal jurisdiction has jurisdiction to try any indictable offence.

Court of criminal jurisdiction — Accessories — Corrupting justice — Attempts — Conspiracy.

469. Every court of criminal jurisdiction has jurisdiction to try an indictable offence other than

(*a*) an offence under any of the following sections:

(i) section 47 (treason),

(ii) section 49 (alarming Her Majesty),

(iii) section 51 (intimidating Parliament or a legislature),

(iv) section 53 (inciting to mutiny),

(v) section 61 (seditious offences),

(vi) section 74 (piracy),

(vii) section 75 (piratical acts), or

(viii) section 235 (murder),

(*b*) the offence of being an accessory after the fact to high treason or treason or murder,

(*c*) an offence under section 119 (bribery) by the holder of a judicial office,

(*d*) the offence of attempting to commit any offence mentioned in subparagraphs (*a*)(i) to (vii), or

(*e*) the offence of conspiring to commit any offence mentioned in paragraph (*a*). R.S. 1985, c. 27 (1st Supp.), s. 62.

Jurisdiction over person.

470. Subject to this Act, every superior court of criminal jurisdiction and every court of criminal jurisdiction that has power to try an indictable offence is competent to try an accused for that offence

(*a*) if the accused is found, is arrested or is in custody within the territorial jurisdiction of the court; or

(*b*) if the accused has been ordered to be tried by

(i) that court, or

(ii) any other court, the jurisdiction of which has by lawful authority been transferred to that court. R.S. 1985, c. 27 (1st Supp.), s. 101(3).

Trial by jury compulsory.

471. Except where otherwise expressly provided by law, every accused who is charged with an indictable offence shall be tried by a court composed of a judge and jury.

472. [Repealed R.S. 1985, c. 27 (1st Supp.), s. 63.]

Trial without jury — Withdrawal of consent.

473. (1) Notwithstanding anything in this Act, an accused charged with an offence listed in section 469 may, with the consent of the accused and the Attorney General, be tried without a jury by a judge of a superior court of criminal jurisdiction.

(2) Notwithstanding anything in this Act, where the consent of an accused and the Attorney General is given in accordance with subsection (1), such consent shall not be withdrawn unless both the accused and the Attorney General agree to the withdrawal. R.S. 1985, c. 27 (1st Supp.), s. 63.

Adjournment when no jury summoned.

474. Where the competent authority has determined that a panel of jurors is not to be summoned for a term or sittings of the court for the trial of criminal cases in any territorial division, the clerk of the court may, on the day of the opening of the term or sittings, if a judge is not present to preside over the court, adjourn the court and the business of the court to a subsequent day.

Accused absconding during trial — Adverse inference — Accused not entitled to re-opening — Counsel for accused may continue to act.

475. (1) Notwithstanding any other provision of this Act, where an accused, whether or not he is charged jointly with another, absconds during the course of his trial,

(*a*) he shall be deemed to have waived his right to be present at his trial, and

(*b*) the court may

(i) continue the trial and proceed to a judgment or verdict and, if it finds the accused guilty, impose a sentence on him in his absence, or

(ii) if a warrant in Form 7 is issued for the arrest of the accused, adjourn the trial to await his appearance,

but where the trial is adjourned pursuant to subparagraph (*b*)(ii), the court may, at any time, continue the trial if it is satisfied that it is no longer in the interests of justice to await the appearance of the accused.

(2) Where a court continues a trial pursuant to subsection (1), it may draw an inference adverse to the accused from the fact that he has absconded.

(3) Where an accused reappears at his trial that is continuing pursuant to subsection (1), he is not entitled to have any part of the proceedings that was conducted in his absence re-opened unless the court is satisfied that because of exceptional circumstances it is in the interests of justice to re-open the proceedings.

(4) Where an accused has absconded during the course of his trial and the court continues the trial, counsel for the accused is not thereby deprived of any authority he may have to continue to act for the accused in the proceedings.

Special Jurisdiction

Special jurisdictions.

476. For the purposes of this Act,

(*a*) where an offence is committed in or on any water or on a bridge between two or more territorial divisions, the offence shall be deemed to have been committed in any of the territorial divisions;

(*b*) where an offence is committed on the boundary of two or more territorial divisions or within five hundred metres of any such boundary, or the offence was commenced within one territorial division and completed within another, the offence shall be deemed to have been committed in any of the territorial divisions;

(*c*) where an offence is committed in or on a vehicle employed in a journey, or on board a vessel employed on a navigable river, canal or inland water, the offence shall be deemed to have been committed in any territorial division through which the vehicle or vessel passed in the course of the journey or voyage on which the offence was committed, and where the center or other part of the road, or navigable river, canal or inland water on which the vehicle or vessel passed in the course of the journey or voyage is the boundary of two or more territorial divisions, the offence shall be deemed to have been committed in any of the territorial divisions;

(*d*) where an offence is committed in an aircraft in the course of a flight of that aircraft, it shall be deemed to have been committed

(i) in the territorial division in which the flight commenced,

(ii) in any territorial division over which the aircraft passed in the course of the flight, or

(iii) in the territorial division in which the flight ended; and

(*e*) where an offence is committed in respect of the mail in the course of its door-to-door delivery, the offence shall be deemed to have been committed in any territorial division through which the mail was carried on that delivery. R.S. 1985, c. 27 (1st Supp.), s. 186; 1992, c. 1, s. 58(1), Sch. I, item 8.

Words and expressions — Saving.

477. (1) In this section and sections 477.1 to 477.4,

(*a*) "fishing zone of Canada" has the same meaning as in the *Territorial Sea and Fishing Zones Act*, but does not include any portion of the internal waters or territorial sea; and

(*b*) unless the context otherwise requires, other words and expressions have the same meaning as in the *Canadian Laws Offshore Application Act*.

(2) Nothing in sections 477.1 to 477.4 limits the operation of any other Act of Parliament or the jurisdiction that a court may exercise apart from those sections.

Offences in, above or beyond continental shelf — Restriction.

477.1 (1) Every person who commits an act or omission that would be an offence under a federal law if it occurred in Canada shall be deemed to have committed that act or omission in Canada if it occurred.

(*a*) in a place in or above the continental shelf or in any exclusive economic zone created by Canada, where the act or omission is an offence in that place by virtue of section 5 of the *Canadian Laws Offshore Application Act*;
(*b*) in any fishing zone of Canada;
(*c*) outside Canada, on board or by means of a ship registered or licensed, or for which an identification number has been issued, pursuant to any Act of Parliament;
(*d*) outside Canada, in the course of hot pursuit; or
(*e*) in the case of a Canadian citizen, outside the territory of any state.

(2) Paragraph (1)(*b*) applies only where

(*a*) the act or omission is committed by a person who is in a fishing zone of Canada in connection with the exploration, exploitation, management or conservation of the living resources thereof; and
(*b*) the act or omission is committed by or in relation to a person who is a Canadian citizen or a permanent resident within the meaning of the *Immigration Act*.

Consent of Attorney General — Idem — Idem.

477.2 (1) Where an offence is committed by a person in or on the territorial sea, no proceedings in respect of that offence, other than proceedings on summary conviction, shall be instituted without the consent of the Attorney General of Canada if the accused is not a Canadian citizen and the offence is alleged to have been committed on board any ship registered outside Canada.

(2) Proceedings in respect of which courts have jurisdiction by virtue only of paragraph 477.1(1)(*a*) or (*b*) shall not be instituted without the consent of the Attorney General of Canada if the accused is not a Canadian citizen and the offence is alleged to have been committed on board any ship registered outside Canada.

(3) Proceedings in respect of which courts have jurisdiction by virtue only of paragraph 477.1(1)(*d*) or (*e*) shall not be instituted without the consent of the Attorney General of Canada.

Exercising powers of arrest, entry, etc. — Arrest, Search, Seizure, etc. — Limitation.

477.3 (1) Every power of arrest, entry, search or seizure or other power that could be exercised in Canada in respect of an act or omission referred to in subsection 477.1(1), and in the circumstances referred to in that subsection, may be exercised

(*a*) at the place or on board the ship or marine installation or structure where the act or omission occurred; or

(*b*) where hot pursuit has been commenced, at any place on the seas, other than a place that is part of the territorial sea of any other state.

(2) A justice or a judge in any territorial division in Canada has jurisdiction to authorize an arrest, entry, search or seizure or an investigation or other ancillary matter related to an offence

(*a*) committed in or on the territorial sea or any area of the sea that forms part of the internal waters, or

(*b*) referred to in subsection 477.1(1)

in the same manner as if the offence had been committed in that territorial division.

(3) Where an act or omission that is an offence by virtue only of subsection 477.1(1) is alleged to have been committed on board any ship registered outside Canada, the powers referred to in subsection (1) shall not be exercised outside Canada with respect to that act or omission without the consent of the Attorney General of Canada.

Territorial division for prosecution — Appearance of accused at trial — Evidence — Certificate cannot be compelled.

477.4 (1) Proceedings in respect of an offence

(*a*) committed in or on the territorial sea or any area of the sea that forms part of the internal waters, or

(*b*) referred to in subsection 477.1(1)

may, whether or not the accused is in Canada, be commenced in any territorial division in Canada and the accused may be tried and punished in respect of that offence in the same manner as if the offence had been committed in that territorial division.

(2) For greater certainty, the provisions of this Act relating to

(*a*) the requirement of the appearance of an accused at proceedings, and

(*b*) the exceptions to that requirement,

apply to proceedings commenced in any territorial division pursuant to subsection (1) or section 481.

(3) In proceedings in respect of an offence,

(*a*) a certificate referred to in subsection 10(1) of the *Canadian Laws Offshore Application Act*, or

(*b*) a certificate issued by or under the authority of the Secretary of State for External Affairs containing a statement that any geographical location specified in the certificate was, at any time material to the proceedings, in a fishing zone of Canada or outside the territory of any state,

is conclusive proof of the truth of the statement without proof of the signature or official character of the person appearing to have issued the certificate.

(4) A certificate referred to in subsection (3) is admissible in evidence in proceedings referred to in that subsection but its production cannot be compelled. 1990, c. 44, s. 15.

Offence committed entirely in one province — Exception — Idem — Where accused committed to stand trial — "Newspaper".

478. (1) Subject to this Act, a court in a province shall not try an offence committed entirely in another province.

(2) Every proprietor, publisher, editor or other person charged with the publication of a defamatory libel in a newspaper or with conspiracy to publish a defamatory libel in a newspaper shall be dealt with, indicted, tried and punished in the province where he resides or in which the newspaper is printed.

(3) Where an accused is charged with an offence that is alleged to have been committed in Canada outside the province in which he is, he may, if the offence is not an offence mentioned in section 469 and

(*a*) in the case of proceedings instituted at the instance of the Government of Canada and conducted by or on behalf of that Government, the Attorney General of Canada consents, or

(*b*) in any other case, the Attorney General of the province where the offence is alleged to have been committed consents,

appear before a court or judge that would have had jurisdiction to try that offence if it had been committed in the province where the accused is, and where the accused signifies his consent to plead guilty and pleads guilty to that offence, the court or judge shall determine the accused to be guilty of the offence and impose the punishment warranted by law, but where the accused does not signify his consent to plead guilty and plead guilty, the accused shall, if he was in custody prior to his appearance, be returned to custody and shall be dealt with according to law.

(4) Notwithstanding that an accused described in subsection (3) has been ordered to stand trial or that an indictment has been preferred against the accused in respect of the offence to which he desires to plead guilty, the accused shall be deemed simply to stand charged of that offence without a preliminary inquiry having been conducted or an indictment having been preferred with respect thereto.

(5) In this section "newspaper" has the same meaning that it has in section 297. R.S. 1985, c. 27 (1st Supp.), ss. 64, 101(3).

Offence outstanding in same province.

479. Where an accused is charged with an offence that is alleged to have been committed in the province in which he is, he may, if the offence is not an offence mentioned in section 469, and

(*a*) in the case of proceedings instituted at the instance of the Government of Canada and conducted by or on behalf of that Government, the Attorney General of Canada consents, or

(*b*) in any other case, the Attorney General of the province where the offence is alleged to have been committed consents,

appear before a court or judge that would have had jurisdiction to try that offence if it had been committed in the place where the accused is, and where the accused signifies his consent to plead guilty and pleads guilty to that offence, the court or judge shall determine the accused to be guilty of the offence and impose the punishment warranted by law, but where he does not signify his consent to plead guilty and plead guilty, the accused shall, if he was in custody prior to his appearance, be returned to custody and shall be dealt with according to law. R.S. 1985, c. 27 (1st Supp.), s. 65.

Offence in unorganized territory — New territorial division.

480. (1) Where an offence is committed in an unorganized tract of country in any province or on a lake, river or other water therein, not included in a territorial division or in a provisional judicial district, proceedings in respect thereof may be commenced and an accused may be charged, tried and punished in respect thereof within any territorial division or provisional judicial district of the province in the same manner as if the offence had been committed within that territorial division or provisional judicial district.

(2) Where a provisional judicial district or a new territorial division is constituted in an unorganized tract referred to in subsection (1), the jurisdiction conferred by that subsection continues until appropriate provision is made by law for the administration of criminal justice within the provisional judicial district or new territorial division.

Offence not in a province.

481. Where an offence is committed in a part of Canada not in a province, proceedings in respect thereof may be commenced and the accused may be charged, tried and punished within any territorial division in any province in the same manner as if that offence had been committed in that territorial division.

Rules of Court

Power to make rules — Idem — Purpose of rules — Publication — Regulations to secure uniformity.

482. (1) Every superior court of criminal jurisdiction and every court of appeal, respectively, may, with the concurrence of a majority of the judges thereof present at a meeting held for the purpose, make rules of court not inconsistent with this Act or any other Act of the Parliament, and any rules so made apply to any prosecution, proceeding, action or appeal, as the case may be, within the jurisdiction of that court, instituted in relation to any matter of a criminal nature or arising from or incidental to any such prosecution, proceeding, action or appeal.

(2) Every court of criminal jurisdiction for a province and every appeal court within the meaning of section 812 that is not a court referred to in subsection (1) may, subject to the approval of the lieutenant governor in council of the province, make rules of court not inconsistent with this Act or any other Act of Parliament, and any rules so made apply to any prosecution, proceeding, action or appeal, as the case may be, within the jurisdiction of that court, instituted in relation to any matter of a criminal nature or arising from or incidental to any such prosecution, proceeding, action or appeal.

(3) Rules under subsection (1) or (2) may be made

(*a*) generally to regulate the duties of the officers of the court and any other matter considered expedient to attain the ends of justice and carry into effect the provisions of the law;

(*b*) to regulate the sittings of the court or any division thereof, or of any judge of the court sitting in chambers, except in so far as they are regulated by law;

(*c*) to regulate in criminal matters the pleading, practice and procedure in the court including pre-hearing conferences held pursuant to section 625.1 and proceedings with respect to judicial interim release and, in the case of rules under subsection (1), proceedings with respect to *mandamus, certiorari, habeas corpus,* prohibition and *procedendo* and proceedings on an appeal under section 830; and

(*d*) to carry out the provisions of this Act relating to appeals from conviction, acquittal or sentence and, without restricting the generality of this paragraph,

(i) for furnishing necessary forms and instructions in relation to notices of appeal or applications for leave to appeal to officials or other persons requiring or demanding them,

(ii) for ensuring the accuracy of notes taken at a trial and the verification of any copy or transcript,

(iii) for keeping writings, exhibits or other things connected with the proceedings on the trial,

(iv) for securing the safe custody of property during the period in which the operation of an order with respect to that property is suspended under subsection 689(1), and

(v) for providing that the Attorney General and counsel who acted for the Attorney General at the trial be supplied with certified copies of writings, exhibits and things connected with the proceedings that are required for the purposes of their duties.

(4) Rules of court that are made under the authority of this section shall be published in the *Canada Gazette.*

(5) Notwithstanding anything in this section, the Governor in Council may make such provision as he considers proper to secure uniformity in the rules of court in criminal matters, and all uniform rules made under the authority of this subsection prevail and have effect as if enacted by this Act. R.S. 1985, c. 27 (1st Supp.), s. 66.

PART XV

SPECIAL PROCEDURE AND POWERS

General Powers of Certain Officials

Officials with powers of two justices.

483. Every judge or provincial court judge authorized by the law of the province in which he is appointed to do anything that is required to be done by two or more justices may do alone anything that this Act or any other Act of the Parliament authorizes two or more justices to do. R.S. 1985, c. 27 (1st Supp.), s. 203.

Preserving order in court.

484. Every judge or provincial court judge has the same power and authority to preserve order in a court over which he presides as may be exercised by the superior court of criminal jurisdiction of the province during the sittings thereof. R.S. 1985, c. 27 (1st Supp.), s. 203.

Procedural irregularities — Summons or warrant — Dismissal for want of prosecution — Adjournment and order — Part XVI to apply.

485. (1) Jurisdiction over an offence is not lost by reason of the failure of any court, judge, provincial court judge or justice to act in the exercise of that jurisdiction at any particular time, or by reason of a failure to comply with any of the provisions of this Act respecting adjournments or remands.

(2) Where jurisdiction over an accused or a defendant is lost and has not been regained, a court, judge, provincial court judge or justice may, within three months after the loss of jurisdiction, issue a summons, or if it or he considers it necessary in the public interest, a warrant for the arrest of the accused or defendant.

(3) Where no summons or warrant is issued under subsection (2) within the period provided therein, the proceedings shall be deemed to be dismissed for want of prosecution and shall not be recommenced except in accordance with section 485.1.

(4) Where, in the opinion of the court, judge, provincial court judge or justice, an accused or a defendant who appears at a proceeding has been misled or prejudiced by reason of any matter referred to in subsection (1), the court, judge, provincial court judge or justice may adjourn the proceeding and may make such order as it or he considers appropriate.

(5) The provisions of Part XVI apply with such modifications as the circumstances require where a summons or warrant is issued under subsection (2). R.S. 1985, c. 27 (1st Supp.), ss. 67, 203.

Recommencement where dismissal for want of prosecution.

485.1 Where an indictment in respect of a transaction is dismissed or deemed by any provision of this Act to be dismissed for want of prosecution, a new information shall not be laid and a new indictment shall not be preferred before any court in respect of the same transaction without

(*a*) the personal consent in writing of the Attorney General or Deputy Attorney General, in any prosecution conducted by the Attorney General or in which the Attorney General intervenes; or

(*b*) the written order of a judge of that court, in any prosecution conducted by a prosecutor other than the Attorney General and in which the Attorney General does not intervene. R.S. 1985, c. 27 (1st Supp.), s. 67.

Exclusion of public in certain cases — Reasons to be stated — Testimony outside court room — Condition of exclusion — Order restricting publication — Mandatory order on application — Failure to comply with order.

486. (1) Any proceedings against an accused shall be held in open court, but where the presiding judge, provincial court judge or justice, as the case may be, is of the opinion that it is in the interest of public morals, the maintenance of order or the proper administration of justice to exclude all or any members of the public from the court room for all or part of the proceedings, he may so order.

(2) Where an accused is charged with an offence mentioned in section 274 and the prosecutor or the accused makes an application for an order under subsection (1), the presiding judge, provincial court judge or justice, as the case may be, shall, if no such order is made, state, by reference to the circumstances of the case, the reason for not making an order.

(2.1) Notwithstanding section 650, where an accused is charged with an offence under section 151, 152, 153, 155 or 159, subsection 160(2) or (3), or section 170, 171, 172, 173, 271, 272 or 273 and the complainant is, at the time of the trial or preliminary inquiry, under the age of eighteen years, the presiding judge or justice, as the case may be, may order that the complainant testify outside the court room or behind a screen or other device that would allow the complainant not to see the accused, if the judge or justice is of the opinion that the exclusion is necessary to obtain a full and candid account of the acts complained of from the complainant.

[1992, c. 21, s. 9 will repeal subsection 486(2.1) and substitute the following.]

Testimony outside court room.

(2.1) Notwithstanding section 650, where an accused is charged with an offence under section 151, 152, 153, 155 or 159, subsection 160(2) or (3), or section 170, 171, 172, 173, 271, 272 or 273 and the complainant, at the time of the trial or preliminary inquiry, is under the age of eighteen years or is able to communicate evidence but may have difficulty doing so by reason of a mental or physical disability, the presiding judge or justice, as the case may be, may order that the complainant testify outside the court room or behind a screen or other device that would allow the complainant not to see the accused, if the judge or justice is of the opinion that the exclusion is necessary to obtain a full and candid account of the acts complained of from the complainant.

(2.2) A complainant shall not testify outside the court room pursuant to subsection (2.1) unless arrangements are made for the accused, the judge or justice and the jury to watch the testimony of the complainant by means of closed-circuit television or otherwise and the accused is permitted to communicate with counsel while watching the testimony.

(3) Subject to subsection (4), where an accused is charged with an offence under section 151, 152, 153, 155, 159, 160, 170, 171, 172, 173, 271, 272, 273, 346 or 347, the presiding judge or justice may make an order directing that the identity of the complainant or of a witness and any information that could disclose the identity of the complainant or witness shall not be published in any document or broadcast in any way.

(4) The presiding judge or justice shall

(*a*) at the first reasonable opportunity, inform any witness under the age of eighteen years and the complainant to proceedings in respect of an offence mentioned in subsection (3) of the right to make an application for an order under subsection (3); and

(*b*) on application made by the complainant, the prosecutor or any such witness, make an order under that subsection.

(5) Every one who fails to comply with an order made pursuant to subsection (3) is guilty of an offence punishable on summary conviction. R.S. 1985, c. 27 (1st Supp.), s. 203; c. 19 (3rd Supp.), s. 14; c. 23 (4th Supp.), s. 1.

(6) [Repealed R.S. 1985, c. 19 (3rd Supp.), s. 14(2).]

Information for search warrant — Endorsement of search warrant — Form — Effect of endorsement.

487. (1) A justice who is satisfied by information on oath in Form 1 that there are reasonable grounds to believe that there is in a building, receptacle or place

(*a*) anything on or in respect of which any offence against this Act or any other Act of Parliament has been or is suspected to have been committed,

(*b*) anything that there is reasonable ground to believe will afford evidence with respect to the commission of an offence against this Act or any other Act of Parliament, or

(*c*) anything that there are reasonable grounds to believe is intended to be used for the purpose of committing any offence against the person for which a person may be arrested without warrant,

may at any time issue a warrant under his hand authorizing a person named therein or a peace officer (*d*) to search the building, receptacle or place for any such thing and to seize it, and

(*e*) subject to any other Act of Parliament, to, as soon as practicable, bring the thing seized before, or make a report in respect thereof to, the justice or some other justice for the same territorial division in accordance with section 489.1.

(2) Where the building, receptacle, or place in which anything mentioned in subsection (1) is believed to be is in any other territorial division, the justice may issue his warrant in like form modified according to the circumstances, and the warrant may be executed in the other territorial division after it has been endorsed, in Form 28, by a justice having jurisdiction in that territorial division.

(3) A search warrant issued under this section may be in the form set out as Form 5 in Part XXVIII, varied to suit the case.

(4) An endorsement that is made on a warrant as provided for in subsection (2) is sufficient authority to the peace officers or such persons to whom it was originally directed and to all peace officers within the jurisdiction of the justice by whom it is endorsed to execute the warrant and to deal with the things seized in accordance with section 489.1 or as otherwise provided by law. R.S. 1985, c. 27 (1st Supp.), s. 68.

Telewarrants — Information on oath and record — Administration of oath — Contents of information — Issuing warrant — Formalities respecting warrant and facsimiles — Providing facsimile — Affixing facsimile — Report of peace officer — Bringing before justice — Proof of authorization.

487.1 (1) Where a peace officer believes that an indictable offence has been committed and that it would be impracticable to appear personally before a justice to make application for a warrant in accordance with section 256 or 487, the peace officer may submit an information on oath by telephone or other means of telecommunication to a justice designated for the purpose by the chief judge of the provincial court having jurisdiction in the matter.

(2) An information submitted by telephone or other means of telecommunication shall be on oath and shall be recorded verbatim by the justice who shall, as soon as practicable, cause to be filed with the clerk of the court for the territorial division in which the warrant is intended for execution the record or a transcription thereof, certified by the justice as to time, date and contents.

(3) For the purposes of subsection (2), an oath may be administered by telephone or other means of telecommunication.

(4) An information on oath submitted by telephone or other means of telecommunication shall include

(*a*) a statement of the circumstances that make it impracticable for the peace officer to appear personally before a justice;

(*b*) a statement of the indictable offence alleged, the place or premises to be searched and the items alleged to be liable to seizure;

(*c*) a statement of the peace officer's grounds for believing that items liable to seizure in respect of the offence alleged will be found in the place or premises to be searched; and

(*d*) a statement as to any prior application for a warrant under this section or any other search warrant, in respect of the same matter, of which the peace officer has knowledge.

(5) A justice referred to in subsection (1) who is satisfied that an information on oath submitted by telephone or other means of telecommunication

(*a*) is in respect of an indictable offence and conforms to the requirements of subsection (4),

(*b*) discloses reasonable grounds for dispensing with an information presented personally and in writing, and

(*c*) discloses reasonable grounds, in accordance with subsection 256(1) or paragraph 487(1)(*a*), (*b*) or (*c*), as the case may be, for the issuance of a warrant in respect of an indictable offence,

may issue a warrant to a peace officer conferring the same authority respecting search and seizure as may be conferred by a warrant issued by a justice before whom the peace officer appears personally pursuant to subsection 256(1) or 487(1), as the case may be, and may require that the warrant be executed within such period as the justice may order.

(6) Where a justice issues a warrant by telephone or other means of telecommunication,

(*a*) the justice shall complete and sign the warrant in Form 5.1, noting on its face the time, date and place of issuance;

(*b*) the peace officer, on the direction of the justice, shall complete, in duplicate, a facsimile of the warrant in Form 5.1, noting on its face the name of the issuing justice and the time, date and place of issuance; and

(*c*) the justice shall, as soon as practicable after the warrant has been issued, cause the warrant to be filed with the clerk of the court for the territorial division in which the warrant is intended for execution.

(7) A peace officer who executes a warrant issued by telephone or other means of telecommunication, other than a warrant issued pursuant to subsection 256(1), shall, before entering the place or premises to be searched or as soon as practicable thereafter, give a facsimile of the warrant to any person present and ostensibly in control of the place or premises.

(8) A peace officer who, in any unoccupied place or premises, executes a warrant issued by telephone or other means of telecommunication, other than a warrant issued pursuant to subsection 256(1), shall, on entering the place or premises or as soon as practicable thereafter, cause a facsimile of

the warrant to be suitably affixed in a prominent place within the place or premises.

(9) A peace officer to whom a warrant is issued by telephone or other means of telecommunication shall file a written report with the clerk of the court for the territorial division in which the warrant was intended for execution as soon as practicable but within a period not exceeding seven days after the warrant has been executed, which report shall include

(*a*) a statement of the time and date the warrant was executed or, if the warrant was not executed, a statement of the reasons why it was not executed;

(*b*) a statement of the things, if any, that were seized pursuant to the warrant and the location where they are being held; and

(*c*) a statement of the things, if any, that were seized in addition to the things mentioned in the warrant and the location where they are being held, together with a statement of the peace officer's grounds for believing that those additional things had been obtained by, or used in, the commission of an offence.

(10) The clerk of the court with whom a written report is filed pursuant to subsection (9) shall, as soon as practicable, cause the report, together with the information on oath and the warrant to which it pertains, to be brought before a justice to be dealt with, in respect of the things seized referred to in the report, in the same manner as if the things were seized pursuant to a warrant issued, on an information presented personally by a peace officer, by that justice or another justice for the same territorial division.

(11) In any proceeding in which it is material for a court to be satisfied that a search or seizure was authorized by a warrant issued by telephone or other means of telecommunication, the absence of the information on oath, transcribed and certified by the justice as to time, date and contents, or of the original warrant, signed by the justice and carrying on its face a notation of the time, date and place of issuance, is, in the absence of evidence to the contrary, proof that the search or seizure was not authorized by a warrant issued by telephone or other means of telecommunication. R.S. 1985, c. 27 (1st Supp.), s. 69; 1992, c. 1, s. 58(1), Sch.I, item 9(1)-9(3); 1992, c. 1, s. 59, Sch. I, item 18.

Restriction on publicity — Definition of "newspaper".

487.2 (1) Where a search warrant is issued under section 487 or 487.1 or a search is made under such a warrant, every one who publishes in any newspaper or broadcasts any information with respect to

(*a*) the location of the place searched or to be searched, or

(*b*) the identity of any person who is or appears to occupy or be in possession or control of that place or who is suspected of being involved in any offence in relation to which the warrant was issued,

without the consent of every person referred to in paragraph (*b*) is, unless a charge has been laid in respect of any offence in relation to which the warrant was issued, guilty of an offence punishable on summary conviction.

(2) In this section, "newspaper" has the same meaning as in section 297. R.S. 1985, c. 27 (1st Supp.), s. 69.

Execution of search warrant.

488. A warrant issued under section 487 or 487.1 shall be executed by day, unless the justice, by the warrant, authorizes execution of it by night. R.S. 1985, c. 27 (1st Supp.), s. 70.

Definitions — "custodian" — "document" — "judge" — "lawyer" — "officer" — Examination or seizure of certain documents where privilege claimed — Application to judge — Disposition of application — Privilege continues — Order to custodian to deliver — Application to another judge — Prohibition — Authority to make copies — Hearing in private — Exception.

488.1 (1) In this section,

"custodian" means a person in whose custody a package is placed pursuant to subsection (2);

"document", for the purposes of this section, has the same meaning as in section 321;

"judge" means a judge of a superior court of criminal jurisdiction of the province where the seizure was made;

"lawyer" means, in the Province of Quebec, an advocate, lawyer or notary and, in any other province, a barrister or solicitor;

"officer" means a peace officer or public officer.

(2) Where an officer acting under the authority of this or any other Act of Parliament is about to examine, copy or seize a document in the possession of a lawyer who claims that a named client of his has a solicitor-client privilege in respect of that document, the officer shall, without examining or making copies of the document,

(*a*) seize the document and place it in a package and suitably seal and identify the package; and

(*b*) place the package in the custody of the sheriff of the district or county in which the seizure was made or, if there is agreement in writing that a specified person act as custodian, in the custody of that person.

(3) Where a document has been seized and placed in custody under subsection (2), the Attorney General or the client or the lawyer on behalf of the client, may

(*a*) within fourteen days from the day the document was so placed in custody, apply, on two days notice of motion to all other persons entitled to make application, to a judge for an order

(i) appointing a place and a day, not later than twenty-one days after the date of the order, for the determination of the question whether the document should be disclosed, and

(ii) requiring the custodian to produce the document to the judge at that time and place;

(*b*) serve a copy of the order on all other persons entitled to make application and on the custodian within six days of the date on which it was made; and

(*c*) if he has proceeded as authorized by paragraph (*b*), apply, at the appointed time and place, for an order determining the question.

(4) On an application under paragraph (3)(*c*), the judge

(*a*) may, if the judge considers it necessary to determine the question whether the document should be disclosed, inspect the document;

(*b*) where the judge is of the opinion that it would materially assist him in deciding whether or not the document is privileged, may allow the Attorney General to inspect the document;

(*c*) shall allow the Attorney General and the person who objects to the disclosure of the document to make representations; and

(*d*) shall determine the question summarily and,

(i) if he is of the opinion that the document should not be disclosed, ensure that it is repackaged and resealed and order the custodian to deliver the document to the lawyer who claimed the solicitor-client privilege or to his client, or

(ii) if he is of the opinion that the document should be disclosed, order the custodian to deliver the document to the officer who seized the document or some other person designated by the Attorney General, subject to such restrictions or conditions as the judge deems appropriate,

and shall, at the same time, deliver concise reasons for the determination in which the nature of the document is described without divulging the details thereof.

(5) Where the judge determines pursuant to paragraph (4)(*d*) that a solicitor-client privilege exists in respect of a document, whether or not he has, pursuant to paragraph (4)(*b*), allowed the Attorney General to inspect the document, the document remains privileged and inadmissible as evidence unless the client consents to its admission in evidence or the privilege is otherwise lost.

(6) Where a document has been seized and placed in custody under subsection (2) and a judge, on the application of the Attorney General, is satisfied that no application has been made under paragraph (3)(*a*) or that following such an application no further application has been made under paragraph (3)(*c*), the judge shall order the custodian to deliver the document to the officer who seized the document or to some other person designated by the Attorney General.

(7) Where the judge to whom an application has been made under paragraph

(3)(*c*) cannot act or continue to act under this section for any reason, subsequent applications under that paragraph may be made to another judge.

(8) No officer shall examine, make copies of or seize any document without affording a reasonable opportunity for a claim of solicitor-client privilege to be made under subsection (2).

(9) At any time while a document is in the custody of a custodian under this section, a judge may, on an *ex parte* application of a person claiming a solicitor-client privilege under this section, authorize that person to examine the document or make a copy of it in the presence of the custodian or the judge, but any such authorization shall contain provisions to ensure that the document is repackaged and that the package is resealed without alteration or damage.

(10) An application under paragraph (3)(*c*) shall be heard in private.

(11) This section does not apply in circumstances where a claim of solicitor-client privilege may be made under the *Income Tax Act.* R.S. 1985, c. 27 (1st Supp.), s. 71.

Seizure of things not specified.

489. Every person who executes a warrant issued under section 462.32, 487 or 487.1 may seize, in addition to the things mentioned in the warrant, any thing that the person believes on reasonable grounds has been obtained by or has been used in the commission of an offence. R.S. 1985, c. 27 (1st Supp.), s. 72; c. 42 (4th Supp.), s. 3.

Restitution of property or report by peace officer — Idem — Form.

489.1 (1) Subject to this or any other Act of Parliament, where a peace officer has seized anything under a warrant issued pursuant to section 258, 487 or 487.1 or under section 489 or otherwise in the execution of his duties under this or any other Act of Parliament, the peace officer shall, as soon as practicable,

(*a*) where the peace officer is satisfied,

(i) that there is no dispute as to who is lawfully entitled to possession of the thing seized, and

(ii) that the continued detention of the thing seized is not required for the purposes of any investigation or a preliminary inquiry, trial or other proceeding,

return the thing seized, on being issued a receipt therefor, to the person lawfully entitled to its possession and report to the justice who issued the warrant or some other justice for the same territorial division or, if no warrant was issued, a justice having jurisdiction in respect of the matter, that he has done so; or

(*b*) where the peace officer is not satisfied as described in subparagraphs (*a*)(i) and (ii),

(i) bring the thing seized before the justice referred to in paragraph (*a*), or

(ii) report to the justice that he has seized the thing and is detaining it or causing it to be detained

to be dealt with by the justice in accordance with subsection 490(1).

(2) Subject to this or any other Act of Parliament, where a person, other than a peace officer, has seized anything under a warrant issued pursuant to section 487 or under section 489 or otherwise in the execution of his duties under this or any other Act of Parliament, that person shall, as soon as practicable,

(*a*) bring the thing seized before the justice who issued the warrant or some other justice for the same territorial division or, if no warrant was issued, before a justice having jurisdiction in respect of the matter, or

(*b*) report to the justice referred to in paragraph (*a*) that he has seized the thing and is detaining it or causing it to be detained,

to be dealt with by the justice in accordance with subsection 490(1).

(3) A report to a justice under this section shall be in the form set out as Form 5.2 in Part XXVIII, varied to suit the case and shall include, in the case of a report in respect of a warrant issued by telephone or other means of telecommunication, the statements referred to in subsection 487.1(9). R.S. 1985, c. 27 (1st Supp.), s. 72.

Detention of things seized — Further detention — Idem — When accused ordered to stand trial — Where continued detention no longer required — Idem — Application for order of return — Exception — Disposal of things seized — Application by lawful owner — Order — Detention pending appeal, etc. — Copies of documents returned — Probative force — Access to anything seized — Conditions — Appeal.

490. (1) Subject to this or any other Act of Parliament, where, pursuant to paragraph 489.1(1)(*b*) or subsection 489.1(2), anything that has been seized is brought before a justice or a report in respect of anything seized is made to a justice, he shall,

(*a*) where the lawful owner or person who is lawfully entitled to possession of the thing seized is known, order it to be returned to him, unless the prosecutor satisfies the justice that the detention of the thing seized is required for the purposes of any investigation or a preliminary inquiry, trial or other proceeding; or

(*b*) where the prosecutor satisfies the justice that the thing seized should be detained for a reason set out in paragraph (*a*), detain the thing seized or order that it be detained, taking reasonable care to ensure that it is preserved until the conclusion of any investigation or until it is required to be produced for the purposes of a preliminary inquiry, trial or other proceeding.

(2) Nothing shall be detained under the authority of paragraph (1)(*b*) for

a period of more than three months after the day of the seizure unless, before the expiration of that period,

(*a*) a justice, on the making of a summary application to him after three clear days notice thereof to the person from whom the thing detained was seized, is satisfied that, having regard to the nature of the investigation, its further detention for a specified period is warranted and he so orders; or

(*b*) proceedings are instituted in which the thing detained may be required.

(3) More than one order for further detention may be made under paragraph (2)(*a*) but the cumulative period of detention shall not exceed one year from the day of the seizure unless before the expiration of that year,

(*a*) a judge of a superior court of criminal jurisdiction or a judge as defined in section 552, on the making of a summary application to him after three clear days notice thereof to the person from whom the thing detained was seized, is satisfied, having regard to the complex nature of the investigation, that the further detention of the thing seized is warranted for a specified period and subject to such other conditions as the judge considers just, and he so orders; or

(*b*) proceedings are instituted in which the thing detained may be required.

(4) When an accused has been ordered to stand trial, the justice shall forward anything detained pursuant to subsections (1) to (3) to the clerk of the court to which the accused has been ordered to stand trial to be detained by the clerk and disposed of as the court directs.

(5) Where at any time before the expiration of the periods of detention provided for or ordered under subsections (1) to (3) in respect of anything seized, the prosecutor determines that the continued detention of the thing seized is no longer required for any purpose mentioned in subsection (1) or (4), he shall apply to

(*a*) a judge of a superior court of criminal jurisdiction or a judge as defined in section 552, where a judge ordered its detention under subsection (3), or

(*b*) a justice, in any other case,

who shall, after affording the person from whom the thing was seized or the person who claims to be the lawful owner thereof or person entitled to its possession, if known, an opportunity to establish that he is lawfully entitled to the possession thereof, make an order in respect of the property under subsection (9).

(6) Where the periods of detention provided for or ordered under subsections (1) to (3) in respect of anything seized have expired and proceedings have not been instituted in which the thing detained may be required, the prosecutor shall apply to a judge or justice referred to in paragraph (5)(*a*) or (*b*) in the circumstances set out therein, for an order in respect of the property under subsection (9).

(7) A person from whom anything has been seized may, after the expiration

of the periods of detention provided for or ordered under subsections (1) to (3) and on three clear days notice to the Attorney General, apply summarily to

(*a*) a judge of a superior court of criminal jurisdiction or a judge as defined in section 552, where a judge ordered the detention of the thing seized under subsection (3), or

(*b*) a justice, in any other case,

for an order under paragraph (9)(*c*) that the thing seized be returned to the applicant.

(8) A judge of a superior court of criminal jurisdiction or a judge as defined in section 552, where a judge ordered the detention of the thing seized under subsection (3), or a justice, in any other case, may allow an application to be made under subsection (7) prior to the expiration of the periods referred to therein where he is satisfied that hardship will result unless such application is so allowed.

(9) Subject to this or any other Act of Parliament, if

(*a*) a judge referred to in subsection (7), where a judge ordered the detention of anything seized under subsection (3), or

(*b*) a justice, in any other case,

is satisfied that the periods of detention provided for or ordered under subsections (1) to (3) in respect of anything seized have expired and proceedings have not been instituted in which the thing detained may be required or, where such periods have not expired, that the continued detention of the thing seized will not be required for any purpose mentioned in subsection (1) or (4), he shall

(*c*) if possession of it by the person from whom it was seized is lawful, order it to be returned to that person; or

(*d*) if possession of it by the person from whom it was seized is unlawful and the lawful owner or person who is lawfully entitled to its possession is known, order it to be returned to the lawful owner or to the person who is lawfully entitled to its possession,

and he may, if possession of it by the person from whom it was seized is unlawful and the lawful owner or person who is lawfully entitled to its possession is not known, order it to be forfeited to Her Majesty, to be disposed of as the Attorney General directs, or otherwise dealt with in accordance with the law.

(10) Subject to this or any other Act of Parliament, a person, other than a person who may make an application under subsection (7), who claims to be the lawful owner or person lawfully entitled to possession of anything seized and brought before or reported to a justice under section 489.1 may, at any time, on three clear days notice to the Attorney General and the person from whom the thing was seized, apply summarily to

(*a*) a judge referred to in subsection (7), where a judge ordered the detention of the thing seized under subsection (3), or (*b*) a justice, in any other case,

for an order that the thing detained be returned to the applicant.

(11) Subject to this or any other Act of Parliament, on an application under subsection (10), where a judge or justice is satisfied that

(*a*) the applicant is the lawful owner or lawfully entitled to possession of the thing seized, and

(*b*) the periods of detention provided for or ordered under subsections (1) to (3) in respect of the thing seized have expired and proceedings have not been instituted in which the thing detained may be required or, where such periods have not expired, that the continued detention of the thing seized will not be required for any purpose mentioned in subsection (1) or (4),

the judge shall order that

(*c*) the thing seized be returned to the applicant; or

(*d*) except as otherwise provided by law, where, pursuant to subsection (9), the thing seized was forfeited, sold or otherwise dealt with in such a manner that it cannot be returned to the applicant, the applicant be paid the proceeds of sale or the value of the thing seized.

(12) Notwithstanding anything in this section, nothing shall be returned, forfeited or disposed of under this section pending any application made, or appeal taken, thereunder in respect of the thing or proceeding in which the right of seizure thereof is questioned or within thirty days after an order in respect of the thing is made under this section.

(13) Where any document is returned or ordered to be returned, forfeited or otherwise dealt with under subsection (1), (9) or (11), the Attorney General may, before returning the document or complying with the order, make or cause to be made, and may retain, a copy of the document.

(14) Every copy made under subsection (13) shall, if certified as a true copy by the Attorney General, be admissible in evidence and, in the absence of evidence to the contrary, shall have the same probative force as the original document would have if it had been proved in the ordinary way.

(15) Where anything is detained pursuant to subsections (1) to (3), a judge of a superior court of criminal jurisdiction or a judge as defined in section 552 may, on summary application on behalf of a person who has an interest in what is detained, after three clear days notice to the Attorney General, order that the person by or on whose behalf the application is made be permitted to examine anything so detained.

(16) An order that is made under subsection (15) shall be made on such terms as appear to the judge to be necessary or desirable to ensure that anything in respect of which the order is made is safeguarded and preserved for any purpose for which it may subsequently be required.

(17) A person who considers himself aggrieved by an order made under subsection (8), (9) or (11) may appeal from the order to the appeal court,

as defined in section 812, and for the purposes of the appeal the provisions of sections 814 to 828 apply with such modifications as the circumstances require. R.S. 1985, c. 27 (1st Supp.), s. 73.

Forfeiture of weapons — Return of weapons to lawful owners — Application of proceeds.

491. (1) Where it is determined by a court that a weapon was used in the commission of an offence and that weapon has been seized and detained, the weapon is, subject to subsection (2), forfeited and may be dealt with as the court that makes the determination directs.

(2) If the court by which a determination referred to in subsection (1) is made is satisfied that the lawful owner of a weapon that, but for this subsection, would be forfeited by virtue of the determination, was not a party to the offence and had no reason to believe that the weapon would or might be used in the commission of an offence, the court shall order the weapon returned to the lawful owner thereof or the proceeds of any sale thereof to be paid to him.

(3) Where any weapon to which this section applies is sold, the proceeds of the sale shall be paid to the Attorney General or, where an order is made under subsection (2), to the person who was, immediately prior to the sale, the lawful owner of the weapon.

[1991, c. 40, s. 30 will repeal section 491 and substitute the following.]

Forfeiture of weapons and ammunition — Return to lawful owners — Application of proceeds.

491. (1) Subject to subsection (2), where it is determined by a court that a weapon or ammunition was used in the commission of an offence or that a person has committed an offence under section 91 with respect to a restricted weapon, and the weapon or ammunition has been seized and detained, the weapon or ammunition is forfeited and may be dealt with as the court that makes the determination directs.

(2) If the court by which a determination referred to in subsection (1) is made is satisfied that the lawful owner of the weapon or ammunition was not a party to the offence and had no reason to believe that the weapon or ammunition would or might be used in the commission of an offence, the court shall order the weapon or ammunition returned to the lawful owner thereof or the proceeds of any sale thereof to be paid to that owner.

(3) Where any weapon or ammunition in respect of whih this section applies is sold, the proceeds of the sale shall be paid to the Attorney General or, where an order is made under subsection (2), to the person who was, immediately prior to the sale, the lawful owner of the weapon or ammunition.

Order for restitution or forfeiture of property obtained by crime — Idem — When certain orders not to be made — By whom order executed.

491.1 (1) Where an accused or defendant is tried for an offence and the court determines that an offence has been committed, whether or not the accused has been convicted or discharged under section 736 of the offence, and at the time of the trial any property obtained by the commission of the offence

(*a*) is before the court or has been detained so that it can be immediately dealt with, and

(*b*) will not be required as evidence in any other proceedings,

section 490 does not apply in respect of the property and the court shall make an order under subsection (2) in respect of the property.

(2) In the circumstances referred to in subsection (1), the court shall order, in respect of any property,

(*a*) if the lawful owner or person lawfully entitled to possession of the property is known, that it be returned to that person; and

(*b*) if the lawful owner or person lawfully entitled to possession of the property is not known, that it be forfeited to Her Majesty, to be disposed of as the Attorney General directs or otherwise dealt with in accordance with the law.

(3) An order shall not be made under subsection (2)

(*a*) in the case of proceedings against a trustee, banker, merchant, attorney, factor, broker or other agent entrusted with the possession of goods or documents of title to goods, for an offence under section 330, 331, 332 or 336; or

(*b*) in respect of

(i) property to which a person acting in good faith and without notice has acquired lawful title for valuable consideration,

(ii) a valuable security that has been paid or discharged in good faith by a person who was liable to pay or discharge it,

(iii) a negotiable instrument that has, in good faith, been taken or received by transfer or delivery for valuable consideration by a person who had no notice and no reasonable cause to suspect that an offence had been committed, or

(iv) property in respect of which there is a dispute as to ownership or right of possession by claimants other than the accused or defendant.

(4) An order made under this section shall, on the direction of the court, be executed by the peace officers by whom the process of the court is ordinarily executed. R.S. 1985, c. 27 (1st Supp.), s. 74.

Photographic evidence — Certified photograph admissible in evidence — Statements made in certificate — Secondary evidence of peace officer — Notice of intention to produce certified photograph — Attendance for examination — Production of property in court — Definition of "photograph".

491.2 (1) Before any property that would otherwise be required to be produced for the purposes of a preliminary inquiry, trial or other proceeding in respect of an offence under section 334, 344, 348, 354, 362 or 380 is returned or ordered to be returned, forfeited or otherwise dealt with under section 489.1 or 490 or is otherwise returned, a peace officer or any person under the direction of a peace officer may take and retain a photograph of the property.

(2) Every photograph of property taken under subsection (1), accompanied by a certificate of a person containing the statements referred to in subsection (3), shall be admissible in evidence and, in the absence of evidence to the contrary, shall have the same probative force as the property would have had if it had been proved in the ordinary way.

(3) For the purposes of subsection (2), a certificate of a person stating that

(*a*) the person took the photograph under the authority of subsection (1),

(*b*) the person is a peace officer or took the photograph under the direction of a peace officer, and

(*c*) the photograph is a true photograph

shall be admissible in evidence and, in the absence of evidence to the contrary, is evidence of the statements contained in the certificate without proof of the signature of the person appearing to have signed the certificate.

(4) An affidavit or solemn declaration of a peace officer or other person stating that the person has seized property and detained it or caused it to be detained from the time that person took possession of the property until a photograph of the property was taken under subsection (1) and that property was not altered in any manner before the photograph was taken shall be admissible in evidence and, in the absence of evidence to the contrary, is evidence of the statements contained in the affidavit or solemn declaration without proof of the signature or official character of the person appearing to have signed the affidavit or solemn declaration.

(5) Unless the court orders otherwise, no photograph, certificate, affidavit or solemn declaration shall be received in evidence at a trial or other proceeding pursuant to subsection (2), (3) or (4) unless the prosecutor has, before the trial or other proceeding, given to the accused a copy thereof and reasonable notice of intention to produce it in evidence.

(6) Notwithstanding subsection (3) or (4), the court may require the person who appears to have signed a certificate, an affidavit or a solemn declaration referred to in that subsection to appear before it for examination or cross-examination in respect of the issue of proof of any of the facts contained in the certificate, affidavit or solemn declaration.

(7) A court may order any property seized and returned pursuant to section 489.1 or 490 to be produced in court or made available for examination by all parties to a proceeding at a reasonable time and place, notwithstanding that a photograph of the property has been received in evidence pursuant to subsection (2), where the court is satisfied that the interests of justice so require and that it is possible and practicable to do so in the circumstances.

(8) In this section, "photograph" includes a still photograph, a photographic

film or plate, a microphotographic film, a photostatic negative, an X-ray film, a motion picture and a videotape. R.S. 1985, c. 23 (4th Supp.), s. 2; 1992, c. 1, s. 58(1), Sch. I, item 10.

Seizure of explosives — Forfeiture — Application of proceeds.

492. (1) Every person who executes a warrant issued under section 487, 487.1 may seize any explosive substance that he suspects is intended to be used for an unlawful purpose, and shall, as soon as possible, remove to a place of safety anything that he seizes by virtue of this section and detain it until he is ordered by a judge of a superior court to deliver it to some other person or an order is made pursuant to subsection (2).

(2) Where an accused is convicted of an offence in respect of anything seized by virtue of subsection (1), it is forfeited and shall be dealt with as the court that makes the conviction may direct.

(3) Where anything to which this section applies is sold, the proceeds of the sale shall be paid to the Attorney General. R.S. 1985, c. 27 (1st Supp.), s. 70.

PART XVI

COMPELLING APPEARANCE OF ACCUSED BEFORE A JUSTICE AND INTERIM RELEASE

Interpretation

Definitions — "Accused" — "Appearance notice" — "Judge" — "Officer in charge" — "Promise to appear" — "Recognizance" — "Summons" — "Undertaking" — "Warrant".

493. In this Part

"accused" includes

(*a*) a person to whom a peace officer has issued an appearance notice under section 496, and

(*b*) a person arrested for a criminal offence;

"appearance notice" means a notice in Form 9 issued by a peace officer;

"judge" means

(*a*) in the Province of Ontario, a judge of the superior court of criminal jurisdiction of the Province,

(*b*) in the Province of Quebec, a judge of the superior court of criminal jurisdiction of the province or three judges of the Court of Quebec,

(*c*) in the Province of Nova Scotia, a judge of the superior court of criminal jurisdiction of the Province or a judge of a county court,

(*d*) in the Provinces of New Brunswick, Manitoba, British Columbia, Prince Edward Island, Saskatchewan, Alberta and Newfoundland, a judge of the superior court of criminal jurisdiction of the province, and

(*e*) in the Yukon Territory and the Northwest Territories, a judge of the Supreme Court;

"officer in charge" means the officer for the time being in command of the police force responsible for the lock-up or other place to which an accused is taken after arrest or a peace officer designated by him for the purposes of this Part who is in charge of that place at the time an accused is taken to that place to be detained in custody;

"promise to appear" means a promise in Form 10 given to an officer in charge;

"recognizance", when used in relation to a recognizance entered into before an officer in charge, means a recognizance in Form 11, and when used in relation to a recognizance entered into before a justice or judge, means a recognizance in Form 32;

"summons" means a summons in Form 6 issued by a justice or a judge;

"undertaking" means an undertaking in Form 12 given to a justice or a judge;

"warrant", when used in relation to a warrant for the arrest of a person, means a warrant in Form 7 and, when used in relation to a warrant for the committal of a person, means a warrant in Form 8. R.S. 1985, c. 11 (1st Supp.), Schedule; R.S. 1985, c. 27, (2d Supp.), Sched., item 6; c. 40 (4th Supp.), Schedule, item; 1990, c. 16, s. 5; 1990, c. 17, s. 12.

Arrest without Warrant and Release from Custody

Arrest without warrant by any person — Arrest by owner, etc., of property — Delivery to peace officer.

494. (1) Any one may arrest without warrant

(*a*) a person whom he finds committing an indictable offence; or

(*b*) a person who, on reasonable grounds, he believes

(i) has committed a criminal offence, and

(ii) is escaping from and freshly pursued by persons who have lawful authority to arrest that person.

(2) Any one who is

(*a*) the owner or a person in lawful possession of property, or

(*b*) a person authorized by the owner or by a person in lawful possession of property

may arrest without warrant a person whom he finds committing a criminal offence on or in relation to that property.

(3) Any one other than a peace officer who arrests a person without warrant shall forthwith deliver the person to a peace officer.

Arrest without warrant by peace officer — Limitation — Consequences of arrest without warrant.

495. (1) A peace officer may arrest without warrant

(*a*) a person who has committed an indictable offence or who, on reasonable grounds, he believes has committed or is about to commit an indictable offence,

(*b*) a person whom he finds committing a criminal offence, or

(*c*) a person in respect of whom he has reasonable grounds to believe that a warrant of arrest or committal, in any form set out in Part XXVIII in relation thereto, is in force within the territorial jurisdiction in which the person is found.

(2) A peace officer shall not arrest a person without warrant for

(*a*) an indictable offence mentioned in section 553,

(*b*) an offence for which the person may be prosecuted by indictment or for which he is punishable on summary conviction, or

(*c*) an offence punishable on summary conviction,

in any case where

(*d*) he believes on reasonable grounds that the public interest, having regard to all the circumstances including the need to

(i) establish the identity of the person,

(ii) secure or preserve evidence of or relating to the offence, or

(iii) prevent the continuation or repetition of the offence or the commission of another offence,

may be satisfied without so arresting the person, and

(*e*) he has no reasonable grounds to believe that, if he does not so arrest the person, the person will fail to attend court in order to be dealt with according to law.

(3) Notwithstanding subsection (2), a peace officer acting under subsection (1) is deemed to be acting lawfully and in the execution of his duty for the purposes of

(*a*) any proceedings under this or any other Act of Parliament; and

(*b*) any other proceedings, unless in any such proceedings it is alleged and established by the person making the allegation that the peace officer did not comply with the requirements of subsection (2). R.S. 1985, c. 27 (1st Supp.), s. 75.

Issue of appearance notice by peace officer.

496. Where, by virtue of subsection 495(2), a peace officer does not arrest a person, he may issue an appearance notice to the person if the offence is

(*a*) an indictable offence mentioned in section 553,

(*b*) an offence for which the person may be prosecuted by indictment or for which he is punishable on summary conviction, or

(*c*) an offence punishable on summary conviction.

Release from custody by peace officer — Where subsection (1) does not apply — Consequences of non-release.

497. (1) Where a peace officer arrests a person without warrant for

(*a*) an indictable offence mentioned in section 553,

(*b*) an offence for which the person may be prosecuted by indictment or for which he is punishable on summary conviction, or

(*c*) an offence punishable on summary conviction,

he shall, as soon as practicable,

(*d*) release the person from custody with the intention of compelling his appearance by way of summons, or

(*e*) issue an appearance notice to the person and thereupon release him,

unless

(*f*) he believes on reasonable grounds that it is necessary in the public interest, having regard to all the circumstances including the need to

(i) establish the identity of the person,

(ii) secure or preserve evidence of or relating to the offence, or

(iii) prevent the continuation or repetition of the offence or the commission of another offence,

that the person be detained in custody or that the matter of his release from custody be dealt with under another provision of this Part, or

(*g*) he believes on reasonable grounds that, if the person is released by him from custody, the person will fail to attend court in order to be dealt with according to law.

(2) Subsection (1) does not apply in respect of a person who has been arrested without warrant by a peace officer for an offence described in subsection 503(3).

(3) A peace officer who has arrested a person without warrant for an offence described in subsection (1) and who does not release the person from custody as soon as practicable in the manner described in paragraph (*d*) or (*e*) of that subsection shall be deemed to be acting lawfully and in the execution of his duty for the purposes of

(*a*) any proceedings under this or any other Act of Parliament; and

(*b*) any other proceedings, unless in any such proceedings it is alleged and established by the person making the allegation that the peace officer did not comply with the requirements of subsection (1).

Release from custody by officer in charge — Where subsection (1) does not apply — Consequences of non-release.

498. (1) Where a person who has been arrested without warrant by a peace officer is taken into custody, or where a person who has been arrested without warrant and delivered to a peace officer under subsection 494(3) is detained in custody under subsection 503(1) for

(*a*) an indictable offence mentioned in section 553,

(*b*) an offence for which the person may be prosecuted by indictment or for which he is punishable on summary conviction,

(*c*) an offence punishable on summary conviction, or

(*d*) any other offence that is punishable by imprisonment for five years or less,

and has not been taken before a justice or released from custody under any other provision of this Part, the officer in charge shall, as soon as practicable,

(*e*) release the person with the intention of compelling his appearance by way of summons,

(*f*) release the person on his giving his promise to appear,

(*g*) release the person on his entering into a recognizance before the officer in charge without sureties in such amount not exceeding five hundred dollars as the officer in charge directs, but without deposit of money or other valuable security, or (*h*) if the person is not ordinarily resident in the province in which the person is in custody or does not ordinarily reside within two hundred kilometres of the place in which he is in custody, release the person on his entering into a recognizance before the officer in charge without sureties in such amount not exceeding five hundred dollars as the officer in charge directs and, if the officer in charge so directs, on his depositing with the officer in charge such sum of money or other valuable security not exceeding in amount or value five hundred dollars as the officer in charge directs,

unless

(*i*) he believes on reasonable grounds that it is necessary in the public interest, having regard to all the circumstances including the need to

(i) establish the identity of the person,

(ii) secure or preserve evidence of or relating to the offence, or

(iii) prevent the continuation or repetition of the offence or the commission of another offence,

that the person be detained in custody or that the matter of his release from custody be dealt with under another provision of this Part, or

(*j*) he believes on reasonable grounds that, if the person is released by him from custody, the person will fail to attend court in order to be dealt with according to law.

(2) Subsection (1) does not apply in respect of a person who has been arrested without warrant by a peace officer for an offence described in subsection 503(3).

(3) An officer in charge who has the custody of a person taken into or detained in custody for an offence described in subsection (1) and who does not release the person from custody as soon as practicable in the manner described in paragraph (*e*), (*f*), (*g*) or (*h*) of that subsection shall be deemed to be acting lawfully and in the execution of his duty for the purposes of

(*a*) any proceedings under this or any other Act of Parliament; or

(*b*) any other proceedings, unless in any such proceedings it is alleged and established by the person making the allegation that the officer in charge did not comply with the requirements of subsection (1). R.S. 1985, c. 27 (1st Supp.), s. 186.

Release from custody by officer in charge where arrest made with warrant.

499. Where a person who has been arrested with a warrant by a peace officer is taken into custody for

(*a*) an indictable offence mentioned in section 553,

(*b*) an offence for which the person may be prosecuted by indictment or for which he is punishable on summary conviction,

(*c*) an offence punishable on summary conviction, or

(*d*) any other offence that is punishable by imprisonment for five years or less,

the officer in charge may, if the warrant has been endorsed by a justice under subsection 507(6), (*e*) release the person on his giving his promise to appear,

(*f*) release the person on his entering into a recognizance before the officer in charge without sureties in such amount not exceeding five hundred dollars as the officer in charge directs, but without deposit of money or other valuable security, or

(*g*) if the person is not ordinarily resident in the province in which the person is in custody or does not ordinarily reside within two hundred kilometres of the place in which he is in custody, release the person on his entering into a recognizance before the officer in charge without sureties in such amount not exceeding five hundred dollars as the officer in charge directs and, if the officer in charge so directs, on his depositing with the officer in charge such sum of money or other valuable security not exceeding in amount or value five hundred dollars, as the officer in charge directs. R.S. 1985, c. 27 (1st Supp.), s. 186.

Money or other valuable security to be deposited with justice.

500. Where a person has, pursuant to paragraph 498(1)(*h*) or paragraph 499(*g*), deposited any sum of money or other valuable security with the officer in charge, the officer in charge shall, forthwith after the deposit thereof, cause the money or valuable security to be delivered to a justice for deposit with the justice.

Contents of appearance notice, promise to appear and recognizance — Idem — Attendance for purposes of *Identification of Criminals Act* — Signature of accused — Proof of issue of appearance notice.

501. (1) An appearance notice issued by a peace officer or a promise to appear given to, or a recognizance entered into before, an officer in charge shall

(*a*) set out the name of the accused;

(*b*) set out the substance of the offence that the accused is alleged to have committed; and

(*c*) require the accused to attend court at a time and place to be stated therein and to attend thereafter as required by the court in order to be dealt with according to law.

(2) An appearance notice issued by a peace officer or a promise to appear given to, or a recognizance entered into before, an officer in charge shall set out the text of subsections 145(5) and (6) and section 502.

(3) An appearance notice issued by a peace officer or a promise to appear given to, or a recognizance entered into before, an officer in charge may, where the accused is alleged to have committed an indictable offence, require the accused to appear at a time and place stated therein for the purposes of the *Identification of Criminals Act*, and a person so appearing is deemed, for the purposes only of that Act, to be in lawful custody charged with an indictable offence.

(4) An accused shall be requested to sign in duplicate his appearance notice, promise to appear or recognizance and, whether or not he complies with that request, one of the duplicates shall be given to the accused, but if the accused fails or refuses to sign, the lack of his signature does not invalidate the appearance notice, promise to appear or recognizance, as the case may be.

(5) The issue of an appearance notice by any peace officer may be proved by the oral evidence, given under oath, of the officer who issued it or by the officer's affidavit made before a justice or other person authorized to administer oaths or to take affidavits. R.S. 1985, c. 27 (1st Supp.), s. 76.

Failure to appear.

502. Where an accused who is required by an appearance notice or promise to appear or by a recognizance entered into before an officer in charge to appear at a time and place stated therein for the purposes of the *Identification of Criminals Act* does not appear at that time and place, a justice may, where the appearance notice, promise to appear or recognizance has been confirmed by a justice under section 508, issue a warrant for the arrest of the accused for the offence with which he is charged.

Appearance of Accused Before Justice

Taking before justice — Conditional release — Remand in custody for return to province where offence alleged to have been committed — Interim release — Release of person about to commit indictable offence — Consequences of non-release.

503. (1) A peace officer who arrests a person with or without warrant or to whom a person is delivered under subsection 494(3) shall cause the person to be detained in custody and, in accordance with the following provisions, to be taken before a justice to be dealt with according to law, namely:

(*a*) where a justice is available within a period of twenty-four hours after the person has been arrested by or delivered to the peace officer, the person shall be taken before a justice without unreasonable delay and in any event within that period, and

(*b*) where a justice is not available within a period of twety-four hours after the person has been arrested by or delivered to the peace officer, the person shall be taken before a justice as soon as possible,

unless, at any time before the expiration of the time prescribed in paragraph (*a*) or (*b*) for taking the person before a justice,

(*c*) the peace officer or officer in charge releases the person under any other provision of this Part, or

(*d*) the peace officer or officer in charge is satisfied that the person should be released from custody, whether unconditionally under subsection (4) or otherwise conditionally or unconditionally, and so releases him.

(2) Where a peace officer or an officer in charge is satisfied that a person described in subsection (1) should be released from custody conditionally, he may, unless the person is detained in custody for an offence mentioned in section 522, release that person in accordance with paragraphs 498(1)(*f*) to (*h*).

(3) Where a person has been arrested without warrant for an indictable offence alleged to have been committed in Canada outside the province in which he was arrested, he shall, within the time prescribed in paragraph (1)(*a*) or (*b*), be taken before a justice within whose jurisdiction he was arrested and the justice,

(*a*) if he is not satisfied that there are reasonable grounds to believe that the person arrested is the person alleged to have committed the offence, shall release him; or

(*b*) if he is satisfied that there are reasonable grounds to believe that the person arrested is the person alleged to have committed the offence, may remand him to the custody of a peace officer to await execution of a warrant for his arrest in accordance with section 528, but if no warrant for his arrest is so executed within a period of six days after the time he is remanded to such custody, the person in whose custody he then is shall release him.

(3.1) Notwithstanding paragraph (3)(*b*), a justice may, with the consent of the prosecutor, order that the person referred to in subsection (3), pending the execution of a warrant for arrest of that person, be released

(*a*) unconditionally, or

(*b*) on any of the following terms to which the prosecutor consents, namely,

(i) giving an undertaking, or

(ii) entering into a recognizance described in any of paragraphs 515(2)(*a*) to (*e*)

with such conditions described in subsection 515(4) as the justice considers desirable and to which the prosecutor consents.

(4) A peace officer or officer in charge having the custody of a person who has been arrested without warrant as a person about to commit an indictable offence shall release that person unconditionally as soon as practicable after he is satisfied that the continued detention of that person in custody is no longer necessary in order to prevent the commission by him of an indictable offence.

(5) Notwithstanding subsection (4), a peace officer or officer in charge having the custody of a person referred to in that subsection who does not release the person before the expiration of the time prescribed in paragraph (1)(*a*) or (*b*) for taking the person before the justice shall be deemed to be acting lawfully and in the execution of his duty for the purposes of

(*a*) any proceedings under this or any other Act of Parliament; or

(*b*) any other proceedings, unless in such proceedings it is alleged and established by the person making the allegation that the peace officer or officer in charge did not comply with the requirements of subsection (4). R.S. 1985, c. 27 (1st Supp.), s. 77.

Information, Summons and Warrant

In what cases justice may receive information.

504. Any one who, on reasonable grounds, believes that a person has committed an indictable offence may lay an information in writing and under oath before a justice, and the justice shall receive the information, where it is alleged

(*a*) that the person has committed, anywhere, an indictable offence that may be tried in the province in which the justice resides, and that the person

(i) is or is believed to be, or

(ii) resides or is believed to reside,

within the territorial jurisdiction of the justice;

(*b*) that the person, wherever he may be, has committed an indictable offence within the territorial jurisdiction of the justice;

(*c*) that the person has, anywhere, unlawfully received property that was unlawfully obtained within the territorial jurisdiction of the justice; or

(*d*) that the person has in his possession stolen property within the territorial jurisdiction of the justice.

Time within which information to be laid in certain cases.

505. Where

(*a*) an appearance notice has been issued to an accused under section 496, or

(*b*) an accused has been released from custody under section 497 or 498,

an information relating to the offence alleged to have been committed by the accused or relating to an included or other offence alleged to have been committed by him shall be laid before a justice as soon as practicable thereafter and in any event before the time stated in the appearance notice, promise to appear or recognizance issued to or given or entered into by the accused for his attendance in court.

Form.

506. An information laid under section 504 or 505 may be in Form 2.

Justice to hear informant and witnesses — Process compulsory — Procedure when witnesses attend — Summons to be issued except in certain cases — No process in blank — Endorsement of warrant by justice — Promise to appear or recognizance deemed to have been confirmed — Issue of summons or warrant.

507. (1) Subject to subsection 523(1.1), a justice who receives an information, other than an information laid before the justice under section 505, shall, except where an accused has already been arrested with or without a warrant,

(*a*) hear and consider, *ex parte*,

(i) the allegations of the informant, and

(ii) the evidence of witnesses, where he considers it desirable or necessary to do so; and

(*b*) where he considers that a case for so doing is made out, issue, in accordance with this section, either a summons or a warrant for the arrest of the accused to compel the accused to attend before him or some other justice for the same territorial division to answer to a charge of an offence.

(2) No justice shall refuse to issue a summons or warrant by reason only that the alleged offence is one for which a person may be arrested without warrant.

(3) A justice who hears the evidence of a witness pursuant to subsection (1) shall

(*a*) take the evidence on oath; and

(*b*) cause the evidence to be taken in accordance with section 540 in so far as that section is capable of being applied.

(4) Where the justice considers that a case is made out for compelling an accused to attend before him to answer to a charge of an offence, he shall issue a summons to the accused unless the allegations of the informant or the evidence of any witness or witnesses taken in accordance with subsection (3) disclose reasonable grounds to believe that it is necessary in the public interest to issue a warrant for the arrest of the accused.

(5) A justice shall not sign a summons or warrant in blank.

(6) Where a justice issues a warrant under this section or section 508 or 512, the justice may, where the offence is

(*a*) an indictable offence mentioned in section 553,

(*b*) an offence for which the person may be prosecuted by indictment or for which he is punishable on summary conviction,

(*c*) an offence punishable on summary conviction, or

(*d*) any other offence that is punishable by imprisonment for five years or less,

authorize the release of the accused pursuant to section 499 by making an endorsement on the warrant in Form 29.

(7) Where, pursuant to subsection (6), a justice authorizes the release of an accused pursuant to section 499, a promise to appear given by the accused or a recognizance entered into by the accused pursuant to that section shall be deemed, for the purposes of subsection 145(5), to have been confirmed by a justice under section 508.

(8) Where, on an appeal from or review of any decision or matter of jurisdiction, a new trial or hearing or a continuance or renewal of a trial or hearing is ordered, a justice may issue either a summons or a warrant for the arrest of the accused in order to compel the accused to attend at the new or continued or renewed trial or hearing. R.S. 1985, c. 27 (1st Supp.), s. 78.

Justice to hear informant and witnesses — Procedure when witnesses attend.

508. (1) A justice who receives an information laid before him under section 505 shall

(*a*) hear and consider, *ex parte*,

(i) the allegations of the informant, and

(ii) the evidence of witnesses, where he considers it desirable or necessary to do so;

(*b*) where he considers that a case for so doing is made out, whether the information relates to the offence alleged in the appearance notice, promise to appear or recognizance or to an included or other offence,

(i) confirm the appearance notice, promise to appear or recognizance, as the case may be, and endorse the information accordingly, or

(ii) cancel the appearance notice, promise to appear or recognizance, as the case may be, and issue, in accordance with section 507, either a summons or a warrant for the arrest of the accused to compel the accused to attend before him or some other justice for the same territorial division to answer to a charge of an offence and endorse on the summons or warrant that the appearance notice, promise to appear or recognizance, as the case may be, has been cancelled; and

(*c*) where he considers that a case is not made out for the purposes of paragraph (*b*), cancel the appearance notice, promise to appear or recognizance, as the case may be, and cause the accused to be notified forthwith of such cancellation.

(2) A justice who hears the evidence of a witness pursuant to subsection (1) shall

(*a*) take the evidence upon oath; and

(*b*) cause the evidence to be taken in accordance with section 540 in so far as that section is capable of being applied. R.S. 1985, c. 27 (1st Supp.), s. 79.

Summons — Service on individual — Proof of service — Content of summons — Attendance for purposes of *Identification of Criminals Act*.

509. (1) A summons issued under this Part shall

(*a*) be directed to the accused;

(*b*) set out briefly the offence in respect of which the accused is charged; and

(*c*) require the accused to attend court at a time and place to be stated therein and to attend thereafter as required by the court in order to be dealt with according to law.

(2) A summons shall be served by a peace officer who shall deliver it personally to the person to whom it is directed or, if that person cannot conveniently be found, shall leave it for him at his latest or usual place of abode with an inmate thereof who appears to be at least sixteen years of age.

(3) Service of a summons may be proved by the oral evidence, given under oath, of the peace officer who served it or by his affidavit made before a justice or other person authorized to administer oaths or to take affidavits.

(4) There shall be set out in every summons the text of subsection 145(4) and section 510.

(5) A summons may, where the accused is alleged to have committed an indictable offence, require the accused to appear at a time and place stated therein for the purposes of the *Identification of Criminals Act*, and a person so appearing is deemed, for the purposes only of that Act, to be in lawful custody charged with an indictable offence. R.S. 1985, c. 27 (1st Supp.), s. 80.

Failure to appear.

510. Where an accused who is required by a summons to appear at a time and place stated therein for the purposes of the *Identification of Criminals Act*, does not appear at that time and place, a justice may issue a warrant for the arrest of the accused for the offence with which he is charged.

Contents of warrant to arrest — No return day.

511. (1) A warrant issued under this Part shall

(*a*) name or describe the accused;

(*b*) set out briefly the offence in respect of which the accused is charged; and

(*c*) order that the accused be forthwith arrested and brought before the judge or justice who issued the warrant or before some other judge or justice having jurisdiction in the same territorial division, to be dealt with according to law.

(2) A warrant issued under this Part remains in force until it is executed, and need not be made returnable at any particular time. R.S. 1985, c. 27 (1st Supp.), s. 81.

Certain actions not to preclude issue of warrant — Warrant in default of appearance.

512. (1) A justice may, where the justice has reasonable and probable grounds to believe that it is necessary in the public interest to issue a summons or a warrant for the arrest of the accused, issue a summons or a warrant notwithstanding that

(*a*) an appearance notice or promise to appear or a recognizance entered into before an officer in charge has been confirmed or cancelled under subsection 508(1);

(*b*) a summons has previously been issued under subsection 507(4); or

(*c*) the accused has been released unconditionally or with the intention of compelling his appearance by way of summons.

(2) Where

(*a*) service of a summons is proved and the accused fails to attend court in accordance with the summons,
(*b*) an appearance notice or promise to appear or a recognizance entered into before an officer in charge has been confirmed under subsection 508(1) and the accused fails to attend court in accordance therewith in order to be dealt with according to law, or
(*c*) it appears that a summons cannot be served because the accused is evading service,

a justice may issue a warrant for the arrest of the accused. R.S. 1985, c. 27 (1st Supp.), s. 82.

Formalities of warrant.

513. A warrant in accordance with this Part shall be directed to the peace officers within the territorial jurisdiction of the justice, judge or court by whom or by which it is issued.

Execution of warrant — By whom warrant may be executed.

514. (1) A warrant in accordance with this Part may be executed by arresting the accused
(*a*) wherever he is found within the territorial jurisdiction of the justice, judge or court by whom or by which the warrant was issued; or
(*b*) wherever he is found in Canada, in the case of fresh pursuit.

(2) A warrant in accordance with this Part may be executed by a person who is one of the peace officers to whom it is directed, whether or not the place in which the warrant is to be executed is within the territory for which the person is a peace officer.

Judicial Interim Release

Order of release — Release on undertaking with conditions, etc. — Power of justice to name sureties in order — Release on undertaking with conditions etc. — Conditions authorized — Detention in custody — Order of detention — Order of release — Idem — Sufficiency of record — Justification for detention in custody — Detention in custody for offence mentioned in s. 469.

515. (1) Subject to this section, where an accused who is charged with an offence other than an offence listed in section 469 is taken before a justice the justice shall, unless a plea of guilty by the accused is accepted, order, in respect of that offence, that the accused be released on his giving an undertaking without conditions, unless the prosecutor, having been given a reasonable opportunity to do so, shows cause, in respect of that offence, why the detention of the accused in custody is justified or why an order under any other provision of this section should be made and where the justice makes an order under any other provision of this section, the order shall refer only to the particular offence for which the accused was taken before the justice.

(2) Where the justice does not make an order under subsection (1), he shall, unless the prosecutor shows cause why the detention of the accused is justified, order that the accused be released

(*a*) on his giving an undertaking with such conditions as the justice directs;

(*b*) on his entering into a recognizance before the justice, without sureties, in such amount and with such conditions, if any, as the justice directs but without deposit of money or other valuable security;

(*c*) on his entering into a recognizance before the justice with sureties in such amount and with such conditions, if any, as the justice directs but without deposit of money or other valuable security;

(*d*) with the consent of the prosecutor, on his entering into a recognizance before the justice, without sureties, in such amount and with such conditions, if any, as the justice directs and on his depositing with the justice such sum of money or other valuable security as the justice directs, or

(*e*) if the accused is not ordinarily resident in the province in which the accused is in custody or does not ordinarily reside within one hundred kilometres of the place in which he is in custody, on his entering into a recognizance before the justice with or without sureties in such amount and with such conditions, if any, as the justice directs, and on his depositing with the justice such sum of money or other valuable security as the justice directs.

(2.1) Where, pursuant to subsection (2) or any other provision of this Act, a justice, judge or court orders that an accused be released on his entering into a recognizance with sureties, the justice, judge or court may, in the order, name particular persons as sureties.

(3) The justice shall not make an order under any of paragraphs (2)(*b*) to (*e*) unless the prosecution shows cause why an order under the immediately preceding paragraph should not be made.

(4) The justice may direct as conditions under subsection (2) that the accused shall do any one or more of the following things as specified in the order:

(*a*) report at times to be stated in the order to a peace officer or other person designated in the order;

(*b*) remain within a territorial jurisdiction specified in the order;

(*c*) notify the peace officer or other person designated under paragraph (*a*) of any change in his address or his employment or occupation;

(*d*) abstain from communicating with any witness or other person expressly named in the order except in accordance with such conditions specified in the order as the justice deems necessary;

(*e*) where the accused is the holder of a passport, deposit his passport as specified in the order; and

(*f*) comply with such other reasonable conditions specified in the order as the justice considers desirable.

[1991, c. 40, s. 31(1) will add the following immediately after subsection 515(4).]

Additional conditions.

(4.1) Before making an order under subsection (2), in the case of an accused who is charged with an offence in the commission of which violence against a person was used, threatened or attempted or an offence described in subsection 39(1) or (2) or 48(1) or (2) of the *Food and Drugs Act* or in subsection 4(1) or (2) of the *Narcotic Control Act*, the justice shall consider whether it is desirable, in the interests of the safety of the accused or of any other person, to include as a condition of the order that the accused be prohibited from possessing any firearm or any ammunition or explosive substance for any period of time specified in the order and that the accused surrender any firearms acquisition certificate that the accused possesses, and where the justice decides that it is not desirable, in the interests of the safety of the accused or of any other person, for the accused to possess any of those things, the justice may add the appropriate condition to the order.

(5) Where the prosecutor shows cause why the detention of the accused in custody is justified, the justice shall order that the accused be detained in custody until he is dealt with according to law and shall include in the record a statement of his reasons for making the order.

(6) Notwithstanding any provision of this section, where an accused is charged

(*a*) with an indictable offence, other than an offence listed in section 469, that is alleged to have been committed while he was at large after being released in respect of another indictable offence pursuant to the provisions of this Part or section 679 or 680,

(*b*) with an indictable offence, other than an offence listed in section 469 and is not ordinarily resident in Canada,

(*c*) with an offence under any of subsections 145(2) to (5) that is alleged to have been committed while he was at large after being released in respect of another offence pursuant to the provisions of this Part or section 679, 680 or 816, or

(*d*) with having committed an offence under section 4 or 5 of the *Narcotic Control Act* or the offence of conspiring to commit an offence under section 4 or 5 of that Act,

the justice shall order that the accused be detained in custody until he is dealt with according to law, unless the accused, having been given a reasonable opportunity to do so, shows cause why his detention in custody is not justified, but where the justice orders that the accused be released, he shall include in the record a statement of his reasons for making the order.

(7) Where an accused to whom paragraph (6)(*a*), (*c*) or (*d*) applies shows cause why his detention in custody is not justified, the justice shall order that he be released on his giving an undertaking or entering into a recognizance

described in any of paragraphs (2)(*a*) to (*e*) with such conditions described in subsection (4) or, where the accused was at large on an undertaking or recognizance with conditions, such additional conditions described in subsection (4), as the justice considers desirable, unless the accused, having been given a reasonable opportunity to do so, shows cause why such conditions or additional conditions should not be imposed.

(8) Where an accused to whom paragraph (6)(*b*) applies shows cause why his detention in custody is not justified, the justice shall order that he be released on his giving an undertaking or entering into a recognizance described in any of paragraphs (2)(*a*) to (*e*) with such conditions, described in subsection (4), as the justice considers desirable.

[1991, c. 40, s. 31(2) will repeal subsections 515(7) and (8) and substitute the following.]

Order of release — Idem.

(7) Where an accused to whom paragraph 6(*a*), (*c*) or (*d*) applies shows cause why the accused's detention in custody is not justified, the justice shall order that the accused be released on giving an undertaking or entering into a recognizance described in any of paragraphs (2)(*a*) to (*e*) with such conditions described in subsections (4) and (4.1) or, where the accused was at large on an undertaking or recognizance with conditions, such additional conditions described in subsections (4) and (4.1), as the justice considers desirable, unless the accused, having been given a reasonable opportunity to do so, shows cause why such conditions or additional conditions should not be imposed.

(8) Where an accused to whom paragraph (6)(*b*) applies shows cause why the accused's detention in custody is not justified, the justice shall order that the accused be released on giving an undertaking or entering into a recognizance described in any of paragraphs (2)(*a*) to (*e*) with such conditions, described in subsections (4) and (4.1), as the justice considers desirable.

(9) For the purposes of subsections (5) and (6), it is sufficient if a record is made of the reasons in accordance with the provisions of Part XVIII relating to the taking of evidence at preliminary inquiries.

(10) For the purposes of this section, the detention of an accused in custody is justified only on either of the following grounds:

(*a*) on the primary ground that his detention is necessary to ensure his attendance in court in order to be dealt with according to law; and

(*b*) on the secondary ground (the applicability of which shall be determined only in the event that and after it is determined that his detention is not justified on the primary ground referred to in paragraph (*a*)) that his detention is necessary in the public interest or for the protection or safety of the public, having regard to all the circumstances including any substantial likelihood that the accused will, if he is released from custody, commit a criminal offence or an interference with the administration of justice.

(11) Where an accused who is charged with an offence mentioned in section 469 is taken before a justice, the justice shall order that the accused be detained in custody until he is dealt with according to law and shall issue a warrant in Form 8 for the committal of the accused. R.S. 1985, c. 27 (1st Supp.), ss. 83, 186.

Remand in custody.

516. A justice may, before or at any time during the course of any proceedings under section 515, on application by the prosecutor or the accused, adjourn the proceedings and remand the accused to custody in prison by warrant in Form 19, but no adjournment shall be for more than three clear days except with the consent of the accused.

Order directing matters not to be published for specified period — Failure to comply — "Newspaper".

517. (1) Where the prosecutor or the accused intends to show cause under section 515, he shall so state to the justice and the justice may, and shall on application by the accused, before or at any time during the course of the proceedings under that section, make an order directing that the evidence taken, the information given or the representations made and the reasons, if any, given or to be given by the justice shall not be published in any newspaper or broadcast before such time as

(*a*) if a preliminary inquiry is held, the accused in respect of whom the proceedings are held is discharged; or

(*b*) if the accused in respect of whom the proceedings are held is tried or committed for trial, the trial is ended.

(2) Every one who fails without lawful excuse, the proof of which lies on him, to comply with an order made under subsection (1) is guilty of an offence punishable on summary conviction.

(3) In this section, "newspaper" has the same meaning as in section 297. R.S. 1985, c. 27 (1st Supp.), s. 101(2).

Inquiries to be made by justice and evidence — Release pending sentence.

518. (1) In any proceedings under section 515,

(*a*) the justice may, subject to paragraph (*b*), make such inquiries, on oath or otherwise, of and concerning the accused as he considers desirable;

(*b*) the accused shall not be examined or cross-examined by the justice or any other person respecting the offence with which he is charged, and no inquiry shall be made of him respecting that offence;

(*c*) the prosecutor may, in addition to any other relevant evidence, lead evidence

(i) to prove that the accused has previously been convicted of a criminal offence,

(ii) to prove that the accused has been charged with and is awaiting trial for another criminal offence,

(iii) to prove that the accused has previously committed an offence under section 145, or

(iv) to show the circumstances of the alleged offence, particularly as they relate to the probability of conviction of the accused;

(*d*) the justice may take into consideration any relevant matters agreed on by the prosecutor and the accused or his counsel;

(*d*.1) the justice may receive evidence obtained as a result of an interception of a private communication under and within the meaning of Part VI.1, in writing, orally or in the form of a recording and, for the purposes of this section, subsection 189(5) does not apply to such evidence; and

(*e*) the justice may receive and base his decision on evidence considered credible or trustworthy by him in the circumstances of each case.

(2) Where, before or at any time during the course of any proceedings under section 515, the accused pleads guilty and that plea is accepted, the justice may make any order provided for in this Part for the release of the accused until the accused is sentenced. R.S. 1985, c. 27 (1st Supp.), s. 84.

Release of accused — Discharge from custody — Warrant for committal.

519. (1) Where a justice makes an order under subsection 515(1), (2), (7) or (8),

(*a*) if the accused thereupon complies with the order, the justice shall direct that the accused be released

(i) forthwith, if the accused is not required to be detained in custody in respect of any other matter, or

(ii) as soon thereafter as the accused is no longer required to be detained in custody in respect of any other matter; and

(*b*) if the accused does not thereupon comply with the order, the justice who made the order or another justice having jurisdiction shall issue a warrant for the committal of the accused and may endorse thereon an authorization to the person having the custody of the accused to release the accused when the accused complies with the order

(i) forthwith after the compliance, if the accused is not required to be detained in custody in respect of any other matter, or

(ii) as soon thereafter as the accused is no longer required to be detained in custody in respect of any other matter

and if the justice so endorses the warrant, he shall attach to it a copy of the order.

(2) Where the accused complies with an order referred to in paragraph (1)(*b*), and is not required to be detained in custody in respect of any other matter, the justice who made the order or another justice having jurisdiction shall, unless the accused has been or will be released pursuant to an authorization referred to in that paragraph, issue an order for discharge in Form 39.

(3) Where the justice makes an order under subsection 515(5) or (6) for the detention of the accused, he shall issue a warrant for the committal of the accused. R.S. 1985, c. 27 (1st Supp.), s. 85.

Review of order of justice — Notice to prosecutor — Accused to be present — Adjournment of proceedings — Failure of accused to attend — Execution — Evidence and powers of judge on review — Limitation of further applications — Application of ss. 517, 518 and 519.

520. (1) Where a justice makes an order under subsection 515(2), (5), (6), (7) or (8) or makes or vacates any order under paragraph 523(2)(*b*), the accused may, at any time before the trial of the charge, apply to a judge for a review of the order made by the justice.

(2) An application under this section shall not, unless the prosecutor otherwise consents, be heard by a judge unless the accused has given to the prosecutor at least two clear days notice in writing of the application.

(3) If the judge so orders or the prosecutor or the accused or his counsel so requests, the accused shall be present at the hearing of an application under this section and, where the accused is in custody, the judge may order, in writing, the person having the custody of the accused to bring him before the court.

(4) A judge may, before or at any time during the hearing of an application under this section, on application by the prosecutor or the accused, adjourn the proceedings, but if the accused is in custody no adjournment shall be for more than three clear days except with the consent of the accused.

(5) Where an accused, other than an accused who is in custody, has been ordered by a judge to be present at the hearing of an application under this section and does not attend the hearing, the judge may issue a warrant for the arrest of the accused.

(6) A warrant issued under subsection (5) may be executed anywhere in Canada.

(7) On the hearing of an application under this section, the judge may consider

(*a*) the transcript, if any, of the proceedings heard by the justice and by any judge who previously reviewed the order made by the justice,

(*b*) the exhibits, if any, filed in the proceedings before the justice, and

(*c*) such additional evidence or exhibits as may be tendered by the accused or the prosecutor,

and shall either

(*d*) dismiss the application, or

(*e*) if the accused shows cause, allow the application, vacate the order previously made by the justice and make any other order provided for in section 515 that he considers is warranted.

(8) Where an application under this section or section 521 has been heard, a further or other application under this section or section 521 shall not be

made with respect to that same accused, except with leave of a judge, prior to the expiration of thirty days from the date of the decision of the judge who heard the previous application.

(9) The provisions of sections 517, 518 and 519 apply with such modifications as the circumstances require in respect of an application under this section. R.S. 1985, c. 27 (1st Supp.), s. 86.

Review of order of justice — Notice to accused — Accused to be present — Adjournment of proceedings — Failure of accused to attend — Warrant for detention — Execution — Evidence and powers of judge on review — Limitation of further applications — Application of ss. 517, 518 and 519.

521. (1) Where a justice makes an order under subsection 515(1), (2), (7) or (8) or makes or vacates any order under paragraph 523(2)(*b*), the prosecutor may, at any time before the trial of the charge, apply to a judge for a review of the order made by the justice.

(2) An application under this section shall not be heard by a judge unless the prosecutor has given to the accused at least two clear days notice in writing of the application.

(3) If the judge so orders or the prosecutor or the accused or his counsel so requests, the accused shall be present at the hearing of an application under this section and, where the accused is in custody, the judge may order, in writing, the person having the custody of the accused to bring him before the court.

(4) A judge may, before or at any time during the hearing of an application under this section, on application of the prosecutor or the accused, adjourn the proceedings, but if the accused is in custody no such adjournment shall be for more than three clear days except with the consent of the accused.

(5) Where an accused, other than an accused who is in custody, has been ordered by a judge to be present at the hearing of an application under this section and does not attend the hearing, the judge may issue a warrant for the arrest of the accused.

(6) Where, pursuant to paragraph (8)(*e*), the judge makes an order that the accused be detained in custody until he is dealt with according to law, he shall, if the accused is not in custody, issue a warrant for the committal of the accused.

(7) A warrant issued under subsection (5) or (6) may be executed anywhere in Canada.

(8) On the hearing of an application under this section, the judge may consider

(*a*) the transcript, if any, of the proceedings heard by the justice and by any judge who previously reviewed the order made by the justice,

(*b*) the exhibits, if any, filed in the proceedings before the justice, and (*c*) such additional evidence or exhibits as may be tendered by the prosecutor or the accused,

and shall either

(*d*) dismiss the application, or

(*e*) if the prosecutor shows cause, allow the application, vacate the order previously made by the justice and make any other order provided for in section 515 that he considers to be warranted.

(9) Where an application under this section or section 520 has been heard, a further or other application under this section or section 520 shall not be made with respect to the same accused, except with leave of a judge, prior to the expiration of thirty days from the date of the decision of the judge who heard the previous application.

(10) The provisions of sections 517, 518 and 519 apply with such modifications as the circumstances require in respect of an application under this section. R.S. 1985, c. 27 (1st Supp.), s. 87.

Interim release by judge only — Idem — Release of accused — Order not reviewable except under s. 680 — Application of ss. 517, 518 and 519 — Other offences.

522. (1) Where an accused is charged with an offence listed in section 469, no court, judge or justice, other than a judge of or a judge presiding in a superior court of criminal jurisdiction for the province in which the accused is so charged, may release the accused before or after the accused has been ordered to stand trial.

(2) Where an accused is charged with an offence listed in section 469, a judge of or a judge presiding in a superior court of criminal jurisdiction for the province in which the accused is charged shall order that the accused be detained in custody unless the accused, having been given a reasonable opportunity to do so, shows cause why his detention in custody is not justified within the meaning of subsection 515(10).

(3) Where the judge does not order that the accused be detained in custody pursuant to subsection (2), he may order that the accused be released on his giving an undertaking or entering into a recognizance described in any of paragraphs 515(2)(*a*) to (*e*) with such conditions described in subsection 515(4) as the judge considers desirable.

[1991, c. 40, s. 32 will repeal subsection 522(3) and substitute the following.]

Release of accused.

(3) Where the judge does not order that the accused be detained in custody pursuant to subsection (2), the judge may order that the accused be released on giving an undertaking or entering into a recognizance described in any of paragraphs 512(2)(*a*) to (*e*) with such conditions described in subsections 515(4) and (4.1) as the judge considers desirable.

(4) An order made under this section is not subject to review, except as provided in section 680.

(5) The provisions of sections 517, 518 except subsection (2) thereof, and 519 apply with such modification as the circumstances require in respect of an application for an order under subsection (2).

(6) Where an accused is charged with an offence mentioned in section 469 and with any other offence, a judge acting under this section may apply the provisions of this Part respecting judicial interim release to that other offence. R.S. 1985, c. 27 (1st Supp.), s. 88.

Period for which appearance notice, etc., continues in force — Where new information charging same offence — Order vacating previous order for release or detention — Provisions applicable to proceedings under subsection (2).

523. (1) Where an accused, in respect of an offence with which he is charged, has not been taken into custody or has been released from custody under or by virtue of any provision of this Part, the appearance notice, promise to appear, summons, undertaking or recognizance issued to, given or entered into by the accused continues in force, subject to its terms, and applies in respect of any new information charging the same offence or an included offence that was received after the appearance notice, promise to appear, summons, undertaking or recognizance was issued, given or entered into,

(*a*) where the accused was released from custody pursuant to an order of a judge made under subsection 522(3), until his trial is completed; or

(*b*) in any other case,

(i) until his trial is completed, and

(ii) where the accused is, at his trial, determined to be guilty of the offence, until a sentence within the meaning of section 673 is imposed on the accused unless, at the time the accused is determined to be guilty, the court, judge or justice orders that the accused be taken into custody pending such sentence.

(1.1) Where an accused, in respect of an offence with which he is charged, has not been taken into custody or is being detained or has been released from custody under or by virtue of any provision of this Part and after the order for interim release or detention has been made, or the appearance notice, promise to appear, summons, undertaking or recognizance has been issued, given or entered into, a new information charging the same offence or an included offence, is received, section 507 or 508, as the case may be, does not apply in respect of the new information and the order for interim release or detention of the accused and the appearance notice, promise to appear, summons, undertaking or recognizance, if any, applies in respect of the new information.

(2) Notwithstanding subsections (1) and (1.1),

(*a*) the court, judge or justice before whom an accused is being tried, at any time,

(*b*) the justice, on completion of the preliminary inquiry in relation to an offence for which an accused is ordered to stand trial, other than an offence listed in section 469, or

(*c*) with the consent of the prosecutor and the accused or, where the accused or the prosecutor applies to vacate an order that would otherwise apply pursuant to subsection (1.1), without such consent, at any time

(i) where the accused is charged with an offence other than an offence listed in section 469, the justice by whom an order was made under this Part or any other justice,

(ii) where the accused is charged with an offence listed in section 469, a judge of or a judge presiding in a superior court of criminal jurisdiction for the province, or

(iii) the court, judge or justice before which or whom an accused is to be tried,

may, on cause being shown, vacate any order previously made under this Part for the interim release or detention of the accused and make any other order provided for in this Part for the detention or release of the accused until his trial is completed that the court, judge or justice considers to be warranted.

(3) The provisions of sections 517, 518 and 519 apply, with such modifications as the circumstances require, in respect of any proceedings under subsection (2), except that subsection 518(2) does not apply in respect of an accused who is charged with an offence listed in section 469. R.S. 1985, c. 27 (1st Supp.), s. 89.

Arrest of Accused on Interim Release

Issue of warrant for arrest of accused — Arrest of accused without warrant — Hearing — Retention of accused — Release of accused — Order not reviewable — Release of accused — Powers of justice after hearing — Release of accused — Reasons — Where justice to order that accused be released — Provisions applicable to proceedings under this section — Certain provisions applicable to order under this section.

524. (1) Where a justice is satisfied that there are reasonable grounds to believe that an accused

(*a*) has contravened or is about to contravene any summons, appearance notice, promise to appear, undertaking or recognizance that was issued or given to him or entered into by him, or

(*b*) has committed an indictable offence after any summons, appearance notice, promise to appear, undertaking or recognizance was issued or given to him or entered into by him,

he may issue a warrant for the arrest of the accused.

(2) Notwithstanding anything in this Act, a peace officer who believes on reasonable grounds that an accused

(*a*) has contravened or is about to contravene any summons, appearance notice, promise to appear, undertaking or recognizance that was issued or given to him or entered into by him, or

(*b*) has committed an indictable offence after any summons, appearance notice, promise to appear, undertaking or recognizance was issued or given to him or entered into by him,

may arrest the accused without warrant.

(3) Where an accused who has been arrested with a warrant issued under subsection (1), or who has been arrested under subsection (2), is taken before a justice, the justice shall

(*a*) where the accused was released from custody pursuant to an order made under subsection 522(3) by a judge of the superior court of criminal jurisdiction of any province, order that the accused be taken before a judge of that court; or

(*b*) in any other case, hear the prosecutor and his witnesses, if any, and the accused and his witnesses, if any.

(4) Where an accused described in paragraph (3)(*a*) is taken before a judge and the judge finds

(*a*) that the accused has contravened or had been about to contravene his summons, appearance notice, promise to appear, undertaking or recognizance, or

(*b*) that there are reasonable grounds to believe that the accused has committed an indictable offence after any summons, appearance notice, promise to appear, undertaking or recognizance was issued or given to him or entered into by him,

he shall cancel the summons, appearance notice, promise to appear, undertaking or recognizance and order that the accused be detained in custody unless the accused, having been given a reasonable opportunity to do so, shows cause why his detention in custody is not justified within the meaning of subsection 515(10).

(5) Where the judge does not order that the accused be detained in custody pursuant to subsection (4), he may order that the accused be released upon his giving an undertaking or entering into a recognizance described in any of paragraphs 515(2)(*a*) to (*e*) with such conditions described in subsection 515(4) or, where the accused was at large on an undertaking or a recognizance with conditions, such additional conditions, described in subsection 515(4), as the judge considers desirable.

(6) Any order made under subsection (4) or (5) is not subject to review, except as provided in section 680.

(7) Where the judge does not make a finding under paragraph (4)(*a*) or (*b*), he shall order that the accused be released from custody.

(8) Where an accused described in subsection (3), other than an accused to whom paragraph (*a*) of that subsection applies, is taken before the justice and the justice finds

(*a*) that the accused has contravened or had been about to contravene his summons, appearance notice, promise to appear, undertaking or recognizance, or

(*b*) that there are reasonable grounds to believe that the accused has committed an indictable offence after any summons, appearance notice, promise to appear, undertaking or recognizance was issued or given to him or entered into by him,

he shall cancel the summons, appearance notice, promise to appear, undertaking or recognizance and order that the accused be detained in custody unless the accused, having been given a reasonable opportunity to do so, shows cause why his detention in custody is not justified within the meaning of subsection 515(10).

(9) Where the accused shows cause why his detention in custody is not justified within the meaning of subsection 515(10), the justice shall order that the accused be released on his giving an undertaking or entering into a recognizance described in any of paragraphs 515(2)(*a*) to (*e*) with such conditions, described in subsection 515(4), as the justice considers desirable.

(10) Where the justice makes an order under subsection (9), he shall include in the record a statement of his reasons for making the order, and subsection 515(9) is applicable with such modification as the circumstances require in respect thereof.

(11) Where the justice does not make a finding under paragraph (8)(*a*) or (*b*), he shall order that the accused be released from custody.

(12) The provisions of sections 517, 518 and 519 apply with such modification as the circumstances require in respect of any proceedings under this section, except that subsection 518(2) does not apply in respect of an accused who is charged with an offence mentioned in section 522.

(13) Section 520 applies in respect of any order made under subsection (8) or (9) as though the order were an order made by a justice under subsection 515(2) or (5), and section 521 applies in respect of any order made under subsection (9) as though the order were an order made by a justice under subsection 515(2).

Review of Detention where Trial Delayed

Time for application to judge — Notice of hearing — Matters to be considered on hearing — Order — Warrant of judge for arrest — Arrest without warrant by peace officer — Hearing and order — Provisions applicable to proceedings — Directions for expediting trial.

525. (1) Where an accused who has been charged with an offence other than an offence listed in section 469 and who is not required to be detained in custody in respect of any other matter is being detained in custody pending his trial for that offence and the trial has not commenced

(*a*) in the case of an indictable offence, within ninety days from

(i) the day on which the accused was taken before a justice under section 503, or

(ii) where an order that the accused be detained in custody has been made under section 521 or 524, the day on which he was taken into custody under that order, or

(*b*) in the case of an offence for which the accused is being prosecuted in proceedings by way of summary conviction, within thirty days from

(i) the day on which the accused was taken before a justice under subsection 503(1), or

(ii) where an order that the accused be detained in custody has been made under section 521 or 524, the day on which he was taken into custody under that order,

the person having the custody of the accused shall, forthwith on the expiration of those ninety or thirty days, as the case may be, apply to a judge having jurisdiction in the place in which the accused is in custody to fix a date for a hearing to determine whether or not the accused should be released from custody.

(2) On receiving an application under subsection (1), the judge shall

(*a*) fix a date for the hearing described in subsection (1) to be held in the jurisdiction

(i) where the accused is in custody, or

(ii) where the trial is to take place; and

(*b*) direct that notice of the hearing be given to such persons, including the prosecutor and the accused, and in such manner, as the judge may specify.

(3) On the hearing described in subsection (1), the judge may, in deciding whether or not the accused should be released from custody, take into consideration whether the prosecutor or the accused has been responsible for any unreasonable delay in the trial of the charge.

(4) If, following the hearing described in subsection (1), the judge is not satisfied that the continued detention of the accused in custody is justified within the meaning of subsection 515(10), the judge shall order that the accused be released from custody pending the trial of the charge on his giving an

undertaking or entering into a recognizance described in any of paragraphs 515(2)(*a*) to (*e*) with such conditions described in subsection 515(4) as the judge considers desirable.

(5) Where a judge having jurisdiction in the province where an order under subsection (4) for the release of an accused has been made is satisfied that there are reasonable grounds to believe that the accused

(*a*) has violated or is about to violate the undertaking or recognizance on which he has been released, or

(*b*) has, after his release from custody on his undertaking or recognizance, committed an indictable offence,

he may issue a warrant for the arrest of the accused.

(6) Notwithstanding anything in this Act, a peace officer who believes on reasonable grounds that an accused who has been released from custody under subsection (4)

(*a*) has contravened or is about to contravene the undertaking or recognizance on which he has been released, or

(*b*) has, after his release from custody on his undertaking or recognizance, committed an indictable offence,

may arrest the accused without warrant and take him or cause him to be taken before a judge having jurisdiction in the province where the order for his release was made.

(7) A judge before whom an accused is taken pursuant to a warrant issued under subsection (5) or pursuant to subsection (6) may, where the accused shows cause why his detention in custody is not justified within the meaning of subsection 515(10), order that the accused be released on his giving an undertaking or entering into a recognizance described in any of paragraphs 515(2)(*a*) to (*e*) with such conditions, described in subsection 515(4), as the judge considers desirable.

(8) The provisions of sections 517, 518 and 519 apply with such modification as the circumstances require in respect of any proceedings under this section.

(9) Where an accused is before a judge under any of the provisions of this section, the judge shall give directions for expediting the trial of the accused. 1985, c. 27 (1st Supp.), s. 90.

Directions for expediting proceedings.

526. Subject to subsection 525(9), a court, judge or justice before which or whom an accused appears pursuant to this Part may give directions for expediting any proceedings in respect of the accused. R.S. 1985, c. 27 (1st Supp.), s. 91.

Procedure to Procure Attendance of a Prisoner

Procuring attendance — Provincial court judge's order — Conveyance of prisoner — Detention of prisoner required as witness — Detention in other cases — Application of sections respecting sentence — Transfer of prisoner — Conveyance of prisoner — Return.

527. (1) Where a person who is confined in a prison is required

(*a*) to attend at a preliminary inquiry into a charge against him,

(*b*) to stand his trial on a charge that may be tried by indictment or on summary conviction, or

(*c*) to attend to give evidence in a proceeding to which this Act applies,

a judge of a superior court of criminal jurisdiction or of a county or district court may order in writing that the prisoner be brought before the court, judge, justice or provincial court judge before whom his attendance is required, from day to day as may be necessary, if

(*d*) the applicant for the order sets out the facts of the case in an affidavit and produces the warrant, if any, and

(*e*) the judge is satisfied that the ends of justice require that an order be made.

(2) A provincial court judge has the same powers for the purposes of subsection (1) as a judge has under that subsection where the person whose attendance is required is confined in a prison within the province in which the provincial court judge has jurisdiction.

(3) An order that is made under subsection (1) or (2) shall be addressed to the person who has custody of the prisoner, and on receipt thereof that person shall

(*a*) deliver the prisoner to any person who is named in the order to receive him; or

(*b*) bring the prisoner before the court, judge, justice or provincial court judge, as the case may be, upon payment of his reasonable charges in respect thereof.

(4) Where the prisoner is required as a witness, the judge or provincial court judge shall direct, in the order, the manner in which the prisoner shall be kept in custody and returned to the prison from which he is brought.

(5) Where the appearance of the prisoner is required for the purposes of paragraph (1)(*a*) or (*b*), the judge or provincial court judge shall give appropriate directions in the order with respect to the manner in which the prisoner is

(*a*) to be kept in custody, if he is committed for trial; or

(*b*) to be returned, if he is discharged upon a preliminary inquiry or if he is acquitted of the charge against him.

(6) Sections 717 and 731 apply where a prisoner to whom this section applies is convicted and sentenced to imprisonment by the court, judge, justice or provincial court judge.

(7) On application by the prosecutor, a judge of a superior court of criminal jurisdiction or of a county or district court may, if the prisoner consents in writing, order the transfer of a prisoner to the custody of a peace officer named in the order for a period specified in the order where the judge is satisfied that the transfer is required for the purpose of assisting a peace officer acting in the execution of his duties.

(8) An order under subsection (7) shall be addressed to the person who has custody of the prisoner and on receipt thereof that person shall deliver the prisoner to the peace officer who is named in the order to receive him.

(9) When the purposes of any order made under this section have been carried out, the prisoner shall be returned to the place where he was confined at the time the order was made. R.S. 1985, c. 27 (1st Supp.), ss. 92, 101(2), 203.

Endorsement of Warrant

Endorsing warrant — Effect of endorsement.

528. (1) Where a warrant for the arrest or committal of an accused, in any form set out in Part XXVIII in relation thereto, cannot be executed in accordance with section 514 or 703, a justice within whose jurisdiction the accused is or is believed to be shall, on application and proof on oath or by affidavit of the signature of the justice who issued the warrant, authorize the arrest of the accused within his jurisdiction by making an endorsement, which may be in Form 28, on the warrant.

(2) An endorsement that is made upon a warrant pursuant to subsection (1) is sufficient authority to the peace officers to whom it was originally directed, and to all peace officers within the territorial jurisdiction of the justice by whom it is endorsed, to execute the warrant and to take the accused before the justice who issued the warrant or before any other justice for the same territorial division. R.S. 1985, c. 27 (1st Supp.), s. 93.

Coroner's Warrant

Coroner's warrant and recognizance — Transmitting depositions.

529. (1) Where a person is alleged, by a verdict on a coroner's inquisition, to have committed murder or manslaughter but he has not been charged with the offence, the coroner shall

(*a*) direct, by warrant under his hand, that the person be taken into custody and be conveyed, as soon as possible, before a justice, or

(*b*) direct the person to enter into a recognizance before him, with or without sureties, to appear before a justice.

(2) Where a coroner makes a direction under subsection (1) he shall transmit to the justice the evidence taken before him in the matter.

PART XVII

LANGUAGE OF ACCUSED

Language of accused — Idem — Accused to be advised of right — Remand — Variation of order.

530. (1) On application by an accused whose language is one of the official languages of Canada, made not later than

(*a*) the time of the appearance of the accused at which his trial date is set, if

(i) he is accused of an offence mentioned in section 553 or punishable on summary conviction, or

(ii) the accused is to be tried on an indictment preferred under section 557,

(*b*) the time of his election, if the accused elects under section 536 to be tried by a provincial court judge, or

(*c*) the time when the accused is ordered to stand trial, if the accused

(i) is charged with an offence listed in section 469,

(ii) has elected to be tried by a court composed of a judge or a judge and jury, or

(iii) is deemed to have elected to be tried by a court composed of a judge and jury,

a justice of the peace or provincial court judge shall grant an order directing that the accused be tried before a justice of the peace, provincial court judge, judge or judge and jury, as the case may be, who speak the official language of Canada that is the language of the accused or, if the circumstances warrant, who speak both official languages of Canada.

(2) On application by an accused whose language is not one of the official languages of Canada, made not later than whichever of the times referred to in paragraphs (1)(*a*) to (*c*) is applicable, a justice of the peace or provincial court judge may grant an order directing that the accused be tried before a justice of the peace, provincial court judge, judge or judge and jury, as the case may be, who speak the official language of Canada in which the accused, in the opinion of the justice or provincial court judge, can best give testimony or, if the circumstances warrant, who speak both official languages of Canada.

(3) The justice of the peace or provincial court judge before whom an accused first appears shall, if the accused is not represented by counsel, advise the accused of his right to apply for an order under subsection (1) or (2) and of the time before which such an application must be made.

(4) Where an accused fails to apply for an order under subsection (1) or (2) and the justice of the peace, provincial court judge or judge before whom the accused is to be tried, in this Part referred to as "the court", is satisfied that it is in the best interests of justice that the accused be tried before a justice of the

peace, provincial court judge, judge or judge and jury who speak the official language of Canada that is the language of the accused or, if the language of the accused is not one of the official languages of Canada, the official language of Canada in which the accused, in the opinion of the court, can best give testimony, the court may, if it does not speak that language, by order remand the accused to be tried by a justice of the peace, provincial court judge, judge or judge and jury, as the case may be, who speak that language or, if the circumstances warrant, who speak both official languages of Canada.

(5) An order under this section that an accused be tried before a justice of the peace, provincial court judge, judge or judge and jury who speak the official language of Canada that is the language of the accused or the official language of Canada in which the accused can best give testimony may, if the circumstances warrant, be varied by the court to require that the accused be tried before a justice of the peace, provincial court judge, judge or judge and jury who speak both official languages of Canada. R.S. 1985, c. 27 (1st Supp.), ss. 94, 203.

[R.S. 1985, c. 31 (4th Supp.), s. 94 will add immediately after section 530 the following.]

Where order granted under section 530.

530.1 Where an order is granted under section 530 directing that an accused be tried before a justice of the peace, provincial court judge, judge or judge and jury who speak the official language that is the language of the accused or in which the accused can best give testimony,

(*a*) the accused and his counsel have the right to use either official language for all purposes during the preliminary inquiry and trial of the accused;

(*b*) the accused and his counsel may use either official language in written pleadings or other documents used in any proceedings relating to the preliminary inquiry or trial of the accused;

(*c*) any witness may give evidence in either official language during the preliminary inquiry or trial;

(*d*) the accused has a right to have a justice presiding over the preliminary inquiry who speaks the official language that is the language of the accused;

(*e*) except where the prosecutor is a private prosecutor, the accused has a right to have a prosecutor who speaks the official language that is the language of the accused;

(*f*) the court shall make interpreters available to assist the accused, his counsel or any witness during the preliminary inquiry or trial;

(g) the record of proceedings during the preliminary inquiry or trial shall include

(i) a transcript of everything that was said during those proceedings in the official language in which it was said,

(ii) a transcript of any interpretation into the other language of what was said, and

(iii) any documentary evidence that was tendered during those proceedings in the official language in which it was tendered; and

(*h*) any trial judgment, including any reasons given therefor, issued in wrting in either official langauge, shall be made available by the court in the official language that is the language of the accused.

[NOTE: 1988, c. 38, s. 94(2) states:

This section shall come into force in a province

(a) in respect of offences punishable on summary conviction,

(i) on the day this Act is assented to, in the case of a province in which sections 1 and 5 of An Act to amend the Criminal Code, *being chapter 36 of the Statutes of Canada, 1977-78, as amended by section 188 of the* Criminal Law Amendment Act, 1985, *being chapter 19 of the Statutes of Canada, 1985, are in force in the province in respect of offences punishable on summary conviction, or*

(ii) on the day on which those sections come into force in respect of offences punishable on summary conviction, in the case of a province in which those sections are not in force in respect of offences punishable on summary conviction on the day this Act is assented to; and

(b) in respect of indictable offences,

(i) on the day this Act is assented to, in the case of a province in which those sections are in force in respect of indictable offences on that day, or

(ii) on the day on which those sections come into force in respect of indictable offences, in the case of a province in which those sections are not in force in respect of indictable offences on the day this Act is assented to.]

Change of venue.

531. Notwithstanding any other provision of this Act but subject to any regulations made pursuant to section 533, the court shall order that the trial of an accused be held in a territorial division in the same province other than that in which the offence would otherwise be tried if an order has been made that the accused be tried before a justice of the peace, provincial court judge, judge or judge and jury who speak the official language of Canada that is the language of the accused or the official language of Canada in which the accused can best give testimony or both official languages of Canada and such order cannot be conveniently complied with in the territorial division in which the offence would otherwise be tried. R.S. 1985, c. 27 (1st Supp.), s. 203.

Saving.

532. Nothing in this Part or the *Official Languages Act* derogates from or otherwise adversely affects any right afforded by a law of a province in force on the coming into force of this Part in that province or thereafter coming into force relating to the language of proceedings or testimony in criminal matters that is not inconsistent with this Part or that Act.

Regulations.

533. The Lieutenant Governor in Council of a province may make regulations generally for carrying into effect the purposes and provisions of this Part in the province and the Commissioner of the Yukon Territory and the Commissioner of the Northwest Territories may make regulations generally for carrying into effect the purposes and provisions of this Part in the Yukon Territory and the Northwest Territories, respectively.

Coming into force — Idem — Idem.

534. (1) Sections 530 and 531 to 533 shall come into force in any of the Provinces of Quebec, Nova Scotia, British Columbia, Prince Edward Island, Saskatchewan, Alberta and Newfoundland, in respect of

(*a*) offences punishable on summary conviction, or

(*b*) indictable offences,

on a day fixed by a proclamation declaring those sections to be in force in that Province with respect to those offences.

(2) Section 530.1 shall come into force in a province

(*a*) in respect of offences punishable on summary conviction,

(i) on the day the *Official Languages Act* is assented to, in the case of a province in which sections 530 and 531 to 533 and paragraph 638(1)(*f*) are in force on that day in respect of offences punishable on summary conviction, or

(ii) on the day on which those sections and that paragraph come into force in respect of offences punishable on summary conviction, in the case of a province in which they are not in force in respect of offences punishable on summary conviction on the day this Act is assented to; and

(*b*) in respect of indictable offences,

(i) on the day the *Official Languages Act* is assented to, in the case of a province in which those sections and that paragraph are in force in respect of indictable offences on that day, or

(ii) on the day on which those sections and that paragraph come into force in respect of indictable offences, in the case of a province in which they are not in force in respect of indictable offences on the day this Act is assented to.

(3) Notwithstanding any other provision in this section, sections 530 and 531 to 533 shall come into force on January 1, 1990

(*a*) in respect of offences punishable on summary conviction, in any province in which those sections are not in force in respect of offences punishable on summary conviction immediately prior to that date; and

(*b*) in respect of indictable offences, in any province in which those sections are not in force in respect of indictable offences immediately prior to that date. R.S. 1985, c. 27 (1st Supp.), s. 95, c. 31 (4th Supp.), s. 95.

PART XVIII

PROCEDURE ON PRELIMINARY INQUIRY

Jurisdiction

Inquiry by justice.

535. Where an accused who is charged with an indictable offence is before a justice, the justice shall, in accordance with this Part, inquire into that charge and any other indictable offence, in respect of the same transaction, founded on the facts that are disclosed by the evidence taken in accordance with this Part. R.S. 1985, c. 27 (1st Supp.) s. 96.

Remand by justice to provincial court judge in certain cases — Election before justice in certain cases — Procedure where accused elects trial by provincial court judge — Procedure where accused elects trial by judge alone or by judge and jury or deemed election — Jurisdiction.

536. (1) Where an accused is before a justice other than a provincial court judge charged with an offence over which a provincial court judge has absolute jurisdiction under section 553, the justice shall remand the accused to appear before a provincial court judge having jurisdiction in the territorial division in which the offence is alleged to have been committed.

(2) Where an accused is before a justice charged with an offence, other than an offence listed in section 469, and the offence is not one over which a provincial court judge has absolute jurisdiction under section 553, the justice shall, after the information has been read to the accused, put the accused to his election in the following words:

You have the option to elect to be tried by a provincial court judge without a jury and without having had a preliminary inquiry; or you may elect to have a preliminary inquiry and to be tried by a judge without a jury; or you may elect to have a preliminary inquiry and to be tried by a court composed of a judge and jury. If you do not elect now, you shall be deemed to have elected to have a preliminary inquiry and to be tried by a court composed of a judge and jury. How do you elect to be tried?

(3) Where an accused elects to be tried by a provincial court judge, the justice shall endorse on the information a record of the election and shall

(*a*) where the justice is not a provincial court judge, remand the accused to appear and plead to the charge before a provincial court judge having jurisdiction in the territorial division in which the offence is alleged to have been committed; or

(*b*) where the justice is a provincial court judge, call on the accused to plead to the charge and if the accused does not plead guilty, proceed with the trial or fix a time for the trial.

(4) Where an accused elects to have a preliminary inquiry and to be tried by a judge without a jury or by a court composed of a judge and jury or does not elect when put to his election, the justice shall hold a preliminary inquiry into the charge and if the accused is ordered to stand trial, the justice shall endorse on the information and, where the accused is in custody, on the warrant of committal, a statement showing the nature of the election of the accused or that the accused did not elect, as the case may be.

(5) Where a justice before whom a preliminary inquiry is being or is to be held has not commenced to take evidence, any justice having jurisdiction in the province where the offence with which the accused is charged is alleged to have been committed has jurisdiction for the purposes of subsection (4). R.S. 1985, c. 27 (1st Supp.), ss. 96, 203.

Powers of Justice

Powers of justice.

537. (1) A justice acting under this Part may

(*a*) adjourn the inquiry from time to time and change the place of hearing, where it appears to be desirable to do so by reason of the absence of a witness, the inability of a witness who is ill to attend at the place where the justice usually sits or for any other sufficient reason, but no adjournment shall be for more than eight clear days unless

(i) the accused, whether or not he is in custody, and the prosecutor consent to the proposed adjournment, or

(ii) the accused is remanded for observation under subparagraph (*b*)(ii);

(*b*) [Repealed S.C. 1991, c. 43, s. 9, Sch., item 3(1)],

(*c*) except where the accused is authorized pursuant to Part XVI to be at large, remand the accused to custody in a prison by warrant in Form 19;

(*d*) resume an inquiry before the expiration of a period for which it has been adjourned with the consent of the prosecutor and the accused or his counsel;

(*e*) order in writing, in Form 30, that the accused be brought before him, or any other justice for the same territorial division, at any time before the expiration of the time for which the accused has been remanded;

(*f*) grant or refuse permission to the prosecutor or his counsel to address him in support of the charge, by way of opening or summing up or by way of reply on any evidence that is given on behalf of the accused;

(*g*) receive evidence on the part of the prosecutor or the accused, as the case may be, after hearing any evidence that has been given on behalf of either of them;

(*h*) order that no person other than the prosecutor, the accused and their counsel shall have access to or remain in the room in which the inquiry is held, where it appears to him that the ends of justice will be best served by so doing; and

(*i*) regulate the course of the inquiry in any way that appears to him to be desirable and that is not inconsistent with this Act.

(2) [Repealed S.C. 1991, c. 43, s. 9, Sch., item 3(2)]

(3) [Repealed S.C. 1991, c. 43, s. 9, Sch., item 3(2)]

(4) [Repealed S.C. 1991, c. 43, s. 9, Sch., item 3(2)]

Corporation.

538. Where an accused is a corporation, subsections 556(1) and (2) apply, with such modifications as the circumstances require.

Taking Evidence of Witnesses

Order restricting publication of evidence taken at preliminary inquiry — Accused to be informed of right to apply for order — Failure to comply with order — "Newspaper".

539. (1) Prior to the commencement of the taking of evidence at a preliminary inquiry, the justice holding the inquiry

(*a*) may, if application therefor is made by the prosecutor, and

(*b*) shall, if application therefor is made by any of the accused,

make an order directing that the evidence taken at the inquiry shall not be published in any newspaper or broadcast before such time as, in respect of each of the accused,

(*c*) he is discharged; or

(*d*) if he is ordered to stand trial, the trial is ended.

(2) Where an accused is not represented by counsel at a preliminary inquiry, the justice holding the inquiry shall, prior to the commencement of the taking of evidence at the inquiry, inform the accused of his right to make application under subsection (1).

(3) Every one who fails to comply with an order made pursuant to subsection (1) is guilty of an offence punishable on summary conviction.

(4) In this section, "newspaper" has the same meaning as in section 297. R.S. 1985, c. 27 (1st Supp.), s. 97.

Taking evidence — Reading and signing depositions — Authentication by justice — Stenographer to be sworn — Authentication of transcript — Transcription of record taken by sound recording apparatus.

540. (1) Where an accused is before a justice holding a preliminary inquiry, the justice shall

(*a*) take the evidence under oath, in the presence of the accused, of the witnesses called on the part of the prosecution and allow the accused or his counsel to cross-examine them; and

(*b*) cause a record of the evidence of each witness to be taken

(i) in legible writing in the form of a deposition, in Form 31, or by a stenographer appointed by him or pursuant to law, or

(ii) in a province where a sound recording apparatus is authorized by or under provincial legislation for use in civil cases, by the type of apparatus so authorized and in accordance with the requirements of the provincial legislation.

(2) Where a deposition is taken down in writing, the justice shall, in the presence of the accused, before asking the accused if he wishes to call witnesses,

(*a*) cause the deposition to be read to the witness;

(*b*) cause the deposition to be signed by the witness; and

(*c*) sign the deposition himself.

(3) Where depositions are taken down in writing, the justice may sign

(*a*) at the end of each deposition; or

(*b*) at the end of several or of all the depositions in a manner that will indicate that his signature is intended to authenticate each disposition.

(4) Where the stenographer appointed to take down the evidence is not a duly sworn court stenographer, he shall make oath that he will truly and faithfully report the evidence.

(5) Where the evidence is taken down by a stenographer appointed by the justice or pursuant to law, it need not be read to or signed by the witnesses, but shall be transcribed by the stenographer and the transcript shall be accompanied by

(*a*) an affidavit of the stenographer that it is a true report of the evidence; or

(*b*) a certificate that it is a true report of the evidence if the stenographer is a duly sworn court stenographer.

(6) Where, in accordance with this Act, a record is taken in any proceedings under this Act by a sound recording apparatus, the record so taken shall be dealt with and transcribed and the transcription certified and used in accordance with the provincial legislation with such modifications as the circumstances require mentioned in subsection (1). R.S. 1985, c. 27 (1st Supp.), s. 98.

Accused to be addressed — Statement of accused — Witnesses for accused — Depositions of such witnesses.

541. (1) When the evidence of the witnesses called on the part of the prosecution has been taken down and, where required by this Part, has been read, the justice shall address the accused as follows or to the like effect:

Having heard the evidence, do you wish to say anything in answer to the charge or any other indictable offence, in respect of the same transaction, founded on the facts that are disclosed by the evidence? You are not bound to say anything, but whatever you do say will be taken down in writing and may be given in evidence against you at your trial. You must clearly understand that you have nothing to hope from any promise of favour and nothing to fear from any threat that may have been held out to you to induce you to make any admission or confession of guilt, but whatever you now say may be given in evidence against you at your trial notwithstanding the promise or threat.

(2) Where the accused says anything in answer to the address made by the justice pursuant to subsection (1), his answer shall be taken down in writing and shall be signed by the justice and kept with the evidence of the witnesses and dealt with in accordance with this Part.

(3) When subsections (1) and (2) have been complied with, the justice shall ask the accused if he wishes to call any witnesses.

(4) The justice shall hear each witness called by the accused who testifies to any matter relevant to the inquiry, and for the purposes of this subsection, section 540 applies, with such modifications as the circumstances require. R.S. 1985, c. 27 (1st Supp.), s. 99.

Confession or admission of accused — Restriction of publication of reports of preliminary inquiry — "Newspaper".

542. (1) Nothing in this Act prevents a prosecutor giving in evidence at a preliminary inquiry any admission, confession or statement made at any time by the accused that by law is admissible against him.

(2) Every one who publishes in any newspaper, or broadcasts, a report that any admission or confession was tendered in evidence at a preliminary inquiry or a report of the nature of such admission or confession so tendered in evidence unless

(*a*) the accused has been discharged, or

(*b*) if the accused has been committed for trial, the trial has ended,

is guilty of an offence punishable on summary conviction.

(3) In this section "newspaper" has the same meaning as in section 297. R.S.C. 1985, c. 27 (1st Supp.), s. 101(2).

Remand Where Offence Committed in Another Jurisdiction

Order that accused appear or be taken before justice where offence committed — Transmission of transcript and documents and effect of order or warrant.

543. (1) Where an accused is charged with an offence alleged to have been committed out of the limits of the jurisdiction in which he has been charged, the justice before whom he appears or is brought may, at any stage of the inquiry after hearing both parties,

(*a*) order the accused to appear, or

(*b*) if the accused is in custody, issue a warrant in Form 15 to convey the accused

before a justice having jurisdiction in the place where the offence is alleged to have been committed, who shall continue and complete the inquiry.

(2) Where a justice makes an order or issues a warrant pursuant to subsection (1), he shall cause the transcript of any evidence given before him in the inquiry and all documents that were then before him and that are relevant to the inquiry to be transmitted to a justice having jurisdiction in the place where the offence is alleged to have been committed and

(*a*) any evidence the transcript of which is so transmitted shall be deemed to have been taken by the justice to whom it is transmitted; and

(*b*) any appearance notice, promise to appear, undertaking or recognizance issued to or given or entered into by the accused under Part XVI shall be deemed to have been issued, given or entered into in the jurisdiction where the offence is alleged to have been committed and to require the accused to appear before the justice to whom the transcript and documents are transmitted at the time provided in the order made in respect of the accused under paragraph (1)(*a*).

Absconding Accused

Accused absconding during inquiry — Adverse inference — Accused not entitled to re-opening — Counsel for accused may continue to act — Provisions of subsections 541(1) and (2) not applicable.

544. (1) Notwithstanding any other provision of this Act, where an accused, whether or not he is charged jointly with another, absconds during the course of a preliminary inquiry into an offence with which he is charged,

(*a*) he shall be deemed to have waived his right to be present at the inquiry; and

(*b*) the justice

(i) may continue the inquiry and, when all the evidence has been taken, shall dispose of the inquiry in accordance with section 548, or

(ii) if a warrant is issued for the arrest of the accused, may adjourn the inquiry to await his appearance,

but where the inquiry is adjourned pursuant to subparagraph (*b*)(ii), the justice may continue it at any time pursuant to subparagraph (*b*)(i) if he is satisfied that it would no longer be in the interests of justice to await the appearance of the accused.

(2) Where the justice continues a preliminary inquiry pursuant to subsection (1), he may draw an inference adverse to the accused from the fact that he has absconded.

(3) Where an accused reappears at a preliminary inquiry that is continuing pursuant to subsection (1), he is not entitled to have any part of the proceedings

that was conducted in his absence re-opened unless the justice is satisfied that because of exceptional circumstances it is in the interests of justice to re-open the inquiry.

(4) Where the accused has absconded during the course of a preliminary inquiry and the justice continues the inquiry, counsel for the accused is not thereby deprived of any authority he may have to continue to act for the accused in the proceedings.

(5) Where, at the conclusion of the evidence on the part of the prosecution at a preliminary inquiry that has been continued pursuant to subsection (1), the accused is absent, the provisions of subsections 541(1) and (2) do not apply but, if counsel for the accused is present, he shall be given an opportunity to call witnesses on behalf of the accused and the provisions of subsection 541(4) apply with such modifications as the circumstances require.

Procedure where Witness Refuses to Testify

Witness refusing to be examined — Further commitment — Saving.

545. (1) Where a person, being present at a preliminary inquiry and being required by the justice to give evidence,

(*a*) refuses to be sworn,

(*b*) having been sworn, refuses to answer the questions that are put to him,

(*c*) fails to produce any writings that he is required to produce, or

(*d*) refuses to sign his deposition,

without offering a reasonable excuse for his failure or refusal, the justice may adjourn the inquiry and may, by warrant in Form 20, commit the person to prison for a period not exceeding eight clear days or for the period during which the inquiry is adjourned, whichever is the lesser period.

(2) Where a person to whom subsection (1) applies is brought before the justice on the resumption of the adjourned inquiry and again refuses to do what is required of him, the justice may again adjourn the inquiry for a period not exceeding eight clear days and commit him to prison for the period of adjournment or any part thereof, and may adjourn the inquiry and commit the person to prison from time to time until the person consents to do what is required of him.

(3) Nothing in this section shall be deemed to prevent the justice from sending the case for trial on any other sufficient evidence taken by him.

Remedial Provisions

Irregularity or variance not to affect validity.

546. The validity of any proceeding at or subsequent to a preliminary inquiry is not affected by (*a*) any irregularity or defect in the substance or form of the summons or warrant,

(*b*) any variance between the charge set out in the summons or warrant and the charge set out in the information, or

(*c*) any variance between the charge set out in the summons, warrant or information and the evidence adduced by the prosecution at the inquiry.

Adjournment if accused misled.

547. Where it appears to the justice that the accused has been deceived or misled by any irregularity, defect or variance mentioned in section 546, he may adjourn the inquiry and may remand the accused or grant him interim release in accordance with Part XVI.

Inability of justice to continue.

547.1 Where a justice acting under this Part has commenced to take evidence and dies or is unable to continue for any reason, another justice may

(*a*) continue taking the evidence at the point at which the interruption in the taking of the evidence occurred, where the evidence was recorded pursuant to section 540 and is available; or

(*b*) commence taking the evidence as if no evidence had been taken, where no evidence was recorded pursuant to section 540 or where the evidence is not available. R.S. 1985, c. 27 (1st Supp.), s. 100.

Adjudication and Recognizances

Order to stand trial or discharge — Endorsing charge — Defect not to affect validity.

548. (1) When all the evidence has been taken by the justice, he shall,

(*a*) if in his opinion there is sufficient evidence to put the accused on trial for the offence charged or any other indictable offence in respect of the same transaction, order the accused to stand trial; or

(*b*) discharge the accused, if in his opinion on the whole of the evidence no sufficient case is made out to put the accused on trial for the offence charged or any other indictable offence in respect of the same transaction.

(2) Where the justice orders the accused to stand trial for an indictable offence, other than or in addition to the one with which the accused was charged, the justice shall endorse on the information the charges on which he orders the accused to stand trial.

(3) The validity of an order to stand trial is not affected by any defect apparent on the face of the information in respect of which the preliminary inquiry is held or in respect of any charge on which the accused is ordered to stand trial unless, in the opinion of the court before which an objection to the information or charge is taken, the accused has been misled or prejudiced in his defence by reason of that defect. R.S. 1985, c. 27 (1st Supp.), s. 101(1).

Order to stand trial at any stage of inquiry with consent — Procedure.

549. (1) Notwithstanding any other provision of this Act, the justice may, at any stage of a preliminary inquiry, with the consent of the accused and the prosecutor, order the accused to stand trial in the court having criminal jurisdiction, without taking or recording any evidence or further evidence.

(2) Where an accused is ordered to stand trial under subsection (1), the justice shall endorse on the information a statement of the consent of the accused and the prosecutor, and the accused shall thereafter be dealt with in all respects as if ordered to stand trial under section 548. R.S. 1985, c. 27 (1st Supp.), s. 101(3).

Recognizance of witness — Form — Sureties or deposit for appearance of witness — Witness refusing to be bound — Discharge.

550. (1) Where an accused is ordered to stand trial, the justice who held the preliminary inquiry may require any witness whose evidence is, in his opinion, material to enter into a recognizance to give evidence at the trial of the accused and to comply with such reasonable conditions prescribed in the recognizance as the justice considers desirable for securing the attendance of the witness to give evidence at the trial of the accused.

(2) The recognizance entered into pursuant to this section may be in Form 32, and may be set out at the end of a deposition or be separate therefrom.

(3) A justice may, for any reason satisfactory to him, require any witness entering into a recognizance pursuant to this section

(*a*) to produce one or more sureties in such amount as he may direct; or

(*b*) to deposit with him a sum of money sufficient in his opinion to ensure that the witness will appear and give evidence.

(4) Where a witness does not comply with subsection (1) or (3) when required to do so by a justice, he may be committed by the justice, by warrant in Form 24, to a prison in the territorial division where the trial is to be held, there to be kept until he does what is required of him or until the trial is concluded.

(5) Where a witness has been committed to prison pursuant to subsection (4), the court before which the witness appears or a justice having jurisdiction in the territorial division where the prison is situated may, by order in Form 39, discharge the witness from custody when the trial is concluded. R.S. 1985, c. 27 (1st Supp.), s. 101(3).

Transmission of Record

Transmitting record.

551. Where a justice orders an accused to stand trial, the justice shall forthwith send to the clerk or other proper officer of the court by which the accused is to be tried, the information, the evidence, the exhibits, the statement if any of the accused taken down in writing under section 541, any promise to appear, undertaking or recognizance given or entered into in accordance with Part XVI, or any evidence taken before a coroner, that is in the possession of the justice. R.S. 1985, c. 27 (1st Supp.), s. 102.

PART XIX

INDICTABLE OFFENCES — TRIAL WITHOUT JURY

Interpretation

Definitions — "Judge".

552. In this Part

"judge" means,

(*a*) in the Province of Ontario, a judge of the superior court of criminal jurisdiction of the Province,

(*b*) in the Province of Quebec, a judge of the Court of Quebec

(*c*) in the Province of Nova Scotia, a judge of the superior court of criminal jurisdiction of the province or a judge of a county court,

(*d*) in the Province of New Brunswick, a judge of the Court of Queen's Bench,

(*e*) in the Province of British Columbia, the Chief Justice or a puisne judge of the Supreme Court,

(*f*) in the Provinces of Prince Edward Island and Newfoundland, a judge of the Supreme Court,

(*g*) in the Province of Manitoba, the Chief Justice, or a puisne judge of the Court of Queen's Bench,

(*h*) in the Provinces of Saskatchewan and Alberta, a judge of the superior court of criminal jurisdiction of the province,

(*i*) in the Yukon Territory and the Northwest Territories, a judge of the Supreme Court. R.S. 1985, c. 11 (1st Supp.), s. 2; c. 27 (1st Supp.), s. 103(1); R.S. 1985, c. 27 (2d Supp.), Schedule, item 6; c. 40 (4th Supp.) Schedule, item 1; 1990, c. 6, s. 6; 1990, c. 17, s. 13.

"magistrate" [Repealed R.S. 1985, c. 27 (1st Supp.), s. 103(2)].

Jurisdiction of Provincial Court Judges

Absolute Jurisdiction

Absolute jurisdiction.

553. The jurisdiction of a provincial court judge to try an accused is absolute and does not depend on the consent of the accused where the accused is charged in an information

(*a*) with

(i) theft, other than theft of cattle,

(ii) obtaining money or property by false pretences,

(iii) unlawfully having in his possession any property or thing or any proceeds of any property or thing knowing that all or a part of the property or thing or of the proceeds was obtained by or derived directly or indirectly from the commission in Canada of an offence punishable by indictment or an act or omission anywhere that, if it had occurred in Canada, would have constituted an offence punishable by indictment,

(iv) having, by deceit, falsehood or other fraudulent means, defrauded the public or any person, whether ascertained or not, of any property, money or valuable security, or

(v) mischief under subsection 430(4),

where the subject-matter of the offence is not a testamentary instrument and where the alleged value of the subject-matter of the offence does not exceed one thousand dollars;

(*b*) with counselling or with an attempt to commit or with being an accessory after the fact to the commission of

(i) any offence referred to in paragraph (*a*) in respect of the subject-matter and value thereof referred to in that paragraph, or

(ii) any offence referred to in paragraph (*c*); or

(*c*) with an offence under

(i) section 201 (keeping gaming or betting house),

(ii) section 202 (betting, pool-selling, book-making, etc.),

(iii) section 203 (placing bets),

(iv) section 206 (lotteries and games of chance),

(v) section 209 (cheating at play),

(vi) section 210 (keeping common bawdy-house),

(vii) subsection 259(4) (driving while disqualified), or

(viii) section 393 (fraud in relation to fares). R.S. 1985, c. 27 (1st Supp.), s. 104; 1992, c. 1, s. 58(1), Sch. I, item 11.

Provincial Court Judge's Jurisdiction with Consent

Trial by provincial court judge with consent.

554. (1) Where an accused is charged in an information with an indictable offence other than an offence that is mentioned in section 469, and the offence is not one over which a provincial court judge has absolute jurisdiction under section 553, a provincial court judge may try the accused if the accused elects to be tried by a provincial court judge. R.S. 1985, c. 27 (1st Supp.), ss. 105, 203.

(2) [Repealed R.S. 1985, c. 27 (1st Supp.), s. 105.]

(3) [Repealed R.S. 1985, c. 27 (1st Supp.), s. 105.]

(4) [Repealed R.S. 1985, c. 27 (1st Supp.), s. 105.]

Provincial court judge may decide to hold preliminary inquiry — Where subject-matter is a testamentary instrument or exceeds $1,000 in value — Continuing proceedings.

555. (1) Where in any proceedings under this Part an accused is before a provincial court judge and it appears to the provincial court judge that for any reason the charge should be prosecuted by indictment, he may, at any time before the accused has entered upon his defence, decide not to adjudicate and shall thereupon inform the accused of his decision and continue the proceedings as a preliminary inquiry.

(2) Where an accused is before a provincial court judge charged with an offence mentioned in paragraph 553(*a*) or subparagraph 553(*b*)(i), and, at any time before the provincial court judge makes an adjudication, the evidence establishes that the subject-matter of the offence is a testamentary instrument or that its value exceeds one thousand dollars, the provincial court judge shall put the accused to his election in accordance with subsection 536(2).

(3) Where an accused is put to his election pursuant to subsection (2), the following provisions apply, namely,

(*a*) if the accused elects to be tried by a judge without a jury or a court composed of a judge and jury or does not elect when put to his election, the provincial court judge shall continue the proceedings as a preliminary inquiry under Part XVIII and, if he orders the accused to stand trial, the provincial court judge shall comply with subsection 536(4); and

(*b*) if the accused elects to be tried by a provincial court judge, the provincial court judge shall endorse on the information a record of the election and continue with the trial. R.S. 1985, c. 27 (1st Supp.), ss. 106, 203.

Corporation — Non-appearance — Corporation not electing.

556. (1) An accused corporation shall appear by counsel or agent.

(2) Where an accused corporation does not appear pursuant to a summons and service of the summons on the corporation is proved, the provincial court judge

(*a*) may, if the charge is one over which he has absolute jurisdiction, proceed with the trial of the charge in the absence of the accused corporation; and

(*b*) shall, if the charge is not one over which he has absolute jurisdiction, hold a preliminary inquiry in accordance with Part XVIII in the absence of the accused corporation.

(3) Where an accused corporation appears but does not elect when put to an election under subsection 536(2), the provincial court judge shall hold a preliminary inquiry in accordance with Part XVIII. R.S. 1985, c. 27 (1st Supp.), s. 107.

Taking evidence.

557. Where an accused is tried by a provincial court judge in accordance with this Part, the evidence of witnesses for the prosecutor and the accused shall be taken in accordance with the provisions of Part XVIII relating to preliminary inquiries. R.S. 1985, c. 27 (1st Supp.), s. 203.

Jurisdiction of Judges
Judges Jurisdiction with Consent

Trial by judge without a jury.

558. Where an accused who is charged with an indictable offence, other than an offence listed in section 469, elects under section 536 or re-elects under section 561 to be tried by a judge without a jury, the accused shall, subject to this Part, be tried by a judge without a jury. R.S. 1985, c. 27 (1st Supp.), s. 108.

Court of record — Custody of records.

559. (1) A judge who holds a trial under this Part shall, for all purposes thereof and proceedings connected therewith or relating thereto, be a court of record.

(2) The record of a trial that a judge holds under this Part shall be kept in the court over which the judge presides.

Election

Duty of judge — Notice by sheriff, when given — Duty of sheriff when date set for trial — Duty of accused when not in custody.

560. (1) Where an accused elects, under section 536, to be tried by a judge without a jury, a judge having jurisdiction shall,

(*a*) on receiving a written notice from the sheriff or other person having custody of the accused stating that the accused is in custody and setting out the nature of the charge against him, or

(*b*) on being notified by the clerk of the court that the accused is not in custody and of the nature of the charge against him,

fix a time and place for the trial of the accused.

(2) The sheriff or other person having custody of the accused shall give the notice mentioned in paragraph (1)(*a*) within twenty-four hours after the accused is ordered to stand trial, if he is in custody pursuant to that order or if, at the time of the order, he is in custody for any other reason.

(3) Where, pursuant to subsection (1), a time and place is fixed for the trial of an accused who is in custody, the accused

(*a*) shall be notified forthwith by the sheriff or other person having custody of the accused of the time and place so fixed; and

(*b*) shall be produced at the time and place so fixed.

(4) Where an accused is not in custody, the duty of ascertaining from the clerk of the court the time and place fixed for the trial, pursuant to subsection (1), is on the accused, and he shall attend for his trial at the time and place so fixed. R.S. 1985, c. 27 (1st Supp.), ss. 101(3), 109.

(5) [Repealed R.S. 1985, c. 27 (1st Supp.), s. 109(2).]

Right to re-elect — Idem — Notice — Idem — Notice and transmitting record — Time and place for re-election — Proceedings on re-election.

561. (1) An accused who elects or is deemed to have elected a mode of trial other than trial by a provincial court judge may re-elect,

(*a*) at any time before or after the completion of the preliminary inquiry, with the written consent of the prosecutor, to be tried by a provincial court judge;

(*b*) at any time before the completion of the preliminary inquiry or before the fifteenth day following the completion of the preliminary inquiry, as of right, another mode of trial other than trial by a provincial court judge; and

(*c*) on or after the fifteenth day following the completion of the preliminary inquiry, any mode of trial with the written consent of the prosecutor.

(2) An accused who elects to be tried by a provincial court judge may, not later than fourteen days before the day first appointed for the trial, re-elect as of right another mode of trial, and may do so thereafter with the written consent of the prosecutor.

(3) Where an accused wishes to re-elect under subsection (1) before the completion of the preliminary inquiry, the accused shall give notice in writing that he wishes to re-elect, together with the written consent of the prosecutor, where that consent is required, to the justice presiding at the preliminary inquiry who shall on receipt of the notice,

(*a*) in the case of a re-election under paragraph (1)(*b*), put the accused to his re-election in the manner set out in subsection (7); or

(*b*) where the accused wishes to re-elect under paragraph (1)(*a*) and the justice is not a provincial court judge, notify a provincial court judge or clerk of the court of the accused's intention to re-elect and send to the provincial court judge or clerk the information and any promise to appear, undertaking or recognizance given or entered into in accordance with Part XVI, or any evidence taken before a coroner, that is in the possession of the justice.

(4) Where an accused wishes to re-elect under section (2), the accused shall give notice in writing that he wishes to re-elect together with the written consent of the prosecutor, where that consent is required, to the provincial court judge before whom the accused appeared and pleaded or to a clerk of the court.

(5) Where an accused wishes to re-elect under subsection (1) after the completion of the preliminary inquiry, the accused shall give notice in writing

that he wishes to re-elect, together with the written consent of the prosecutor, where such consent is required, to a judge or clerk of the court of his original election who shall, on receipt of the notice, notify the judge or provincial court judge or clerk of the court by which the accused wishes to be tried of the accused's intention to re-elect and send to that judge or provincial court judge or clerk the information, the evidence, the exhibits and the statement, if any, of the accused taken down in writing under section 541 and any promise to appear, undertaking or recognizance given or entered into in accordance with Part XVI, or any evidence taken before a coroner, that is in the possession of the first-mentioned judge or clerk.

(6) Where a provincial court judge or judge or clerk of the court is notified under paragraph (3)(*b*) or subsection (4) or (5) that the accused wishes to re-elect, the provincial court judge or judge shall forthwith appoint a time and place for the accused to re-elect and shall cause notice thereof to be given to the accused and the prosecutor.

(7) The accused shall attend or, if he is in custody, shall be produced at the time and place appointed under subsection (6) and shall, after

(*a*) the charge on which he has been ordered to stand trial or the indictment, where an indictment has been preferred pursuant to section 566, 574 or 577 or is filed with the court before which the indictment is to be preferred pursuant to section 577, or

(*b*) in the case of a re-election under subsection (1) before the completion of the preliminary inquiry or under subsection (2), the information

has been read to the accused, be put to his re-election in the following words or in words to the like effect:

> You have given notice of your wish to re-elect the mode of your trial. You now have the option to do so. How do you wish to re-elect? R.S. 1985, c. 27 (1st Supp.), s. 110.

Proceedings following re-election — Idem.

562. (1) Where the accused re-elects under paragraph 561(1)(*a*) before the completion of the preliminary inquiry or under subsection 561(1) after the completion of the preliminary inquiry, the provincial court judge or judge, as the case may be, shall proceed with the trial or appoint a time and place for the trial.

(2) Where the accused re-elects under paragraph 561(1)(*b*) before the completion of the preliminary inquiry or under subsection 561(2), the justice shall proceed with the preliminary inquiry. R.S. 1985, c. 27 (1st Supp.), s. 110.

Proceedings on re-election to be tried by provincial court judge without jury.

563. Where an accused re-elects under section 561 to be tried by a provincial court judge,

(*a*) the accused shall be tried on the information that was before the justice at the preliminary inquiry, subject to any amendments thereto that may be allowed by the provincial court judge by whom the accused is tried; and

(*b*) the provincial court judge before whom the re-election is made shall endorse on the information a record of the re-election. R.S. 1985, c. 27 (1st Supp.), s. 110.

564. [Repealed R.S. 1985, c. 27 (1st Supp.), s. 110.]

Election deemed to have been made — Where direct indictment preferred — Notice of re-election — Application.

565. (1) Where an accused is ordered to stand trial for an offence that, under this Part, may be tried by a judge without a jury, the accused shall, for the purposes of the provisions of this Part relating to election and re-election, be deemed to have elected to be tried by a court composed of a judge and jury if

(*a*) he was ordered to stand trial by a provincial court judge who, pursuant to subsection 555(1), continued the proceedings before him as a preliminary inquiry;

(*b*) the justice, provincial court judge or judge, as the case may be, declined pursuant to section 567 to record the election or re-election of the accused; or

(*c*) the accused does not elect when put to an election under section 536.

(2) Where an accused is to be tried after an indictment has been preferred against him pursuant to a consent or order given under section 577, the accused shall, for the purposes of the provisions of this Part relating to election and re-election, be deemed to have elected to be tried by a court composed of a judge and jury and may, with the written consent of the prosecutor, re-elect to be tried by a judge without a jury.

(3) Where an accused wishes to re-elect under subsection (2), he shall give notice in writing that he wishes to re-elect, together with the written consent of the prosecutor, to a judge or clerk of the court where the indictment has been filed or preferred who shall, on receipt of the notice, notify a judge having jurisdiction or clerk of the court by which the accused wishes to be tried of the accused's intention to re-elect and send to that judge or clerk the indictment and any promise to appear, undertaking or recognizance given or entered into in accordance with Part XVI, any summons or warrant issued under section 578, or any evidence taken before a coroner, that is in the possession of the first-mentioned judge or clerk.

(4) Subsections 561(6) and (7) apply to a re-election made under subsection (3). R.S. 1985, c. 27 (1st Supp.), s. 111.

Trial

Indictment — Preferring indictment — What counts may be included and who may prefer indictment.

566. (1) The trial of an accused for an indictable offence, other than a trial before a provincial court judge, shall be on an indictment in writing setting forth the offence with which he is charged.

(2) Where an accused elects under section 536 or re-elects under section 561 to be tried by a judge without a jury, an indictment in Form 4 may be preferred.

(3) Section 574 and subsection 576(1) apply, with such modifications as the circumstances require, and section 577 does not apply, to the preferring of an indictment pursuant to subsection (2). R.S. 1985, c. 27 (1st Supp.), s. 111.

General

Mode of trial where two or more accused.

567. Notwithstanding any other provision of this Part, where two or more persons are charged with the same offence, unless all of them elect or re-elect or are deemed to have elected, as the case may be, the same mode of trial, the justice, provincial court judge or judge

(*a*) may decline to record any election, re-election or deemed election for trial by a provincial court judge or a judge without a jury; and

(*b*) if he declines to do so, shall hold a preliminary inquiry unless a preliminary inquiry has been held prior to the election, re-election or deemed election. R.S. 1985, c. 27 (1st Supp.), s. 111.

Attorney General may require trial by jury.

568. The Attorney General may, notwithstanding that an accused elects under section 536 or re-elects under section 561 to be tried by a judge or provincial court judge, as the case may be, require the accused to be tried by a court composed of a judge and jury, unless the alleged offence is one that is punishable with imprisonment for five years or less, and where the Attorney General so requires, a judge or provincial court judge has no jurisdiction to try the accused under this Part and a preliminary inquiry shall be held before a justice unless a preliminary inquiry has been held prior to the requirement by the Attorney General that the accused be tried by a court composed of a judge and jury. R.S. 1985, c. 27 (1st Supp.), s. 111.

569. [Repealed R.S. 1985, c. 27 (1st Supp.), s. 111.]

Record of conviction or order — Acquittal and record of acquittal — Transmission of record — Proof of conviction order or acquittal — Warrant of committal.

570. (1) Where an accused who is tried under this Part is determined by a judge or provincial court judge to be guilty of an offence on acceptance of a plea of guilty or on a finding of guilt, the judge or provincial court judge, as the case may be, shall endorse the information accordingly and shall sentence the accused or otherwise deal with the accused in the manner authorized by law and, on request by the accused, the prosecutor or a peace officer, shall cause a conviction in Form 35 and a certified copy thereof, or an order in Form 36 and a certified copy thereof, to be drawn up and shall deliver the certified copy to the person making the request.

(2) Where an accused who is tried under this Part is found not guilty of an offence with which the accused is charged, the judge or provincial court judge, as the case may be, shall immediately acquit the accused in respect of that offence and shall cause an order in Form 37 to be drawn up, and on request shall make out and deliver to the accused a certified copy of the order.

(3) Where an accused elects to be tried by a provincial court judge under this Part, the provincial court judge shall transmit the written charge, the memorandum of adjudication and the conviction, if any, into such custody as the Attorney General may direct.

(4) A copy of a conviction in Form 35 or of an order in Form 36 or 37, certified by the judge or by the clerk or other proper officer of the court, or by the provincial court judge, as the case may be, or proved to be a true copy, is, on proof of the identity of the person to whom the conviction or order relates, sufficient evidence in any legal proceedings to prove the conviction of that person or the making of the order against that person or his acquittal, as the case may be, for the offence mentioned in the copy of the conviction or order.

(5) Where an accused other than a corporation is convicted, the judge or provincial court judge, as the case may be, shall issue or cause to be issued a warrant of committal in Form 21, and section 528 applies in respect of a warrant of committal issued under this subsection. R.S. 1985, c. 27 (1st Supp.), ss. 112, 203.

Adjournment.

571. A judge or provincial court judge acting under this Part may from time to time adjourn a trial until it is finally terminated. R.S. 1985, c. 27 (1st Supp.), s. 203.

Application of Parts XVI, XVIII, XX and XXIII.

572. The provisions of Part XVI, the provisions of Part XVIII relating to transmission of the record by a provincial court judge where he holds a preliminary inquiry, and the provisions of Parts XX and XXIII, in so far as they are not inconsistent with this Part, apply, with such modifications as the circumstances require to proceedings under this Part. R.S. 1985, c. 27 (1st Supp.), s. 203.

PART XX

PROCEDURE IN JURY TRIALS AND GENERAL PROVISIONS

Preferring Indictment

573. [Repealed R.S. 1985, c. 27 (1st Supp.), s. 113.]

Prosecutor may prefer indictment — Consent to inclusion of other charges — Private prosecutor requires consent.

574. (1) Subject to subsection (3) and section 577, the prosecutor may prefer an indictment against any person who has been ordered to stand trial in respect of

(*a*) any charge on which that person was ordered to stand trial, or

(*b*) any charge founded on the facts disclosed by the evidence taken on the preliminary inquiry, in addition to or in substitution for any charge on which that person was ordered to stand trial,

whether or not the charges were included in one information.

(2) An indictment preferred under subsection (1) may, if the accused consents, include any charge that is not referred to in paragraph (1)(*a*) or (*b*), and the offence charged may be dealt with, tried and determined and punished in all respects as if it were an offence in respect of which the accused had been ordered to stand trial, but if the offence was committed wholly in a province other than that in which the accused is before the court, subsection 478(3) applies.

(3) In any prosecution conducted by a prosecutor other than the Attorney General and in which the Attorney General does not intervene, an indictment shall not be preferred under subsection (1) before any court without the written order of a judge of that court. R.S. 1985, c. 27 (1st Supp.), s. 113.

575. [Repealed 1985 R.S., c. 27 (1st Supp.), s. 113.]

Indictment — Criminal information and bill of indictment — Coroner's inquisition.

576. (1) Except as provided in this Act, no indictment shall be preferred.

(2) No criminal information shall be laid or granted and no bill of indictment shall be preferred before a grand jury.

(3) No person shall be tried on a coroner's inquisition. R.S. 1985, c. 27 (1st Supp.), s. 114.

Direct indictments.

577. In any prosecution,

(*a*) where a preliminary inquiry has not been held, an indictment shall not be preferred, or

(*b*) where a preliminary inquiry has been held and the accused has been discharged, an indictment shall not be preferred or a new information shall not be laid

before any court without,

(*c*) where the prosecution is conducted by the Attorney General or the Attorney General intervenes in the prosecution, the personal consent in writing of the Attorney General or Deputy Attorney General, or

(*d*) where the prosecution is conducted by a prosecutor other than the Attorney General and the Attorney General does not intervene in the prosecution, the written order of a judge of that court. R.S. 1985, c. 27 (1st Supp.), s. 115.

Summons or warrant — Part XVI to apply.

578. (1) Where notice of the recommencement of proceedings has been given pursuant to subsection 579(2) or an indictment has been filed with the court before which the proceedings are to commence or recommence, the court, if it considers it necessary, may issue

(*a*) a summons addressed to, or

(*b*) a warrant for the arrest of,

the accused or defendant, as the case may be, to compel him to attend before the court to answer the charge described in the indictment.

(2) The provisions of Part XVI apply with such modifications as the circumstances require where a summons or warrant is issued under subsection (1). R.S. 1985, c. 27 (1st Supp.), s. 116.

Attorney General may direct stay — Recommencement of proceedings.

579. (1) The Attorney General or counsel instructed by him for that purpose may, at any time after any proceedings in relation to an accused or a defendant are commenced and before judgment, direct the clerk or other proper officer of the court to make an entry on the record that the proceedings are stayed by his direction, and such entry shall be made forthwith thereafter, whereupon the proceedings shall be stayed accordingly and any recognizance relating to the proceedings is vacated.

(2) Proceedings stayed in accordance with subsection (1) may be recommenced, without laying a new information or preferring a new indictment, as the case may be, by the Attorney General or counsel instructed by him for that purpose giving notice of the recommencement to the clerk of the court in which the stay of the proceedings was entered, but where no such notice is given within one year after the entry of the stay of proceedings, or before the expiration of the time within which the proceedings could have been commenced, whichever is the earlier, the proceedings shall be deemed never to have been commenced. R.S. 1985, c. 27 (1st Supp.), s. 117.

Form of indictment.

580. An indictment is sufficient if it is on paper and is in Form 4. R.S. 1985, c. 27 (1st Supp.), s. 117.

General Provisions respecting Counts

Substance of offence — Form of statement — Details of circumstances — Indictment for treason — Reference to section — General provisions not restricted.

581. (1) Each count in an indictment shall in general apply to a single transaction and shall contain in substance a statement that the accused or defendant committed an indictable offence therein specified.

(2) The statement referred to in subsection (1) may be

(*a*) in popular language without technical averments or allegations of matters that are not essential to be proved;

(*b*) in the words of the enactment that describes the offence or declares the matters charged to be an indictable offence; or

(*c*) in words that are sufficient to give to the accused notice of the offence with which he is charged.

(3) A count shall contain sufficient detail of the circumstances of the alleged offence to give to the accused reasonable information with respect to the act or omission to be proved against him and to identify the transaction referred to, but otherwise the absence or insufficiency of details does not vitiate the count.

(4) Where an accused is charged with an offence under section 47 or sections 49 to 53, every overt act that is to be relied on shall be stated in the indictment.

(5) A count may refer to any section, subsection, paragraph or subparagraph of the enactment that creates the offence charged, and for the purpose of determining whether a count is sufficient, consideration shall be given to any such reference.

(6) Nothing in this Part relating to matters that do not render a count insufficient shall be deemed to restrict or limit the application of this section. R.S. 1985, c. 27 (1st Supp.), s. 118.

High treason and first degree murder.

582. No person shall be convicted for the offence of high treason or first degree murder unless in the indictment charging the offence he is specifically charged with that offence.

Certain omissions not grounds for objection.

583. No count in an indictment is insufficient by reason of the absence of details where, in the opinion of the court, the count otherwise fulfils the requirements of section 581 and, without restricting the generality of the foregoing, no count in an indictment is insufficient by reason only that

(*a*) it does not name the person injured or intended or attempted to be injured,

(*b*) it does not name the person who owns or has a special property or interest in property mentioned in the count;

(*c*) it charges an intent to defraud without naming or describing the person whom it was intended to defraud;

(*d*) it does not set out any writing that is the subject of the charge;

(*e*) it does not set out the words used where words that are alleged to have been used are the subject of the charge;

(*f*) it does not specify the means by which the alleged offence was committed;

(*g*) it does not name or describe with precision any person, place or thing; or

(*h*) it does not, where the consent of a person, official or authority is required before proceedings may be instituted for an offence, state that the consent has been obtained.

Special Provisions respecting Counts

Sufficiency of count charging libel — Specifying sense — Proof.

584. (1) No count for publishing a blasphemous, seditious or defamatory libel, or for selling or exhibiting an obscene book, pamphlet, newspaper or other written matter, is insufficient by reason only that it does not set out the words that are alleged to be libellous or the writing that is alleged to be obscene.

(2) A count for publishing a libel may charge that the published matter was written in a sense that by innuendo made the publication thereof criminal, and may specify that sense without any introductory assertion to show how the matter was written in that sense.

(3) It is sufficient, on the trial of a count for publishing a libel, to prove that the matter published was libellous, with or without innuendo.

Sufficiency of count charging perjury, etc.

585. No count that charges

(*a*) perjury,

(*b*) the making of a false oath or a false statement,

(*c*) fabricating evidence, or

(*d*) procuring the commission of an offence mentioned in paragraph (*a*), (*b*) or (*c*),

is insufficient by reason only that it does not state the nature of the authority of the tribunal before which the oath or statement was taken or made, or the subject of the inquiry, or the words used or the evidence fabricated, or that it does not expressly negative the truth of the words used.

Sufficiency of count relating to fraud.

586. No count that alleges false pretences, fraud or any attempt or conspiracy by fraudulent means is insufficient by reason only that it does not set out in detail the nature of the false pretence, fraud or fraudulent means.

Particulars

What may be ordered — Regard to evidence — Particular.

587. (1) A court may, where it is satisfied that it is necessary for a fair trial, order the prosecutor to furnish particulars and, without restricting the generality of the foregoing, may order the prosecutor to furnish particulars

(*a*) of what is relied on in support of a charge of perjury, the making of a false oath or of a false statement, fabricating evidence or counselling the commission of any of those offences;

(*b*) of any false pretence or fraud that is alleged;

(*c*) of any alleged attempt or conspiracy by fraudulent means;

(*d*) setting out the passages in a book, pamphlet, newspaper or other printing or writing that are relied on in support of a charge of selling or exhibiting an obscene book, pamphlet, newspaper, printing or writing;

(*e*) further describing any writing or words that are the subject of a charge;

(*f*) further describing the means by which an offence is alleged to have been committed; or

(*g*) further describing a person, place or thing referred to in an indictment.

(2) For the purpose of determining whether or not a particular is required, the court may give consideration to any evidence that has been taken.

(3) Where a particular is delivered pursuant to this section,

(*a*) a copy shall be given without charge to the accused or his counsel,

(*b*) the particular shall be entered in the record, and

(*c*) the trial shall proceed in all respects as if the indictment had been amended to conform with the particular. R.S. 1985, c. 27 (1st Supp.), s. 7(2).

Ownership of Property

Ownership.

588. The real and personal property of which a person has, by law, the management, control or custody shall, for the purposes of an indictment or proceeding against any other person for an offence committed on or in respect of the property, be deemed to be the property of the person who has the management, control or custody of it.

Joinder or Severance of Counts

Count for murder.

589. No count that charges an indictable offence other than murder shall be joined in an indictment to a count that charges murder unless

(*a*) the count that charges the offence other than murder arises out of the same transaction as a count that charges murder; or

(*b*) the accused signifies consent to the joinder of the counts. 1991, c. 4, s. 2.

Offences may be charged in the alternative — Application to amend or divide counts — Order.

590. (1) A count is not objectionable by reason only that

(*a*) it charges in the alternative several different matters, acts or omissions that are stated in the alternative in an enactment that describes as an indictable offence the matters, acts or omissions charged in the count; or

(*b*) it is double or multifarious.

(2) An accused may at any stage of his trial apply to the court to amend or to divide a count that

(*a*) charges in the alternative different matters, acts or omissions that are stated in the alternative in the enactment that describes the offence or declares that the matters, acts or omissions charged are an indictable offence, or

(*b*) is double or multifarious,

on the ground that, as framed, it embarrasses him in his defence.

(3) The court may, where it is satisfied that the ends of justice require it, order that a count be amended or divided into two or more counts, and thereupon a formal commencement may be inserted before each of the counts into which it is divided.

Joinder of counts — Each count separate — Severance of accused and counts — Order for severance — Subsequent procedure — Idem.

591. (1) Subject to section 589, any number of counts for any number of offences may be joined in the same indictment, but the counts shall be distinguished in the manner shown in Form 4.

(2) Where there is more than one count in an indictment, each count may be treated as a separate indictment.

(3) The court may, where it is satisfied that the interests of justice so require, order

(*a*) that the accused or defendant be tried separately on one or more of the counts; and

(*b*) where there is more than one accused or defendant, that one or more of them be tried separately on one of more of the counts.

(4) An order under subsection (3) may be made before or during the trial

but, if the order is made during the trial, the jury shall be discharged from giving a verdict on the counts

(*a*) on which the trial does not proceed; or

(*b*) in respect of the accused or defendant who has been granted a separate trial.

(5) The counts in respect of which a jury is discharged pursuant to paragraph (4)(*a*) may subsequently be proceeded on in all respects as if they were contained in a separate indictment.

(6) Where an order is made in respect of an accused or defendant under paragraph (3)(*b*), the accused or defendant may be tried separately on the counts in relation to which the order was made as if they were contained in a separate indictment. R.S. 1985, c. 27 (1st Supp.), s. 119.

Joinder of Accused in Certain Cases

Accessories after the fact.

592. Any one who is charged with being an accessory after the fact to any offence may be indicted, whether or not the principal or any other party to the offence has been indicted or convicted or is or is not amenable to justice.

Trial of persons jointly for having in possession — Conviction of one or more.

593. (1) Any number of persons may be charged in the same indictment with an offence under section 354 or paragraph 356(1)(*b*), notwithstanding that

(*a*) the property was had in possession at different times; or

(*b*) the person by whom the property was obtained

(i) is not indicted with them, or

(ii) is not in custody or is not amenable to justice.

(2) Where, pursuant to subsection (1), two or more persons are charged in the same indictment with an offence referred to in that subsection, any one or more of those persons who separately committed the offence in respect of the property or any part of it may be convicted.

594. [Repealed, R.S. 1985, c. 27 (1st Supp.), s. 120.]

595. [Repealed, R.S. 1985, c. 27 (1st Supp.), s. 120.]

596. [Repealed, R.S. 1985, c. 27 (1st Supp.), s. 120.]

Proceedings when Person Indicted is at Large

Bench warrant — Execution — Interim release.

597. (1) Where an indictment has been preferred against a person who is at large, and that person does not appear or remain in attendance for his trial, the court before which the accused should have appeared or remained in attendance may issue a warrant in Form 7 for his arrest.

(2) A warrant issued under subsection (1) may be executed anywhere in Canada.

(3) Where an accused is arrested under a warrant issued under subsection (1), a judge of the court that issued the warrant may order that the accused be released on his giving an undertaking that he will do any one or more of the following things as specified in the order, namely,

(*a*) report at times to be stated in the order to a peace officer or other person designated in the order;

(*b*) remain within a territorial jurisdiction specified in the order;

(*c*) notify the peace officer or other person designated under paragraph (*a*) of any change in his address or his employment or occupation;

(*d*) abstain from communicating with any witness or other person expressly named in the order except in accordance with such conditions specified in the order as the judge deems necessary;

(*e*) where the accused is the holder of a passport, deposit his passport as specified in the order; and

(*f*) comply with such other reasonable conditions specified in the order as the judge considers desirable. R.S. 1985, c. 27 (1st Supp), s. 121.

Election deemed to be waived — Idem.

598. (1) Notwithstanding anything in this Act, where a person to whom subsection 597(1) applies has elected or is deemed to have elected to be tried by a court composed of a judge and jury and, at the time he failed to appear or to remain in attendance for his trial, he had not re-elected to be tried by a court composed of a judge without a jury or a provincial court judge without a jury, he shall not be tried by a court composed of a judge and jury unless

(*a*) he establishes to the satisfaction of a judge of the court in which he is indicted that there was a legitimate excuse for his failure to appear or remain in attendance for his trial; or

(*b*) the Attorney General requires pursuant to section 568 that the accused be tried by a court composed of a judge and jury.

(2) An accused who, pursuant to subsection (1), may not be tried by a court composed of a judge and jury is deemed to have elected under section 536 to be tried by a judge of the court in which he is indicted without a jury and section 561 does not apply in respect of the accused. R.S. 1985, c. 27 (1st Supp.), ss. 122, 203.

Change of Venue

Reasons for change of venue — Conditions as to expense — Transmission of record — Idem.

599. (1) A court before which an accused is or may be indicted, at any term or sittings thereof, or a judge who may hold or sit in that court, may at any time before or after an indictment is found, on the application of the prosecutor or the accused, order the trial to be held in a territorial division in the same province other than that in which the offence would otherwise be tried if

(*a*) it appears expedient to the ends of justice; or

(*b*) a competent authority has directed that a jury is not to be summoned at the time appointed in a territorial division where the trial would otherwise by law be held.

(2) [Repealed R.S. 1985, c. 1(4th Supp.), s. 16]

(3) The court or judge may, in an order made on an application by the prosecutor under subsection (1), prescribe conditions that he thinks proper with respect to the payment of additional expenses caused to the accused as a result of the change of venue.

(4) Where an order is made under subsection (1), the officer who has custody of the indictment, if any, and the writings and exhibits relating to the prosecution, shall transmit them forthwith to the clerk of the court before which the trial is ordered to be held, and all proceedings in the case shall be held or, if previously commenced, shall be continued in that court.

(5) Where the writings and exhibits referred to in subsection (4) have not been returned to the court in which the trial was to be held at the time an order is made to change the place of trial, the person who obtains the order shall serve a true copy thereof on the person in whose custody they are and that person shall thereupon transmit them to the clerk of the court before which the trial is to be held. R.S. 1985, c. 1(4th Supp.) s. 16.

Order is authority to remove prisoner.

600. An order that is made under section 599 is sufficient warrant, justification and authority to all sheriffs, keepers of prisons and peace officers for the removal, disposal and reception of an accused in accordance with the terms of the order, and the sheriff may appoint and authorize any peace officer to convey the accused to a prison in the territorial division in which the trial is ordered to be held.

Amendment

Amending defective indictment or count — Amendment where variance — Amending indictment — Matters to be considered by the court — Variance not material — Adjournment if accused prejudiced — Question of law — Endorsing indictment — Mistakes not material — Limitation — Definition of "court" — Application.

601. (1) An objection to an indictment or to a count in an indictment for a defect apparent on the face thereof shall be taken by motion to quash the indictment or count before the accused has pleaded, and thereafter only by leave of the court before which the proceedings take place, and the court before which an objection is taken under this section may, if it considers it necessary, order the indictment or count to be amended to cure the defect.

(2) Subject to this section, a court may, on the trial of an indictment, amend the indictment or a count therein or a particular that is furnished under section 587, to make the indictment, count or particular conform to the evidence, where there is a variance between the evidence and

(*a*) a count in the indictment as preferred; or

(*b*) a count in the indictment

(i) as amended, or

(ii) as it would have been if it had been amended in conformity with any particular that has been furnished pursuant to section 587.

(3) Subject to this section, a court shall, at any stage of the proceedings, amend the indictment or a count therein as may be necessary where it appears

(*a*) that the indictment has been preferred under a particular Act of Parliament instead of another Act of Parliament;

(*b*) that the indictment or a count thereof

(i) fails to state or states defectively anything that is requisite to constitute the offence,

(ii) does not negative an exception that should be negatived,

(iii) is in any way defective in substance,

and the matters to be alleged in the proposed amendment are disclosed by the evidence taken on the preliminary inquiry or on the trial; or

(*c*) that the indictment or a count thereof is in any way defective in form.

(4) The court shall, in considering whether or not an amendment should be made to the indictment or a count thereof under subsection (3), consider

(*a*) the matters disclosed by the evidence taken on the preliminary inquiry;

(*b*) the evidence taken on the trial, if any;

(*c*) the circumstances of the case;

(*d*) whether the accused has been misled or prejudiced in his defence by any variance, error or omission mentioned in subsection (2) or (3); and

(*e*) whether, having regard to the merits of the case, the proposed amendment can be made without injustice being done.

(4.1) A variance between the indictment or a count therein and the evidence taken is not material with respect to

(*a*) the time when the offence is alleged to have been committed, if it is proved that the indictment was preferred within the prescribed period of limitation, if any; or

(*b*) the place where the subject-matter of the proceedings is alleged to have arisen, if it is proved that it arose within the territorial jurisdiction of the court.

(5) Where, in the opinion of the court, the accused has been misled or prejudiced in his defence by a variance, error or omission in an indictment or a count therein, the court may, if it is of the opinion that the misleading

or prejudice may be removed by an adjournment, adjourn the proceedings to a specified day or sittings of the court and may make such an order with respect to the payment of costs resulting from the necessity for amendment as it considers desirable.

(6) The question whether an order to amend an indictment or a count thereof should be granted or refused is a question of law.

(7) An order to amend an indictment or a count therein shall be endorsed on the indictment as part of the record and the proceedings shall continue as if the indictment or count had been originally preferred as amended.

(8) A mistake in the heading of an indictment shall be corrected as soon as it is discovered but, whether corrected or not, is not material.

(9) The authority of a court to amend indictments does not authorize the court to add to the overt acts stated in an indictment for high treason or treason or for an offence against any provision in sections 49, 50, 51 and 53.

(10) In this section, "court" means a court, judge, justice or provincial court judge acting in summary conviction proceedings or in proceedings on indictment.

(11) This section applies to all proceedings, including preliminary inquiries, with such modifications as the circumstances require. R.S. 1985, c. 27 (1st Supp.), s. 123.

602. [Repealed R.S. 1985, c. 27 (1st Supp.), s. 124.]

Inspection and Copies of Documents

Right of accused.

603. An accused is entitled, after he has been ordered to stand trial or at his trial,

(*a*) to inspect without charge the indictment, his own statement, the evidence and the exhibits, if any; and

(*b*) to receive, on payment of a reasonable fee determined in accordance with a tariff of fees fixed or approved by the Attorney General of the province, a copy

(i) of the evidence,

(ii) of his own statement, if any, and

(iii) of the indictment;

but the trial shall not be postponed to enable the accused to secure copies unless the court is satisfied that the failure of the accused to secure them before the trial is not attributable to lack of diligence on the part of the accused. R.S. 1985, c. 27 (1st Supp.), s. 101(2).

Delivery of documents in case of treason, etc. — Details — Witnesses to delivery — Exception.

604. (1) An accused who is indicted for high treason or treason or for being an accessory after the fact to high treason or treason is entitled to receive, after the indictment has been found and at least ten days before his arraignment,

(*a*) a copy of the indictment;

(*b*) a list of the witnesses to be produced on the trial to prove the indictment; and

(*c*) a copy of the panel of jurors who are to try him, returned by the sheriff.

(2) The list of the witnesses and the copy of the panel of the jurors referred to in subsection (1) shall mention the names, occupations and places of abode of the witnesses and jurors respectively.

(3) The writings referred to in subsection (1) shall be given to the accused at the same time and in the presence of at least two witnesses.

(4) This section does not apply to the offence of high treason by killing Her Majesty, or to the offence of high treason where the overt act alleged is an attempt to injure the person of Her Majesty in any manner or to the offence of being an accessory after the fact in such a case of high treason.

Release of exhibits for testing — Disobeying orders.

605. (1) A judge of a superior court of criminal jurisdiction or a court of criminal jurisdiction may, on summary application on behalf of the accused or the prosecutor, after three days notice to the accused or prosecutor, as the case may be, order the release of any exhibit for the purpose of a scientific or other test or examination, subject to such terms as appear to be necessary or desirable to ensure the safeguarding of the exhibit and its preservation for use at the trial.

(2) Every one who fails to comply with the terms of an order made under subsection (1) is guilty of contempt of court and may be dealt with summarily by the judge or provincial court judge who made the order or before whom the trial of the accused takes place. R.S. 1985, c. 27 (1st Supp.), s. 203.

Pleas

Pleas permitted — Refusal to plead — Allowing time — Included or other defence.

606. (1) An accused who is called on to plead may plead guilty or not guilty, or the special pleas authorized by this Part and no others.

(2) Where an accused refuses to plead or does not answer directly, the court shall order the clerk of the court to enter a plea of not guilty.

(3) An accused is not entitled as of right to have his trial postponed but the court may, if it considers that the accused should be allowed further time

to plead, move to quash, or prepare for his defence or for any other reason, adjourn the trial to a later time in the session or sittings of the court, or to the next of any subsequent session or sittings of the court, on such terms as the court considers proper.

(4) Notwithstanding any other provision of this Act, where an accused or defendant pleads not guilty of the offence charged but guilty of any other offence arising out of the same transaction, whether or not it is an included offence, the court may, with the consent of the prosecutor, accept that plea of guilty and, if the plea is accepted, the court shall find the accused or defendant not guilty of the offence charged and find him guilty of the offence in respect of which the plea of guilty was accepted and enter those findings in the record of the court. R.S. 1985, c. 27 (1st Supp.), s. 125.

Special pleas — In case of libel — Disposal — Pleading over — Statement sufficient — Exceptions: foreign trials *in absentia*.

607. (1) An accused may plead the special pleas of

(*a*) *autrefois acquit*;

(*b*) *autrefois convict*; and

(*c*) pardon.

(2) An accused who is charged with defamatory libel may plead in accordance with sections 611 and 612.

(3) The pleas of *autrefois acquit, autrefois convict* and pardon shall be disposed of by the judge without a jury before the accused is called on to plead further.

(4) When the pleas referred to in subsection (3) are disposed of against the accused, he may plead guilty or not guilty.

(5) Where an accused pleads *autrefois acquit* or *autrefois convict*, it is sufficient if he

(*a*) states that he has been lawfully acquitted, convicted or discharged under subsection 736(1), as the case may be, of the offence charged in the count to which the plea relates; and

(*b*) indicates the time and place of the acquittal, conviction or discharge under subsection 736(1).

(6) A person who is alleged to have committed an act or omission outside Canada that is an offence in Canada by virtue of any of subsections 7(2) to (3.4) or subsection 7(3.7) or (3.71), and in respect of which that person has been tried and convicted outside Canada, may not plead *autrefois convict* with respect to a count that charges that offence if

(a) at the trial outside Canada the person was not present and was not represented by counsel acting under the person's instructions, and

(b) the person was not punished in accordance with the sentence imposed upon conviction in respect of the act or omission,

notwithstanding that the person is deemed by virtue of subsection 7(6) to have been tried and convicted in Canada in respect of the act or omission. R.S. 1985, c. 27 (1st Supp.), s. 126; c. 30 (3rd Supp.), s. 2.

Evidence of identity of charges.

608. Where an issue on a plea of *autrefois acquit* or *autrefois convict* is tried, the evidence and adjudication and the notes of the judge and official stenographer on the former trial and the record transmitted to the court pursuant to section 551 on the charge that is pending before that court are admissible in evidence to prove or to disprove the identity of the charges.

What determines identity — Allowance of special plea in part.

609. (1) Where an issue on a plea of *autrefois acquit* or *autrefois convict* to a count is tried and it appears

(*a*) that the matter on which the accused was given in charge on the former trial is the same in whole or in part as that on which it is proposed to give him in charge, and

(*b*) that on the former trial, if all proper amendments had been made that might then have been made, he might have been convicted of all the offences of which he may be convicted on the count to which the plea of *autrefois acquit* or *autrefois convict* is pleaded,

the judge shall give judgment discharging the accused in respect of that count.

(2) The following provisions apply where an issue on a plea of *autrefois acquit* or *autrefois convict* is tried:

(*a*) where it appears that the accused might on the former trial have been convicted of an offence of which he may be convicted on the count in issue, the judge shall direct that the accused shall not be found guilty of any offence of which he might have been convicted on the former trial; and

(*b*) where it appears that the accused may be convicted on the count in issue of an offence of which he could not have been convicted on the former trial, the accused shall plead guilty or not guilty with respect to that offence.

Circumstances of aggravation — Effect of previous charge of murder or manslaughter — Previous charges of first degree murder — Effect of previous charge of infanticide or manslaughter.

610. (1) Where an indictment charges substantially the same offence as that charged in an indictment on which an accused was previously convicted or acquitted, but adds a statement of intention or circumstances of aggravation tending, if proved, to increase the punishment, the previous conviction or acquittal bars the subsequent indictment.

(2) A conviction or an acquittal on an indictment for murder bars a subsequent indictment for the same homicide charging it as manslaughter or infanticide, and a conviction or acquittal on an indictment for manslaughter or infanticide bars a subsequent indictment for the same homicide charging it as murder.

(3) A conviction or an acquittal on an indictment for first degree murder bars a subsequent indictment for the same homicide charging it as second degree murder, and a conviction or acquittal on an indictment for second degree murder bars a subsequent indictment for the same homicide charging it as first degree murder.

(4) A conviction or an acquittal on an indictment for infanticide bars a subsequent indictment for the same homicide charging it as manslaughter, and a conviction or acquittal on an indictment for manslaughter bars a subsequent indictment for the same homicide charging it as infanticide.

Libel, plea of justification — Where more than one sense alleged — Plea in writing — Reply.

611. (1) An accused who is charged with publishing a defamatory libel may plead that the defamatory matter published by him was true, and that it was for the public benefit that the matter should have been published in the manner in which and at the time when it was published.

(2) A plea that is made under subsection (1) may justify the defamatory matter in any sense in which it is specified in the count, or in the sense that the defamatory matter bears without being specified, or separate pleas justifying the defamatory matter in each sense may be pleaded separately to each count as if two libels had been charged in separate counts.

(3) A plea that is made under subsection (1) shall be in writing and shall set out the particular facts by reason of which it is alleged to have been for the public good that the matter should have been published.

(4) The prosecutor may in his reply deny generally the truth of a plea that is made under this section.

Plea of justification necessary — Not guilty, in addition — Effect of plea on punishment.

612. (1) The truth of the matters charged in an alleged libel shall not be inquired into in the absence of a plea of justification under section 611 unless the accused is charged with publishing the libel knowing it to be false, in which case evidence of the truth may be given to negative the allegation that the accused knew that the libel was false.

(2) The accused may, in addition to a plea that is made under section 611, plead not guilty and the pleas shall be inquired into together.

(3) Where a plea of justification is pleaded and the accused is convicted, the court may, in pronouncing sentence, consider whether the guilt of the accused is aggravated or mitigated by the plea.

Plea of not guilty.

613. Any ground of defence for which a special plea is not provided by this Act may be relied on under the plea of not guilty.

Insanity of accused when offence committed — Custody after finding.

614. (1) Where, on the trial of an accused who is charged with an indictable offence, evidence is given that the accused was insane at the time the offence was committed and the accused is acquitted,

(*a*) the jury, or

(*b*) the judge or provincial court judge, where there is no jury,

shall find whether the accused was insane at the time the offence was committed and shall declare whether he is acquitted on account of insanity.

(2) Where the accused is found to have been insane at the time the offence was committed, the court, judge or provincial court judge before whom the trial is held shall order that he be kept in strict custody in the place and in the manner that the court, judge or provincial court judge directs, until the pleasure of the lieutenant governor of the province is known. R.S. 1985, c. 27 (1st Supp.), s. 203.

Insanity at time of trial — Direction or remand for observation — Idem — Court shall assign counsel — Trial of issue — If sane, trial proceeds — If insane, order for custody — Where accused acquitted — Subsequent trial.

615. (1) A court, judge or provincial court judge may, at any time before verdict, where it appears that there is sufficient reason to doubt that the accused is, on account of insanity, capable of conducting his defence, direct that an issue be tried whether the accused is then, on account of insanity, unfit to stand his trial.

(2) A court, judge or provincial court judge may, at any time before verdict or sentence, when of the opinion, supported by the evidence or, where the prosecutor and the accused consent, by the report in writing, of at least one duly qualified medical practitioner, that there is reason to believe that

(*a*) an accused is mentally ill, or

(*b*) the balance of the mind of an accused is disturbed, where the accused is a female person charged with an offence arising out of the death of her newly-born child,

by order in writing

(*c*) direct the accused to attend, at a place or before a person specified in the order and within a time specified therein, for observation, or

(*d*) remand the accused to such custody as the court, judge or provincial court judge directs for observation for a period not exceeding thirty days.

(3) Notwithstanding subsection (2), a court, judge or provincial court judge may remand an accused in accordance with that subsection

(*a*) for a period not exceeding thirty days without having heard the evidence or considered the report of a duly qualified medical practitioner where compelling circumstances exist for so doing and where a medical practitioner is not readily available to examine the accused and give evidence or submit a report; and

(*b*) for a period of more than thirty days but not exceeding sixty days where he is satisfied that observation for such a period is required in all the circumstances of the case and his opinion is supported by the evidence or, where the prosecutor and the accused consent, by the report in writing, of at least one duly qualified medical practitioner.

(4) Where it appears that there is sufficient reason to doubt that the accused is, on account of insanity, capable of conducting his defence, the court, judge or provincial court judge shall, if the accused is not represented by counsel, assign counsel to act on behalf of the accused.

(5) For the purposes of subsection (1), the following provisions apply:

(*a*) where the issue arises before the close of the case of the prosecution, the court, judge or provincial court judge may postpone directing the trial of the issue until any time up to the opening of the case for the defence;

(*b*) where the trial is held or is to be held before a court composed of a judge and jury,

(i) if the judge directs the issue to be tried before the accused is given in charge to a jury for trial on the indictment, it shall be tried by twelve jurors, or in the Yukon Territory and the Northwest Territories, by six jurors, and

(ii) if the judge directs the issue to be tried after the accused has been given in charge to a jury for trial on the indictment, the jury shall be sworn to try that issue in addition to the issue on which they are already sworn; and

(*c*) where the trial is held before a judge or provincial court judge, he shall try the issue and render a verdict.

(6) Where the verdict is that the accused is not unfit on account of insanity to stand his trial, the arraignment or the trial shall proceed as if no such issue had been directed.

(7) Where the verdict is that the accused is unfit on account of insanity to stand his trial, the court, judge or provincial court judge shall order that the accused be kept in custody until the pleasure of the lieutenant governor of the province is known, and any plea that has been pleaded shall be set aside and the jury shall be discharged.

(8) Where the court, judge or provincial court judge has postponed directing the trial of the issue pursuant to paragraph (5)(*a*) and the accused is acquitted at the close of the case for the prosecution, the issue shall not be tried.

(9) No proceeding pursuant to this section shall prevent the accused from being tried subsequently on the indictment unless the trial of the issue was postponed pursuant to paragraph (5)(*a*) and the accused was acquitted at the close of the case for the prosecution. R.S. 1985, c. 27 (1st Supp.), s. 203.

Insanity of accused to be discharged for want of prosecution.

616. Where an accused who is charged with an indictable offence is brought before a court, judge or provincial court judge to be discharged for want of prosecution and the accused appears to be insane, the court, judge or provincial court judge shall proceed in accordance with section 615 in so far as that section may be applied. R.S. 1985, c. 27 (1st Supp.), s. 203.

Supervision of insane persons — Warrant for transfer — Transfer of accused — Arrest of accused — Taking before a justice — Order of justice.

617. (1) Where an accused is, pursuant to this Part, found to be insane, the lieutenant governor of the province in which he is detained may make an order

(*a*) for the safe custody of the accused in a place and manner directed by him; or

(*b*) if in his opinion it would be in the best interest of the accused and not contrary to the interest of the public, for the discharge of the accused either absolutely or subject to such conditions as he prescribes.

(2) An accused to whom paragraph (1)(*a*) applies may, by warrant signed by an officer authorized for that purpose by the lieutenant governor of the province in which he is detained, be transferred for the purposes of his rehabilitation to any other place in Canada specified in the warrant with the consent of the person in charge of that other place.

(3) A warrant mentioned in subsection (2) is sufficient authority for any person who has custody of the accused to deliver the accused to the person in charge of the place specified in the warrant and for the last mentioned person to detain the accused in the manner specified in the order mentioned in subsection (1).

(4) A peace officer who believes on reasonable and probable grounds that an accused to whom paragraph (1)(*b*) applies has contravened any condition prescribed in the order for his discharge may arrest the accused without warrant.

(5) Where an accused has been arrested pursuant to subsection (4), he shall be dealt with in accordance with the following provisions:

(*a*) where a justice having jurisdiction in the territorial division in which the accused has been arrested is available within a period of twenty-four hours after the arrest of the accused by a peace officer, the accused shall be taken before a justice without unreasonable delay and in any event within that period; and

(*b*) where a justice having jurisdiction in the territorial division in which the accused has been arrested is not available within a period of twenty-four hours after the arrest of the accused by a peace officer, the accused shall be taken before a justice as soon as possible.

(6) A justice before whom an accused is taken pursuant to subsection (5) may make any order that to him seems desirable in the circumstances respecting

the detention of the accused pending a decision of the lieutenant governor of the province referred to in subsection (1) and shall cause notice of the order to be given to that lieutenant governor.

Prisoner mentally ill — Custody in safe-keeping — Order for imprisonment or discharge — Order for transfer to custody of minister of health — Definition of "prison".

618. (1) The lieutenant governor of a province may, on evidence satisfactory to him that a person who is insane, mentally ill, mentally deficient or feeble-minded is serving a sentence in a prison in that province, order that the person be removed to a place of safe-keeping to be named in the order.

(2) A person who is removed to a place of safe-keeping under an order made pursuant to subsection (1) shall, subject to subsections (3) and (4), be kept in that place or in any other place of safe-keeping in which he may be ordered by the lieutenant governor to be kept.

(3) Where the lieutenant governor is satisfied that a person to whom subsection (2) applies has recovered, he may order that the person

(*a*) be returned to the prison from which he was removed pursuant to subsection (1), if he is liable to further custody in prison; or

(*b*) be discharged, if he is not liable to further custody in prison.

(4) Where the lieutenant governor is satisfied that a person to whom subsection (2) applies has partially recovered, he may, where the person is not liable to further custody in prison, order that the person shall be subject to the direction of the minister of health for the province, or such other person as the lieutenant governor may designate, and the minister of health or other person designated may make any order or direction in respect of the custody and care of the person that he considers proper.

(5) In this section, "prison" means a prison other than a penitentiary, and includes a reformatory school or industrial school.

Appointment of board of review — Constitution of board — Idem — Quorum — Periodic review and report to be made on case of each person in custody — Review and report to be made when requested by lieutenant governor — Powers.

619. (1) The lieutenant governor of a province may appoint a board to review the case of every person in custody in a place in that province by virtue of an order made pursuant to section 617 or subsection 618(1) or (2).

(2) The board shall consist of not less than three and not more than five members of whom one member shall be designated chairman by the members of the board, if no chairman has been designated by the lieutenant governor.

(3) At least two members of the board shall be duly qualified psychiatrists entitled to engage in the practice of medicine under the laws of the province

for which the board is appointed, and at least one member of the board shall be a member of the bar of the province.

(4) Three members of the board, at least one of whom is a psychiatrist described in subsection (3) and one of whom is a member of the bar of the province, constitute a quorum of the board.

(5) The board shall review the case of every person referred to in subsection (1)

(*a*) not later than six months after the making of the order referred to in that subsection relating to that person, and

(*b*) at least once in every twelve month period following the review required pursuant to paragraph (*a*) so long as the person remains in custody under the order,

and forthwith after each review the board shall report to the lieutenant governor setting out fully the results of the review and stating

(*c*) where the person in custody was found unfit on account of insanity to stand trial, whether, in the opinion of the board, that person has recovered sufficiently to stand trial,

(*d*) where the person in custody was found not guilty on account of insanity, whether, in the opinion of the board, that person has recovered and, if so, whether in its opinion it is in the interest of the public and of that person for the lieutenant governor to order that he be discharged absolutely or subject to such conditions as the lieutenant governor may prescribe,

(*e*) where the person in custody was removed from a prison pursuant to subsection 618(1), whether, in the opinion of the board, that person has recovered or partially recovered, or

(*f*) any recommendations that it considers desirable in the interests of recovery of the person to whom such review relates and that are not contrary to the public interest.

(6) In addition to any review required to be made under subsection (5), the board shall review any case referred to in subsection (1) when requested to do so by the lieutenant governor and shall forthwith after the review report to the lieutenant governor in accordance with subsection (5).

(7) For the purposes of a review under this section, the chairman of a board has all the powers that are conferred by sections 4 and 5 of the *Inquiries Act* on commissioners appointed under Part I of that Act.

Corporations

Appearance by attorney.

620. Every corporation against which an indictment is found shall appear and plead by counsel or agent.

Notice to corporation — Contents of notice.

621. (1) The clerk of the court shall, where an indictment is found against a corporation, cause a notice of the indictment to be served on the corporation.

(2) A notice of an indictment referred to in subsection (1) shall set out the nature and purport of the indictment and advise that, unless the corporation appears and pleads within seven days after service of the notice, a plea of not guilty will be entered for the accused by the court, and that the trial of the indictment will be proceeded with as though the corporation had appeared and pleaded.

Procedure on default of appearance.

622. Where a corporation does not appear in the court in which an indictment is found and plead within the time specified in the notice referred to in section 621, the presiding judge may, on proof by affidavit of service of the notice, order the clerk of the court to enter a plea of not guilty on behalf of the corporation, and the plea has the same force and effect as if the corporation had appeared by its counsel or agent and pleaded that plea.

Trial of corporation.

623. Where a corporation appears and pleads to the indictment or a plea of not guilty is entered by order of the court pursuant to section 622, the court shall proceed with the trial of the indictment and, where the corporation is convicted, section 719 applies.

Record of Proceedings

How recorded — Record of proceedings.

624. (1) It is sufficient, in making up the record of a conviction or acquittal on an indictment, to copy the indictment and the plea that was pleaded, without a formal caption or heading.

(2) The court shall keep a record of every arraignment and of proceedings subsequent to arraignment.

Form of record in case of amendment.

625. Where it is necessary to draw up a formal record in proceedings in which the indictment has been amended, the record shall be drawn up in the form in which the indictment remained after the amendment, without reference to the fact that the indictment was amended.

Pre-hearing Conference

Pre-hearing conference — Mandatory pre-trial hearing for jury trials.

625.1 (1) Subject to subsection (2), on application by the prosecutor or the accused or on its own motion, the court before which, or the judge, provincial court judge or justice before whom, any proceedings are to be held may, with the consent of the prosecutor and the accused, order that a conference between the prosecutor and the accused or counsel for the accused, to be presided over by the court, judge, provincial court judge or justice, be held prior to the proceedings to consider such matters as will promote a fair and expeditious hearing.

(2) In any case to be tried with a jury, a judge of the court before which the accused is to be tried shall, prior to the trial, order that a conference between the prosecutor and the accused or counsel for the accused, to be presided over by a judge of that court, be held in accordance with the rules of court made under section 482 to consider such matters as will promote a fair and expeditious trial. R.S. 1985, c. 27 (1st Supp.), s. 127.

Juries

Qualification of jurors — No disqualification based on sex.

626. (1) A person who is qualified as a juror according to, and summoned as a juror in accordance with, the laws of a province is qualified to serve as a juror in criminal proceedings in that province.

(2) Notwithstanding any law of a province referred to in subsection (1), no person may be disqualified, exempted or excused from serving as a juror in criminal proceedings on the grounds of his or her sex. R.S. 1985, c. 27 (1st Supp.), s. 128.

Mixed Juries

Mixed juries in Quebec — Motion by accused — Order for panel.

627. (1) In those districts in the Province of Quebec in which the sheriff is required by law to return a panel of petit jurors composed one-half of persons who speak the English language and one-half of persons who speak the French language, he shall in his return specify in separate lists those jurors whom he returns as speaking the English language and those whom he returns as speaking the French language, and the names of the jurors summoned shall be called alternately from those lists.

(2) In any district referred to in subsection (1) the accused may, upon arraignment, move that he be tried by a jury composed entirely of jurors who speak the language of the accused if that language is English or French.

(3) Where a motion is made under subsection (2), the judge may order the sheriff to summon a sufficient panel of jurors who speak the language of the

accused unless, in his discretion, it appears that the ends of justice are better served by empanelling a mixed jury.

[NOTE: R.S. 1985, c. 2 (1st Supp.), ss. 1 and 3 [am. by R.S. 1985, c. 27 (1st Supp.), s. 188] state that the repeal of section 627 of the Criminal Code shall come into force on the day on which ss. 530 to 533 and s. 638(1)(f) of the Criminal Code come into force in the Province of Quebec in respect of offences other than offences punishable on summary conviction.]

628. [Repealed R.S. 1985, c. 27 (1st Supp.), s. 129.]

Challenging the jury panel — In writing — Form.

629. (1) The accused or the prosecutor may challenge the jury panel only on the ground of partiality, fraud or wilful misconduct on the part of the sheriff or other officer by whom the panel was returned.

(2) A challenge under subsection (1) shall be in writing and shall state that the person who returned the panel was partial or fraudulent or that he wilfully misconducted himself, as the case may be.

(3) A challenge under this section may be in Form 40. R.S. 1985, c. 27 (1st Supp.), s. 130.

Trying ground of challenge.

630. Where a challenge is made under section 629, the judge shall determine whether the alleged ground of challenge is true or not, and where he is satisfied that the alleged ground of challenge is true, he shall direct a new panel to be returned.

Empanelling Jury

Names of jurors on cards — To be placed in box — To be drawn by clerk of court — Juror to be sworn — Drawing additional names if necessary.

631. (1) The name of each juror on a panel of jurors that has been returned, his number on the panel and his address shall be written on a separate card, and all the cards shall, as far as possible, be of equal size.

(2) The sheriff or other officer who returns the panel shall deliver the cards referred to in subsection (1) to the clerk of the court who shall cause them to be placed together in a box to be provided for the purpose and to be thoroughly shaken together.

(3) Where

(*a*) the array of jurors is not challenged, or

(*b*) the array of jurors is challenged but the judge does not direct a new panel to be returned,

the clerk of the court shall, in open court, draw out the cards referred to in subsection (1), one after another, and shall call out the name and number on each card as it is drawn, until the number of persons who have answered to their names is, in the opinion of the judge, sufficient to provide a full jury after allowing for orders to excuse, challenges and directions to stand by.

(4) The clerk of the court shall swear each member of the jury in the order in which the names of the jurors were drawn.

(5) Where the number of persons who answer to their names under subsection (3) is not sufficient to provide a full jury, the clerk of the court shall proceed in accordance with subsections (3) and (4) until twelve jurors are sworn. R.S. 1985, c. 27 (1st Supp.), s. 131.1992, c. 41, s. 1.

Excusing jurors.

632. The judge may, at any time before the commencement of a trial, order that any juror be excused from jury service, whether or not the juror has been called pursuant to subsection 631(3) or any challenge has been made in relation to the juror, for reasons of

(*a*) personal interest in the matter to be tried;

(*b*) relationship with the judge, prosecutor, accused, counsel for the accused or a prospective witness; or

(*c*) personal hardship or any other reasonable cause that, in the opinion of the judge, warrants that the juror be excused. 1992, c. 41, s. 2.

Stand by.

633. The judge may direct a juror whose name has been called pursuant to subsection 631(3) to stand by for reasons of personal hardship or any other reasonable cause. 1992, c. 41, s. 2.

Peremptory challenges — Maximum number — Where there are multiple counts — Where there are joint trials.

634. (1) A juror may be challenged peremptorily whether or not the juror has been challenged for cause pursuant to section 638.

(2) Subject to subsections (3) and (4), the prosecutor and the accused are each entitled to

(*a*) twenty peremptory challenges, where the accused is charged with high treason or first degree murder;

(*b*) twelve peremptory challenges, where the accused is charged with an offence, other than an offence mentioned in paragraph (*a*), for which the accused may be sentenced to imprisonment for a term exceeding five years; or

(*c*) four peremptory challenges, where the accused is charged with an offence that is not referred to in paragraph (*a*) or (*b*).

(3) Where to or more counts in an indictment are to be tried together, the prosecutor and the accused are each entitled only to the number of peremptory

challenges provided in respect of the count for which the greatest number of peremptory challenges is available.

(4) Where two or more accused are to be tried together,

(*a*) each accused is entitled to the number of peremptory challenges to which the accused would be entitled if tried alone; and

(*b*) the prosecutor is entitled to the total number of peremptory challenges available to all the accused. 1992, c. 41, s. 2.

Order of challenges — Where there are joint trials.

635. (1) The accused shall be called on before the prosecutor is called on to declare whether the accused challenges the first juror, for cause or peremptorily, and thereafer the prosecutor and the accused shall be called on alternately, in respect of each of the remaining jurors, to first make such a declaration.

(2) Subsection (1) applies where two or more accused are to be tried together, but all of the accused shall exercise the challenges of the defence in turn, in the order in which their names appear in the indictment or in any other order agreed on by them,

(*a*) in respect of the first juror, before the prosecutor; and

(*b*) in respect of each of the remaining jurors, either before or after the prosecutor, in accordance with subsection (1). 1992, c. 41, s. 2.

[NOTE: Sections 634 and 635 do not apply in respect of a jury properly constituted and consisting of jurors duly sworn before July 23, 1992.]

636. [Repealed 1992, c. 41, s. 2.]

637. [Repealed 1992, c. 41, s. 2.]

Challenge for cause — No other ground — Coming into force — Consultation — Where no agreement reached.

638. (1) A prosecutor or an accused is entitled to any number of challenges on the ground that

(*a*) the name of a juror does not appear on the panel, but no misnomer or misdescription is a ground of challenge where it appears to the court that the description given on the panel sufficiently designates the person referred to;

(*b*) a juror is not indifferent between the Queen and the accused;

(*c*) a juror has been convicted of an offence for which he was sentenced to death or to a term of imprisonment exceeding twelve months;

(*d*) a juror is an alien;

(*e*) a juror is physically unable to perform properly the duties of a juror; or

(*f*) a juror does not speak the official language of Canada that is the language of the accused or the official language of Canada in which the accused can best give testimony or both official languages of Canada, where the accused is required by reason of an order under section 530 to be tried before a judge and jury who speak the official language of Canada that is the language of the accused or the official language of Canada in which the accused can best give testimony or who speak both official languages of Canada, as the case may be.

(2) No challenge for cause shall be allowed on a ground not mentioned in subsection (1).

(3) Paragraph (1)(*f*) shall come into force in any of the Provinces of Quebec, Nova Scotia, British Columbia, Prince Edward Island, Saskatchewan, Alberta and Newfoundland, in respect of

(*a*) offences punishable on summary conviction, or

(*b*) indictable offences,

only on a day to be fixed in a proclamation declaring that paragraph to be in force in that Province with respect to those offences.

(4) Notwithstanding any other provision in this section, paragraph 638(1)(*f*) shall come into force on January 1, 1990

(*a*) in respect of offences punishable on summary conviction, in any province in which that paragraph is not in force in respect of offences punishable on summary conviction immediately prior to that date; and

(*b*) in respect of indictable offences, in any province in which that paragraph is not in force in respect of indictable offences immediately prior to that date. R.S. 1985, c. 27 (1st Supp.), s. 132; c. 31 (4th Supp.), s. 96.

[NOTE: S. 638(1)(f) has been proclaimed in force in the provinces of Manitoba, New Brunswick, Ontario and in Yukon Territory and Northwest Territories.]

Challenge in writing — Form — Denial.

639. (1) Where a challenge is made on a ground mentioned in section 638, the court may, in its discretion, require the party that challenges to put the challenge in writing.

(2) A challenge may be in Form 41.

(3) A challenge may be denied by the other party to the proceedings on the ground that it is not true.

Objection that name not on panel — Other grounds — If challenge not sustained, or if sustained — Disagreement of triers.

640. (1) Where the ground of a challenge is that the name of a juror does not appear on the panel, the issue shall be tried by the judge on the *voir dire* by the inspection of the panel, and such other evidence that the judge thinks fit to receive.

(2) Where the ground of a challenge is one not mentioned in subsection (1), the two jurors who were last sworn, or if no jurors have then been sworn, two persons present whom the court may appoint for the purpose, shall be sworn to determine whether the ground of challenge is true.

(3) Where the finding, pursuant to subsection (1) or (2) is that the ground of challenge is not true, the juror shall be sworn, but if the finding is that the ground of challenge is true, the juror shall not be sworn.

(4) Where, after what the court considers to be a reasonable time, the two persons who are sworn to determine whether the ground of challenge is true are unable to agree, the court may discharge them from giving a verdict and may direct two other persons to be sworn to determine whether the ground of challenge is true.

Calling jurors who have stood by — Other jurors becoming available.

641. (1) Where a full jury has not been sworn and no names remain to be called, the names of those who have been directed to stand by shall be called again in the order in which their names were drawn and they shall be sworn, unless excused by the judge or challenged by the accused or the prosecutor.

(2) Where, before a juror is sworn pursuant to subsection (1), other jurors in the panel become available, the prosecutor may require the names of those jurors to be put into and drawn from the box in accordance with section 631, and those jurors shall be challenged, directed to stand by, excused or sworn, as the case may be, before the names of the jurors who were originally directed to stand by are called again. 1992, c. 41, s. 3.

Summoning other jurors when panel exhausted — Orally — Adding names to panel.

642. (1) Where a full jury cannot be provided notwithstanding that the relevant provisions of this Part have been complied with, the court may, at the request of the prosecutor, order the sheriff or other proper officer forthwith to summon as many persons, whether qualified jurors or not, as the court directs for the purpose of providing a full jury.

(2) Jurors may be summoned under subsection (1) by word of mouth, if necessary.

(3) The names of the persons who are summoned under this section shall be added to the general panel for the purposes of the trial, and the same proceedings shall be taken with respect to calling and challenging those persons, excusing them and directing them to stand by as are provided in this Part with respect to the persons named in the original panel. 1992, c. 41, s. 4.

Who shall be jury — Same jury may try another issue by consent — Sections directory.

643. (1) The twelve jurors whose names are drawn and who are sworn in accordance with this Part shall be the jury to try the issues of the indictment, and the names of the jurors so drawn and sworn shall be kept apart until the jury gives its verdict or until it is discharged, whereupon the names shall be returned to the box as often as occasion arises, as long as an issue remains to be tried before a jury.

(2) The court may try an issue with the same jury in whole or in part that previously tried or was drawn to try another issue, without the jurors being sworn again, but if the prosecutor or the accused objects to any of the jurors or the court excuses any of the jurors, the court shall order those persons to withdraw and shall direct that the required number of names to make up a full jury be drawn and, subject to the provisions of this Part relating to challenges, orders to excuse and directions to stand by, the persons whose names are drawn shall be sworn.

(3) Failure to comply with the directions of this section or section 631, 635 or 641 does not affect the validity of a proceeding. 1992, c. 41, s. 5.

Discharge of juror — Trial may continue.

644. (1) Where in the course of a trial the judge is satisfied that a juror should not, by reason of illness or other reasonable cause, continue to act, the judge may discharge the juror.

(2) Where in the course of a trial a member of the jury dies or is discharged pursuant to subsection (1), the jury shall, unless the judge otherwise directs and if the number of jurors is not reduced below ten, be deemed to remain properly constituted for all purposes of the trial and the trial shall proceed and a verdict may be given accordingly. 1992, c. 41, s. 6.

Trial

Trial continuous — Adjournment — Formal adjournment unnecessary — Questions reserved for decision — Questions reserved for decision in a trial with a jury.

645. (1) The trial of an accused shall proceed continuously subject to adjournment by the court.

(2) The judge may adjourn the trial from time to time in the same sittings.

(3) No formal adjournment of trial or entry thereof is required.

(4) The judge, in any case tried without a jury, may reserve his final decision on any question raised at the trial, and his decision, when given, shall be deemed to have been given at the trial.

(5) In any case to be tried with a jury, the judge before whom an accused is or is to be tried has jurisdiction, before any juror on a panel of jurors is called pursuant to subsection 631(3) and in the absence of any such juror, to deal with any matter that would ordinarily or necessarily be dealt with in the absence of the jury after it has been sworn. R.S. 1985, c. 27 (1st Supp.), s. 133.

Taking evidence.

646. On the trial of an accused for an indictable offence, the evidence of the witnesses for the prosecutor and the accused and the addresses of the prosecutor and the accused or counsel for the accused by way of summing up shall be taken in accordance with the provisions of Part XVIII relating to the taking of evidence at preliminary inquiries.

Separation of jurors — Keeping in charge — Non-compliance with subsection (2) — Empanelling new jury in certain cases — Refreshment and accommodation.

647. (1) The judge may, at any time before the jury retires to consider its verdict, permit the members of the jury to separate.

(2) Where permission to separate under subsection (1) cannot be given or is not given, the jury shall be kept under the charge of an officer of the court as the judge directs, and that officer shall prevent the jurors from communicating with anyone other than himself or another member of the jury without leave of the judge.

(3) Failure to comply with subsection (2) does not affect the validity of the proceedings.

(4) Where the fact that there has been a failure to comply with this section or section 648 is discovered before the verdict of the jury is returned, the judge may, if he considers that the failure to comply might lead to a miscarriage of justice, discharge the jury and

(*a*) direct that the accused be tried with a new jury during the same session or sittings of the court; or

(*b*) postpone the trial on such terms as justice may require.

(5) The judge shall direct the sheriff to provide the jurors who are sworn with suitable and sufficient refreshment, food and lodging while they are together until they have given their verdict.

Restriction on publication — Offence — "Newspaper".

648. (1) Where permission to separate is given to members of a jury under subsection 647(1), no information regarding any portion of the trial at which the jury is not present shall be published, after the permission is granted, in any newspaper or broadcast before the jury retires to consider its verdict.

(2) Every one who fails to comply with subsection (1) is guilty of an offence punishable on summary conviction.

(3) In this section, "newspaper" has the same meaning as in section 297.

Disclosure of jury proceedings.

649. Every member of a jury who, except for the purposes of

(*a*) an investigation of an alleged offence under subsection 139(2) in relation to a juror, or

(*b*) giving evidence in criminal proceedings in relation to such an offence,

discloses any information relating to the proceedings of the jury when it was absent from the courtroom that was not subsequently disclosed in open court is guilty of an offence punishable on summary conviction.

Accused to be present — Exceptions — To make defence.

650. (1) Subject to subsection (2), an accused other than a corporation shall be present in court during the whole of his trial.

(2) The court may

(*a*) cause the accused to be removed and to be kept out of court, where he misconducts himself by interrupting the proceedings so that to continue the proceedings in his presence would not be feasible;

(*b*) permit the accused to be out of court during the whole or any part of his trial on such conditions as the court considers proper; or

(*c*) cause the accused to be removed and to be kept out of court during the trial of an issue as to whether the accused is unfit to stand trial, where it is satisfied that failure to do so might have an adverse effect on the mental condition of the accused.

(3) An accused is entitled, after the close of the case for the prosecution, to make full answer and defence personally or by counsel. S.C. 1991, c. 43, s. 9, Sch., item 4.

Summing up by prosecutor — Summing up by accused — Accused's right of reply — Prosecutor's right of reply where more than one accused.

651. (1) Where an accused, or any one of several accused being tried together, is defended by counsel, the counsel shall, at the end of the case for the prosecution, declare whether or not he intends to adduce evidence on behalf of the accused for whom he appears and if he does not announce his intention to adduce evidence, the prosecutor may address the jury by way of summing up.

(2) Counsel for the accused or the accused, where he is not defended by counsel, is entitled, if he thinks fit, to open the case for the defence, and after the conclusion of that opening to examine such witnesses as he thinks fit, and when all the evidence is concluded to sum up the evidence.

(3) Where no witnesses are examined for an accused, he or his counsel is entitled to address the jury last, but otherwise counsel for the prosecution is entitled to address the jury last.

(4) Where two or more accused are tried jointly and witnesses are examined for any of them, all the accused or their respective counsel are required to address the jury before it is addressed by the prosecutor.

View — Directions to prevent communication — Who shall attend.

652. (1) The judge may, where it appears to be in the interests of justice, at any time after the jury has been sworn and before it give its verdict, direct the jury to have a view of any place, thing or person, and shall give directions respecting the manner in which, and the persons by whom, the place, thing or person shall be shown to the jury, and may for that purpose adjourn the trial.

(2) Where a view is ordered under subsection (1), the judge shall give any directions that he considers necessary for the purpose of preventing undue communication by any person with members of the jury, but failure to comply with any directions given under this subsection does not affect the validity of the proceedings.

(3) Where a view is ordered under subsection (1) the accused and the judge shall attend.

Disagreement of jury — Discretion not reviewable.

653. (1) Where the judge is satisfied that the jury is unable to agree on its verdict and that further detention of the jury would be useless, he may in his discretion discharge that jury and direct a new jury to be empanelled during the sittings of the court, or may adjourn the trial on such terms as justice may require.

(2) A discretion that is exercised under subsection (1) by a judge is not reviewable.

Proceeding on Sunday, etc., not invalid.

654. The taking of the verdict of a jury and any proceeding incidental thereto is not invalid by reason only that it is done on Sunday or on a holiday.

Evidence on Trial

Admissions at trial.

655. Where an accused is on trial for an indictable offence, he or his counsel may admit any fact alleged against him for the purpose of dispensing with proof thereof.

Evidence of stealing ores or minerals.

656. In any proceeding in respect of theft of ores or minerals, the possession, contrary to any law in that behalf, of smelted gold or silver, gold-bearing quartz, or unsmelted or unmanufactured gold or silver, by an operator, workman or labourer actively engaged in or on a mine, is, in the absence of any evidence to the contrary, proof that the gold, silver or quartz was stolen by him.

Use in evidence of statement by accused.

657. A statement made by an accused under subsection 541(2) and purporting to be signed by the justice before whom it was made may be given in evidence against the accused at his trial without proof of the signature of the justice, unless it is proved that the justice by whom the statement purports to be signed did not sign it.

Proof of ownership and value of property — Statements to be made — Notice of intention to produce affidavit or solemn declaration — Attendance for examination.

657.1 (1) In any proceedings in respect of an offence under section 334, 348, 354, 362 or 380, an affidavit or a selmn declaration of a person who claims to be the lawful owner or person lawfully entitled to possession of property that was the subject-matter of the offence, containing the statement referred to in subsection (2), shall be admissible in evidence and, in the absence of evidence to the contrary, is evidence of the statements contained in the affidavit or solemn declaration without proof of the signature of the person appearing to have signed the affidavit or solemn declaration.

(2) For the purposes of subsection (1), a person shall state in an affidavit or a solemn declaration

(*a*) that the person is the lawful owner or is lawfully entitled to possession of the property;

(*b*) the value of the property;

(*c*) that the person has been deprived of the property by fraudulent means or otherwise without the lawful consent of the person; and

(*d*) any facts within the personal knowledge of the person relied on to justify the statements referred to in paragraphs (*a*) to (*c*).

(3) Unless the court orders otherwise, no affidavit or solemn declaration shall be received in evidence pursuant to subsection (1) unless the prosecutor has, before the trial or other proceeding, given to the accused a copy of the affidavit or solemn declaration and reasonable notice of intention to produce it in evidence.

(4) Notwithstanding subsection (1), the court may require the person who appears to have signed an affidavit or solemn declaration referred to in that subsection to appear before it for examination or cross-examination in respect of the issue of proof of any of the statements contained in the affidavit or solemn declaration. R.S. 1985, c. 23 (4th Supp.), s. 3.

Children and Young Persons

Proof of age — Inference from appearance.

658. (1) In any proceedings to which this Act applies, an entry or record of an incorporated society or its officers who have had the control or care of a child or young person at or about the time the child or young person was brought to Canada is evidence of the age of the child or young person if the entry or record was made before the time when the offence is alleged to have been committed.

(2) In the absence of other evidence, or by way of corroboration of other

evidence, a jury, judge, justice or magistrate, as the case may be, may infer the age of a child or young person from his appearance.

Corroboration

659. [Repealed R.S. 1985, c. 19 (3rd Supp.), s. 15.]

Verdicts

Full offence charged, attempt proved.

660. Where the complete commission of an offence charged is not proved but the evidence establishes an attempt to commit the offence, the accused may be convicted of the attempt.

Attempt charged, full offence proved — Conviction a bar.

661. (1) Where an attempt to commit an offence is charged but the evidence establishes the commission of the complete offence, the accused is not entitled to be acquitted, but the jury may convict him of the attempt unless the judge presiding at the trial, in his discretion, discharges the jury from giving a verdict and directs that the accused be indicted for the complete offence.

(2) An accused who is convicted under this section is not liable to be tried again for the offence that he was charged with attempting to commit.

Offence charged, part only proved — First degree murder charged — Conviction for infanticide or manslaughter on charge of murder — Conviction for concealing body of child where murder or infanticide charged — Conviction for dangerous driving where manslaughter charged — Conviction for break and enter with intent.

662. (1) A count in an indictment is divisible and where the commission of the offence charged, as described in the enactment creating it or as charged in the count, includes the commission of another offence, whether punishable by indictment or on summary conviction, the accused may be convicted

(*a*) of an offence so included that is proved, notwithstanding that the whole offence that is charged is not proved; or

(*b*) of an attempt to commit an offence so included.

(2) For greater certainty and without limiting the generality of subsection (1), where a count charges first degree murder and the evidence does not prove first degree murder but proves second degree murder or an attempt to commit second degree murder, the jury may find the accused not guilty of first degree murder but guilty of second degree murder or an attempt to commit second degree murder, as the case may be.

(3) Subject to subsection (4), where a count charges murder and the evidence proves manslaughter or infanticide but does not prove murder, the jury may

find the accused not guilty of murder but guilty of manslaughter or infanticide, but shall not on that count find the accused guilty of any other offence.

(4) Where a count charges the murder of a child or infanticide and the evidence proves the commission of an offence under section 243 but does not prove murder or infanticide, the jury may find the accused not guilty of murder or infanticide, as the case may be, but guilty of an offence under section 243.

(5) For greater certainty, where a count charges an offence under section 220, 221 or 236 arising out of the operation of a motor vehicle or the navigation or operation of a vessel or aircraft, and the evidence does not prove such offence but does prove an offence under section 249, the accused may be convicted of an offence under section 249.

(6) Where a count charges an offence under paragraph 348(1)(*b*) and the evidence does not prove such offence but does prove an offence under paragraph 348(1)(*a*), the accused may be convicted of an offence under paragraph 348(1)(*a*). R.S. 1985, c. 27 (1st Supp.), s. 134.

No acquittal unless act or omission not wilful.

663. Where a female person is charged with infanticide and the evidence establishes that she caused the death of her child but does not establish that, at the time of the act or omission by which she caused the death of the child,

(*a*) she was not fully recovered from the effects of giving birth to the child or from the effect of lactation consequent on the birth of the child, and

(*b*) the balance of her mind was, at that time, disturbed by reason of the effect of giving birth to the child or of the effect of lactation consequent on the birth of the child,

she may be convicted unless the evidence establishes that the act or omission was not wilful.

Previous Convictions

No reference to previous conviction.

664. No indictment in respect of an offence for which, by reason of previous convictions, a greater punishment may be imposed shall contain any reference to previous convictions.

Previous conviction — Procedure — Where hearing ex parte — Corporations — Section does not apply.

665. (1) Subject to subsections (3) and (4), where an accused or a defendant is convicted of an offence for which a greater punishment may be imposed by reason of previous convictions, no greater punishment shall be imposed on him by reason thereof unless the prosecutor satisfies the court that the accused or defendant, before making his plea, was notified that a greater punishment would be sought by reason thereof.

(2) Where an accused or a defendant is convicted of an offence for which a greater punishment may be imposed by reason of previous convictions, the court shall, on application by the prosecutor and on being satisfied that the accused or defendant was notified in accordance with subsection (1), ask the accused or defendant whether he was previously convicted and, if he does not admit that he was previously convicted, evidence of previous convictions may be adduced.

(3) Where a summary conviction court holds a trial pursuant to subsection 803(2) and convicts the defendant, the court may, whether or not the defendant was notified that a greater punishment would be sought by reason of a previous conviction, make inquiries and hear evidence with respect to previous convictions of the defendant and if any such conviction is proved may impose a greater punishment by reason thereof.

(4) Where, pursuant to section 623, the court proceeds with the trial of a corporation that has not appeared and pleaded and convicts the corporation, the court may, whether or not the corporation was notified that a greater punishment would be sought by reason of a previous conviction, make inquiries and hear evidence with respect to previous convictions of the corporation and if any such conviction is proved may impose a greater punishment by reason thereof.

(5) This section does not apply to a person referred to in paragraph 742(*a*.1). R.S. 1985, c. 27 (1st Supp.), s. 135.

Evidence of character.

666. Where, at a trial, the accused adduces evidence of his good character, the prosecutor may, in answer thereto, before a verdict is returned, adduce evidence of the previous conviction of the accused for any offences, including any previous conviction by reason of which a greater punishment may be imposed.

Proof of previous conviction — Idem — Proof of identity — Attendance and right to cross-examine — Notice of intention to produce certificate — "Fingerprint examiner".

667. (1) In any proceedings,

(*a*) a certificate setting out with reasonable particularity the conviction, discharge under section 736 or the conviction and sentence in Canada of an offender signed by

(i) the person who made the conviction or order for the discharge,

(ii) the clerk of the court in which the conviction or order for the discharge was made, or

(iii) a fingerprint examiner,

is, on proof that the accused or defendant is the offender referred to in the certificate, evidence that the accused or defendant was so convicted, so discharged or so convicted and sentenced without proof of the signature or the official character of the person appearing to have signed the certificate;

(*b*) evidence that the fingerprints of the accused or defendant are the same as the fingerprints of the offender whose fingerprints are reproduced in or attached to a certificate issued under subparagraph (*a*)(iii) is, in the absence of evidence to the contrary, proof that the accused or defendant is the offender referred to in that certificate;

(*c*) a certificate of a fingerprint examiner stating that he has compared the fingerprints reproduced in or attached to that certificate with the fingerprints reproduced in or attached to a certificate issued under subparagraph (*a*)(iii) and that they are those of the same person is evidence of the statements contained in the certificate without proof of the signature or the official character of the person appearing to have signed the certificate; and

(*d*) a certificate under subparagraph (*a*)(iii) may be in Form 44, and a certificate under paragraph (*c*) may be in Form 45.

(2) In any proceedings, a copy of the summary conviction or discharge under section 736 in Canada of an offender, signed by the person who made the conviction or order for the discharge or by the clerk of the court in which the conviction or order for the discharge was made, is, on proof that the accused or defendant is the offender referred to in the copy of the summary conviction, evidence of the conviction or discharge under section 736 of the accused or defendant, without proof of the signature or the official character of the person appearing to have signed it.

(2.1) In any summary conviction proceedings, where the name of a defendant is similar to the name of an offender referred to in a certificate made under subparagraph (1)(*a*)(i) or (ii) in respect of a summary conviction or referred to in a copy of a summary conviction mentioned in subsection (2), that similarity of name is, in the absence of evidence to the contrary, evidence that the defendant is the offender referred to in the certificate or the copy of the summary conviction.

(3) An accused against whom a certificate issued under subparagraph (1)(*a*)(iii) or paragraph (1)(*c*) is produced may, with leave of the court, require the attendance of the person who signed the certificate for the purposes of cross-examination.

(4) No certificate issued under subparagraph (1)(*a*)(iii) or paragraph (1)(*c*) shall be received in evidence unless the party intending to produce it has given to the accused reasonable notice of his intention together with a copy of the certificate.

(5) In this section "fingerprint examiner" means a person designated as such for the purposes of this section by the Solicitor General of Canada. R.S. 1985, c. 27 (1st Supp.), s. 136.

Sentence

Accused found guilty may speak to sentence.

668. Where a jury finds an accused guilty, or where an accused pleads guilty, the judge presiding at the trial shall ask the accused whether he has anything to say before sentence is passed upon him, but an omission to comply with this section does not affect the validity of the proceedings.

Sentence justified by any count.

669. Where one sentence is passed on a verdict of guilty on two or more counts of an indictment, the sentence is good if any of the counts would have justified the sentence.

Jurisdiction

Jurisdiction — Adjournment.

669.1 (1) Where any judge, court or provincial court judge by whom or which the plea of the accused or defendant to an offence was taken has not commenced to hear evidence, any judge, court or provincial court judge having jurisdiction to try the accused or defendant has jurisdiction for the purpose of the hearing and adjudication.

(2) Any court, judge or provincial court judge having jurisdiction to try an accused or a defendant, or any clerk or other proper officer of the court, or in the case of an offence punishable on summary conviction, any justice, may, at any time before or after the plea of the accused or defendant is taken, adjourn the proceedings. R.S. 1985, c. 27 (1st Supp.), s. 137.

Continuation of proceedings — Where adjudication is made — Where no adjudication is made.

669.2 (1) Subject to this section, where an accused or a defendant is being tried by

(*a*) a judge or provincial court judge,

(*b*) a justice or other person who is, or is a member of, a summary conviction court, or

(*c*) a court composed of a judge and jury,

as the case may be, and the judge, provincial court judge, justice or other person dies or is for any reason unable to continue, the proceedings may be continued before another judge, provincial court judge, justice or other person, as the case may be, who has jurisdiction to try the accused or defendant.

(2) Where a verdict was rendered by a jury or an adjudication was made by a judge, provincial court judge, justice or other person before whom the trial was commenced, the judge, provincial court judge, justice or other person before whom the proceedings are continued shall, without further election by

an accused, impose the punishment or make the order that is authorized by law in the circumstances.

(3) Where the trial was commenced but no adjudication was made or verdict rendered, the judge, provincial court judge, justice or other person before whom the proceedings are continued shall, without further election by an accused, commence the trial again as if no evidence had been taken. R.S. 1985, c. 27 (1st Supp.), s. 137.

Formal Defects in Jury Process

Judgment not to be stayed on certain grounds.

670. Judgment shall not be stayed or reversed after verdict on an indictment

(*a*) by reason of any irregularity in the summoning or empanelling of the jury; or

(*b*) for the reason that a person who served on the jury was not returned as a juror by a sheriff or other officer.

Directions respecting jury or jurors directory.

671. No omission to observe the directions contained in any Act with respect to the qualification, selection, balloting or distribution of jurors, the preparation of the jurors' book, the selecting of jury lists or the drafting of panels from the jury lists is a ground for impeaching or quashing a verdict rendered in criminal proceedings.

Saving powers of court.

672. Nothing in this Act alters, abridges or affects any power or authority that a court or judge had immediately before April 1, 1955, or any practice or form that existed immediately before April 1, 1955, with respect to trials by jury, jury process, juries or jurors, except where the power or authority, practice or form is expressly altered by or is inconsistent with this Act.

PART XX.1

MENTAL DISORDER

Interpretation

Definitions — "accused" — "assessment" — "chairperson" — "court" — "disposition" — "dual status offender" — "hospital" — "medical practitioner" — "party" — "placement decision" — "prescribed" — "Review Board" — "Verdict of not criminally responsible on account of mental disorder".

672.1 In this Part,

"accused" includes a defendant in summary conviction proceedings and an accused in respect of whom a verdict of not criminally responsible on account of mental disorder has been rendered;

"assessment" means an assessment by a medical practitioner of the mental condition of the accused pursuant to an assessment order made under section 672.11, and any incidental observation or examination of the accused;

"chairperson" includes any alternate that the chairperson of a Review Board may designate to act on the chairperson's behalf;

"court" includes a summary conviction court as defined in section 785, a judge, a justice and a judge of the court of appeal as defined in section 673;

"disposition" means an order made by a court or Review Board under section 672.54 or an order made by a court under section 672.58;

"dual status offender" means an offender who is subject to a sentence of imprisonment in respect of one offence and a custodial disposition under paragraph 672.54(*c*) in respect of another offence;

"hospital" means a place in a province that is designated by the Minister of Health for the province for the custody, treatment or assessment of an accused in respect of whom an assessment order, a disposition or a placement decision is made.

"medical practitioner" means a person who is entitled to practise medicine by the laws of a province;

"party", in relation to proceedings of a court or Review Board to make or review a disposition, means

(*a*) the accused,

(*b*) the person in charge of the hospital where the accused is detained or is to attend pursuant to an assessment order or a disposition,

(*c*) an Attorney General designated by the court or Review Board under subsection 672.5(3),

(*d*) any interested person designated by the court or Review Board under subsection 672.5(4), or

(*e*) where the disposition is to be made by a court, the prosecutor of the charge against the accused;

"placement decision" means a decision by a Review Board under subsection 672.68(2) as to the place of custody of a dual status offender;

"prescribed" means prescribed by regulations made by the Governor in Council under section 672.95;

"Review Board" means the Review Board established or designated for a province pursuant to subsection 672.38(1);

"verdict of not criminally responsible on account of mental disorder" means a verdict that the accused committed the act or made the omission that formed the basis of the offence with which the accused is charged but is not criminally responsible on account of mental disorder. 1991, c. 43, s. 4.

Assessment Orders

Assessment order.

672.11 A court having jurisdiction over an accused in respect of an offence may order an assessment of the mental condition of the accused, if it has reasonable grounds to believe that such evidence is necessary to determine

(*a*) whether the accused is unfit to stand trial;

(*b*) whether the accused was, at the time of the commission of the alleged offence, suffering from a mental disorder so as to be exempt from criminal responsibility by virtue of subsection 16(1);

(*c*) whether the balance of the mind of the accused was disturbed at the time of commission of the alleged offence, where the accused is a female person charged with an offence arising out of the death of her newly-born child;

(*d*) the appropriate disposition to be made, where a verdict of not criminally responsible on account of mental disorder or unfit to stand trial has been rendered in respect of the accused; or

(*e*) whether an order should be made under subsection 736.11(1) to detain the accused in a treatment facility, where the accused has been convicted of the offence. 1991, c. 43, s. 4.

Where court may order assessment — Limitation on prosecutor's application for assessment of fitness — Limitation on prosecutor's application for assessment.

672.12 (1) The court may make an assessment order at any stage of proceedings against the accused of its own motion, on application of the accused or, subject to subsections (2) and (3), on application of the prosecutor.

(2) Where the prosecutor applies for an assessment in order to determine whether the accused is unfit to stand trial for an offence that is prosecuted by way of summary conviction, the court may only order the assessment if

(*a*) the accused raised the issue of fitness; or

(*b*) the prosecutor satisfies the court that there are reasonable grounds to doubt that the accused is fit to stand trial.

(3) Where the prosecutor applies for an assessment in order to determine whether the accused was suffering from a mental disorder at the time of the offence so as to be exempt from criminal responsibility, the court may only order the assessment if

(*a*) the accused puts his or her mental capacity for criminal intent into issue; or

(*b*) the prosecutor satisfies the court that there are reasonable grounds to doubt that the accused is criminally responsible for the alleged offence, on account of mental disorder. 1991, c. 43, s. 4.

Contents of assessment order — Form.

672.13 (1) An assessment order must specify

(*a*) the service that or the person who is to make the assessment, or the hospital where it is to be made;

(*b*) whether the accused is to be detained in custody while the order is in force; and

(*c*) the period that the order is to be in force, including the time required for the assessment and for the accused to travel to and from the place where the assessment is to be made.

(2) An assessment order may be in Form 48. 1991, c. 43, s. 4.

General rule for period — Exception in fitness cases — Exception for compelling circumstances.

672.14 (1) An assessment order shall not be in force for more than thirty days.

(2) No assessment order to determine whether the accused is unfit to stand trial shall be in force for more than five days, excluding holidays and the time required for the accused to travel to and from the place where the assessment is to be made, unless the accused and the prosecutor agree to a longer period not exceeding thirty days.

(3) Notwithstanding subsections (1) and (2), a court may make an assessment order that remains in force for sixty days where the court is satisfied that compelling circumstances exist that warrant it. 1991, c 43, s. 4.

Extensions — Maximum duration of extensions — Presumption of custody in certain circumstances.

672.15 (1) Subject to subsection (2), a court may extend an assessment order, of its own motion or on the application of the accused or the prosecutor made during or after the period that the order is in force, for any further period that is required, in its opinion, to complete the assessment of the accused.

(2) No extension of an assessment order shall exceed thirty days, and the period of the initial order together with all extensions shall not exceed sixty days.

(3) An accused who is charged with an offence described in any of paragraphs 515(6)(*a*) to (*d*) in the circumstances described in that paragraph, or an offence described in subsection 522(2), shall be detained in custody pursuant to an assessment order, unless the accused shows that custody is not justified under the terms of that paragraph or subsection. 1991, c. 43, s. 4.

Presumption against custody — Report of medical practitioner.

672.16 (1) Subject to subsection (3), an accused shall not be detained in custody pursuant to an assessment order unless

(*a*) the court is satisfied that on the evidence custody is necessary to assess the accused, or that on the evidence of a medical practitioner custody is desirable to assess the accused and the accused consents to custody;

(*b*) custody of the accused is required in respect of any other matter or by virtue of any other provision of this Act; or

(*c*) the prosecutor, having been given a reasonable opportunity to do so, shows that detention of the accused in custody is justified on either of the grounds set out in subsection 515(10).

(2) For the purposes of paragraph (1)(*a*), where the prosecutor and the accused agree, the evidence of a medical practitioner may be received in the form of a report in writing. 1991, c. 43, s. 4.

Assessment order takes precedence over bail hearing.

672.17 During the period that an assessment order of an accused charged with an offence is in force, no order for the interim release or detention of the accused may be made by virtue of Part XVI or section 679 in respect of that offence or an included offence. 1991, c. 43, s. 4.

Application to vary assessment order.

672.18 Where at any time while an assessment order made by a court is in force the prosecutor or an accused shows cause, the court may vary the terms of the order respecting the interim release or detention of the accused in such manner as it considers appropriate in the circumstances. 1991, c. 43, s. 4.

No treatment order on assessment.

672.19 No assessment order may direct that psychiatric or any other treatment of the accused be carried out, or direct the accused to submit to such treatment. 1991, c. 43, s. 4.

Assessment Reports

Assessment reports — Assessment report to be filed with court — Court to send assessment report to Review Board — Copies of reports to accused and prosecutor.

672.2 (1) An assessment order may require the person who makes the assessment to submit in writing an assessment report on the mental condition of the accused.

(2) An assessment report shall be filed with the court that ordered it, within the period fixed by the court.

(3) The court shall send to the Review Board without delay a copy of any report filed with it pursuant to subsection (2), to assist in determining the appropriate disposition to be made in respect of the accused.

(4) Subject to subsection 672.51(3), copies of any report filed with a court pursuant to subsection (2) shall be provided without delay to the prosecutor, the accused and any counsel representing the accused. 1991, c. 43, s. 4.

Protected Statements

Definition of "protected statement" — Protected statements not admissible against accused — Exceptions.

672.21 (1) In this section, "protected statement" means a statement made by the accused during the course and for the purposes of an assessment or treatment directed by a disposition, to the person specified in the assessment order or the disposition, or to anyone acting under that person's direction.

(2) No protected statement or reference to a protected statement made by an accused is admissible in evidence, without the consent of the accused, in any proceeding before a court, tribunal, body or person with jurisdiction to compel the production of evidence.

(3) Notwithstanding subsection (2), evidence of a protected statement is admissible for the purpose of

(*a*) determining whether the accused is unfit to stand trial;

(*b*) making a disposition or placement decision respecting the accused;

(*c*) finding whether the accused is a dangerous mentally disordered accused under section 672.65;

(*d*) determining whether the balance of the mind of the accused was disturbed at the time of commission of the alleged offence, where the accused is a female person charged with an offence arising out of the death of her newly-born child;

(*e*) determining whether the accused was, at the time of the commission of an alleged offence, suffering from automatism or a mental disorder so as to be exempt from criminal responsibility by virtue of subsection 16(1), if the accused puts his or her mental capacity for criminal intent into issue, or if the prosecutor raises the issue after verdict;

(*f*) challenging the credibility of an accused in any proceeding where the testimony of the accused is inconsistent in a material particular with a protected statement that the accused made previously; or

(*g*) establishing the perjury of an accused who is charged with perjury in respect of a statement made in any proceeding. 1991, c. 43, s. 4.

Fitness to Stand Trial

Presumption of fitness.

672.22 An accused is presumed fit to stand trial unless the court is satisfied on the balance of probabilities that the accused is unfit to stand trial. 1991, c. 43, s. 4.

Court may direct issue to be tried — Burden of proof.

672.23 (1) Where the court has reasonable grounds, at any stage of the proceedings before a verdict is rendered, to believe that the accused is unfit to stand trial, the court may direct, of its own motion or on application of the accused or the prosecutor, that the issue of fitness of the accused be tried.

(2) An accused or a prosecutor who makes an application under subsection (1) has the burden of proof that the accused is unfit to stand trial. 1991, c. 43, s. 4.

Counsel.

672.24 Where the court has reasonable grounds to believe that an accused is unfit to stand trial and the accused is not represented by counsel, the court shall order that the accused be represented by counsel. 1991, c. 43, s. 4.

Postponing trial of issue — Idem.

672.25 (1) The court shall postpone directing the trial of the issue of fitness of an accused in proceedings for an offence for which the accused may be prosecuted by indictment or that is punishable on summary conviction, until the prosecutor has elected to proceed by way of indictment or summary conviction.

(2) The court may postpone directing the trial of the issue of fitness of an accused

(*a*) where the issue arises before the close of the case for the prosecution at a preliminary inquiry, until a time that is not later than the time the accused is called on to answer to the charge; or

(*b*) where the issue arises before the close of the case for the prosecution at trial, until a time not later than the opening of the case for the defence or, on motion of the accused, any later time that the court may direct. 1991, c. 43, s. 4.

Trial of issue by judge and jury.

672.26 Where an accused is tried or is to be tried before a court composed of a judge and jury,

(*a*) if the judge directs that the issue of fitness of the accused be tried before the accused is given in charge to a jury for trial on the indictment, a jury composed of the number of jurors required in respect of the indictment in the province where the trial is to be held shall be sworn to try that issue and, with the consent of the accused, the issues to be tried on the indictment; and

(*b*) if the judge directs that the issue of fitness of the accused be tried after the accused has been given in charge to a jury for trial on the indictment, the jury shall be sworn to try that issue in addition to the issues in respect of which it is already sworn. 1991, c. 43, s. 4.

Trial of issue by court.

672.27 The court shall try the issue of fitness of an accused and render a verdict where the issue arises

(*a*) in respect of an accused who is tried or is to be tried before a court other than a court composed of a judge and jury; or

(*b*) before a court at a preliminary inquiry or at any other stage of the proceedings. 1991, c. 43, s. 4.

Proceeding continues where accused is fit.

672.28 Where the verdict on trial of the issue is that an accused is fit to stand trial, the arraignment, preliminary inquiry, trial or other stage of the proceeding shall continue as if the issue of fitness of the accused had never arisen. 1991, c. 43, s. 4.

Where continued detention in custody.

672.29 Where an accused is detained in custody on delivery of a verdict that the accused is fit to stand trial, the court may order the accused to be detained in a hospital until the completion of the trial, if the court has reasonable grounds to believe that the accused would become unfit to stand trial if released. 1991, c. 43, s. 4.

Acquittal.

672.3 Where the court has postponed directing the trial of the issue of fitness of an accused pursuant to subsection 672.25(2) and the accused is discharged or acquitted before the issue is tried, it shall not be tried. 1991, c. 43, s. 4.

Verdict of unfit to stand trial.

672.31 Where the verdict on trial of the issue is that an accused is unfit to stand trial, any plea that has been made shall be set aside and any jury shall be discharged. 1991, c. 43, s. 4.

Subsequent proceedings — Burden of proof.

672.32 (1) A verdict of unfit to stand trial shall not prevent the accused from being tried subsequently where the accused becomes fit to stand trial.

(2) The burden of proof that the accused has subsequently become fit to stand trial is on the party who asserts it, and is discharged by proof on the balance of probabilities. 1991, c. 43, s. 4.

***Prima facie* case to be made every two years — Court may order inquiry to be held — Burden of proof — Admissible evidence at an inquiry — Conduct of inquiry — Where *prima facie* case not made.**

672.33 (1) The court that has jurisdiction in respect of the offence charged against an accused who is found unfit to stand trial shall hold an inquiry, not later than two years after the verdict is rendered and every two years thereafter until the accused is acquitted pursuant to subsection (6) or tried, to decide whether sufficient evidence can be adduced at that time to put the accused on trial.

(2) On application of the accused, the court may order an inquiry under this section to be held at any time if it is satisfied, on the basis of the application and any written material submitted by the accused, that there is reason to doubt that there is a *prima facie* case against the accused.

(3) At an inquiry under this section, the burden of proof that sufficient evidence can be adduced to put the accused on trial is on the prosecutor.

(4) In an inquiry under this section, the court shall admit as evidence

(*a*) any affidavit containing evidence that would be admissible if given by the person making the affidavit as a witness in court; or

(*b*) any certified copy of the oral testimony given at a previous inquiry or hearing held before a court in respect of the offence with which the accused is charged.

(5) The court may determine the manner in which an inquiry under this section is conducted and may follow the practices and procedures in respect of a preliminary inquiry under Part XVIII where it concludes that the interests of justice so require.

(6) Where, on the completion of an inquiry under this section, the court is satisfied that sufficient evidence cannot be adduced to put the accused on trial, the court shall acquit the accused. 1991, c. 43, s. 4.

Verdict of Not Criminally Responsible on Account of Mental Disorder

Verdict of not criminally responsible on account of mental disorder.

672.34 Where the jury, or the judge or provincial court judge where there is no jury, finds that an accused committed the act or made the omission that formed the basis of the offence charged, but was at the time suffering from mental disorder so as to be exempt from criminal responsibility by virtue of subsection 16(1), the jury or the judge shall render a verdict that the accused committed the act or made the omission but is not criminally responsible on account of mental disorder. 1991, c. 43, s. 4.

Effect of verdict of not criminally responsible on account of mental disorder.

672.35 Where a verdict of not criminally responsible on account of mental disorder is rendered, the accused shall not be found guilty or convicted of the offence, but

(*a*) the accused may plead *autrefois acquit* in respect of any subsequent charge relating to that offence;

(*b*) any court may take the verdict into account in considering an application for judicial interim release or in considering what dispositions to make or sentence to impose for any other offence; and

(*c*) the National Parole Board or any provincial parole board may take the verdict into account in considering an application by the accused for parole or pardon in respect of any other offence. 1991, c. 43, s. 4.

Verdict not a previous conviction.

672.36 A verdict of not criminally responsible on account of mental disorder is not a previous conviction for the purposes of any offence under any Act of Parliament for which a greater punishment is provided by reason of previous convictions. 1991, c. 43, s. 4.

Definition of "application for federal employment" — Application for federal employment — Punishment.

672.37 (1) In this section, "application for federal employment" means an application form relating to

(*a*) employment in any department, as defined in section 2 of the *Financial Administration Act*;

(*b*) employment by any Crown corporation as defined in subsection 83(1) of the *Financial Administration Act*;

(*c*) enrolment in the Canadian Forces; or

(*d*) employment in connection with the operation of any work, undertaking or business that is within the legislative authority of Parliament.

(2) No application for federal employment shall contain any question that requires the applicant to disclose any charge or finding that the applicant committed an offence that resulted in a finding or a verdict of not criminally responsible on account of mental disorder if the applicant was discharged absolutely or is no longer subject to any disposition in respect of that offence.

(3) Any person who uses or authorizes the use of an application for federal employment that contravenes subsection (2) is guilty of an offence punishable on summary conviction. 1991, c. 43, s. 4.

Review Boards

Review boards to be established — Treated as provincial Board.

672.38 (1) A Review Board shall be established or designated for each province to make or review dispositions concerning any accused in respect of whom a verdict of not criminally responsible by reason of mental disorder or unfit to stand trial is rendered, and shall consist of not fewer than five members appointed by the lieutenant governor in council of the province.

(2) A Review Board shall be treated as having been established under the laws of the province. 1991, c. 43, s. 4.

Members of review board.

672.39 A Review Board must have at least one member who is entitled under the laws of a province to practise psychiatry and, where only one member is so entitled, at least one other member must have training and experience in the field of mental health, and be entitled under the laws of a province to practise medicine or psychology. 1991, c. 43, s. 4.

Chairperson of a review board — Transitional.

672.4 (1) Subject to subsection (2), the chairperson of a Review Board shall be a judge of the Federal Court or of a superior, district or county court of a province, or a person who is qualified for appointment to, or has retired from, such a judicial office.

(2) Where the chairperson of a Review Board that was established before the coming into force of subsection (1) is not a judge or other person referred to therein, the chairperson may continue to act until the expiration of his or her term of office if at least one other member of the Review Board is a judge or other person referred to in subsection (1) or is a member of the bar of the province. 1991, c. 43, s. 4.

Quorum of review board — Transitional.

672.41 (1) Subject to subsection (2), the quorum of a Review Board is constituted by the chairperson, a member who is entitled under the laws of a province to practise psychiatry, and any other member.

(2) Where the chairperson of a Review Board that was established before the coming into force of this section is not a judge or other person referred to in subsection 672.4(1), the quorum of the Review Board is constituted by the chairperson, a member who is entitled under the laws of a province to practise psychiatry, and a member who is a person referred to in that subsection or a member of the bar of the province. 1991, c. 43, s. 4.

Majority vote.

672.42 A decision of a majority of the members present and voting is the decision of a Review Board. 1991, c. 43, s. 4.

Powers of review boards.

672.43 At a hearing held by a Review Board to make a disposition or review a disposition in respect of an accused, the chairperson has all the powers that are conferred by sections 4 and 5 of the *Inquiries Act* on persons appointed as commissioners under Part I of that Act. 1991, c. 43, s. 4.

Rules of review board — Application and publication of rules — Regulations.

672.44 (1) A Review Board may, subject to the approval of the lieutenant governor in council of the province, make rules providing for the practice and procedure before the Review Board.

(2) The rules made by a Review Board under subsection (1) apply to any proceeding within its jurisdiction, and shall be published in the *Canada Gazette*.

(3) Notwithstanding anything in this section, the Governor in Council may make regulations to provide for the practice and procedure before Review Boards, in particular to make the rules of Review Boards uniform, and all regulations made under this subsection prevail over any rules made under subsection (1). 1991, c. 43, s. 4.

Disposition Hearings

Hearing to be held by a court — Disposition to be made.

672.45 (1) Where a verdict of not criminally responsible on account of mental disorder or unfit to stand trial is rendered in respect of an accused, the court may of its own motion, and shall on application by the accused or the prosecutor, hold a disposition hearing.

(2) At a disposition hearing, the court shall make a disposition in respect of the accused, if it is satisfied that it can readily do so and that a disposition should be made without delay. 1991, c. 43, s. 4.

Status quo pending review board hearing — Variation of order.

672.46 (1) Where the court does not make a disposition in respect of the accused at a disposition hearing, any order for the interim release or detention of the accused or any appearance notice, promise to appear, summons, undertaking or recognizance in respect of the accused that is in force at the time the verdict of not criminally responsible on account of mental disorder or unfit to stand trial is rendered continues in force, subject to its terms, until the Review Board makes a disposition.

(2) Notwithstanding subsection (1), a court may, on cause being shown, vacate any order, appearance notice, promise to appear, summons, undertaking or recognizance referred to in that subsection and make any other order for the interim release to detention of the accused that the court considers to be appropriate in the circumstances, including an order directing that the accused be detained in custody in a hospital pending a disposition by the Review Board in respect of the accused. 1991, c. 43, s. 4.

Review board to make disposition where court does not — Extension of time for hearing — Where disposition made by court.

672.47 (1) Where a verdict of not criminally responsible on account of mental disorder or unfit to stand trial is rendered and the court makes no disposition in respect of an accused, the Review Board shall, as soon as is practicable but not later than forty-five days after the verdict was rendered, hold a hearing and make a disposition.

(2) Where the court is satisfied that there are exceptional circumstances that warrant it, the court may extend the time for holding a hearing under subsection (1) to a maximum of ninety days after the verdict was rendered.

(3) Where a court makes a disposition under section 672.54 other than an absolute discharge in respect of an accused, the Review Board shall hold a hearing on a day not later than the day on which the disposition ceases to be in force, and not later than ninety days after the disposition was made, and shall make a disposition in respect of the accused. 1991, c. 43, s. 4.

Review board to determine fitness — Review Board shall send accused to court — Chairperson may send accused to court.

672.48 (1) Where a Review Board holds a hearing to make or review a disposition in respect of an accused who has been found unfit to stand trial, it shall determine whether in its opinion the accused is fit to stand trial at the time of the hearing.

(2) If a Review Board determines that the accused is fit to stand trial, it shall order that the accused be sent back to court, and the court shall try the issue and render a verdict.

(3) The chairperson of a Review Board may, with the consent of the accused and the person in charge of the hospital where an accused is being detained, order that the accused be sent back to court for trial of the issue of whether the accused is unfit to stand trial, where the chairperson is of the opinion that

(*a*) the accused is fit to stand trial, and

(*b*) the Review Board will not hold a hearing to make or review a disposition in respect of the accused within a reasonable period. 1991, c. 43, s. 4.

Continued detention in hospital — Copy of disposition to be sent to court.

672.49 (1) In a disposition made pursuant to section 672.47 the Review Board or chairperson may require the accused to continue to be detained in a hospital until the court determines whether the accused is fit to stand trial, if the Review Board or chairperson has reasonable grounds to believe that the accused would become unfit to stand trial if released.

(2) The Review Board or chairperson shall send a copy of a disposition made pursuant to section 672.47 without delay to the court having jurisdiction over the accused and to the Attorney General of the province where the accused is to be tried. 1991, c. 43, s. 4.

Procedure at disposition hearing — Hearing to be informal — Attorneys General may be parties — Interested person may be a party — Notice of hearing — Order excluding the public — Right to counsel — Assigning counsel — Right of accused to be present — Removal or absence of accused — Rights of parties at hearing — Request to compel attendance of witnesses.

672.5 (1) A hearing held by a court or Review Board to make or review a disposition in respect of an accused shall be held in accordance with this section.

(2) The hearing may be conducted in as informal a manner as is appropriate in the circumstances.

(3) On application, the court or Review Board shall designate as a party the Attorney General of the province where the disposition is to be made and, where an accused is transferred from another province, the Attorney General of the province from which the accused is transferred.

(4) The court or Review Board may designate as a party any person who has a substantial interest in protecting the interests of the accused, if the court or Review Board is of the opinion that it is just to do so.

(5) Notice of the hearing shall be given to the parties, the Attorney General of the province where the diposition is to be made and, where the accused is transferred to another province, the Attorney General of the province from which the accused is transferred, within the time and in the manner prescribed, or within the time and in the manner fixed by the rules of the court or Review Board.

(6) Where the court or Review Board considers it to be in the best interests of the accused and not contrary to the public interest, the court or Review Board may order the public or any members of the public to be excluded from the hearing or any part of the hearing.

(7) The accused or any other party has the right to be represented by counsel.

(8) The court or Review Board shall, if an accused is not represented by counsel, assign counsel to act for any accused

(*a*) who has been found unfit to stand trial; or

(*b*) wherever the interests of justice so require.

(9) Subject to subsection (10), the accused has the right to be present during the whole of the hearing.

(10) The court or the chairperson of the Review Board may

(*a*) permit the accused to be absent during the whole or any part of the hearing on such conditions as the court or chairperson considers proper; or

(*b*) cause the accused to be removed and barred from re-entry for the whole or any part of the hearing

(i) where the accused interrupts the hearing so that to continue in the presence of the accused would not be feasible,

(ii) on being satisfied that failure to do so would likely endanger the life or safety of another person or would seriously impair the treatment or recovery of the accused, or

(iii) in order to hear, in the absence of the accused, evidence, oral or written submissions, or the cross-examination of any witness concerning whether grounds exist for removing the accused pursuant to subparagraph (ii).

(11) Any party may adduce evidence, make oral or written submissions, call witnesses and cross-examine any witness called by any other party and, on application, cross-examine any person who made an assessment report that was submitted to the court or Review Board in writing.

(12) A party may not compel the attendance of witnesses, but may request the court or the chairperson of the Review Board to do so. 1991, c. 43, s. 4.

Definition of "disposition information" — Disposition information to be made available to parties — Exception where disclosure dangerous to any person — Idem — Exception where disclosure unnecessary or prejudicial — Exclusion of certain persons from hearing — Prohibition of disclosure in certain cases — Idem — Information to be made available to specified persons — Disclosure for research or statistical purposes — Prohibition on publication — Powers of courts not limited.

672.51 (1) In this section, "disposition information" means all or part of an assessment report submitted to the court or Review Board and any other written information before the court or Review Board about the accused that is relevant to making a disposition.

(2) Subject to this section, all disposition information shall be made available for inspection by, and the court or Review Board shall provide a copy of it to, each party and any counsel representing the accused.

(3) The court or Review Board shall withhold some or all of the disposition information from an accused where it is satisfied, on the basis of that information and the evidence or report of the medical practitioner responsible for the assessment or treatment of the accused, that disclosure of the information would be likely to endanger the life or safety of another person or would seriously impair the treatment or recovery of the accused.

(4) Notwithstanding subsection (3), the court or Review Board may release some or all of the disposition information to an accused where the interests of justice make disclosure essential in its opinion.

(5) The court or Review Board shall withold disposition information from a party other than the accused or an Attorney General, where disclosure to that party, in the opinion of the court or Review Board, is not necessary to the proceeding and may be prejudicial to the accused.

(6) A court of Review Board that withholds disposition information from

the accused or any other party pursuant to subsection (3) or (5) shall exclude the accused or the other party, as the case may be, from the hearing during

(*a*) the oral presentation of that disposition information; or

(*b*) the questioning by the court or Review Board or the cross-examination of any person concerning that disposition information.

(7) No disposition information shall be made available for inspection or disclosed to any person who is not a party to the proceedings

(*a*) where the disposition information has been withheld from the accused or any other party pursuant to subsection (3) or (5); or

(*b*) where the court or Review Board is of the opinion that disclosure of the disposition information would be seriously prejudicial to the accused and that, in the circumstances, protection of the accused takes precedence over the public interest in disclosure.

(8) No part of the record of the proceedings in respect of which the accused was excluded pursuant to subparagraph 672.5(10)(*b*)(ii) or (iii) shall be made available for inspection to the accused or to any person who is not a party to the proceedings.

(9) Notwithstanding subsections (7) and (8), the court or Review Board may make any disposition information, or a copy of it, available on request to any person or member of a class of persons

(*a*) that has a valid interest in the information for research or statistical purposes, where the court or Review Board is satisfied that disclosure is in the public interest;

(*b*) that has a valid interest in the information for the purposes of the proper administration of justice; or

(*c*) that the accused requests or authorizes in writing to inspect it, where the court or Review Board is satisfied that the person will not disclose or give to the accused a copy of any disposition information withheld from the accused pursuant to subsection (3) or (5), or of any part of the record of proceedings referred to in subsection (8), or that the reasons for withholding that information from the accused no longer exist.

(10) A person to whom the court or Review Board makes disposition information available under paragraph (9)(*a*) may disclose it for research or statistical purposes, but not in any form or manner that could reasonably be expected to identify any person to whom it relates.

(11) No person shall publish in any newspaper within the meaning of section 297 or broadcast

(*a*) any disposition information that is prohibited from being disclosed pursuant to subsection (7); or

(*b*) any part of the record of the proceedings in respect of which the accused was excluded pursuant to subparagraph 672.5(10)(*b*)(ii) or (iii).

(12) Except as otherwise provided in this section, nothing in this section

limits the powers that a court may exercise apart from this section. 1991, c. 43, s. 4.

Record of proceedings — Transmittal of transcript to Review Board — Reasons for disposition and copies to be provided.

672.52 (1) The court or Review Board shall cause a record of the proceedings of its disposition hearings to be kept, and include in the record any assessment report submitted.

(2) Where a court makes a disposition, it shall send without delay a transcript of the disposition hearing, any document or information relating thereto in the possession of the court, and all exhibits filed with the court or copies of those exhibits, to the Review Board that has jurisdiction in respect of the matter.

(3) The court or Review Board shall state its reasons for making a disposition in the record of the proceedings, and shall provide every party with a copy of the disposition and those reasons. 1991, c. 43, s. 4.

Proceedings not invalid.

672.53 Any procedural irregularity in relation to a disposition hearing does not affect the validity of the hearing unless it causes the accused substantial prejudice. 1991, c. 43, s. 4.

Dispositions by a Court or Review Board

Terms of Dispositions

Dispositions that may be made.

672.54 Where a court or Review Board makes a disposition pursuant to subsection 672.45(2) or section 672.47, it shall, taking into consideration the need to protect the public from dangerous persons, the mental condition of the accused, the reintegration of the accused into society and the other needs of the accused, make one of the following dispositions that is the least onerous and least restrictive to the accused:

(*a*) where a verdict of not criminally responsible on account of mental disorder has been rendered in respect of the accused and, in the opinion of the court or Review Board, the accused is not a signficant threat to the safety of the public, by order, direct that the accused be discharged absolutely;

(*b*) by order, direct that the accused be discharged subject to such conditions as the court or Review Board considers appropriate; or

(*c*) by order, direct that the accused be detained in custody in a hospital, subject to such conditions as the court or Review Board considers appropriate. 1991, c. 43, s. 4.

Treatment not a condition — Effective period of disposition.

672.55 (1) No disposition made under section 672.54 shall direct that any psychiatric or other treatment of the accused be carried out or that the accused submit to such treatment.

(2) No disposition made under paragraph 672.54(*c*) by a court shall continue in force for more than ninety days after the day that it is made. 1991, c. 43, s. 4.

Delegated authority to vary restrictions on liberty of accused — Notice to accused and Review Board of increase in restrictions.

672.56 (1) A Review Board that makes a disposition in respect of an accused under paragraph 672.54(*b*) or (*c*) may delegate to the person in charge of the hospital authority to direct that the restrictions on the liberty of the accused be increased or decreased within any limits and subject to any conditions set out in that disposition, and any direction so made is deemed for the purposes of this Act to be a disposition made by the Review Board.

(2) A person who increases the restrictions on the liberty of the accused significantly pursuant to authority delegated to the person by a Review Board shall

(*a*) make a record of the increased restrictions on the file of the accused; and

(*b*) give notice of the increase as soon as is practicable to the accused and, if the increased restrictions remain in force for a period exceeding seven days, to the Review Board. 1991, c. 43, s. 4.

Warrant of committal.

672.57 Where the court or Review Board makes a disposition under paragraph 672.54(*c*), it shall issue a warrant of committal of the accused, which may be in Form 49. 1991, c. 43, s. 4.

Treatment disposition.

672.58 Where a verdict of unfit to stand trial is rendered and the court has not made a disposition under section 672.54 in respect of an accused, the court may, on application by the prosecutor, by order, direct that treatment of the accused be carried out for a specified period not exceeding sixty days, subject to such conditions as the court considers appropriate and, where the accused is not detained in custody, direct that the accused submit to that treatment by the person or at the hospital specified. 1991, c. 43, s. 4.

Criteria for disposition — Evidence required.

672.59 (1) No disposition may be made under section 672.58 unless the court is satisfied, on the basis of the testimony of a medical practitioner, that a specific treatment should be administered to the accused for the purpose of making the accused fit to stand trial.

(2) The testimony required by the court for the purposes of subsection (1)

shall include a statement that the medical practitioner has made an assessment of the accused and is of the opinion, based on the grounds specified, that

(*a*) the accused, at the time of the assessment, was unfit to stand trial;

(*b*) the psychiatric treatment and any other related medical treatment specified by the medical practitioner will likely make the accused fit to stand trial within a period not exceeding sixty days and that without that treatment the accused is likely to remain unfit to stand trial;

(*c*) the risk of harm to the accused from the psychiatric and other related medical treatment specified is not disproportionate to the benefit anticipated to be derived from it; and

(*d*) the psychiatric and other related medical treatment specified is the least restrictive and least intrusive treatment that could, in the circumstances, be specified for the purpose referred to in subsection (1), considering the opinions referred to in paragraphs (*b*) and (*c*). 1991, c. 43, s. 4.

Notice required — Challenge by accused.

672.6 (1) The court shall not make a disposition under section 672.58 unless the prosecutor notifies the accused of the application, within the time and in the manner prescribed.

(2) On receiving the notice referred to in subsection (1), the accused may challenge the application and adduce evidence for that purpose. 1991, c. 43, s. 4.

Exception — Definitions — "electro-convulsive therapy" — "psychosurgery".

672.61 (1) The court shall not direct, and no disposition made under section 672.58 shall include, the performance of psychosurgery or electro-convulsive therapy or any other prohibited treatment that is prescribed.

(2) In this section,

"electro-convulsive therapy" means a procedure for the treatment of certain mental disorders that induces, by electrical stimulation of the brain, a series of generalized convulsions;

"psychosurgery" means any procedure that by direct or indirect access to the brain removes, destroys or interrupts the continuity of histologically normal brain tissue, or inserts indwelling electrodes for pulsed electrical stimulation for the purpose of altering behaviour or treating psychiatric illness, but does not include neurological procedures used to diagnose or treat intractable physical pain, organic brain conditions, or epilepsy, where any of those conditions is clearly demonstrable. 1991, c. 43, s. 4.

Consent of hospital required for treatment — Consent of accused not required for treatment.

672.62 (1) No court shall make a disposition under section 672.58 without the consent of (*a*) the person in charge of the hospital where the accused is to be treated; or

(*b*) the person to whom responsibility for the treatment of the accused is assigned by the court.

(2) The court may direct that treatment of an accused be carried out pursuant to a disposition made under section 672.58 without the consent of the accused or a person who, according to the laws of the province where the disposition is made, is authorized to consent for the accused. 1991, c. 43, s. 4.

Effective date of disposition.

672.63 A disposition shall come into force on the day that it is made or on any later day that the court or Review Board specifies in it, and shall remain in force until the date of expiration that the disposition specifies or until the Review Board holds a hearing pursuant to section 672.47 or 672.81. 1991, c. 43, s. 4.

[Sections 672.64 to 672.66 are not in force at time of publication.]

Capping of Dispositions

Definitions — "Designated offence" — "Cap" — Additional designated offences under the National Defence Act — Cap for various offences — Longest cap applies where two or more offences — Offence committed where subject to previous disposition.

672.64 (1) In this section, section 672.65, 672.79 and 672.8,

"designated offence" means an offence included in the schedule to this Part, an offence under the *National Defence Act* referred to in subsection (2), or any conspiracy or attempt to commit, being an accessory after the fact in relation to, or any counselling in relation to, such an offence;

"cap" means the maximum period during which an accused is subject to one or more dispositions in respect of an offence, beginning at the time when the verdict is rendered.

(2) An offence contrary to any of the following sections of the *National Defence Act* is a designated offence if it is committed in the circumstances described:

(*a*) section 73 (offences by commanders when in action), where the accused person acted from cowardice;

(*b*) section 74 (offences by any person in presence of enemy), 75 (offences related to security) or 76 (offences related to prisoners of war), where the accused person acted otherwise than traitorously;

(*c*) section 77 (offences related to operations), where the accused person committed the offence on active service;

(*d*) section 107 (wrongful acts in relation to aircraft or aircraft material) or 127 (injurious or destructive handling of dangerous substances), where the accused person acted wilfully;

(*e*) section 130 (service trial of civil offences), where the civil offence is included in the schedule to this Part; and

(*f*) section 132 (offences under law applicable outside Canada), where a court martial determines that the offence is substantially similar to an offence included in the schedule to this Part.

(3) Where a verdict of not criminally responsible on account of mental disorder or unfit to stand trial is rendered in respect of an accused, the cap is

(*a*) life, where the offence is

(i) high treason under subsection 47(1) or first or second degree murder under section 229,

(ii) an offence under section 73 (offences by commanders when in action), section 74 (offences by any person in presence of enemy), section 75 (offences related to security) or section 76 (offences related to prisoners of war) of the *National Defence Act*, if the accused person acted traitorously, or first or second degree murder punishable under section 130 of that Act,

(iii) any other offence under any Act of Parliament for which a minimum punishment of imprisonment for life is provided by law;

(*b*) ten years, or the maximum period during which the accused is liable to imprisonment in respect of the offence, whichever is shorter, where the offence is a designated offence that is prosecuted by indictment; or

(*c*) two years, or the maximum period during which the accused is liable to imprisonment in respect of the offence, whichever is shorter, where the offence is an offence under this Act or any other Act of Parliament, other than an offence referred to in paragraph (*a*) or (*b*).

(4) Subject to subsection (5), where an accused is subject to a verdict in relation to two or more offences, even if they arise from the same transaction, the offence with the longest maximum period of imprisonment as a punishment shall be used to determine the cap that applies to the accused in respect of all the offences.

(5) Where a verdict of not criminally responsible on account of mental disorder or unfit to stand trial is rendered in respect of an accused who is subject to a disposition other than an absolute discharge in respect of a previous offence, the court may order that any disposition that it makes in respect of the offence be consecutive to the previous disposition, even if the duration of all the dispositions exceeds the cap for the offences determined pursuant to subsections (3) and (4).

Dangerous Mentally Disordered Accused

Definition of "serious personal injury offence" — Application for a finding that accused is a dangerous mentally disordered accused — Grounds for finding — Court may increase duration of disposition.

672.65 (1) In this section, "serious personal injury offence" means

(*a*) an offence or attempt to commit an offence mentioned in section 271 (sexual assault), 272 (sexual assault with a weapon, threats to a third party or causing bodily harm) or 273 (aggravated sexual assault); or

(*b*) any designated offence prosecuted by indictment involving

(i) the use or attempted use of violence against another person, or

(ii) conduct endangering or likely to endanger the life or safety of another person or inflicting or likely to inflict severe psychological damage on another person,

and for which the accused is liable to imprisonment for ten years or more.

(2) Where a verdict of not criminally responsible on account of mental disorder is rendered in respect of an accused, the prosecutor may, before any disposition is made, apply to the court that rendered the verdict or to a superior court of criminal jurisdiction for a finding that the accused is a dangerous mentally disordered accused.

(3) On an application made under this section, the court may find the accused to be a dangerous mentally disordered accused where it is satisfied that

(*a*) the offence that resulted in the verdict is a serious personal injury offence described in paragraph (1)(*b*), and the accused constitutes a threat to the life, safety, physical or mental well-being of other persons on the basis of evidence establishing

(i) a pattern of repetitive behaviour by the accused, of which the offence that resulted in the verdict is a part, that shows a failure to exercise behavioural restraint and a likelihood that the accused will cause death or injury to other persons or inflict severe psychological damage on other persons, through failure in the future to exercise restraint,

(ii) a pattern of persistent aggressive behaviour by the accused, of which the offence that resulted in the verdict is a part, or

(iii) any behaviour by the accused, associated with the offence that resulted in the verdict, that is of such a brutal nature as to compel the conclusion that the behaviour of the accused in future is unlikely to be inhibited by normal standards of behavioural restraint; or

(*b*) the offence that resulted in the verdict is a serious personal injury offence described in paragraph (1)(*a*), and the accused, by conduct in any sexual matter including the conduct in the commission of the offence that resulted in the verdict, has shown a failure to control sexual impulses and a likelihood that the accused will cause injury, pain or other harm to other persons through failure in the future to control such impulses.

(4) Where the court finds the accused to be a dangerous mentally disordered

accused under this section, it may increase the cap in respect of the offence to a maximum of life.

Sections 754 to 758 apply — Transmittal of transcript to Review Board.

672.66 (1) Sections 754 to 758 apply, with such modifications as the circumstances require, to an application under section 672.65 as if it were made under Part XXIV and the accused were an offender.

(2) Where a court makes a finding that the accused is a dangerous mentally disordered accused, it shall send without delay to the Review Board that has jurisdiction in respect of the matter a transcript of the hearing of the application, any document or information relating to it in the possession of the court, and all exhibits filed with the court or copies of them.

Dual Status Offenders

Where court imposes a sentence — Custodial disposition by court.

672.67 (1) Where a court imposes a sentence of imprisonment on an offender who is, or thereby becomes, a dual status offender, that sentence takes precedence over any prior custodial disposition, pending any placement decision by the Review Board.

(2) Where a court imposes a custodial disposition on an accused who is, or thereby becomes, a dual status offender, the disposition takes precedence over any prior sentence of imprisonment except a hospital order, as defined in section 736.1, pending any placement decision by the Review Board. 1991, c. 43, s. 4.

Definition of "minister" — Placement decision by Review Board — Idem — Time for making placement decision — Effects of placement decision.

672.68 (1) In this section and in sections 672.69 and 672.7, "Minister" means the Solicitor General of Canada or the Minister responsible to which a dual status offender may be sent pursuant to a sentence of imprisonment.

(2) On application by the Minister or of its own motion, where the Review Board is of the opinion that the place of custody of a dual status offender pursuant to a sentence or custodial disposition made by the court is inappropriate to meet the mental health needs of the offender or to safeguard the well-being of other persons, the Review Board shall, after giving the offender and the Minister reasonable notice, decide whether to place the offender in custody in a hospital or in a prison.

(3) In making a placement decision, the Review Board shall take into consideration

(*a*) the need to protect the public from dangerous persons;

(*b*) the treatment needs of the offender and the availability of suitable treatment resources to address those needs;

(*c*) whether the offender would consent to or is a suitable candidate for treatment;

(*d*) any submissions made to the Review Board by the offender or any other party to the proceedings and any assessment report submitted in writing to the Review Board; and

(*e*) any other factors that the Review Board considers relevant.

(4) The Review Board shall make its placement decision as soon as practicable but not later than thirty days after receiving an application from, or giving notice to, the Minister under subsection (2), unless the Review Board and the Minister agree to a longer period not exceeding sixty days.

(5) Where the offender is detained in a prison pursuant to the placement decision of the Review Board, the Minister is responsible for the supervision and control of the offender. 1991, c. 43, s. 4.

Minister and review board entitled to access — Review of placement decisions — Idem — Minister shall be a party.

672.69 (1) The Minister and the Review Board are entitled to have access to any dual status offender in respect of whom a placement decision has been made, for the purpose of conducting a review of the sentence or disposition imposed.

(2) The Review Board shall hold a hearing as soon as is practicable to review a placement decision, on application by the Minister or the dual status offender who is the subject of the decision, where the Review Board is satisfied that a significant change in circumstances requires it.

(3) The Review Board may of its own motion hold a hearing to review a placement decision after giving the Minister and the dual status offender who is subject to it reasonable notice.

(4) The Minister shall be a party in any proceedings relating to the placement of a dual status offender. 1991, c. 43, s. 4.

Notice of discharge — Warrant of committal.

672.7 (1) Where the Minister or the Review Board intends to discharge a dual status offender from custody, each shall give written notice to the other indicating the time, place and conditions of the discharge.

(2) A Review Board that makes a placement decision shall issue a warrant of committal of the accused, which may be in Form 50. 1991, c. 43, s. 4.

Detention to count as service of term — Disposition takes precedence over probation orders.

672.71 (1) Each day of detention of a dual status offender pursuant to a placement decision or a custodial disposition shall be treated as a day of service of the term of imprisonment, and the accused shall be deemed, for all purposes, to be lawfully confined in a prison.

(2) When a dual status offender is convicted or discharged on the conditions set out in a probation order made under section 736 in respect of an offence but is not sentenced to a term of imprisonment, the custodial disposition in respect of the accused comes into force and, notwithstanding subsection 738(1), takes precedence over any probation order made in respect of the offence. 1991, c. 43, s. 4.

Appeals

Grounds for appeal — Limitation period for appeal — Appeal to be heard expeditiously.

672.72 (1) Any party may appeal against a disposition or placement decision made by a court or Review Board to the court of appeal of the province where the disposition or placement decision was made on any ground of appeal that raises a question of law or fact alone or of mixed law and fact.

(2) Notice of an appeal against a disposition or placement decision shall be given in the manner directed by the applicable rules of court within fifteen days after the day on which the parties are provided with a copy of the placement decision or disposition and the reasons for it or within any further time that the court of appeal, or a judge of that court, may direct.

(3) The court of appeal shall hear an appeal against a disposition or placement decision in or out of the regular sessions of the court, as soon as practicable after the day on which the notice of appeal is given, within any period that may be fixed by the court of appeal, a judge of the court of appeal, or the rules of that court. 1991, c. 43, s. 4.

Appeal on the transcript — Additional evidence.

672.73 (1) An appeal against a disposition by a court or Review Board or placement decision by a Review Board shall be based on a transcript of the proceedings and any other evidence that the court of appeal finds necessary to admit in the interests of justice.

(2) For the purpose of admitting additional evidence under this section, subsections 683(1) and (2) apply, with such modifications as the circumstances require. 1991, c. 43, s. 4.

Notice of appeal to be given to court or review board — Transmission of records to court of appeal — Record to be kept by court of appeal — Appellant to provide transcript of evidence — Saving.

672.74 (1) The clerk of the court of appeal, on receiving notice of an appeal against a disposition or placement decision, shall notify the court or Review Board that made the disposition.

(2) On receipt of notification under subsection (1), the court or Review Board shall transmit to the court of appeal, before the time that the appeal is to

be heard or within any time that the court of appeal or a judge of that court may direct,

(*a*) a copy of the disposition or placement decision;

(*b*) all exhibits filed with the court or Review Board or a copy of them; and

(*c*) all other material in its possession respecting the hearing.

(3) The clerk of the court of appeal shall keep the material referred to in subsection (2) with the records of the court of appeal.

(4) Unless it is contray to an order of the court of appeal or any applicable rules of court, the appellant shall provide the court of appeal and the respondent with a transcript of any evidence taken before a court or Review Board by a stenographer or a sound recording apparatus, certified by the stenographer or in accordance with subsection 540(6), as the case may be.

(5) An appeal shall not be dismissed by the court of appeal by reason only that a person other than the appellant failed to comply with this section. 1991, c. 43, s. 4.

Automatic suspension of certain dispositions.

672.75 The filing of a notice of appeal against a disposition made under paragraph 672.54(*a*) or section 672.58 suspends the application of the disposition pending the determination of the appeal. 1991, c. 43, s. 4.

Application respecting dispositions under appeal — Discretionary powers respecting suspension of dispositions — Copy of order to parties.

672.76 (1) Any party who gives notice to each of the other parties, within the time and in the manner prescribed, may apply to a judge of the court of appeal for an order under this section respecting a disposition or placement decision that is under appeal.

(2) On receipt of an application made pursuant to subsection (1) a judge of the court of appeal may, if satisfied that the mental condition of the accused justifies it,

(*a*) by order, direct that a disposition made under paragraph 672.54(*a*) or section 672.58 be carried out pending the determination of the appeal, notwithstanding section 672.75;

(*b*) by order, direct that the application of a placement decision or a disposition made under paragraph 672.54(*b*) or (*c*) be suspended pending the determination of the appeal;

(*c*) where the application of a disposition is suspended pursuant to section 672.75 or paragraph (*b*), make any other disposition in respect of the accused that is appropriate in the circumstances, other than a disposition under paragraph 672.54(*a*) or section 672.58, pending the determination of the appeal;

(*d*) where the application of a placement decision is supsended pursuant to an order made under paragraph (*b*), make any other placement decision that is appropriate in the circumstances, pending the determination of the appeal; and

(*e*) give any directions that the judge considers necessary for expediting the appeal.

(3) A judge of the court of appeal who makes an order under this section shall send a copy of the order to each of the parties without delay. 1991, c. 43, s. 4.

Effect of suspension of disposition.

672.77 Where the application of a disposition or placement decision appealed from is suspended, a disposition, or in the absence of a disposition any order for the interim release or detention of the accused, that was in effect immediately before the disposition or placement decision appealed from took effect, shall be in force pending the determination of the appeal, subject to any disposition made under paragraph 672.76(2)(*c*). 1991, c. 43, s. 4.

Powers of court of appeal — Idem — Orders that the court may make.

672.78 (1) The court of appeal may allow an appeal against a disposition or placement decision and set aside an order made by the court or Review Board, where the court of appeal is of the opinion that

(*a*) it is unreasonable or cannot be supported by the evidence;

(*b*) it is based on a wrong decision on a question of law; or

(*c*) there was a miscarriage of justice.

(2) The court of appeal may dismiss an appeal against a disposition or placement decision where the court is of the opinion

(*a*) that paragraphs (1)(*a*), (*b*) and (*c*) do not apply; or

(*b*) that paragraph (1)(*b*) may apply, but the court finds that no substantial wrong or miscarriage of justice has occurred.

(3) Where the court of appeal allows an appeal against a disposition or placement decision, it may

(*a*) make any disposition under section 672.54 or any placement decision that the court or Review Board could have made;

(*b*) refer the matter back to the court or Review Board for rehearing, in whole or in part, in accordance with any directions that the court of appeal considers appropriate; or

(*c*) make any other order that justice requires. 1991, c. 43, s. 4.

Appeal by dangerous mentally disordered accused — Disposition of appeal.

672.79 (1) Where a court finds an accused to be a dangerous mentally disordered accused and increases the cap applicable to the accused pursuant to section 672.65, the accused may appeal to the court of appeal against the increase in the cap on any ground of law or fact or mixed law and fact.

(2) On an appeal by an accused under subsection (1), the court of appeal may

(*a*) quash any increase in the cap and impose any other cap that might have been imposed in respect of the offence, or order a new hearing; or

(*b*) dismiss the appeal. 1991, c. 43, s. 4.

Appeal by Attorney General — Disposition of appeal — Part XXI applies to appeal.

672.8 (1) The Attorney General may appeal against the dismissal of an application for a finding that the accused is a dangerous mentally disordered accused on any ground of law.

(2) On an appeal by the Attorney General under subsection (1), the court of appeal may

(*a*) allow the appeal, designate the accused as a dangerous mentally disordered accused, and increase the cap in respect of the offence to a maximum of life, or order a new hearing; or

(*b*) dismiss the appeal.

(3) The provisions of Part XXI with respect to procedure on appeals apply, with such modifications as the circumstances require, to appeals under this section or section 672.79. 1991, c. 43, s. 4.

Review of Dispositions

Mandatory review of dispositions — Additional mandatory reviews in custody cases — Idem.

672.81 (1) A Review Board shall hold a hearing not later than twelve months after making a disposition and every twelve months thereafter for as long as the disposition remains in force, to review any disposition that it has made in respect of an accused, other than an absolute discharge under paragraph 672.54(*a*).

(2) The Review Board shall hold a hearing to review any disposition made under paragraph 672.54(*b*) or (*c*) as soon as is practicable after receiving notice that the person in charge of the place where the accused is detained or directed to attend

(*a*) has increased the restrictions on the liberty of the accused significantly for a period exceeding seven days; or

(*b*) requests a review of the disposition.

(3) Where an accused is detained in custody pursuant to a disposition made under paragraph 672.54(*c*) and a sentence of imprisonment is subsequently imposed on the accused in respect of another offence, the Review Board shall hold a hearing to review the disposition as soon as is practicable after receiving notice of that sentence. 1991, c. 43, s. 4.

Discretionary review on request — Review cancels appeal.

672.82 (1) A Review Board may hold a hearing to review any of its dispositions at any time, at the request of the accused or any other party.

(2) Where a party requests a review of a disposition under this section, the party is deemed to abandon any appeal against the disposition taken under section 672.72. 1991, c. 43, s. 4.

Disposition by review board — Idem.

672.83 (1) At a hearing held pursuant to section 672.81 or 672.82, the Review Board shall, except where a determination is made under subsection 672.48(1) that the accused is fit to stand trial, review the disposition made in respect of the accused and make any other disposition that the Review Board considers to be appropriate in the circumstances.

(2) Subsection 672.52(2), and sections 672.64 and 672.71 to 672.82 apply to a disposition made under this section, with such modifications as the circumstances require. 1991, c. 43, s. 4.

Prcoedure for review.

672.84 The Review Board shall hold a hearing to review a disposition under section 672.81 or 672.82 in accordance with the procedures described in section 672.5. 1991, c. 43, s. 4.

Bringing accused before review board.

672.85 For the purpose of bringing the accused in respect of whom a hearing under section 672.81 is to be held before the Review Board, the chairperson

(*a*) shall order the person having custody of the accused to bring the accused to the hearing at the time and place fixed for it; or

(*b*) may issue a summons or warrant to compel the accused to appear at the time and place fixed for the hearing, if the accused is not in custody. 1991, c. 43, s. 4.

Interprovincial Transfers

Interprovincial transfers — Transfer where accused in custody — Transfer where accused not in custody.

672.86 (1) An accused who is detained in custody or directed to attend at a hospital pursuant to a disposition made by a court or Review Board under paragraph 672.54(*c*) or a court under section 672.58 may be transferred to any other place in Canada where

(*a*) the Review Board of the province where the accused is detained or directed to attend recommends a transfer for the purpose of the reintegration of the accused into society or the recovery, treatment or custody of the accused; and (*b*) the Attorneys General of the provinces to and from which the accused is to be transferred give their consent.

(2) Where an accused who is detained in custody is to be transferred, an officer authorized by the Attorney General of the province where the accused is being detained shall sign a warrant specifying the place in Canada to which the accused is to be transferred.

(3) Where an accused who is not detained in custody is to be transferred, the Review Board of the province where the accused is directed to attend shall, by order,

(*a*) direct that the accused be taken into custody and transferred pursuant to a warrant described in subsection (2); or

(*b*) direct the accused to attend at a specified place in Canada, subject to any conditions that the Review Board considers appropriate. 1991, c. 43, s. 4.

Delivery and detention of accused.

672.87 A warrant described in subsection 672.86(2) is sufficient authority

(*a*) for any person who is responsible for the custody of an accused to have the accused taken into custody and conveyed to the person in charge of the place specified in the warrant; and

(*b*) for the person specified in the warrant to detain the accused in accordance with any disposition made in respect of the accused under paragraph 672.54(*c*). 1991, c. 43, s. 4.

Review board of receiving province has jurisdiction over transferee — Agreement.

672.88 (1) The Review Board of the province to which an accused is transferred pursuant to section 672.86 has exclusive jurisdiction over the accused, and may exercise the powers and shall perform the duties mentioned in sections 672.5 and 672.81 to 672.83 as if that Review Board had made the disposition in respect of the accused.

(2) Notwithstanding subsection (1), the Attorney General of the province to which an accused is transferred may enter into an agreement subject to this Act with the Attorney General of the province from which the accused is transferred, enabling the Review Board of that province to exercise the powers and perform the duties referred to in subsection (1) in respect of the accused, in the circumstances and subject to the terms and conditions set out in agreement. 1991, c. 43, s. 4.

Other interprovincial transfers — Agreement.

672.89 (1) Where an accused who is detained in custody pursuant to a disposition made by a Review Board is transferred to another province otherwise than pursuant to section 672.86, the Review Board of the province from which the accused is transferred has exclusive jurisdiction over the accused and may continue to exercise the powers and shall continue to perform the duties mentioned in sections 672.5 and 672.81 to 672.83.

(2) Notwithstanding subsection (1), the Attorneys General of the provinces to and from which the accused is to be transferred as described in that subsection may, after the transfer is made, enter into an agreement subject to this Act, enabling the Review Board of the province to which an accused is transferred to exercise the powers and perform the duties referred to in subsection (1) in respect of the accused, subject to the terms and conditions and in the circumstances set out in the agreement. 1991, c. 43, s. 4.

Enforcement of Orders and Regulations

Execution of warrant anywhere in Canada.

672.9 Any warrant or process issued in relation to an assessment order or disposition made in respect of an accused may be executed or served in any place in Canada outside the province where the order or disposition was made as if it had been executed or served in that province. 1991, c. 43, s. 4.

Arrest without warrant for contravention of disposition.

672.91 A peace officer may arrest an accused without a warrant at any place in Canada if the peace officer has reasonable grounds to believe that the accused has contravened or wilfully failed to comply with the disposition or any condition of it, or is about to do so. 1991, c. 43, s. 4.

Accused to be brought before justice — Idem.

672.92 (1) An accused who is arrested pursuant to section 672.91 shall be taken before a justice having jurisdiction in the territorial division in which the accused is arrested, without unreasonable delay and in any event within twenty-four hours after the arrest.

(2) If a justice described in subsection (1) is not available within twenty-four hours after the arrest, the accused shall be taken before a justice as soon as is practicable. 1991, c. 43, s. 4.

Where Justice to release accused — Order of justice pending decision of Review Board.

672.93 (1) A justice shall release an accused who is brought before the justice pursuant to section 672.92 unless the justice is satisfied that there are reasonable grounds to believe that the accused has contravened or failed to comply with a disposition.

(2) If the justice is satisfied that there are reasonable grounds to believe that the accused has contravened or failed to comply with a disposition, the justice may make an order that is appropriate in the circumstances in relation to the accused, pending a hearing of the Review Board of the province where

the disposition was made, and shall cause notice of that order to be given to that Review Board. 1991, c. 43, s. 4.

Powers of review board.

672.94 Where a Review Board receives a notice given pursuant to subsection 672.93(2), it may exercise the powers and shall perform the duties mentioned in sections 672.5 and 672.81 to 672.83 as if the Review Board were reviewing a disposition. 1991, c. 43, s. 4.

Regulations.

672.95 The Governor in Council may make regulations

(*a*) prescribing anything that may be prescribed under this Part; and

(*b*) generally to carry out the purposes and provisions of this Part.

PART XXI

APPEALS — INDICTABLE OFFENCES

Interpretation

Definitions — "Court of appeal" — "Indictment" — "Registrar" — "Sentence" — "Trial court".

673. In this Part,

"court of appeal" means the court of appeal, as defined by the definition "court of appeal" in section 2, for the province or territory in which the trial of a person by indictment is held;

"indictment" includes an information or charge in respect of which a person has been tried for an indictable offence under Part XIX;

"registrar" means the registrar or clerk of the court of appeal;

"sentence" includes

(*a*) a declaration made under subsection 199(3).

(*b*) an order made under subsection 100(1) or (2), 194(1) or 259(1) or (2), section 261 or 462.37, subsection 491.1(2), section 725, 726 or 727.9, subsection 736(1) or 744, and

(*c*) a disposition made under subsection 737(1) or 738(3) or (4);

"trial court" means the court by which an accused was tried and includes a judge or a provincial court judge acting under Part XIX. R.S. 1985, c. 27 (1st Supp.), ss. 138, 203; c. 1 (4th Supp.), s. 24; c. 23 (4th Supp.), s. 4; c. 42 (4th Supp.), s. 4; 1991, c. 43, s. 5; 1992, c. 1, s. 58(1), Sch. I, item 12.

Right of Appeal

Procedure abolished.

674. No proceedings other than those authorized by this Part and Part XXVI shall be taken by way of appeal in proceedings in respect of indictable offences.

Right of appeal of person convicted — Appeal against absolute term in excess of 10 years — Appeal against verdicts based on mental disorder — Where application for leave to appeal refused by judge.

675. (1) A person who is convicted by a trial court in proceedings by indictment may appeal to the court of appeal

(*a*) against his conviction

(i) on any ground of appeal that involves a question of law alone,

(ii) on any ground of appeal that involves a question of fact or a question of mixed law and fact, with leave of the court of appeal or a judge thereof or on the certificate of the trial judge that the case is a proper case for appeal, or

(iii) on any ground of appeal not mentioned in subparagraph (i) or (ii) that appears to the court of appeal to be a sufficient ground of appeal, with leave of the court of appeal; or

(*b*) against the sentence passed by the trial court, with leave of the court of appeal or a judge thereof unless that sentence is one fixed by law.

(2) A person who has been convicted of second degree murder and sentenced to imprisonment for life without eligibility for parole for a specified number of years in excess of ten may appeal to the court of appeal against the number of years in excess of ten of his imprisonment without eligibility for parole.

(3) Where a verdict of not criminally responsible on account of mental disorder or unfit to stand trial is rendered in respect of a person, that person may appeal to the court of appeal against that verdict on any ground of appeal mentioned in subparagraph (1)(*a*)(i), (ii) or (iii) and subject to the conditions described therein.

(4) Where a judge of the court of appeal refuses leave to appeal under this section otherwise than under paragraph (1)(*b*), the appellant may, by filing notice in writing with the court of appeal within seven days after refusal, have the application for leave to appeal determined by the court of appeal. 1991, c. 43, s. 9, Sch., item 5.

Right of Attorney General to appeal — Acquittal — Appeal against verdicts based on mental disorder — Appeal against ineligible parole period.

676. (1) The Attorney General or counsel instructed by him for the purpose may appeal to the court of appeal

(*a*) against a judgment or verdict of acquittal of a trial court in proceedings by indictment on any ground of appeal that involves a question of law alone;

(*b*) against an order of a superior court of criminal jurisdiction that quashes an indictment or in any manner refuses or fails to exercise jurisdiction on an indictment;

(*c*) against an order of a trial court that stays proceedings on an indictment or quashes an indictment; or

(*d*) with leave of the court of appeal or a judge thereof, against the sentence passed by a trial court in proceedings by indictment, unless that sentence is one fixed by law.

(2) For the purposes of this section, a judgment or verdict of acquittal includes an acquittal in respect of an offence specifically charged where the accused has, on the trial thereof, been convicted or discharged under section 736 of any other offence.

(3) Where a verdict of not criminally responsible on account of mental disorder or unfit to stand trial is rendered in respect of a person, that person may appeal to the court of appeal against that verdict on any ground of appeal

mentioned in subparagraph 1(*a*)(i), (ii) or (iii) and subject to the conditions described therein.

[1991, c. 43, s. 9, Sch., item 5 will repeal subsection 676(3) and substitute the following.]

(3) The Attorney General or counsel instructed by the Attorney General for the purpose may appeal to the court of appeal against a verdict that an accused is unfit to stand trial, on any ground of appeal that involves a question of law alone.

(4) The Attorney General or counsel instructed by him for the purpose may appeal to the court of appeal in respect of a conviction for second degree murder, against the number of years of imprisonment without eligibility for parole, being less than twenty-five, that has been imposed as a result of that conviction. R.S. 1985, c. 27 (1st Supp.), s. 139; 1991, c. 43, s. 9, Sch., item 5.

Specifying grounds of dissent.

677. Where an appeal is dismissed by the court of appeal and a judge of that court expresses an opinion dissenting from the judgment of the court, the formal judgment of the court shall specify any grounds in law on which the dissent, in whole or in part, is based.

Procedure on Appeals

Notice of appeal — Extension of time.

678. (1) An appellant who proposes to appeal to the court of appeal or to obtain the leave of that court to appeal shall give notice of appeal or notice of his application for leave to appeal in such manner and within such period as may be directed by rules of court.

(2) The court of appeal or a judge thereof may at any time extend the time within which notice of appeal or notice of an application for leave to appeal may be given.

Service where respondent cannot be found.

678.1 Where a respondent cannot be found after reasonable efforts have been made to serve him with a notice of appeal or notice of an application for leave to appeal, service of the notice of appeal or the notice of the application for leave to appeal may be effected substitutionally in the manner and within the period directed by a judge of the court of appeal. R.S. 1985, c. 27 (1st Supp.), s. 140.

Release pending determination of appeal — Notice of application for release — Circumstances in which appellant may be released — Idem — Conditions of order — Application of certain provisions of s. 525 — Release or detention pending new trial, new hearing or hearing of reference — Application to appeals on summary conviction proceedings — Form of undertaking or recognizance — Directions for expediting appeal, new trial, etc.

679. (1) A judge of the court of appeal may, in accordance with this section, release an appellant from custody pending the determination of his appeal if,

(*a*) in the case of an appeal to the court of appeal against conviction, the appellant has given notice of appeal or, where leave is required, notice of his application for leave to appeal pursuant to section 678;

(*b*) in the case of an appeal to the court of appeal against sentence only, the appellant has been granted leave to appeal; or

(*c*) in the case of an appeal or an application for leave to appeal to the Supreme Court of Canada, the appellant has filed and served his notice of appeal or, where leave is required, his application for leave to appeal.

(2) Where an appellant applies to a judge of the court of appeal to be released pending the determination of his appeal, he shall give written notice of the application to the prosecutor or to such other person as a judge of the court of appeal directs.

(3) In the case of an appeal referred to in paragraph (1)(*a*) or (*c*), the judge of the court of appeal may order that the appellant be released pending the determination of his appeal if the appellant establishes that

(*a*) the appeal or application for leave to appeal is not frivolous,

(*b*) he will surrender himself into custody in accordance with the terms of the order, and

(*c*) his detention is not necessary in the public interest.

(4) In the case of an appeal referred to in paragraph (1)(*b*), the judge of the court of appeal may order that the appellant be released pending the determination of his appeal or until otherwise ordered by a judge of the court of appeal if the appellant establishes that

(*a*) the appeal has sufficient merit that, in the circumstances, it would cause unnecessary hardship if he were detained in custody;

(*b*) he will surrender himself into custody in accordance with the terms of the order; and

(*c*) his detention is not necessary in the public interest.

(5) Where the judge of the court of appeal does not refuse the application of the appellant, he shall order that the appellant be released

(*a*) on his giving an undertaking to the judge, without conditions or with such conditions as the judge directs, to surrender himself into custody in accordance with the order, or

(*b*) on his entering into a recognizance

(i) with one or more sureties,
(ii) with deposit of money or other valuable security,
(iii) with both sureties and deposit, or
(iv) with neither sureties nor deposit,

in such amount, subject to such conditions, if any, and before such justice as the judge directs,

and the person having the custody of the appellant shall, where the appellant complies with the order, forthwith release the appellant.

(6) The provisions of subsections 525(5), (6) and (7) apply with such modification as the circumstances require in respect of a person who has been released from custody under subsection (5) of this section.

(7) Where, with respect to any person, the court of appeal or the Supreme Court of Canada orders a new trial or new hearing or the Minister of Justice gives a direction or makes a reference under section 690, this section applies to the release or detention of that person pending the new trial or new hearing or the hearing and determination of the reference, as the case may be, as though that person were an appellant in an appeal described in paragraph (1)(*a*).

(8) This section applies to applications for leave to appeal and appeals to the Supreme Court of Canada in summary conviction proceedings.

(9) An undertaking under this section may be in Form 12 and a recognizance under this section may be in Form 32.

(10) A judge of the court of appeal, where on the application of an appellant he does not make an order under subsection (5) or where he cancels an order previously made under this section, or a judge of the Supreme Court of Canada on application by an appellant in the case of an appeal to that Court, may give such directions as he thinks necessary for expediting the hearing of the appellant's appeal or for expediting the new trial or new hearing or the hearing of the reference, as the case may be. R.S. 1985, c. 27 (1st Supp.), s. 141.

Review by court of appeal — Single judge acting — Enforcement of decision.

680. (1) A decision made by a judge under section 522 or subsection 524(4) or (5) or a decision made by a judge of the court of appeal under section 679 may, on the direction of the chief justice or acting chief justice of the court of appeal, be reviewed by that court and that court may, if it does not confirm the decision,

(*a*) vary the decision; or

(*b*) substitute such other decision as, in its opinion, should have been made.

(2) On consent of the parties, the powers of the court of appeal under subsection (1) may be exercised by a judge of that court.

(3) A decision as varied or substituted under this section shall have effect and may be enforced in all respects as though it were the decision originally made. R.S. 1985, c. 27 (1st Supp.), 142.

Direction or remand for observation — Idem.

681. [Repealed 1991, c. 43, s. 9, Sch., item 7.]

Report by judge — Transcript of evidence — Notes of proceedings — Copies to interested parties — Copy for Minister of Justice.

682. (1) Where, under this Part, an appeal is taken or an application for leave to appeal is made, the judge or provincial court judge who presided at the trial shall, at the request of the court of appeal or a judge thereof, in accordance with rules of court, furnish it or him with a report on the case or on any matter relating to the case that is specified in the request.

(2) A copy or transcript of

(*a*) the evidence taken at the trial,

(*b*) the charge to the jury, if any,

(*c*) the reasons for judgment, if any, and

(*d*) the addresses of the prosecutor and the accused, if a ground for the appeal is based on either of the addresses,

shall be furnished to the court of appeal, except in so far as it is dispensed with by order of a judge of that court.

(3) A copy of the charge to the jury, if any, and any objections that were made to it shall, before the copy or transcript is transmitted to the court of appeal pursuant to subsection (2), be submitted to the judge who presided at the trial, and if the judge refuses to certify that the charge and objections are accurately set out, he shall immediately certify to the court of appeal

(*a*) the reasons for his refusal; and

(*b*) the charge that was given to the jury, if any, and any objections that were made to it.

(4) A party to an appeal is entitled to receive, on payment of any charges that are fixed by rules of court, a copy or transcript of any material that is prepared under subsections (1) to (3).

(5) The Minister of Justice is entitled, on request, to receive a copy or transcript of any material that is prepared under subsections (1) to (3). R.S. 1985, c. 27 (1st Supp.), ss. 143, 203.

Powers of court of appeal — Parties entitled to adduce evidence and be heard — Other powers — Execution of process — Power to order suspension — Revocation of suspension order.

683. (1) For the purposes of an appeal under this Part, the court of appeal may, where it considers it in the interests of justice,

(*a*) order the production of any writing, exhibit, or other thing connected with the proceedings;

(*b*) order any witness who could have been a compellable witness at the trial, whether or not he was called at the trial,

(i) to attend and be examined before the court of appeal, or

(ii) to be examined in the manner provided by rules of court before a judge of the court of appeal, or before any officer of the court of appeal or justice of the peace or other person appointed by the court of appeal for the purpose;

(*c*) admit, as evidence, an examination that is taken under subparagraph (*b*)(ii);

(*d*) receive the evidence, if tendered, of any witness, including the appellant, who is a competent but not compellable witness;

(*e*) order that any question arising on the appeal that

(i) involves prolonged examination of writings or accounts, or scientific or local investigation,

(ii) cannot in the opinion of the court of appeal conveniently be inquired into before the court of appeal,

be referred for inquiry and report, in the manner provided by rules of court, to a special commissioner appointed by the court of appeal; and

(*f*) act upon the report of a commissioner who is appointed under paragraph (*e*) in so far as the court of appeal thinks fit to do so.

(*g*) amend the indictment, unless it is of the opinion that the accused has been misled or prejudiced in his defence or appeal.

(2) In proceedings under this section, the parties or their counsel are entitled to examine or cross-examine witnesses and, in an inquiry under paragraph (1)(*e*), are entitled to be present during the inquiry, and to adduce evidence and to be heard.

(3) A court of appeal may exercise in relation to proceedings in the court, any powers not mentioned in subsection (1) that may be exercised by the court on appeals in civil matters, and may issue any process that is necessary to enforce the orders or sentences of the court, but no costs shall be allowed to the appellant or respondent on the hearing and determination of an appeal or on any proceedings preliminary or incidental thereto.

(4) Any process that is issued by the court of appeal under this section may be executed anywhere in Canada.

(5) Where an appeal or an application for leave to appeal has been filed in the court of appeal, that court may, where it considers it to be in the interests of justice, order that

(*a*) any obligation to pay a fine,

(*b*) any order of forfeiture or disposition of forfeited property,

(*c*) any order to make restitution under section 725 or 726, or

(*d*) any order to pay a victim fine surcharge under section 727.9

be suspended until the appeal has been determined.

(6) The court of appeal may revoke any order it makes under subsection (5) where it considers the revocation to be in the interests of justice. R.S. 1985, c. 27 (1st Supp.), s. 144; c. 23 (4th Supp.), s. 5.

Legal assistance for appellant — Counsel fees and disbursements — Taxation of fees and disbursements.

684. (1) A court of appeal or a judge of that court may, at any time, assign counsel to act on behalf of an accused who is a party to an appeal or to proceedings preliminary or incidental to an appeal where, in the opinion of the court or judge, it appears desirable in the interests of justice that the accused should have legal assistance and where it appears that the accused has not sufficient means to obtain that assistance.

(2) Where counsel is assigned pursuant to subsection (1) and legal aid is not granted to the accused pursuant to a provincial legal aid program, the fees and disbursements of counsel shall be paid by the Attorney General who is the appellant or respondent, as the case may be, in the appeal.

(3) Where subsection (2) applies and where counsel and the Attorney General cannot agree on fees or disbursements of counsel, the Attorney General or the counsel may apply to the registrar of the court of appeal and the registrar may tax the disputed fees and disbursements. R.S. 1985, c. 34 (3rd Supp.), s. 9.

Summary determination of frivolous appeals.

685. Where it appears to the registrar that a notice of appeal, which purports to be on a ground of appeal that involves a question of law alone, does not show a substantial ground of appeal, the registrar may refer the appeal to the court of appeal for summary determination, and, where an appeal is referred under this section, the court of appeal may, if it considers that the appeal is frivolous or vexatious and can be determined without being adjourned for a full hearing, dismiss the appeal summarily, without calling on any person to attend the hearing or to appear for the respondent on the hearing.

Powers of the Court of Appeal

Powers — Order to be made — Substituting verdict — Appeal from acquittal — New trial under Part XIX — Where appeal allowed against verdict of unfit to stand trial — Appeal court may set aside verdict of unfit to stand trial — Additional powers.

686. (1) On the hearing of an appeal against a conviction or against a verdict that the appellant is unfit to stand trial or not criminally responsible on account of mental disorder, the court of appeal

(*a*) may allow the appeal where it is of the opinion that

(i) the verdict should be set aside on the ground that it is unreasonable or cannot be supported by the evidence,

(ii) the judgment of the trial court should be set aside on the ground of a wrong decision on a question of law, or

(iii) on any ground there was a miscarriage of justice;

(*b*) may dismiss the appeal where

(i) the court is of the opinion that the appellant, although he was not properly convicted on a count or part of the indictment, was properly convicted on another count or part of the indictment,

(ii) the appeal is not decided in favour of the appellant on any ground mentioned in paragraph (*a*),

(iii) notwithstanding that the court is of the opinion that on any ground mentioned in subparagraph (*a*)(ii) the appeal might be decided in favour of the appellant, it is of the opinion that no substantial wrong or miscarriage of justice has occurred; or

(iv) notwithstanding any procedural irregularity at trial, the trial court had jurisdiction over the class of offence of which the appellant was convicted and the court of appeal is of the opinion that the appellant suffered no prejudice thereby;

(*c*) may refuse to allow the appeal where it is of the opinion that the trial court arrived at a wrong conclusion respecting the effect of a special verdict, may order the conclusion to be recorded that appears to the court to be required by the verdict, and may pass a sentence that is warranted in law in substitution for the sentence passed by the trial court; or

(*d*) may set aside a conviction and find the appellant unfit to stand trial or not criminally responsible on account of mental disorder and may exercise any of the powers of the trial court conferred by or referred to in section 672.45 in any manner deemed appropriate to the court of appeal in the circumstances.

(2) Where a court of appeal allows an appeal under paragraph (1)(*a*), it shall quash the conviction and

(*a*) direct a judgment or verdict of acquittal to be entered; or

(*b*) order a new trial.

(3) Where a court of appeal dismisses an appeal under subparagraph (1)(*b*)(i), it may substitute the verdict that in its opinion should have been found and

(*a*) affirm the sentence passed by the trial court; or

(*b*) impose a sentence that is warranted in law or remit the matter to the trial court and direct the trial court to impose a sentence that is warranted in law.

(4) Where an appeal is from an acquittal, the court of appeal may

(*a*) dismiss the appeal; or

(*b*) allow the appeal, set aside the verdict and

(i) order a new trial, or

(ii) except where the verdict is that of a court composed of a judge and jury, enter a verdict of guilty with respect to the offence of which, in its opinion, the accused should have been found guilty but for the error in law, and pass a sentence that is warranted in law, or remit the matter to the trial court and direct the trial court to impose a sentence that is warranted in law..

(5) Where an appeal is taken in respect of proceedings under Part XIX and the court of appeal orders a new trial under this Part, the following provisions apply:

(*a*) if the accused, in his notice of appeal or notice of application for leave to appeal, requested that the new trial, if ordered, should be held before a court composed of a judge and jury, the new trial shall be held accordingly;

(*b*) if the accused, in his notice of appeal or notice of application for leave to appeal, did not request that the new trial, if ordered, should be held before a court composed of a judge and jury, the new trial shall, without further election by the accused, be held before a judge or provincial court judge, as the case may be, acting under Part XIX, other than a judge or provincial court judge who tried the accused in the first instance, unless the court of appeal directs that the new trial be held before the judge or provincial court judge who tried the accused in the first instance;

(*c*) if the court of appeal orders that the new trial shall be held before a court composed of a judge and jury the new trial shall be commenced by an indictment in writing setting forth the offence in respect of which the new trial was ordered; and

(*d*) notwithstanding paragraph (*a*), if the conviction against which the accused appealed was for an offence mentioned in section 553 and was made by a provincial court judge, the new trial shall be held before a provincial court judge acting under Part XIX, other than the provincial court judge who tried the accused in the first instance, unless the court of appeal directs that the new trial be held before the provincial court judge who tried the accused in the first instance.

(6) Where a court of appeal allows an appeal against a verdict that the accused is unfit to stand trial, it shall, subject to subsection (7), order a new trial.

(7) Where a verdict that the accused is unfit to stand trial was returned after the close of the case for the prosecution, the court of appeal may, notwithstanding that the verdict is proper, if it is of the opinion that the accused should have been acquitted at the close of the case for the prosecution, allow the appeal, set aside the verdict and direct a judgment or verdict of acquittal to be entered.

(8) Where a court of appeal exercises any of the powers conferred by subsection (2), (4), (6) or (7), it may make any order, in addition, that justice requires. R.S. 1985, c. 27 (1st Supp.), ss. 145, 203; 1991, c. 43, s. 9, Sch., items 8(1) to (3).

Powers of court on appeal against sentence — Effect of judgment.

687. (1) Where an appeal is taken against sentence the court of appeal shall, unless the sentence is one fixed by law, consider the fitness of the sentence appealed against, and may on such evidence, if any, as it thinks fit to require or to receive,

(*a*) vary the sentence within the limits prescribed by law for the offence of which the accused was convicted; or

(*b*) dismiss the appeal.

(2) A judgment of a court of appeal that varies the sentence of an accused who was convicted has the same force and effect as if it were a sentence passed by the trial court.

Right of appellant to attend — Appellant represented by counsel — Argument may be oral or in writing — Sentence in absence of appellant.

688. (1) Subject to subsection (2), an appellant who is in custody is entitled, if he desires, to be present at the hearing of the appeal.

(2) An appellant who is in custody and who is represented by counsel is not entitled to be present

(*a*) at the hearing of the appeal, where the appeal is on a ground involving a question of law alone,

(*b*) on an application for leave to appeal, or

(*c*) on any proceedings that are preliminary or incidental to an appeal,

unless rules of court provide that he is entitled to be present or the court of appeal or a judge thereof gives him leave to be present.

(3) An appellant may present his case on appeal and his argument in writing instead of orally, and the court of appeal shall consider any case of argument so presented.

(4) A court of appeal may exercise its power to impose sentence notwithstanding that the appellant is not present.

Restitution or forfeiture of property — Annulling or varying order.

689. (1) Where the trial court makes an order for compensation for the restitution of property under section 725, 726 or 727 or an order of forfeiture of property under subsection 462.37(1), the operation of the order is suspended.

(*a*) until the expiration of the period prescribed by rules of court for the giving of notice of appeal or of notice of application for leave to appeal, unless the accused waives an appeal; and

(*b*) until the appeal or application for leave to appeal has been determined, where an appeal is taken or application for leave to appeal is made.

(2) The court of appeal may by order annul or vary an order made by the trial court with respect to compensation or the restitution of property within the limits prescribed by the provision under which the order was made by the trial court, whether or not the conviction is quashed. R.S. 1985, c. 42 (4th Supp.), s. 5.

Powers of Minister of Justice

Powers of Minister of Justice.

690. The Minister of Justice may, on an application for the mercy of the Crown by or on behalf of a person who has been convicted in proceedings by indictment or who has been sentenced to preventive detention under Part XXIV,

(*a*) direct, by order in writing, a new trial or, in the case of a person under sentence of preventive detention, a new hearing, before any court that he thinks proper, if after inquiry he is satisfied that in the circumstances a new trial or hearing, as the case may be, should be directed;

(*b*) refer the matter at any time to the court of appeal for hearing and determination by that court as if it were an appeal by the convicted person or the person under sentence of preventive detention, as the case may be; or

(*c*) refer to the court of appeal at any time, for its opinion, any question on which he desires the assistance of that court, and the court shall furnish its opinion accordingly.

Appeals to the Supreme Court of Canada

Appeal from conviction — Appeal where acquittal set aside.

691. (1) A person who is convicted of an indictable offence and whose conviction is affirmed by the court of appeal may appeal to the Supreme Court of Canada

(*a*) on any question of law on which a judge of the court of appeal dissents; or

(*b*) on any question of law, if leave to appeal is granted by the Supreme Court of Canada.

(2) A person

(*a*) who is acquitted of an indictable offence other than by reason of a verdict of not criminally responsible on account of mental disorder and whose acquittal is set aside by the court of appeal, or

(*b*) who is tried jointly with a person referred to in paragraph (*a*) and is convicted and whose conviction is sustained by the court of appeal,

may appeal to the Supreme Court of Canada on a question of law. R.S. 1985, c. 34 (3rd Supp.), s. 10; 1991, c. 43, s. 9, Sch., item 9.

Appeal against affirmation of verdict of not criminally responsible on account of mental disorder — Appeal against affirmation of verdict of unfit to stand trial — Grounds of appeal.

692. (1) A person who has been found not criminally responsible on account of mental disorder and (*a*) whose verdict is affirmed on that ground by the court of appeal, or

(*b*) against whom a verdict of guilty is entered by the court of appeal under subparagraph 686(4)(*b*)(ii),

may appeal to the Supreme Court of Canada.

(2) A person who is found unfit to stand trial and against whom that verdict is affirmed by the court of appeal may appeal to the Supreme Court of Canada.

(3) An appeal under subsection (1) or (2) may be

(*a*) on any question of law on which a judge of the court of appeal dissents; or

(*b*) on any question of law, if leave to appeal is granted by the Supreme Court of Canada. R.S. 1985, c. 34 (3rd Supp.), s. 11; 1991, c. 43, s. 9, Sch.; items 10(1), (2).

Appeal by Attorney General — Terms.

693. (1) Where a judgment of a court of appeal sets aside a conviction pursuant to an appeal taken under section 675 or dismisses an appeal taken pursuant to paragraph 676(1)(*a*), (*b*) or (*c*) or subsection 676(3), the Attorney General may appeal to the Supreme Court of Canada

(*a*) on any question of law on which a judge of the court of appeal dissents, or

(*b*) on any question of law, if leave to appeal is granted by the Supreme Court of Canada.

(2) Where leave to appeal is granted under paragraph (1)(*b*), the Supreme Court of Canada may impose such terms as it sees fit. R.S. 1985, c. 27 (1st Supp.), s. 146; c. 34 (3rd Supp.), s. 12.

Notice of appeal.

694. No appeal lies to the Supreme Court of Canada unless notice of appeal in writing is served by the appellant on the respondent in accordance with the *Supreme Court Act*. R.S. 1985, c. 34 (3rd Supp.), s. 13.

Legal assistance for accused — Counsel fees and disbursements — Taxation of fees and disbursements.

694.1 (1) The Supreme Court of Canada or a judge thereof may, at any time, assign counsel to act on behalf of an accused who is a party to an appeal to the Court or to proceedings preliminary or incidental to an appeal to the Court where, in the opinion of the Court or judge, it appears desirable in the interests of justice that the accused should have legal assistance and where it appears that the accused has not sufficient means to obtain that assistance.

(2) Where counsel is assigned pursuant to subsection (1) and legal aid is not granted to the accused pursuant to a provincial legal aid program, the fees and disbursements of counsel shall be paid by the Attorney General who is the appellant or respondent, as the case may be, in the appeal.

(3) Where subsection (2) applies and counsel and the Attorney General cannot agree on fees or disbursements of counsel, the Attorney General or the counsel may apply to the Registrar of the Supreme Court of Canada, and the Registrar may tax the disputed fees and disbursements. R.S. 1985, c. 34 (3rd Supp.), s. 13.

Right of appellant to attend — Appellant represented by counsel

694.2 (1) Subject to subsection (2), an appellant who is in custody and who desires to be present at the hearing of the appeal before the Supreme Court of Canada is entitled to be present at it.

(2) An appellant who is in custody and who is represented by counsel is not entitled to be present before the Supreme Court of Canada

(*a*) on an application for leave to appeal,

(*b*) on any proceedings that are preliminary or incidental to an appeal, or

(*c*) at the hearing of the appeal,

unless rules of court provide that entitlement or the Supreme Court of Canada or a judge thereof gives the appellant leave to be present. R.S. 1985, c. 34 (3rd Supp.), s. 13.

Order of Supreme Court of Canada — When appeal presumed abandoned.

695. (1) The Supreme Court of Canada may, on an appeal under this Part, make any order that the court of appeal might have made and may make any rule or order that is necessary to give effect to its judgment.

(2) An appeal to the Supreme Court of Canada that is not brought on for hearing by the appellant at the session of that court during which the judgment appealed from is pronounced by the court of appeal, or during the next session thereof, shall be deemed to be abandoned, unless otherwise ordered by the Supreme Court of Canada or a judge thereof.

Appeals by Attorney General of Canada

Right of Attorney General of Canada to appeal.

696. The Attorney General of Canada has the same rights of appeal in proceedings instituted at the instance of the Government of Canada and conducted by or on behalf of that Government as the Attorney General of a province has under this Part.

PART XXII

PROCURING ATTENDANCE

Application

Application.

697. Except where section 527 applies, this Part applies where a person is required to attend to give evidence in a proceeding to which this Act applies. R.S. 1985, c. 27 (1st Supp.), s. 147.

Process

Subpoena — Warrant in Form 17 — Subpoena issued first.

698. (1) Where a person is likely to give material evidence in a proceeding to which this Act applies, a subpoena may be issued in accordance with this Part requiring that person to attend to give evidence.

(2) Where it is made to appear that a person who is likely to give material evidence

(*a*) will not attend in response to a subpoena if a subpoena is issued, or

(*b*) is evading service of a subpoena,

a court, justice or provincial court judge having power to issue a subpoena to require the attendance of that person to give evidence may issue a warrant in Form 17 to cause that person to be arrested and to be brought to give evidence.

(3) Except where paragraph (2)(*a*) applies, a warrant in Form 17 shall not be issued unless a subpoena has first been issued. R.S. 1985, c. 27 (1st Supp.), s. 203.

How subpoena issued — Who may issue — Order of judge — Seal — Signature — Form.

699. (1) Where a person is required to attend to give evidence before a superior court of criminal jurisdiction, a court of appeal, an appeal court or a court of criminal jurisdiction other than a provincial court judge acting under Part XIX, a subpoena directed to that person shall be issued out of the court before which the attendance of that person is required.

(2) Where a person is required to attend to give evidence before a provincial court judge acting under Part XIX, or a summary conviction court under Part XXVII or in proceedings over which a justice has jurisdiction, a subpoena directed to that person shall be issued

(*a*) by a justice or provincial court judge, as the case may be, where the person whose attendance is required is within the province in which the proceedings were instituted; or

(*b*) out of a superior court of criminal jurisdiction or a county or district court of the province in which the proceedings were instituted, where the person whose attendance is required is not within the province.

(3) A subpoena shall not be issued pursuant to paragraph (2)(*b*), except pursuant to an order of a judge of the court made on application by a party to the proceedings.

(4) A subpoena or warrant that is issued by a court under this Part shall be under the seal of the court and shall be signed by a judge of the court or by the clerk of the court.

(5) A subpoena or warrant that is issued by a justice or provincial court judge under this Part shall be signed by the justice or provincial court judge.

(6) A subpoena issued under this Part may be in Form 16. R.S. 1985, c. 27 (1st Supp.), s. 203.

Contents of subpoena — Witness to appear and remain.

700. (1) A subpoena shall require the person to whom it is directed to attend, at a time and place to be stated in the subpoena, to give evidence and, if required, to bring with him anything that he has in his possession or under his control relating to the subject-matter of the proceedings.

(2) A person who is served with a subpoena issued under this Part shall attend and shall remain in attendance throughout the proceedings unless he is excused by the presiding judge, justice or provincial court judge. R.S. 1985, c. 27 (1st Supp.), ss. 148, 203.

Execution or Service of Process

Service — Personal service — Proof of service.

701. (1) Subject to subsection (2), a subpoena shall be served in accordance with subsection 509(2).

(2) A subpoena that is issued pursuant to paragraph 699(2)(*b*) shall be served personally on the person to whom it is directed.

(3) Service of a subpoena may be proved by the affidavit of the person who effected service.

Subpoena effective throughout Canada — Subpoena effective throughout province.

702. (1) A subpoena that is issued out of a superior court of criminal jurisdiction, a court of appeal, an appeal court or a court of criminal jurisdiction other than a provincial court judge acting under Part XIX has effect anywhere in Canada according to its terms.

(2) A subpoena that is issued by a justice or provincial court judge has effect anywhere in the province in which it is issued. R.S. 1985, c. 27 (1st Supp.), s. 203.

Warrant effective throughout Canada — Warrant effective in a province.

703. (1) Notwithstanding any other provision of this Act, a warrant of arrest or committal that is issued out of a superior court of criminal jurisdiction, a court of appeal, an appeal court within the meaning of section 812 or a court of criminal jurisdiction other than a provincial court judge acting under Part XIX may be executed anywhere in Canada.

(2) Notwithstanding any other provision of this Act but subject to subsection 705(3), a warrant of arrest or committal that is issued by a justice or provincial court judge may be executed anywhere in the province in which it is issued. R.S. 1985, c. 27 (1st Supp.), s. 149.

Summons effective throughout Canada.

703.1 A summons may be served anywhere in Canada and, if served, is effective notwithstanding the territorial jurisdiction of the authority that issued the summons. R.S. 1985, c. 27 (1st Supp.), s. 149.

Service of process on a corporation.

703.2 Where any summons, notice or other process is required to be or may be served on a corporation, and no other method of service is provided, service may be effected by delivery

(*a*) in the case of a municipal corporation, to the mayor, warden, reeve or other chief officer of the corporation, or to the secretary, treasurer or clerk of the corporation; and

(*b*) in the case of any other corporation, to the manager, secretary or other executive officer of the corporation or of a branch thereof. R.S. 1985, c. 27 (1st Supp.), s. 149.

Defaulting or Absconding Witness

Warrant for absconding witness — Endorsement of warrant — Copy of information.

704. (1) Where a person is bound by recognizance to give evidence in any proceedings, a justice who is satisfied on information being made before him in writing and under oath that the person is about to abscond or has absconded may issue his warrant in Form 18 directing a peace officer to arrest that person and to bring him before the court, judge, justice or provincial court judge before whom he is bound to appear.

(2) Section 528 applies, with such modifications as the circumstances require, to a warrant issued under this section.

(3) A person who is arrested under this section is entitled, on request, to receive a copy of the information upon which the warrant for his arrest was issued. R.S. 1985, c. 27 (1st Supp.), s. 203.

Warrant when witness does not attend — Warrant where witness bound by recognizance — Warrant effective throughout Canada.

705. (1) Where a person who has been served with a subpoena to give evidence in a proceeding does not attend or remain in attendance, the court, judge, justice or provincial court judge before whom that person was required to attend may, if it is established

(*a*) that the subpoena has been served in accordance with this Part, and

(*b*) that the person is likely to give material evidence,

issue or cause to be issued a warrant in Form 17 for the arrest of that person.

(2) Where a person who has been bound by a recognizance to attend to give evidence in any proceeding does not attend or does not remain in attendance, the court, judge, justice or provincial court judge before whom that person was bound to attend may issue or cause to be issued a warrant in Form 17 for the arrest of that person.

(3) A warrant that is issued by a justice or provincial court judge pursuant to subsection (1) or (2) may be executed anywhere in Canada. R.S. 1985, c. 27 (1st Supp.), s. 203.

Order where witness arrested under warrant.

706. Where a person is brought before a court, judge, justice or provincial court judge under a warrant issued pursuant to subsection 698(2), or section 704 or 705, the court, judge, justice or provincial court judge may order that the person

(*a*) be detained in custody, or

(*b*) be released on recognizance in Form 32, with or without sureties,

to appear and give evidence when required. R.S. 1985, c. 27 (1st Supp.), s. 203.

Maximum period for detention of witness — Application by witness to judge — Review of detention.

707. (1) No person shall be detained in custody under the authority of any provision of this Act, for the purpose only of appearing and giving evidence when required as a witness, for any period exceeding thirty days unless prior to the expiration of those thirty days he has been brought before a judge of a superior court of criminal jurisdiction in the province in which he is being detained.

(2) Where at any time prior to the expiration of the thirty days referred to in subsection (1), a witness being detained in custody as described in that subsection applies to be brought before a judge of a court described therein, the judge before whom the application is brought shall fix a time prior to the expiration of those thirty days for the hearing of the application and shall cause notice of the time so fixed to be given to the witness, the person having custody of the witness and such other persons as the judge may specify, and

at the time so fixed for the hearing of the application the person having custody of the witness shall cause the witness to be brought before a judge of the court for that purpose.

(3) If the judge before whom a witness is brought under this section is not satisfied that the continued detention of the witness is justified, he shall order him to be discharged, or to be released on recognizance in Form 32, with or without sureties, to appear and to give evidence when required, but if the judge is satisfied that the continued detention of the witness is justified, he may order his continued detention until the witness does what is required of him pursuant to section 550 or the trial is concluded, or until the witness appears and gives evidence when required, as the case may be, except that the total period of detention of the witness from the time he was first detained in custody shall not in any case exceed ninety days.

Contempt — Punishment — Form.

708. (1) A person who, being required by law to attend or remain in attendance for the purpose of giving evidence, fails, without lawful excuse, to attend or remain in attendance accordingly is guilty of contempt of court.

(2) A court, judge, justice or provincial court judge may deal summarily with a person who is guilty of contempt of court under this section and that person is liable to a fine not exceeding one hundred dollars or to imprisonment for a term not exceeding ninety days or to both, and may be ordered to pay the costs that are incident to the service of any process under this Part and to his detention, if any.

(3) A conviction under this section may be in Form 38 and a warrant of committal in respect of a conviction under this section may be in Form 25. R.S. 1985, c. 27 (1st Supp.), s. 203.

Evidence on Commission

Order appointing commissioner.

709. A party to proceedings by way of indictment or summary conviction may apply for an order appointing a commissioner to take the evidence of a witness who

(*a*) is, by reason of

(i) physical disability arising out of illness, or

(ii) any other good and sufficient cause,

not likely to be able to attend at the time the trial is held; or

(*b*) is out of Canada. R.S. 1985, c. 27 (1st Supp.), s. 150.

Application where witness is ill — Evidence of medical practitioner.

710. (1) An application under paragraph 709(*a*) shall be made (*a*) to a judge of a superior court of the province in which the proceedings are taken,

(*b*) to a judge of a county or district court in the territorial division in which the proceedings are taken, or

(*c*) to a provincial court judge, where

(i) at the time the application is made, the accused is before a provincial court judge presiding over a preliminary inquiry under Part XVIII, or

(ii) the accused or defendant is to be tried by a provincial court judge acting under Part XIX or XXVII.

(2) An application under subparagraph 709(*a*)(i) may be granted on the evidence of a registered medical practitioner. R.S. 1985, c. 27 (1st Supp.), s. 151.

Reading evidence of witness who is ill.

711. Where the evidence of a witness mentioned in paragraph 709(*a*) is taken by a commissioner appointed under section 710, it may be read in evidence in the proceedings if

(*a*) it is proved by oral evidence or by affidavit that the witness is unable to attend by reason of death or physical disability arising out of illness or some other good and sufficient cause,

(*b*) the transcript of the evidence is signed by the commissioner by or before whom it purports to have been taken; and

(*c*) it is proved to the satisfaction of the court that reasonable notice of the time for taking the evidence was given to the other party, and that the accused or his counsel, or the prosecutor or his counsel, as the case may be, had or might have had full opportunity to cross-examine the witness. R.S. 1985, c. 27 (1st Supp.), s. 152.

Application for order when witness out of Canada — Reading evidence of witness out of Canada.

712. (1) An application that is made under paragraph 709(*b*) shall be made

(*a*) to a judge of a superior court of criminal jurisdiction or of a court of criminal jurisdiction before which the accused is to be tried; or

(*b*) to a provincial court judge, where the accused or defendant is to be tried by a provincial court judge acting under Part XIX or XXVII.

(2) Where the evidence of a witness is taken by a commissioner appointed under this section, it may be read in evidence in the proceedings. 1985, c. 27 (1st Supp.), s. 153.

(3) [Repealed R.S. 1985, c. 27 (1st Supp.), s. 153.]

Providing for presence of accused counsel — Return of evidence.

713. (1) A judge or provincial court judge who appoints a commissioner may make provision in the order to enable an accused to be present or represented by counsel when the evidence is taken, but failure of the accused to be present or to be represented by counsel in accordance with the order does not prevent the reading of the evidence in the proceedings if the evidence has otherwise been taken in accordance with the order and with this Part.

(2) An order for the taking of evidence by commission shall indicate the officer of the court to whom the evidence that is taken under the order shall be returned. R.S. 1985, c. 27 (1st Supp.), s. 203.

Rules and practice same as in civil cases.

714. Except where otherwise provided by this Part or by rules of court, the practice and procedure in connection with the appointment of commissioners under this Part, the taking of evidence by commissioners, the certifying and return thereof and the use of the evidence in the proceedings shall, as far as possible, be the same as those that govern like matters in civil proceedings in the superior court of the province in which the proceedings are taken.

Evidence Previously Taken

Evidence at preliminary inquiry may be read at trial in certain cases — Idem — Absconding accused deemed present.

715. (1) Where, at the trial of an accused, a person whose evidence was given at a previous trial on the same charge, or whose evidence was taken in the investigation of the charge against the accused or on the preliminary inquiry into the charge, refuses to be sworn or to give evidence, or if facts are proved on oath from which it can be inferred reasonably that the person

(*a*) is dead,

(*b*) has since become and is insane,

(*c*) is so ill that he is unable to travel or testify, or

(*d*) is absent from Canada,

and where it is proved that his evidence was taken in the presence of the accused, it may be read as evidence in the proceedings without further proof, if the evidence purports to be signed by the judge or justice before whom it purports to have been taken, unless the accused proves that it was not in fact signed by that judge or justice or that he did not have full opportunity to cross-examine the witness.

(2) Evidence that has been taken on the preliminary inquiry or other investigation of a charge against an accused may be read as evidence in the prosecution of the accused for any other offence on the same proof and in the same manner in all respects, as it might, according to law, be read in the prosecution of the offence with which the accused was charged when the evidence was taken.

(3) For the purposes of this section, where evidence was taken at a previous trial of an accused in the absence of the accused, who was absent by reason

of having absconded, he shall be deemed to have been present during the taking of the evidence and to have had full opportunity to cross-examine the witness.

Videotaped Evidence

Evidence of complainant.

715.1 In any proceeding relating to an offence under section 151, 152, 153, 155 or 159, subsection 160(2) or (3), or section 170, 171, 172, 173, 271, 272, or 273, in which the complainant was under the age of eighteen years at the time the offence is alleged to have been committed, a videotape made within a reasonable time after the alleged offence, in which the complainant describes the acts complained of, is admissible in evidence if the complainant while testifying adopts the contents of the videotape. R.S. 1985, c. 19 (3rd Supp.), s. 16.

PART XXIII

PUNISHMENTS, FINES, FORFEITURES, COSTS AND RESTITUTION OF PROPERTY

Punishment Generally

Definitions — "accused" — "court".

716. In this Part,

"accused" includes a defendant;

"court" means

(*a*) a superior court of criminal jurisdiction,

(*b*) a court of criminal jurisdiction,

(*c*) a justice or provincial court judge acting as a summary conviction court under Part XXVII, or

(*d*) a court that hears an appeal. R.S., 1985, c. 27 (1st Supp.), s. 154.

Degrees of punishment — Discretion respecting punishment — Imprisonment in default where term not specified — Cumulative punishments.

717. (1) Where an enactment prescribes different degrees or kinds of punishment in respect of an offence, the punishment to be imposed is, subject to the limitations prescribed in the enactment, in the discretion of the court that convicts a person who commits the offence.

(2) Where an enactment prescribes a punishment in respect of an offence, the punishment to be imposed is, subject to the limitations prescribed in the enactment, in the discretion of the court that convicts a person who commits the offence, but no punishment is a minimum punishment unless it is declared to be a minimum punishment.

(3) Where an accused is convicted of an offence punishable with both fine and imprisonment and a term of imprisonment in default of payment of the fine is not specified in the enactment that prescribed the punishment to be imposed, the imprisonment that may be imposed in default of payment shall not exceed the term of imprisonment that is prescribed in respect of the offence.

(4) Where an accused

(*a*) is convicted while under sentence for an offence, and a term of imprisonment, whether in default of payment of a fine or otherwise, is imposed,

(*b*) is convicted of an offence punishable with both fine and imprisonment, and both are imposed with a direction that, in default of payment of the fine, the accused shall be imprisoned for a term certain, or

(*c*) is convicted of more offences than one before the same court at the same sittings, and

(i) more than one fine is imposed with a direction in respect of each of them that, in default of payment thereof, the accused shall be imprisoned for a term certain,

(ii) terms of imprisonment for the respective offences are imposed, or

(iii) a term of imprisonment is imposed in respect of one offence and a fine is imposed in respect of another offence with a direction that, in default of payment, the accused shall be imprisoned for a term certain,

the court that convicts the accused may direct that the terms of imprisonment shall be served one after the other.

Fine in lieu of other punishment — Fine in addition to other punishment — Imprisonment in default of payment — Time for payment — What to be considered — Idem — Warrant of committal — Reasons for committal — Surrender by accused — Young offenders — Extension of time — Definition of "fine".

718. (1) An accused who is convicted of an indictable offence punishable with imprisonment for five years or less may be fined in addition to or in lieu of any other punishment that is authorized, but an accused shall not be fined in lieu of imprisonment where the offence of which he is convicted is punishable by a minimum term of imprisonment.

(2) An accused who is convicted of an indictable offence punishable with imprisonment for more than five years may be fined in addition to, but not in lieu of, any other punishment that is authorized.

(3) Where a fine is imposed under this section, a term of imprisonment may be imposed in default of payment of the fine, but no such term shall exceed

(*a*) two years, where the term of imprisonment that may be imposed for the offence is less than five years, or

(*b*) five years, where the term of imprisonment that may be imposed for the offence is five years or more.

(4) Subject to this section, where an accused is convicted of an offence and is fined, the court that convicts the accused may direct that the fine

(*a*) be paid forthwith; or

(*b*) be paid at such time and on such terms as the court may fix.

(5) Where a court imposes a fine, the court shall not, at the time the sentence is imposed, direct that the fine be paid forthwith, unless

(*a*) the court is satisfied that the convicted person is possessed of sufficient means to enable him to pay the fine forthwith;

(*b*) on being asked by the court whether he desires time for payment, or for discharging the fine in accordance with section 718.1, where a program has been established for that purpose, the convicted person does not request such time, or

(*c*) for any other special reason, the court deems it expedient that no time should be allowed.

(6) The court, in considering whether time should be allowed for payment

of a fine and, if so, for what period, shall consider any representation made by the accused but any time allowed shall be not less than fourteen clear days from the date sentence is imposed.

(7) Where time has been allowed for payment of a fine, the court shall not issue a warrant of committal in default of payment of the fine until the expiration of the time allowed for payment.

(8) Where no time has been allowed for payment of a fine and a warrant committing the accused to prison for default of payment of the fine is issued, the court shall state in the warrant the reason for immediate committal.

(9) Notwithstanding subsection (7), where, before the expiration of the time allowed for payment, the accused appears before a court and signifies in writing that he prefers to be committed immediately rather than to await the expiration of the time allowed, the court may forthwith issue a warrant committing the accused to prison.

(10) Where a person who has been allowed time for payment of a fine appears to the court to be not less than sixteen nor more than twenty-one years of age, the court shall, before issuing a warrant committing the person to prison for default of payment of the fine, obtain and consider a report concerning the conduct and means to pay of the accused.

(11) Where time has been allowed for payment under subsection (4), the court that imposed the sentence may, on an application by or on behalf of the accused, allow further time for payment, subject to any rules made by the court under section 482.

(12) In this section, "fine" includes a pecuniary penalty or other sum of money. R.S. 1985, c. 27 (1st Supp.), s. 155.

Fine option program — Credits and other matters — Deemed payment — Federal-provincial agreement.

718.1 (1) An offender, other than a corporation, against whom a fine is imposed in respect of an offence may, whether or not the offender is serving a term of imprisonment imposed in default of payment of the fine, discharge the fine in whole or in part by earning credits for work performed during a period not greater than two years in a program established for that purpose by the Lieutenant Governor in Council

(*a*) of the province in which the fine was imposed; or

(*b*) of the province in which the offender resides, where an appropriate agreement is in effect between the government of that province and the government of the province in which the fine was imposed.

(2) A program referred to in subsection (1) shall determine the rate at which credits are earned and may provide for the manner of crediting any amounts earned against the fine and any other matters necessary for or incidental to carrying out the program.

(3) Credits earned for work performed as provided by subsection (1) shall, for the purposes of this Act, be deemed to be payment in respect of a fine.

(4) Where, by virtue of section 723, the proceeds of a fine belong to Her Majesty in right of Canada, an offender may discharge the fine in whole or in part in a fine option program of a province pursuant to subsection (1), where an appropriate agreement is in effect between the government of the province and the Government of Canada. R.S. 1985, c. 27 (1st Supp.), s. 156.

Fines on corporations.

719. Notwithstanding section 718, a corporation that is convicted of an offence is liable, in lieu of any imprisonment that is prescribed as punishment for that offence, to be fined in an amount, except where otherwise provided by law,

(*a*) that is in the discretion of the court, where the offence is an indictable offence; or

(*b*) not exceeding twenty-five thousand dollars, where the offence is a summary conviction offence. R.S. 1985, c. 27 (1st Supp.), s. 157.

Enforcement of fines on corporations.

720. Where a fine that is imposed on a corporation is not paid forthwith the prosecutor may, by filing the conviction, enter as a judgment the amount of the fine and costs, if any, in the superior court of the province in which the trial was held, and that judgment is enforceable against the corporation in the same manner as if it were a judgment rendered against the corporation in that court in civil proceedings.

Commencement of sentence — Convicted person lawfully at large — Determination of sentence — When time begins to run — Where fine imposed — Application for leave to appeal.

721. (1) A sentence commences when it is imposed, except where a relevant enactment otherwise provides.

(2) Any time during which a convicted person is lawfully at large on interim release granted pursuant to any provision of this Act does not count as part of any term of imprisonment imposed pursuant to his conviction.

(3) In determining the sentence to be imposed on a person convicted of an offence, a justice, provincial court judge or judge may take into account any time spent in custody by the person as a result of the offence.

(4) Notwithstanding subsection (1), a term of imprisonment, whether imposed by a trial court or the court appealed to, commences or shall be deemed to be resumed, as the case requires, on the day on which the convicted person is arrested and taken into custody under the sentence.

(5) Notwithstanding subsection (1), where the sentence that is imposed is a fine with a term of imprisonment in default of payment, no time prior to

the day of execution of the warrant of committal counts as part of the term of imprisonment.

(6) An application for leave to appeal is an appeal for the purposes of this section. R.S. 1985, c. 27 (1st Supp.), s. 203.

Reduction of imprisonment on part payment — Minimum that can be accepted — To whom payment made — Application of money paid — "Penalty".

722. (1) Where a term of imprisonment is imposed in default of payment of a penalty, the term shall, on payment of a part of the penalty, whether the payment was made before or after the issue of a warrant of committal, be reduced by the number of days that bears the same proportion to the number of days in the term as the part paid bears to the total penalty.

(2) No amount offered in part payment of a penalty shall be accepted unless it is sufficient to secure reduction of sentence of one day, or a multiple thereof, and where a warrant of committal has been issued, no part payment shall be accepted until any fee that is payable in respect of the warrant or its execution has been paid.

(3) Payment may be made under this section to the person who has lawful custody of the prisoner or to such other person as the Attorney General directs.

(4) A payment under this section shall, unless the order imposing the penalty otherwise provides, be applied to the payment in full of costs and charges, and thereafter to payment in full of compensation or damages that are included in the penalty, and finally to payment in full of any part of the penalty that remains unpaid.

(5) In this section, "penalty" means all the sums of money, including fines, in default of payment of which a term of imprisonment is imposed and includes the costs and charges of committing the defaulter and of conveying him to prison.

Fines and penalties go to provincial treasurer — Exception — Direction for payment to municipality.

723. (1) Where a fine, penalty or forfeiture is imposed or a recognizance is forfeited and no provision, other than this section, is made by law for the application of the proceeds thereof, the proceeds belong to Her Majesty in right of the province in which the fine, penalty or forfeiture was imposed or the recognizance was forfeited, and shall be paid by the person who receives them to the treasurer of that province.

(2) Where

(*a*) a fine, penalty or forfeiture is imposed

(i) in respect of a contravention of a revenue law of Canada,

(ii) in respect of a breach of duty or malfeasance in office by an officer or employee of the Government of Canada, or

(iii) in respect of any proceedings instituted at the instance of the

Government of Canada in which that government bears the costs of prosecution, or

(*b*) a recognizance in connection with proceedings mentioned in paragraph (*a*) is forfeited,

the proceeds of the fine, penalty, forfeiture or recognizance belong to Her Majesty in right of Canada and shall be paid by the person who receives them to the Receiver General.

(3) Where a provincial, municipal or local authority bears, in whole or in part, the expense of administering the law under which a fine, penalty or forfeiture is imposed or under which proceedings are taken in which a recognizance is forfeited,

(*a*) the lieutenant governor in council may, direct that the proceeds of a fine, penalty, forfeiture or recognizance that belongs to Her Majesty in right of the province shall be paid to that authority; and

(*b*) the Governor in Council may, direct that the proceeds of a fine, penalty, forfeiture or recognizance that belongs to Her Majesty in right of Canada shall be paid to that authority.

Recovery of penalties — Limitation.

724. (1) Where a fine, pecuniary penalty or forfeiture is imposed by law and no other mode is prescribed for the recovery thereof, the fine, pecuniary penalty or forfeiture is recoverable or enforceable in civil proceedings by Her Majesty, but by no other person.

(2) No proceedings under subsection (1) shall be instituted more than two years after the time when the cause of action arose or the offence was committed in respect of which the fine, pecuniary penalty or forfeiture was imposed.

Compensation for loss of property — Enforcement — Moneys found on accused.

725. (1) A court that convicts or discharges under section 736 an accused of an offence may, on the application of a person aggrieved, at the time sentence is imposed, order the accused to pay to that person an amount by way of satisfaction or compensation for loss of or damage to property suffered by that person as a result of the commission of the offence.

(2) Where an amount that is ordered to be paid under subsection (1) is not paid forthwith, the applicant may, by filing the order, enter as a judgment, in the superior court of the province in which the trial was held, the amount ordered to be paid, and that judgment is enforceable against the accused in the same manner as if it were a judgment rendered against the accused in that court in civil proceedings.

(3) All or any part of an amount that is ordered to be paid under subsection (1) may, if the court making the order is satisfied that ownership of or right to possession of those moneys is not disputed by claimants other than the

accused and the court so directs, be taken out of moneys found in the possession of the accused at the time of his arrest. R.S., c. C-34, s. 653; R.S. 1985, c. 27 (1st Supp.), s. 158.

[R.S. 1985, c. 23 (4th Supp.), s. 6 will repeal section 725 and substitute the following.]

Restitution to victims of offences.

725. Where an offender is convicted or discharged under section 736 of an offence, the court imposing sentence on or discharging the offender shall, on application of the Attorney General or on its own motion, in addition to any other punishment imposed on the offender, if it is applicable and appropriate in the circumstances, order that the offender shall, on such terms and conditions as the court may fix, make restitution to another person as follows:

(*a*) in the case of damage to, or the loss or destruction of, the property of any person as a result of the commission of the offence or the arrest or attempted arrest of the offender, by paying to the person an amount not exceeding the replacement value of the property as of the date the order is imposed, less the value of any part of the property that is returned to that person as of the date it is returned, where the amount is readily ascertainable; or

(*b*) in the case of bodily injury to any person as a result of the commission of the offence or the arrest or attempted arrest of the offender, by paying to the person an amount equal to all pecuniary damages, including loss of income or support, incurred as a result of the bodily injury, where the amount is readily ascertainable.

[1992, c. 1, s. 58(1), Sch. I, item 13 will repeal paragraph 725(b) and substitute the following.]

(*b*) in the case of bodily injury to any person as a result of the commission of the offence or the arrest or attempted arrest of the offender, by paying to the person an amount not exceeding all pecuniary damages, including loss of income or support, incurred as a result of the bodily injury, where the amount is readily ascertainable.

Compensation to *bona fide* purchasers — Moneys found on accused.

726. (1) Where an accused is convicted or discharged under section 736 of an offence and any property obtained as a result of the commission of the offence has been sold to an innocent purchaser, the court may, on the application of the purchaser after restitution of the property to its owner, order the accused to pay to the purchaser an amount not exceeding the amount paid by the purchaser for the property.

(2) Where an amount that is ordered to be paid under subsection (1) is not paid forthwith, the applicant may, by filing the order, enter as a judgment, in the superior court of the province in which the trial was held, the amount ordered to be paid, and that judgment is enforceable against the accused in

the same manner as if it were a judgment rendered against the accused in that court in civil proceedings.

(3) All or any part of an amount that is ordered to be paid under subsection (1) may, if the court making the order is satisfied that ownership of or right to possession of those moneys is not disputed by claimants other than the accused and the court so directs, be taken out of moneys found in the possession of the accused at the time of his arrest. R.S., c. C-34, s. 654; R.S. 1985, c. 27 (1st Supp.), s. 159.

[R.S. 1985, c. 23 (4th Supp.), s. 6 will repeal section 726 and substitute the following.]

Restitution to persons acting in good faith.

726. Where an offender is convicted or discharged under section 736 of an offence and

(*a*) any property obtained as a result of the commission of the offence has been conveyed or transferred for valuable consideration to a person acting in good faith and without notice, or

(*b*) the offender has borrowed money on the security of that property from a person acting in good faith and without notice,

the court may, where that property has been returned to the lawful owner or the person who had lawful possession of that property at the time the offence was committed, order the offender to pay as restitution to the person referred to in paragraph (*a*) or (*b*), on such terms as the court may fix, an amount not exceeding the amount of consideration for that propoerty or the total amount outstanding in respect of the loan, as the case may be.

727. [Repealed R.S. 1985, c. 27 (1st Supp.), s. 160.]

[R.S. 1985, c. 23 (4th Supp.), s. 6 will further amend this Act by adding the following sections.]

Inquiry concerning amount of loss and ability of offender to pay — Offender to disclose finances — Report concerning offender's ability to make restitution — Copies of report provided to parties — Time within which restitution to be made — Payment to estate.

727. (1) Before making an order to pay an amount as restitution under section 725 or 726 and for the purpose of determining the amount to be paid, the time for payment and the method of payment, the court shall, unless the offender acknowledges the ability to pay, conduct or cause to be conducted an inquiry concerning the present or future ability of the offender to pay the amount and, in so doing, the court shall consider

(*a*) the employment, earning ability and financial resources of the offender at the present or in the future and any other circumstances that may affect the ability of the offender to make restitution;

(*b*) any benefit, financial or otherwise, derived, directly or indirectly, by the offender as a result of the commission of the offence; and

(*c*) any harm done to, or loss suffered by, any person to whom restitution may be ordered to be made.

(2) The court may require the offender, for the purpose of subsection (1), to disclose to the court, orally or in writing, particulars of the financial circumstances of the offender in the manner and form prescribed by the court and that information shall not be used for any other purpose, except in a prosecution for perjury or giving contradictory evidence in any proceeding.

(3) A court may require that a written report be prepared and filed with the court containing information concerning

(*a*) the financial status of the offender and, in particular, the ability of the offender to make restitution; and

(*b*) the amount to be paid to any person by the offender.

(4) Where a report is filed with the court under subsection (3), the clerk of the court shall forthwith cause a copy of the report to be provided to the offender or counsel for the offender and the prosecutor.

(5) Where a court makes an order of restitution under section 725 or 726 in relation to an offender, the court may require the offender to comply with the order forthwith or within a specified period ending not later than, or in specified instalments ending not later than, three years after the day on which the order is made.

(6) Where a person to whom an amount is ordered to be paid under section 725 or 726 dies before the order is fully complied with, the amount shall be paid to the estate of such person.

Moneys found on offender.

727.1 All or part of an amount that is ordered to be paid under section 725 or 726 may be taken out of moneys found in the possession of the offender at the time of the arrest of the offender if the court making the order, on being satisfied that ownership of or right to possession of those moneys is not disputed by claimants other than the offender, so directs.

Notice to interested persons — Notice of orders under sections 725 and 726 — Service of notices — Order of restitution to be recorded.

727.2 (1) Before making an order of restitution under section 725 or 726, the court may direct that notice be given to any person who may be the beneficiary of such an order and to such other persons having an interest in the order as the court thinks fit.

(2) Where a court makes an order of restitution under section 725 or 726, it shall cause notice of the terms of the order or a copy of the order to be given to the person who is to be beneficiary of the order.

(3) Any notice or copy of an order required to be given pursuant to this

section or section 727.4 shall be given or served in such manner as the court directs or as may be prescribed by rules of court made under section 482.

(4) Where a court makes an order of restitution under section 725 or 726, it shall enter the terms of the order in the record of the proceedings or, where the proceedings are not recorded, the order and the terms thereof shall be in writing.

Priority to restitution.

727.3 Where the court finds it applicable and appropriate in the circumstances of a case to make, in relation to an offender, an order of restitution under section 725 or 726, and

(*a*) an order of forfeiture under this or any other Act of Parliament may be made in respect of property that is the same as property in respect of which the order of restitution may be made, or

(*b*) the court is considering ordering the offender to pay a fine and it appears to the court that the offender would not have the means and ability to comply with both the order of restitution and the order to pay the fine.

the court shall first make the order of restitution and shall then consider whether and to what extent an order of forfeiture or an order to pay a fine is appropriate in the circumstances.

Extension of time for payment of orders of restitution — Notice to beneficiary — Maximum extension for payment of restitution.

727.4 (1) Subject to subsection (2), where an order of restitution made under section 725 or 726 specifies a period within which or instalments in which payment is to be made, the court that made the order may, unless an information has been laid under section 727.6 on an application by or on behalf of the offender, extend the period or vary the instalments, subject to rules of court made under section 482.

(2) Before extending the period within which or varying the instalments in which payment is to be made pursuant to an order of restitution made under section 725 or 726, the court may direct that notice be given to, and may hear, the beneficiary of the order.

(3) A court shall not extend the period within which payment of restitution is to be made pursuant to subsection (1) to a date later than the expiration of the fourth year after the day on which the order of restitution was made under section 725 or 726, as the case may be.

Enforcement of orders of restitution.

727.5 Where an order of restitution made under section 725 or 726 is not complied with forthwith, the beneficiary of the order may, by filing the order, enter it as a judgment in the superior court of the province in which the trial was held and that judgment is enforceable against the offender in the same manner as if it were a judgment rendered against the offender in that court in civil proceedings.

Idem — When default in payment of restitution — Limitation — Hearing — Disposition after hearing — Effect of judgment — Where reasonable excuse — Notice — Maximum extension for period of restitution — Service of term of imprisonment — Endorsement of order as varied.

727.6 (1) Any person who, on reasonable grounds, believes that an offender has failed or refused to comply with, or defaulted under, an order of restitution made under section 725 or 726 may lay an information in writing and under oath before a justice who shall receive the information, and the matter shall be dealt with by the court that made the order or any other court that would, having regard to the mode of trial of the offender, have had jurisdiction to make the order or, with the consent of the prosecutor and the offender, by any other court of criminal jurisdiction or superior court of criminal jurisdiction.

(2) The payment of an amount by way of restitution is in default when any part of the amount is due and unpaid on the day fixed or provided for payment under the terms of the order of restitution.

(3) No proceedings under subsection (1) shall be instituted more than six years after the date of the alleged failure or refusal to comply or alleged default.

(4) The justice who receives an information under subsection (1) shall require the offender to appear before the court that, pursuant to subsection (1), is to deal with the matter.

(5) At a hearing held pursuant to this section, the court shall hear the prosecutor and the offender and, where the court is satisfied that the offender has failed or refused, without reasonable excuse, the proof of which lies on the offender, to comply with the order of restitution made in relation to that offender, the court shall

(*a*) direct that the order be filed and entered as a judgment for the unpaid amount of the order in the superior court of the province in which the trial was held; and

(*b*) if it is appropriate in the circumstances, impose on the offender a term of imprisonment not exceeding two years, where the order was made in respect of an indictable offence, or not exceeding six months, where the order was made in respect of a summary conviction offence.

(6) A judgment entered in a court pursuant to paragraph (5)(*a*) is enforceable against the offender in the same manner as if it were a judgment rendered against the offender in that court in civil proceedings.

(7) At a hearing held pursuant to this section, where an offender establishes that the offender had a reasonable excuse for failing or refusing to comply with the order of restitution made in relation to that offender, the court may, subject to subsections (7.1) and (8), extend any term of the order, including

the period within which payment of restitution is to be made, and vary any other term of the order except the amount ordered to be paid.

(7.1) Before exercising any of the powers provided for in subsection (7), the court may direct that notice be given to, any may hear, the beneficiary of the order of restitution.

(8) A court shall not extend the period within which payment of restitution is to be made pursuant to subsection (7) to a date later than the expiration of the fourth year after the day on which the order of restitution was made under section 725 or 726, as the case may be.

(9) Any term of imprisonment imposed under this section shall be served consecutively to any other term of imprisonment that is being or is to be served by the offender unless the court orders otherwise.

(10) Where, under subsection (7), the court makes any changes or additions to an order or the terms or conditions thereof or changes the period for which an order is to remain in force, it shall endorse the order accordingly and cause the offender to be informed of its action and to be given a copy of the order so endorsed.

Compelling appearance.

727.7 The provisions of Parts XVI and XVIII with respect to compelling the appearance of an accused before a justice and with respect to release and detention apply, with such modifications as the circumstances require, to proceedings under section 727.6 and in particular, but without limiting the generality of the foregoing,

(*a*) a peace officer may arrest withou warrant a person bound by an order made under section 725 or 726 who has contravened the order or who, on reasonable grounds, is believed to have contravened the order, where the peace officer has reasonable grounds to believe that, if the person is not so arrested, the person will fail to attend court in order to be dealt with according to law; and

(*b*) as if the references in those provisions of Parts XVI and XVIII to an "offence" were references to a "contravention of an order to make restitution."

Reduction of imprisonment on partial payment — Minimum that can be accepted — To whom payment made — Application of money paid — Priority to restitution.

727.8 (1) Where a term of imprisonment is imposed under section 727.6 for failure or refusal to pay an amount by way of restitution pursuant to an order made under section 725 or 726, the term shall, on the payment of part of the amount, whether the payment was made before or after the issue of a warrant of committal, be reduced by the number of days that bears the same proportion to the number of days in the term as the part paid bears to the total amount in respect of which the offender was imprisoned.

(2) No amount offered in partial payment shall be accepted unless it is sufficient to secure a reduction of sentence of one day, or a multiple thereof, and where a warrant of committal has been issued, no partial payment shall be received until any fee that is payable in respect of the warrant or its execution has been paid.

(3) Payment may be made under this section to the person who has lawful custody of the offender or to such other person as the Attorney General directs.

(4) Subject to subsection (5), a payment under this section shall be applied first to the payment in full of the amount by way of restitution and thereafter to the payment in full of the costs and charges of committing and conveying the offender to prison.

(5) Where a term of imprisonment is imposed for failure or refusal to pay both a fine and an amount by way of restitution, a payment under this section shall be applied first to the payment in full of any part of the amount to be paid by way of restitution that remains unpaid, and thereafter to payment in full of any part of the fine that remains unpaid.

Victim fine surcharge — Exception — Written reasons for not making order — Amounts applied to aid victims — Regulations — Enforcement.

727.9 (1) Subject to subsection (2), where an offender is convicted or discharged under section 736 of an offence under this Act, Part III or IV of the *Food and Drugs Act* or the *Narcotic Control Act*, the court imposing sentence on or discharging the offender shall, in addition to any other punishment imposed on the offender, order the offender to pay a victim fine surcharge in an amount not exceeding

(*a*) fifteen per cent of any fine that is imposed on the offender for that offence or, where no fine is imposed on the offender for that offence, ten thousand dollars, or

(*b*) such lesser amount as may be prescribed by, or calculated in the manner prescribed by, regulations made by the Governor in Council,

subject to such terms and conditions as may be prescribed by regulations made by the Governor in Council.

(2) Where the offender establishes to the satisfaction of the court that undue hardship to the offender or the dependants of the offender would result from the making of an order under subsection (1), the court is not required to make the order.

(3) Where the court does not make an order under subsection (1), the court shall

(*a*) provide the reasons why the order is not being made; and

(*b*) enter the reasons in the record of the proceedings or, where the proceedings are not recorded, provide written reasons.

(4) A victim fine surcharge imposed under subsection (1) shall be applied

for the purposes of providing such assistance to victims of offences as the Lieutenant Governor in Council of the province in which the surcharge is imposed may direct from time to time.

(5) The Governor in Council may, for the purposes of subsection (1), make regulations prescribing the maximum amount or the manner of calculating the maximum amount of a victim fine surchage to be imposed under that subsection, not exceeding the amount referred to in paragraph (1)(*a*), and any terms and conditions subject to which the victim fine surcharge is to be imposed.

(6) Subsections 718(3) to (11) apply and section 718.1 does not apply in respect of a victim fine surcharge imposed under subsection (1). R.S. 1985, c. 23 (4th Supp.), s. 6.

[NOTE: 1988, c. 30, s. 8 states:

Section 727.9 of the Criminal Code, *as enacted by section 6 of this Act, does not apply to any proceedings in respect of an offence committed before the coming into force of that section.]*

Costs to successful party in case of libel.

728. The person in whose favour judgment is given in proceedings by indictment for defamatory libel is entitled to recover from the opposite party costs in a reasonable amount to be fixed by order of the court.

How recovered.

729. Where costs that are fixed under section 728 are not paid forthwith, the party in whose favour judgment is given may enter judgment for the amount of the costs by filing the order in the superior court of the province in which the trial was held, and that judgment is enforceable against the opposite party in the same manner as if it were a judgment rendered against him in that court in civil proceedings.

Imprisonment

Imprisonment when no other provision.

730. Every one who is convicted of an indictable offence for which no punishment is specially provided is liable to imprisonment for a term not exceeding five years.

Imprisonment for life or more than two years — Subsequent term less than two years — Imprisonment for term less than two years — Sentence to penitentiary of person serving sentence elsewhere — Transfer to penitentiary — Only definite portion of certain sentences to be counted — Idem — Exemptions.

731. (1) Except where otherwise provided, a person who is sentenced to imprisonment for

(*a*) life,

(*b*) a term of two years or more, or

(*c*) two or more terms of less than two years each that are to be served one after the other and that, in the aggregate, amount to two years or more,

shall be sentenced to imprisonment in a penitentiary.

(2) Where a person who is sentenced to imprisonment in a penitentiary is, before the expiration of that sentence, sentenced to imprisonment for a term of less than two years, he shall be sentenced to and shall serve that term in a penitentiary, but if the previous sentence of imprisonment in a penitentiary is set aside, he shall serve that term in accordance with subsection (3).

(3) A person who is sentenced to imprisonment and who is not required to be sentenced as provided in subsection (1) or (2) shall, unless a special prison is prescribed by law, be sentenced to imprisonment in a prison or other place of confinement within the province in which he is convicted, other than a penitentiary, in which the sentence of imprisonment may be lawfully executed.

(4) Where a person is sentenced to imprisonment in a penitentiary while he is lawfully imprisoned in a place other than a penitentiary he shall, except where otherwise provided, be sent immediately to the penitentiary and shall serve in the penitentiary the unexpired portion of the term of imprisonment that he was serving when he was sentenced to the penitentiary as well as the term of imprisonment for which he was sentenced to the penitentiary.

(5) Where, at any time, a person who is imprisoned in a prison or place of confinement other than a penitentiary is subject to two or more terms of imprisonment, each of which is for less than two years, that are to be served one after the other, and the aggregate of the unexpired portions of those terms at that time amounts to two years or more, he shall be transferred to a penitentiary to serve those terms, but if any one or more of those terms is set aside and the unexpired portions of the remaining term or terms on the day on which he was transferred under this section amounted to less than two years, he shall serve that term or terms in accordance with subsection (3).

(6) For the purposes of this section, where a person is sentenced to imprisonment for a definite term and an indeterminate period thereafter, such sentence shall be deemed to be for a term of less than two years and only the definite term thereof shall be taken into account in determining whether he is required to be sentenced to imprisonment in a penitentiary or to be committed or transferred to a penitentiary under subsection (5).

(7) Where a person has been sentenced, committed or transferred to a penitentiary, otherwise than pursuant to an agreement made under subsection 18(1) of the *Penitentiary Act,* any indeterminate portion of his sentence shall, for all purposes, be deemed not to have been imposed.

[1992, c. 20, s. 200(1) will repeal subsections 731(6) and (7).]

(8) For the purposes of subsection (3) "penitentiary" does not, until a day to be fixed by order of the Governor in Council, include the pentitentiary

mentioned in subsection 16(1) of the Penitenitiry Act. 1992, c. 1, s. 58(1), Sch. I, item 14.

[1992, c. 20, s. 200(2) will repeal subsection 731(8) and substitute the following.]

Newfoundland.

(8) For the purposes of subsection (3), "pentitentiary" does not, until a day to be fixed by order of the Governor in Council, include the facility mentioned in subsection 15(2) of the *Corrections and Conditional Release Act.*

[1992, c. 20, s. 201 will add the following immediately after section 731.]

Report by court to Correctional Service.

731.1 A court that sentences or commits a person to pentitentiary shall forward to the Correctional Service of Canada its reasons and recommendations relating to the sentence or committal, any relevant reports that were submitted to the court, and any other information relevant to administering the sentence or committal.

Sentence served according to regulations — Hard labour improperly ordered.

732. (1) A sentence of imprisonment shall be served in accordance with the enactments and rules that govern the institution to which the prisoner is sentenced, and a reference to hard labour in a conviction or sentence shall be deemed to be a reference to the employment of prisoners that is provided for in the enactments or rules.

(2) A conviction or sentence that imposes hard labour shall not be quashed or set aside on the ground only that the enactment that creates the offence does not authorize the imposition of hard labour, but shall be amended accordingly.

Transfer of young person to place of custody — Removal of young person from place of custody — Definitions.

733. (1) Where a young person is sentenced to imprisonment under this or any other Act of Parliament, the young person may, with the consent of the provincial director, be transferred to a place of custody for any portion of his term of imprisonment, but in no case shall the young person be kept in a place of custody under this section after he attains the age of twenty years.

(2) Where the provincial director certifies that a young person transferred to a place of custody under subsection (1) can no longer be held therein without significant danger of escape or of detrimentally affecting the rehabilitation or reformation of other young persons held therein, the young person may be imprisoned during the remainder of his term of imprisonment in any place where he might, but for subsection (1), have been imprisoned.

(3) For the purposes of this section, the expressions "adult", "provincial director" and "young person" have the meanings assigned by subsection 2(1)

of the *Young Offenders Act* and the expression "place of custody" means "open custody" or "secure custody" within the meaning assigned by subsection 24(1) of that Act. R.S. 1985 (2d Supp.), c. 24, s. 46.

Delivery of Accused to Keeper of Prison

Execution of warrant of committal.

734. A peace officer or other person to whom a warrant of committal authorized by this or any other Act of Parliament is directed shall arrest the person named or described therein, if it is necessary to do so in order to take that person into custody, convey that person to the prison mentioned in the warrant and deliver him, together with the warrant, to the keeper of the prison who shall thereupon give to the peace officer or other person who delivers the prisoner a receipt in Form 43 setting out the state and condition of the prisoner when delivered into his custody. R.S. 1985, c. 27 (1st Supp.), s. 161.

Report by probation officer — Victim impact statement — Procedure for victim impact statement — Other evidence concerning victim admissible — Definition of "victim" — Copies to be provided.

735. (1) Where an accused, other than a corporation, pleads guilty to or is found guilty of an offence, a probation officer shall, if required to do so by a court, prepare and file with the court a report in writing relating to the accused for the purpose of assisting the court in imposing sentence or in determining whether the accused should be discharged pursuant to section 736.

(1.1) For the purpose of determining the sentence to be imposed on an offender or whether the offender should be discharged pursuant to section 662.1 in respect of any offence, the court may consider a statement, prepared in accordance with subsection (1.2), of a victim of the offence describing the harm done to, or loss suffered by, the victim arising from the commission of the offence.

(1.2) A statement referred to in subsection (1.1) shall be

(*a*) prepared in writing in the form and in accordance with the procedures established by a program designated for the purpose by the Lieutenant Governor in Council of the province in which the court is exercising its jurisdiction; and

(*b*) filed with the court.

(1.3) A statement of a victim of an offence prepared and filed in accordance with subsection (1.2) does not prevent the court from considering any other evidence concerning any victim of the offence for the purpose of determining the sentence to be imposed on the offender or whether the offender should be discharged pursuant to section 662.1.

(1.4) For the purpose of this section, "victim", in relation to an offence,

(*a*) means the person to whom harm is done or who suffers physical or emotional loss as a result of the commission of the offence, and
(*b*) where the person described in paragraph (*a*) is dead, ill or otherwise incapable of making a statement referred to in subsection (1.1), includes the spouse or any relative of that person, anyone who has in law or in fact the custody of that person or is responsible for the care or support of that person or any dependant of that person.

(2) Where a report of statement is filed with the court under subsection (1) or (1.2), the clerk of the court shall forthwith cause a copy of the report or statement to be provided to the offender or counsel for the offender and to the prosecutor. R.S. 1985, c. 23 (4th Supp.), s. 7.

Conditional and absolute discharge — Period for which appearance notice, etc. continues in force — Effect of discharge — Where person bound by probation order convicted of offence.

736. (1) Where an accused, other than a corporation, pleads guilty to or is found guilty of an offence, other than an offence for which a minimum punishment is prescribed by law or an offence punishable, in the proceedings commenced against him, by imprisonment for fourteen years or for life, the court before which he appears may, if it considers it to be in the best interests of the accused and not contrary to the public interest, instead of convicting the accused, by order direct that the accused be discharged absolutely or on the conditions prescribed in a probation order.

(2) Subject to the provisions of Part XVI, where an accused who has not been taken into custody or who has been released from custody under or by virtue of any provision of Part XVI pleads guilty to or is found guilty of an offence but is not convicted, the appearance notice, promise to appear, summons, undertaking or recognizance issued to or given or entered into by him continues in force, subject to its terms, until a disposition in respect of him is made under subsection (1) unless, at the time he pleads guilty or is found guilty, the court, judge or justice orders that he be taken into custody pending such a disposition.

(3) Where a court directs under subsection (1) that an offender be discharged of an offence, the offender shall be deemed not to have been convicted of the offence except that
(*a*) the offender may appeal from the determination of guilt as if it were a conviction in respect of the offence;
(*b*) the Attorney General and, in the case of summary conviction proceedings, the informant or the informant's agent may appeal from the decision of the court not to convict the offender of the offence as if that decision were a judgment or verdict of acquittal of the offence or a dismissal of the information against the offender; and
(*c*) the offender may plead *autrefois convict* in respect of any subsequent charge relating to the offence.

(4) Where an accused who is bound by the conditions of a probation order made at a time when he was directed to be discharged under this section is convicted of an offence, including an offence under section 740, the court that made the probation order may, in addition to or in lieu of exercising its authority under subsection 738(4), at any time when it may take action under that subsection, revoke the discharge, convict the accused of the offence to which the discharge relates and impose any sentence that could have been imposed if the accused had been convicted at the time he was discharged, and no appeal lies from a conviction under this subsection where an appeal was taken from the order directing that the accused be discharged. R.S. 1985, c. 27 (1st Supp.), s. 162.

[1991, c. 43, s. 6 will add the following immediately after section 736.]

Definitions — "assessment report" — "hospital order" — "medical practitioner" — "treatment facility".

736.1 In this section and sections 736.11 to 736.18,

"assessment report" means a written report made pursuant to an assessment order made under section 672.11 by a psychiatrist who is entitled under the laws of a province to practise psychiatry or, where a psychiatrist is not practicably available, by a medical practitioner;

"hospital order" means an order by a court under section 736.11 that an offender be detained in a treatment facility;

"medical practitioner" means a person who is entitled to practise medicine by the laws of a province;

"treatment facility" means any hospital or place for treatment of the mental disorder of an offender, or a place within a class of such places, designated by the Governor in Council, the lieutenant governor in council of the province in which the offender is sentenced or a person to whom authority has been delegated in writing for that purpose by the Governor in Council or that lieutenant governor in council.

Court may make a hospital order — Limitation on hospital order — Form — Warrant of committal.

736.11 (1) A court may order that an offender be detained in a treatment facility as the initial part of a sentence of imprisonment where it finds, at the time of sentencing, that the offender is suffering from a mental disorder in an acute phase and the court is satisfied, on the basis of an assesment report and any other evidence, that immediate treatment of the mental disorder is urgently required to prevent further significant deterioration of the mental or physical health of the offender, or to prevent the offender from causing serious bodily harm to any person.

(2) A hospital order shall be for a single period of treatment not exceeding

sixty days, subject to any terms and conditions that the court considers appropriate.

(3) A hospital order may be in Form 51.

(4) A court that makes a hospital order shall issue a warrant for committal of the offender, which may be in Form 8.

Recommended treatment facility — Court chooses treatment facility.

736.12 (1) In a hospital order, the court shall specify that the offender be detained in a particular treatment facility recommended by the central administration of any penitentiary, prison or other institution to which the offender has been sentenced to imprisonment, unless the court is satisfied, on the evidence of a medical practitioner, that serious harm to the mental or physical health of the offender would result from travelling to that treatment facility or from the delay occasioned in travelling there.

(2) Where the court does not follow a recommendation referred to in subsection (1), it shall order that the offender be detained in a treatment facility that is reasonably accessible to the place where the accused is detained when the hospital order is made or to the place where the court is located.

Condition.

736.13 No hospital order may be made unless the offender and the person in charge of the treatment facility where the offender is to be detained consent to the order and its terms and conditions, but nothing in this section shall be construed as making unnecessary the obtaining of any authorization or consent to treatment from any other person that is or may be required otherwise than under this Act.

Exception.

736.14 No hospital order may be made in respect of an offender

(*a*) who is convicted of or is serving a sentence imposed in respect of a conviction for an offence for which a minimum punishment of imprisonment for life is prescribed by law;

(*b*) who has been found to be a dangerous offender pursuant to section 753;

(*c*) where the term of imprisonment to be served by the offender does not exceed sixty days;

(*d*) where the term of imprisonment is imposed

(i) on the offender in default of payment of a fine or of a victim fine surcharge imposed under subsection 727.9(1), or

(ii) under section 727.6 for failure or refusal to pay an amount by way of restitution pursuant to an order made under section 725 or 726; or

(*e*) where the sentence of imprisonment imposed on the offender is ordered under paragraph 737(1)(*c*) to be served intermittently.

Offender to serve remainder of sentence — Transfer from one treatment facility to another.

736.15 (1) An offender shall be sent or returned to a prison to serve the portion of the offender's sentence that remains unexpired where

(*a*) the hospital order expires before the expiration of the sentence; or

(*b*) the consent to the detention of the offender in the treatment facility pursuant to the hospital order is withdrawn either by the offender or by the person in charge of the treatment facility.

(2) Before the expiration of a hospital order in respect of an offender, the offender may be transferred from the treatment facility specified in the hospital order to another treatment facility where treatment of the offender's mental disorder is available, if the court authorizes the transfer in writing and the person in charge of the treatment facility consents.

Detention to count as service of term.

736.16 Each day that an offender is detained under a hospital order shall be treated as a day of service of the term of imprisonment of the offender and the offender shall be deemed, for all purposes, to be lawfully confined in a prison during that detention.

Application of subsection 19(1) of Penitentiary Act.

736.17 Notwithstanding subsection 19(1) of the *Penitentiary Act*, an offender in respect of whom a hospital order is made and who is sentenced or committed to a penitentiary shall be detained in the treatment facility specified in the order during the period that it is in force, and may be received in a penitentiary for the purpose of the order before the expiration of the time limited by law for an appeal.

[1992, c. 20, s. 229 will repeal section 736.17 and substitute the following upon the coming into force of 1991, c. 43, s. 6.]

Application of section 12 of *Corrections and Conditional Release Act*.

736.17 Notwithstanding section 12 of the *Corrections and Conditional Release Act*, an offender in respect of whom a hospital order is made and who is sentenced or committed to a pentitentiary may, during the period for which that order is in force, be received in a pentitentiary before the expiration of the time limited by law for an appeal and shall be detained in the treatment facility specified in the order during that period.

Copy of warrant and order given to prison and hospital.

736.18 Where a court makes a hospital order in respect of an offender, the court shall cause a copy of the order and of the warrant of committal issued pursuant to subsection 736.11(4) to be sent to the central administration of the penitentiary, prison or other institution where the term of imprisonment imposed on the offender is to be served and to the treatment facility where the offender is to be detained for treatment.

Making of probation order — Conditions in probation order — Form and period of order — Proceedings on making of order.

737. (1) Where an accused is convicted of an offence, the court may, having regard to the age and character of the accused, the nature of the offence and the circumstances surrounding its commission,

(*a*) in the case of an offence other than one for which a minimum punishment is prescribed by law, suspend the passing of sentence and direct that the accused be released on the conditions prescribed in a probation order;

(*b*) in addition to fining the accused or sentencing him to imprisonment, whether in default of payment of a fine or otherwise, for a term not exceeding two years, direct that the accused comply with the conditions prescribed in a probation order; or

(*c*) where it imposes a sentence of imprisonment on the accused, whether in default of payment of a fine or otherwise, that does not exceed ninety days, order that the sentence be served intermittently at such times as are specified in the order and direct that the accused, at all times when he is not in confinement pursuant to such order, comply with the conditions prescribed in a probation order.

(2) The following conditions shall be deemed to be prescribed in a probation order, namely, that the accused shall keep the peace and be of good behaviour and shall appear before the court when required to do so by the court, and, in addition, the court may prescribe as conditions in a probation order that the accused shall do any one or more of the following things as specified in the order, namely,

(*a*) report to and be under the supervision of a probation officer or other person designated by the court;

(*b*) provide for the support of his spouse or any other dependants whom he is liable to support;

(*c*) abstain from the consumption of alcohol either absolutely or on such terms as the court may specify;

(*d*) abstain from owning, possessing or carrying a weapon;

(*e*) make restitution or reparation to any person aggrieved or injured by the commission of the offence for the actual loss or damage sustained by that person as a result thereof;

(*f*) remain within the jurisdiction of the court and notify the court or the probation officer or other person designated under paragraph (*a*) of any change in his address or his employment or occupation;

(*g*) make reasonable efforts to find and maintain suitable employment; and

(*h*) comply with such other reasonable conditions as the court considers desirable for securing the good conduct of the accused and for preventing a repetition by him of the same offence or the commission of other offences.

(3) A probation order may be in Form 46, and the court that makes the probation order shall specify therein the period for which it is to remain in force.

(4) Where the court makes a probation order, it shall

(*a*) cause the order to be read by or to the accused;

(*b*) cause a copy of the order to be given to the accused; and

(*c*) inform the accused of the provisions of subsection 738(4) and of section 740.

Coming into force of order — Duration of order and limit on term of order — Modification of order — Modification of order where person bound convicted of offence — Compelling appearance of person bound.

738. (1) A probation order comes into force

(*a*) on the date on which the order is made; or

(*b*) where the accused is sentenced to imprisonment under paragraph 737(1)(*b*) otherwise than in default of payment of a fine, on the expiration of that sentence.

(2) Subject to subsection (4),

(*a*) where an accused who is bound by a probation order is convicted of an offence, including an offence under section 740, or is imprisoned under paragraph 737(1)(*b*) in default of payment of a fine, the order continues in force except in so far as the sentence renders it impossible for the accused for the time being to comply with the order; and

(*b*) no probation order shall continue in force for more than three years from the date on which the order came into force.

(3) Where a court has made a probation order, the court may at any time, on application by the accused or the prosecutor, require the accused to appear before it and, after hearing the accused and the prosecutor,

(*a*) make any changes in or additions to the conditions prescribed in the order that in the opinion of the court are rendered desirable by a change in the circumstances since the conditions were prescribed,

(*b*) relieve the accused, either absolutely or on such terms or for such period as the court deems desirable, of compliance with any condition described in any of paragraphs 737(2)(*a*) to (*h*) that is prescribed in the order, or

(*c*) decrease the period for which the order is to remain in force,

and the court shall thereupon endorse the probation order accordingly and, if it changes or adds to the conditions prescribed in the order, inform the accused of its action and give him a copy of the order so endorsed.

(4) Where an accused who is bound by a probation order is convicted of an offence, including an offence under section 740, and

(*a*) the time within which an appeal may be taken against that conviction has expired and he has not taken an appeal, (*b*) he has taken an appeal against that conviction and the appeal has been dismissed, or

(*c*) he has given written notice to the court that convicted him that he elects not to appeal his conviction or has abandoned his appeal, as the case may be,

in addition to any punishment that may be imposed for that offence, the court that made the probation order may, on application by the prosecutor, require the accused to appear before it and, after hearing the prosecutor and the accused,

(*d*) where the probation order was made under paragraph 737(1)(*a*), revoke the order and impose any sentence that could have been imposed if the passing of sentence had not been suspended, or

(*e*) make such changes in or additions to the conditions prescribed in the order as the court deems desirable or extend the period for which the order is to remain in force for such period, not exceeding one year, as the court deems desirable,

and the court shall thereupon endorse the probation order accordingly and, if it changes or adds to the conditions prescribed in the order or extends the period for which the order is to remain in force, inform the accused of its action and give him a copy of the order so endorsed.

(5) The provisions of Parts XVI and XVIII with respect to compelling the appearance of an accused before a justice apply with such modifications as the circumstances require to proceedings under subsections (3) and (4).

Transfer of order — Where court unable to act.

739. (1) Where an accused who is bound by a probation order becomes a resident of, or is convicted or discharged under section 736 of an offence including an offence under section 740 in a territorial division, other than the territorial division where the order was made, the court that made the order may, on the application of the prosecutor, and, if both such territorial divisions are not in the same province, with the consent of

(*a*) the Attorney General of Canada, in the case of proceedings in relation to an offence that were instituted at the instance of the Government of Canada and conducted by or on behalf of that Government, or

(*b*) in any other case, the Attorney General of the province in which the order was made,

transfer the order to a court in that other territorial division that would, having regard to the mode of trial of the accused, have had jurisdiction to make the order in that other territorial division if the accused had been tried and convicted there of the offence in respect of which the order was made, and the order may thereafter be dealt with and enforced by the court to which it is so transferred in all respects as if that court had made the order.

(2) Where a court that has made a probation order or to which a probation order has been transferred pursuant to subsection (1) is for any reason unable to act, the powers of that court in relation to the probation order may be

exercised by any other court that has equivalent jurisdiction in the same province. R.S. 1985, c. 27 (1st Supp.), s. 163.

Failure to comply with order — Where accused may be tried and punished.

740. (1) An accused who is bound by a probation order and who wilfully fails or refuses to comply with that order is guilty of an offence punishable on summary conviction.

(2) An accused who is charged with an offence under subsection (1) may be tried and punished by any court having jurisdiction to try that offence in the place where the offence is alleged to have been committed or in the place where the accused is found, is arrested or is in custody, but where the place where the accused is found, is arrested or is in custody is outside the province in which the offence is alleged to have been committed, no proceedings in respect of that offence shall be instituted in that place without the consent of the Attorney General of that province.

741. [Repealed R.S. 1985, c. 27 (1st Supp.), s. 164.]

Dispositions Against Young Persons

Transfer of jurisdiction — Whether sentence to be served concurrently or consecutively — Remaining portion deemed to constitute one sentence.

741.1 (1) Where a person is sentenced for an offence while subject to a disposition made under paragraph 20(1)(*j*), (*k*), or (*k*.1) of the *Young Offenders Act*, on the application of the Attorney General or the Attorney General's agent, the court that sentences the person may, unless to so order would bring the administration of justice into disrepute, order that the remaining portion of the disposition made under that Act be dealt with, for all purposes under this Act or any other Act of Parliament, as if it had been a sentence imposed under this Act.

(2) Where an order is made under subsection (1), in respect of a disposition made under paragraph 20(1)(*k*) or (*k*.1) or the *Young Offenders Act*, the remaining portion of the disposition to be served pursuant to the order shall be served concurrently with the sentence referred to in subsection (1), where it is a term of imprisonment, unless the court making the order orders that it be served consecutively.

(3) For greater certainty, the remaining portion of the disposition referred to in subsection (2) shall, for the purposes of section 20 of the *Parole Act* and section 731 of this Act, be deemed to constitute one sentence of imprisonment imposed on the day the order is made. R.S. 1985, c. 24 (2d Supp.), s. 47; 1992, c. 11, s. 14.

[1992, c. 20, s. 202 will repeal subsection 741.1(3) and subsitute the following.]

Remaining portion deemed to constitute one sentence.

(3) For greater certainty, the remaining portion of the disposition referred

to in subsection (2) shall, for the purposes of section 139 of the *Corrections and Conditional Release Act* and section 731 of this Act, be deemed to constitute one sentence of imprisonment imposed on the day the order is made.

[1992, c. 20, s. 203 will add the following immediately after section 741.1.]

Eligibility for Parole

Power of court to delay parole.

741.2 Notwithstanding subsection 120(1) of the *Corrections and Conditional Release Act*, where an offender is sentenced, after the coming into force of this section, to a term of imprisonment of two years or more on conviction for one or more offences set out in Schedules I and II to that Act that were prosecuted by way of indictment, the court may, if satisfied, having regard to the circumstances of the commission of the offences and the character and circumstances of the offender, that the expression of society's denunciation of the offences or the objective of specific or general deterrence so requires, order that the portion of the sentence that must be served before the offender may be released on full parole is one half of the sentence or ten years, whichever is less.

Imprisonment for Life

Sentence of life imprisonment.

742. Subject to section 742.1, the sentence to be pronounced against a person who is to be sentenced to imprisonment for life shall be

(*a*) in respect of a person who has been convicted of high treason or first degree murder, that he be sentenced to imprisonment for life without eligibility for parole until he has served twenty-five years of his sentence;

(*a*.1) in respect of a person who has been convicted of second degree murder where that person has previously been convicted of culpable homicide that is murder, however described under this Act, that he be sentenced to imprisonment for life without eligibility for parole until he has served twenty-five years of his sentence;

(*b*) in respect of a person who has been convicted of second degree murder, that he be sentenced to imprisonment for life without eligibility for parole until he has served at least ten years of his sentence or such greater number of years, not being more than twenty-five years, as has been substituted therefor pursuant to section 744; and

(*c*) in respect of a person who has been convicted of any other offence, that he be sentenced to imprisonment for life with normal eligibility for parole. R.S. 1985, c. 27 (1st Supp.), s. 165; 1992, c. 11, s. 15.

Persons under eighteen.

742.1 The sentence to be pronounced against a person who was under the age of eighteen at the time of the commission of the offence for which the person was convicted of first degree murder or second degree murder and who is to be sentenced to imprisonment for life shall be that the person be sentenced to imprisonment for life without eligibility for parole until the person has served such period between five and ten years of the sentence as is specified by the judge presiding at the trial. 1992, c. 11, s. 16.

Recommendation by jury.

743. Subject to section 743.1, where a jury finds an accused guilty of second degree murder, the judge presiding at the trial shall, before discharging the jury, put to them the following question:

> You have found the accused guilty of second degree murder and the law requires that I now pronounce a sentence of imprisonment for life against the accused. Do you wish to make any recommendation with respect to the number of years that the accused must serve before the accused is eligible for release on parole? You are not required to make any recommendation but if you do, your recommendation will be considered by me when I am determining whether I should substitute for the ten year period, which the law would otherwise require the accused to serve befoe the accused is eligible to be considered for release on parole, a number of years that is more than ten but not more than twenty-five. 1992, c. 11, s. 16.

Person under eighteen.

743.1 Where a jury finds an accused guilty of first degree murder or second degree murder and the accused was under the age of eighteen at the time of the commission of the offence, the judge presiding at the trial shall, before discharging the jury, put to them the following question:

> You have found the accused guilty of first degree murder (or second degree murder) and the law requires that I now pronounce a sentence of imprisonment for life against the accused. Do you wish to make any recommendation with respect to the period of imprisonment that the accused must serve before the accused is eligible for release on parole? You are not required to make any recommendation but if you do, your recommendation will be considered by me when I am determining the period of imprisonment that is between five years and ten years that the law would require the accused to serve before the accused is eligible to be considered for release on parole. 1992, c. 11, s. 16.

Ineligibility for parole.

744. Subject to section 744.1, at the time of the sentencing under paragraph 742(*b*) of an offender who is convicted of second degree murder, the judge who presided at the trial of the offender or, if that judge is unable to do so, any judge of the same court may, having regard to the character of the offender, the nature of the offence and the circumstances surrounding its commission, and to the recommendation, if any, made pursuant to section 743, by order, substitute for ten years a number of years of imprisonment (being more than ten but not more than twenty-five) without eligibility for parole, as the judge deems fit in the circumstances. R.S. 1985, c. 27 (1st Supp.), s. 166; 1992, c. 11, s. 16.

Idem.

744.1 At the time of the sentencing under section 742.1 of an offender who is convicted of first degree murder or second degree murder and who was under the age of eighteen at the time of the commission of the offence, the judge who presided at the trial of the offender or, if that judge is unable to do so, any judge of the same court may, having regard to the age and character of the offender, the nature of the offence and the circumstances surrounding its commission, and to the recommendation, if any, made pursuant to section 743.1, by order, decide the period of imprisonment the offender is to serve that is between five years and ten years without eligibility for parole, as the judge deems fit in the circumstances. 1992, c. 11, s. 16.

Application for judicial review — Judicial hearing — Renewal of application — Reduction — Rules — Appropriate Chief Justice — Territories.

745. (1) Where a person has served at least fifteen years of his sentence

(*a*) in the case of a person who has been convicted of high treason or first degree murder, or

(*b*) in the case of a person convicted of second degree murder who has been sentenced to imprisonment for life without eligibility for parole until he has served more than fifteen years of his sentence,

he may apply to the appropriate Chief Justice in the province in which the conviction took place for a reduction in his number of years of imprisonment without eligibility for parole.

(2) Upon receipt of an application under subsection (1), the appropriate Chief Justice shall designate a judge of the superior court of criminal jurisdiction to empanel a jury to hear the application and determine whether the applicant's number of years of imprisonment without eligibility for parole ought to be reduced having regard to the character of the applicant, his conduct while serving his sentence, the nature of the offence for which he was convicted and such other matters as the judge deems relevant in the circumstances and the determination shall be made by not less than two-thirds of the jury.

(3) Where the jury hearing an application under subsection (1) determines that the applicant's number of years of imprisonment without eligibility for parole ought not to be reduced, the jury shall set another time at or after which an application may again be made by the applicant to the appropriate Chief Justice for a reduction in his number of years of imprisonment without eligibility for parole.

(4) Where the jury hearing an application under subsection (1) determines

that the applicant's number of years of imprisonment without eligibility for parole ought to be reduced, the jury may, by order,

(*a*) substitute a lesser number of years of imprisonment without eligibility for parole than that then applicable; or

(*b*) terminate the ineligibility for parole.

(5) The appropriate Chief Justice in each province may make such rules in respect of applications and hearings under this section as are required for the purposes of this section.

(6) For the purposes of this section, the "appropriate Chief Justice" is

(*a*) in relation to the Province of Ontario, the Chief Justice of the Ontario Court;

(*b*) in relation to the Province of Quebec, the Chief Justice of the Superior Court;

(*c*) in relation to the Provinces of Nova Scotia, Prince Edward Island and Newfoundland, respectively, the Chief Justice of the Supreme Court, Trial Division;

(*d*) in relation to the Provinces of New Brunswick, Manitoba, Saskatchewan and Alberta, respectively, the Chief Justice of the Court of Queen's Bench;

(*e*) in relation to the Province of British Columbia, the Chief Justice of the Supreme Court; and

(*f*) in relation to the Yukon Territory and the Northwest Territories, respectively, the Chief Justice of the Court of Appeal thereof.

(7) For the purposes of this section, when the appropriate Chief Justice is designating a judge of the superior court of criminal jurisdiction to empanel a jury to hear an application in respect of a conviction that took place in the Yukon Territory or the Northwest Territories, the appropriate Chief Justice may designate the judge from the Court of Appeal or the Supreme Court of the Yukon Territory or Northwest Territories, as the case may be. R.S. 1985, c. 27 (2d Supp.), Schedule, item 6; 1990, c. 17, s. 14.

Time spent in custody.

746. In calculating the period of imprisonment served for the purposes of section 742, 744 or 745, there shall be included any time spent in custody between,

(*a*) in the case of a sentence of imprisonment for life imposed after July 25, 1976, the day on which that person was arrested and taken into custody in respect of the offence for which he was sentenced to imprisonment for life and the day the sentence was imposed; or

(*b*) in the case of a sentence of death that has been or is deemed to have been commuted to a sentence of imprisonment for life, the day on which that person was arrested and taken into custody in respect of the offence for which he was sentenced to death and the day the sentence was commuted or deemed to have been commuted to a sentence of imprisonment for life.

Parole prohibited — Temporary absence or day parole — Idem.

747. (1) Unless Parliament otherwise provides by an enactment making express reference to this section, no person who has been sentenced to imprisonment for life without eligibility for parole for a specified number of years pursuant to this Act shall be considered for parole or released pursuant to the terms of a grant of parole under the *Parole Act* or any other Act of Parliament until the expiration or termination of his specified number of years of imprisonment without eligibility for parole.

(2) Subject to subsection (2.1), notwithstanding the *Penitentiary Act* and the *Parole Act*, in the case of any person sentenced to imprisonment for life without eligibility for parole for a specified number of years pursuant to this Act, until the expiration of all but three years of the number of years of imprisonment the person is to serve without eligibility for parole, no absence without escort may be authorized under the *Penitentiary Act*, no absence with escort for humanitarian and rehabilitative reasons may be authorized under the *Penitentiary Act* without the approval of the National Parole Board and no day parole may be granted under the *Parole Act*.

(2.1) Notwithstanding the *Penitentiary Act* and the *Parole Act*, in the case of any person convicted of first degree murder or second degree murder who was under the age of eighteen at the time of the commission of the offence and who is sentenced to imprisonment for life without eligibility for parole for a specified number of years pursuant to this Act, until the expiration of all but one fifth of the period of imprisonment the person is to serve without eligibility for parole, no absence without escort may be authorized under the *Penitentiary Act*, no absence with escort for humanitarian and rehabilitative reasons may be authorized under the *Penitentiary Act* without the approval of the National Parole Board and no day parole may be granted under the *Parole Act*. 1992, c. 11, s. 17.

[1992, c. 20, s. 204 will repeal section 747 and substitute the following.]

Parole prohibited — Absences and day parole.

747. (1) Unless Parliament otherwise provides by an enactment making express reference to this section, a person who has been sentenced to imprisonment for life without eligibility for parole for a specified number of years pursuant to ths Act shall not be considered for parole or released pursuant to a grant of parole under the *Corrections and Conditional Release Act* or any other Act of Parliament until the expiration or termination of the specified number of years of imprisonment.

(2) In respect of a person sentenced to imprisonment for life without eligibility for parole for a specified number of years pursuant to this Act, until the expiration of all but three years of the specified number of years of imprisonment,

(*a*) no day parole may be granted under the *Corrections and Conditional Release Act*;

(*b*) no absence without escort may be authorized under that Act or the *Prisons and Reformatories Act*; and

(*c*) except with the approval of the National Parole Board, no absence with escort otherwise than for medical reasons may be authorized under either of those Acts.

[1992, c. 20, s. 228 will repeal subsections 747(2) and (2.1) and will substitute the following.]

Temporary absences and day parole — Idem.

(2) Subject to subsection (2.1), in respect of a person sentenced to imprisonment for life without eligibility for parole for a specified number of years pursuant to this Act, until the expiration of all but three years of the specified number of years of imprisonment,

(*a*) no day parole may be granted under the *Corrections and Conditional Release Act*;

(*b*) no absence without escort may be authorized under that Act or the *Prisons and Reformatories Act*; and

(*c*) except with the approval of the National Parole Board, no absence with escort otherwise than for medical reasons may be authorized under either of those Acts.

(2.1) Notwithstanding the *Corrections and Conditional Release Act*, in the case of any person convicted of first degree murder or second degree murder who was under the age of eighteen at the time of the commission of the offence and who is sentenced to imprisonment for life without eligibility for parole for a specified number of years pursuant to this Act, until the expiration of all but one fifth of the period of imprisonment the person is to serve without eligibility for parole,

(*a*) no day parole may be granted under the *Corrections and Conditional Release Act*;

(*b*) no absence without escort may be authorized under that Act or the *Prisons and Reformatories Act*; and

(*c*) except with the approval of the National Parole Board, no absence with escort otherwise than for medical reasons may be authorized under either of those Acts.

Disabilities

Public office vacated on conviction — When disability ceases — Disability to contract — Application for restoration of privileges — Order of restoration — Removal of disability.

748. (1) Where a person is convicted of an indictable offence for which he is sentenced to imprisonment for a term exceeding five years and holds, at the time he is convicted, an office under the Crown or other public employment, the office or employment forthwith becomes vacant.

(2) A person to whom subsection (1) applies is, until he undergoes the punishment imposed on him or the punishment substituted therefor by competent authority or receives a free pardon from Her Majesty, incapable of holding any office under the Crown or other public employment, or of being elected or sitting or voting as a member of Parliament or of a legislature or of exercising any right of suffrage.

(3) No person who is convicted of an offence under section 121, 124 or 418 has, after that conviction, capacity to contract with Her Majesty or to receive any benefit under a contract between Her Majesty and any other person or to hold office under Her Majesty.

(4) A person to whom subsection (3) applies may, at any time before a pardon is granted to him under section 4 of the *Criminal Records Act*, apply to the Governor in Council for the restoration of one or more of the capacities lost by him by virtue of that subsection.

[1992, c. 22, s. 12 will repeal subsection 748(4) and substitute the following.]

Application for restoration of privileges.

(4) A person to whom subsection (3) applies may, at any time before a pardon is granted to the person under section 4.1 of the *Criminal Records Act*, apply to the Governor in Council for the restoration of one or more of the capacities lost by the person by virtue of that subsection.

(5) Where an application is made under subsection (4), the Governor in Council may order that the capacities lost by the applicant by virtue of subsection (3) be restored to him in whole or in part and subject to such conditions as he considers desirable in the public interest.

(6) Where a conviction is set aside by competent authority, any disability imposed by this section is removed.

Pardon

To whom pardon may be granted — Free or conditional pardon — Effect of free pardon — Punishment for subsequent offence not affected.

749. (1) Her Majesty may extend the royal mercy to a person who is sentenced to imprisonment under the authority of an Act of Parliament, even if the person is imprisoned for failure to pay money to another person.

(2) The Governor in Council may grant a free pardon or a conditional pardon to any person who has been convicted of an offence.

(3) Where the Governor in Council grants a free pardon to a person, that person shall be deemed thereafter never to have committed the offence in respect of which the pardon is granted.

(4) No free pardon or conditional pardon prevents or mitigates the punishment to which the person might otherwise be lawfully sentenced on a subsequent conviction for an offence other than that for which the pardon was granted.

Remission by Governor in Council — Terms of remission.

750. (1) The Governor in Council may order the remission, in whole or in part, of a pecuniary penalty, fine or forfeiture imposed under an Act of Parliament, whoever the person may be to whom it is payable or however it may be recoverable.

(2) An order for remission under subsection (1) may include the remission of costs incurred in the proceedings, but no costs to which a private prosecutor is entitled shall be remitted.

Royal prerogative.

751. Nothing in this Act in any manner limits or affects Her Majesty's royal prerogative of mercy.

PART XXIV

DANGEROUS OFFENDERS

Interpretation

Definitions — "Court" — "Serious personal injury offence".

752. In this Part,

"court" means the court by which an offender in relation to whom an application under this Part is made was convicted, or a superior court of criminal jurisdiction;

"serious personal injury offence" means

(*a*) an indictable offence, other than high treason, treason, first degree murder or second degree murder, involving

(i) the use or attempted use of violence against another person, or

(ii) conduct endangering or likely to endanger the life or safety of another person or inflicting or likely to inflict severe psychological damage upon another person,

and for which the offender may be sentenced to imprisonment for ten years or more, or

(*b*) an offence or attempt to commit an offence mentioned in section 271 (sexual assault), 272 (sexual assault with a weapon, threats to a third party or causing bodily harm) or 273 (aggravated sexual assault).

Dangerous Offenders

Application for finding.

753. Where, upon an application made under this Part following the conviction of a person for an offence but before the offender is sentenced therefor, it is established to the satisfaction of the court

(*a*) that the offence for which the offender has been convicted is a serious personal injury offence described in paragraph (*a*) of the definition of that expression in section 752 and the offender constitutes a threat to the life, safety or physical or mental well-being of other persons on the basis of evidence establishing

(i) a pattern of repetitive behaviour by the offender, of which the offence for which he has been convicted forms a part, showing a failure to restrain his behaviour and a likelihood of his causing death or injury to other persons, or inflicting severe psychological damage on other persons, through failure in the future to restrain his behaviour,

(ii) a pattern of persistent aggressive behaviour by the offender, of which the offence for which he has been convicted forms a part, showing a substantial degree of indifference on the part of the offender respecting the reasonably foreseeable consequences to other persons of his behaviour, or

(iii) any behaviour by the offender, associated with the offence for which he has been convicted, that is of such a brutal nature as to compel the conclusion that his behaviour in the future is unlikely to be inhibited by normal standards of behavioural restraint, or

(*b*) that the offence for which the offender has been convicted is a serious personal injury offence described in paragraph (*b*) of the definition of that expression in section 752 and the offender, by his conduct in any sexual matter including that involved in the commission of the offence for which he has been convicted, has shown a failure to control his sexual impulses and a likelihood of his causing injury, pain or other evil to other persons through failure in the future to control his sexual impulses,

the court may find the offender to be a dangerous offender and may thereupon impose a sentence of detention in a penitentiary for an indeterminate period, in lieu of any other sentence that might be imposed for the offence for which the offender has been convicted.

Hearing of application — By court alone — When proof unnecessary — Proof of consent.

754. (1) Where an application under this Part has been made, the court shall hear and determine the application except that no such application shall be heard unless

(*a*) the Attorney General of the province in which the offender was tried has, either before or after the making of the application, consented to the application;

(*b*) at least seven days notice has been given to the offender by the prosecutor, following the making of the application, outlining the basis on which it is intended to found the application; and

(*c*) a copy of the notice has been filed with the clerk of the court or the provincial court judge, as the case may be.

(2) An application under this Part shall be heard and determined by the court without a jury.

(3) For the purposes of an application under this Part, where an offender admits any allegations contained in the notice referred to in paragraph (1)(*b*), no proof of those allegations is required.

(4) The production of a document purporting to contain any nomination or consent that may be made or given by the Attorney General under this Part and purporting to be signed by the Attorney General is, in the absence of any evidence to the contrary, proof of that nomination or consent without proof of the signature or the official character of the person appearing to have signed the document. R.S. 1985, c. 27 (1st Supp.), s. 203.

Evidence of dangerous offender status — Nomination of psychiatrists — Nomination by court — Saving.

755. (1) On the hearing of an application under this Part, the court shall hear the evidence of at least two psychiatrists and all other evidence that, in its opinion, is relevant, including the evidence of any psychologist or criminologist called as a witness by the prosecution or the offender.

(2) One of the psychiatrists referred to in subsection (1) shall be nominated by the prosecution and one shall be nominated by the offender.

(3) If the offender fails or refuses to nominate a psychiatrist pursuant to this section, the court shall nominate a psychiatrist on behalf of the offender.

(4) Nothing in this section shall be construed to enlarge the number of expert witnesses that may be called without the leave of the court or judge under section 7 of the *Canada Evidence Act.*

Direction or remand for observation — Idem.

756. (1) A court to which an application is made under this part may, by order in writing,

(*a*) direct the offender in relation to whom the application is made to attend, at a place or before a person specified in the order and within a time specified therein, for observation, or

(*b*) remand the offender in such custody as the court directs, for a period not exceeding thirty days, for observation,

where in its opinion, supported by the evidence of, or where the prosecutor and the offender consent, supported by the report in writing of, at least one duly qualified medical practitioner, there is reason to believe that evidence might be obtained as a result of the observation that would be relevant to the application.

(2) Notwithstanding subsection (1), a court to which an application is made under this Part may remand the offender to which that application relates in accordance with that subsection

(*a*) for a period not exceeding thirty days without having heard the evidence or considered the report of a duly qualified medical practitioner where compelling circumstances exist for so doing and where a medical practitioner is not readily available to examine the offender and give evidence or submit a report; and

(*b*) for a period of more than thirty but not more than sixty days where it is satisfied that observation for that period is required in all the circumstances of the case and its opinion is supported by the evidence of, or where the prosecutor and the offender consent, by the report in writing of, at least one duly qualified medical practitioner.

Evidence of character.

757. Without prejudice to the right of the offender to tender evidence respecting his character and repute, evidence of character and repute may, if the court thinks fit, be admitted on the question whether the offender is or is not a dangerous offender.

Presence of accused at hearing of application — Exception.

758. (1) The offender shall be present at the hearing of the application under this Part and if at the time the application is to be heard

(*a*) he is confined in a prison, the court may order, in writing, the person having the custody of the accused to bring him before the court; or

(*b*) he is not confined in a prison, the court shall issue a summons or a warrant to compel the accused to attend before the court and the provisions of Part XVI relating to summons and warrant are applicable with such modifications as the circumstances require.

(2) Notwithstanding subsection (1), the court may

(*a*) cause the offender to be removed and to be kept out of court, where he misconducts himself by interrupting the proceedings so that to continue the proceedings in his presence would not be feasible; or

(*b*) permit the offender to be out of court during the whole or any part of the hearing on such conditions as the court considers proper.

Appeal — Appeal by Attorney General — Disposition of appeal — Idem — Effect of judgment — Commencement of sentence — Part XXI applies re appeals.

759. (1) A person who is sentenced to detention in a penitentiary for an indeterminate period under this Part may appeal to the court of appeal against that sentence on any ground of law or fact or mixed law and fact.

(2) The Attorney General may appeal to the court of appeal against the dismissal of an application for an order under this Part on any ground of law.

(3) On an appeal against a sentence of detention in a penitentiary for an indeterminate period, the court of appeal may

(*a*) quash such sentence and impose any sentence that might have been imposed in respect of the offence for which the appellant was convicted, or order a new hearing; or

(*b*) dismiss the appeal.

(4) On an appeal against the dismissal of an application for an order under this Part, the court of appeal may

(*a*) allow the appeal, set aside any sentence imposed in respect of the offence for which the respondent was convicted and impose a sentence of detention in a penitentiary for an indeterminate period, or order a new hearing; or

(*b*) dismiss the appeal.

(5) A judgment of the court of appeal imposing a sentence pursuant to this section has the same force and effect as if it were a sentence passed by the trial court.

(6) Notwithstanding subsection 721(1), a sentence imposed on an offender by the court of appeal pursuant to this section shall be deemed to have commenced when the offender was sentenced by the court by which he was convicted.

(7) The provisions of Part XXI with respect to procedure on appeals apply, with such modifications as the circumstances require, to appeals under this section.

Disclosure to Solicitor General.

760. Where a court, pursuant to section 753, finds an offender to be a dangerous offender and imposes a sentence of detention in a penitentiary for an indeterminate period, the court shall order that a copy of all reports or testimony given by psychiatrists, psychologists or criminologists and any observations of the court with respect to the reasons for the sentence, together with a transcript of the trial of the dangerous offender, be forwarded to the Solicitor General of Canada for his information.

Review for parole — Idem.

761. (1) Subject to subsection (2), where a person is in custody under a sentence of detention in a penitentiary for an indeterminate period, the National Parole Board shall, forthwith after the expiration of three years from the day on which that person was taken into custody and not later than every two years thereafter, review the condition, history and circumstances of that person for the purpose of determining whether he should be granted parole under the *Parole Act* and, if so, on what conditions.

(2) Where a person is in custody under a sentence of detention in a penitentiary for an indeterminate period that was imposed before October 15, 1977, the National Parole Board shall, at least once in every year, review the condition, history and circumstances of that person for the purpose of determining whether he should be granted parole under the *Parole Act* and, if so, on what conditions.

[1992, c. 20, s. 215(1)(*a*) will repeal the expression "*Parole Act*" wherever it occurs in section 761 and substitute the expression "Part II of the *Corrections and Conditional Release Act*".]

PART XXV

EFFECT AND ENFORCEMENT OF RECOGNIZANCES

Applications for forfeiture of recognizances — Definitions — "Clerk of the court" — "Schedule".

762. (1) Applications for the forfeiture of recognizances shall be made to the courts, designated in column II of the schedule, of the respective provinces designated in column I of the schedule.

(2) In this Part

"clerk of the court" means the officer designated in column III of the schedule in respect of the court designated in column II of the schedule;

"schedule" means the schedule to this Part.

Recognizance binding.

763. Where a person is bound by recognizance to appear before a court, justice or provincial court judge for any purpose and the session or sittings of that court or the proceedings are adjourned or an order is made changing the place of trial, that person and his sureties continue to be bound by the recognizance in like manner as if it had been entered into with relation to the resumed proceedings or the trial at the time and place at which the proceedings are ordered to be resumed or the trial is ordered to be held. R.S. 1985, c. 27 (1st Supp.), s. 203.

Responsibility of sureties — Committal or new sureties — Effect of committal — Endorsement on recognizance.

764. (1) Where an accused is bound by recognizance to appear for trial, his arraignment or conviction does not discharge the recognizance, but it continues to bind him and his sureties, if any, for his appearance until he is discharged or sentenced, as the case may be.

(2) Notwithstanding subsection (1), the court, justice or provincial court judge may commit an accused to prison or may require him to furnish new or additional sureties for his appearance until he is discharged or sentenced, as the case may be.

(3) The sureties of an accused who is bound by recognizance to appear for trial are discharged if he is committed to prison pursuant to subsection (2).

(4) The provisions of section 763 and subsections (1) to (3) of this section shall be endorsed on any recognizance entered into pursuant to this Act. R.S. 1985, c. 27 (1st Supp.), s. 203.

Effect of subsequent arrest.

765. Where an accused is bound by recognizance to appear for trial, his arrest on another charge does not vacate the recognizance, but it continues to bind him and his sureties, if any, for his appearance until he is discharged or sentenced, as the case may be, in respect of the offence to which the recognizance relates.

Render of accused by sureties — Arrest — Certificate and entry of render — Discharge of sureties.

766. (1) A surety for a person who is bound by recognizance to appear may, by an application in writing to a court, justice or provincial court judge, apply to be relieved of his obligation under the recognizance, and the court, justice or provincial court judge shall thereupon issue an order in writing for committal of that person to the prison nearest to the place where he was, under the recognizance, bound to appear.

(2) An order under subsection (1) shall be given to the surety and upon receipt thereof he or any peace officer may arrest the person named in the order and deliver that person with the order to the keeper of the prison named herein, and the keeper shall receive and imprison that person until he is discharged according to law.

(3) Where a court, justice or provincial court judge issues an order under subsection (1) and receives from the sheriff a certificate that the person named in the order has been committed to prison pursuant to subsection (2), the court, justice or provincial court judge shall order an entry of the committal to be endorsed on the recognizance.

(4) An endorsement under subsection (3) vacates the recognizance and discharges the sureties. R.S. 1985, c. 27 (1st Supp.), s. 203.

Render of accused in court by sureties.

767. A surety for a person who is bound by recognizance to appear may bring that person into the court at which he is required to appear at any time during the sittings thereof and before his trial and the surety may discharge his obligation under the recognizance by giving that person into the custody of the court, and the court shall thereupon commit that person to prison until he is discharged according to law.

Substitution of surety — Signing of recognizance by new sureties.

767.1 (1) Notwithstanding subsection 766(1) and section 767, where a surety for a person who is bound by a recognizance has rendered the person into the custody of a court pursuant to section 767 or applies to be relieved of his obligation under the recognizance pursuant to subsection 766(1), the court, justice or provincial court judge, as the case may be, may, instead of committing or issuing an order for the committal of the person to prison, substitute any other suitable person for the surety under the recognizance.

(2) Where a person substituted for a surety under a recognizance pursuant to subsection (1) signs the recognizance, the original surety is discharged, but

the recognizance and the order for judicial interim release pursuant to which the recognizance was entered into are not otherwise affected. R.S. 1985, c. 27 (1st Supp.), s. 167.

Rights of surety preserved.

768. Nothing in this Part limits or restricts any right that a surety has of taking and giving into custody any person for whom, under a recognizance, he is a surety.

Application of judicial interim release provisions.

769. Where a surety for a person has rendered him into custody and that person has been committed to prison, the provisions of Parts XVI, XXI and XXVII relating to judicial interim release apply, with such modifications as the circumstances require, in respect of him and he shall forthwith be taken before a justice or judge as an accused charged with an offence or as an appellant, as the case may be, for the purposes of those provisions.

Default to be endorsed — Transmission to clerk of court — Certificate is evidence — Transmission of deposit.

770. (1) Where, in proceedings to which this Act applies, a person who is bound by recognizance does not comply with a condition of the recognizance, a court, justice or provincial court judge having knowledge of the facts shall endorse or cause to be endorsed on the back of the recognizance a certificate in Form 33 setting out

(*a*) the nature of the default,

(*b*) the reason for the default, if it is known,

(*c*) whether the ends of justice have been defeated or delayed by reason of the default, and

(*d*) the names and addresses of the principal and sureties.

(2) A recognizance that has been endorsed pursuant to subsection (1) shall be sent to the clerk of the court and shall be kept by him with the records of the court.

(3) A certificate that has been endorsed on a recognizance pursuant to subsection (1) is evidence of the default to which it relates.

(4) Where, in proceedings to which this section applies, the principal or surety has deposited money as security for the performance of a condition of a recognizance, that money shall be sent to the clerk of the court with the defaulted recognizance, to be dealt with in accordance with this Part. R.S. 1985, c. 27 (1st Supp.), s. 203.

Proceedings in case of default — Order of judge — Judgment debtors of the Crown — Order may be filed — Transfer of deposit.

771. (1) Where a recognizance has been endorsed with a certificate pursuant to section 770 and has been received by the clerk of the court pursuant to that section,

(*a*) a judge of the court shall, on the request of the clerk of the court or the Attorney General or counsel acting on his behalf, fix a time and place for the hearing of an application for the forfeiture of the recognizance; and

(*b*) the clerk of the court shall, not less than ten days before the time fixed under paragraph (*a*) for the hearing, send by registered mail to each principal and surety named in the recognizance, directed to him at the address set out in the certificate, a notice requiring him to appear at the time and place fixed by the judge to show cause why the recognizance should not be forfeited.

(2) Where subsection (1) has been complied with, the judge may, after giving the parties an opportunity to be heard, in his discretion grant or refuse the application and make any order with respect to the forfeiture of the recognizance that he considers proper.

(3) Where, pursuant to subsection (2), a judge orders forfeiture of a recognizance, the principal and his sureties become judgment debtors of the Crown, each in the amount that the judge orders him to pay.

(3.1) An order made under subsection (2) may be filed with the clerk of the superior court or, in the Province of Quebec, the prothonotary and, where an order is filed, the clerk or the prothonotary shall issue a writ of *fieri facias* in Form 34 and deliver it to the sheriff of each of the territorial divisions in which the principal or any of his sureties resides, carries on business or has property.

(4) Where a deposit has been made by a person against whom an order for forfeiture of a recognizance has been made, no writ of *fieri facias* shall issue, but the amount of the deposit shall be transferred by the person who has custody of it to the person who is entitled by law to receive it. R.S. 1985, c. 27 (1st Supp.), s. 168.

Levy under writ — Costs.

772. (1) Where a writ of *fieri facias* is issued pursuant to section 771, the sheriff to whom it is delivered shall execute the writ and deal with the proceeds thereof in the same manner in which he is authorized to execute and deal with the proceeds of writs of *fieri facias* issued out of superior courts in the province in civil proceedings.

(2) Where this section applies, the Crown is entitled to the costs of execution and of proceedings incidental thereto that are fixed, in the Province of Quebec, by any tariff applicable in the Superior Court in civil proceedings, and in any other province, by any tariff applicable in the superior court of the province in civil proceedings, as the judge may direct.

Committal when writ not satisfied — Notice — Hearing — Warrant to committal — "Attorney General".

773. (1) Where a writ of *fieri facias* has been issued under this Part and it appears from a certificate in a return made by the sheriff that sufficient goods and chattels, lands and tenements cannot be found to satisfy the writ, or that the proceeds of the execution of the writ are not sufficient to satisfy it, a judge of the court may, upon the application of the Attorney General or counsel acting on his behalf, fix a time and place for the sureties to show cause why a warrant of committal should not be issued in respect of them.

(2) Seven clear days notice of the time and place fixed for the hearing pursuant to subsection (1) shall be given to the sureties.

(3) The judge shall, at the hearing held pursuant to subsection (1), inquire into the circumstances of the case and may in his discretion

(*a*) order the discharge of the amount for which the surety is liable; or

(*b*) make any order with respect to the surety and to his imprisonment that he considers proper in the circumstances and issue a warrant of committal in Form 27.

(4) A warrant of committal issued pursuant to this section authorizes the sheriff to take into custody the person in respect of whom the warrant was issued and to confine him in a prison in the territorial division in which the writ was issued or in the prison nearest to the court, until satisfaction is made or until the period of imprisonment fixed by the judge has expired.

(5) In this section and in section 771, "Attorney General" means, where subsection 723(2) applies, the Attorney General of Canada.

SCHEDULE

(*Section 762*)

Column I.	Column II.	Column III.
Ontario	The Supreme Court in repsect of a recognizance for the appearance of a person before that Court.	The Registrar or Local Registrar of the Supreme Court.
	A judge of the Court of Appeal in respect of a recognizance for the appearance of a person before that Court	The Registrar of the Supreme Court.

	The District Court in respect of a recognizance for the appearance of a person before that Court, a judge acting under Part XIX, a justice or a provincial court judge.	The Local Registrar of the District Court.
Quebec	The Superior Court, exercising civil jurisdiction.	The Clerk of the Peace.
Nova Scotia	A judge of the Supreme Court in respect of a recognizance for the appearance of a person before the Appeal Division.	The Prothonotary at Halifax.
	A judge of the County Court in respect of a recognizance for the appearance of a person before a judge of the Supreme Court, a judge of the County Court, a judge acting under Part XIX, a justice or a provincial court judge.	The Clerk of the County Court.
New Brunswick	The Court of Queen's Bench.	The Registrar of the Court of Queen's Bench.
British Columbia	The Supreme Court in respect of a recognizance for the appearance of a person before that court or the Court of Appeal.	The District Registrar of the Supreme Court.
	A County Court in respect of a recognizance for the appearance of a person before that Court or a judge acting under Part XIX.	The Clerk of the County Court.
	A Provincial Court in respect of a recognizance for the appearance of a person before a judge of that Court or a justice.	The Clerk of the Provincial Court.

Prince Edward Island	The Supreme Court, Trial Division.	The Prothonotary.
Manitoba	The Court of Queen's Bench.	The Clerk or Deputy Clerk of the Crown and Pleas.
Saskatchewan	The Court of Queen's Bench.	The Local Registrar of the Court of Queen's Bench.
Alberta	The Court of Queen's Bench.	The Clerk of the Court of Queen's Bench.
Newfoundland	The Supreme Court.	The Registrar of the Supreme Court.
Yukon Territory	The Supreme Court.	The Clerk of the Supreme Court.
Northwest Territories	The Supreme Court.	The Clerk of the Supreme Court.

R.S. 1985, c. 11 (1st Supp.), s. 2; c. 27 (1st Supp.) Schedule, item 6.

PART XXVI

EXTRAORDINARY REMEDIES

Application of Part.

774. This Part applies to proceedings in criminal matters by way of *certiorari, habeas corpus, mandamus, procedendo* and prohibition. R.S. 1985, c. 27 (1st Supp.), s. 169.

Detention on inquiry to determine legality of imprisonment.

775. Where proceedings to which this Part applies have been instituted before a judge or court having jurisdiction, by or in respect of a person who is in custody by reason that he is charged with or has been convicted of an offence, to have the legality of his imprisonment determined, the judge or court may, without determiniing the question, make an order for the further detention of that person and direct the judge, justice or provincial court judge under whose warrant he is in custody, or any other judge, justice or provincial court judge to take any proceedings, hear such evidence or do any other thing that, in the opinion of the judge or court, will best further the ends of justice. R.S. 1985, c. 27 (1st Supp.), s. 203.

Where conviction of order not reviewable.

776. No conviction or order shall be removed by *certiorari*

(*a*) where an appeal was taken, whether or not the appeal has been carried to a conclusion; or

(*b*) where the defendant appeared and pleaded and the merits were tried, and an appeal might have been taken, but the defendant did not appeal.

Conviction or order remediable, when — Correcting punishment — Amendment — Sufficiency of statement.

777. (1) No conviction, order or warrant for enforcing a conviction or order shall, on being removed by *certiorari*, be held to be invalid by reason of any irregularity, informality or insufficiency therein, where the court before which or the judge before whom the question is raised, on perusal of the evidence, is satisfied

(*a*) that an offence of the nature described in the conviction, order or warrant, as the case may be, was committed,

(*b*) that there was jurisdiction to make the conviction or order or issue the warrant, as the case may be, and

(*c*) that the punishment imposed, if any, was not in excess of the punishment that might lawfully have been imposed,

but the court or judge has the same powers to deal with the proceedings in the manner that the court or judge considers proper that are conferred on a court to which an appeal might have been taken.

(2) Where, in proceedings to which subsection (1) applies, the court or judge is satisfied that a person was properly convicted of an offence but the punishment that was imposed is greater than the punishment that might lawfully have been imposed, the court or judge

(*a*) shall correct the sentence,

(i) where the punishment is a fine, by imposing a fine that does not exceed the maximum fine that might lawfully have been imposed,

(ii) where the punishment is imprisonment, and the person has not served a term of imprisonment under the sentence that is equal to or greater than the term of imprisonment that might lawfully have been imposed, by imposing a term of imprisonment that does not exceed the maximum term of imprisonment that might lawfully have been imposed, or

(iii) where the punishment is a fine and imprisonment, by imposing a punishment in accordance with subparagraph (i) or (ii), as the case requires; or

(*b*) shall remit the matter to the convicting judge, justice or provincial court judge and direct him to impose a punishment that is not greater than the punishment that may be lawfully imposed.

(3) Where an adjudication is varied pursuant to subsection (1) or (2), the conviction and warrant of committal, if any, shall be amended to conform with the adjudication as varied.

(4) Any statement that appears in a conviction and is sufficient for the purpose of the conviction is sufficient for the purposes of an information, summons, order or warrant in which it appears in the proceedings. R.S. 1985, c. 27 (1st Supp.), s. 203.

Irregularities within section 777.

778. Without restricting the generality of section 777, that section shall be deemed to apply where

(*a*) the statement of the adjudication or of any other matter or thing is in the past tense instead of in the present tense;

(*b*) the punishment imposed is less than the punishment that might by law have been imposed for the offence that appears by the evidence to have been committed; or

(*c*) there has been an omission to negative circumstances, the existence of which would make the act complained of lawful, whether those circumstances are stated by way of exception or otherwise in the provision under which the offence is charged or are stated in another provision.

General order for security by recognizance — Provisions of Part XXV.

779. (1) A court that has authority to quash a conviction, order or other proceeding on *certiorari* may prescribe by general order that no motion to quash any such conviction, order or other proceeding removed to the court by *certiorari*, shall be heard unless the defendant has entered into a recognizance with one or more sufficient sureties, before one or more justices of the territorial division in which the conviction or order was made or before a judge or other officer, or has made a deposit to be prescribed with a condition that the defendant will prosecute the writ of *certiorari* at his own expense, without wilful delay, and, if ordered, will pay to the person in whose favour the conviction, order or other proceeding is affirmed his full costs and charges to be taxed according to the practice of the court where the conviction, order or proceeding is affirmed.

(2) The provisions of Part XXV relating to forfeiture of recognizances apply to a recognizance entered into under this section.

Effect of order dismissing application to quash.

780. Where a motion to quash a conviction, order or other proceeding is refused, the order of the court refusing the application is sufficient authority for the clerk of the court forthwith to return the conviction, order or proceeding to the court from which or the person from whom it was removed, and for proceedings to be taken with respect thereto for the enforcement thereof.

Want of proof of order in council — Judicial notice.

781. (1) No order, conviction or other proceeding shall be quashed or set aside, and no defendant shall be discharged, by reason only that evidence has not been given

(*a*) of a proclamation or order of the Governor in Council or the lieutenant governor in council;

(*b*) of rules, regulations or by-laws made by the Governor in Council under an Act of Parliament or by the lieutenant governor in council under an Act of the legislature of the province; or

(*c*) of the publication of a proclamation, order, rule, regulation or by-law in the *Canada Gazette* or in the official gazette for the province.

(2) Proclamations, orders, rules, regulations and by-laws mentioned in subsection (1) and the publication thereof shall be judicially noticed.

Defect in form.

782. No warrant of committal shall, on *certiorari* or *habeas corpus*, be held to be void by reason only of any defect therein, where

(*a*) it is alleged in the warrant that the defendant was convicted; and

(*b*) there is a valid conviction to sustain the warrant.

No action against official when conviction, etc., quashed.

783. Where an application is made to quash a conviction, order or other proceeding made or held by a provincial court judge acting under Part XIX or a justice on the ground that he exceeded his jurisdiction, the court to which or the judge to whom the application is made may, in quashing the conviction, order or other proceeding, order that no civil proceedings shall be taken against the justice or provincial court judge or against any officer who acted under the conviction, order or other proceeding or under any warrant issued to enforce it.

Appeal in mandamus, etc. — Application of Part XXI — Refusal of application, and appeal — Where writ granted — Appeal from judgment on return of writ —Hearing of appeal.

784. (1) An appeal lies to the court of appeal from a decision granting or refusing the relief sought in proceedings by way of *mandamus, certiorari* or prohibition.

(2) Except as provided in this section, Part XXI applies, with such modifications as the circumstances require, to appeals under this section.

(3) Where an application for a writ of *habeas corpus ad subjiciendum* is refused by a judge of a court having jurisdiction therein, no application may again be made on the same grounds, whether to the same or to another court or judge, unless fresh evidence is adduced, but an appeal from such refusal shall lie to the court of appeal, and where on the appeal the application is refused a further appeal shall lie to the Supreme Court of Canada.

(4) Where a writ of *habeas corpus ad subjiciendum* is granted by any judge, no appeal therefrom shall lie at the instance of any party including the Attorney General of the province concerned or the Attorney General of Canada.

(5) Where a judgment is issued on the return of a writ of *habeas corpus ad subjiciendum*, an appeal therefrom lies to the court of appeal, and from a judgment of the court of appeal to the Supreme Court of Canada, with the leave of that court, at the instance of the applicant or the Attorney General of the province concerned or the Attorney General of Canada, but not at the instance of any other party.

(6) An appeal in *habeas corpus* matters shall be heard by the court to which the appeal is directed at an early date, whether in or out of the prescribed sessions of the court.

PART XXVII

SUMMARY CONVICTIONS

Interpretation

Definitions — "Clerk of the appeal court" — "Informant" — "Information" — "Order" — "Proceedings" — "Prosecutor" — "Sentence" — "Summary conviction court" — "Trial".

785. (1) In this Part

"clerk of the appeal court" includes a local clerk of the appeal court;

"informant" means a person who lays an information;

"information" includes

(*a*) a count in an information, and

(*b*) a complaint in respect of which a justice is authorized by an Act of Parliament or an enactment made thereunder to make an order;

"order" means any order, including an order for the payment of money;

"proceedings" means

(*a*) proceedings in respect of offences that are declared by an Act of Parliament or an enactment made thereunder to be punishable on summary conviction, and

(*b*) proceedings where a justice is authorized by an Act of Parliament or an enactment made thereunder to make an order;

"prosecutor" means the Attorney General or where the Attorney General does not intervene, the informant, and includes counsel or an agent acting on behalf of either of them;

"sentence" includes

(*a*) a declaration made under subsection 199(3),

(*b*) an order made under subsection 100(2) or 259(1) or (2), section 261 or subsection 736(1), and

(*c*) a disposition made under subsection 737(1) or 738(3) or (4);

"summary conviction court" means a person who has jurisdiction in the territorial division where the subject-matter of the proceedings is alleged to have arisen and who

(*a*) is given jurisdiction over the proceedings by the enactment under which the proceedings are taken,

(*b*) is a justice or provincial court judge, where the enactment under which the proceedings are taken does not expressly give jurisdiction to any person or class of persons, or

(*c*) is a provincial court judge, where the enactment under which the proceedings are taken gives jurisdiction in respect thereof to two or more justices;

"trial" includes the hearing of a complaint. R.S. 1985, c. 27 (1st Supp.), ss. 170, 203; 1992, c. 1, s. 58(1), Sch. I, item 16.

Application of Part — Limitation.

786. (1) Except where otherwise provided by law, this Part applies to proceedings as defined in this Part.

(2) No proceedings shall be instituted more than six months after the time when the subject-matter of the proceedings arose.

Punishment

General penalty — Imprisonment in default where not otherwise specified.

787. (1) Except where otherwise provided by law, every one who is convicted of an offence punishable on summary conviction is liable to a fine of not more than two thousand dollars or to imprisonment for six months or to both.

(2) Where the imposition of a fine or the making of an order for the payment of money is authorized by law, but the law does not provide that imprisonment may be imposed in default of payment of the fine or compliance with the order, the court may order that in default of payment of the fine or compliance with the order, as the case may be, the defendant shall be imprisoned for a term not exceeding six months. R.S. 1985, c. 27 (1st Supp.), s. 171.

(3) to (11) [Repealed R.S. 1985, c. 27 (1st Supp.), s. 171.]

Information

Commencement of proceedings — One justice may act before the trial.

788. (1) Proceedings under this Part shall be commenced by laying an information in Form 2.

(2) Notwithstanding any other law that requires an information to be laid before or to be tried by two or more justices, one justice may

(*a*) receive the information;

(*b*) issue a summons or warrant with respect to the information; and

(*c*) do all other things preliminary to the trial.

Formalities of information — No reference to previous convictions.

789. (1) In proceedings to which this Part applies, an information

(*a*) shall be in writing and under oath; and

(*b*) may charge more than one offence or relate to more than one matter of complaint, but where more than one offence is charged or the information relates to more than one matter of complaint, each offence or matter of complaint, as the case may be, shall be set out in a separate count.

(2) No information in respect of an offence for which, by reason of previous convictions, a greater punishment may be imposed shall contain any reference to previous convictions.

Any justice may act before and after trial — Two or more justices.

790. (1) Nothing in this Act or any other law shall be deemed to require a justice before whom proceedings are commenced or who issues process before or after the trial to be the justice or one of the justices before whom the trial is held.

(2) Where two or more justices have jurisdiction with respect to proceedings, they shall be present and act together at the trial, but one justice may thereafter do anything that is required or is authorized to be done in connection with the proceedings. R.S. 1985, c. 27 (1st Supp.), s. 172.

(3) and (4) [Repealed R.S. 1985, c. 27 (1st Supp.), s. 172.]

791. [Repealed R.S. 1985, c. 27 (1st Supp.), s. 173.]

792. [Repealed R.S. 1985, c. 27 (1st Supp.), s. 174.]

793. [Repealed R.S. 1985, c. 27 (1st Supp.), s. 175.]

No need to negative exception, etc. — Burden of proving exception, etc.

794. (1) No exception, exemption, proviso, excuse or qualification prescribed by law is required to be set out or negatived, as the case may be, in an information.

(2) The burden of proving that an exception, exemption, proviso, excuse or qualification prescribed by law operates in favour of the defendant is on the defendant, and the prosecutor is not required, except by way of rebuttal, to prove that the exception, exemption, proviso, excuse or qualification does not operate in favour of the defendant, whether or not it is set out in the information.

Application

Application of Parts XVI, XVIII, XX and XX.I.

795. The provisions of Parts XVI and XVIII with respect to compelling the appearance of an accused before a justice, and the provisions of Parts XX and XX.1, in so far as they are not inconsistent with this Part, apply, with such modifications as the circumstances require, to proceedings under this Part. R.S. 1985, c. 27 (1st Supp.), s. 176; 1991, c. 43, s. 7.

796. [Repealed R.S. 1985, c. 27 (1st Supp.), s. 176.]

797. [Repealed R.S. 1985, c. 27 (1st Supp.), s. 176.]

Trial

Jurisdiction.

798. Every summary conviction court has jurisdiction to try, determine and adjudge proceedings to which this Part applies in the territorial division over which the person who constitutes that court has jurisdiction.

Non-appearance of prosecutor.

799. Where, in proceedings to which this Part applies, the defendant appears for the trial and the prosecutor, having had due notice, does not appear, the summary conviction court may dismiss the information or may adjourn the trial to some other time on such terms as it considers proper.

When both parties appear — Counsel or agent — Appearance by corporation.

800. (1) Where the prosecutor and defendant appear for the trial, the summary conviction court shall proceed to hold the trial.

(2) A defendant may appear personally or by counsel or agent, but the summary conviction court may require the defendant to appear personally and may, if it thinks fit, issue a warrant in Form 7 for the arrest of the defendant and adjourn the trial to await his appearance pursuant thereto.

(3) Where the defendant is a corporation, it shall appear by counsel or agent, and if it does not appear, the summary conviction court may, on proof of service of the summons, proceed *ex parte* to hold the trial.

Arraignment — Finding of guilt, conviction or order if charge admitted — Procedure if charge not admitted.

801. (1) Where the defendant appears for the trial, the substance of the information laid against him shall be stated to him, and he shall be asked,

(*a*) whether he pleads guilty or not guilty to the information, where the proceedings are in respect of an offence that is punishable on summary conviction; or

(*b*) whether he has cause to show why an order should not be made against him, in proceedings where a justice is authorized by law to make an order.

(2) Where the defendant pleads guilty or does not show sufficient cause why an order should not be made against him, as the case may be, the summary conviction court shall convict the defendant, discharge the defendant under section 736 or make an order against the defendant accordingly.

(3) Where the defendant pleads not guilty or states that he has cause to show why an order should not be made against him, as the case may be, the summary conviction court shall proceed with the trial, and shall take the evidence of witnesses for the prosecutor and the defendant in accordance with the provisions of Part XVIII relating to preliminary inquiries. R.S. 1985, c. 27 (1st Supp.), s. 177.

(4) and (5) [Repealed R.S. 1985, c. 27 (1st Supp.), s. 177].

Right to make full answer and defence — Examination of witnesses — On oath.

802. (1) The prosecutor is entitled personally to conduct his case and the defendant is entitled to make his full answer and defence.

(2) The prosecutor or defendant, as the case may be, may examine and cross-examine witnesses personally or by counsel or agent.

(3) Every witness at a trial in proceedings to which this Part applies shall be examined under oath.

Adjournment — Non-appearance of defendant — Consent of Attorney General required — Non-appearance of prosecutor.

803. (1) The summary conviction court may, in its discretion, before or during the trial, adjourn the trial to a time and place to be appointed and stated in the presence of the parties or their counsels or agents, but no adjournment shall be for more than eight clear days unless both parties or their counsel or agents consent to the proposed adjournment whether or not the defendant is in custody.

(2) Where a defendant to whom an appearance notice that has been confirmed by a justice under section 508 has been issued or who has been served with a summons does not appear at the time and place appointed for the trial and the issue of the appearance notice or service of the summons within a reasonable time before the appearance was required is proved, or where a defendant does not appear for the resumption of a trial that has been adjourned in accordance with subsection (1), the summary conviction court

(*a*) may proceed *ex parte* to hear and determine the proceedings in the absence of the defendant as fully and effectually as if the defendant had appeared; or

(*b*) may, if it thinks fit, issue a warrant in Form 7 for the arrest of the defendant and adjourn the trial to await his appearance pursuant thereto.

(3) Where, at the trial of a defendant, the summary conviction court proceeds in the manner described in paragraph (2)(*a*), no proceedings under section 145 arising out of the failure of the defendant to appear at the time and place appointed for the trial or for the resumption of the trial shall be instituted or if instituted shall be proceeded with, except with the consent of the Attorney General.

(4) Where the prosecutor does not appear at the time and place appointed for the resumption of an adjourned trial, the summary conviction court may dismiss the information with or without costs.

(5) [Repealed 1991, c. 43, s. 9, Sch., item 11.]

(6) [Repealed 1991, c. 43, s. 9, Sch., item 11.]

(7) [Repealed 1991, c. 43, s. 9, Sch., item 11.]

(8) [Repealed 1991, c. 43, s. 9, Sch., item 11.]

Adjudication

Finding of guilt, conviction, order or dismissal.

804. When the summary conviction court has heard the prosecutor, defendant and witnesses, it shall, after considering the matter, convict the defendant, discharge the defendant under section 736, make an order against the defendant or dismiss the information, as the case may be. R.S. 1985, c. 27 (1st Supp.), s. 178.

805. [Repealed R.S. 1985, c. 27 (1st Supp.), s. 179.]

Memo of conviction or order — Warrant of committal.

806. (1) Where a defendant is convicted or where an order is made in relation to him, a minute or memorandum of the conviction or order shall be made by the summary conviction court, without fee, indicating that the matter was dealt with under this Part and, on request by the defendant or the prosecutor, the court shall cause a conviction or order in Form 35 or 36, as the case may be, and a certified copy thereof to be drawn up and shall deliver the certified copy to the person making the request.

(2) Where a defendant is convicted or an order is made against him, the summary conviction court shall issue a warrant of committal in Form 21 or 22, and section 528 applies in respect of a warrant of committal issued under this subsection.

Disposal of penalties when joint offenders.

807. Where several persons join in committing the same offence and upon conviction each is adjudged to pay an amount to a person aggrieved, no more shall be paid to that person than an amount equal to the value of the property destroyed or injured or the amount of the injury done, together with costs, if any, and the residue of the amount adjudged to be paid shall be applied in the manner in which other penalties imposed by law are directed to be applied.

Order of dismissal — Effect of certificate.

808. (1) Where the summary conviction court dismisses an information, it may, if requested by the defendant, draw up an order of dismissal, and shall give to the defendant a certified copy of the order of dismissal.

(2) A copy of an order of dismissal, certified in accordance with subsection (1) is, without further proof, a bar to any subsequent proceedings against the defendant in respect of the same cause.

Costs — Order set out — Costs are part of fine — Where no fine imposed — Definition of "costs".

809. (1) The summary conviction court may in its discretion award and order such costs as it considers reasonable and not inconsistent with such of the fees established by section 840 as may be taken or allowed in proceedings before that summary conviction court, to be paid

(*a*) to the informant by the defendant, where the summary conviction court convicts or makes an order against the defendant; or

(*b*) to the defendant by the informant, where the summary conviction court dismisses an information.

(2) An order under subsection (1) shall be set out in the conviction, order or order of dismissal, as the case may be.

(3) Where a fine or sum of money or both are adjudged to be paid by a defendant and a term of imprisonment in default of payment is imposed, the defendant is, in default of payment, liable to serve the term of imprisonment imposed, and for the purposes of this subsection, any costs that are awarded against the defendant shall be deemed to be part of the fine or sum of money adjudged to be paid.

(4) Where no fine or sum of money is adjudged to be paid by a defendant, but costs are awarded against the defendant or informant, the person who is liable to pay them is, in default of payment, liable to imprisonment for one month.

(5) In this section, "costs" includes the costs and charges, after they have been ascertained, of committing and conveying to prison the person against whom costs have been awarded.

Sureties to Keep the Peace

Where injury or damage feared — Duty of justice — Adjudication — Forms — Procedure.

810. (1) Any person who fears that another person will cause personal injury to him or his spouse or child or will damage his property may lay an information before a justice.

(2) A justice who receives an informatton under subsection (1) shall cause the parties to appear before him or before a summary conviction court having jurisdiction in the same territorial division.

(3) The justice or the summary conviction court before which the parties appear may, if satisfied by the evidence adduced that the informant has reasonable grounds for his fears,

(*a*) order that the defendant enter into a recognizance, with or without sureties, to keep the peace and be of good behaviour for any period that does not exceed twelve months, and comply with such other reasonable conditions prescribed in the recognizance as the court considers desirable for securing the good conduct of the defendant; or

(*b*) commit the defendant to prison for a term not exceeding twelve months if he fails or refuses to enter into the recognizance.

[1991, c. 40, s. 33 will add the following immediately after subsection 810(3).]

Conditions

(3.1) Before making an order under subsection (3), the justice or the summary conviction court shall consider whether it is desirable, in the interests of the safety of the defendant or of any other person, to include as a condition of the recognizance that the defendant be prohibited from possessing any firearm or any ammunition or explosive substance for any period of time specified in the recognizance and that the defendant surrender any firearms acquisition certificate that the accused possesses and, where the justice or summary conviction court decides that it is not desirable, in the interests of the safety of the defendant or of any other person, for the defendant to possess any of those things, the justice or summary conviction court may add the appropriate condition to the reecognizance.

(4) A recognizance and committal to prison in default of recognizance under subsection (3) may be in Forms 32 and 23, respectively.

(5) The provisions of this Part apply, with such modifications as the circumstances require, to proceedings under this section.

Breach of recognizance.

811. A person bound by recognizance under section 810 who commits a breach of the recognizance is guilty of an offence punishable on summary conviction.

Appeal

Definition of "appeal court".

812. For the purposes of sections 813 to 828 "appeal court" means
(*a*) in the Province of Ontario, the Ontario Court (General Division) sitting in the region, district or county or group of counties where the adjudication was made;
(*b*) in the Province of Quebec, the Superior Court;
(*c*) in the Province of Nova Scotia, the county court of the district or county where the cause of the proceedings arose;
(*d*) in the Provinces of New Brunswick, Manitoba, Saskatchewan and Alberta, the Court of Queen's Bench;
(*e*) in the Province of British Columbia, the Supreme Court;
(*f*) in the Province of Prince Edward Island, the Trial Division of the Supreme Court;
(*g*) in the Province of Newfoundland, the Trial Division of the Supreme Court; and
(*h*) in the Yukon Territory and Northwest Territories, a judge of the Supreme Court thereof. R.S. 1985, c. 11 (1st Supp.), s. 2; c. 27 (2d Supp.), Schedule, item 6; 1990, c. 16, s. 7; 1990, c. 17, s. 15.

Appeal by defendant, informant or Attorney General.

813. Except where otherwise provided by law,

(*a*) the defendant in proceedings under this Part may appeal to the appeal court

(i) from a conviction or order made against him;

(ii) against a sentence passed on him; or

(iii) against a verdict of unfit to stand trial or not criminally responsible on account of mental disorder; and

(*b*) the informant, the Attorney General or his agent in proceedings under this Part may appeal to the appeal court

(i) from an order that stays proceedings on an information or dismisses an information,

(ii) against a sentence passed upon a defendant, or

(iii) against a verdict of not criminally responsible on account of mental disorder or unfit to stand trial,

and the Attorney General of Canada or his agent has the same rights of appeal in proceedings instituted at the instance of the Government of Canada and conducted by or on behalf of that government as the Attorney General of a province or his agent has under this paragraph. R.S. 1985, c. 27 (1st Supp.), s. 180; 1991, c. 43, s. 9, Sch., item 12(1), (2).

Manitoba and Alberta — Saskatchewan — British Columbia — Yukon and Northwest Territories.

814. (1) In the Provinces of Manitoba and Alberta, an appeal under section 813 shall be heard at the sittings of the appeal court that is held nearest to the place where the cause of the proceedings arose, but the judge of the appeal court may, on the application of one of the parties, appoint another place for the hearing of the appeal.

(2) In the Province of Saskatchewan, an appeal under section 813 shall be heard at the sittings of the appeal court at the judicial centre nearest to the place where the adjudication was made, but the judge of the appeal court may, on the application of one of the parties, appoint another place for the hearing of the appeal.

(3) In the Province of British Columbia, an appeal under section 813 shall be heard at the sittings of the appeal court that is held nearest to the place where the adjudication was made, but the judge of the appeal court may, on the application of one of the parties, appoint another place for the hearing of the appeal.

(4) In the Yukon Territory and the Northwest Territories, an appeal under section 813 shall be heard at the place where the cause of the proceedings arose or at the place nearest thereto where a court is appointed to be held.

Notice of appeal — Extension of time.

815. (1) An appellant who proposes to appeal to the appeal court shall give notice of appeal in such manner and within such period as may be directed by rules of court.

(2) The appeal court or a judge thereof may extend the time within which notice of appeal may be given.

Interim Release of Appellant

Undertaking or recognizance of appellant — Application of certain provisions of section 525.

816. (1) A person who was the defendant in proceedings before a summary conviction court and by whom an appeal is taken under section 813 shall, if he is in custody, remain in custody unless the appeal court at which the appeal is to be heard orders that the appellant be released

(*a*) on his giving an undertaking to the appeal court, without conditions or with such conditions as the appeal court directs, to surrender himself into custody in accordance with the order,

(*b*) on his entering into a recognizance without sureties in such amount, with such conditions, if any, as the appeal court directs, but without deposit of money or other valuable security, or

(*c*) on his entering into a recognizance with or without sureties in such amount, with such conditions, if any, as the appeal court directs, and on his depositing with that appeal court such sum of money or other valuable security as the appeal court directs,

and the person having the custody of the appellant shall, where the appellant complies with the order, forthwith release the appellant.

(2) The provisions of subsections 525(5), (6) and (7) apply with such modifications as the circumstances require in respect of a person who has been released from custody under subsection (1). R.S. 1985, c. 27 (1st Supp.), s. 181.

Undertaking or recognizance of prosecutor — Condition — Appeals by Attorney General — Form of undertaking or recognizance.

817. (1) The prosecutor in proceedings before a summary conviction court by whom an appeal is taken under section 813 shall, forthwith after filing the notice of appeal and proof of service thereof in accordance with section 815, appear before a justice, and the justice shall, after giving the prosecutor and the respondent a reasonable opportunity to be heard, order that the prosecutor

(*a*) give an undertaking as prescribed in this section; or

(*b*) enter into a recognizance in such amount, with or without sureties and with or without deposit of money or other valuable security, as the justice directs.

(2) The condition of an undertaking or recognizance given or entered into

under this section is that the prosecutor will appear personally or by counsel at the sittings of the appeal court at which the appeal is to be heard.

(3) This section does not apply in respect of an appeal taken by the Attorney General or by counsel acting on behalf of the Attorney General.

(4) An undertaking under this section may be in Form 14 and a recognizance under this section may be in Form 32.

Application to appeal court for review — Disposition of application by appeal court — Effect of order.

818. (1) Where a justice makes an order under section 817, either the appellant or the respondent may, before or at any time during the hearing of the appeal, apply to the appeal court for a review of the order made by the justice.

(2) On the hearing of an application under this section, the appeal court, after giving the appellant and the respondent a reasonable opportunity to be heard, shall

(*a*) dismiss the application; or

(*b*) if the person applying for the review shows cause, allow the application, vacate the order made by the justice and make the order that in the opinion of the appeal court should have been made.

(3) An order made under this section shall have the same force and effect as if it had been made by the justice.

Application to fix date for hearing of appeal — Order fixing date.

819. (1) Where, in the case of an appellant who has been convicted by a summary conviction court and who is in custody pending the hearing of his appeal, the hearing of his appeal has not commenced within thirty days from the day on which notice of his appeal was given in accordance with the rules referred to in section 815, the person having the custody of the appellant shall, forthwith on the expiration of those thirty days, apply to the appeal court to fix a date for the hearing of the appeal.

(2) On receiving an application under subsection (1), the appeal court shall, after giving the prosecutor a reasonable opportunity to be heard, fix a date for the hearing of the appeal and give such directions as it thinks necessary for expediting the hearing of the appeal.

Payment of fine not a waiver of appeal — Presumption.

820. (1) A person does not waive his right of appeal under section 813 by reason only that he pays the fine imposed on conviction, without in any way indicating an intention to appeal or reserving the right to appeal.

(2) A conviction, order or sentence shall be deemed not to have been appealed against until the contrary is shown.

Procedure on Appeal

Notification and transmission of conviction, etc. — Saving — Appellant to furnish transcript of evidence.

821. (1) Where a notice of appeal has been given in accordance with the rules referred to in section 815, the clerk of the appeal court shall notify the summary conviction court that made the conviction or order appealed from or imposed the sentence appealed against of the apeal and on receipt of the notification that summary conviction court shall transmit the conviction, order or order of dismissal and all other material in its possession in connection with the proceedings to the appeal court before the time when the appeal is to be heard, or within such further time as the appeal court may direct, and the material shall be kept by the clerk of the appeal court with the records of the appeal court.

(2) An appeal shall not be dismissed by the appeal court by reason only that a person other than the appellant failed to comply with the provisions of this Part relating to appeals.

(3) Where the evidence on a trial before a summary conviction court has been taken by a stenographer duly sworn or by a sound recording apparatus, the appellant shall, unless the appeal court otherwise orders or the rules referred to in section 815 otherwise provide, cause a transcript thereof, certified by the stenographer or in accordance with subsection 540(6), as the case may be, to be furnished to the appeal court and the respondent for use on the appeal.

Certain sections applicable to appeals — New trial — Order of detention or release — Trial de novo — Former evidence — Appeal against sentence — General provisions re appeals.

822. (1) Where an appeal is taken under section 813 in respect of any conviction, acquittal, sentence verdict, or order, sections 683 to 689, with the exception of subsections 683(3) and 686(5), apply with such modifications as the circumstances require.

(2) Where an appeal court orders a new trial, it shall be held before a summary conviction court other than the court that tried the defendant in the first instance, unless the appeal court directs that the new trial be held before the summary conviction court that tried the accused in the first instance.

(3) Where an appeal court orders a new trial, it may make such order for the release or detention of the appellant pending the trial as may be made by a justice pursuant to section 515 and the order may be enforced in the same manner as if it had been made by a justice under that section, and the provisions of Part XVI apply with such modifications as the circumstances require to the order.

(4) Notwithstanding subsections (1) to (3), where an appeal is taken under section 813 and where, because of the condition of the record of the trial in

the summary conviction court or for any other reason, the appeal court, upon application of the defendant, the informant, the Attorney General or his agent, is of the opinion that the interests of justice would be better served by hearing and determining the appeal by holding a trial *de novo*, the appeal court may order that the appeal shall be heard by way of trial *de novo* in accordance with such rules as may be made under section 482 and for this purpose the provisions of sections 793 to 809 apply with such modifications as the circumstances require.

(5) The appeal court may, for the purpose of hearing and determining an appeal under subsection (4), permit the evidence of any witness taken before the summary conviction court to be read if that evidence has been authenticated in accordance with section 540 and if

(*a*) the appellant and respondent consent,

(*b*) the appeal court is satisfied that the attendance of the witness cannot reasonably be obtained, or

(*c*) by reason of the formal nature of the evidence or otherwise the court is satisfied that the opposite party will not be prejudiced,

and any evidence that is read under the authority of this subsection has the same force and effect as if the witness had given the evidence before the appeal court.

(6) Where an appeal is taken under subsection (4) against sentence, the appeal court shall, unless the sentence is one fixed by law, consider the fitness of the sentence appealed against and may, on such evidence, if any, as it thinks fit to require or receive, by order,

(*a*) dismiss the appeal, or

(*b*) vary the sentence within the limits prescribed by law for the offence of which the defendant was convicted;

and in making any order under paragraph (*b*) the appeal court may take into account any time spent in custody by the defendant as a result of the offence.

(7) The following provisions apply in respect of appeals under subsection (4):

(*a*) where an appeal is based on an objection to an information or any process, judgment shall not be given in favour of the appellant

(i) for any alleged defect therein in substance or in form, or

(ii) for any variance between the information or process and the evidence adduced at the trial,

unless it is shown

(iii) that the objection was taken at the trial, and

(iv) that an adjournment of the trial was refused notwithstanding that the variance referred to in subparagraph (ii) had deceived or misled the appellant; and

(*b*) where an appeal is based on a defect in a conviction or an order, judgment shall not be given in favour of the appellant, but the court shall make an order curing the defect. 1991, c. 43, s. 9, Sch., item 13.

823. [Repealed S.C. 1991, c. 43, s. 9, Sch., item 15.]

Adjournment.

824. The appeal court may adjourn the hearing of an appeal from time to time as may be necessary.

Dismissal for failure to appear or want of prosecution.

825. The appeal court may, on proof that notice of an appeal has been given and that

(*a*) the appellant has failed to comply with any order made under section 816 or 817 or with the conditions of any undertaking or recognizance given or entered into as prescribed in either of those sections, or

(*b*) the appeal has not been proceeded with or has been abandoned,

order that the appeal be dismissed.

Costs.

826. Where an appeal is heard and determined or is abandoned or is dismissed for want of prosecution, the appeal court may make any order with respect to costs that it considers just and reasonable.

To whom costs payable, and when — Certificate of non-payment of costs — Committal.

827. (1) Where the appeal court orders the appellant or respondent to pay costs, the order shall direct that the costs be paid to the clerk of the court, to be paid by him to the person entitled to them, and shall fix the period within which the costs shall be paid.

(2) Where costs are not paid in full within the period fixed for payment and the person who has been ordered to pay them has not been bound by a recognizance to pay them, the clerk of the court shall, on application by the person entitled to the costs, or by any person on his behalf, and on payment of any fee to which the clerk of the court is entitled, issue a certificate in Form 42 certifying that the costs or a part thereof, as the case may be, have not been paid.

(3) A justice having jurisdiction in the territorial division in which a certificate has been issued under subsection (2) may, upon production of the certificate, by warrant in Form 26, commit the defaulter to imprisonment for a term not exceeding one month, unless the amount of the costs and, where the justice thinks fit so to order, the costs of the committal and of conveying the defaulter to prison are sooner paid.

Enforcement of conviction or order by court of appeal — Enforcement by justice — Duty of clerk of court.

828. (1) A conviction or order made by the appeal court may be enforced

(*a*) in the same manner as if it had been made by the summary conviction court; or

(*b*) by process of the appeal court.

(2) Where an appeal taken against a conviction or order adjudging payment of a sum of money is dismissed, the summary conviction court that made the conviction or order or a justice for the same territorial division may issue a warrant of committal as if no appeal had been taken.

(3) Where a conviction or order that has been made by an appeal court is to be enforced by a justice, the clerk of the appeal court shall send to the justice the conviction or order and all writings relating thereto, except the notice of intention to appeal and any recognizance.

Summary Appeal on Transcript or Agreed Statement of Facts

Definition of "appeal court".

829. For the purposes of sections 830 to 838, "appeal court" means, in any province, the superior court of criminal jurisdiction for the province. R.S. 1985, c. 27 (1st Supp.), s. 182.

Appeals — Form of appeal — Rules for appeals — Rights of Attorney General of Canada.

830. (1) A party to proceedings to which this Part applies or the Attorney General may appeal against a conviction, judgment, verdict of acquittal or verdict of not criminally responsible on account of mental disorder or of unfit to stand trial or other final order or determination of a summary conviction court on the ground that

(*a*) it is erroneous in point of law;

(*b*) it is in excess of jurisdiction; or

(*c*) it constitutes a refusal or failure to exercise jurisdiction.

(2) An appeal under this section shall be based on a transcript of the proceedings appealed from unless the appellant files with the appeal court, within fifteen days of the filing of the notice of appeal, a statement of facts agreed to in writing by the respondent.

(3) An appeal under this section shall be made within the period and in the manner directed by any applicable rules of court and where there are no such rules otherwise providing, a notice of appeal in writing shall be served on the respondent and a copy thereof, together with proof of service, shall be filed with the appeal court within thirty days after the date of the conviction,

judgment or verdict of acquittal or other final order or determination that is the subject of the appeal.

(4) The Attorney General of Canada has the same rights of appeal in proceedings instituted at the instance of the Government of Canada and conducted by or on behalf of that Government as the Attorney General of a province has under this section. R.S. 1985, c. 27 (1st Supp.), s. 182; 1991, c. 43, s. 9, Sch., item 15.

Application.

831. The provisions of sections 816, 817, 819 and 825 apply, with such modifications as the circumstances require, in respect of an appeal under section 830, except that on receiving an application by the person having the custody of an appellant described in section 819 to appoint a date for the hearing of the appeal, the appeal court shall, after giving the prosecutor a reasonable opportunity to be heard, give such directions as it thinks necessary for expediting the hearing of the appeal. R.S. 1985, c. 27 (1st Supp.), s. 182.

Undertaking or recognizance — Attorney General.

832. (1) When a notice of appeal is filed pursuant to section 830, the appeal court may order that the appellant appear before a justice and give an undertaking or enter into a recognizance as provided in section 816 where the defendant is the appellant, or as provided in section 817, in any other case.

(2) Subsection (1) does not apply where the appellant is the Attorney General or counsel acting on behalf of the Attorney General. R.S. 1985, c. 27 (1st Supp.), s. 182.

No writ required.

833. No writ of *certiorari* or other writ is required to remove any conviction, judgment, verdict or other final order or determination of a summary conviction court for the purpose of obtaining the judgment, determination or opinion of the appeal court. R.S. 1985, c. 27 (1st Supp.), s. 182; 1991, c. 43, s. 9, Sch., item 16.

Powers of appeal court — Authority of judge.

834. (1) When a notice of appeal is filed pursuant to section 830, the appeal court shall hear and determine the grounds of appeal and may

(*a*) affirm, reverse or modify the conviction, judgment, verdict or other final order or determination, or

(*b*) remit the matter to the summary conviction court with the opinion of the appeal court,

and may make any other order in relation to the matter or with respect to costs that it considers proper.

(2) Where the authority and jurisdiction of the appeal court may be exercised by a judge of that court, the authority and jurisdiction may, subject to any

applicable rules of court, be exercised by a judge of the court sitting in chambers as well in vacation as in term time. R.S. 1985, c. 27 (1st Supp.), s. 182; 1991, c. 43, s. 9, Sch., item 17.

Enforcement — Idem.

835. (1) Where the appeal court renders its decision on an appeal, the summary conviction court from which the appeal was taken or a justice exercising the same jurisdiction has the same authority to enforce a conviction, order or determination that has been affirmed, modified or made by the appeal court as the summary conviction court would have had if no appeal had been taken.

(2) An order of the appeal court may be enforced by its own process. R.S. 1985, c. 27 (1st Supp.), s. 182.

Appeal under section 830.

836. Every person who appeals under section 830 from any conviction, judgment, verdict or other final order or determination in respect of which that person is entitled to an appeal under section 813 shall be taken to have abandoned all the person's rights of appeal under section 813. R.S. 1985, c. 27 (1st Supp.), s. 182; 1991, c. 43, s. 9, Sch., item 18.

Appeal barred.

837. Where it is provided by law that no appeal lies from a conviction or order, no appeal under section 830 lies from such a conviction or order. R.S. 1985, c. 27 (1st Supp.), s. 182.

Extension of time.

838. The appeal court or a judge thereof may at any time extend any time period referred to in section 830, 831 or 832. R.S. 1985, c. 27 (1st Supp.), s. 182.

Appeals to Court of Appeal

Appeal on question of law — Sections applicable — Costs — Enforcement of decision — Right of Attorney General of Canada to appeal.

839. (1) An appeal to the court of appeal, as defined in section 673 may, with leave of that court or a judge thereof, be taken on any ground that involves a question of law alone, against

(*a*) a decision of a court in respect of an appeal under section 822; or

(*b*) a decision of an appeal court under section 834, except where that court is the court of appeal.

(2) Sections 673 to 689 apply with such modifications as the circumstances require to an appeal under this section.

(3) Notwithstanding subsection (2), the court of appeal may make any order

with respect to costs that it considers proper in relation to an appeal under this section.

(4) The decision of the court of appeal may be enforced in the same manner as if it had been made by the summary conviction court before which the proceedings were originally heard and determined.

(5) The Attorney General of Canada has the same rights of appeal in proceedings instituted at the instance of the Government of Canada and conducted by or on behalf of that Government as the Attorney General of a province has under this Part. R.S. 1985, c. 27 (1st Supp.), s. 183.

Fees and Allowances

Fees and allowances — Order of lieutenant governor in council.

840. (1) Subject to subsection (2), the fees and allowances mentioned in the schedule to this Part are the fees and allowances that may be taken or allowed in proceedings before summary conviction courts and justices under this Part.

(2) The lieutenant governor in council of a province may order that all or any of the fees and allowances mentioned in the schedule to this Part shall not be taken or allowed in proceedings before summary conviction courts and justices under this Part in that province.

SCHEDULE

(*Section 840*)

FEES AND ALLOWANCES THAT MAY BE CHARGED BY SUMMARY CONVICTION COURTS AND JUSTICES

1.	Information	$1.00
2.	Summons or warrant	0.50
3.	Warrant where summons issued in first instance	0.30
4.	Each necessary copy of summons or warrant	0.30
5.	Each subpoena or warrant to or for witnesses (A subpoena may contain any number of names. Only one subpoena may be issued on behalf of a party in any proceeding, unless the summary conviction court or the justice considers it necessary or desirable that more than one subpoena be issued.)	0.30
6.	Information for warrant for witness and warrant for witness	1.00
7.	Each necessary copy of subpoena to or warrant for witness	0.20
8.	Each recognizance	1.00
9.	Hearing and determining proceeding	1.00
10.	Where hearing lasts more than two hours	2.00
11.	Where two or more justices hear and determine a proceeding, each is entitled to the fee authorized by item 9.	

12. Each warrant of committal 0.50
13. Making up record of conviction or order on request of a party to the proceedings 1.00
14. Copy of a writing other than a conviction or order, on request of a party to the proceedings; for each folio of one hundred words... 0.10
15. Bill of costs, when made out in detail on request of a party to the proceedings 0.20
(Items 14 and 15 may be charged only where there has been an adjudication.)
16. Attending to remand prisoner 1.00
17. Attending to take recognizance of bail 1.00

FEES AND ALLOWANCES THAT MAY BE ALLOWED TO PEACE OFFICERS

18. Arresting a person on a warrant or without a warrant $1.50
19. Serving summons or subpoena 0.50
20. Mileage to serve summons or subpoena or to make an arrest, both ways, for each mile 0.10
(Where a public conveyance is not used, reasonable costs of transportation may be allowed.)
21. Mileage where service cannot be effected, on proof of a diligent attempt to effect service, each way, for each mile 0.10
22. Returning with prisoner after arrest to take him before a summary conviction court or justice at a place different from the place where the peace officer received the warrant to arrest, if the journey is of necessity over a route different from that taken by the peace officer to make the arrest, each way, for each mile 0.10
23. Taking a prisoner to prison on remand or committal, each way, for each mile 0.10
(Where a public conveyance is not used, reasonable costs of transportation may be allowed. No charge may be made under this item in respect of a service for which a charge is made under item 22.)
24. Attending summary conviction court or justice on summary conviction proceedings, for each day necessarily employed 2.00
(No more than $2.00 may be charged under this item in respect of any day notwithstanding the number of proceedings that the peace officer attended on that day before that summary conviction court or justice.)

FEES AND ALLOWANCES THAT MAY BE ALLOWED TO WITNESSES

25. Each day attending trial $4.00

26. Mileage travelled to attend trial, each way, for each mile......... 0.10

FEES AND ALLOWANCES THAT MAY BE ALLOWED TO INTERPRETERS

27. Each half day attending trial.................................. $2.50
28. Actual living expenses when away from ordinary place of residence, not to exceed per day.................................... 10.00
29. Mileage travelled to attend trial, each way, for each mile......... 0.10

PART XXVIII

FORMS

Forms — Seal not required — Official language.

841. (1) The forms set out in this Part varied to suit the case or forms to the like effect shall be deemed to be good, valid and sufficient in the circumstances for which, respectively, they are provided.

(2) No justice is required to attach or affix a seal to any writing or process that he is authorized to issue and in respect of which a form is provided by this Part.

(3) Any pre-printed portions of a form set out in this Part varied to suit the case or of a form to the like effect shall be printed in both official languages. R.S. 1985, c. 31 (4th Supp.), s. 97.

Form 1

INFORMATION TO OBTAIN A SEARCH WARRANT
(Section 487)

Canada,

Province of ....,
(*territorial division*).

This is the information of A.B., of .... in the said (*territorial division*), (*occupation*), hereinafter called the informant, taken before me.

The informant says that (*describe things to be searched for and offence in respect of which search is to be made*), and that he believes on reasonable grounds that the said things, or some part of them, are in the (*dwelling-house, etc.*), of C.D., of .... in the said (*territorial division*) (*Here add the grounds of belief, whatever they may be*).

Wherefore the informant prays that a search warrant may be granted to search the said (*dwelling-house, etc.*) for the said things.

Sworn before me
this .... day of
..........., A.D. ...., ...
at .... (*Signature of Informant*)
....
A Justice of the Peace in and for
....

FORM 2

INFORMATION (Sections 506 and 788)

Canada,

Province of ....,
(*territorial division*).

This is the information of C.D., of ...., (*occupation*), hereinafter called the informant.

The informant says that (*if the informant has no personal knowledge state that he believes on reasonable grounds and state the offence.*)

Sworn before me
this .... day of
..........., A.D. ...., ...
at .... (*Signature of Informant*)
....
A Justice of the Peace in and for
....

[*Note:* The date of birth of the accused may be mentioned on the information or indictment.]

R.S. 1985, c. 27 (1st Supp.), s. 184(1).

FORM 3

Repealed, R.S., c. 27 (1st Supp.), s. 184(2).

FORM 4

HEADING OF INDICTMENT (Sections 566, 580 and 591)

Canada,

Province of ....,
(*territorial division*).

In the (*set out name of the court*)

Her Majesty the Queen

against

(*name of accused*)

(*Name of accused*) stands charged

1. That he (*state offence*).
2. That he (*state offence*).

Dated this .... day of .... A.D. ...., at ....

....
(*Signature of signing officer, Agent of Attorney General etc., as the case may be*)

[*Note:* The date of birth of the accused may be mentioned on the information or indictment.]

R.S. 1985, c. 27 (1st Supp.), s. 184(1).

FORM 5

WARRANT TO SEARCH (Section 487)

Canada,

Province of .... ,
(*territorial division*).

To the peace officers in the said (*territorial division*):

Whereas it appears on the oath of A.B., of .... that there are reasonable grounds for believing that (*describe things to be searched for and offence in respect of which search is to be made*) are in .... at .... , hereinafter called the premises:

This is, therefore, to authorize and require you between the hours of (*as the justice may direct*) to enter into the said premises and to search for the said things and to bring them before me or some other justice.

Dated this .... day of .... A.D. ...., at ....

....
A Justice of the Peace in and for
....

FORM 5.1

WARRANT TO SEARCH (Section 487.1)

Canada,

Province of .... ,
(*specify province*).

To A.B., and other peace officers in the (*territorial division in which the warrant is intended for execution*):

Whereas it appears on the oath of A.B., a peace officer in the (*territorial division in which the warrant is intended for execution*), that there are reasonable grounds for dispensing with an information presented personally and in writing; and that there are reasonable grounds for believing that the following things

(*describe things to be searched for*)

relevant to the investigation of the following indictable offence

(*describe offence in respect of which search is to be made*)

are to be found in the following place or premises

(*describe place or premises to be searched*):

This is, therefore, to authorize you to enter the said place or premises between the hours of (*as the justice may direct*) and to search for and seize the said things and to report thereon as soon as practicable but within a period not exceeding seven days after the execution of the warrant to the clerk of the court for the (*territorial division in which the warrant is intended for execution*).

Issued at (*time*) on the (*day*) of (*month*) A.D. (*year*) at (*place*).

....

A Judge of the Provincial
Court in and for the
Province of (specify province).

To the Occupant: This search warrant was issued by telephone or other means of telecommunication. If you wish to know the basis on which this warrant was issued, you may apply to the clerk of the court for the territorial division in which the warrant was executed, at [*address*], to obtain a copy of the information on oath.

You may obtain from the clerk of the court a copy of the report filed by the peace officer who executed this warrant. That report will indicate the things, if any, that were seized and the location where they are being held.

R.S. 1985, c. 27 (1st Supp.), s. 184(3); c. 1(4th Supp.), s. 17.

FORM 5.2

REPORT TO A JUSTICE (Section 489.1)

Canada,

Province of .... ,

(*territorial division*).

To the justice who issued a warrant to the undersigned pursuant to section 256, 487 or 487.1 of the *Criminal Code* (*or another justice for the same territorial division or, if no warrant was issued, any justice having jurisdiction in respect of the matter*).

I, (*name of the peace officer or other person*) have (*state here whether you have acted under a warrant issued pursuant to section 256, 487 or 487.1 of the Criminal Code or under section 489 of the Criminal Code or otherwise in the execution of duties under the Criminal Code or another Act of Parliament to be specified*)

1. searched the premises situated at .... ; and
2. seized the following things and dealt with them as follows:

Property Seized (*describe each thing seized*)	Disposition (*state, in respect of each thing seized, whether* (*a*) *it was returned to the person lawfully entitled to its possession, in which case the receipt therefor shall be attached hereto, or* (*b*) *it is being detained to be dealt with according to law, and the location and manner in which, or where applicable, the person by whom it is being detained*).
1.	....
2.	....
3.	....
4.	....

In the case of a warrant issued by telephone or other means of telecommunication, the statements referred to in subsection 487.1(9) of the *Criminal Code* shall be specified in the report.

Dated this .... day of .... A.D. ...., at ....

....
Signature of peace officer or other person

R.S. 1985, c. 27 (1st Supp.), s. 184(3).

Form 5.3

REPORT TO A JUDGE OF PROPERTY SEIZED
(Section 462.32)

Canada,
Province of .... ,
(*territorial division*).

To a judge of the court from which the warrant was issued (*specify court*):

I, (*name of the peace officer or other person*) have acted under a warrant issued under section 462.32 of the Criminal Code and have

1. searched the premises situated at .... ; and

2. seized the following property:

Property Seized	Location
(*describe each item of property seized*)	(*state, in respect of each item of property seized, the location where it is being detained*).
1.	....
2.	....
3.	....
4.	....

Dated this .... day of .... A.D. ...., at ....

....
Signature of peace officer or other person

R.S. 1985, c. 42(4th Supp.), s. 6.

FORM 6

SUMMONS TO A PERSON CHARGED WITH AN OFFENCE

(Sections 493, 508 and 512)

Canada,
Province of .... ,
(*territorial division*).

To A.B., of .... (*occupation*):

Whereas you have this day been charged before me that (*set out briefly the offence in respect of which the accused is charged*);

This is therefore to command you, in Her Majesty's name:

(*a*) to attend court on .... , the .... day of .... A.D. .... , at .... o'clock in the .... noon, at .... or before any justice for the said (*territorial division*) who is there, and to attend thereafter as required by the court, in order to be dealt with according to law; and

(*b*) to appear on .... , the .... day of .... A.D. ...., at .... o'clock in the .... noon, at .... , for the purposes of the *Identification of Criminals Act*. (*Ignore, if not filled in*).

You are warned that failure without lawful excuse to attend court in accordance with this summons is an offence under subsection 145(4) of the *Criminal Code*.

Subsection 145(4) of the *Criminal Code* states as follows:

"(4) Every one who is served with a summons and who fails, without lawful excuse, the proof of which lies upon him, to appear at a time and place stated therein, if any, for the purposes of the *Identification of Criminals Act* or to attend court in accordance therewith, is guilty of
accordance therewith, is guilty of

(*a*) an indictable offence and is liable to imprisonment for a term not exceeding two years, or

(*b*) an offence punishable on summary conviction."

Section 510 of the *Criminal Code* states as follows:

"**510.** Where an accused who is required by a summons to appear at a time and place stated therein for the purposes of the *Identification of Criminals Act* does not appear at that time and place, a justice may issue a warrant for the arrest of the accused for the offence with which he is charged."

Dated this .... day of .... A.D. ...., at ....

....
A Justice of the Peace in
and for .... *or* Judge
R.S. 1985, c. 27 (1st Supp.), s. 184(4).

FORM 7

WARRANT FOR ARREST
(Sections 475, 493, 597, 800 and 803)

Canada,
Province of .... ,
(*territorial division*).

To the peace officers in the said (*territorial division*):

This warrant is issued for the arrest of A.B., of .... , (*occupation*), hereinafter called the accused.

Whereas the accused has been charged that (*set out briefly the offence in respect of which the accused is charged*):

And whereas:*

(*a*) there are reasonable and probable grounds to believe that it is necessary in the public interest to issue this warrant for the arrest of the accused [507(4); 512(1)];

(*b*) the accused failed to attend court in accordance with the summons served on him [512(2)];

(*c*) (an appearance notice *or* a promise to appear *or* a recognizance entered into before an officer in charge) was confirmed and the accused failed to attend court in accordance therewith [512(2)];

(*d*) it appears that a summons cannot be served because the accused is evading service [512(2)];

(*e*) the accused was ordered to be present at the hearing of an application for a review of an order made by a justice and did not attend the hearing [520(5), 521(5)];

(*f*) there are reasonable grounds to believe that the accused has contravened or is about to contravene the (promise to appear *or* undertaking *or* recognizance) on which he was released [524(1), 525(5), 679(6)];

(*g*) there are reasonable grounds to believe that the accused has since his release from custody on (a promise to appear *or* an undertaking *or* a recognizance) committed an indictable offence [524(1), 525(5), 679(6)];

(*h*) the accused was required by (an appearance notice *or* a promise to appear *or* a recognizance entered into before an officer in charge *or* a summons) to attend at a time and place stated therein for the purposes of the *Identification of Criminals Act* and did not appear at that time and place [502, 510];

(*i*) an indictment has been found against the accused and the accused has not appeared or remained in attendance before the court for his trial [597];

(*j*) **

This is, therefore, to command you, in Her Majesty's name, forthwith to arrest the said accused and to bring him before (*state court, judge or justice*), to be dealt with according to law.

Dated this .... day of .... A.D. .... , at ....

....
Judge, Clerk of the Court,
Provincial Court Judge or Justice

* *Initial applicable recital.*

** *For any case not covered by recitals (a) to (i), insert recital in the words of the statute authorizing the warrant.*

FORM 8

WARRANT FOR COMMITTAL

(Sections 493 and 515)

Canada,

Province of .... ,
(*territorial division*).

To the peace officers in the said (*territorial division*) and to the keeper of the (*prison*) at .... :

This warrant is issued for the committal of A.B., of ...., (*occupation*), hereinafter called the accused.

Whereas the accused has been charged that (*set out briefly the offence in respect of which the accused is charged*);

And whereas:*

(*a*) the prosecutor has shown cause why the detention of the accused in custody is justified [515(5)];

(*b*) an order has been made that the accused be released on (giving an undertaking *or* entering into a recognizance) but the accused has not yet complied with the order [519(1), 520(9), 524(12), 525(8)];**

(*c*) the application by the prosecutor for a review of the order of a justice in respect of the interim release of the accused has been allowed and that order has been vacated, and the prosecutor has shown cause why the detention of the accused in custody is justified [521];

(*d*) the accused has contravened or was about to contravene his (promise to appear *or* undertaking *or* recognizance) and the same was cancelled, and the detention of the accused in custody is justified or seems proper in the circumstances [524(4), 524(8)];

(*e*) there are reasonable and probable grounds to believe that the accused has after his release from custody on (a promise to appear *or* an undertaking *or* a recognizance) committed an indictable offence and the detention of the accused in custody is justified or seems proper in the circumstances [524(4), 524(8)];

(*f*) the accused has contravned or was about to contravene the (undertaking *or* recognizance) on which he was released and the detention of the accused in custody seems proper in the circumstances [525(7), 679(6)];

(*g*) there are reasonable grounds to believe that the accused has after his release from custody on (an undertaking *or* a recognizance) committed an indictable offence and the detention of the accused in custody seems proper in the circumstances [525(7), 679(6)];

(*h*) ***

This is, therefore, to command you, in Her Majesty's name, to take the accused and convey him safely to the (*prison*) at ...., and there deliver him to the keeper thereof, with the following precept:

I do hereby command you the said keeper to receive the accused in your custody in the said prison and keep him safely there until he is delivered by due course of law.

Dated this .... day of .... A.D. ...., at ....

....

Judge, Clerk of the Court,
Provincial Court Judge *or* Justice

---

* *Initial applicable recital.*

** *If the person having custody of the accused is authorized under paragraph 519(1)(b) to release him upon his complying with an order, endorse the authorization on this warrant and attach a copy of the order.*

*** *For any case not covered by recitals (a) to (g), insert recital in the words of the statute authorizing the warrant.*

FORM 9

APPEARANCE NOTICE ISSUED BY A PEACE OFFICER TO A PERSON NOT YET CHARGED WITH AN OFFENCE
(Section 493)

Canada,

Province of .... ,
(*territorial division*).

To A.B., of .... , (*occupation*):

You are alleged to have committed (*set out substance of offence*).

1. You are required to attend court on .... day, the .... day of .... A.D. .... , at .... o'clock in the .... noon, in courtroom No. .... , at .... court, in the municipality of .... , and to attend thereafter as required by the court, in order to be dealt with according to law.

2. You are also required to appear on .... day, the .... day of .... A.D. .... , at .... o'clock in the .... noon, at (*police station*), (*address*), for the purposes of the *Identification of Criminals Act*. (*Ignore, if not filled in*).

You are warned that failure to attend court in accordance with this appearance notice is an offence under subsection 145(5) of the *Criminal Code*.

Subsections 145(5) and (6) of the *Criminal Code* state as follows:

"(5) Every one who is named in an appearance notice or promise to appear, or in a recognizance entered into before an officer in charge, that has been confirmed by a justice under section 508 and who fails, without lawful excuse, the proof of which lies on him to appear at a time and place stated therein, if any, for the purposes of the *Identification of Criminals Act*, or to attend court in accordance therewith, is guilty of

(*a*) an indictable offence and is liable to imprisonment for a term not exceeding two years, or

(*b*) an offence punishable on summary conviction.

(6) For the purposes of subsection (5), it is not a lawful excuse that an

appearance notice, promise to appear or recognizance states defectively the substance of the alleged offence."

Section 502 of the *Criminal Code* states as follows:

"**502** Where an accused who is required by an appearance notice or promise to appear or by a recognizance entered into before an officer in charge to appear at a time and place stated therein for the purposes of the *Identification of Criminals Act* does not appear at that time and place, a justice may, where the appearance notice, promise to appear or recognizance has been confirmed by a justice under section 508, issue a warrant for the arrest of the accused for the offence with which he is charged."

Issued at .... a.m./p.m. this .... day of .... A.D. ...., at ....

....
(*Signature of peace officer*)

....
(*Signature of accused*)

R.S. 1985, c. 27 (1st Supp.), s. 184(5).

Form 10

PROMISE TO APPEAR (Section 493)

Canada,

Province of .... ,
(*territorial division*).

I, A.B., of .... , (*occupation*), understand that it is alleged that I have committed (*set out substance of offence*).

In order that I may be released from custody,

1. I promise to attend court on .... day, the .... day of .... A.D. ...., at .... o'clock in the .... noon, in courtroom No. .... , at court in the municipality of .... , and to attend thereafter as required by the court, in order to be dealt with according to law.

2. I also promise to appear on .... day, the .... day of .... A.D. ...., at .... o'clock in the .... noon, at (*police station*), (*address*), for the purposes of the *Identification of Criminals Act*. (*Ignore if not filled in*).

I understand that failure without lawful excuse to attend court in accordance with this promise to appear is an offence under subsection 145(5) of the *Criminal Code*.

Subsections 145(5) and (6) of the *Criminal Code* state as follows:

"(5) Every one who is named in an appearance notice or promise to appear, or in a recognizance entered into before an officer in charge, that has been confirmed by a justice under section 508 and who fails, without lawful excuse, the proof of which lies on him, to appear at a time and place stated therein, if any, for the purposes of the *Identification of Criminals Act*, or to attend court in accordance therewith, is guilty of

(*a*) an indictable offence and is liable to imprisonment for a term not exceeding two years, or

(*b*) an offence punishable on summary conviction.

(6) For the purposes of subsection (5), it is not a lawful excuse that an appearance notice, promise to appear or recognizance states defectively the substance of the alleged offence."

Section 502 of the *Criminal Code* states as follows:

"**502.** Where an accused who is required by an appearance notice or promise to appear or by a recognizance, entered into before an officer in charge to appear at a time and place stated therein for the purposes of the *Identification of Criminals Act* does not appear at that time and place, a justice may, where the appearance notice, promise to appear or recognizance has been confirmed by a justice under section 508, issue a warrant for the arrest of the accused for the offence with which he is charged."

Dated this .... day of .... A.D.
.........., at ....

....
(*Signature of accused*)

FORM 11

RECOGNIZANCE ENTERED INTO BEFORE AN OFFICER IN CHARGE
(Section 493)

Canada,

Province of .... ,
(*territorial division*).

I, A.B., of .... , (*occupation*), understand that it is alleged that I have committed (*set out substance of offence*).

In order that I may be released from custody, I hereby acknowledge that I owe $ (*not exceeding $500*) to Her Majesty the Queen to be levied on my real and personal property if I fail to attend court as hereinafter required.

(*or, for a person not ordinarily resident in the province in which he is in custody or within two hundred kilometres of the place in which he is in custody*:)

In order that I may be released from custody, I hereby acknowledge that I owe $ (*not exceeding $500*) to Her Majesty the Queen and deposit herewith (*money or other valuable security not exceeding in amount or value $500*) to be forfeited if I fail to attend court as hereinafter required.

1. I acknowledge that I am required to attend court on .... day, the .... day of .... A.D. .... , at .... o'clock in the .... noon, in courtroom No. .... , at .... court, in the municipality of .... , and to attend thereafter as required by the court, in order to be dealt with according to law.

2. I acknowledge that I am also required to appear on .... day, the .... day of .... A.D. .... , at .... o'clock in the .... noon, at (*police station*), (*address*), for the purposes of the *Identification of Criminals Act*. (*Ignore if not filled in*).

I understand that failure without lawful excuse to attend court in accordance with this recognizance to appear is an offence under subsection 145(5) of the *Criminal Code*.

Subsections 145(5) and (6) of the *Criminal Code* state as follows:

"(5) Every one who is named in an appearance notice or promise to appear, or in a recognizance entered into before an officer in charge, that has been confirmed by a justice under section 508 and who fails, without lawful excuse, the proof of which lies on him, to appear at a time and place stated therein, if any, for the purposes of the *Identification of Criminals Act*, or to attend court in accordance therewith, is guilty of

(*a*) an indictable offence and is liable to imprisonment for a term not exceeding two years, or

(*b*) an offence punishable on summary conviction.

(6) For the purposes of subsection (5), it is not a lawful excuse that an appearance notice, promise to appear or recognizance states defectively the substance of the alleged offence."

Section 502 of the *Criminal Code* states as follows:

"**502** Where an accused who is required by an appearance notice or promise to appear or by a recognizance entered into before an officer in charge to appear at a time and place stated therein for the purposes of the *Identification of Criminals Act* does not appear at that time and place, a justice may, where the appearance notice, promise to appear or recognizance has been confirmed by a justice under section 508, issue a warrant for the arrest of the accused for the offence with which he is charged."

Dated this .... day of .... A.D. .... , at ....

....
(*Signature of accused*)

1992, c. 1, s. 58(1), Sch. I, item 17

FORM 12

UNDERTAKING GIVEN TO A JUSTICE OR A JUDGE

(Sections 493 and 679)

Canada,

Province of .... ,

(*territorial division*).

I, A.B., of .... , (*occupation*), understand that I have been charged that (*set out briefly the offence in respect of which accused is charged*).

In order that I may be released from custody, I undertake to attend court on .... day, the .... day of .... A.D. .... , and to attend thereafter as required by the court in order to be dealt with according to law *or* (*where date and place of appearance before court are not known at the time undertaking is given* to attend at the time and place fixed by the court and thereafter as required by the court in order to be dealt with according to law).

(*and where applicable*)

I also undertake to (*insert any conditions that are directed*)

(*a*) report at (*state times*) to (*name of peace officer or other person designated*),

(*b*) remain within (*designated territorial jurisdiction*),

(*c*) notify (*name of peace officer or other person designated*) of any change in my address, employment or occupation,

(*d*) abstain from communication with (*name of witness or other person*) except in accordance with the following conditions: (*as the justice or judge specifies*),

(*e*) deposit my passport (*as the justice or judge directs*); and

(*f*) (*any other reasonable conditions*).

I understand that failure without lawful excuse to attend court in accordance with this undertaking is an offence under subsection 145(2) of the *Criminal Code.*

Subsections 145(2) and (3) of the *Criminal Code* state as follows:

"(2) Every one who,

(*a*) being at large on his undertaking or recognizance given to or entered into before a justice or judge, fails, without lawful excuse, the proof of which lies on him, to attend court in accordance with the undertaking or recognizance, or

(*b*) having appeared before a court, justice or judge, fails, without lawful excuse, the proof of which lies on him, to attend court as thereafter required by the court, justice or judge,

or to surrender himself in accordance with an order of the court, justice or judge, as the case may be, is guilty of an indictable offence and liable to imprisonment for a term not exceeding two years or is guilty of an offence punishable on summary conviction.

(3) Every one who, being at large on his undertaking or recognizance given to or entered into before a justice or a judge and being bound to comply with a condition of that undertaking or recognizance directed by a justice or a judge, fails, without lawful excuse, the proof of which lies on him, to comply with that condition, is guilty of

(*a*) an indictable offence and is liable to imprisonment for a term not exceeding two years, or

(*b*) an offence punishable on summary conviction."

Dated this .... day of .... A.D. ...., at ....

....

(*Signature of accused*)

R.S. 1985, c. 27 (1st Supp.), s. 184(6).

FORM 13

UNDERTAKING BY APPELLANT (DEFENDANT)
(Sections 832 and 834)

Canada,

Province of .... ,
(*territorial division*).

I, A.B., of .... , (*occupation*), being the appellant against conviction (*or* against sentence *or* against an order *or* by way of stated case) in respect of the following matter (*set out the offence, subject matter of order or question of law*)

undertake to appear personally at the sittings of the appeal court at which the appeal is to be heard.

(*and where applicable*)

I also undertake to (*insert any conditions that are directed*)

(*a*) report at (*state times*) to (*name of peace officer or other person designated*),

(*b*) remain within (*designated territorial jurisdiction*),

(*c*) notify (*name of peace officer or other person designated*) of any change in my address, employment or occupation,

(*d*) abstain from communicating with (*name of witness or other person*) except in accordance with the following conditions: (*as the justice or judge specifies*),

(*e*) deposit my passport (*as the justice or judge directs*); and

(*f*) (*any other reasonable conditions*).

Dated this .... day of .... A.D. ...., at ....

....

(*Signature of appellant*)

FORM 14

UNDERTAKING BY APPELLANT (PROSECUTOR)
(Section 817)

Canada,

Province of ....,
(*territorial division*).

I, A.B., of ...., (*occupation*), being the appellant against an order of dismissal (*or* against sentence) in respect of the following charge (*set out the name of the defendant and the offence, subject matter of order or question of law*)

undertake to appear personally or by counsel at the sittings of the appeal court at which the appeal is to be heard.

Dated this .... day of .... A.D. ...., at ....

....
(*Signature of appellant*)

FORM 15

WARRANT TO CONVEY ACCUSED BEFORE JUSTICE OF ANOTHER TERRITORIAL DIVISION (Section 543)

Canada,

Province of ....,
(*territorial division*).

To the peace officers in the said (*territorial division*):

Whereas A.B., of .... hereinafter called the accused, has been charged that (*state place of offence and charge*);

And Whereas I have taken the deposition of X.Y. in respect of the said charge;

And Whereas the charge is for an offence committed in the (*territorial division*):

This is to command you, in Her Majesty's name, to convey the said A.B., before a justice of the (*last mentioned territorial division*).

Dated this .... day of .... A.D. ...., at ....

....
A Justice of the Peace in and for
....

FORM 16

SUBPOENA TO A WITNESS (Section 699)

Canada,

Province of ....,
(*territorial division*).

To E.F., of ...., (*occupation*):

Whereas A.B. has been charged that (*state offence as in the information*), and it has been made to appear that you are likely to give material evidence for (the prosecution *or* the defence):

This is therefore to command you to attend before (*set out court or justice*), on .... the .... day of .... A.D. ...., at .... o'clock in the .... noon at .... to give evidence concerning the said charge.*

Dated this .... day of .... A.D. ...., at ....

....
A Justice *or* Clerk of the court

(*Seal, if required*) ....

**Where a witness is required to produce anything add the following:*

and to bring with you anything in your possession or under your control that relates to the said charge, and more particularly the following: (*specify any documents, objects or other things required*).

R.S. 1985, c. 27 (1st Supp.), s. 184(7).

FORM 17

WARRANT FOR WITNESS (Sections 698 and 705)

Canada,

Province of ....,
(*territorial division*).

To the peace officers in the (*territorial division*):

Whereas A.B. of ...., has been charged that (*state offence as in the information*);

And Whereas it has been made to appear that E.F. of ...., hereinafter called the witness, is likely to give material evidence for (the prosecution *or* the defence) and that*

This is therefore to command you, in Her Majesty's name, to arrest and bring the witness forthwith before (*set out court or justice*) to be dealt with in accordance with section 706 of the *Criminal Code*.

Dated this .... day of .... A.D. ...., at ....

....
A Justice *or* Clerk of the Court

(*Seal, if required*)

**Insert whichever of the following is appropriate*:
(*a*) the said E.F. will not attend unless compelled to do so;
(*b*) the said E.F. is evading service of a subpoena;
(*c*) the said E.F. was duly served with a subpoena and has neglected (to attend at the time and place appointed therein *or* to remain in attendance);
(*d*) the said E.F. was bound by a recognizance to attend and give evidence and has neglected (to attend *or* to remain in attendance).

R.S. 1985, c. 27 (1st Supp.), s. 184(8).

FORM 18

WARRANT TO ARREST AN ABSCONDING WITNESS
(Section 704)

Canada,
Province of .... ,
(*territorial division*).

To the peace officers in the (*territorial division*):

Whereas A.B. of .... , has been charged that (*state offence as in the information*);

And Whereas I am satisfied by information in writing and under oath that C.D. of .... , hereinafter called the witness, is bound by recognizance to give evidence on the trial of the accused on the said charge, and that the witness (has absconded *or* is about to abscond):

This is therefore to command you, in Her Majesty's name, to arrest the witness and bring him forthwith before (*the court, judge, justice or provincial court judge before whom the witness is bound to appear*) to be dealt with in accordance with section 706 of the *Criminal Code*.

Dated this .... day of .... A.D. ...., at ....

....
A Justice of the Peace in and for
....

Form 19

WARRANT REMANDING A PRISONER
(Sections 516 and 537)

Canada,

Province of .... ,
(*territorial division).*

To the peace officers in the (*territorial division*):

You are hereby commanded forthwith to arrest, if necessary, and convey to the (*prison*) at .... the persons named in the following schedule each of whom has been remanded to the time mentioned in the schedule:

Person charged	Offence	Remanded to

And I hereby command you, the keeper of the said prison, to receive each of the said persons into your custody in the prison and keep him safely until the day when his remand expires and then to have him before me or any other justice at .... at .... o'clock in the .... noon of the said day, there to answer to the charge and to be dealt with according to law, unless you are otherwise ordered before that time.

Dated this .... day of .... A.D. ...., at ....

....
A Justice of the Peace in and for
....

R.S. 1985, c. 27 (1st Supp.), s. 184(9).

Form 20

WARRANT OF COMMITTAL OF WITNESS FOR REFUSING TO BE SWORN OR TO GIVE EVIDENCE
(Section 545)

Canada,

Province of .... ,
(*territorial division*).

To the peace officers in the (*territorial division*):

Whereas A.B. of .... , hereinafter called the accused, has been charged that (*set out offence as in the information*);

And Whereas E.F. of .... , hereinafter called the witness, attending before me to give evidence for (the prosecution *or* the defence) concerning the charge against the accused (refused to be sworn *or* being duly sworn as a witness refused to answer certain questions concerning the charge that were put to him *or* refused or neglected to produce the following writings, namely

. . . . *or* refused to sign his deposition) having been ordered to do so, without offering any just excuse for such refusal or neglect:

This is therefore to command you, in Her Majesty's name, to arrest, if necessary, and take the witness and convey him safely to the prison at . . . . , and there deliver him to the keeper thereof, together with the following precept:

I do hereby command you, the said keeper, to receive the said witness into your custody in the said prison and safely keep him there for the term of . . . . . days, unless he sooner consents to do what was required of him, and for so doing this is a sufficient warrant.

Dated this . . . . day of . . . . A.D. . . . . , at . . . .

. . . .
A Justice of the Peace in and for
. . . .

R.S. 1985, c. 27 (1st Supp.), s. 184(19).

FORM 21

WARRANT OF COMMITTAL ON CONVICTION
(Sections 570 and 806)

Canada,
Province of . . . . ,
(*territorial division*).

To the peace officers in the territorial division of (*name*) and to the keeper of a federal penitentiary (or provincial correctional institution for the province of . . . . , as the case may be):

Whereas (*name*), hereinafter called the offender was on the . . . . day of . . . . 19 . . . . , convicted by (name of judge and court) of having committed the following offence(s) and it was adjudged that the offender be sentenced as follows:

Offence	*Sentence*	*Remarks*
(state offence of which offender was convicted)	*(state term of imprisonment for the offence and, in case of imprisonment for default of payment of fine, so indicate together with the amount thereof and costs applicable and whether payable forthwith or within a time fixed)*	*(state whether concurrent or consecutive to any other sentence imposed at the same time or presently being served by the offender)*

1. ....
2. ....
3. ....
4. ....

You are hereby commanded, in her Majesty's name, to arrest the offender if it is necessary to do so in order to take the offender into custody, and to take and convey him safely to a federal penitentiary (or provincial correctional institution for the province of ...., as the case may be) and deliver him to the keeper thereof, who is hereby commanded to receive the accused into custody and to imprison him there for the term(s) of his sentence, unless, where a term of imprisonment was imposed only in default of payment of a fine or costs, the said amounts and the costs and charges of the committal and of conveying the offender to the said prison are sooner paid, and this is a sufficient warrant for so doing.

Dated this .... day of .... A.D. ...., at ....

....
Clerk of the Court,
Justice, Judge or
Provincial Court Judge

R.S. 1985, c. 27 (1st Supp.), s. 184(10).

FORM 22

WARRANT OF COMMITTAL ON AN ORDER FOR THE PAYMENT OF MONEY (Section 806)

Canada,
Province of ....,
(*territorial division*).

To the peace officers in the (*territorial division*) and to the keeper of the (*prison*) at .... :

Whereas A.B., hereinafter called the defendant, was tried on an information alleging that (*set out matter of complaint*), and it was ordered that (*set out the order made*), and in default that the defendant be imprisoned in the (*prison*) at .... for a term of .... :

I hereby command you, in Her Majesty's name, to arrest, if necessary, and take the defendant and convey him safely to the (*prison*) at ...., and deliver him to the keeper thereof, together with the following precept:

I hereby command you, the keeper of the said prison, to receive the defendant into your custody in the said prison and imprison him there for the term of ...., unless the said amounts and the costs and charges of the committal and of conveying the defendant to the said prison are sooner paid, and for so doing this is a sufficient warrant.

Dated this .... day of .... A.D. ...., at ....

....
A Justice of the Peace in and for
....
R.S. 1985, c. 27 (1st Supp.), s. 184(19).

FORM 23

WARRANT OF COMMITTAL FOR FAILURE TO FURNISH RECOGNIZANCE TO KEEP THE PEACE
(Section 810)

Canada,
Province of .... ,
(*territorial division*).

To the peace officers in the (*territorial division*) and to the keeper of the (*prison*) at .... :

Whereas A.B., hereinafter called the accused, has been ordered to enter into a recognizance to keep the peace and be of good behaviour, and has (refused *or* failed) to enter into a recognizance accordingly:

You are hereby commanded, in Her Majesty's name, to arrest, if necessary, and take the accused and convey him safely to the (*prison*) at .... and deliver him to the keeper thereof, together with the following precept:

You, the said keeper, are hereby commanded to receive the accused into your custody in the said prison and imprison him there until he enters into a recognizance as aforesaid or until he is discharged in due course of law.

Dated this .... day of .... A.D. ...., at ....

....
Clerk of the Court, Justice
or Provincial Court Judge
R.S. 1985, c. 27 (1st Supp.), ss. 184(19), 206.

(*Seal, if required*)

Form 24

WARRANT OF COMMITTAL OF WITNESS FOR FAILURE TO ENTER INTO RECOGNIZANCE (Section 550)

Canada,

Province of .... ,
(*territorial division*).

To the peace officers in the (*territorial division*) and to the keeper of the (*prison*) at .... :

Whereas A.B., hereinafter called the accused, was committed for trial on a charge that (*state offence as in the information*);

And Whereas E.F., hereinafter called the witness, having appeared as a witness on the preliminary inquiry into the said charge, and being required to enter into a recognizance to appear as a witness on the trial of the accused on the said charge, has (failed *or* refused) to do so:

This is therefore to command you, in Her Majesty's name, to arrest, if necessary, and take and safely convey the said witness to the (*prison*) at .... and there deliver him to the keeper thereof, together with the following precept:

I do hereby command you, the said keeper, to receive the witness into your custody in the said prison and keep him there safely until the trial of the accused on the said charge, unless before that time the witness enters into the said recognizance.

Dated this .... day of .... A.D. .... , at ....

....
A Justice of the Peace in and for
....

R.S. 1985, c. 27 (1st Supp.), s. 184(19).

Form 25

WARRANT OF COMMITTAL FOR CONTEMPT (Section 708)

Canada,

Province of .... ,
(*territorial division*).

To the peace officers in the said (*territorial division*) and to the keeper of the (*prison*) at .... :

Whereas E.F. of .... , hereinafter called the defaulter, was on the .... day of .... A.D.. .... , at .... , convicted before .... for contempt in that he did not attend before .... to give evidence on the trial of a charge that (*state offence as in the information*) against A.B. of ...., although (duly subpoenaed *or* bound by recognizance to appear and give evidence in that behalf, *as the case may be*) and did not show any sufficient excuse for his default;

And Whereas in and by the said conviction it was adjudged that the defaulter (*set out punishment adjudged*);

And Whereas the defaulter has not paid the amounts adjudged to be paid; (*delete if not applicable*)

This is therefore to command you, in Her Majesty's name, to arrest, if necessary, and take the defaulter and convey him safely to the prison at .... and there deliver him to the keeper thereof, together with the following precept:

I do hereby command you, the said keeper, to receive the defaulter into your custody in the said prison and imprison him there* and for so doing this is a sufficient warrant.

Dated this .... day of .... A.D. ...., at ....

....
A Justice *or* Clerk of the Court

(*Seal, if required*)

**Insert whichever of the following is applicable:*

(*a*) for the term of ....,

(*b*) for the term of .... unless the said sums and the costs and charges of the committal and of conveying the defaulter to the said prison are sooner paid, *or*

(*c*) for the term of .... and for the term of (*if consecutive so state*) unless the said sums and costs and charges of the committal and of conveying the defaulter to the said prison are sooner paid.

R.S. 1985, c. 27 (1st Supp.), s. 184(19).

FORM 26

WARRANT OF COMMITTAL IN DEFAULT OF PAYMENT OF COSTS OF AN APPEAL (Section 827)

Canada,

Province of ....,
(*territorial division*).

To the peace officers of (*territorial division*) and to the keeper of the (*prison*) at . . . . :

Whereas it appears that on the hearing of an appeal before the (*set out court*), it was adjudged that A.B., of . . . . , hereinafter called the defaulter, should pay to the Clerk of the Court the sum of . . . . dollars in respect of costs;

And Whereas the Clerk of the Court has certified that the defaulter has not paid the sum within the time limited therefor:

I do hereby command you, the said peace officers, in Her Majesty's name, to take the defaulter and safely convey him to the (*prison*) at . . . . and deliver him to the keeper thereof, together with the following precept:

I do hereby command you, the said keeper, to receive the defaulter into your custody in the said prison and imprison him for the term of . . . . , unless the said sum and the costs and charges of the committal and of conveying the defaulter to the said prison are sooner paid, and for so doing this is a sufficient warrant.

Dated this . . . . day of . . . . A.D. . . . . , at . . . .

. . . .
A Justice of the Peace in and for
. . . .

FORM 27

WARRANT OF COMMITTAL ON FORFEITURE OF A RECOGNIZANCE
(Section 773)

Canada,
Province of . . . . ,
(*territorial division*).

To the sheriff of (*territorial division*) and to the keeper of the (*prison*) at . . . . :

You are hereby commanded to arrest, if necessary, and take (A.B. and C.D. *as the case may be*) hereinafter called the defaulters, and to convey them safely to the (*prison*) at . . . . and deliver them to the keeper thereof, together with the following precept:

You, the said keeper, are hereby commanded to receive the defaulters into your custody in the said prison and imprison them for a period of . . . . or until satisfaction is made of a judgment debt of . . . . dollars due to Her Majesty the Queen in respect of the forfeiture of a recognizance entered into by . . . . on the . . . . day of . . . . A.D. . . . .

Dated this .... day of .... A.D. ...., at ....

....

Clerk of the

....

R.S. 1985, c. 27 (1st Supp.), s. 184(11).

(*Seal*)

FORM 28

ENDORSEMENT OF WARRANT
(Sections 487 and 528)

Canada,

Province of ...., (*territorial division*).

Pursuant to application this day made to me, I hereby authorize the arrest of the accused (*or defendant*) (*or execution of this warrant, in the case of a warrant issued pursuant to section 487*), within the said (*territorial division*).

Dated this .... day of .... A.D. ...., at ....

....

A Justice of the Peace in and for

....

R.S. 1985, c. 27 (1st Supp.), s. 184(12).

FORM 29

ENDORSEMENT OF WARRANT
(Section 507)

Canada,

Province of ...., (*territorial division*).

Whereas this warrant is issued in respect of an offence mentioned in subsection 498(1) of the *Criminal Code* I hereby authorize the release of the accused pursuant to section 499 thereof.

Dated this .... day of .... A.D. ...., at ....

....

A Justice of the Peace in and for

....

Form 30

ORDER FOR ACCUSED TO BE BROUGHT BEFORE JUSTICE PRIOR TO EXPIRATION OF PERIOD OF REMAND

(Section 537)

Canada,

Province of ....,
(*territorial division*).

To the keeper of the (*prison*) at ....:

Whereas by warrant dated the .... day of .... A.D. ...., I committed A.B., hereinafter called the accused, to your custody and required you safely to keep [him] until the .... day of .... A.D. ...., and then to have him before me or any other justice at .... at .... o'clock in the .... noon to answer to the charge against him and to be dealt with according to law unless you should be ordered otherwise before that time:

Now, therefore, I order and direct you to have the accused before .... at .... at .... o'clock in the .... noon to answer to the charge against him and to be dealt with according to law.

Dated this .... day of .... A.D. ...., at ....

....
A Justice of the Peace in and for
....

Form 31

DEPOSITION OF A WITNESS

(Section 540)

Canada,

Province of ....,
(*territorial division*).

These are the depositions of X.Y., of ...., and M.N., of ...., taken before me, this .... day of .... A.D., ... at ...., in the presence and hearing of A.B., hereinafter called the accused, who stands charged (*state offence as in the information*).

X.Y., having been duly sworn, deposes as follows: (*insert deposition as nearly as possible in words of witness*).

M.N., having been duly sworn, deposes as follows:

I certify that the depositions of X.Y., and M.N., written on the several sheets of paper hereto annexed to which my signature is affixed, were taken in the presence and hearing of the accused (and signed by them respectively, in is presence, *where they are required to be signed by witness*). In witness whereof I have hereto signed my name.

. . . .
A Justice of the Peace in and for
. . . .

Form 32

RECOGNIZANCE

(Sections 493, 550, 679, 706, 707, 810 and 817)

Canada,
Province of . . . . ,
(*territorial division*).

Be it remembered that on this day the persons named in the following schedule personally came before me and severally acknowledged themselves to owe to Her Majesty the Queen the several amounts set opposite their respective names, namely,

Name	Address	Occupation	Amount
A.B.			
C.D.			
E.F.			

to be made and levied of their several goods and chattels, lands and tenements, respectively, to the use of Her Majesty the Queen, if the said A.B. fails in any of the conditions hereunder written.

Taken and acknowledged before me on the . . . . day of . . . . . . A.D. . . . . , at . . . .

. . . .
Judge, Clerk of the Court,
Provincial Court Judge *or* Justice

1. Whereas the said . . . . , hereinafter called the accused, has been charged that (*set out the offence in respect of which the accused has been charged*);

Now, therefore, the condition of this recognizance is that if the accused attends court on . . . . day, the . . . . day of . . . . A.D. . . . . , at . . . . o'clock in the . . . . noon and attends thereafter as required by the court in order to be dealt with according to law *or* (*where date and place of appearance before court are not known at the time recognizance is entered into*) if the accused attends at the time and place fixed by the court and attends thereafter as required by the court in order to be dealt with according to law [515, 520, 521, 522, 523, 524, 525, 680].

And further, if the accused (*insert in Schedule of Conditions any additional conditions that are directed*),

the said recognizance is void, otherwise it stands in full force and effect.

2. Whereas the said ...., hereinafter called the appellant, is an appellant against his conviction (*or* against his sentence) in respect of the following charge (*set out the offence for which the appellant was convicted*) [679, 680]:

Now, therefore, the condition of this recognizance is that if the appellant attends as required by the court in order to be dealt with according to law;

And further, if the appellant (*insert in Schedule of Conditions any additional conditions that are directed*),

the said recognizance is void, otherwise it stands in full force and effect.

3. Whereas the said .... , hereinafter called the appellant, is an appellant against his conviction (*or* against his sentence *or* against an order *or* by way of stated case) in respect of the following matter (*set out offence, subject-matter of order or question of law*) [816, 831, 832, 834];

Now, therefore, the condition of this recognizance is that if the appellant appears personally at the sittings of the appeal court at which the appeal is to be heard;

And further, if the appellant (*insert in Schedule of Conditions any additional conditions that are directed*),

the said recognizance is void, otherwise it stands in full force and effect.

4. Whereas the said .... , hereinafter called the appellant, is an appellant against an order of dismissal (*or* against sentence) in respect of the following charge (*set out the name of the defendant and the offence, subject-matter of order or question of law*) [817, 831, 832, 834];

Now, therefore, the condition of this recognizance is that if the appellant appears personally or by counsel at the sittings of the appeal court at which the appeal is to be heard the said recognizance is void, otherwise it stands in full force and effect.

5. Whereas the said ...., hereinafter called the accused, was ordered to stand trial on a charge that (*set out the offence in respect of which the accused has been charged*);

And whereas A.B. appeared as a witness on the preliminary inquiry into the said charge [550, 706, 707];

Now, therefore, the condition of this recognizance is that if the said A.B. appears at the time and place fixed for the trial of the accused to give evidence on the indictment that is found against the accused, the said recognizance is void, otherwise it stands in full force and effect.

6. The condition of the above written recognizance is that if A.B. keeps

the peace and is of good behaviour for the term of . . . . commencing on . . . . , the said recognizance is void, otherwise it stands in full force and effect [810].

7. Whereas a warrant was issued under section 462.32 or a restraint order was made under subsection 462.33(3) of the *Criminal Code* in relation to any property (*set out a description of the property and its location*);

Now, therefore, the condition of this recognizance is that A.B. shall not do or cause anything to be done that would result, directly or indirectly, in the disappearance, dissipaton or reduction in value of the property or otherwise affect the property so that all or a part thereof could not be subject to an order of forfeiture under section 462.37 or 462.38 of the *Criminal Code* or any other provision of the *Criminal Code* or any other Act of Parliament *[*462.34*]*. R.S. 1985, c. 42 (4th Supp.), s. 7.

Schedule of Conditions

(*a*) reports at (*state times*) to (*name of peace officer or other person designated*),
(*b*) remains within (*designated territorial jurisdiction*),
(*c*) notifies (*name of peace officer or other person designated*) of any change in his address, employment or occupation,
(*d*) abstains from communicating with (*name of witness or other person*) except in accordance with the following conditions: (*as the justice or judge specifies*),
(*e*) deposits his passport (*as the justice or judge directs*), and
(*f*) (*any other reasonable conditions*).

Note: Section 763 and subsections 764(1) to (3) of the *Criminal Code* state as follows:

"**763.** Where a person is bound by recognizance to appear before a court, justice or provincial court judge for any purpose and the session or sittings of that court or the proceedings are adjourned or an order is made changing the place of trial, that person and his sureties continue to be bound by the recognizance in like manner as if it had been entered into with relation to the resumed proceedings or the trial at the time and place at which the proceedings are ordered to be resumed or the trial is ordered to be held.

764. (1) Where an accused is bound by recognizance to appear for trial, his arraignment or conviction does not discharge the recognizance, but it continues to bind him and his sureties, if any, for his appearance until he is discharged or sentenced, as the case may be.

(2) Notwithstanding subsection (1), the court, justice or provincial court judge may commit an accused to prison or may require him to furnish new or additional sureties for his appearance until he is discharged or sentenced, as the case may be.

(3) The sureties of an accsued who is bound by recognizance to appear for trial are discharged if he is committed to prison pursuant to subsection (2).

R.S. 1985, c. 27 (1st Supp.), ss. 101(2), 184(13), 206; c. 42 (4th Supp.), s. 7.

FORM 33

CERTIFICATE OF DEFAULT TO BE ENDORSED ON RECOGNIZANCE
(Section 770)

I hereby certify that A.B. has not appeared as required by this recognizance and that by reason thereof the ends of justice have been (defeated *or* delayed, *as the case may be*).

The reason for the default is (*state reason if known*).

The names and addresses of the principal and sureties are as follows:

Dated this .... day of .... A.D. ...., at ....

....
Clerk of the Court, Judge,
Justice *or* Provincial Court Judge

(*Seal, if required*)

R.S. 1985, c. 27 (1st Supp.), s. 206.

FORM 34

WRIT OF FIERI FACIAS
(Section 771)

Elizabeth II by the Grace of God, etc.

To the sheriff of (*territorial division*), GREETING.

You are hereby commanded to levy of the goods and chattels, lands and tenements of each of the following persons the amount set opposite the name of each:

Name	Address	Occupation	Amount

And you are further commanded to make a return of what you have done in execution of this writ.

Dated this .... day of .... A.D. ...., at ....

....
Clerk of the ....

(*Seal*)

FORM 35

CONVICTION
(Sections 570 and 806)

Canada,

Province of ....,
(*territorial division*).

Be it remembered that on the .... day of .... at ...., A.B., (*date of birth*) hereinafter called the accused, was tried under Part (XIX *or* XXVII) of the *Criminal Code* on the charge that (*state fully the offence of which accused was convicted*), was convicted of the said offence and the following punishment was imposed on him, namely,*

Dated this .... day of .... A.D. ...., at ....

....
Clerk of the Court, Justice
or Provincial Court Judge

(*Seal, if required*)

---

* *Use whichever of the following forms of sentence is applicable*:

(*a*) That the said accused be imprisoned in the (*prison*) at .... for the term of ....

(*b*) That the said accused forfeit and pay the sum of .... dollars to be applied according to law and also pay to .... the sum of .... dollars in respect of costs and in default of payment of the said sums (forthwith *or within a time fixed, if any*) to be imprisoned in the (*prison*) at .... for the term of .... unless the said sums and costs and charges of the committal and of conveying the accused to the said prison are sooner paid.

(*c*) That the said accused be imprisoned in the (*prison*) at .... for the term of .... and in addition forfeit and pay the sum of .... dollars to be applied according to law and also pay to .... the sum of .... dollars in respect of costs and in default of payment of the said sums (forthwith *or within a time fixed, if any*) to be imprisoned in the (*prison*) at .... for the term of .... (*if sentence to be consecutive, state accordingly*) unless the said sums and costs and charges of the committal and of conveying the accused to the said prison are sooner paid.

R.S. 1985, c. 27 (1st Supp.), ss. 184(14), 206.

Form 36

ORDER AGAINST AN OFFENDER
(Sections 570 and 806)

Canada,

Province of .... ,
(*territorial division*).

Be it remembered that on the .... day of .... A.D. .... , at .... , A.B., (*date of birth*) of .... , was tried on an information (*indictment*) alleging that (*set out matter of complaint*, *or alleged offence*), and it was ordered and adjudged that (*set out the order made*).

Dated this .... day of .... A.D. .... , at ....

....
Justice *or* Clerk
of the Court

R.S. 1985, c. 27 (1st Supp.), s. 184(15).

Form 37

ORDER ACQUITTING ACCUSED
(Section 570)

Canada,

Province of .... ,
(*territorial division*).

Be it remembered that on the .... day of .... A.D. .... , at .... , A.B., of .... , (*occupation*), (*date of birth*) was tried on the charge that (*state fully the offence of which accused was acquitted*) and was found not guilty of the said offence.

Dated this .... day of .... A.D. .... , at ....

....
Provincial Court Judge *or* Clerk of the Court

(*Seal, if required*)

R.S. 1985, c. 27 (1st Supp.), ss. 184(16), 203, 206.

FORM 38

CONVICTION FOR CONTEMPT
(Section 708)

Canada,
Province of .... ,
(*territorial division*).

Be it remembered that on the .... day of .... A.D. .... , at .... in the (*territorial division*), E.F. of .... , hereinafter called the defaulter, is convicted by me for contempt in that he did not attend before (set out court *or* justice) to give evidence on the trial of a charge that (*state fully offence with which accused was charged*), although (duly subpoenaed *or* bound by recognizance to attend to give evidence, *as the case may be*) and has not shown before me any sufficient excuse for his default;

Wherefore I adjudge the defaulter for his said default, (*set out punishment as authorized and determined in accordance with section 708 of the Criminal Code*).

Dated this .... day of .... A.D. .... , at ....

....
A Justice *or* Clerk of the Court

(*Seal, if required*)

FORM 39

ORDER FOR DISCHARGE OF A PERSON IN CUSTODY
(Sections 519 and 550)

Canada,
Province of .... ,
(*territorial division*).

To the keeper of the (*prison*) at .... :

I hereby direct you to release E.F., detained by you under a (warrant of committal *or* order) dated the .... day of .... A.D. .... , if the said E.F. is detained by you for no other cause.

....
A Judge, Justice *or* Clerk of the Court

(*Seal, if required*)

Form 40

CHALLENGE TO ARRAY
(Section 629)

Canada,

Province of .... ,
(*territorial division*).

The Queen
v.
C.D.

The (prosecutor *or* accused) challenges the array of the panel on the ground that X.Y., (sheriff *or* deputy sheriff), who returned the panel, was guilty of (partiality *or* fraud *or* wilful misconduct) on returning it.

Dated this .... day of .... A.D. .... , at ....

....
Counsel for (prosecutor *or* accused)

Form 41

CHALLENGE FOR CAUSE
(Section 639)

Canada,

Province of .... ,
(*territorial division*).

The Queen
v.
C.D.

The (prosecutor *or* accused) challenges G.H. on the ground that (*set out ground of challenge in accordance with subsection 638 (1) of the Criminal Code*).

....
Counsel for (prosecutor *or* accused)

Form 42

CERTIFICATE OF NON-PAYMENT OF COSTS OF APPEAL
(Section 827)

In the Court of ....

(*Style of Cause*)

I hereby certify that A.B. (the appellant *or* respondent, *as the case may be*) in this appeal, having been ordered to pay costs in the sum of .... dollars, has failed to pay the said costs within the time limited for the payment thereof.

Dated this .... day of .... A.D. ...., at ....

....
Clerk of the Court of

(*Seal*) ....

FORM 43

JAILER'S RECEIPT TO PEACE OFFICER FOR PRISONER
(Section 734)

I hereby certify that I have received from X.Y., a peace officer for (*territorial division*) one A.B., together with a (warrant *or* order) issued by (*set out court or justice, as the case may be*).*

Dated this .... day of .... A.D. ...., at ....

....
Keeper of (*prison*)

**Add a statement of the condition of the prisoner*

FORM 44

(Section 667)

I, (*name*), a fingerprint examiner designated as such for the purposes of section 667 of the *Criminal Code* by the Solicitor General of Canada, do hereby certify that (*name*) also known as (*aliases if any*), FPS Number ...., whose fingerprints are shown reproduced below (*reproduction of fingerprints*) or attached hereto, has been convicted, discharged under section 736 of the *Criminal Code* or convicted and sentenced in Canada as follows:

(*record*)

Dated this .... day of .... A.D. ...., at ....

....
Fingerprint Examiner

R.S. 1985, c. 27 (1st Supp.), s. 184(17).

FORM 45

(Section 667)

I, (*name*), a fingerprint examiner designated as such for the purposes of section 667 of the *Criminal Code* by the Solicitor General of Canada, do hereby certify that I have compared the fingerprints reproduced in or attached to exhibit A with the fingerprints reproduced in or attached to the certificate in Form 44 attached marked exhibit B and that they are those of the same person.

Dated this .... day of .... A.D. ...., at ....

....
Fingerprint Examiner

R.S. 1985, c. 27 (1st Supp.), s. 184(18).

FORM 46

PROBATION ORDER

(Section 737)

Canada,
Province of ....,
(*territorial division*).

Whereas on the .... day of .... at ...., A.B., hereinafter called the accused, (pleaded guilty to or was tried under (*here insert Part XIX, XX or XXVII, as the case may be*) of the Criminal Code and was (*here insert convicted or found guilty, as the case may be*) on the charge that (*here state the offence to which the accused pleaded guilty or for which the accused was convicted or found guilty, as the case may be*));

And whereas on the .... day of .... the court adjudged*

*(*Use whichever of the following forms of disposition is applicable*):

(*a*) that the accused be discharged on the conditions hereinafter prescribed:

(*b*) that the passing of sentence on the accused be suspended and that the said accused be released on the conditions hereinafter prescribed:

(*c*) that the accused forfeit and pay the sum of .... dollars to be applied according to law and in default of payment of the said sum (*forthwith or within a time fixed, if any*) be imprisoned in the (*prison*) at .... for the term of .... unless the said sum and charges of the committal and of conveying the said accused to the said prison are sooner paid, and in addition thereto, that the said accused comply with the conditions hereinafter prescribed:

(*d*) that the accused be imprisoned in the (*prison*) at .... for the term of .... and, in addition thereto, that the said accused comply with the conditions hereinafter prescribed:

Now therefore the said accused shall, for the period of .... from the date of this order or, where paragraph (*d*) is applicable, the date of expiration of his sentence of imprisonment, comply with the following conditions, namely, that the said accused shall keep the peace and be of good behaviour and appear before the court when required to do so by the court, and, in addition, (*here state any additional conditions prescribed pursuant to subsection 737(2) of the Criminal Code*).

Dated this .... day of .... A.D. ...., at ....

....
Clerk of the Court, Justice
or Provincial Court Judge
R.S. 1985, c. 27 (1st Supp.), s. 206.

FORM 47

ORDER TO DISCLOSE INCOME TAX INFORMATION
(Section 462.48)

Canada,

Province of ....,
(*territorial division*)

To A.B., of ...., (*office or occupation*):

Whereas, it appears on the oath of C.D., of ...., that there are reasonable grounds for believing that E.F., of ...., has committed or benefited from the commission of the offence of .... and that the information or documents (*describe information or documents*) are likely to be of substantial value to an investigation of that offence or a related matter; and

Whereas there are reasonable grounds for believing that it is in the public interest to allow access to the information or documents, having regard to the benefit likely to accrue to the investigation if the access is obtained;

This is, therefore, to authorize and require you between the hours of (*as the judge may direct*), during the period commencing on .... and ending on ...., to produce all the above-mentioned information and documents to one of the following police officers, namely, (*here name police officers*) and allow the police officer to remove the information or documents, or to allow the police officer access to the above-mentioned information and documents and to examine them, as the judge directs, subject to the following conditions (*state conditions*): . . . .

Dated this . . . . day of . . . . A.D. . . . . , at . . . .

. . . .
Signature of judge
R.S. 1985, c. 42 (4th Supp.), s. 8.

FORM 48
(*Section 672.13*)
ASSESSMENT ORDER

Canada,
Province of
(*territorial division*)

Whereas I have reasonable grounds to believe that evidence of the mental condition of (*name of accused*), who has been charged with . . . . . ., may be necessary to determine*

☐ whether the accused is unfit to stand trial
☐ whether the accused suffered from a mental disorder so as to exempt the accused from criminal responsibility by virtue of subsection 16(1) of the *Criminal Code* at the time of the act or omission charged against the accused
☐ whether the accused is a dangerous mentally disordered accused under section 672.65 of the *Criminal Code*
☐ whether the balance of the mind of the accused was disturbed at the time of commission of the allged offence, where the accused is a female person charged with an offence arising out of the death of her newly-born child
☐ where a verdict of unfit to stand trial or a verdict of not criminally responsible on account of mental disorder has been rendered in respect of the accused, the appropriate disposition to be made in respect of the accused pursuant to section 672.54 or 672.58 of the *Criminal Code*
☐ where the accused has been convicted of the offence, whether an order under subsection 736.11(1) of the *Criminal Code* should be made in respect of the accused

I hereby order an assessment of the mental condition of (*name of accused*) to be conducted by/at (*name of person or service by whom or place where assessment is to be made*) for a period of . . . . days.

This order is to be in force for a total of . . . . days, including travelling time, during which time the accused is to remain*

☐ in custody at (*place where accused is to be detained*)
☐ out of custody, on the following conditions:

(*set out conditions, where applicable*)

* Check applicable option.

Dated this .... day of .... A.D. ......, at ....

....
(Signature of justice or judge or clerk of the court, as the case may be)

1992, c. 1, s. 58(1), Sch. I, item 17

FORM 49
(*Section 672.57*)
WARRANT OF COMMITTAL
DISPOSITION OF DETENTION

Canada,
Province of
(*territorial division*)

To the peace officers in the said (*territorial division*) and to the keeper (*administrator, warden*) of the (*prison, hospital or other appropriate place where the accused is detained*).

This warrant is issued for the committal of A.B., of ...., (*occupation*), hereinafter called the accused.

Whereas the accused has been charged that (*set out briefly the offence in respect of which the accused was charged*);

And whereas the accused was found*

☐ unfit to stand trial
☐ not criminally responsible on account of mental disorder

This is, therefore, to command you, in Her Majesty's name, to take the accused in custody and convey the accused safely to the (*prison, hospital or other appropriate place*) at ....., and there deliver the accused to the keeper (*administrator, warden*) with the following precept:

I do therefore command you the said keeper (*administrator, warden*) to receive the accused in your custody in the said (*prison, hospital or other appropriate place*) and to keep the accused safely there until the accused is delivered by due course of law.

The following are the conditions to which the accused shall be subject while in your (*prison, hospital or other appropriate place*):

The following are the powers regarding the restrictions (*and the limits and conditions on those restrictions*) on the liberty of the accused that are hereby delegated to you the said keeper (*administrator, warden*) of the said (*prison, hospital or other appropriate place*):

*Check applicable option.

Dated this .... day of ..... A.D. ...., at ....

....
(Signature of judge, clerk of the court, provincial court judge or chairperson of the Review Board)
1992, c. 1, s. 58(1), Sch. I, item 17

FORM 50
(*Subsection 672.7(2)*)
WARRANT OF COMMITTAL
PLACEMENT DECISION

Canada,
Province of
(*territorial division*)

To the peace officers in the said (*territorial division*) and to the keeper (*administrator, warden*) of the (*prison, hospital or other appropriate place where the accused is detained*).

This warrant is issued for the committal of A.B., of .... , (*occupation*), hereinafter called the accused.

Whereas the accused has been charged that (*set out briefly the offence in respect of which the accused was charged*);

And whereas the accused was found*

☐ unfit to stand trial
☐ not criminally responsible on account of mental disorder

And whereas the Review Board has held a hearing and decided that the accused shall be detained in custody;

And whereas the accused is required to be detained in custody pursuant to a warrant of committal issued by (*set out the name of the Judge, Clerk of the Court, Provincial Court Judge or Justice as well as the name of the court and territorial division*), dated the .... day of .... , in respect of the offence that (*set out briefly the offence in respect of which the accused was charged or convicted*);

This is, therefore, to command you, in Her Majesty's name, to *

☐ execute the warrant of committal issued by the court, according to its terms
☐ execute the warrant of committal issued herewith by the Review Board
* Check applicable option.

Dated this .... day of .... A.D. ...., at ....

....
(Signature of chairperson of the Review Board)
1992, c. 1, s. 58(1), Sch. I, item 17

FORM 51
(*Subsection 736.11(3)*)
HOSPITAL ORDER

Canada,
Province of
(*territorial division*)

Whereas (*name of offender*), who has been convicted of (*offence*) and sentenced to a term of imprisonment of (*length of term of imprisonment*), is suffering from a mental disorder in an acute phase and immediate treatment of the mental disorder is urgently required to prevent significant deterioration of the mental or physical health of the offender or to prevent the offender from causing serious bodily harm to any person;

And whereas (*name of offender*) and (*name of treatment facility*) have consented to this order and its terms and conditions;

I hereby order that (*name of offender*) be detained for treatment at (*name of treatment facility*) for a period not to exceeed (*length of period not to exceed sixty days*) subject to the following terms and conditions:

(*set out terms and conditions, where applicable*)

Dated this .... day of .... A.D. .... at ....

....
(Signature of justice or judge or clerk of the court, as the case may be)

1992, c. 1, s. 58(1), Sch. I, item 17

CANADA EVIDENCE ACT

TABLE OF CONCORDANCE

R.S.C. 1970, c. E-10	R.S.C. 1985, c. C-5	R.S.C. 1970, c. E-10	R.S.C. 1985, c. C-5
E-10	**C-5**	**E-10**	**C-5**
1	1	28	28
2	2	29	29
3	3	30	30
4	4	31	31
5	5	32	32
6	6	33	33
7	7	34	34
8	8	35	35
9	9	36	36
10	10	36.1	37
11	11	36.2	38
12	12	36.3	39
13	13	37	40
14	14	38	41
15	15	39	42
16	16	40	43
17	17	41	44
18	18	42	45
19	19	43	46
20	20	44	47
21	21	45	48
22	22	46	49
23	23	47	50
24	24	48	51
25	25	49	52
26	26	50	53
27	27	51	54

CEA

CANADA EVIDENCE ACT

R.S.C. 1985, c. C-5

An Act respecting witnesses and evidence
As amended by R.S. 1985, c. 19 (3rd Supp.), s. 17, 18; 1992, c. 1, Sch. V, item 9(1).

SHORT TITLE

Short Title.

1. This Act may be cited as the *Canada Evidence Act.*

PART I
APPLICATION

Application.

2. This Part applies to all criminal proceedings and to all civil proceedings and other matters whatever respecting which Parliament has jurisdiction.

WITNESSES

Interest or crime.

3. A person is not incompetent to give evidence by reason of interest or crime.

Accused and spouse — Idem — Communications during marriage — Offences against young persons — Saving — Failure to testify.

4. (1) Every person charged with an offence, and, except as otherwise provided in this section, the wife or husband, as the case may be, of the person so charged, is a competent witness for the defence whether the person so charged is charged solely or jointly with any other person.

(2) The wife or husband of a person charged with an offence against subsection 50(1) of the *Young Offenders Act* or with an offence against any of sections 151, 152, 153, 155 or 159, subsection 160(2) or (3), or sections 170 to 173, 179, 212, 215, 218, 271 to 273, 280 to 283, 291 to 294 or 329 of the *Criminal Code,* or an attempt to commit any such offence, is a competent and compellable witness for the prosecution without the consent of the person charged.

(3) No husband is compellable to disclose any communication made to him by his wife during their marriage, and no wife is compellable to disclose any communication made to her by her husband during their marriage.

(4) The wife or husband of a person charged with an offence against any of sections 220, 221, 235, 236, 237, 239, 240, 266, 267, 268 or 269 of the

Criminal Code where the complainant or victim is under the age of fourteen years is a competent and compellable witness for the prosecution without the consent of the person charged.

(5) Nothing in this section affects a case where the wife or husband of a person charged with an offence may at common law be called as a witness without the consent of that person.

(6) The failure of the person charged, or of the wife or husband of such person, to testify shall not be made the subject of comment by the judge or by counsel for the prosecution. R.S., c. 19 (3rd Supp.), s. 17.

Incriminating questions — Answer not admissible against witness.

5. (1) No witness shall be excused from answering any question on the ground that the answer to the question may tend to criminate him, or may tend to establish his liability to a civil proceeding at the instance of the Crown or of any person.

(2) Where with respect to any question a witness objects to answer on the ground that his answer may tend to criminate him, or may tend to establish his liability to a civil proceeding at the instance of the Crown or of any person, and if but for this Act, or the Act of any provincial legislature, the witness would therefore have been excused from answering the question, then although the witness is by reason of this Act or the provincial Act compelled to answer, the answer so given shall not be used or admissible in evidence against him in any criminal trial or other criminal proceeding against him thereafter taking place, other than a prosecution for perjury in the giving of that evidence.

Evidence of mute.

6. A witness who is unable to speak may give his evidence in any other manner in which he can make it intelligible.

Expert witnesses.

7. Where, in any trial or other proceeding, criminal or civil, it is intended by the prosecution or the defence, or by any party, to examine as witnesses professional or other experts entitled according to the law or practice to give opinion evidence, not more than five of such witnesses may be called on either side without the leave of the court or judge or person presiding.

Handwriting comparison.

8. Comparison of a disputed writing with any writing proved to the satisfaction of the court to be genuine shall be permitted to be made by witnesses, and such writings, and the evidence of witnesses respecting those writings, may be submitted to the court and jury as proof of the genuineness or otherwise of the writing in dispute.

Adverse witnesses — Previous statements in writing by witness not proved adverse.

9. (1) A party producing a witness shall not be allowed to impeach his credit by general evidence of bad character, but if the witness, in the opinion of the court, proves adverse, the party may contradict him by other evidence, or, by leave of the court, may prove that the witness made at other times a statement inconsistent with his present testimony, but before the last mentioned proof can be given the circumstances of the supposed statement, sufficient to designate the particular occasion, shall be mentioned to the witness, and he shall be asked whether or not he did make the statement.

(2) Where the party producing a witness alleges that the witness made at other times a statement in writing, or reduced to writing, inconsistent with his present testimony, the court may, without proof that the witness is adverse, grant leave to that party to cross-examine the witness as to the statement and the court may consider the cross-examination in determining whether in the opinion of the court the witness is adverse.

Cross-examination as to previous statements in writing — Deposition of witness in criminal investigation.

10. (1) On any trial a witness may be cross-examined as to previous statements made by him in writing, or reduced to writing, relative to the subject-matter of the case, without the writing being shown to him, but, if it is intended to contradict the witness by the writing, his attention must, before the contradictory proof can be given, be called to those parts of the writing that are to be used for the purpose of so contradicting him, and the judge, at any time during the trial, may require the production of the writing for his inspection, and thereupon make such use of it for the purposes of the trial as he thinks fit.

(2) A deposition of a witness, purporting to have been taken before a justice on the investigation of a criminal charge and to be signed by the witness and the justice, returned to and produced from the custody of the proper officer shall be presumed, in the absence of evidence to the contrary, to have been signed by the witness.

Cross-examination as to previous oral statements.

11. Where a witness, on cross-examination as to a former statement made by him relative to the subject-matter of the case and inconsistent with his present testimony, does not distinctly admit that he did make the statement, proof may be given that he did in fact make it, but before the proof can be given the circumstances of the supposed statement, sufficient to designate the particular occasion, shall be mentioned to the witness, and he shall be asked whether or not he did make the statement.

Examination as to previous conviction — How conviction proved.

12. (1) A witness may be questioned as to whether he has been convicted of any offence, and on being so questioned, if he either denies the fact or refuses to answer, the opposite party may prove the conviction.

(2) A conviction may be proved by producing

(*a*) a certificate containing the substance and effect only, omitting the formal part, of the indictment and conviction, if it is for an indictable offence, or a copy of the summary conviction, if it is for an offence punishable on summary conviction, purporting to be signed by the clerk of the court or other officer having the custody of the records of the court in which the conviction, if on indictment, was had, or to which the conviction, if summary, was returned; and

(*b*) proof of identity.

OATHS AND SOLEMN AFFIRMATIONS

Who may administer oaths.

13. Every court and judge, and every person having, by law or consent of parties, authority to hear and receive evidence, has power to administer an oath to every witness who is legally called to give evidence before that court, judge or person.

Solemn affirmation by witness instead of oath — Effect.

14. (1) Where a person called or desiring to give evidence objects, on grounds of conscientious scruples, to take an oath, or is objected to as incompetent to take an oath, that person may make the following solemn affirmation:

I do solemnly affirm that the evidence to be given by me shall be the truth, the whole truth, and nothing but the truth.

(2) Where a person makes a solemn affirmation in accordance with subsection (1), his evidence shall be taken and have the same effect as if taken under oath.

Solemn affirmation by deponent — Effect.

15. (1) Where a person who is required or who desires to make an affidavit or deposition in a proceeding or on an occasion on which or concerning a matter respecting which an oath is required or is lawful, whether on the taking of office or otherwise, refuses or is unwilling to be sworn, on grounds of conscientious scruples, the court or judge, or other officer or person qualified to take affidavits or depositions, shall permit that person, instead of being sworn, to make his solemn affirmation in the words following, namely, "I do solemnly affirm, etc.", and that solemn affirmation shall be of the same force and effect as if that person had taken an oath in the usual form.

(2) Any witness whose evidence is admitted or who makes a solemn affirmation under this section or section 14 is liable to indictment and punishment for perjury in all respects as if he had been sworn.

Witness whose capacity is in question — Testimony under oath or solemn affirmation — Testimony on promise to tell truth — Inability to testify — Burden as to capacity of witness.

16. (1) Where a proposed witness is a person under fourteen years of age or a person whose mental capacity is challenged, the court shall, before permitting the person to give evidence, conduct an inquiry to determine

(*a*) whether the person understands the nature of an oath or a solemn affirmation; and

(*b*) whether the person is able to communicate the evidence.

(2) A person referred to in subsection (1) who understands the nature of an oath or a solemn affirmation and is able to communicate the evidence shall testify under oath or solemn affirmation.

(3) A person referred to in subsection (1) who does not understand the nature of an oath or a solemn affirmation but is able to communicate the evidence may testify on promising to tell the truth.

(4) A person referred to in subsection (1) who neither understands the nature of an oath or a solemn affirmation nor is able to communicate the evidence shall not testify.

(5) A party who challenges the mental capacity of a proposed witness of fourteen years of age or more has the burden of satisfying the court that there is an issue as to the capacity of the proposed witness to testify under an oath or a solemn affirmation. R.S., c. 19 (3rd Supp.), s. 18.

JUDICIAL NOTICE

Imperial Acts, etc.

17. Judicial notice shall be taken of all Acts of the Imperial Parliament, of all ordinances made by the Governor in Council, or the lieutenant governor in council of any province or colony that, or some portion of which, now forms or hereafter may form part of Canada, and of all the Acts of the legislature of any such province or colony, whether enacted before or after the passing of the *Constitution Act, 1867*.

Acts of Canada.

18. Judicial notice shall be taken of all Acts of Parliament, public or private, without being specially pleaded.

DOCUMENTARY EVIDENCE

Copies by Queen's Printer.

19. Every copy of any Act of Parliament, public or private, printed by the Queen's Printer, is evidence of that Act and of its contents and every copy purporting to be printed by the Queen's Printer shall be deemed to be so printed, unless the contrary is shown.

Imperial proclamations, etc.

20. Imperial proclamations, orders in council, treaties, orders, warrants, licences, certificates, rules, regulations, or other Imperial official records, Acts or documents may be proved

(*a*) in the same manner as they may from time to time be provable in any court in England;

(*b*) by the production of a copy of the *Canada Gazette*, or a volume of the Acts of Parliament purporting to contain a copy of the same or a notice thereof; or

(*c*) by the production of a copy thereof purporting to be printed by the Queen's Printer.

Proclamations, etc., of Governor General.

21. Evidence of any proclamation, order, regulation or appointment, made or issued by the Governor General or by the Governor in Council, or by or under the authority of any minister or head of any department of the Government of Canada and evidence of a treaty to which Canada is a party, may be given in all or any of the following ways:

(*a*) by the production of a copy of the *Canada Gazette*, or a volume of the Acts of Parliament purporting to contain a copy of the treaty, proclamation, order, regulation or appointment or a notice thereof;

(*b*) by the production of a copy of the proclamation, order, regulation or appointment, purporting to be printed by the Queen's Printer;

(*c*) by the production of a copy of the treaty purporting to be printed by the Queen's Printer;

(*d*) by the production, in the case of any proclamation, order, regulation or appointment made or issued by the Governor General or by the Governor in Council, of a copy or extract purporting to be certified to be true by the clerk or assistant or acting clerk of the Queen's Privy Council for Canada; and

(*e*) by the production, in the case of any order, regulation or appointment made or issued by or under the authority of any minister or head of a department of the Government of Canada, of a copy or extract purporting to be certified to be true by the minister, by his deputy or acting deputy, or by the secretary or acting secretary of the department over which he presides.

Proclamations, etc., of lieutenant governor — In the case of the Territories.

22. (1) Evidence of any proclamation, order, regulation or appointment made or issued by a lieutenant governor or lieutenant governor in council of any province, or by or under the authority of any member of the executive council, being the head of any department of the government of the province, may be given in all or any of the following ways:

(*a*) by the production of a copy of the official gazette for the province, purporting to contain a copy of the proclamation, order, regulation or appointment, or a notice thereof;

(*b*) by the production of a copy of the proclamation, order, regulation or appointment purporting to be printed by the government or Queen's Printer for the province; and

(*c*) by the production of a copy or extract of the proclamation, order, regulation or appointment purporting to be certified to be true by the clerk or assistant or acting clerk of the executive council, by the head of any department of the government of a province, or by his deputy or acting deputy, as the case may be.

(2) Evidence of any proclamation, order, regulation or appointment made by the Lieutenant Governor or Lieutenant Governor in Council of the Northwest Territories, as constituted prior to September 1, 1905, or of the Commissioner in Council of the Yukon Territory or of the Commissioner in Council of the Northwest Territories, may be given by the production of a copy of the *Canada Gazette* purporting to contain a copy of the proclamation, order, regulation or appointment, or a notice thereof.

Evidence of judicial proceedings, etc. — Certificate where court has no seal.

23. (1) Evidence of any proceeding or record whatever of, in or before any court in Great Britain, the Supreme Court or Federal Court of Canada, any court in any province, any court in any British colony or possession or any court of record of the United States, of any state of the United States or of any other foreign country, or before any justice of the peace or coroner in any province, may be given in any action or proceeding by an exemplification or certified copy thereof, purporting to be under the seal of the court or under the hand or seal of the justice or coroner, as the case may be, without any proof of the authenticity of the seal or of the signature of the justice or coroner, or other proof whatever.

(2) Where any court, justice or coroner referred to in subsection (1), has no seal, or so certifies, the evidence may be given by a copy purporting to be certified under the signature of a judge or presiding magistrate of the court or of the justice or coroner, without any proof of the authenticity of the signature or other proof whatever.

Certified copies.

24. In every case in which the original record could be admitted in evidence,

(*a*) a copy of any official or public document of Canada or of any province, purporting to be certified under the hand of the proper officer or person in whose custody the official or public document is placed, or
(*b*) a copy of a document, by-law, rule, regulation or proceeding, or a copy of any entry in any register or other book of any municipal or other corporation, created by charter or Act of Parliament or the legislature of any province, purporting to be certified under the seal of the corporation, and the hand of the presiding officer, clerk or secretary thereof,

is admissible in evidence without proof of the seal of the corporation, or of the signature or official character of the person or persons appearing to have signed it, and without further proof thereof.

Books and documents.

25. Where a book or other document is of so public a nature as to be admissible in evidence on its mere production from the proper custody, and no other Act exists that renders its contents provable by means of a copy, a copy thereof or extract therefrom is admissible in evidence in any court of justice or before a person having, by law or by consent of parties, authority to hear, receive and examine evidence, if it is proved that it is a copy or extract purporting to be certified to be true by the officer to whose custody the original has been entrusted.

Books kept in offices under Government of Canada — Proof of non-issue of licence or document — Proof of mailing departmental matter — Proof of official character.

26. (1) A copy of any entry in any book kept in any office or department of the Government of Canada, or in any commission, board or other branch of the public service of Canada, shall be admitted as evidence of that entry, and of the matters, transactions and accounts therein recorded, if it is proved by the oath or affidavit of an officer of the office or department, commission, board or other branch of the public service of Canada that the book was, at the time of the making of the entry, one of the ordinary books kept in the office, department, commission, board or other branch of the public service of Canada, that the entry was made in the usual and ordinary course of business of the office, department, commission, board or other branch of the public service of Canada and that the copy is a true copy thereof.

(2) Where by any Act of Parliament or regulation made thereunder provision is made for the issue by a department, commission, board or other branch of the public service of Canada of a licence requisite to the doing or having of any act or thing or for the issue of any other document, an affidavit of an officer of the department, commission, board or other branch of the public service, sworn before any commissioner or other person authorized to take affidavits, setting out that he has charge of the appropriate records and that after careful examination and search of those records he has been unable to

find in any given case that any such licence or other document has been issued, shall be admitted in evidence as proof, in the absence of evidence to the contrary, that in that case no licence or other document has been issued.

(3) Where by any Act of Parliament or regulation made thereunder provision is made for sending by mail any request for information, notice or demand by a department or other branch of the public service of Canada an affidavit of an officer of the department or other branch of the public service, sworn before any commissioner or other person authorized to take affidavits, setting out that he has charge of the appropriate records, that he has a knowledge of the facts in the particular case, that the request, notice or demand was sent by registered letter on a named date to the person or firm to whom it was addressed (including that address) and that he identifies as exhibits attached to the affidavit the post office certificate of registration of the letter and a true copy of the request, notice or demand, shall, on production and proof of the post office receipt for the delivery of the registered letter to the addressee, be admitted in evidence as proof, in the absence of evidence to the contrary, of the sending and of the request, notice or demand.

(4) Where proof is offered by affidavit pursuant to this section it is not necessary to prove the official character of the person making the affidavit if that information is set out in the body of the affidavit.

Notarial acts in Quebec.

27. Any document purporting to be a copy of a notarial act or instrument made, filed or registered in the Province of Quebec, and to be certified by a notary or prothonotary to be a true copy of the original in his possession as such notary or prothonotary, shall be admitted in evidence in the place and stead of the original and has the same force and effect as the original would have if produced and proved, but it may be proved in rebuttal that there is no original, that the copy is not a true copy of the original in some material particular or that the original is not an instrument of such nature as may, by the law of the Province of Quebec, be taken before a notary or be filed, enrolled or registered by a notary in that Province.

Notice of production of book or document — Not less than 7 days.

28. (1) No copy of any book or other document shall be admitted in evidence, under the authority of section 23, 24, 25, 26 or 27, on any trial, unless the party intending to produce the copy has before the trial given to the party against whom it is intended to be produced reasonable notice of that intention.

(2) The reasonableness of the notice referred to in subsection (1) shall be determined by the court, judge or other person presiding, but the notice shall not in any case be less than seven days.

Copies of entries — Admission in evidence — Cheques, proof of "no account" — Proof of official character — Compulsion of production or appearance — Order to inspect and copy — Warrants to search — Computation of time — Definitions.

29. (1) Subject to this section, a copy of any entry in any book or record kept in any financial institution shall in all legal proceedings be admitted in evidence as proof, in the absence of evidence to the contrary, of the entry and of the matters, transactions and accounts therein recorded.

(2) A copy of an entry in the book or record described in subsection (1) shall not be admitted in evidence under this section unless it is first proved that the book or record was, at the time of the making of the entry, one of the ordinary books or records of the financial institution, that the entry was made in the usual and ordinary course of business, that the book or record is in the custody or control of the financial institution and that the copy is a true copy thereof, and such proof may be given by the manager or accountant of the financial institution and may be given orally or by affidavit sworn before any commissioner or other person authorized to take affidavits.

(3) Where a cheque has been drawn on any financial institution or branch thereof by any person, an affidavit of the manager or accountant of the financial institution or branch, sworn before any commissioner or other person authorized to take affidavits, setting out that he is the manager or accountant, that he has made a careful examination and search of the books and records for the purpose of ascertaining whether or not that person has an account with the financial institution or branch and that he has been unable to find such an account, shall be admitted in evidence as proof, in the absence of evidence to the contrary, that that person has no account in the financial institution or branch.

(4) Where evidence is offered by affidavit pursuant to this section, it is not necessary to prove the signature or official character of the person making the affidavit if the official character of that person is set out in the body of the affidavit.

(5) A financial institution or officer of a financial institution is not in any legal proceedings to which the financial institution is not a party compellable to produce any book or record, the contents of which can be proved under this section, or to appear as a witness to prove the matters, transactions and accounts therein recorded unless by order of the court made for special cause.

(6) On the application of any party to a legal proceeding, the court may order that that party be at liberty to inspect and take copies of any entries in the books or records of a financial institution for the purposes of the legal proceeding, and the person whose account is to be inspected shall be notified of the application at least two clear days before the hearing thereof, and if it is shown to the satisfaction of the court that he cannot be notified personally, the notice may be given by addressing it to the financial institution.

(7) Nothing in this section shall be construed as prohibiting any search of the premises of a financial institution under the authority of a warrant to search issued under any other Act of Parliament, but unless the warrant is expressly endorsed by the person under whose hand it is issued as not being limited by this section, the authority conferred by any such warrant to search the premises of a financial institution and to seize and take away anything therein shall, with respect to the books or records of the institution, be construed as limited to the searching of those premises for the purpose of inspecting and taking copies of entries in those books or records.

(8) Holidays shall be excluded from the computation of time under this section.

(9) In this section,

"court" means the court, judge, arbitrator or person before whom a legal proceeding is held or taken;

"financial institution" means the Bank of Canada, the Federal Business Development Bank and any institution incorporated in Canada that accepts deposits of money from its members or the public, and includes a branch, agency or office of any such Bank or institution;

"legal proceeding" means any civil or criminal proceeding or inquiry in which evidence is or may be given, and includes an arbitration.

Business records to be admitted in evidence — Inference where information not in business record — Copy of records — Where record kept in form requiring explanation — Court may order other part of record to be produced — Court may examine record and hear evidence — Notice of intention to produce record or affidavit — Not necessary to prove signature and official character — Examination on record with leave of court — Evidence inadmissible under this section — Construction of this section — Definitions.

30. (1) Where oral evidence in respect of a matter would be admissible in a legal proceeding, a record made in the usual and ordinary course of business that contains information in respect of that matter is admissible in evidence under this section in the legal proceeding on production of the record.

(2) Where a record made in the usual and ordinary course of business does not contain information in respect of a matter the occurrence or existence of which might reasonably be expected to be recorded in that record, the court may on production of the record admit the record for the purpose of establishing that fact and may draw the inference that the matter did not occur or exist.

(3) Where it is not possible or reasonably practicable to produce any record described in subsection (1) or (2), a copy of the record accompanied by an affidavit setting out the reasons why it is not possible or reasonably practicable to produce the record and an affidavit of the person who made the copy setting out the source from which the copy was made and attesting to its authenticity,

each affidavit having been sworn before a commissioner or other person authorized to take affidavits, is admissible in evidence under this section in the same manner as it if were the original of the record.

(4) Where production of any record or of a copy of any record described in subsection (1) or (2) would not convey to the court the information contained in the record by reason of its having been kept in a form that requires explanation, a transcript of the explanation of the record or copy prepared by a person qualified to make the explanation, accompanied by an affidavit of that person setting out his qualifications to make the explanation, attesting to the accuracy of the explanation and sworn before any commissioner or other person authorized to take affidavits, is admissible in evidence under this section in the same manner as if it were the original of the record.

(5) Where part only of a record is produced under this section by any party, the court may examine any other part of the record and direct that, together with the part of the record previously so produced, the whole or any part of the other part thereof be produced by that party as the record produced by him.

(6) For the purpose of determining whether any provision of this section applies, or for the purpose of determining the probative value, if any, to be given to information contained in any record admitted in evidence under this section, the court may, on production of any record, examine the record, admit any evidence in respect thereof given orally or by affidavit including evidence as to the circumstances in which the information contained in the record was written, recorded, stored or reproduced, and draw any reasonable inference from the form or content of the record.

(7) Unless the court orders otherwise, no record or affidavit shall be admitted in evidence under this section unless the party producing the record or affidavit has, at least seven days before its production, given notice of his intention to produce it to each other party to the legal proceeding and has, within five days after receiving any notice in that behalf given by any such party, produced it for inspection by that party.

(8) Where evidence is offered by affidavit under this section, it is not necessary to prove the signature or official character of the person making the affidavit if the official character of that person is set out in the body of the affidavit.

(9) Subject to section 4, any person who has or may reasonably be expected to have knowledge of the making or contents of any record produced or received in evidence under this section may, with leave of the court, be examined or cross-examined thereon by any party to the legal proceeding.

(10) Nothing in this section renders admissible in evidence in any legal proceeding

(*a*) such part of any record as is proved to be

(i) a record made in the course of an investigation or inquiry,

(ii) a record made in the course of obtaining or giving legal advice or in contemplation of a legal proceeding.

(iii) a record in respect of the production of which any privilege exists and is claimed, or

(iv) a record of or alluding to a statement made by a person who is not, or if he were living and of sound mind would not be, competent and compellable to disclose in the legal proceeding a matter disclosed in the record;

(*b*) any record the production of which would be contrary to public policy; or

(*c*) any transcript or recording of evidence taken in the course of another legal proceeding.

(11) The provisions of this section shall be deemed to be in addition to and not in derogation of

(*a*) any other provision of this or any other Act of Parliament respecting the admissiblity in evidence of any record or the proof of any matter; or

(*b*) any existing rule of law under which any record is admissible in evidence or any matter may be proved.

(12) In this section,

"business" means any business, profession, trade, calling, manufacture or undertaking of any kind carried on in Canada or elsewhere whether for profit or otherwise, including any activity or operation carried on or performed in Canada or elsewhere by any government, by any department, branch, board, commission or agency of any government, by any court or other tribunal or by any other body or authority performing a function of government;

"copy", in relation to any record, includes a print, whether enlarged or not, from a photographic film of the record, and "photographic film" includes a photographic plate, microphotographic film or photostatic negative;

"court" means the court, judge, arbitrator or person before whom a legal proceeding is held or taken;

"legal proceeding" means any civil or criminal proceeding or inquiry in which evidence is or may be given, and includes an arbitration;

"record" includes the whole or any part of any book, document, paper, card, tape or other thing on or in which information is written, recorded, stored or reproduced, and, except for the purposes of subsections (3) and (4), any copy or transcript admitted in evidence under this section pursuant to subsection (3) or (4).

Definitions — When print admissible in evidence — Evidence of compliance with conditions — Proof by notarial copy.

31. (1) In this section,

"corporation" means any bank, including the Bank of Canada and the Federal

Business Development Bank, and each of the following carrying on business in Canada, namely, every railway, express, telegraph and telephone company (except a street railway and tramway company), insurance company or society, trust company and loan company (except a company subject to Part II of the *Small Loans Act*, chapter S-11 of the Revised Statutes of Canada, 1970);

[1992, c. 1, Sch. V, item 9(2) will repeal the definition "corporation" in subsection 31(1) and substitute the following.]

"corporation" means any bank, including the Bank of Canada and the Federal Business Development Bank, and each of the following carrying on business in Canada, namely, every railway, express, telegraph and telephone company (except a street railway and tramway company), insurance company or society, trust company and loan company;

"government" means the government of Canada or of any province and includes any department, commission, board or branch of any such government; and

"photographic film" includes any photographic plate, microphotographic film and photostatic negative.

(2) A print, whether enlarged or not, from any photographic film of

(*a*) an entry in any book or record kept by any government or corporation and destroyed, lost or delivered to a customer after the film was taken,

(*b*) any bill of exchange, promissory note, cheque, receipt, instrument or document held by any government or corporation and destroyed, lost or delivered to a customer after the film was taken, or

(*c*) any record, document, plan, book or paper belonging to or deposited with any government or corporation,

is admissible in evidence in all cases in which and for all purposes for which the object photographed would have been admitted on proof that

(*d*) while the book, record, bill of exchange, promissory note, cheque, receipt, instrument or document, plan, book or paper was in the custody or control of the government or corporation, the photographic film was taken thereof in order to keep a permanent record thereof, and

(*e*) the object photographed was subsequently destroyed by or in the presence of one or more of the employees of the government or corporation, or was lost or was delivered to a customer.

(3) Evidence of compliance with the conditions prescribed by this section may be given by any one or more of the employees of the government or corporation, having knowledge of the taking of the photographic film, of the destruction, loss or delivery to a customer, or of the making of the print, as the case may be, either orally or by affidavit sworn in any part of Canada before any notary public or commissioner for oaths.

(4) Unless the court otherwise orders, a notarial copy of an affidavit under subsection (3) is admissible in evidence in lieu of the original affidavit. S.C. 1992, c. 1, Sch. V, item 9(1).

Order signed by Secretary of State — Copies printed in Canada Gazette.

32. (1) An order signed by the Secretary of State of Canada and purporting to be written by command of the Governor General shall be admitted in evidence as the order of the Governor General.

(2) All copies of official and other notices, advertisements and documents printed in the *Canada Gazette* are admissible in evidence as proof, in the absence of evidence to the contrary, of the originals and of the contents thereof.

Proof of handwriting of person certifying — Printed or written.

33. (1) No proof shall be required of the handwriting or official position of any person certifying, in pursuance of this Act, to the truth of any copy of or extract from any proclamation, order, regulation, appointment, book or other document.

(2) Any copy or extract referred to in subsection (1) may be in print or in writing, or partly in print and partly in writing.

Attesting witness — Instrument, how proved.

34. (1) It is not necessary to prove by the attesting witness any instrument to the validity of which attestation is not requisite.

(2) Any instrument referred to in subsection (1) may be proved by admission or otherwise as if there had been no attesting witness thereto.

Impounding of forged instrument.

35. Where any instrument that has been forged or fraudulently altered is admitted in evidence, the court or the judge or person who admits the instrument may, at the request of any person against whom it is admitted in evidence, direct that the instrument shall be impounded and be kept in the custody of an officer of the court or other proper person for such period and subject to such conditions as to the court, judge or person admitting the instrument seem meet.

Construction.

36. This Part shall be deemed to be in addition to and not in derogation of any powers of proving documents given by any existing Act or existing at law.

DISCLOSURE OF GOVERNMENT INFORMATION

Objection to disclosure of information — Where objection made to superior court — Where objection not made to superior court — Limitation period — Appeal to court of appeal — Limitation period for appeal under subsection (5) — Limitation periods for appeals to Supreme Court of Canada.

37. (1) A minister of the Crown in right of Canada or other person interested may object to the disclosure of information before a court, person or body with jurisdiction to compel the production of information by certifying orally or in writing to the court, person or body that the information should not be disclosed on the grounds of a specified public interest.

(2) Subject to sections 38 and 39, where an objection to the disclosure of information is made under subsection (1) before a superior court, that court may examine or hear the information and order its disclosure, subject to such restrictions or conditions as it deems appropriate, if it concludes that, in the circumstances of the case, the public interest in disclosure outweighs in importance the specified public interest.

(3) Subject to sections 38 and 39, where an objection to the disclosure of information is made under subsection (1) before a court, person or body other than a superior court, the objection may be determined, on application, in accordance with subsection (2) by

(*a*) the Federal Court-Trial Division, in the case of a person or body vested with power to compel production by or pursuant to an Act of Parliament if the person or body is not a court established under a law of a province; or

(*b*) the trial division or trial court of the superior court of the province within which the court, person or body exercises its jurisdiction, in any other case.

(4) An application pursuant to subsection (3) shall be made within ten days after the objection is made or within such further or lesser time as the court having jurisdiction to hear the application considers appropriate in the circumstances.

(5) An appeal lies from a determination under subsection (2) or (3)

(*a*) to the Federal Court of Appeal from a determination of the Federal Court-Trial Division; or

(*b*) to the court of appeal of a province from a determination of a trial division or trial court of a superior court of a province.

(6) An appeal under subsection (5) shall be brought within ten days from the date of the determination appealed from or within such further time as the court having jurisdiction to hear the appeal considers appropriate in the circumstances.

(7) Notwithstanding any other Act of Parliament,

(*a*) an application for leave to appeal to the Supreme Court of Canada from a judgment made pursuant to subsection (5) shall be made within ten days from the date of the judgment appealed from or within such further time as the court having jurisdiction to grant leave to appeal considers appropriate in the circumstances; and

(*b*) where leave to appeal is granted, the appeal shall be brought in the manner set out in subsection 60(1) of the *Supreme Court Act* but within such time as the court that grants leave specifies.

Objection relating to international relations or national defence or security — Limitation period — Appeal to Federal Court of Appeal — Subsections 37(6) and (7) apply — Special rules for hearings — Ex parte representations.

38. (1) Where an objection to the disclosure of information is made under subsection 37(1) on grounds that the disclosure would be injurious to international relations or national defence or security, the objection may be determined, on application, in accordance with subsection 37(2) only by the Chief Justice of the Federal Court, or such other judge of that court as the Chief Justice may designate to hear such applications.

(2) An application under subsection (1) shall be made within ten days after the objection is made or within such further or lesser time as the Chief Justice of the Federal Court, or such other judge of that Court as the Chief Justice may designate to hear such applications, considers appropriate.

(3) An appeal lies from a determination under subsection (1) to the Federal Court of Appeal.

(4) Subsection 37(6) applies in respect of appeals under subsection (3), and subsection 37(7) applies in respect of appeals from judgments made pursuant to subsection (3), with such modifications as the circumstances require.

(5) An application under subsection (1) or an appeal brought in respect of the application shall

(*a*) be heard *in camera*; and

(*b*) on the request of the person objecting to the disclosure of information, be heard and determined in the National Capital Region described in the schedule to the *National Capital Act.*

(6) During the hearing of an application under subsection (1) or an appeal brought in respect of the application, the person who made the objection in respect of which the application was made or the appeal was brought shall, on the request of that person, be given the opportunity to make representations *ex parte.*

Objection relating to a confidence of the Queen's Privy Council — Definition — Definition of "Council" — Exception.

39. (1) Where a minister of the Crown or the Clerk of the Privy Council objects to the disclosure of information before a court, person or body with jurisdiction to compel the production of information by certifying in writing that the information constitutes a confidence of the Queen's Privy Council for Canada, disclosure of the information shall be refused without examination or hearing of the information by the court, person or body.

(2) For the purpose of subsection (1), "a confidence of the Queen's Privy Council for Canada" includes, without restricting the generality thereof, information contained in

(*a*) a memorandum the purpose of which is to present proposals or recommendations to Council;

(*b*) a discussion paper the purpose of which is to present background explanations, analyses of problems or policy options to Council for consideration by Council in making decisions;

(*c*) an agendum of Council or a record recording deliberations or decisions of Council;

(*d*) a record used for or reflecting communications or discussions between ministers of the Crown on matters relating to the making of government decisions or the formulation of government policy;

(*e*) a record the purpose of which is to brief ministers of the Crown in relation to matters that are brought before, or are proposed to be brought before, Council or that are the subject of communications or discussions referred to in paragraph (*d*); and

(*f*) draft legislation.

(3) For the purposes of subsection (2), "Council" means the Queen's Privy Council for Canada, committees of the Queen's Privy Council for Canada, Cabinet and committees of Cabinet.

(4) Subsection (1) does not apply in respect of

(*a*) a confidence of the Queen's Privy Council for Canada that has been in existence for more than twenty years; or

(*b*) a discussion paper described in paragraph (2)(*b*)

(i) if the decisions to which the discussion paper relates have been made public, or

(ii) where the decisions have not been made public, if four years have passed since the decisions were made.

PROVINCIAL LAWS OF EVIDENCE

How applicable.

40. In all proceedings over which Parliament has legislative authority, the laws of evidence in force in the province in which those proceedings are taken, including the laws of proof of service of any warrant, summons, subpoena or other document, subject to this Act and other Acts of Parliament, apply to those proceedings.

STATUTORY DECLARATIONS

Solemn declaration.

41. Any judge, notary public, justice of the peace, police or provincial court judge, recorder, mayor or commissioner authorized to take affidavits to be used either in the provincial or federal courts, or any other functionary authorized by law to administer an oath in any matter, may receive the solemn declaration of any person voluntarily making the declaration before him, in the following form, in attestation of the execution of any writing, deed or instrument, or of the truth of any fact, or of any account rendered in writing:

I, . . . , solemnly declare that (*state the fact or facts declared to*), and I make this solemn declaration conscientiously believing it to be true, and knowing that it is of the same force and effect as if made under oath.

Declared before me . . . . . at . . . . . this . . . . . day of . . . . . 19 . . .

INSURANCE PROOFS

Affidavits, etc.

42. Any affidavit, solemn affirmation or declaration required by any insurance company authorized by law to do business in Canada, in regard to any loss of or injury to person, property or life insured or assured therein, may be taken before any commissioner or other person authorized to take affidavits, before any justice of the peace or before any notary public for any province, and the commissioner, person, justice of the peace or notary public is required to take the affidavit, solemn affirmation or declaration.

PART II

APPLICATION

Foreign courts.

43. This Part applies to the taking of evidence relating to proceedings in courts out of Canada.

INTERPRETATION

Definitions.

44. In this Part,

"cause" includes a proceeding against a criminal;

"court" means any superior court in any province;

"judge" means any judge of any superior court in any province;

"oath" includes a solemn affirmation in cases in which, by the law of Canada, or of a province, as the case may be, a solemn affirmation is allowed instead of an oath.

Construction.

45. This Part shall not be so construed as to interfere with the right of legislation of the legislature of any province requisite or desirable for the carrying out of the objects hereof.

PROCEDURE

Order for examination of witness in Canada.

46. Where, on an application for that purpose, it is made to appear to any court or judge that any court or tribunal of competent jurisdiction in the Commonwealth and Dependent Territories or in any foreign country, before which any civil, commercial or criminal matter is pending, is desirous of obtaining the testimony in relation to that matter of a party or witness within the jurisdiction of the first mentioned court, of the court to which the judge belongs or of the judge, the court or judge may, in its or his discretion, order the examination on oath on interrogatories, or otherwise, before any person or persons named in the order, of that party or witness accordingly, and by the same or any subsequent order may command the attendance of such party or witness for the purpose of being examined, and for the production of any writings or other documents mentioned in the order, and of any other writings or documents relating to the matter in question that are in the possession or power of that party or witness.

Enforcement of the order.

47. On the service on the party or witness of an order referred to in section 46, and of an appointment of a time and place for the examination of the party or witness signed by the person named in the order for taking the examination, or, if more than one person is named, by one of the persons named, and on payment or tender of the like conduct money as is properly payable on attendance at a trial, the order may be enforced in like manner as an order made by the court or judge in a cause pending in that court or before that judge.

Expenses and conduct money.

48. Every person whose attendance is required in manner described in section 47 is entitled to the like conduct money and payment for expenses and loss of time as on attendance at a trial.

Administering oath.

49. On any examination of parties or witnesses, under the authority of any order made in pursuance of this Part, the oath shall be administered by the person authorized to take the examination, or, if more than one person is authorized, by one of those persons.

Right of refusal to answer or produce document — Nature of right.

50. (1) Any person examined under any order made under this Part has the like right to refuse to answer questions tending to criminate himself, or other questions, as a party or witness, as the case may be, would have in any cause pending in the court by which, or by a judge whereof, the order is made.

(2) No person shall be compelled to produce, under any order referred to in subsection (1), any writing or other document that he could not be compelled to produce at a trial of such a cause.

Rules of court — Letters rogatory.

51. (1) The court may frame rules and orders in relation to procedure and to the evidence to be produced in support of the application for an order for examination of parties and witnesses under this Part, and generally for carrying this Part into effect.

(2) In the absence of any order in relation to the evidence to be produced in support of the application referred to in subsection (1), letters rogatory from any court of justice in the Commonwealth and Dependent Territories, or from any foreign tribunal, in which the civil, commercial or criminal matter is pending, shall be deemed and taken to be sufficient evidence in support of the application.

PART III

APPLICATION

Application of this Part.

52. This Part extends to the following classes of persons:

(*a*) officers of any of Her Majesty's diplomatic or consular services while performing their functions in any foreign country, including ambassadors, envoys, ministers, charges d'affaires, counsellors, secretaries, attaches, consuls general, consuls, vice-consuls, pro-consuls, consular agents, acting consuls general, acting consuls, acting vice-consuls and acting consular agents;

(*b*) officers of the Canadian diplomatic, consular and representative services while performing their functions in any foreign country or in any part of the Commonwealth and Dependent Territories other than Canada, including, in addition to the diplomatic and consular officers mentioned in paragraph (*a*), high commissioners, permanent delegates, acting high commissioners, acting permanent delegates, counsellors and secretaries;

(*c*) Canadian Government Trade Commissioners and Assistant Canadian Government Trade Commissioners while performing their functions in any foreign country or in any part of the Commonwealth and Dependent Territories other than Canada; and

(*d*) honorary consular officers of Canada while performing their functions in any foreign country or in any part of the Commonwealth and Dependent Territories other than Canada. 1984, c. 40, s. 27(3).

OATHS AND SOLEMN AFFIRMATIONS

Oaths taken abroad.

53. Oaths, affidavits, solemn affirmations or declarations administered, taken or received outside Canada by any person mentioned in section 52, are as valid and effectual and are of the like force and effect to all intents and purposes as if they had been administered, taken or received in Canada by a person authorized to administer, take or receive oaths, affidavits, solemn affirmations or declarations therein that are valid and effectual under this Act.

DOCUMENTARY EVIDENCE

Documents to be admitted in evidence.

54. Any document that purports to have affixed, impressed, or subscribed thereon or thereto the signature of any person authorized by this Part to administer, take or receive oaths, affidavits, solemn affirmations or declarations, together with his seal or with the seal or stamp of his office, or the office to which he is attached, in testimony of any oath, affidavit, solemn affirmation or declaration being administered, taken or received by him, shall be admitted in evidence, without proof of the seal or stamp or of his signature or official character.

CANADIAN BILL OF RIGHTS

R.S.C. 1985, Appendix III

An Act for the Recognition and Protection of Human Rights and Fundamental Freedoms, S.C. 1960, c. 44

Preamble.

The Parliament of Canada, affirming that the Canadian Nation is founded upon principles that acknowledge the supremacy of God, the dignity and worth of the human person and the position of the family in a society of free men and free institutions;

Affirming also that men and institutions remain free only when freedom is founded upon respect for moral and spiritual values and the rule of law;

And being desirous of enshrining these principles and the human rights and fundamental freedoms derived from them, in a Bill of Rights which shall reflect the respect of Parliament for its constitutional authority and which shall ensure the protection of these rights and freedoms in Canada:

Therefore, Her Majesty, by and with the advice and consent of the Senate and House of Commons of Canada, enacts as follows:

PART I

BILL OF RIGHTS

Recognition and declaration of rights and freedoms.

1. It is hereby recognized and declared that in Canada there have existed and shall continue to exist without discrimination by reason of race, national origin, colour, religion or sex, the following human rights and fundamental freedoms, namely,

(*a*) the right of the individual to life, liberty, security of the person and enjoyment of property, and the right not to be deprived thereof except by due process of law;

(*b*) the right of the individual to equality before the law and the protection of the law;

(*c*) freedom of religion;

(*d*) freedom of speech;

(*e*) freedom of assembly and association; and

(*f*) freedom of the press.

Construction of law.

2. Every law of Canada shall, unless it is expressly declared by an Act of the Parliament of Canada that it shall operate notwithstanding the *Canadian Bill of Rights*, be so construed and applied as not to abrogate, abridge or infringe or to authorize the abrogation, abridgment or infringement of any of the rights or freedoms herein recognized and declared, and in particular, no law of Canada shall be construed or applied so as to

(*a*) authorize or effect the arbitrary detention, imprisonment or exile of any person;

(*b*) impose or authorize the imposition of cruel and unusual treatment or punishment;

(*c*) deprive a person who has been arrested or detained

(i) of the right to be informed promptly of the reason for his arrest or detention,

(ii) of the right to retain and instruct counsel without delay, or

(iii) of the remedy by way of *habeas corpus* for the determination of the validity of his detention and for his release if the detention is not lawful;

(*d*) authorize a court, tribunal, commission, board or other authority to compel a person to give evidence if he is denied counsel, protection against self crimination or other constitutional safeguards;

(*e*) deprive a person of the right to a fair hearing in accordance with the principles of fundamental justice for the determination of his rights and obligations;

(*f*) deprive a person charged with a criminal offence of the right to be presumed innocent until proved guilty according to the law in a fair and public hearing by an independent and impartial tribunal, or of the right to reasonable bail without just cause; or

(*g*) deprive a person of the right to the assistance of an interpreter in any proceedings in which he is involved or in which he is a party or a witness, before a court, commission, board or other tribunal, if he does not understand or speak the language in which such proceedings are conducted.

Duties of Minister of Justice — Exception.

3. (1) Subject to subsection (2), the Minister of Justice shall, in accordance with such regulations as may be prescribed by the Governor in Council, examine every regulation transmitted to the Clerk of the Privy Council for registration pursuant to the *Statutory Instruments Act* and every Bill introduced in or presented to the House of Commons by a Minister of the Crown in order to ascertain whether any of the provisions thereof are inconsistent with the purposes and provisions of this Part and he shall report any such inconsistency to the House of Commons at the first convenient opportunity.

(2) A regulation need not be examined in accordance with subsection (1) if prior to being made it was examined as a proposed regulation in accordance with section 3 of the *Statutory Instruments Act* to ensure that it was not inconsistent with the purposes and provisions of this Part.

Short title.

4. The provisions of this Part shall be known as the *Canadian Bill of Rights*.

PART II

Savings — "Law of Canada" defined — Jurisdiction of Parliament.

5. (1) Nothing in Part I shall be construed to abrogate or abridge any human right or fundamental freedom not enumerated therein that may have existed in Canada at the commencement of this Act.

(2) The expression "law of Canada" in Part I means an Act of the Parliament of Canada enacted before or after the coming into force of this Act, any order, rule or regulation thereunder, and any law in force in Canada or in any part of Canada at the commencement of this Act that is subject to be repealed, abolished or altered by the Parliament of Canada.

(3) The provisions of Part I shall be construed as extending only to matters coming within the legislative authority of the Parliament of Canada.

CONSTITUTION ACT, 1982

R.S.C. 1985, Appendix II, No. 44

Enacted by the Canada Act 1982 (U.K.), c. 11
As amended by the Constitution Amendment Proclamation, 1983, SI/84-102, Schedule, in force June 21, 1984

SCHEDULE B

PART I

CANADIAN CHARTER OF RIGHTS AND FREEDOMS

Whereas Canada is founded upon principles that recognize the supremacy of God and the rule of law:

Guarantee of Rights and Freedoms

Rights and freedoms in Canada.

1. The *Canadian Charter of Rights and Freedoms* guarantees the rights and freedoms set out in it subject only to such reasonable limits prescribed by law as can be demonstrably justified in a free and democratic society.

Fundamental Freedoms

Fundamental freedoms.

2. Everyone has the following fundamental freedoms:

(*a*) freedom of conscience and religion;

(*b*) freedom of thought, belief, opinion and expression, including freedom of the press and other media of communication;

(*c*) freedom of peaceful assembly; and

(*d*) freedom of association.

Democratic Rights

Democratic rights of citizens.

3. Every citizen of Canada has the right to vote in an election of members of the House of Commons or of a legislative assembly and to be qualified for membership therein.

Maximum duration of legislative bodies — Continuation in special circumstances.

4. (1) No House of Commons and no legislative assembly shall continue for longer than five years from the date fixed for the return of the writs at a general election of its members.

(2) In time of real or apprehended war, invasion or insurrection, a House of Commons may be continued by Parliament and a legislative assembly may be continued by the legislature beyond five years if such continuation is not opposed by the votes of more than one-third of the members of the House of Commons or the legislative assembly, as the case may be.

Annual sitting of legislative bodies.

5. There shall be a sitting of Parliament and of each legislature at least once every twelve months.

Mobility Rights

Mobility of citizens — Rights to move and gain livelihood — Limitation — Affirmative action programs.

6. (1) Every citizen of Canada has the right to enter, remain in and leave Canada.

(2) Every citizen of Canada and every person who has the status of a permanent resident of Canada has the right

(*a*) to move to and take up residence in any province; and

(*b*) to pursue the gaining of a livelihood in any province.

(3) The rights specified in subsection (2) are subject to

(*a*) any laws or practices of general application in force in a province other than those that discriminate among persons primarily on the basis of province of present or previous residence; and

(*b*) any laws providing for reasonable residency requirements as a qualification for the receipt of publicly provided social services.

(4) Subsections (2) and (3) do not preclude any law, program or activity that has as its object the amelioration in a province of conditions of individuals in that province who are socially or economically disadvantaged if the rate of employment in that province is below the rate of employment in Canada.

Legal Rights

Life, liberty and security of person.

7. Everyone has the right to life, liberty and security of the person and the right not to be deprived thereof except in accordance with the principles of fundamental justice.

Search or seizure.

8. Everyone has the right to be secure against unreasonable search or seizure.

Detention or imprisonment.

9. Everyone has the right not to be arbitrarily detained or imprisoned.

Arrest or detention.

10. Everyone has the right on arrest or detention

(*a*) to be informed promptly of the reasons therefor;

(*b*) to retain and instruct counsel without delay and to be informed of that right; and

(*c*) to have the validity of the detention determined by way of *habeas corpus* and to be released if the detention is not lawful.

Proceedings in criminal and penal matters.

11. Any person charged with an offence has the right

(*a*) to be informed without unreasonable delay of the specific offence;

(*b*) to be tried within a reasonable time;

(*c*) not to be compelled to be a witness in proceedings against that person in respect of the offence;

(*d*) to be presumed innocent until proven guilty according to law in a fair and public hearing by an independent and impartial tribunal;

(*e*) not to be denied reasonable bail without just cause;

(*f*) except in the case of an offence under military law tried before a military tribunal, to the benefit of trial by jury where the maximum punishment for the offence is imprisonment for five years or a more severe punishment;

(*g*) not to be found guilty on account of any act or omission unless, at the time of the act or omission, it constituted an offence under Canadian or international law or was criminal according to the general principles of law recognized by the community of nations;

(*h*) if finally acquitted of the offence, not to be tried for it again and, if finally found guilty and punished for the offence, not to be tried or punished for it again; and

(*i*) if found guilty of the offence and if the punishment for the offence has been varied between the time of commission and the time of sentencing, to the benefit of the lesser punishment.

Treatment or punishment.

12. Everyone has the right not to be subjected to any cruel and unusual treatment or punishment.

Self-crimination.

13. A witness who testified in any proceedings has the right not to have any incriminating evidence so given used to incriminate that witness in any other proceedings, except in a prosecution for perjury or for the giving of contradictory evidence.

Interpreter.

14. A party or witness in any proceedings who does not understand or speak the language in which the proceedings are conducted or who is deaf has the right to the assistance of an interpreter.

Equality Rights

Equality before and under law and equal protection and benefit of law — Affirmative action programs.

15. (1) Every individual is equal before and under the law and has the right to the equal protection and equal benefit of the law without discrimination and, in particular, without discrimination based on race, national or ethnic origin, colour, religion, sex, age or mental or physical disability.

(2) Subsection (1) does not preclude any law, program or activity that has as its object the amelioration of conditions of disadvantaged individuals or groups including those that are disadvantaged because of race, national or ethnic origin, colour, religion, sex, age or mental or physical disability.

Official Languages of Canada

Official languages of Canada — Official languages of New Brunswick — Advancement of status and use.

16. (1) English and French are the official languages of Canada and have equality of status and equal rights and privileges as to their use in all institutions of the Parliament and government of Canada.

(2) English and French are the official languages of New Brunswick and have equality of status and equal rights and privileges as to their use in all institutions of the legislature and government of New Brunswick.

(3) Nothing in this Charter limits the authority of Parliament or a legislature to advance the equality of status or use of English and French.

Proceedings of Parliament — Proceedings of New Brunswick legislature.

17. (1) Everyone has the right to use English or French in any debates and other proceedings of Parliament.

(2) Everyone has the right to use English or French in any debates and other proceedings of the legislature of New Brunswick.

Parliamentary statutes and records — New Brunswick statutes and records.

18. (1) The statutes, records and journals of Parliament shall be printed and published in English and French and both language versions are equally authoritative.

(2) The statutes, records and journals of the legislature of New Brunswick shall be printed and published in English and French and both language versions are equally authoritative.

Proceedings in courts established by Parliament — Proceedings in New Brunswick courts.

19. (1) Either English or French may be used by any person in, or in any pleading in or process issuing from, any court established by Parliament.

(2) Either English or French may be used by any person in, or in any pleading in or process issuing from, any court of New Brunswick.

Communications by public with federal institutions — Communications by public with New Brunswick institutions.

20. (1) Any member of the public in Canada has the right to communicate with, and to receive available services from, any head or central office of an institution of the Parliament or government of Canada in English or French, and has the same right with respect to any other office of any such institution where

(*a*) there is a significant demand for communications with and services from that office in such language; or

(*b*) due to the nature of the office, it is reasonable that communications with and services from that office be available in both English and French.

(2) Any member of the public in New Brunswick has the right to communicate with, and to receive available services from, any office of an institution of the legislature or government of New Brunswick in English or French.

Continuation of existing constitutional provisions.

21. Nothing in sections 16 to 20 abrogates or derogates from any right, privilege or obligation with respect to the English and French languages, or either of them, that exists or is continued by virtue of any other provision of the Constitution of Canada.

Rights and privileges preserved.

22. Nothing in sections 16 to 20 abrogates or derogates from any legal or customary right or privilege acquired or enjoyed either before or after the coming into force of this Charter with respect to any language that is not English or French.

Minority Language Educational Rights

Language of instruction — Continuity of language instruction — Application where numbers warrant.

23. (1) Citizens of Canada

(*a*) whose first language learned and still understood is that of the English or French linguistic minority population of the province in which they reside, or

(*b*) who have received their primary school instruction in Canada in English or French and reside in a province where the language in which they received that instruction is the language of the English or French linguistic minority population of the province,

have the right to have their children receive primary and secondary school instruction in that language in that province.

(2) Citizens of Canada of whom any child has received or is receiving primary or secondary school instruction in English or French in Canada, have the right to have all their children receive primary and secondary school instruction in the same language.

(3) The right of citizens of Canada under subsections (1) and (2) to have their children receive primary and secondary school instruction in the language of the English or French linguistic minority population of a province

(*a*) applies wherever in the province the number of children of citizens who have such a right is sufficient to warrant the provision to them out of public funds of minority language instruction; and

(*b*) includes, where the number of those children so warrants, the right to have them receive that instruction in minority language educational facilities provided out of public funds.

Enforcement

Enforcement of guaranteed rights and freedoms — Exclusion of evidence bringing administration of justice into disrepute.

24. (1) Anyone whose rights or freedoms, as guaranteed by this Charter, have been infringed or denied may apply to a court of competent jurisdiction to obtain such remedy as the court considers appropriate and just in the circumstances.

(2) Where, in proceedings under subsection (1), a court concludes that evidence was obtained in a manner that infringed or denied any rights or freedoms guaranteed by this Charter, the evidence shall be excluded if it is established that, having regard to all the circumstances, the admission of it in the proceedings would bring the administration of justice into disrepute.

General

Aboriginal rights and freedoms not affected by Charter.

25. The guarantee in this Charter of certain rights and freedoms shall not be construed so as to abrogate or derogate from any aboriginal treaty or other rights or freedoms that pertain to the aboriginal peoples of Canada including

(*a*) any rights or freedoms that have been recognized by the Royal Proclamation of October 7, 1763; and

(*b*) any rights or freedoms that now exist by way of land claims agreements or may be so acquired.

Other rights and freedoms not affected by Charter.

26. The guarantee in this Charter of certain rights and freedoms shall not be construed as denying the existence of any other rights or freedoms that exist in Canada.

Multicultural heritage.

27. This Charter shall be interpreted in a manner consistent with the preservation and enhancement of the multicultural heritage of Canadians.

Rights guaranteed equally to both sexes.

28. Notwithstanding anything in this Charter, the rights and freedoms referred to in it are guaranteed equally to male and female persons.

Rights respecting certain schools preserved.

29. Nothing in this Charter abrogates or derogates from any rights or privileges guaranteed by or under the Constitution of Canada in respect of denominational, separate or dissentient schools.

Application to territories and territorial authorities.

30. A reference in this Charter to a province or to the legislative assembly or legislature of a province shall be deemed to include a reference to the Yukon Territory and the Northwest Territories, or to the appropriate legislative authority thereof, as the case may be.

Legislative powers not extended.

31. Nothing in this Charter extends the legislative powers of any body or authority.

Application of Charter

Application of Charter — Exception.

32. (1) This Charter applies

(*a*) to the Parliament and government of Canada in respect of all matters within the authority of Parliament including all matters relating to the Yukon Territory and Northwest Territories; and

(*b*) to the legislature and government of each province in respect of all matters within the authority of the legislature of each province.

(2) Notwithstanding subsection (1), section 15 shall not have effect until three years after this section comes into force.

Exception where express declaration — Operation of exception — Five year limitation — Re-enactment — Five year limitation.

33. (1) Parliament or the legislature of a province may expressly declare in an Act of Parliament or of the legislature, as the case may be, that the

Act or a provision thereof shall operate notwithstanding a provision included in section 2 or sections 7 to 15 of this Charter.

(2) An Act or a provision of an Act in respect of which a declaration made under this section is in effect shall have such operation as it would have but for the provision of this Charter referred to in the declaration.

(3) A declaration made under subsection (1) shall cease to have effect five years after it comes into force or on such earlier date as may be specified in the declaration.

(4) Parliament or a legislature of a province may re-enact a declaration made under subsection (1).

(5) Subsection (3) applies in respect of a re-enactment made under subsection (4).

Citation

Citation.

34. This Part may be cited as the *Canadian Charter of Rights and Freedoms.*

CRIMINAL RECORDS ACT

TABLE OF CONCORDANCE

R.S.C. 1970, c. 12 (1st Supp.)	R.S.C. 1985, c. C-47	Remarks
12	**C-47**	
1	1	
2	2, part. 4	
3	3	
4	part. 4	
5	5	
6	6	
7	7	
8	8	
9	9	part. OM
10	10	
Sch/Ann	Sch/Ann	

CRA

CRIMINAL RECORDS ACT

R.S.C. 1985, c. C-47

An Act to provide for the relief of persons who have been convicted of offences and have subsequently rehabilitated themselves

SHORT TITLE

Short title.

1. This Act may be cited as the *Criminal Records Act.*

INTERPRETATION

Definitions — Termination of period of probation — Absolute and conditional discharges.

2. (1) In this Act,

"Board" means the National Parole Board;

"Commissioner" means the Commissioner of the Royal Canadian Mounted Police;

"Minister" means the Solicitor General of Canada;

"pardon" means a pardon granted by the Governor in Council under subsection 4(8);

[1992, c, 22, s. 1(1) will repeal the definition "pardon" in subsection 2(1) and substitute the following.]

"pardon" means a pardon granted or issued by the Board under section 4.1;

"period of probation" means a period during which a person convicted of an offence was directed by the court that convicted him

(*a*) to be released on his own recognizance to keep the peace and be of good behaviour, or

(*b*) to be released on or comply with the conditions prescribed in a probation order.

[1992, c. 22, s. 1(2) will amend subsection 2(1) by adding the following definition.]

"sentence" has the same meaning as in the *Criminal Code*, but does not include an order made under section 100 or 259 of that Act.

(2) For the purposes of this Act, the period of probation shall be deemed to have terminated at the time the recognizance or the probation order that relates to the period of probation ceased to be in force.

(3) Subject to subsection 4(3), for the purposes of this Act, a person who has been directed by a court, under section 736 of the *Criminal Code*, to be discharged in respect of an offence absolutely or on the conditions prescribed in a probation order shall be deemed to have been convicted of the offence.

[1992, c. 22, s. 1(3) will repeal subsection 2(3).]

[1992, c. 22, s. 2(1) will add the following immediately after section 2.]

Jurisdiction of the Board.

2.1. The Board has exclusive jurisdiction to grant or issue or refuse to grant or issue or to revoke a pardon.

Quorum — Idem.

2.2. (1) Applications for pardons referred to in subsection 4.1(1) shall be determined, and decisions whether to revoke pardons under section 7 shall be made, by a panel that consists of one member of the Board.

(2) The Chairman of the Board may direct that the number of members of the Board required to constitute a panel for the determination of an application for a pardon referred to in subsection 4.1(1) or to decide whether to revoke a pardon under section 7 or for the determination of any class of those applications or for the making of any class of those decisions shall be greater than one.

[1992, c. 22, s. 2(2) will repeal subsection 2.2(2) and substitute the following upon the coming into force of 1992, c. 20, s. 104.]

Idem.

(2) The Chairperson of the Board may direct that the number of members of the Board required to constitute a panel for the determination of an application for a pardon referred to in subsection 4.1(1) or to decide whether to revoke a pardon under section 7 or for the determination of any class of those applications or for the making of any class of those decisions shall be greater than one.

APPLICATION FOR PARDON

Application for pardon.

3. A person who has been convicted of an offence under an Act of Parliament or a regulation made thereunder may apply to the Minister for a pardon in respect of that offence.

[1992, c. 22, s. 3 will repeal section 3 and substiute the following.]

Application for pardon — Transfer of offenders.

3. (1) A person who has been convicted of an offence under an Act of Parliament or a regulation made under an Act of Parliament may apply to the Board for a pardon in respect of that offence and a Canadian offender within the meaning of the *Transfer of Offenders Act* who has been transferred to Canada under that Act may apply to the Board for a pardon in respect of the offence of which the offender has been found guilty.

(2) For the purposes of this Act, the offence of which a Canadian offender within the meaning of the *Transfer of Offenders Act* who has been transferred to Canada under that Act has been found guilty is deemed to be an offence that was prosecuted by indictment.

PROCEDURE

Referral to Board — Inquiries by Board — Delay periods for inquiries — Calculation of period of sentence — Report by Board — Notification to applicant — Board to consider representations — Grant of pardon — Form.

4. (1) On receipt of an application for a pardon, the Minister shall refer the application to the Board.

(2) The Board shall, after the expiration of the period set out in subsection (3), cause proper inquiries to be made in order to ascertain the behaviour of the applicant for a pardon since the date of the conviction of the applicant.

(3) For the purposes of subsection (2), the period after which inquiries shall be made in respect of an applicant for a pardon is,

(*a*) in the case of an offence punishable on summary conviction in proceedings under Part XXVII of the *Criminal Code*,

(i) where the applicant was convicted of the offence, two years after the latest of the termination of any period of imprisonment, the period of probation and the payment of any fine imposed on the applicant in respect of the offence, or

(ii) where the applicant was directed by a court under section 736 of the *Criminal Code* to be discharged absolutely in respect of the offence, one year after the direction of the court and where the applicant was so directed to be discharged on the conditions presented in a probation order, one year after the termination of the period of probation; or

(*b*) in any other case,

(i) five years after the date after which the two year period set out in subparagraph (*a*)(i) would have been computed, if that subparagraph had been applicable to the applicant, or

(ii) three years after the date after which the one year period set out in subparagraph (*a*)(ii) would have been computed, if that subparagraph had been applicable to the applicant.

(4) For the purposes of this section, in calculating any term of imprisonment imposed on an applicant, there shall be included, in addition to any time spent by him in custody pursuant to that term, any period of statutory remission granted to him in respect thereof.

(5) Subject to subsections (6) and (7), on completion of its inquiries under subsection (2), the Board shall report the result thereof to the Minister with its recommendation as to whether a pardon should be granted.

(6) If the Board proposes to recommend that a pardon should not be granted to an applicant therefor, it shall, before making the recommendation, forthwith notify the applicant of its proposal and advise him that he is entitled to make any representations to the Board that he believes relevant.

(7) The Board shall, before making a report under subsection (5), consider any oral or written representations made to it by or on behalf of the applicant within a reasonable time after the notification is given to the applicant pursuant to subsection (6).

(8) On receipt of a recommendation from the Board that a pardon should be granted, the Minister shall refer the recommendation to the Governor in Council who may grant the pardon.

(9) A pardon shall be in the form set out in the schedule.

[1992, c. 22, s. 4(1) will repeal section 4 and substitute the following.]

Conviction-free period.

4. Before an application for a pardon may be considered, the following period must have elapsed after the expiration according to law of any sentence, including a sentence of imprisonment, a period of probation and the payment of any fine, imposed for an offence, namely,

(*a*) five years, in the case of

(i) an offence prosecuted by indictment, or

(ii) a service offence within the meaning of the *National Defence Act* for which the offender was punished by a fine of more than two thousand dollars, detention for more than six months, dismissal from Her Majesty's service, imprisonment for more than six months or a punishment that is greater than imprisonment for less than two years in the scale of punishments set out in subsection 139(1) of that Act; or

(*b*) three years, in the case of

(i) an offence punishable on summary conviction, or

(ii) a service offence within the meaning of the *National Defence Act*, other than a service offence referred to in subparagraph (*a*)(ii).

Grant of pardon-indictable offences — Summary conviction offences.

4.1. (1) The Board may grant a pardon for an offence prosecuted by indictment or a service offence referred to in subparagraph 4(*a*)(ii) if the Board is satisfied that the applicant, during the period of five years referred to in paragraph 4(*a*),

(*a*) has been of good conduct; and

(*b*) has not been convicted of an offence under an Act of Parliament or a regulation made under an Act of Parliament.

(2) A pardon for an offence punishable on summary conviction or a service offence referred to in subparagraph 4(*b*)(ii) shall be issued if the offender has not been convicted of an offence under an Act of Parliament or a regulation

made under an Act of Parliament during the period of three years referred to in paragraph 4(*b*).

Inquiries — Opportunity to make representations — Board to consider representations.

4.2 (1) On receipt of an application for a pardon for an offence referred to in paragraph 4(*a*), the Board shall cause inquiries to be made to ascertain the conduct of the applicant since the date of the conviction.

(2) If the Board proposes to refuse to grant a pardon, it shall notify the applicant of its proposal and advise the applicant that he or she is entitled to make any representations to the Board that he or she believes relevant.

(3) The Board shall, before deciding whether to refuse to grant a pardon, consider any oral or written representations made to it by or on behalf of the applicant within a reasonable time after the notification is given to the applicant pursuant to subsection (2).

Expiration of sentence.

4.3 For the purposes of section 4, in calculating any sentence of imprisonment imposed on an applicant, there shall be included any period of remission standing to the credit of the applicant in respect of that sentence of imprisonment.

[1992, c. 22, s. 4(2) will repeal section 4.3 and substitute the following upon the coming into force of 1992, c. 20, s. 99(2).]

Expiration of sentence.

4.3 For the purposes of section 4, a reference to the expiration according to law of a sentence of imprisonment imposed for an offence shall be read as a reference to the day on which the sentence expires, without taking into account

(*a*) any period during which the offender could be entitled to statutory release or any period following a statutory release date; or

(*b*) any remission that stands to the credit of the offender in respect of the offence.

EFFECT OF GRANT OF PARDON

Effect of grant.

5. The grant of a pardon

(*a*) is evidence of the fact that the Board, after making proper inquiries, was satisfied that the applicant for the pardon was of good behaviour and that the conviction in respect of which the pardon is granted should no longer reflect adversely on his character; and

(*b*) unless the pardon is subsequently revoked, vacates the conviction in respect of which it is granted and, without restricting the generality of the foregoing, removes any disqualification to which the person so convicted is, by reason of the conviction, subject by virtue of any Act of Parliament or a regulation made thereunder.

[1992, c. 22, s. 5 will repeal section 5 and sbustitute the following.]

Effect of pardon.

5. The pardon

(*a*) is evidence of the fact

(i) that, in the case of a pardon for an offence referred to in paragraph 4(*a*), the Board, after making inquiries, was satisfied that the applicant for the pardon was of good conduct, and

(ii) that, in the case of any pardon, the conviction in respect of which the pardon is granted or issued should no longer reflect adversely on the applicant's character; and

(*b*) unless the pardon is subsequently revoked or ceases to have effect, vacates the conviction in respect of which it is granted and, without restricting the generality of the foregoing, removes any disqualification to which the person so convicted is, by reason of the conviction, subject by virtue of the provisions of any Act of Parliament, other than section 100 or 259 of the *Criminal Code*, or of a regulation made under an Act of Parliament.

CUSTODY OF RECORDS

Order respecting custody of records — Records to be kept separate and not to be disclosed — Approval for disclosure.

6. (1) The Minister may, by order in writing addressed to any person having the custody or control of any judicial record of a conviction in respect of which a pardon has been granted, require that person to deliver that record into the custody of the Commissioner.

(2) Any record of a conviction in respect of which a pardon has been granted that is in the custody of the Commissioner or of any department or agency of the Government of Canada shall be kept separate and apart from other criminal records, and no such record shall be disclosed to any person, nor shall the existence of the record or the fact of the conviction be disclosed to any person, without the prior approval of the Minister.

(3) The Minister shall, before granting the approval for disclosure referred to in subsection (2), satisfy himself that the disclosure is desirable in the interests of the administration of justice or for any purpose related to the safety or security of Canada or any state allied or associated with Canada.

[1992, c. 22, s. 6 will add the following immediately after section 6.]

Discharges — Purging C.P.I.C.

6.1 (1) No record of a discharge under section 736 of the *Criminal Code* that is in the custody of the Commissioner or of any department or agency of the Government of Canada shall be disclosed to any person, nor shall the existence of the record or the fact of the discharge be disclosed to any person, without the prior approval of the Minister, if

(*a*) more than one year has elapsed since the offender was discharged absolutely; or

(*b*) more than three years have elapsed since the offender was discharged on the conditions prescribed in a probation order.

(2) The Commissioner shall remove all references to a discharge under section 736 of the *Criminal Code* from the automated criminal conviction records retrieval system maintained by the Royal Canadian Mounted Police on the expiration of the relevant period referred to in subsection (1).

Disclosure to police forces.

6.2 Notwithstanding sections 6 and 6.1, the name, date of birth and last known address of a person who has received a pardon or a discharge referred to in section 6.1 may be disclosed to a police force if a fingerprint, identified as that of the person, is found

(*a*) at the scene of a crime during an investigation of the crime; or

(*b*) during an attempt to identify a deceased person or a person suffering from amnesia.

REVOCATION

Revocation of pardon.

7. A pardon may be revoked by the Governor in Council

(*a*) if the person to whom it is granted is subsequently convicted of a further offence under an Act Parliament or a regulation made thereunder; or

(*b*) on evidence establishing to the satisfaction of the Governor in Council

(i) that the person to whom it was granted is no longer of good conduct, or

(ii) that the person knowingly made a false or deceptive statement in relation to his application for the pardon, or knowingly concealed some material particular in relation to that application.

[1992, c. 22, s. 7 will repeal section 7 and substitute the following.]

Revocation of pardon.

7. A pardon may be revoked by the Board

(*a*) if the person to whom it is granted or issued is subsequently convicted of an offence punishable on summary conviction under an Act of Parliament or a regulation made under an Act of Parliament;

(*b*) on evidence establishing to the satisfaction of the Board that the person to whom it was granted or issued is no longer of good conduct; or

(*c*) on evidence establishing to the satisfaction of the Board that the person to whom it was granted or issued knowingly made a false or deceptive statement in relation to the application for the pardon, or knowingly concealed some material particular in relation to that application.

Opportunity to make representations — Board to consider representation.

7.1 (1) If the Board proposes to revoke a pardon, it shall notify the person to whom the pardon was granted or issued of its proposal and advise that person that he or she is entitled to make any representations to the Board that he or she believes relevant.

(2) The Board shall, before deciding whether to revoke a pardon, consider any oral or written representations made to it by or on behalf of the person to whom the pardon was granted or issued within a reasonable time after the notification is given to that person pursuant to subsection (1).

Cessation of pardon's effect.

7.2 A pardon ceases to have effect if the peson to whom it is granted or issued is subsequently convicted of an offence prosecuted by indictment under an Act of Parliament or a regulation made under an Act of Parliament.

GENERAL

Applications for employment.

8. No application form for or relating to

[1992, c. 22, s. 8(1) will repeal all that portion of section 8 preceding paragraph (*a*) and substitute the following.]

Applications for employment.

8. No person shall use or authorize the use of an application form for or relating to any of the following matters that contains a question that by its terms requires the applicant to disclose a conviction in respect of which a pardon that has not been revoked or ceased to have effect has been granted or issued to the applicant:

(*a*) employment in any department as defined in section 2 of the *Financial Administration Act,*

(*b*) employment by any Crown corporation as defined in section 83 of the *Financial Administration Act,*

(*c*) enrolment in the Canadian Forces, or

(*d*) employment on or in connection with the operation of any work, undertaking or business that is within the legislative authority of Parliament,

shall contain any question that by its terms requires the applicant to disclose a conviction in respect of which he has been granted a pardon that has not been revoked.

[1992, c. 22, s. 8(2) will repeal all that portion of section 8 following paragraph (*d*).]

Saving provision.

9. Nothing in this Act in any manner limits or affects the provisions of the *Criminal Code,* or of the Letters Patent Constituting the Office of Governor General of Canada, relating to pardons, except that sections 6 and 8 apply in respect of any pardon granted pursuant to any authority conferred by those provisions.

[1992, c. 22, s. 9 will repeal section 9 and substitute the following.]

Saving of other pardons.

9. Nothing in this Act in any manner limits or affects Her Majesty's royal prerogative of mercy or the provisions of the *Criminal Code* relating to pardons, except that sections 6 and 8 apply in respect of any pardon granted pursuant to the royal prerogative of mercy or those provisions.

Regulations.

9.1 The Governor in Council may make regulations for carrying out the purposes and provisions of this Act.

OFFENCES

Offence and punishment.

10. Any person who contravenes any provision of this Act is guilty of an offence punishable on summary conviction.

SCHEDULE
(Section 4)
PARDON

HIS EXCELLENCY THE GOVERNOR GENERAL IN COUNCIL, on the recommendation of the Parole Board, is pleased hereby to grant to ...., a pardon, in respect of the offence of ...., of which he was convicted on the .... day of ...., 19 ....;

And this pardon is evidence of the fact that the Parole Board, after making proper inquiries, was satisfied that the .... was of good behaviour and that the conviction should no longer reflect adversely on his character and, unless subsequently revoked, this pardon vacates the conviction in respect of which it is granted and, without restricting the generality of the foregoing, removes any disqualification to which the .... is, by reason of such conviction, subject by virtue of any Act of Parliament or a regulation made thereunder.

Given at Ottawa, this .... day of ...., 19 ....

By Order,
Deputy Registrar General

EXTRADITION ACT

TABLE OF CONCORDANCE

R.S.C. 1970, c. E-21	R.S.C. 1985, c. E-23	R.S.C. 1970, c. E-21	R.S.C. 1985, c. E-23
E-21	**E-23**	**E-21**	**E-23**
1	1	21	21
2	2	22	22
3	3	23	23
4	4	24	24
5	5	25	25
6	6	26	26
7	7	27	27
8	8	28	28
9	9	29	29
10	10	30	30
11	11	31	31
12	12	32	32
13	13	33	33
14	14	34	34
15	15	35	35
16	16	36	36
17	17	37	37
18	18	38	38
19	19	39	39
20	20	40	40
		Sch/Ann I-III	Sch/Ann I-III

EA

EXTRADITION ACT

R.S.C. 1985, c. E-23

An Act respecting the extradition of fugitive criminals
As amended by R.S. 1985, c. 27 (1st Supp.), ss. 187, 203, Schedule V

SHORT TITLE

Short title.

1. This Act may be cited as the *Extradition Act.*

INTERPRETATION

Definitions.

2. In this Act,

"conviction" or "convicted" does not include the case of a condemnation under foreign law by reason of contumacy; but "accused person" includes a person so condemned;

"extradition arrangement" or "arrangement" means a treaty, convention or arrangement that extends to Canada made by Her Majesty with a foreign state for the surrender of fugitive criminals;

"extradition crime" means

(*a*) any crime that, if committed in Canada, or within Canadian jurisdiction, would be one of the crimes described in Schedule I, and

(*b*) in the application of this Act to the case of an extradition arrangement, any crime described in the arrangement, whether or not it is included in that Schedule;

"foreign state" includes every colony, dependency and constituent part of the foreign state, and every vessel of a foreign state is deemed to be within the jurisdiction of and to be part of the state;

"fugitive" or "fugitive criminal" means a person being or suspected of being in Canada, who is accused or convicted of an extradition crime committed within the jurisdiction of a foreign state;

"judge" includes any person authorized to act judicially in extradition matters;

"warrant", in the case of a foreign state, includes any judicial document that authorizes the arrest of a person accused or convicted of crime.

PART I
EXTRADITION UNDER TREATY

Application of this Part

Existing arrangements.

3. In the case of any foreign state with which there is an extradition arrangement this Part applies during the continuance of the arrangement; but no provision of this Part that is inconsistent with any of the terms of the arrangement has effect to contravene the arrangement, and this Part shall be so read and construed as to provide for the execution of the arrangement.

Orders in council limiting application of U.K. Act and this Part.

4. Where, with respect to a foreign state, an order of Her Majesty in Council makes the application to the United Kingdom of the Act of the Parliament of the United Kingdom entitled *The Extradition Act, 1870*, 33-34 Victoria, chapter 52 and any Act amending that Act subject to any limitation, condition, qualification or exception, the Governor in Council shall, by order, make the application of this Part subject to that limitation, condition, qualification or exception.

Revocation, etc., of orders.

5. The Governor in Council may, by order, revoke or alter, subject to the restrictions of this Part, any order made by the Governor in Council under section 4, and all the provisions of this Part with respect to the original order, in so far as applicable, apply with such modifications as the circumstances require to the new order.

Date when Part applies or is affected.

6. This Part, in so far as its application in the case of any foreign state depends on or is affected by any order in council made under section 4 or 5 or referred to in this Part, shall apply, or its application shall be affected, after the time specified in the order or, if no time is specified, after the date of the publication of the order in the *Canada Gazette*.

Mandatory publication in Canada Gazette.

7. Any order of Her Majesty in Council, referred to in section 4, and any order of the Governor in Council made under section 4 or 5 and any extradition arrangement shall, as soon as possible, be published in the *Canada Gazette* and laid before both Houses of Parliament.

Effect of publication.

8. The publication in the *Canada Gazette* of an extradition arrangement or an order in council is evidence of the arrangement or order, of the terms thereof and of the application of this Part pursuant and subject thereto, any court or judge shall without proof take judicial notice of the arrangement or order, and the validity of the order and the application of this Part, pursuant and subject thereto, shall not be questioned.

Judges and Commissioners

Judges who may act — Habeas corpus.

9. (1) All judges of the superior courts and of the county courts of a province, and all commissioners who are appointed for the purpose in a province by the Governor in Council, under the Great Seal, by virtue of this Part, are authorized to act judicially in extradition matters under this Part within the province, and each of those persons has for the purposes of this Part all the powers and jurisdiction of any judge or provincial court judge of the province.

(2) Nothing in this section shall be construed so as to confer on any judge any jurisdiction in *habeas corpus* matters. R.S., c. 27 (1st Supp.), s. 203.

Extradition from Canada

Grounds for warrant — Report to Minister of Justice.

10. (1) Whenever this Part applies, a judge may issue a warrant for the apprehension of a fugitive on a foreign warrant of arrest, or an information or a complaint laid before the judge, and on such evidence or after such proceedings as in the opinion of the judge would, subject to this Part, justify the issue of the warrant if the crime of which the fugitive is accused or is alleged to have been convicted had been committed in Canada.

(2) The judge shall forthwith send a report of the fact of the issue of the warrant referred to in subsection (1), together with certified copies of the evidence and foreign warrant, information or complaint, to the Minister of Justice.

Execution of warrant.

11. A warrant issued under this Part may be executed in any part of Canada in the same manner as if it had been originally issued, or subsequently endorsed, by a justice of the peace having jurisdiction in the place where it is executed.

Surrender not to depend on time when offence was committed, etc.

12. Every fugitive criminal of a foreign state, to which this Part applies, is liable to be apprehended, committed and surrendered in the manner provided in this Part, whether the crime or conviction, in respect of which the surrender is sought was committed or took place before or after the date of an arrangement, or before or after the time when this Part is made to apply to that state, and whether there is or is not any criminal jurisdiction in any court of Her Majesty's Realms and Territories over the fugitive in respect of the crime.

Fugitive to be brought before judge.

13. The fugitive referred to in section 12 shall be brought before a judge, who shall, subject to this Part, hear the case, in the same manner, as nearly as may be, as if the fugitive was brought before a justice of the peace, charged with an indictable offence committed in Canada.

Evidence of charge.

14. The judge shall receive on oath, or on solemn affirmation, if affirmation is allowed by law, the evidence of any witness tendered to show the truth of the charge or the fact of the conviction.

Evidence that crime is not an extradition crime.

15. The judge shall receive, in the manner set out in section 14, any evidence tendered to show that the crime of which the fugitive is accused or alleged to have been convicted is an offence of a political character, or is, for any other reason, not an extradition crime, or that the proceedings are being taken with a view to prosecute or punish the fugitive for an offence of a political character.

Depositions or statements taken outside Canada.

16. Depositions or statements taken in a foreign state on oath, or on solemn affirmation, where affirmation is allowed by the law of that state, and copies of the depositions or statements and foreign certificates of, or judicial documents stating the fact of, conviction may, if duly authenticated, be received in evidence in proceedings under this Part.

When to be deemed authenticated.

17. The documents referred to in section 16 shall be deemed duly authenticated if authenticated in the manner provided by law, or if

(*a*) the warrant purports to be signed by, the certificate purports to be certified by, or the depositions or statements, or the copies thereof, purport to be certified to be the originals or true copies, by a judge, provincial court judge or officer of the foreign state; and

(*b*) the papers are authenticated by the oath or affirmation of a witness, or by being sealed with the official seal of the Minister of Justice or any other minister of the foreign state, or of a colony, dependency or constituent part of the foreign state, of which seal the judge shall take judicial notice without proof. R.S., c. 27 (1st Supp.), s. 203.

Evidence sufficient to justify committal — Discharge.

18. (1) The judge shall issue a warrant for the committal of the fugitive to the nearest convenient prison, there to remain until surrendered to the foreign state, or discharged according to law,

(*a*) in the case of a fugitive alleged to have been convicted of an extradition crime, if such evidence is produced as would, according to the law of Canada, subject to this Part, prove that the fugitive was so convicted, and

(*b*) in the case of a fugitive accused of an extradition crime, if such evidence is produced as would, according to the law of Canada, subject to this Part, justify the committal of the fugitive for trial, if the crime had been committed in Canada.

(2) If the evidence referred to in subsection (1) is not produced, the judge shall order the fugitive to be discharged.

Information to be given to fugitives.

19. The judge who commits a fugitive to prison, shall, on the committal,

(*a*) inform the fugitive that he will not be surrendered until after the expiration of fifteen days and has a right to apply for a writ of *habeas corpus*; and

(*b*) transmit to the Minister of Justice a certificate of the committal, with a copy of all the evidence taken before the judge not already so transmitted, and such report on the case as the judge thinks fit.

By whom requisition for surrender may be made — By arrangement.

20. (1) A requisition for the surrender of a fugitive criminal of a foreign state who is, or is suspected to be, in Canada, may be made to the Minister of Justice

(*a*) by any person recognized by the Minister of Justice as a consular officer of that state resident at Ottawa; or

(*b*) by any minister of that state communicating with the Minister of Justice through the diplomatic representative of Her Majesty in that state.

(2) If neither of the modes referred to in subsection (1) is convenient, then the requisition shall be made in such other mode as is settled by arrangement.

Fugitive not liable to surrender.

21. No fugitive is liable to surrender under this Part if it appears that

(*a*) the offence in respect of which proceedings are taken under this Part is one of a political character; or

(*b*) the proceedings are being taken with a view to prosecute or punish the fugitive for an offence of a political character.

When Minister may refuse to make order — Discharge of fugitive.

22. The Minister of Justice may at any time refuse to make an order for surrender referred to in section 25 where he determines that

(*a*) the offence in respect of which proceedings are being taken under this Part is one of a political character;

(*b*) the proceedings are, in fact, being taken with a view to try or punish the fugitive for an offence of a political character; or

(*c*) the foreign state does not intend to make a requisition for surrender.

(2) Where the Minster of Justice refuses to make an order for surrender, he may, by order under his hand and seal, cancel any order made by him or any warrant issued by a judge under this Part and order the fugitive to be discharged out of custody on any committal made under this Part, and the fugitive shall be discharged accordingly.

Delay before surrender.

23. A fugitive shall not be surrendered until after the expiration of fifteen days from the date of his committal for surrender, or, if a writ of *habeas corpus* is issued, until after the decision of the court remanding the fugitive.

If fugitive is an offender under Canadian law.

24. A fugitive who has been accused of an offence within Canadian jurisdiction, not being the offence for which the fugitive's surrender is asked, or who is undergoing sentence under a conviction in Canada, shall not be surrendered until after having been discharged, whether by acquittal, by expiration of the sentence or otherwise.

Surrender of fugitive to officer of a foreign state.

25. Subject to this Part, the Minister of Justice, on the requisition of the foreign state, may, under his hand and seal, order a fugitive who has been committed for surrender to be surrendered to the person or persons who are, in the Minister's opinion, duly authorized to receive the fugitive in the name and on behalf of the foreign state, and the fugitive shall be so surrendered accordingly.

Powers of such officers.

26. Any person to whom an order of the Minister of Justice made under section 25 is directed may deliver, and the person thereto authorized by that order may receive, hold in custody and convey, the fugitive within the jurisdiction of the foreign state, and if the fugitive escapes out of any custody to which the fugitive is delivered, on or in pursuance of that order, the fugitive may be retaken in the same manner as any person accused or convicted of any crime against the laws of Canada may be retaken on an escape.

Property found on fugitive.

27. Everything found in the possession of the fugitive at the time of his arrest that may be material as evidence in making proof of the crime may be delivered up with the fugitive on his surrender, subject to all rights of third persons with regard thereto.

Fugitive to be conveyed out of Canada within certain time.

28. Where a fugitive is not surrendered and conveyed out of Canada within two months after committal for surrender, or, if a writ of *habeas corpus* is issued, within two months after the decision of the court on that writ, over and above, in either case, the time required to convey the fugitive from the prison to which he has been committed, by the readiest way out of Canada, any one or more of the judges of the superior courts of the province in which that person is confined, having power to grant a writ of *habeas corpus*, may, on application made by or on behalf of the fugitive, and on proof that reasonable notice of the intention to make the application has been given to the Minister of Justice, order the fugitive to be discharged out of custody, unless sufficient cause is shown against the discharge.

Forms.

29. The Forms set forth in Schedule II, or forms as near thereto as circumstances permit, may be used in the matters to which those Forms refer and, when used, shall be deemed valid.

Extradition from a Foreign State

Requisition for a fugitive out of Canada — By arrangement.

30. (1) A requisition for the surrender of a fugitive criminal from Canada, who is or is suspected to be in any foreign state with which there is an extradition arrangement, may be made by the Minister of Justice

(*a*) to a consular officer of that state resident at Ottawa, or

(*b*) to the Minister of Justice or any other minister of that state, through the diplomatic representative of Her Majesty in that state.

(2) If neither of the modes referred to in subsection (1) is convenient, the requisition shall be made in such other mode as is settled by arrangement.

Depositions for use in a foreign state — Summoning of witnesses — Enforcement of subpoena.

31. (1) Whenever, for the purposes of this Act, it becomes necessary or expedient to secure evidence by depositions taken in Canada to be used in a foreign state, any justice of the peace or any person having authority to issue a warrant for the apprehension of persons accused of offences and to commit those persons for trial may take depositions in the absence of a person accused of an extradition crime in like manner as he might take the depositions if the accused person were present and charged before him with the extradition crime.

(2) The justice of the peace or person having authority referred to in subsection (1) may, by subpoena or order, command the attendance at the time and place therein mentioned of any person or witness for the purpose of being examined respecting any extradition crime charged under this Act, and may require the production of any writings or other documents relating to the charge that are in the possession or power of that person or witness.

(3) After service of a subpoena or order referred to in subsection (2), and on payment or tender of the like conduct money as is properly payable on attendance at the trial of an indictable offence in a superior court, the subpoena or order may be enforced in like manner as a subpoena or order issued by that superior court.

Conveyance of fugitive surrendered.

32. Any person accused or convicted of an extradition crime who is surrendered by a foreign state may, under the warrant for that person's surrender issued in that state, be brought into Canada and delivered to the proper authorities, to be dealt with according to law.

Fugitives surrendered by a foreign state not punishable contrary to arrangement.

33. A person accused or convicted of an extradition crime who is surrendered by a foreign state in pursuance of an extradition arrangement is not, until after having been restored or having had an opportunity of returning to the foreign state within the meaning of the arrangement, subject, in contravention of any of the terms of the arrangement, to a prosecution or punishment in Canada for any other offence committed prior to his surrender, for which that person should not, under the arrangement, be prosecuted.

Schedule I

How list of crimes in Schedule I to be construed.

34. The list of crimes set out in Schedule I shall be construed according to the law existing in Canada at the date of the commission of the alleged crime, whether by common law or by statute, and as including only such crimes, of the description comprised in the list, as are indictable offences under that law.

PART II
EXTRADITION IRRESPECTIVE OF TREATY

Commencement of Part — Proclamation may be revoked.

35. (1) This Part does not come into force, with respect to fugitive offenders from any foreign state, until it has been declared by proclamation of the Governor General to be in force and effect with respect to that foreign state after a day to be named in the proclamation.

(2) Where by proclamation the Governor General declares this Part to be no longer in operation with respect to any foreign state, its provisions shall cease to have any force or effect with respect to fugitive offenders from that state after a day to be named in the proclamation.

Application of Part.

36. This Part applies to any crime mentioned in Schedule III that is committed after the coming into force of this Part with respect to any foreign state to which this Part has, by proclamation pursuant to subsection 35(1), been declared to apply.

Extradition where no arrangement, or where crime not included — Procedure under Part I.

37. (1) Where no extradition arrangement exists between Her Majesty and a foreign state, or where an extradition arrangement extending to Canada exists between Her Majesty and a foreign state but does not include the crimes set out in Schedule III, it is nevertheless lawful for the Minister of Justice to issue his warrant for the surrender to that foreign state of any fugitive offender from that state charged with or convicted of any of the crimes set out in Schedule III.

(2) The arrest, committal, detention, surrender and conveyance out of Canada of a fugitive offender referred to in subsection (1) is governed by Part I, and all the provisions of that Part apply to all steps and proceedings in relation to the arrest, committal, detention, surrender and conveyance out of Canada in the same manner and to the same extent as they would apply if the crimes set out in Schedule III were included and specified in an extradition arrangement between Her Majesty and the foreign state extending to Canada.

Payment of expenses.

38. All expenses connected with the arrest, committal, detention, surrender and conveyance out of Canada of any fugitive offender under this Part shall be borne by the foreign state that applies for the surrender of the fugitive offender.

Interpretation of Schedule III.

39. The list of crimes set out in Schedule III shall be construed according to the law existing in Canada at the date of the commission of the alleged crime, whether by common law or by statute, and as including only such crimes, of the description comprised in the list, as are indictable offences under that law.

When warrant may not be issued.

40. No warrant shall issue under this Part for the extradition of any person to a state or country in which by the law in force in that state or country that person may be tried after the extradition for any other offence than that for which he has been extradited, unless an assurance has first been given by the executive authority of the state or country that the person whose extradition has been claimed will not be tried for any other offence than that in respect of which the extradition has been claimed.

SCHEDULE I

(*Sections 2 and 34*)

LIST OF CRIMES

1. Murder, or attempt or conspiracy to murder
2. Manslaughter
3. Counterfeiting or altering money, and uttering counterfeit or altered money

4. Forgery, counterfeiting or altering, or uttering what is forged, counterfeited or altered

5. Larceny or theft

6. Embezzlement

7. Obtaining money or goods, or valuable securities, by false pretences

8. Crimes against bankruptcy or insolvency law

9. Fraud committed by a bailee, banker, agent, factor, ttustee, or by a director or member or officer of any company, which fraud is made criminal by any Act for the time being in force

10. Sexual assault, sexual assault with a weapon, threats to a third party or causing bodily harm or aggravated sexual assault

11. Abduction

12. Child stealing

13. Kidnapping

14. False imprisonment

15. Burglary, housebreaking or shop-breaking

16. Arson

17. Robbery

18. Threats, by letter or otherwise, with intent to extort

19. Perjury or subornation of perjury

20. Piracy by municipal law or law of nations committed on board of or against a vessel of a foreign state

21. Criminal scuttling or destruction of a vessel of a foreign state at sea, whether on the high seas or on the Great Lakes of North America, or attempting or conspiring to do so

22. Assault on board a vessel of a foreign state at sea, whether on the high seas or on the Great Lakes of North America, with intent to destroy life or to do grievous bodily harm

23. Revolt, or conspiracy to revolt, by two or more persons on board a vessel of a foreign state at sea, whether on the high seas or on the Great Lakes of North America, against the authority of the master

24. Any offence under

(*a*) sections 52, 57, 58, 79 to 81, 153, 154, 178, 280 to 283, 385 to 391, 393 to 396, subsection 397(1), sections 398, 400, 401, 405 and paragraph 465(1)(*a*) of the *Criminal Code*,

(*b*) Part VIII of the *Criminal Code*, except sections 249, 250, 252, 253, 255 and 259 in relation to a vessel and sections 264.1 and 290 to 317,

(*c*) Part IX of the *Criminal Code*, except subsection 339(2), (*d*) Part XI of the *Criminal Code*, except sections 438, 440, 441, 446 and 447,

(*e*) Part XII of the *Criminal Code*, except section 454, that is not included in any foregoing portion of this Schedule

25. Any offence that is, in the case of the principal offender, included in any foregoing portion of this Schedule, and for which the fugitive criminal, though not the principal, is liable to be tried or punished as if he were the principal. R.S., c. 27 (1st Supp.), s. 187, Schedule V, item 4.

SCHEDULE II

(*Section 29*)

FORM 1

FORM OF WARRANT OF APPREHENSION

.... ;

To wit:

To all and each of the constables of ....

Whereas it has been shown to the undersigned, a judge under the *Extradition Act*, that .... late of .... is accused (*or* convicted) of the crime of .... within the jurisdiction of ....

This is therefore to command you, in Her Majesty's name, forthwith to apprehend the said .... and to bring that person before me, or any other judge under the said Act, to be further dealt with according to law, for which this shall be your warrant.

Given under my hand and seal at .... this .... day of ...., 19 ....

FORM 2

FORM OF WARRANT OF COMMITTAL

..........;

To wit:

To .... one of the constables of .... and to the keeper of the .... at ....

Be it remembered that on this .... day of ...., 19 .... at .... is brought before me .... a judge under the *Extradition Act*, ... who has been apprehended under that Act, to be dealt with according to law, and as I have determined that that person should be surrendered in pursuance of that Act, on the ground of his being accused (*or* convicted) of the crime of .... within the jurisdiction of ....

This is therefore to command you the said constable, in Her Majesty's name, forthwith to convey and deliver the said .... into the custody of the keeper of the .... at .... and you, the said keeper to receive the said .... into your custody, and safely to keep that person there until thence delivered pursuant to the provisions of the said Act, for which this shall be your warrant.

Given under my hand and seal at .... this .... day of ...., 19 ....

FORM 3

FORM OF ORDER OF MINISTER OF JUSTICE FOR SURRENDER

To the keeper of the .... at .... and to ....

Whereas .... late of .... accused (*or* convicted) of the crime of .... within the jurisdiction of .... was delivered into the custody of you, the keeper of the .... at .... by warrant dated .... pursuant to the *Extradition Act.*

Now I do hereby, in pursuance of the said Act, order you the said keeper, to deliver the said .... into the custody of the said .... , and I command you, the said .... to receive the said .... into your custody, and to convey him within the jurisdiction of the said .... and there place him in the custody of any person or persons (*or* of ....) appointed by the said .... to receive him, for which this shall be your warrant.

Given under the hand and seal of the undersigned Minister of Justice of Canada, this .... day of ...., 19 ....

SCHEDULE III
(*Sections 36, 37 and 39*)

1. Murder, or attempt or conspiracy to murder

2. Manslaughter

3. Counterfeiting or altering money, and uttering counterfeit or altered money

4. Forgery, counterfeiting or altering, or uttering what is forged, counterfeited or altered

5. Larceny or theft

6. Embezzlement

7. Obtaining money or goods or valuable securities, by false pretences

8. Sexual assault, sexual assault with a weapon, threats to a third party or causing bodily harm or aggravated sexual assault

9. Abduction

10. Child stealing

11. Kidnapping

12. Burglary, housebreaking or shop-breaking

13. Arson

14. Robbery

15. Fraud committed by a bailee, banker, agent, factor, trustee or by a member or public officer of any company or municipal corporation, which fraud is made criminal by any law for the time being in force

16. Any malicious act done with intent to endanger persons in a railway train

17. Piracy by municipal law or law of nations committed on board of or against a vessel of a foreign state

18. Criminal scuttling or destruction of a vessel of a foreign state at sea, whether on the high seas or on the Great Lakes of North America, or attempting or conspiring to do so

19. Assault on board a vessel of a foreign state at sea, whether on the high seas or on the Great Lakes of North America, with intent to destroy life or to do grievous bodily harm

20. Revolt, or conspiracy to revolt, by two or more persons, on board a vessel of a foreign state at sea, whether on the high seas or on the Great Lakes of North America, against the authority of the master

21. Administering drugs or using instruments with intent to procure the miscarriage of a woman

22. Any offence that is, in the case of the principal offender, included in any foregoing portion of this Schedule, and for which the fugitive criminal, though not the principal, is liable to be tried or punished as if he were the principal.

FOOD AND DRUGS ACT

TABLE OF CONCORDANCE

R.S.C. 1970, c. F-27	R.S.C. 1985, c. F-27
F-27	**F-27**
1	1
2	2
3	3
4	4
5	5
6	6
6.1	6.1
7	7
8	8
9	9
10	10
11	11
12	12
13	13
14	14
15	15
16	16
17	17
18	18
19	19
20	20
21	21
21.1	part. 22
22	part. 22, 23 part. 24, 25
23	part. 26, 27
23.1	28
24	29
25	30
26	part. 31
27	32
28	33
29	part. 34
30	35
31	part. 36

R.S.C. 1970, c. F-27	R.S.C. 1985, c. F-27
F-27	**F-27**
32	37
33	38
	38.1
34	39
35	40
36	41
37	part. 24, part. 25, part. 26, part. 27, 42-44
37.1	44.1
37.2	44.2
37.3	44.3
37.4	44.4
38	45
39	part. 31, part. 34, part. 36
40	46
41	47
42	48
43	49
44	50
44.1	50.1
44.2	50.2
44.3	50.3
45	51
46	part. 31, part. 34, part. 36
Sch/Ann A-H	Sch/Ann A-H

FOOD AND DRUGS ACT

R.S.C. 1985, c. F-27

An Act respecting food, drugs, cosmetics and therapeutic devices
As amended by R.S. 1985, c. 27 (1st Supp.), ss. 191-195; c. 31 (1st Supp.), s. 11; c. 27 (3rd Supp.), s. 1; c. 42 (4th Supp.) ss. 9-11.

SHORT TITLE

Short title.

1. This Act may be cited as the *Food and Drugs Act.*

INTERPRETATION

Definitions.

2. In this Act,

"advertisement" includes any representation by any means whatever for the purpose of promoting directly or indirectly the sale or disposal of any food, drug, cosmetic or device;

"analyst" means any person designated as an analyst under section 28;

"contraceptive device" means any instrument, apparatus, contrivance or any substance other than a drug, that is manufactured, sold or represented for use in the prevention of conception;

"cosmetic" includes any substance or mixture of substances manufactured, sold or represented for use in cleansing, improving or altering the complexion, skin, hair or teeth, and includes deodorants and perfumes;

"Department" means the Department of National Health and Welfare;

"device" means any article, instrument, apparatus or contrivance, including any component, part or accessory thereof, manufactured, sold or represented for use in

(*a*) the diagnosis, treatment, mitigation or prevention of a disease, disorder or abnormal physical state, or the symptoms thereof, in man or animal,

(*b*) restoring, correcting or modifying a body function or the body structure of man or animal,

(*c*) the diagnosis of pregnancy in humans or animals, or

(*d*) the care of humans or animals during pregnancy and at and after birth of the offspring, including care of the offspring,

and includes a contraceptive device but does not include a drug;

"drug" includes any substance or mixture of substances manufactured, sold or represented for use in

(*a*) the diagnosis, treatment, mitigation or prevention of a disease, disorder, abnormal physical state, or the symptoms thereof, in man or animal,

(*b*) restoring, correcting or modifying organic functions in man or animal, or (*c*) disinfection in premises in which food is manufactured, prepared or kept;

"food" includes any article manufactured, sold or represented for use as food or drink for man, chewing gum, and any ingredient that may be mixed with food for any purpose whatever;

"inspector" means any person designated as an inspector under subsection 22(1), or pursuant to the Department of Consumer and Corporate Affairs Act for the purpose of the enforcement of this Act;

"label" includes any legend, word or mark attached to, included in, belonging to or accompanying any food, drug, cosmetic, device or package;

"Minister" means the Minister of National Health and Welfare;

"package" includes any thing in which any food, drug, cosmetic or device is wholly or partly contained, placed or packed;

"prescribed" means prescribed by the regulations;

"sell" includes offer for sale, expose for sale, have in possession for sale and distribute, whether or not the distribution is made for consideration;

"unsanitary conditions" means such conditions or circumstances as might contaminate a food, drug or cosmetic with dirt or filth, or render injurious to health a food, drug or cosmetic. R.S., c. 27 (1st Supp.), s. 191.

PART I
FOODS, DRUGS, COSMETICS AND DEVICES

General

Prohibited advertising — Prohibited label or advertisement where sale made — Unauthorized advertising of contraceptive device prohibited.

3. (1) No person shall advertise any food, drug, cosmetic or device to the general public as a treatment, preventative or cure for any of the diseases, disorders or abnormal physical states referred to in Schedule A.

(2) No person shall sell any food, drug, cosmetic or device

(*a*) that is represented by label, or

(*b*) that the person advertises to the general public

as a treatment, preventative or cure for any of the diseases, disorders or abnormal physical states referred to in Schedule A.

(3) Except as authorized by regulation, no person shall advertise to the general public any contraceptive device or any drug manufactured, sold or represented for use in the prevention of conception.

Food

Prohibited sales of food.

4. No person shall sell an article of food that

(*a*) has in or on it any poisonous or harmful substance;

(*b*) is unfit for human consumption;
(*c*) consists in whole or in part of any filthy, putrid, disgusting, rotten, decomposed or diseased animal or vegetable substance;
(*d*) is adulterated; or
(*e*) was manufactured, prepared, preserved, packaged or stored under unsanitary conditions.

Deception, etc., regarding food — Food labelled or packaged in contravention of regulations.

5. (1) No person shall label, package, treat, process, sell or advertise any food in a manner that is false, misleading or deceptive or is likely to create an erroneous impression regarding its character, value, quantity, composition, merit or safety.

(2) An article of food that is not labelled or packaged as required by, or is labelled or packaged contrary to, the regulations shall be deemed to be labelled or packaged contrary to subsection (1).

Importation and interprovincial movement of food — Not applicable to carriers — Labelling, etc., of food that is imported or moved interprovincially.

6. (1) Where a standard for a food has been prescribed, no person shall
(*a*) import into Canada,
(*b*) send, convey or receive for conveyance from one province to another, or
(*c*) have in possession for the purpose of sending or conveying from one province to another

any article that is intended for sale and that is likely to be mistaken for such food unless the article complies with the prescribed standard.

(2) Paragraphs (1)(*b*) and (*c*) do not apply to an operator of a conveyance that is used to carry an article or to a carrier of an article whose sole concern, in respect of the article, is the conveyance of the article unless the operator or carrier could, with reasonable diligence, have ascertained that the conveying or receiving for conveyance of the article or the possession of the article for the purpose of conveyance would be in violation of subsection (1).

(3) Where a standard for a food has been prescribed, no person shall label, package, sell or advertise any article that
(*a*) has been imported into Canada,
(*b*) has been sent or conveyed from one province to another, or
(*c*) is intended to be sent or conveyed from one province to another

in such a manner that it is likely to be mistaken for such food unless the article complies with the prescribed standard. R.S., c. 27 (3rd Supp.), s. 1.

Governor in Council may identify standard or portion thereof — Where standard or portion thereof is identified.

6.1 (1) The Governor in Council may, by regulation, identify a standard or any portion of a standard prescribed for a food as being necessary to prevent injury to the health of the consumer or purchaser of the food.

(2) Where a standard or any portion of a standard prescribed for a food is identified by the Governor in Council pursuant to subsection (1), no person shall label, package, sell or advertise any article in such a manner that it is likely to be mistaken for such food unless the article complies with the standard or portion of a standard so identified. R.S., c. 27 (3rd Supp.), s. 1.

Unsanitary manufacture, etc., of food.

7. No person shall manufacture, prepare, preserve, package or store for sale any food under unsanitary conditions.

Drugs

Prohibited sales of drugs.

8. No person shall sell any drug that

(*a*) was manufactured, prepared, preserved, packaged or stored under unsanitary conditions; or

(*b*) is adulterated.

Deception, etc., regarding drugs — Drugs labelled or packaged in contravention of regulations.

9. (1) No person shall label, package, treat, process, sell or advertise any drug in a manner that is false, misleading or deceptive or is likely to create an erroneous impression regarding its character, value, quantity, composition, merit or safety.

(2) A drug that is not labelled or packaged as required by, or is labelled or packaged contrary to, the regulations shall be deemed to be labelled or packaged contrary to subsection (1).

Where standard prescribed for drug — Trade standards — Where no prescribed or trade standard.

10. (1) Where a standard has been prescribed for a drug, no person shall label, package, sell or advertise any substance in such a manner that it is likely to be mistaken for that drug, unless the substance complies with the prescribed standard.

(2) Where a standard has not been prescribed for a drug, but a standard for the drug is contained in any publication referred to in Schedule B, no person shall label, package, sell or advertise any substance in such a manner that

it is likely to be mistaken for that drug, unless the substance complies with the standard.

(3) Where a standard for a drug has not been prescribed and no standard for the drug is contained in any publication referred to in Schedule B, no person shall sell the drug unless

(*a*) it is in accordance with the professed standard under which it is sold; and

(*b*) it does not resemble, in a manner likely to deceive, any drug for which a standard has been prescribed or is contained in any publication referred to in Schedule B.

Unsanitary manufacture, etc., of drug.

11. No person shall manufacture, prepare, preserve, package or store for sale any drug under unsanitary conditions.

Drugs not to be sold unless safe manufacture indicated.

12. No person shall sell any drug described in Schedule C or D unless the Minister has, in prescribed form and manner, indicated that the premises in which the drug was manufactured and the process and conditions of manufacture therein are suitable to ensure that the drug will not be unsafe for use.

Drugs not to be sold unless safe batch indicated.

13. No person shall sell any drug described in Schedule E unless the Minister has, in prescribed form and manner, indicated that the batch from which the drug was taken is not unsafe for use.

Samples — Exception.

14. (1) No person shall distribute or cause to be distributed any drug as a sample.

(2) Subsection (1) does not apply to the distribution, under prescribed conditions, of samples of drugs to physicians, dentists, veterinary surgeons or pharmacists.

Schedule F drugs not to be sold.

15. No person shall sell any drug described in Schedule F.

Cosmetics

Prohibited sales of cosmetics.

16. No person shall sell any cosmetic that

(*a*) has in or on it any substance that may cause injury to the health of the user when the cosmetic is used,

(i) according to the directions on the label or accompanying the cosmetic, or

(ii) for such purposes and by such methods of use as are customary or usual therefor;

(*b*) consists in whole or in part of any filthy or decomposed substance or of any foreign matter; or

(*c*) was manufactured, prepared, preserved, packaged or stored under unsanitary conditions.

Where standard prescribed for cosmetic.

17. Where a standard has been prescribed for a cosmetic, no person shall label, package, sell or advertise any article in such a manner that it is likely to be mistaken for that cosmetic, unless the article complies with the prescribed standard.

Unsanitary conditions.

18. No person shall manufacture, prepare, preserve, package or store for sale any cosmetic under unsanitary conditions.

Devices

Prohibited sales of devices.

19. No person shall sell any device that, when used according to directions or under such conditions as are customary or usual, may cause injury to the health of the purchaser or user thereof.

Deception, etc., regarding devices — Devices labelled or packaged in contravention of regulations.

20. (1) No person shall label, package, treat, process, sell or advertise any device in a manner that is false, misleading or deceptive or is likely to create an erroneous impression regarding its design, construction, performance, intended use, quantity, character, value, composition, merit or safety.

(2) A device that is not labelled or packaged as required by, or is labelled or packaged contrary to, the regulations shall be deemed to be labelled or packaged contrary to subsection (1).

Where standard prescribed for device.

21. Where a standard has been prescribed for a device, no person shall label, package, sell or advertise any article in such a manner that is likely to be mistaken for such device, unless the article complies with the prescribed standard.

PART II
ADMINISTRATION AND ENFORCEMENT

Inspection, Seizure and Forfeiture

Inspectors — Certificate to be produced.

22. (1) The Minister may designate any person as an inspector for the purpose of the enforcement of this Act.

(2) An inspector shall be furnished with a prescribed certificate of his designation as an inspector and on entering any place pursuant to subsection 23(1) an inspector shall, if so required, produce the certificate to the person in charge of that place.

Powers of inspectors — Warrant required to enter dwelling-house — Authority to issue warrant — Use of force — Definition of "article to which this Act or the regulations apply" — Assistance and information to be given inspector.

23. (1) Subject to subsection (1.1), an inspector may at any reasonable time enter any place where the inspector believes on reasonable grounds any article to which this Act or the regulations apply is manufactured, prepared, preserved, packaged or stored, and may

(*a*) examine any such article and take samples thereof, and examine anything that the inspector believes on reasonable grounds is used or capable of being used for that manufacture, preparation, preservation, packaging or storing;

(*a*.1) enter any conveyance that the inspector believes on reasonable grounds is used to carry any article to which section 6 or 6.1 applies and examine any such article found therein and take samples thereof;

(*b*) open and examine any receptacle or package that the inspector believes on reasonable grounds contains any article to which this Act or the regulations apply;

(*c*) examine and make copies of, or extracts from, any books, documents or other records found in any place referred to in this subsection that the inspector believes on reasonable grounds contain any information relevant to the enforcement of this Act with respect to any article to which this Act or the regulations apply and

(*d*) seize and detain for such time as may be necessary any article by means of or in relation to which the inspector believes on reasonable grounds any provision of this Act or the regulations has been contravened.

(1.1) Where any place mentioned in subsection (1) is a dwelling-house, an inspector may not enter that dwelling-house without the consent of the occupant except under the authority of a warrant issued under subsection (1.2).

(1.2) Where on *ex parte* application a justice of the peace is satisfied by information on oath

(*a*) that the conditions for entry described in subsection (1) exist in relation to a dwelling-house, (*b*) that entry to the dwelling-house is necessary for any purpose relating to the administration or enforcement of this Act, and

(*c*) that entry to the dwelling-house has been refused or that there are reasonable grounds for believing that entry thereto will be refused,

the justice of the peace may issue a warrant under his hand authorizing the inspector named therein to enter that dwelling-house subject to such conditions as may be specified in the warrant.

(1.3) In executing a warrant issued under subsection (1.2), the inspector named therein shall not use force unless the inspector is accompanied by a peace officer and the use of force has been specifically authorized in the warrant.

(2) In subsection (1), "article to which this Act or the regulations apply" includes

(*a*) any food, drug, cosmetic or device;

(*b*) anything used for the manufacture, preparation, preservation, packaging or storing thereof; and

(*c*) any labelling or advertising material.

(3) The owner or person in charge of a place entered by an inspector pursuant to subsection (1) and every person found therein shall give the inspector all reasonable assistance and furnish the inspector with any information he may reasonably require. R.S., c. 31 (1st Supp.), s. 11; c. 27 (3rd Supp.), s. 2.

Obstruction and false statements — Interference.

24. (1) No person shall obstruct or hinder, or knowingly make any false or misleading statement either orally or in writing to, an inspector while the inspector is engaged in carrying out his duties or functions under this Act or the regulations.

(2) Except with the authority of an inspector, no person shall remove, alter or interfere in any way with anything seized under this Part.

Storage and removal.

25. Any article seized under this Act may, at the option of an inspector, be kept or stored in the building or place where it was seized or, at the direction of an inspector, the article may be removed to any other proper place.

Release of seized articles.

26. An inspector who has seized any article under this Part shall release it when he is satisfied that all the provisions of this Act and the regulations with respect thereto have been complied with.

Destruction with consent — Forfeiture on conviction — Order for forfeiture on application of inspector.

27. (1) Where an inspector has seized an article under this Part and the owner thereof or the person in whose possession the article was at the time of seizure consents to its destruction, the article is thereupon forfeited to Her

Majesty and may be destroyed or otherwise disposed of as the Minister or the Minister of Consumer and Corporate Affairs may direct.

(2) Where a person has been convicted of a contravention of this Act or the regulations, the court or judge may order that any article by means of or in relation to which the offence was committed, and any thing of a similar nature belonging to or in the possession of the accused or found with the article, be forfeited and, on the making of the order, the article and thing are forfeited to Her Majesty and may be disposed of as the Minister or the Minister of Consumer and Corporate Affairs may direct.

(3) Without prejudice to subsection (2), a judge of a superior, county or district court of the province in which any article is seized under this Part may, on the application of an inspector and on such notice to such persons as the judge directs, order that the article and any thing of a similar nature found therewith be forfeited to Her Majesty, to be disposed of as the Minister or the Minister of Consumer and Corporate Affairs may direct, if the judge finds, after making such inquiry as he considers necessary, that the article is one by means of or in relation to which any of the provisions of this Act or the regulations have been contravened.

Analysis

Analysts.

28. The Minister may designate any person as an analyst for the purpose of the enforcement of this Act.

Analysis and examination — Certificate or report.

29. (1) An inspector may submit to an analyst for analysis or examination, any article seized by the inspector, any sample therefrom or any sample taken by the inspector.

(2) An analyst who has made an analysis or examination may issue a certificate or report setting out the results of the examination or analysis.

Regulations

Regulations — Regulations respecting drugs manufactured outside Canada.

30. (1) The Governor in Council may make regulations for carrying the purposes and provisions of this Act into effect, and, in particular, but without restricting the generality of the foregoing, may make regulations

(*a*) declaring that any food or drug or class of food or drugs is adulterated if any prescribed substance or class of substances is present therein or has been added thereto or extracted or omitted therefrom;

(*b*) respecting

(i) the labelling and packaging and the offering, exposing and advertising for sale of food, drugs, cosmetics and devices,
(ii) the size, dimensions, fill and other specifications of packages of food, drugs, cosmetics and devices,
(iii) the sale or the conditions of sale of any food, drug, cosmetic or device, and
(iv) the use of any substance as an ingredient in any food, drug, cosmetic or device,

to prevent the purchaser or consumer thereof from being deceived or misled in respect of the design, construction, performance, intended use, quantity, character, value, composition, merit or safety thereof, or to prevent injury to the health of the purchaser or consumer;

(*c*) prescribing standards of composition, strength, potency, purity, quality or other property of any article of food, drug, cosmetic or device;

(*d*) respecting the importation of foods, drugs, cosmetics and devices in order to ensure compliance with this Act and the regulations;

(*e*) respecting the method of manufacture, preparation, preserving, packing, storing and testing of any food, drug, cosmetic or device in the interest of, or for the prevention of injury to, the health of the purchaser or consumer;

(*f*) requiring persons who sell food, drugs, cosmetics or devices to maintain such books and records as the Governor in Council considers necessary for the proper enforcement and administration of this Act and the regulations;

(*g*) respecting the form and manner of the Minister's indication under section 12, including the fees payable therefor, and prescribing what premises or what processes or conditions of manufacture, including qualifications of technical staff, shall or shall not be deemed to be suitable for the purposes of that section;

(*h*) requiring manufacturers of any drugs described in Schedule E to submit test portions of any batch of those drugs and respecting the form and manner of the Minister's indication under section 13, including the fees payable therefor;

(*i*) respecting the powers and duties of inspectors and analysts and the taking of samples and the seizure, detention, forfeiture and disposition of articles;

(*j*) exempting any food, drug, cosmetic or device from all or any of the provisions of this Act and prescribing the conditions of the exemption;

(*k*) prescribing forms for the purposes of this Act and the regulations;

(*l*) providing for the analysis of food, drugs or cosmetics other than for the purposes of this Act and prescribing a tariff of fees to be paid for that analysis;

(*m*) adding anything to any of the schedules, in the interest of, or for the prevention of injury to, the health of the purchaser or consumer, or deleting anything therefrom;

(*n*) respecting the distribution or the conditions of distribution of samples of any drug;

(*o*) respecting

(i) the method of manufacture, preparation, preserving, packing, labelling, storing and testing of any new drug, and

(ii) the sale or the conditions of sale of any new drug,

and defining for the purposes of this Act the expression "new drug"; and

(*p*) authorizing the advertising to the general public of contraceptive devices and drugs manufactured, sold or represented for use in the prevention of conception and prescribing the circumstances and conditions under which, and the persons by whom, those devices and drugs may be so advertised.

(2) Without limiting or restricting the authority conferred by any other provisions of this Act or any Part thereof for carrying into effect the purposes and provisions of this Act or any Part thereof, the Governor in Council may make such regulations governing, regulating or prohibiting

(*a*) the importation into Canada of any drug or class of drugs manufactured outside Canada, or

(*b*) the distribution or sale in Canada, or the offering, exposing or having in possession for sale in Canada, of any drug or class of drugs manufactured outside Canada,

as the Governor in Council deems necessary for the protection of the public in relation to the safety and quality of any such drug or class of drugs.

Offences and Punishment

Contravention of Act, except Parts III and IV, or regulations.

31. Every person who contravenes any of the provisions of this Act, except Parts III and IV, or of the regulations made under this Part is guilty of an offence and liable

(*a*) on summary conviction for a first offence to a fine not exceeding five hundred dollars or to imprisonment for a term not exceeding three months or to both and, for a subsequent offence to a fine not exceeding one thousand dollars or to imprisonment for a term not exceeding six months or to both; and

(*b*) on conviction on indictment to a fine not exceeding five thousand dollars or to imprisonment for a term not exceeding three years or to both.

Limitation period.

32. A prosecution under paragraph 31(*a*) may be instituted at any time within but not later than twelve months from the time the subject-matter of the prosecution arose.

Venue.

33. A prosecution for a contravention of this Act or the regulations may be instituted, heard, tried or determined in the place in which the offence was committed or the subject-matter of the prosecution arose or in any place in which the accused is apprehended or happens to be.

Want of knowledge — Notice of reliance on want of knowledge.

34. (1) Subject to subsection (2), in a prosecution for the sale of any article in contravention of this Act, except Parts III and IV, or of the regulations made under this Part, if the accused proves to the satisfaction of the court or judge that

(*a*) the accused purchased the article from another person in packaged form and sold it in the same package and in the same condition the article was in at the time it was so purchased, and

(*b*) that the accused could not with reasonable diligence have ascertained that the sale of the article would be in contravention of this Act or the regulations,

the accused shall be acquitted.

(2) Subsection (1) does not apply in any prosecution unless the accused, at least ten days before the day fixed for the trial, has given to the prosecutor notice in writing that the accused intends to avail himself of the provisions of subsection (1) and has disclosed to the prosecutor the name and address of the person from whom the accused purchased the article and the date of purchase.

Certificate of analyst — Requiring attendance of analyst — Notice of intention to produce certificate — Proof of service — Attendance for examination.

35. (1) Subject to this section, in any prosecution for an offence under section 31 or an offence referred to in subsection 41(1) or 50(1), a certificate purporting to be signed by an analyst and stating that an article, sample or substance has been submitted to, and analyzed or examined by, the analyst and stating the results of the analysis or examination is admissible in evidence and, in the absence of evidence to the contrary, is proof of the statements contained in the certificate without proof of the signature or official character of the person appearing to have signed the certificate.

(2) The party against whom a certificate of an analyst is produced pursuant to subsection (1) may, with leave of the court, require the attendance of the analyst for the purposes of cross-examination.

(3) No certificate shall be admitted in evidence pursuant to subsection (1) unless, before the trial, the party intending to produce the certificate has given reasonable notice of that intention, together with a copy of the certificate, to the party against whom it is intended to be produced.

(4) For the purposes of this Act, service of any certificate referred to in subsection (1) may be proved by oral evidence given under oath by, or by the affidavit or solemn declaration of, the person claiming to have served it.

(5) Notwithstanding subsection (4), the court may require the person who appears to have signed an affidavit or solemn declaration referred to in that subsection to appear before it for examination or cross-examination in respect of the issue of proof of service. R.S. 1985, c. 27 (1st Supp.), s. 192.

Proof as to manufacturer or packager — Offence by employee or agent — Certified copies and extracts — Where accused had adulterating substances.

36. (1) In a prosecution for a contravention of this Act, except Parts III and IV, or of the regulations under this Part, proof that a package containing any article to which this Act or the regulations apply bore a name or address purporting to be the name or address of the person by whom it was manufactured or packaged is, in the absence of evidence to the contrary, proof that the article was manufactured or packaged, as the case may be, by the person whose name or address appeared on the package.

(2) In a prosecution for a contravention described in subsection (1), it is sufficient proof of the offence to establish that it was committed by an employee or agent of the accused whether or not the employee or agent is identified or has been prosecuted for the offence.

(3) In a prosecution for a contravention described in subsection (1), a copy of a record or an extract therefrom certified to be a true copy by the inspector who made it pursuant to paragraph 23(1)(*c*) is admissible in evidence and is, in the absence of evidence to the contrary, proof of its contents.

(4) Where a person is prosecuted under this Part for having manufactured an adulterated food or drug for sale, and it is established that the person had in his possession or on his premises any substance the addition of which to that food or drug has been declared by regulation to cause the adulteration of the food or drug, the onus of proving that the food or drug was not adulterated by the addition of that substance lies on the accused.

Exports

Conditions under which exports exempt — Definition of "drug".

37. (1) This Act does not apply to any packaged food, drug, cosmetic or device, not manufactured for consumption in Canada and not sold for consumption in Canada, if the package is marked in distinct overprinting with the word "Export" and a certificate that the package and its contents do not contravene any known requirement of the law of the country to which it is or is about to be consigned has been issued in respect thereof in prescribed form and manner.

(2) In subsection (1), "drug" does not include a drug or other substance defined as a controlled drug by Part III or as a restricted drug by Part IV.

PART III
CONTROLLED DRUGS

Definitions.

38. In this Part,

"controlled drug" means any drug or other substance included in Schedule G;

"possession" means possession within the meaning of subsection 4(3) of the *Criminal Code*;

"practitioner" means a person who is registered and entitled under the laws of a province to practise in that province the profession of medicine, dentistry or veterinary medicine;

"prescription" means, in respect of a controlled drug, an authorization given by a practitioner that a stated amount of the controlled drug be dispensed for the person named therein;

"traffic" means to manufacture, sell, export from or import into Canada, transport or deliver, otherwise than under the authority of this Part or the regulations. R.S. 1985, c. 27 (1st Supp.), s. 193.

Failure to disclose previous prescriptions — Offence and punishment — Limitation period.

38.1 (1) No person shall, at any time, seek or obtain a controlled drug or a prescription for a controlled drug from a practitioner unless that person discloses to the practitioner particulars of every controlled drug or prescription for a controlled drug issued to that person by a different practitioner within the preceding thirty days.

(2) Every person who contravenes subsection (1)

(*a*) is guilty of an indictable offence and is liable to a fine not exceeding five thousand dollars or to imprisonment for a term not exceeding three years; or

(*b*) is guilty of an offence punishable on summary conviction and is liable

(i) for a first offence, to a fine not exceeding one thousand dollars or to imprisonment for a term not exceeding six months, and

(ii) for a subsequent offence, to a fine not exceeding two thousand dollars or to imprisonment for a term not exceeding one year.

(3) Summary conviction proceedings in respect of an offence under this section may be instituted at any time within but not later than one year from the time when the subject-matter of the proceedings arose. R.S. 1985, c. 27 (1st Supp), s. 194.

Trafficking in controlled drug — Possession for trafficking — Offence and punishment.

39. (1) No person shall traffic in a controlled drug or any substance represented or held out by the person to be a controlled drug.

(2) No person shall have in possession any controlled drug for the purpose of trafficking.

(3) Every person who contravenes subsection (1) or (2) is guilty of an offence and liable

(*a*) on summary conviction, to imprisonment for a term not exceeding eighteen months; or

(*b*) on conviction on indictment, to imprisonment for a term not exceeding ten years.

Procedure in prosecution for possession for trafficking — Procedure on finding in respect of possession — Acquittal on conviction.

40. (1) In any prosecution for a contravention of subsection 39(2), if the accused does not plead guilty, the trial shall proceed as if the issue to be tried is whether the accused was in possession of a controlled drug.

(2) If, pursuant to subsection (1), the court finds that the accused was not in possession of a controlled drug, the accused shall be acquitted but, if the court finds that the accused was in possession of a controlled drug, the accused shall be given an opportunity of establishing that he was not in possession of the controlled drug for the purpose of trafficking and, thereafter, the prosecutor shall be given an opportunity of adducing evidence to the contrary.

(3) If the accused establishes, pursuant to subsection (2), that he was not in possession of the controlled drug for the purpose of trafficking, the accused shall be acquitted of the offence as charged and, if the accused fails to so establish, the accused shall be convicted of the offence as charged and sentenced accordingly.

Setting out or negativing exception, etc., not required — Burden of proving exception, etc.

41. (1) No exception, exemption, excuse or qualification prescribed by law is required to be set out or negatived, as the case may be, in an information or indictment for an offence under section 39 or under section 463, 464 or 465 of the *Criminal Code* in respect of an offence under section 39.

(2) In any prosecution under this Part, the burden of proving that an exception, exemption, excuse or qualification prescribed by law operates in favour of the accused is on the accused, and the prosecutor is not required, except by way of rebuttal, to prove that the exception, exemption, excuse or qualification does not operate in favour of the accused, whether or not it is set out in the information or indictment.

Entry and search — Search of person and seizure — Warrant to search dwelling-house — Writ of assistance — Powers of peace officer — Application for restoration — Order of immediate restoration — Order of restoration at later time — Where application not made or order refused.

42. (1) A peace officer may, at any time, without a warrant enter and search any place other than a dwelling-house, and under the authority of a warrant issued under subsection (3), enter and search any dwelling-house in which the peace officer believes on reasonable grounds there is a controlled drug by means of or in respect of which an offence under this Part has been committed.

(2) A peace officer may search any person found in a place entered pursuant to subsection (1) and may seize and take away any controlled drug found in that place and any other thing that may be evidence that an offence under this Part has been committed.

(3) A justice who is satisfied by information on oath that there are reasonable grounds for believing that there is a controlled drug, by means of or in respect of which an offence under this Part has been committed, in any dwelling-house may issue a warrant under his hand authorizing a peace officer named therein at any time to enter the dwelling-house and search for controlled drugs.

(4) [Repealed R.S. 1985, c. 27 (1st Supp.), s. 195(2).]

(5) For the purpose of exercising authority under this section, a peace officer may, with such assistance as that officer deems necessary, break open any door, window, lock, fastener, floor, wall, ceiling, compartment, plumbing fixture, box, container or any other thing. R.S. 1985, c. 27 (1st Supp.), s. 195.

Application for restoration — Order of immediate restoration — Order of restoration at later time — Where aplication not made or order refused.

43. (1) Where a controlled drug or other thing has been seized under this section, any person may, within two months after the date of the seizure, where prior notification has been given to the Crown in the manner prescribed by the regulations, apply to a provincial court judge within whose territorial jurisdiction the seizure was made for an order of restoration under subsection (2).

(2) Subject to section 44, where, on the hearing of an application made under subsection (1), the provincial court judge is satisfied that the applicant is entitled to possession of the controlled drug or other thing seized, and that the thing seized is not or will not be required as evidence in any proceedings in respect of an offence under this Part, he shall order that the thing seized be restored forthwith to the applicant.

(3) Where on the hearing of an application made under subsection (1) the provincial court judge is satisfied that the applicant is entitled to possession of the thing seized but is not satisfied that the thing is not or will not be required as evidence in any proceedings in respect of an offence under this Part, he shall order that the thing seized be restored to the applicant

(*a*) on the expiration of four months after the date of seizure, if no proceedings in respect of an offence under this Part have been commenced before that time; or

(*b*) on the final conclusion of any such proceedings, in any other case.

(4) Where no application has been made for the return of any controlled drug or other thing seized pursuant to this section within two months after the date of the seizure, or an application therefor has been made but on the

hearing thereof no order of restoration is made, the thing so seized shall be delivered to the Minister, who may make such disposition thereof as the Minister sees fit. R.S. 1985, c. 27 (1st Supp.), s. 203; 1988, c. 51, s. 9.

Forfeiture on conviction.

44. Where a person has been convicted of an offence under this Part, any controlled drug seized pursuant to subsection 42(2) by means of or in respect of which the offence was committed and any money so seized that was used for the purchase of that controlled drug is forfeited to Her Majesty and shall be disposed of as the Minister directs.

Interpretation.

44.1 For the purposes of sections 44.2 to 44.4, a reference therein to an offence under section 39, 44.2 or 44.3 shall be deemed to include a reference to a conspiracy or an attempt to commit, being an accessory after the fact in relation to, or any counselling in relation to, such an offence. R.S. 1985, c. 42 (4th Supp.), s. 9.

Possession of property obtained by trafficking in controlled drugs — Punishment.

44.2 (1) No person shall possess any property or any proceeds of any property knowing that all or part of the property or of those proceeds was obtained or derived directly or indirectly as a result of

(*a*) the commission in Canada of an offence under section 39; or

(*b*) an act or omission anywhere that, if it had occurred in Canada, would have constituted an offence under section 39.

(2) Every person who contravenes subsection (1)

(*a*) is guilty of an indictable offence and is liable to imprisonment for a term not exceeding ten years, where the value of the subject-matter of the offence exceeds one thousand dollars; or

(*b*) is guilty

(i) of an indictable offence and is liable to imprisonment for a term not exceeding two years, or

(ii) of an offence punishable on summary conviction,

where the value of the subject-matter of the offence does not exceed one thousand dollars. R.S. 1985, c. 42 (4th Supp.), s. 9.

Laundering proceeds of trafficking in controlled drugs — Punishment.

44.3 (1) No person shall use, transfer the possession of, send or deliver to any person or place, transport, transmit, alter, dispose of or otherwise deal with, in any manner or by any means, any property or any proceeds of any property with intent to conceal or convert that property or those proceeds and knowing that all or a part of that property or of those proceeds was obtained or derived directly or indirectly as a result of

(*a*) the commission in Canada of an offence under section 39; or (*b*) an act or omission anywhere that, if it had occurred in Canada, would have constituted an offence under section 39.

(2) Every person who contravenes subsection (1)
(*a*) is guilty of an indictable offence and is liable to imprisonment for a term not exceeding ten years; or
(*b*) is guilty of an offence punishable on summary conviction. R.S. 1985, c. 42 (4th Supp.), s. 9.

Part XII.1 and Part XII.2 of the *Criminal Code* applicable — Idem.

44.4 (1) Sections 462.3 and 462.32 to 462.5 of the *Criminal Code* apply, with such modifications as the circumstances require, in respect of proceedings for an offence under section 39, 44.2 or 44.3.

(2) For the purposes of subsection (1),
(*a*) a reference in section 462.37 or 462.38 or subsection 462.41(2) of the *Criminal Code* to an enterprise crime offence shall be deemed to be a reference to an offence under section 39, 44.2 or 44.3; and
(*b*) a reference, in relation to the manner in which forfeited property is to be disposed of, in subsection 462.37(1) or 462.38(2), paragraph 462.43(*c*) or section 462.5 of the *Criminal Code*, to the Attorney General shall be deemed to be a reference to the Minister. R.S. 1985, c. 42 (4th Supp.), s. 9.

Regulations respecting controlled drugs — Amendment of Schedule G.

45. (1) The Governor in Council may make regulations for carrying out the purposes and provisions of this Part, and, in particular, but without restricting the generality of the foregoing, may make regulations
(*a*) authorizing the manufacture, sale, importation, transportation, delivery or other dealing in controlled drugs and prescribing the circumstances and conditions under which, and the persons by whom, controlled drugs may be manufactured, sold, imported, transported, delivered, or otherwise dealt in;
(*b*) providing for the issue of licences for the importation, manufacture or sale of controlled drugs;
(*c*) prescribing the form, duration and terms and conditions of any licence described in paragraph (*b*) and the fees payable therefor, and providing for the cancellation and suspension of those licences;
(*d*) requiring persons who import, manufacture, sell, administer or deal in controlled drugs to maintain such books and records as the Governor in Council considers necessary for the proper administration and enforcement of this Part and the regulations made under this Part and to make such returns and furnish such information relating to the said controlled drugs as the Governor in Council may require;
(*e*) authorizing the communication of any information obtained under this Part or the regulations to provincial professional licensing authorities; and
(*f*) prescribing a fine not exceeding five hundred dollars or a term of

imprisonment not exceeding six months, or both, to be imposed upon summary conviction as a penalty for the contravention of any regulation.

(2) The Governor in Council may, amend Schedule G by adding thereto or deleting therefrom any substance, the inclusion or exclusion of which, as the case may be, is deemed necessary by the Governor in Council in the public interest.

PART IV
RESTRICTED DRUGS

Definitions.

46. In this Part,

"possession" means possession within the meaning of subsection 4(3) of the *Criminal Code*;

"regulations" means regulations made as provided for by or under section 51;

"restricted drug" means any drug or other substance included in Schedule H;

"traffic" means to manufacture, sell, export from or import into Canada, transport or deliver, otherwise than under the authority of this Part or the regulations.

Possession of restricted drug — Offence.

47. (1) Except as authorized by this Part or the regulations, no person shall have a restricted drug in his possession.

(2) Every person who contravenes subsection (1) is guilty of an offence and liable

(*a*) on summary conviction for a first offence, to a fine not exceeding one thousand dollars or to imprisonment for a term not exceeding six months, or to both and, for a subsequent offence, to a fine two thousand dollars or to imprisonment for a term not exceeding one year or to both; or

(*b*) on conviction on indictment, to a fine not exceeding five thousand dollars or to imprisonment for a term not exceeding three years or to both.

Trafficking in restricted drug — Possession for trafficking — Offence.

48. (1) No person shall traffic in a restricted drug or any substance represented or held out by the person to be a restricted drug.

(2) No person shall have in possession any restricted drug for the purpose of trafficking.

(3) Every person who contravenes subsection (1) or (2) is guilty of an offence and liable

(*a*) on summary conviction, to imprisonment for a term not exceeding eighteen months; or

(*b*) on conviction on indictment, to imprisonment for a term not exceeding ten years.

Procedure in prosecution for possession for trafficking — Procedure on finding in respect of possession — Acquittal and conviction.

49. (1) In any prosecution for a contravention of subsection 48(2), if the accused does not plead guilty, the trial shall proceed as if the issue to be tried is whether the accused was in possession of a restricted drug contrary to subsection 47(1).

(2) If, pursuant to subsection (1), the court finds that the accused was not in possession of a restricted drug contrary to subsection 47(1), the accused shall be acquitted but, if the court finds that the accused was in possession of a restricted drug contrary to subsection 47(1), the accused shall be given an opportunity of establishing that he was not in possession of the restricted drug for the purpose of trafficking, and thereafter, the prosecutor shall be given an opportunity of adducing evidence to the contrary.

(3) If the accused establishes, pursuant to subsection (2), that he was not in possession of the restricted drug for the purpose of trafficking, the accused shall be acquitted of the offence as charged but shall be convicted of an offence under subsection 47(1) and sentenced accordingly, and if the accused fails to so establish, the accused shall be convicted of the offence as charged and sentenced accordingly.

Setting out or negativing exception, etc., not required — Burden of proving exception, etc.

50. (1) No exception, exemption, excuse or qualification prescribed by law is required to be set out or negatived, as the case may be, in an information or indictment for an offence under this Part or under section 463, 464 or 465 of the *Criminal Code* in respect of an offence under this Part.

(2) In any prosecution under this Part, the burden of proving that an exception, exemption, excuse or qualification prescribed by law operates in favour of the accused is on the accused, and the prosecutor is not required, except by way of rebuttal, to prove that the exception, exemption, excuse or qualification does not operate in favour of the accused, whether or not it is set out in the information or indictment.

Interpretation.

50.1 For the purposes of section 44.4, as that section is applicable in respect of this Part by virtue of section 51, and sections 50.2 to 51, a reference therein to an offence under section 48, 50.2 or 50.3 shall be deemed to include a reference to a conspiracy or an attempt to commit, being an accessory after the fact in relation to, or any counselling in relation to, such an offence. R.S. 1985, c. 42 (4th Supp.), s. 10.

Possession of property obtained by trafficking in restricted drugs — Punishment.

50.2 (1) No person shall possess any property or any proceeds of any property knowing that all or part of the property or of those proceeds was obtained or derived directly or indirectly as a result of

(*a*) the commission in Canada of an offence under section 48; or

(*b*) an act or omission anywhere that, if it had occurred in Canada, would have constituted an offence under section 48.

(2) Every person who contravenes subsection (1)

(*a*) is guilty of an indictable offence and is liable to imprisonment for a term not exceeding ten years, where the value of the subject-matter of the offence exceeds one thousand dollars; or

(*b*) is guilty

(i) of an indictable offence and is liable to imprisonment for a term not exceeding two years, or

(ii) of an offence punishable on summary conviction,

where the value of the subject-matter of the offence does not exceed one thousand dollars. R.S. 1985, c. 42 (4th Supp.), s. 10.

Laundering proceeds of trafficking in restricted drugs — Punishment.

50.3 (1) No person shall use, transfer the possession of, send or deliver to any person or place, transport, transmit, alter, dispose of or otherwise deal with, in any manner or by any means, any property or any proceeds of any property with intent to conceal or convert that property or those proceeds and knowing that all or a part of that property or of those proceeds was obtained or derived directly or indirectly as a result of

(*a*) the commission in Canada of an offence under section 48; or

(*b*) an act or omission anywhere that, if it had occurred in Canada, would have constituted an offence under section 48.

(2) Every person who contravenes subsection (1)

(*a*) is guilty of an indictable offence and is liable to imprisonment for a term not exceeding ten years; or

(*b*) is guilty of an offence punishable on summary conviction. R.S. 1985, c. 42 (4th Supp.), s. 10.

Application of certain provisions of Part III — Modification for purpose of application — Additional regulations.

51. (1) Sections 42 to 44, 44.4 and 45 apply in respect of this Part.

(2) For the purposes of subsection (1),

(*a*) there shall be substituted for the expression "controlled drug", wherever it appears in any of the sections referred to in that subsection, the expression "restricted drug";

(*b*) a reference in any of those sections and

(i) to "Schedule G" shall be deemed to be a reference to Schedule H, and

(ii) to "this Part" shall be deemed to be a reference to Part IV; and (*c*) a reference in section 44.4 or in a provision of the *Criminal Code* mentioned therein

(i) to "an offence under section 39, 44.2 or 44.3" shall be deemed to be a reference under section 48, 50.2 or 50.3, and

(ii) to "this Part" shall be deemed to be a reference to Part IV.

(3) In addition to the regulations provided for by subsection (1), the Governor in Council may make regulations authorizing the possession or export of restricted drugs and prescribing the circumstances and conditions under which, and the persons by whom restricted drugs may be had in possession or exported. R.S. 1985, c. 42 (4th Supp.), s. 11.

SCHEDULE G

(*Sections 30, 38, 45 and 51*)

Amphetamine and its salts
Barbituric acid and its salts and derivatives
Benzphetamine and its salts
Butorphanol and its salts
Chlorphentermine and its salts
Diethylpropion and its salts
Methamphetamine and its salts
Methaqualone and its salts
Methylphenidate and its salts
Nalbuphine and its salts
Phendimetrazine and its salts
Phenmetrazine and its salts
Phentermine and its salts
Thiobarbituric acid and its salts and derivatives

SCHEDULE H

(*Sections 30, 46 and 51*)

Lysergic acid diethylamide (LSD) or any salt thereof
N,N-Diethyltryptamine (DET) or any salt thereof
N,N-Dimethyltryptamine (DMT) or any salt thereof
4-Methyl-2,5-dimethoxyamphetamine (STP(DOM)) or any salt thereof
3,4-methylenedioxyamphetamine (MDA) or any salt thereof
N-methyl-3-piperidyl benzilate (LBJ) or any salt thereof
2,3-dimethoxyamphetamine or any salt thereof
2,4-dimethoxyamphetamine or any salt thereof
2,5-dimethoxyamphetamine or any salt thereof
2,6-dimethoxyamphetamine or any salt thereof
3,4-dimethoxyamphetamine or any salt thereof

3,5-dimethoxyamphetamine or any salt thereof

4,9-dihydro-7-methoxy-1-methyl-3H-pyrido (3,4-b) indole (Harmaline) and any salt thereof

4,9-dihydro-1-methyl-3H-pyrido (3,4-b) indol-7-ol (Harmalol) and any salt thereof

4-methoxyamphetamine or any salt thereof

3-[2-(Dimethylamino) ethyl]-4-hydroxyindole (Psilocin) or any salt thereof

3-[2-(Dimethylamino) ethyl]-4-phosphoryloxyindole (Psilocybin) or any salt thereof

2,4,5-Trimethoxyamphetamine or any salt, isomer, or salt of isomer, thereof

3,4-methylenedioxy-N-methylamphetamine or any salt thereof

N-(1-phenycyclohexyl) ethylamine or any salt thereof

4-bromo-2, 5-dimethoxyamphetamine or any salt thereof

1-[1-(2-thienyl) cyclohexyl] piperidine and its salts

1-phenyl-N-propylcyclohexanamine or any salt thereof

3,4,5-trimethoxybenzeneethanamine (Mescaline) or any salt thereof but not including peyote (lophophora)

4-ethoxy-2, 5-dimethoxy-α-methylbenzeneethanamine or any salt, isomer, or salt of isomer, thereof

7-methoxy-α-methyl-1,3-benzodioxole-5-ethanamine (MMDA) or any salt, isomer or salt of isomer thereof

N,N,-α-trimethyl-1,3-benzodioxole-5-ethanamine or any salt, isomer or salt of isomer thereof

N-ethyl-α-methyl-1,3-benzodioxole-5-ethanamine or any salt, isomer or salt of isomer thereof

4-ethyl-2,5-dimethoxy-α-methylbenzeneethanamine (DOET) or any salt, isomer or salt of isomer thereof

4-ethoxy-α-methylbenzeneethanamine or any salt, isomer or salt of isomer thereof

4-chloro-2,5-dimethoxy-α-methylbenzeneethanamine or any salt, isomer or salt of isomer thereof

4,5-dihydro-4-methyl-5-phenyl-2-oxazolamine (4-methylaminorex) or any salt thereof

N-ethyl-α-methylbenzeneethanamine or any salt thereof

α-methyl-N-propyl-1, 3-benzodioxole-5-ethanamine or any salt, isomer or salt of isomer thereof

1-[1-(phenylmethyl)cyclohexyl]piperidine or any salt, isomer or salt of isomer thereof

1-[1-(4-methylphenyl)]cyclohexylpiperidine or any salt, isomer or salt of isomer thereof

2-methylamino-1-phenyl-1-propanone or any salt thereof

IDENTIFICATION OF CRIMINALS ACT

TABLE OF CONCORDANCE

R.S.C. 1970, c. I-1	R.S.C. 1985, c. I-1
I-1	**I-1**
1	1
2	2
3	3

ICA

IDENTIFICATION OF CRIMINALS ACT

R.S.C. 1985, c. I-1

An Act respecting the identification of criminals

SHORT TITLE

Short title.

1. This Act may be cited as the *Identification of Criminals Act*.

IDENTIFICATION OF CRIMINALS

Bertillon Signaletic System — Use of force — Publication of cards.

2. (1) Any person who is in lawful custody, charged with, or under conviction of an indictable offence, or who has been apprehended under the *Extradition Act* or the *Fugitive Offenders Act*, may be subjected, by or under the direction of those in whose custody the person is, to

(*a*) the measurements, processes and operations practised under the system for the identification of criminals commonly known as the Bertillon Signaletic System; or

(*b*) any measurements, processes or operations sanctioned by the Governor in Council that have the same object as the measurements, processes and operations practised under the Bertillon Signaletic System.

(2) Such force may be used as is necessary to the effectual carrying out and application of the measurements, processes and operations described under subsection (1).

(3) The signaletic cards and other results of the measurements, processes and operations to which a person has been subjected pursuant to subsection (1) may be published for the purpose of affording information to officers and others engaged in the execution or administration of the law.

No liability for acting under Act.

3. No liability, civil or criminal, for anything lawfully done under this Act shall be incurred by any person

(*a*) having custody of a person described in subsection 2(1);

(*b*) acting in the aid or under the direction of a person having such custody; or

(*c*) concerned in the publication of signaletic cards and other results under subsection 2(3).

INTERPRETATION ACT

TABLE OF CONCORDANCE

R.S.C. 1970, c. I-23	R.S.C. 1985, c. I-21	R.S.C. 1970, c. I-23	R.S.C. 1985 c. I-21
I-23	**I-21**	**I-23**	**I-21**
1	1	24	25
2	2	25	26
3	3	25	27
4	4	25	28
5	5	25	29
6	6	25	30
7	7	26	31
8	8	26	32
9	9	26	33
10	10	27	34
11	12	28	11, 25, 35, part. 37
12	13	28.1	39
13	14	29	36
14	15	30	38
15	16	31	part. 37
16	17	32	40
17	18	33	41
18	19	34	42
19	20	35	43
20	21	36	44
21	22	37	45
22	23	38	46
23	24	Sch/Ann	Sch/Ann

IA

INTERPRETATION ACT

R.S.C. 1985, c. I-21

An Act respecting the interpretation of statutes and regulations
As amended by R.S. 1985, c. 11 (1st Supp.), s. 2; c. 27 (2nd Supp.), s. 10; SOR/86-532 (Gaz. 28/5/86, p. 2197); 1990, c. 17, s. 26; 1992, c. 1, ss. 87-91

SHORT TITLE

Short title.

1. This Act may be cited as the *Interpretation Act.*

INTERPRETATION

Definitions — Expired enactment.

2. (1) In this Act,

"Act" means an Act of Parliament;

"enact" includes to issue, make or establish;

"enactment" means an Act or regulation or any portion of an Act or regulation;

"public officer" includes any person in the public service of Canada who is authorized by or under an enactment to do or enforce the doing of an act or thing or to exercise a power, or on whom a duty is imposed by or under an enactment;

"regulation" includes an order, regulation, rule, rule of court, form, tariff of costs or fees, letters patent, commission, warrant, proclamation, by-law, resolution or other instrument issued, made or established

(*a*) in the execution of a power conferred by or under the authority of an Act, or

(*b*) by or under the authority of the Governor in Council;

"repeal" includes revoke or cancel.

(2) For the purposes of this Act, an enactment that has expired or lapsed or otherwise ceased to have effect shall be deemed to have been repealed.

APPLICATION

Application — Application to this Act — Rules of construction not excluded.

3. (1) Every provision of this Act applies, unless a contrary intention appears, to every enactment, whether enacted before or after the commencement of this Act.

(2) The provisions of this Act apply to the interpretation of this Act.

(3) Nothing in this Act excludes the application to an enactment of a rule of construction applicable to that enactment and not inconsistent with this Act.

ENACTING CLAUSE OF ACTS

Enacting clause — Order of clauses.

4. (1) The enacting clause of an Act may be in the following form:

"Her Majesty, by and with the advice and consent of the Senate and House of Commons of Canada, enacts as follows:".

(2) The enacting clause of an Act shall follow the preamble, if any, and the various provisions within the purview or body of the Act shall follow in a concise and enunciative form.

OPERATION

Royal Assent

Royal assent — Date of commencement — Commencement provision — Commencement when no date fixed.

5. (1) The Clerk of the Parliaments shall endorse on every Act, immediately after its title, the day, month and year when the Act was assented to in Her Majesty's name and the endorsement shall be a part of the Act.

(2) If no date of commencement is provided for in an Act, the date of commencement of that Act is the date of assent to the Act.

(3) Where an Act contains a provision that the Act or any portion thereof is to come into force on a day later than the date of assent to the Act, that provision is deemed to have come into force on the date of assent to the Act.

(4) Where an Act provides that certain provisions thereof are to come or are deemed to have come into force on a day other than the date of assent to the Act, the remaining provisions of the Act are deemed to have come into force on the date of assent to the Act.

Day Fixed for Commencement or Repeal

Operation when date fixed for commencement or repeal — When no date fixed — Judicial notice.

6. (1) Where an enactment is expressed to come into force on a particular day, it shall be construed as coming into force on the expiration of the previous day, and where an enactment is expressed to expire, lapse or otherwise cease to have effect on a particular day, it shall be construed as ceasing to have effect upon the commencement of the following day.

(2) Every enactment that is not expressed to come into force on a particular day shall be construed as coming into force

(*a*) in the case of an Act, on the expiration of the day immediately before the day the Act was assented to in Her Majesty's name; and

(*b*) in the case of a regulation, on the expiration of the day immediately before the day the regulation was registered pursuant to section 6 of the *Statutory Instruments Act* or, if the regulation is of a class that is exempted from the application of subsection 5(1) of that Act, on the expiration of the day immediately before the day the regulation was made.

(3) Judicial notice shall be taken of a day for the coming into force of an enactment that is fixed by a regulation that has been published in the *Canada Gazette*. 1992, c. 1, s. 87.

Regulation Prior to Commencement

Preliminary proceedings.

7. Where an enactment is not in force and it contains provisions conferring power to make regulations or do any other thing, that power may, for the purpose of making the enactment effective on its commencement, be exercised at any time before its commencement, but a regulation so made or a thing so done has no effect until the commencement of the enactment except in so far as may be necessary to make the enactment effective on its commencement.

Territorial Operation

Territorial operation — Amending enactment — Extra-territorial operation.

8. (1) Every enactment applies to the whole of Canada, unless a contrary intention is expressed in the enactment.

(2) Where an enactment that does not apply to the whole of Canada is amended, no provision in the amending enactment applies to any part of Canada to which the amended enactment does not apply, unless it is provided in the amending enactment that it applies to that part of Canada or to the whole of Canada.

(3) Every Act now in force enacted prior to December 11, 1931 that expressly or by necessary or reasonable implication was intended, as to the whole or any part thereof, to have extra-territorial operation shall be construed as if, at the date of its enactment the Parliament of Canada had full power to make laws having extra-territorial operation as provided by the *Statute of Westminster, 1931*.

RULES OF CONSTRUCTION

Private Acts

Provisions in private Acts.

9. No provision in a private Act affects the rights of any person, except only as therein mentioned or referred to.

Law Always Speaking

Law always speaking.

10. The law shall be considered as always speaking, and where a matter or thing is expressed in the present tense, it shall be applied to the circumstances as they arise, so that effect may be given to the enactment according to its true spirit, intent and meaning.

Imperative and Permissive Construction

"Shall" and "may".

11. The expression "shall" is to be construed as imperative and the expression "may" as permissive.

Enactments Remedial

Enactments deemed remedial.

12. Every enactment shall be deemed remedial, and shall be given such fair, large and liberal construction and interpretation as best ensures the attainment of its objects.

Preambles and Marginal Notes

Preamble.

13. The preamble of an enactment shall be read as a part of the enactment intended to assist in explaining its purport and object.

Marginal notes and historical references.

14. Marginal notes and references to former enactments that appear after the end of a section or other division in an enactment form no part of the enactment, but are inserted for convenience of reference only.

Application of Interpretation Provisions

Application of definitions and interpretation rules — Interpretation sections subject to exceptions.

15. (1) Definitions or rules of interpretation in an enactment apply to all of the provisions of the enactment, including the provisions that contain those definitions or rules of interpretation.

(2) Where an enactment contains an interpretation section or provision, it shall be read and construed

(*a*) as being applicable only if a contrary intention does not appear, and

(*b*) as being applicable to all other enactments relating to the same subject-matter unless a contrary intention appears.

Words in regulations.

16. Where an enactment confers power to make regulations, expressions used in the regulations have the same respective meanings as in the enactment conferring the power.

Her Majesty

Her Majesty not bound or affected unless stated.

17. No enactment is binding on Her Majesty or affects Her Majesty or Her Majesty's rights or prerogatives in any manner, except only as therein mentioned or referred to in the enactment.

Proclamations

Proclamation — Proclamation to be issued on advice — Effective date of proclamations.

18. (1) Where an enactment authorizes the issue of a proclamation, the proclamation shall be understood to be a proclamation of the Governor in Council.

(2) Where the Governor General is authorized to issue a proclamation, the proclamation shall be understood to be a proclamation issued under an order of the Governor in Council, but it is not necessary to mention in the proclamation that it is issued under such an order.

(3) A proclamation that is issued under an order of the Governor in Council may purport to have been issued on the day of the order or on any subsequent day and, if so, takes effect on that day. 1992, c. 1, s. 88.

Oaths

Administration of oaths — Where justice of peace empowered.

19. (1) Where by an enactment or by a rule of the Senate or House of Commons, evidence under oath is authorized or required to be taken, or an oath is authorized or directed to be made, taken or administered, the oath may be administered, and a certificate of its having been made, taken or administered may be given by

(*a*) any person authorized by the enactment or rule to take the evidence; or

(*b*) a judge of any court, a notary public, a justice of the peace, or a commissioner for taking affidavits, having authority or jurisdiction within the place where the oath is administered.

(2) Where power is conferred upon a justice of the peace to administer an oath or solemn affirmation or to take an affidavit or declaration, the power may be exercised by a notary public or a commissioner for taking oaths.

Reports to Parliament

Reports to Parliament.

20. Where an Act requires a report or other document to be laid before Parliament and, in compliance with the Act, a particular report or document has been laid before Parliament at a session thereof, nothing in the Act shall be construed as requiring the same report or document to be laid before Parliament at any subsequent session.

Corporations

Powers vested in corporations — Corporate name — Banking business.

21. (1) Words establishing a corporation shall be construed

(*a*) as vesting in the corporation power to sue and be sued, to contract and be contracted with by its corporate name, to have a common seal and to alter or change it at pleasure, to have perpetual succession, to acquire and hold personal property for the purposes for which the corporation is established and to alienate that property at pleasure;

(*b*) in the case of a corporation having a name consisting of an English and a French form or a combined English and French form, as vesting in the corporation power to use either the English or the French form of its name or both forms and to show on its seal both the English and French forms of its name or have two seals, one showing the English and the other showing the French form of its name;

(*c*) as vesting in a majority of the members of the corporation the power to bind the others by their acts; and (*d*) as exempting from personal liability for its debts, obligations or acts such indiviual members of the corporation who do not contravene the provisions of the enactment establishing the corporation.

(2) Where an enactment establishes a corporation and in each of the English and French versions of the enactment the name of the corporation is in the form only of the language of that version, the name of the corporation shall consist of the form of its name in each of the versions of the enactment.

(3) No corporation is deemed to be authorized to carry on the business of banking unless that power is expressly conferred on it by the enactment establishing the corporation.

Majority and Quorum

Majorities — Quorum of board, court, commission, etc.

22. (1) Where an enactment requires or authorizes more than two persons to do an act or thing, a majority of them may do it.

(2) Where an enactment establishes a board, court, commission or other body consisting of three or more members, in this section called an "association",

(*a*) at a meeting of the association, a number of members of the association equal to,

(i) if the number of members provided for by the enactment is a fixed number, at least one-half of the number of members, and

(ii) if the number of members provided for by the enactment is not a fixed number but is within a range having a maximum or minimum, at least one-half of the number of members in office if that number is within the range,

constitutes a quorum;

(*b*) an act or thing done by a majority of the members of the association present at a meeting, if the members present constitute a quorum, is deemed to have been done by the association; and

(*c*) a vacancy in the membership of the association does not invalidate the constitution of the association or impair the right of the members in office to act, if the number of members in office is not less than a quorum.

Appointment, Retirement and Powers of Officers

Public officers hold office during pleasure — Effective day of appointments — Appointment or engagement otherwise than under Great Seal — Remuneration — Commencement of appointments or retirements

23. (1) Every public officer appointed by or under the authority of an enactment or otherwise is deemed to have been appointed to hold office during pleasure only, unless it is otherwise expressed in the enactment, commission or instrument of appointment.

(2) Where an appointment is made by instrument under the Great Seal, the instrument may purport to have been issued on or after the day its issue was authorized, and the day on which it so purports to have been issued is deemed to be the day on which the appointment takes effect.

(3) Where there is authority in an enactment to appoint a person to a position or to engage the services of a person, otherwise than by instrument under the Great Seal, the instrument of appointment or engagement may be expressed to be effective on or after the day on which that person commenced the performance of the duties of the position or commenced the performance of the services, and the day on which it is so expressed to be effective, unless that day is more than sixty days before the day on which the instrument is issued, is deemed to be the day on which the appointment or engagement takes effect.

(4) Where a person is appointed to an office, the appointing authority may fix, vary or terminate that person's remuneration.

(5) Where a person is appointed to an office effective on a specified day, or where the appointment of a person is terminated effective on a specified day, the appointment or termination is deemed to have been effected immediately on the expiration of the previous day.

Implied powers respecting public officers — Powers to act for Ministers — Restriction to public servants — Successors to and deputy of public officer — Powers of holder of public office.

24. (1) Words authorizing the appointment of a public officer to hold office during pleasure include, in the discretion of the authority in whom the power of appointment is vested, the power to

(*a*) terminate the appointment or remove or suspend the public officer;

(*b*) re-appoint or reinstate the public officer; and

(*c*) appoint another person in the stead of, or to act in the stead of, the public officer.

(2) Words directing or empowering a minister of the Crown to do an act or thing, regardless of whether the act or thing is administrative, legislative or judicial, or otherwise applying to that minister as the holder of the office, include

(*a*) a minister acting for that minister or, if the office is vacant, a minister designated to act in the office by or under the authority of an order in council;

(*b*) the successors of that minister in the office;

(*c*) his or their deputy; and

(*d*) notwithstanding paragraph (*c*), a person apointed to serve, in the department or ministry of state over which the minister presides, in a capacity appropriate to the doing of the act or thing, or to the words so applying.

(3) Nothing in paragraph (2)(*c*) or (*d*) shall be construed as authorizing the exercise of any authority conferred on a minister to make a regulation as defined in the *Statutory Instruments Act.*

(4) Words directing or empowering any other public officer, other than a minister of the Crown, to do any act or thing, or otherwise applying to the public officer by his name of office, include his successors in the office and his or their deputy.

(5) Where a power is conferred or a duty imposed on the holder of an office the power may be exercised and the duty shall be performed by the person for the time being charged with the execution of the powers and duties of the office. 1992, c. 1, s. 89(1), (3), (4).

Evidence

Documentary evidence — Queen's Printer.

25. (1) Where an enactment provides that a document is evidence of a fact without anything in the context to indicate that the document is conclusive evidence, then, in any judicial proceedings, the document is admissible in evidence and the fact is deemed to be established in the absence of any evidence to the contrary.

(2) Every copy of an enactment having printed thereon what purports to be the name or title of the Queen's Printer and Controller of Stationery or the Queen's Printer is deemed to be a copy purporting to be printed by the Queen's Printer for Canada.

Computation of Time

Time limits and holidays.

26. Where the time limited for the doing of a thing expires or falls on a holiday, the thing may be done on the day next following that is not a holiday.

Clear days — Not clear days — Beginning and ending of prescribed periods — After specified day — Within a time.

27. (1) Where there is a reference to a number of clear days or "at least" a number of days between two events, in calculating that number of days the days on which the events happen are excluded.

(2) Where there is a reference to a number of days, not expressed to be clear days, between two events, in calculating that number of days the day on which the first event happens is excluded and the day on which the second event happens is included.

(3) Where a time is expressed to begin or end at, on or with a specified day, or to continue to or until a specified day, the time includes that day.

(4) Where a time is expressed to begin after or to be from a specified day, the time does not include that day.

(5) Where anything is to be done within a time after, from, of or before a specified day, the time does not include that day.

Calculation of a period of months after or before a specified day.

28. Where there is a reference to a period of time consisting of a number of months after or before a specified day, the period is calculated by

(*a*) counting forward or backward from the specified day the number of months, without including the month in which that day falls;

(*b*) excluding the specified day; and

(*c*) including in the last month counted under paragraph (*a*) the day that has the same calendar number as the specified day or, if that month has no day with that number, the last day of that month.

Time of the day.

29. Where there is a reference to time expressed as a specified time of the day, the time is taken to mean standard time.

Time when specified age attained.

30. A person is deemed not to have attained a specified number of years of age until the commencement of the anniversary, of the same number, of the day of that person's birth.

Miscellaneous Rules

Reference to provincial court judge, etc. — Ancillary powers — Powers to be exercised as required — Power to repeal.

31. (1) Where anything is required or authorized to be done by or before a judge, provincial court judge, justice of the peace or any functionary or officer, it shall be done by or before one whose jurisdiction or powers extend to the place where the thing is to be done.

(2) Where power is given to a person, officer or functionary to do or enforce the doing of any act or thing, all such powers as are necessary to enable the person, officer or functionary to do or enforce the doing of the act or thing are deemed to be also given.

(3) Where a power is conferred or a duty imposed, the power may be exercised and the duty shall be performed from time to time as occasion requires.

(4) Where a power is conferred to make regulations, the power shall be construed as including a power, exercisable in the same manner, and subject to the same consent and conditions, if any, to repeal, amend or vary the regulations and make others.

Forms.

32. Where a form is prescribed, deviations from that form, not affecting the substance or calculated to mislead, do not invalidate the form used.

Gender — Number — Parts of speech and grammatical forms.

33. (1) Words importing female persons include male persons and corporations and words importing male persons include female persons and corporations.

(2) Words in the singular include the plural, and words in the plural include the singular.

(3) Where a word is defined, other parts of speech and grammatical forms of the same word have corresponding meanings. 1992, c. 1, s. 90.

Offences

Indictable and summary conviction offences — Criminal Code to apply — Documents similarly construed.

34. (1) Where an enactment creates an offence,

(*a*) the offence is deemed to be an indictable offence if the enactment provides that the offender may be prosecuted for the offence by indictment;

(*b*) the offence is deemed to be one for which the offender is punishable on summary conviction if there is nothing in the context to indicate that the offence is an indictable offence; and

(*c*) if the offence is one for which the offender may be prosecuted by indictment or for which he is punishable on summary conviction, no person shall be considered to have been convicted of an indictable offence by reason only of having been convicted of the offence on summary conviction.

(2) All the provisions of the *Criminal Code* relating to indictable offences apply to indictable offences created by an enactment, and all the provisions of that Code relating to summary conviction offences apply to all other offences created by an enactment, except to the extent that the enactment otherwise provides.

(3) In a commission, proclamation, warrant or other document relating to criminal law or procedure in criminal matters,

(*a*) a reference to an offence for which the offender may be prosecuted by indictment shall be construed as a reference to an indictable offence; and

(*b*) a reference to any other offence shall be construed as a reference to an offence for which the offender is punishable on summary conviction.

DEFINITIONS

ɜeneral definitions — Governor in Council may amend schedule.

35. (1) In every enactment,

"Act", as meaning an Act of a legislature, includes an ordinance of the Yukon Territory or of the Northwest Territories;

"bank" means a bank to which the *Bank Act* applies;

"British Commonwealth" or "British Commonwealth of Nations" has the same meaning as "Commonwealth";

"broadcasting" means any radiocommunication in which the transmissions are intended for direct reception by the general public;

"Clerk of the Privy Council" or "Clerk of the Queen's Privy Council" means the Clerk of the Privy Council and Secretary to the Cabinet;

"commencement", when used with references to an enactment, means the time at which the enactment comes into force;

"Commonwealth" or "Commonwealth of Nations" means the association of countries named in the schedule;

"Commonwealth and Dependent Territories" means the several Commonwealth countries and their colonies, possessions, dependencies, protectorates, protected states, condominiums and trust territories;

"corporation" does not incude a partnership that is considered to be a separate legal entity under provincial law;

"county" includes two or more counties united for purposes to which the enactment relates;

"diplomatic or consular officer" includes an ambassador, envoy, minister, chargé d'affaires, counsellor, secretary, attaché, consul-general, consul, vice-consul, pro-consul, consular agent, acting consul-general, acting consul, acting vice-consul, acting consular agent, high commissioner, permanent delegate, adviser, acting high commissioner, and acting permanent delegate;

"Federal Court" means the Federal Court of Canada;

"Federal Court — Appeal Division" or "Federal Court of Appeal" means that division of the Federal Court of Canada called the Federal Court — Appeal Division or referred to as the Court of Appeal or Federal Court of Appeal by the *Federal Court Act*;

"Federal Court — "Trial Division" means that division of the Federal Court of Canada so named by the *Federal Court Act*;

"Governor", "Governor General", or "Governor of Canada" means the Governor General of Canada, or other chief executive officer or administrator carrying on the Government of Canada on behalf and in the name of the Sovereign, by whatever title that officer is designated;

"Governor General in Council", or "Governor in Council" means the Governor General of Canada acting by and with the advice of, or by and with the advice and consent of, or in conjunction with the Queen's Privy Council for Canada;

"Great Seal" means the Great Seal of Canada;

"Her Majesty", "His Majesty", "the Queen", "the King", or "the Crown" means the Sovereign of the United Kingdom, Canada and Her other Realms and Territories, and Head of the Commonwealth;

"Her Majesty's Realm and Territories" means all realms and territories under the sovereignty of Her Majesty;

"herein" used in any section shall be understood to relate to the whole enactment, and not to that section only;

"holiday" means any of the following days, namely, Sunday; New Year's Day; Good Friday; Easter Monday; Christmas Day; the birthday or the day fixed by proclamation for the celebration of the birthday of the reigning Sovereign; Victoria Day; Canada Day; the first Monday in September designated Labour Day; Remembrance Day; any day appointed by proclamation to be observed as a day of general prayer or mourning or day of public rejoicing or thanksgiving; and any of the following additional days, namely:

(*a*) in any province, any day appointed by proclamation of the lieutenant governor of the province to be observed as a public holiday or as a day of general prayer or mourning or day of public rejoicing or thanksgiving within the province, and any day that is a non-juridical day by virtue of an Act of the legislature of the province, and

(*b*) in any city, town, municipality or other organized district, any day appointed to be observed as a civic holiday by resolution of the council or other authority charged with the administration of the civic or municipal affairs of the city, town, municipality or district;

"legislative assembly", "legislative council" or "legislature", includes the Lieutenant Governor in Council and the Legislative Assembly of the Northwest Territories, as constituted before September 1, 1905, the Commissioner in Council of the Yukon Territory, and the Commissioner in Council of the Northwest Territories;

"lieutenant governor" means the lieutenant governor or other chief executive officer or administrator carrying on the government of the province indicated by the enactment, by whatever title that officer is designated, and, in relation to the Yukon Territory or the Northwest Territories, means the Commissioner thereof;

"lieutenant governor in council" means the lieutenant governor acting by and with the advice of, or by and with the advice and consent of, or in conjunction with the executive council of the province indicated by the enactment and in relation to the Yukon Territory or the Northwest Territories, means the Commissioner thereof;

"local time", in relation to any place, means the time observed in that place for the regulation of business hours;

"military" shall be construed as relating to all or any part of the Canadian Forces;

"month" means a calendar month;

"oath" includes a solemn affirmation or declaration when the context applies to any person by whom and to any case in which a solemn affirmation or declaration may be made instead of an oath, and in the same cases the expression "sworn" includes the expression "affirmed" or "declared";

"Parliament" means the Parliament of Canada;

"person" or any word or expression descriptive of a person, includes a corporation;

"proclamation" means a proclamation under the Great Seal;

"province" means a province of Canada, and includes the Yukon Territory and the Northwest Territories;

"radio" or "radiocommunication" means any transmission, emission or reception of signs, signals, writing, images, sounds or intelligence of any nature by means of electromagnetic waves of frequencies lower than 3,000 GHz propagated in space without artificial guide;

"regular force" means the component of the Canadian Forces that is referred to in the *National Defence Act* as the regular force;

"reserve force" means the component of the Canadian Forces that is referred to in the *National Defence Act* as the reserve force;

"security" means sufficient security, and "sureties" means sufficient sureties, and when those words are used one person is sufficient therefor, unless otherwise expressly required;

"standard time", except as otherwise provided by any proclamation of the Governor in Council that may be issued for the purposes of this definition in relation to any province or territory or any part thereof, means

(*a*) in relation to the Province of Newfoundland, Newfoundland standard time, being three hours and thirty minutes behind Greenwich time,

(*b*) in relation to the Provinces of Nova Scotia, New Brunswick and Prince Edward Island, those parts of the Province of Quebec lying east of the sixty-third meridian of west longitude, and those parts of the Northwest Territories lying east of the sixty-eighth meridian of west longitude, Atlantic standard time, being four hours behind Greenwich time,

(*c*) in relation to those parts of the Province of Quebec lying west of the sixty-third meridian of west longitude, and those parts of the Province of Ontario lying between the sixty-eight and the ninetieth meridians of west longitude, Southampton Island and the islands adjacent to Southampton Island, and that part of the Northwest Territories lying between the sixty-eighth and the eighty-fifty meridians of west longitude, eastern standard time, being five hours behind Greenwich time,

(*d*) in relation to that part of the Province of Ontario lying west of the ninetieth meridian of west longitude, the Province of Manitoba, and that part of the Northwest Territories, except Southampton Island and the islands of adjacent to Southampton Island, lying between the eighty-fifth and the one hundred and second meridians of west longitude, central standard time, being six hours behind Greenwich time,

(*e*) in relation to the Province of Saskatchewan, the Province of Alberta, and that part of the Northwest Territories lying west of the one hundred and second meridian of west longitude, mountain standard time, being seven hours behind Greenwich time,

(*f*) in relation to the Province of British Columbia, Pacific standard time, being eight hours behind Greenwich time, and

(*g*) in relation to the Yukon Territory, Yukon standard time, being nine hours behind Greenwich time;

"statutory declaration" means a solemn declaration made pursuant to section 41 of the *Canada Evidence Act*;

"superior court" means

(*a*) in the Province of Nova Scotia, Prince Edward Island or Newfoundland, the Supreme Court,

(*a*.1) in the Province of Ontario, the Court of Appeal for Ontario and the Ontario Court (General Division),

(*b*) in the Province of Quebec, the Court of Appeal, and the Superior Court in and for the Province,

(*c*) in the Province of New Brunswick, Manitoba, Saskatchewan or Alberta, the Court of Appeal for the Province and the Court of Queen's Bench for the Province,

(*d*) in the Province of British Columbia, the Court of Appeal and the Supreme Court of the Province,

(*e*) in the Yukon Territory or the Northwest Territories, the Supreme Court thereof,

and includes the Supreme Court of Canada and the Exchequer Court of Canada;

"telecommunication" means any transmission, emission or reception of signs, signals, writing, images or sounds or intelligence of any nature by wire, radio, visual or other electromagnetic system;

"two justices" means two or more justices of the peace, assembled or acting together;

"United Kingdom" means the United Kingdom of Great Britain and Northern Ireland;

"United States" means the United States of America;

"writing", or any term of like import, includes words printed, typewritten, painted, engraved, lithographed, photographed, or represented or reproduced by any mode of representing or reproducing words in visible form.

(2) The Governor in Council may, by order, amend the schedule by adding thereto the name of any country recognized by the order to be a member of the Commonwealth or deleting therefrom the name of any country recognized by the order to be no longer a member of the Commonwealth. R.S., c. 27 (2nd Supp.), s. 10; SOR/86-532 (Gaz. 28/5/86, p. 2197); 1990, c. 17, s. 26(1), (2); 1992, c. 1, s. 91.

Construction of "telegraph".

36. The expression "telegraph" and its derivatives, in an enactment or in an Act of the legislature of any province enacted before that province became part of Canada on any subject that is within the legislative powers of Parliament, are deemed not to include the word "telephone" or its derivatives.

Construction of "year" — Governor in Council may define year.

37. (1) The expression "year" means any period of twelve consecutive months, except that a reference

(*a*) to a "calendar year" means a period of twelve consecutive months commencing on January 1;

(*b*) to a "financial year" or "fiscal year" means, in relation to money provided by Parliament, or the Consolidated Revenue Fund, or the accounts, taxes or finances of Canada, the period beginning on April 1 in one calendar year and ending on March 31 in the next calendar year; and

(*c*) by number to a Dominical year means the period of twelve consecutive months commencing on January 1 of that Dominical year.

(2) Where in an enactment relating to the affairs of Parliament or the Government of Canada there is a reference to a period of a year without anything in the context to indicate beyond doubt whether a financial or fiscal year, any period of twelve consecutive months or a period of twelve consecutive months commencing on January 1 is intended, the Governor in Council may prescribe which of those periods of twelve consecutive months shall constitute a year for the purposes of the enactment.

Common names.

38. The name commonly applied to any country, place, body, corporation, society, officer, functionary, person, party or thing means the country, place, body, corporation, society, officer, functionary, person, party or thing to which the name is commonly applied, although the name is not the formal or extended designation thereof.

Affirmative and negative resolutions — Effect of negative resolution.

39. (1) In every Act,

(*a*) the expression "subject to affirmative resolution of Parliament", when used in relation to any regulation, means that the regulation shall be laid before Parliament within fifteen days after it is made or, if Parliament is not then sitting, on any of the first fifteen days next thereafter that Parliament is sitting and shall not come into force unless and until it is affirmed by a resolution of both Houses of Parliament introduced and passed in accordance with the rules of those Houses;

(*b*) the expression "subject to affirmative resolution of the House of Commons", when used in relation to any regulation, means that the regulation shall be laid before the House of Commons within fifteen days after it is made or, if the House is not then sitting, on any of the first fifteen days next thereafter that the House is sitting and shall not come into force unless and until it is affirmed by a resolution of the House of Commons introduced and passed in accordance with the rules of that House;

(*c*) the expression "subject to negative resolution of Parliament", when used in relation to any regulation, means that the regulation shall be laid before Parliament within fifteen days after it is made or, if Parliament is not then sitting, on any of the first fifteen days next thereafter that Parliament is sitting and may be annulled by a resolution of both Houses of Parliament introduced and passed in accordance with the rules of those Houses; and

(*d*) the expression "subject to negative resolution of the House of Commons", when used in relation to any regulation, means that the regulation shall be laid before the House of Commons within fifteen days after it is made or, if the House is not then sitting, on any of the first fifteen days next thereafter that the House is sitting and may be annulled by a resolution of the House of Commons introduced and passed in accordance with the rules of that House.

(2) Where a regulation is annulled by a resolution of Parliament or of the House of Commons, it is deemed to have been revoked on the day the resolution is passed and any law that was revoked or amended by the making of that regulation is deemed to be revived on the day the resolution is passed but the validity of any action taken or not taken in compliance with a regulation so deemed to have been revoked shall not be affected by the resolution.

REFERENCES AND CITATIONS

Citation of enactment — Citation includes amendment.

40. (1) In an enactment or document,

(*a*) an Act may be cited by reference to its chapter number in the Revised Statutes, by reference to its chapter number in the volume of Acts for the year or regnal year in which it was enacted or by reference to its long title or short title, with or without reference to its chapter number; and

(*b*) a regulation may be cited by reference to its long title or short title, by reference to the Act under which it was made or by reference to the number or designation under which it was registered by the Clerk of the Privy Council.

(2) A citation of or reference to an enactment is deemed to be a citation of or reference to the enactment as amended.

Reference to two or more parts, etc. — Reference in enactments to parts, etc. — Reference in enactment to subsections, etc. — Reference to regulations — Reference to another enactment.

41. (1) A reference in an enactment by number or letter to two or more parts, divisions, sections, subsections, paragraphs, subparagraphs, clauses, subclauses, schedules, appendices or forms shall be read as including the number or letter first mentioned and the number or letter last mentioned.

(2) A reference in an enactment to a part, division, section, schedule, appendix or form shall be read as a reference to a part, division, section, schedule, appendix or form of the enactment in which the reference occurs.

(3) A reference in an enactment to a subsection, paragraph, subparagraph, clause or subclause shall be read as a reference to a subsection, paragraph, subparagraph, clause or subclause of the section, subsection, paragraph, subparagraph or clause, as the case may be, in which the reference occurs.

(4) A reference in an enactment to regulations shall be read as a reference to regulations made under the enactment in which the reference occurs.

(5) A reference in an enactment by number or letter to any section, subsection, paragraph, subparagraph, clause, subclause or other division or line of another enactment shall be read as a reference to the section, subsection, paragraph, subparagraph, clause, subclause or other division or line of such other enactment as printed by authority of law.

REPEAL AND AMENDMENT

Power of repeal or amendment reserved — Amendment or repeal at same session — Amendment part of enactment.

42. (1) Every Act shall be construed as to reserve to Parliament the power of repealing or amending it, and of revoking, restricting or modifying any power, privilege or advantage thereby vested in or granted to any person.

(2) An Act may be amended or repealed by an Act passed in the same session of Parliament.

(3) An amending enactment, as far as consistent with the tenor thereof, shall be construed as part of the enactment that it amends.

Effect of repeal.

43. Where an enactment is repealed in whole or in part, the repeal does not (*a*) revive any enactment or anything not in force or existing at the time when the repeal takes effect,

(*b*) affect the previous operation of the enactment so repealed or anything duly done or suffered thereunder,

(*c*) affect any right, privilege, obligation or liability acquired, accrued, accruing or incurred under the enactment so repealed,

(*d*) affect any offence committed against or contravention of the provisions of the enactment so repealed, or any punishment, penalty or forfeiture incurred under the enactment so repealed, or

(*e*) affect any investigation, legal proceeding or remedy in respect of any right, privilege, obligation, or liability, referred to in paragraph (*c*) or in respect of any punishment, penalty or forfeiture or referred to in paragraph (*d*),

and an investigation, legal proceeding or remedy as described in paragraph (*e*) may be instituted, continued or enforced, and the punishment, penalty or forefeiture may be imposed as if the enactment had not been so repealed.

Repeal and substitution.

44. Where an enactment, in this section called the "former enactment", is repealed and another enactment, in this section called the "new enactment", is substituted therefor,

(*a*) every person acting under the former enactment shall continue to act, as if appointed under the new enactment, until another person is appointed in the stead of that person;

(*b*) every bond and security given by a person appointed under the former enactment remains in force, and all books, papers, forms and things made or used under the former enactment shall continue to be used as before the repeal in so far as they are consistent with the new enactment;

(*c*) every proceeding taken under the former enactment shall be taken up and continued under and in conformity with the new enactment in so far as it may be done consistently with the new enactment;

(*d*) the procedure established by the new enactment shall be followed as far as it can be adapted thereto

(i) in the recovery or enforcement of fines, penalties and forfeitures imposed under the former enactment,

(ii) in the enforcement of rights, existing or accruing under the former enactment, and

(iii) in a proceeding in relation to matters that have happened before the repeal;

(*e*) when any punishment, penalty or forfeiture is reduced or mitigated by the new enactment, the punishment, penalty or forfeiture if imposed or adjudged after the repeal shall be reduced or mitigated accordingly;

(*f*) except to the extent that the provisions of the new enactment are not in substance the same as those of the former enactment, the new enactment shall not be held to operate as new law, but shall be construed and have effect as a consolidation and as declaratory of the law as contained in the fomer enactment;

(*g*) all regulations made under the repealed enactment remain in force and are deemed to have been made under the new enactment, in so far as they are not inconsistent with the new enactment, until they are repealed or others made in their stead; and

(*h*) any reference in an unrepealed enactment to the former enactment shall, with respect to a subsequent transaction, matter or thing, be read and construed as a reference to the provisions of the new enactment relating to the same subject-matter as the former enactment, but where there are no provisions in the new enactment relating to the same subject-matter, the former enactment shall be read as unrepealed in so far as is necessary to maintain or give effect to the unrepealed enactment.

Repeal does not imply enactment was in force — Amendment does not imply change in law — Repeal does not declare previous law — Judicial construction not adopted.

45. (1) The repeal of an enactment in whole or in part shall not be deemed to be or to involve a declaration that the enactment was previously in for or was considered by Parliament or other body or person by whom the enactment was enacted to have been previously in force.

(2) The amendment of an enactment shall not be deemed to be or to involve a declaration that the law under that enactment was or was considered by Parliament or other body or person by whom the enactment was enacted to have been different from the law as it is under the enactment as amended.

(3) The repeal or amendment of an enactment in whole or in part shall not be deemed to be or to involve any declaration as to the previous state of the law.

(4) A re-enactment, revision, consolidation or amendment of an enactment shall not be deemed to be or to involve an adoption of the construction that has by judicial decision or otherwise been placed on the language used in the enactment or on similar language.

DEMISE OF CROWN

Effect of demise — Continuation of proceedings.

46. (1) Where there is a demise of the Crown,

(*a*) the demise does not affect the holding of any office under the Crown in right of Canada; and

(*b*) it is not necessary by reason of the demise that the holder of any such office again be appointed thereto or, having taken an oath of office or allegiance before the demise, again take that oath.

(2) No writ, action or other process or proceeding, civil or criminal, in or issuing out of any court established by an Act of the Parliament of Canada is, by reason of a demise of the Crown, determined, abated, discontinued or affected, but every such writ, action, process or proceeding remains in full force and may be enforced, carried on or otherwise proceeded with or completed as though there had been no such demise.

SCHEDULE

(*Section 35*)

Antigua and Barbuda
Australia
The Bahamas
Bangladesh
Barbados
Belize
Botswana
Brunei Darussalam
Canada
Cyprus
Dominica
Fiji
Gambia
Ghana
Grenada
Guyana
India
Jamaica
Kenya
Kiribati
Lesotho
Malawi
Malaysia
Maldives
Malta
Mauritius
Nauru
New Zealand
Nigeria
New Guinea Papua
St. Christopher and Nevis
St. Lucia
St. Vincent and the Grenadines
Seychelles
Sierra Leone
Singapore
Solomon Islands
Sri Lanka
Swaziland
Tanzania
Tonga
Trinidad and Tobago
Tuvalu
Uganda
United Kingdom
Vanuatu
Western Samoa
Zambia
Zimbabwe

MOTOR VEHICLE TRANSPORT ACT, 1987

TABLE OF CONCORDANCE

R.S.C. 1970 c. M-14	R.S.C. 1985, c. M-12	R.S.C. 1985, c. 29 (3d Supp.)	Remarks
M-14	**M-12**	**29**	
1	1	1	
2	2	2	
		3	
3	3	4	
		5	
4	4	6	
		7	
		8	
		9	
		10	
		11	
		12	
		13	
		14	
		15	
5	6	16	
6	5	18	
		19	
		21	
		17	
		22	
		23	
		24	
		25	
		26	
		27	
		28	
		29	
		30	
		31	
		32	
		33	
		34	
		35	

MVTA

MOTOR VEHICLE TRANSPORT ACT, 1987

R.S.C. 1985, c. 29 (3rd Supp.)

An Act respecting motor vehicle transport by extra-provincial undertakings

SHORT TITLE

Short title.

1. This Act may be cited as the *Motor Vehicle Transport Act, 1987.*

INTERPRETATION

Definitions — Interpretation.

2. (1) In this Act,

"extra-provincial bus transport" means the transport of passengers or passengers and goods by means of an extra-provincial bus undertaking;

"extra-provincial bus undertaking" means a work or undertaking for the transport of passengers or passengers and goods by a bus, connecting a province with any other or others of the provinces, or extending beyond the limits of a province;

"extra-provincial truck transport" means the transport of goods by means of an extra-provincial truck undertaking;

"extra-provincial truck undertaking" means a work or undertaking for the transport of goods by a motor vehicle other than a bus, connecting a province with any other or others of the provinces, or extending beyond the limits of a province;

"law of a province" means a law of a province or municipality that provides for the control or regulation of the operation in the province or municipality of local bus undertakings or local truck undertakings;

"local bus transport" means the transport of passengers or passengers and goods by means of a local bus undertaking;

"local bus undertaking" means a work or undertaking for the transport of passengers or passengers and goods by a bus, not being an extra-provincial bus undertaking;

"local truck transport" means the transport of goods by means of a local truck undertaking;

"local truck undertaking" means a work or undertaking for the transport of goods by a motor vehicle other than a bus, not being an extra-provincial truck undertaking;

"Minister" means the Minister of Transport;

"prescribed" means prescribed by regulation under this Act;

"provincial transport board" means a board, commission or other body or person having under the law of a province authority to control or regulate the operation of local bus undertakings or local truck undertakings.

(2) For the purposes of this Act, an extra-provincial bus undertaking or extra-provincial truck undertaking is operated in a province if it is operated into, in, across or out of the province.

SAFETY

Regulations — Incorporation by reference — Prohibition.

3. (1) The Governor in Council may, on the recommendation of the Minister made after consultation by the Minister with the government of each province affected thereby, make regulations respecting the safe operation of extra-provincial bus undertakings or extra-provincial truck undertakings including, without limiting the generality of the foregoing, regulations respecting audit, inspection, entry on premises and the provision of information.

(2) A regulation under subsection (1) may incorporate by reference the law of a province as amended from time to time.

(3) No person shall operate an extra-provincial bus undertaking or extra-provincial truck undertaking in contravention of any regulation made under subsection (1).

PART I
BUS TRANSPORT

Operating Licence

Operation without licence prohibited.

4. Where in any province a licence is by the law of the province required for the operation of a local bus undertaking, no person shall operate an extra-provincial bus undertaking in that province except under and in accordance with a licence issued under the authority of this Part.

Issue of licence.

5. The provincial transport board in each province may in its discretion issue a licence to a person to operate an extra-provincial bus undertaking in the province on the like terms and conditions and in the like manner as if the extra-provincial bus undertaking were a local bus undertaking.

Tariffs and Tolls

Tariffs and tolls.

6. Where in any province tariffs and tolls for local bus transport are determined or regulated by the provincial transport board, the provincial transport board may in its discretion determine or regulate the tariffs and tolls for extra-provincial bus transport on the like terms and conditions and in the like manner as if the extra-provincial bus transport were local bus transport.

PART II

TRUCKING

Operating Licence

Operation without licence prohibited.

7. Where in any province a licence is by the law of the province required for the operation of a local truck undertaking, no person shall operate an extra-provincial truck undertaking in that province except under and in accordance with a licence issued under the authority of this Part.

Issue of licence — Idem — Public hearings — Objection by interested person — Implementation — Limitation.

8. (1) Subject to this section and to any regulations made pursuant to section 9, the provincial transport board in each province may issue a licence to a person to operate an extra-provincial truck undertaking in the province on the like terms and conditions and in the like manner as if the extra-provincial truck undertaking were a local truck undertaking.

(2) The provincial transport board in a province shall, in exercising its powers under subsection (1), issue a licence to operate an extra-provincial truck undertaking in that province to an applicant therefor who submits to the board prescribed evidence that the applicant meets the prescribed criteria relating to the fitness of the applicant to hold such a licence.

(3) Notwithstanding subsection (2), where under the law of a province the provincial transport board is authorized to hold a public hearing with respect to an application for a licence to operate a local truck undertaking, the board shall not hold a public hearing with respect to an application for a licence referred to in subsection (2) unless an interested person who objects to the issue of the licence provides the board with evidence that satisfies the board that, in the absence of evidence to the contrary, the operation of the extra-provincial truck undertaking in respect of which the licence is sought would likely be detrimental to the public interest.

(4) Notwithstanding subsection (2), where under the law of a province an interested person may object to the issue by the provincial transport board of a licence to operate a local truck undertaking, the provincial transport board is not required to issue a licence referred to in subsection (2) if an interested person objects to the issue of the licence and establishes to the satisfaction of the board that the operation of the extra-provincial truck undertaking in

respect of which the licence is sought would likely be detrimental to the public interest.

(5) In applying subsections (3) and (4), a provincial transport board shall

(*a*) give primary emphasis to the interests of users of transportation services, whether those services are provided by the undertaking or not; and

(*b*) have regard to any relevant written expressions of public transportation policy issued by the Government of Canada after consultation with the government of each province affected thereby.

(6) Subject to subsection 10(3) but notwithstanding any other provision of this Part, after the day on which subsections (3) to (5) and paragraphs 9(1)(*a*) to (*d*) cease to have effect,

(*a*) a provincial transport board may not attach any restrictions or conditions to a licence issued under the authority of this Part; and

(*b*) the restrictions and conditions to which any licence issued under the authority of this Part is subject, except the condition referred to in subsection 10(3), shall cease to have effect.

Regulations — Fitness criteria

9. (1) The Governor in Council may, on the recommendation of the Minister made after consultation by the Minister with the government of each province affected thereby, make regulations

(*a*) prescribing restrictions or conditions to which licences issued under the authority of this Part shall be subject;

(*b*) requiring an applicant for a licence under this Part to furnish to the provincial transport board information respecting the applicant's identity and service proposal;

(*c*) exempting corridor operations from the application of subsections 8(3) to (5);

(*d*) exempting from the application of subsections 8(3) to (5) the extra-provincial truck transport of such commodities as may be specified in the regulations;

(*e*) prescribing as the criteria relating to the fitness of an applicant to hold a licence issued under the authority of this Part

(i) the criteria set out in any agreement between the Government of Canada and the governments of all of the provinces, as amended from time to time, or

(ii) in the absence of any agreement referred to in subparagraph (i) or on the failure to renew such an agreement, such criteria as the Governor in Council may consider necessary;

(*f*) authorizing any person or body to determine and certify whether an applicant for a licence under this Part meets, or the holder of a licence issued under the authority of this Part continues to meet, the requirements related to safety that are included in the criteria prescribed pursuant to paragraph (*e*) and to determine and certify the level at which the applicant or holder of the licence meets those requirements;

(*g*) prescribing the type, amount and conditions of insurance and bonding coverage required to be held by an extra-provincial truck undertaking;

(*h*) prescribing any other matter or thing that by this Part is to be prescribed; and

(*i*) generally as may be necessary for the purposes and provisions of this Part.

(2) The criteria relating to the fitness of an applicant referred to in paragraph (1)(*e*) shall include requirements related to safety and insurance, and may include requirements relating to bonding coverage, and any other requirement relating to the fitness of an applicant to hold a licence.

Compliance with fitness criteria — Licence not transferable — Condition.

10. (1) The holder of a licence issued under the authority of this Part shall not operate the undertaking in respect of which the licence was issued during any period during which the holder does not meet the criteria prescribed pursuant to paragraph 9(1)(*e*).

(2) A licence issued under the authority of this Part is not transferable.

(3) It is a condition of every licence issued under the authority of this Part that the holder thereof will comply with subsections (1) and (2) and any regulations made under subsection 3(1).

PART III
INTRA-PROVINCIAL TRUCKING

Interpretation.

11. For the purposes of this Part, "intra-provincial truck transport of goods" means the transport of goods between any two points in a province by means of an extra-provincial truck undertaking.

Prohibition.

12. Where in any province a licence is by the law of the province required for the operation of a local truck undertaking, no person shall engage in the intra-provincial truck transport of goods in that province except under and in accordance with a licence issued under the authority of Part II and a licence issued under the authority of this Part.

Issue of licence.

13. The provincial transport board in each province may in its discretion issue a licence to a person to engage in the intra-provincial truck transport of goods on the like terms and conditions and in the like manner as if that transport were local truck transport.

Tariffs and tolls.

14. Where in any province tariffs and tolls for local truck transport are determined or regulated by the provincial transport board, the provincial transport board may in its discretion determine or regulate the tariffs and tolls for the intra-provincial truck transport of goods on the like terms and conditions and in the like manner as if that transport were local truck transport.

Impartiality.

15. The provincial transport board shall exercise the discretion given to it by sections 12 to 14 by applying, in relation to an extra-provincial truck undertaking, the same criteria as it would apply in relation to a local truck undertaking in like circumstances.

PART IV

EXEMPTIONS AND ENFORCEMENT

Exemption

Exemption.

16. The Governor in Council may, by regulation, on the recommendation of the Minister made after consultation by the Minister with the government of each province affected thereby, exempt from the application of this Act or of any provision of this Act, either generally or for a limited period or in respect of a limited area, any person, the whole or any part of any extra-provincial bus undertaking or extra-provincial truck undertaking, every extra-provincial bus undertaking or extra-provincial truck undertaking, any group or class of such undertakings or any extra-provincial bus transport or extra-provincial truck transport.

Foreign Carriers

Unfair practices — Order in Council.

17. (1) Where the Minister is of the opinion that a government in a foreign country has engaged in unfair, discriminatory or restrictive practices with regard to Canadian carriers that transport goods by motor vehicle in that country or between that country and Canada, the Minister shall, with the concurrence of the Secretary of State for External Affairs, seek elimination of such practices through consultations.

(2) Where the consultations referred to in subsection (1) fail to result in the elimination of the practices referred to in that subsection, the Governor in Council may, on the recommendation of the Minister and the Secretary of State for External Affairs made after consultation by the Minister with the

government of each province affected thereby, notwithstanding this Act or any other Act of Parliament, by order,

(*a*) prohibit or restrict the issuance of any licence under the authority of this Act to any foreign carrier, all foreign carriers or any class of foreign carrier,

(*b*) direct any provincial transport board to amend or suspend any licence issued under the authority of this Act to any foreign carrier, all foreign carriers or any class of foreign carrier, and

(*c*) direct any provincial transport board to reinstate any licence suspended in accordance with a direction issued under paragraph (*b*),

subject to such terms and conditions as may be specified in the order, and a provincial transport board to which the order applies shall comply with the order.

Offence and Punishment

Offence — Limitation.

18. (1) Every person who contravenes or fails to comply with any provision of this Act or any regulation or order made under this Act is guilty of an offence punishable on summary conviction.

(2) Any proceedings in respect of an offence under this Act may be commenced at any time within, but not later than, twelve months after the time when the subject-matter of the proceedings arose.

Punishment re individuals — Punishment re corporations.

19. (1) An individual who is convicted of an offence under this Act is liable to a fine not exceeding five thousand dollars.

(2) A corporation that is convicted of an offence under this Act is liable to a fine not exceeding twenty-five thousand dollars.

Officers, etc., of corporations.

20. Where a corporation commits an offence under this Act, every person who at the time of the commission of the offence was a director or officer of the corporation is guilty of the like offence unless the act or omission constituting the offence took place without the person's knowledge or consent or the person exercised all due diligence to prevent the commission of the offence.

Disposition of fines.

21. A fine imposed under section 19 shall be paid over by the provincial court judge or officer receiving it to the treasurer of the province in which it was imposed.

Proof of documents.

22. In any proceedings for an offence under this Act, any document purporting to be certified by the Secretary of a provincial transport board to be a true copy of any order or direction made by the board is, without proof of the signature or of the official character of the person appearing to have signed the document, evidence of the original document of which it purports to be a copy.

PART V
CONSEQUENTIAL AMENDMENTS AND COMING INTO FORCE

Repeal

23. The *Motor Vehicle Transport Act*, is repealed.

Energy Supplies Emergency Act

24. Section 38 of the *Energy Supplies Emergency Act* is amended by substituting for the references to "extra-provincial undertaking" and "*Motor Vehicle Transport Act*" references to "extra-provincial truck undertaking" and "*Motor Vehicle Transport Act, 1987*", respectively.

Canada Grain Act

25. The definition "public carrier" in section 2 of the *Canada Grain Act* is repealed and the following substituted therefor:

""public carrier" means any railway company, any operator of an extra-provincial truck undertaking within the meaning of the *Motor Vehicle Transport Act, 1987* and any owner or operator of a ship;"

National Transportation Act, 1987

26. If, during the second session of the thirty-third Parliament, Bill C-18 entitled *An Act respecting national transportation* is assented to,

(*a*) subsection 184(1) of that Act is repealed and the following substituted therefor:

Motor Vehicle Transport Act, 1987.

"184. (1) While the *Motor Vehicle Transport Act, 1987* is in force and notwithstanding anything in this Act, this Division applies only in respect of such extra-provincial bus undertaking or such part thereof as is exempted from the application of the *Motor Vehicle Transport Act, 1987* pursuant to section 16 of that Act.";

(*b*) subsection 199(1) of that Act is repealed and the following substituted therefor:

Motor Vehicle Transport Act, 1987.

"199. (1) While the *Motor Vehicle Transport Act, 1987* is in force and notwithstanding anything in this Act, this Division applies only in respect of such extra-provincial truck undertaking or such part thereof as is exempted from the application of the *Motor Vehicle Transport Act, 1987* pursuant to section 16 of that Act.";

(*c*) subsection 266(1) of that Act is repealed and the following substituted therefor:

Comprehensive review.

"266. (1) The Governor in Council shall, in January, 1992, appoint one or more persons to carry out a comprehensive review of the operation of this Act, the provisions of the *Railway Act* amended by this Act, the *Shipping Conferences Exemption Act,* the *Motor Vehicle Transport Act, 1987* and any other Act of Parliament for which the Minister is responsible that pertains to the economic regulation of a mode of transportation."; and

(*d*) subsection 267(1) of that Act is repealed and the following substituted therefor:

For certain years.

"267. (1) After the expiration of each of the years 1988, 1989, 1990 and 1991, the Agency shall make a review in respect of that year of the operation of this Act, the provisions of the *Railway Act* amended by this Act, the *Shipping Conferences Exemption Act,* the *Motor Vehicle Transport Act, 1987* and any other Act of Parliament for which the Minister is responsible that pertains to the economic regulation of a mode of transportation."

Transitional

Continuation of licences respecting bus undertakings.

27. Every licence authorizing the operation of an extra-provincial bus undertaking that has been issued under the authority of the *Motor Vehicle Transport Act* and that is in effect on the day immediately before the day on which this Act, except section 26, comes into force shall be deemed to have been issued under the authority of Part I of this Act.

Intra-provincial bus transport.

28. For greater certainty, every licence authorizing the operation of an extra-provincial bus undertaking between any two points in a province that purports to have been issued under a law of the province prior to the coming into force of this Act, except section 26, and that purports to be in effect on the day immediately before this Act, except section 26, comes into force shall be deemed to have been issued under the authority of Part I of this Act if that licence was issued to a person who at the time of issuance was the holder of a licence issued under the authority of the *Motor Vehicle Transport Act* in respect of the same extra-provincial bus undertaking.

Continuation of licences respecting truck undertakings — Exception.

29. (1) Subject to subsection (2), every licence authorizing the operation of an extra-provincial truck undertaking that has been issued under the authority of the *Motor Vehicle Transport Act* and that is in effect on the day immediately before the day on which this Act, except section 26, comes into force shall be deemed to have been issued under the authority of Part II of this Act.

(2) Where a licence referred to in subsection (1) authorizes the holder thereof to engage in the intra-provincial truck transport of goods, within the meaning of Part III of this Act, that licence shall be deemed to have been issued under the authority of Parts II and III of this Act.

Intra-provincial trucking.

30. For greater certainty, every licence authorizing the operation of an extra-provincial truck undertaking between any two points in a province that purports to have been issued under a law of the province prior to the coming into force of this Act, except section 26, and that purports to be in effect on the day immediately before this Act, except section 26, comes into force shall be deemed to have been issued under the authority of Part III of this Act if that licence was issued to a person who at the time of issuance was the holder of a licence issued under the authority of the *Motor Vehicle Transport Act* in respect of the same extra-provincial truck undertaking.

Pending applications.

31. Every application for a licence made under the *Motor Vehicle Transport Act* and pending on the day immediately before the day on which this Act, except section 26, comes into force shall be deemed to have been made pursuant to section 5, 8 or 13 of this Act, whichever is applicable, and shall be dealt with in accordance with this Act.

Continuation of exemptions.

32. Every exemption granted under section 6 of the *Motor Vehicle Transport Act* and in force on the day immediately before the day on which this Act, except section 26, comes into force shall be deemed to have been granted under section 16 of this Act.

Coming Into Force

Coming into force — Idem.

33. (1) This Act, except section 26, shall come into force on January 1, 1988 or on such earlier day as may be fixed by proclamation.

(2) Section 26 shall come into force on the later of the day on which section 16 comes into force and the day on which sections 184, 199, 266 and 267 of the Bill, mentioned in section 26, come into force.

Repeal

Repeal — Review — Tabling of report — Continuation in force — Idem.

34. (1) Subsections 8(3) to (5) and paragraphs 9(1)(*a*) to (*d*) shall, subject to subsections (2) to (4), cease to have effect five years after the day on which this Act, except section 26, comes into force.

(2) The Minister shall, after the expiration of three years after the coming into force of subsections 8(3) to (5) and before the expiration of four years after the coming into force of those subsections, undertake and complete a comprehensive review of the operation and effect of those subsections.

(2.1) After the completion of the review referred to in subsection (2), the Minister shall cause a copy of a report of the review to be laid before each House of Parliament on any of the first fifteen days on which that House is sitting after the report has been prepared.

(3) The Governor in Council may, by proclamation, on the recommendation of the Minister made after consultation by the Minister with the government of each province, after the completion of the review referred to in subsection (2) and before subsections 8(3) to (5) and paragraphs 9(1)(*a*) to (*d*) cease to have effect pursuant to subsection (1), continue subsections 8(3) to (5) and paragraphs 9(1)(*a*) to (*d*) in force for such further period as is specified in proclamation.

(4) The Governor in Council may, by proclamation, on the recommendation of the Minister made after consultation by the Minister with the government of each province, at any time while subsections 8(3) to (5) and paragraphs 9(1)(*a*) to (*d*) are in force pursuant to subsection (3) or this subsection, continue subsections 8(3) to (5) and paragraphs 9(1)(*a*) to (*d*) in force for such further period as is specified in the proclamation.

ANNUAL REPORT

Annual Report — Contents of report.

35. (1) After the expiration of each of the years 1988 to 1993, the Minister shall prepare the report referred to in subsection (2) and shall cause a copy of the report to be laid before each House of Parliament on any of the first fifteen days on which that House is sitting after the Minister completes it.

(2) The report of the Minister shall contain the following in respect of each year referred to in subsection (1):

(*a*) the available statistical information respecting trends of highway accidents in Canada involving motor vehicles operated by extra-provincial bus undertakings and extra-provincial truck undertakings; and

(*b*) a progress report on the implementation of rules and standards respecting the safe operation of extra-provincial bus undertakings and of extra-provincial truck undertakings.

NARCOTIC CONTROL ACT

TABLE OF CONCORDANCE

R.S.C. 1970, c. N-1	R.S.C. 1985 c. N-1	R.S.C. 1970, c. N-1	R.S.C. 1985 c. N-1
N-1	**N-1**	**N-1**	**N-1**
1	1	11	17
2	2	11	18
3	3	11	19
	3.1	11	19.1
		11	19.2
		11	19.3
4	4	12	20
5	5	13	21
6	6	14	22
7	7	15	23
8	8	16	24
9	9	17	25
10	10 to 16	18	26
		19	27
			28
		Sch/Ann	Sch/Ann

NARCOTIC CONTROL ACT

R.S.C. 1985, c. N-1

An Act to provide for the control of narcotic drugs

As amended by R.S. 1985, c. 27 (1st Supp.), ss. 196-200, 203, 208; c. 27 (2nd Supp.), s. 10; c. 42 (4th Supp.), ss. 12, 13; 1990, c. 16, s. 18; 1990, c. 17, s. 36; 1992, c. 1, s. 98.

SHORT TITLE

Short title.

1. This Act may be cited as the *Narcotic Control Act.*

INTERPRETATION

Definitions.

2. In this Act,

"analyst" means a person designated as an analyst under the *Food and Drugs Act* or this Act;

"conveyance" includes any aircraft, vessel, motor vehicle or other conveyance of any description whatever;

"marihuana" means *Cannabis sativa* L.;

"Minister" means

(*a*) with respect to Part I, the Minister of National Health and Welfare, and

(*b*) with respect to Part II, the Minister of Justice;

"narcotic" means any substance included in the schedule or anything that contains any substance included in the schedule;

"narcotic addict" means a person who through the use of narcotics,

(*a*) has developed a desire or need to continue to take a narcotic, or

(*b*) has developed a psychological or physical dependence upon the effect of a narcotic;

"opium poppy" means *Papaver somniferum* L.;

"possession" means possession as defined in the *Criminal Code*;

"practitioner" means a person who is registered and entitled under the laws of a province to practise in that province the profession of medicine, dentistry or veterinary medicine;

"prescription" means, in respect of a narcotic, an authorization given by a practitioner that a stated amount of the narcotic be dispensed for the person named therein;

"traffic" means

(*a*) to manufacture, sell, give, administer, transport, send, deliver or distribute, or

(*b*) to offer to do anything referred to in paragraph (*a*)

otherwise than under the authority of this Act or the regulations. R.S., c. 27 (1st Supp.), s. 196.

PART I
OFFENCES AND ENFORCEMENT

Particular Offences

Possession of narcotic — Offence and punishment.

3. (1) Except as authorized by this Act or the regulations, no person shall have a narcotic in his possession.

(2) Every person who contravenes subsection (1) is guilty of an offence and liable

(*a*) on summary conviction for a first offence, to a fine not exceeding one thousand dollars or to imprisonment for a term not exceeding six months or to both and, for a subsequent offence, to a fine not exceeding two thousand dollars or to imprisonment for a term not exceeding one year or to both; or

(*b*) on conviction on indictment, to imprisonment for a term not exceeding seven years.

Failure to disclose previous prescriptions — Offence and punishment — Limitation period.

3.1 (1) No person shall, at any time, seek or obtain a narcotic or a prescription for a narcotic from a practitioner unless that person discloses to the practitioner particulars of every narcotic or prescription for a narcotic issued to that person by a different practitioner within the preceding thirty days.

(2) Every person who contravenes subsection (1)

(*a*) is guilty of an indictable offence and liable to imprisonment for a term not exceeding seven years; or

(*b*) is guilty of an offence punishable on summary conviction and liable

(i) for a first offence, to a fine not exceeding one thousand dollars or to imprisonment for a term not exceeding six months, and

(ii) for a subsequent offence, to a fine not exceeding two thousand dollars or to imprisonment for a term not exceeding one year.

(3) Summary conviction proceedings in respect of an offence under this section may be instituted at any time within but not later than one year from the time when the subject-matter of the proceedings arose. R.S., c. 27 (1st Supp.), s. 197.

Trafficking — Possession for purpose of trafficking — Offence and punishment.

4. (1) No person shall traffic in a narcotic or any substance represented or held out by the person to be a narcotic.

(2) No person shall have in his possession any narcotic for the purpose of trafficking.

(3) Every person who contravenes subsection (1) or (2) is guilty of an indictable offence and liable to imprisonment for life.

Importing and exporting — Offence and punishment.

5. (1) Except as authorized by this Act or the regulations, no person shall import into Canada or export from Canada any narcotic.

(2) Every person who contravenes subsection (1) is guilty of an indictable offence and liable to imprisonment for life but not less than seven years.

Cultivation of opium poppy or marihuana — Offence and punishment — Destruction of plant.

6. (1) No person shall cultivate opium poppy or marihuana except under the authority of, and in accordance with, a licence issued to the person under the regulations.

(2) Every person who contravenes subsection (1) is guilty of an indictable offence and liable to imprisonment for a term not exceeding seven years.

(3) The Minister may cause to be destroyed any growing plant of opium poppy or marihuana cultivated otherwise than under authority of and in accordance with a licence issued under the regulations.

Prosecutions

Setting out or negativing exception, etc. not required — Burden of proving exception, etc.

7. (1) No exception, exemption, excuse or qualification prescribed by law is required to be set out or negatived, as the case may be, in an information or indictment for an offence under this Act or under section 463, 464 or 465 of the *Criminal Code* in respect of an offence under this Act.

(2) In any prosecution under this Act the burden of proving that an exception, exemption, excuse or qualification prescribed by law operates in favour of the accused is on the accused, and the prosecutor is not required, except by way of rebuttal, to prove that the exception, exemption, excuse or qualification does not operate in favour of the accused, whether or not it is set out in the information or indictment.

Procedure in prosecution for trafficking — Idem — Conviction of possession or conviction of trafficking.

8. (1) In any prosecution for a contravention of subsection 4(2), if the accused does not plead guilty, the trial shall proceed as if it were a prosecution for an offence under section 3.

(2) After the close of the case for the prosecution pursuant to subsection (1) and after the accused has had an opportunity to make full answer and defence, the court shall make a finding as to whether or not the accused contravened subsection 3(1) and, if the court finds that the accused did not contravene subsection 3(1), the accused shall be acquitted but, if the court finds that the accused contravened subsection 3(1), the accused shall be given an opportunity of establishing that he was not in possession of the narcotic for the purpose of trafficking and, thereafter, the prosecutor shall be given an opportunity of adducing evidence to establish the contrary.

(3) After compliance with subsection (2), in the case of finding a contravention by the accused of subsection 3(1),

(*a*) if the accused establishes that he was not in possession of the narcotic for the purpose of trafficking, the accused shall be acquitted of the offence as charged but shall be convicted of an offence under section 3 and sentenced accordingly; or

(*b*) if the accused fails to establish that he was not in possession of the narcotic for the purpose of trafficking, the accused shall be convicted of the offence as charged and sentenced accordingly.

Certificate of analyst — Requiring attendance of analyst — Notice of intention to produce certificate — Proof of service — Attendance for examination.

9. (1) Subject to this section, a certificate purporting to be signed by an analyst stating that the analyst has analyzed or examined a substance and stating the result of the analysis or examination is admissible in evidence in any prosecution for an offence referred to in subsection 7(1), and, in the absence of evidence to the contrary, is proof of the statements contained in the certificate without proof of the signature or official character of the person appearing to have signed the certificate.

(2) The party against whom a certificate of an analyst is produced pursuant to subsection (1) may, with leave of the court, require the attendance of the analyst for the purposes of cross-examination.

(3) No certificate shall be admitted in evidence pursuant to subsection (1) unless the party intending to produce it has, before the trial, given to the party against whom it is intended to be produced reasonable notice of that intention together with a copy of the certificate.

(4) For the purposes of this Act, service of any certificate referred to in subsection (1) may be proved by oral evidence given under oath by, or by the affidavit or solemn declaration of, the person claiming to have served it.

(5) Notwithstanding subsection (4), the court may require the person who appears to have signed an affidavit or solemn declaration referred to in that subsection to appear before it for examination or cross-examination in respect of the issue of proof of service. R.S., c. 27 (1st Supp.), s. 198.

Search, Seizure and Forfeiture

Entry and search.

10. A peace officer may, at any time, without a warrant enter and search any place other than a dwelling-house, and under the authority of a warrant issued under section 12, enter and search any dwelling-house in which the peace officer believes on reasonable grounds there is a narcotic by means of or in respect of which an offence under this Act has been committed. R.S., c. 27 (1st Supp.), s. 199.

Search of person and seizure.

11. A peace officer may search any person found in a place entered pursuant to section 10 and may seize and, from a place so entered, take away any narcotic found therein, anything therein in which the peace officer reasonably suspects a narcotic is contained or concealed, or any other thing by means of or in respect of which that officer believes on reasonable grounds an offence under this Act has been committed or that may be evidence of the commission of such an offence.

Warrant to search dwelling-house.

12. A justice who is satisfied by information on oath that there are reasonable grounds for believing that there is a narcotic, by means of or in respect of which an offence under this Act has been committed, in any dwelling-house may issue a warrant, under the hand of the justice, authorizing a peace officer named therein at any time to enter the dwelling-house and search for narcotics.

13. [Repealed, R.S. 1985, c. 27 (1st Supp.), s. 200.]

[*NOTE: R.S. 1985, c. 27 (1st Supp.), s. 208 states:*

Nothing in sections 190, 195, 199 and 200 of this Act [Criminal Law Amendments Act, 1985] shall be construed as rendering invalid or inadmissible in any proceedings any evidence obtained by the exercise of a writ of assistance prior to the coming into force of those sections.]

Powers of peace officer.

14. For the purpose of exercising authority pursuant to any of sections 10 to 13, a peace officer may, with such assistance as that officer deems necessary, break open any door, window, lock, fastener, floor, wall, ceiling, compartment, plumbing fixture, box, container or any other thing.

Application for restoration — Order of immediate restoration — Order of restoration at specified time — Where application not made or order refused.

15. (1) Where a narcotic or other thing has been seizied under section 11, any person may, within two months after the date of the seizure, on prior notification being given to the Crown in the manner prescribed by the regulations, apply to a provincial court judge within whose territorial jurisdiction the seizure was made for an order of restoration under this section.

(2) Subject to section 16, where on the hearing of an application made under subsection (1) the provincial court judge is satisfied that the applicant is entitled to possession of the narcotic or other thing seized and that the thing seized is not or will not be required as evidence in any proceedings in respect of an offence under this Act, the provincial court judge shall order that the thing seized be restored forthwith to the applicant.

(3) Where on the hearing of an application made under subsection (1) the provincial court judge is satisfied that the applicant is entitled to possession of the thing seized but is not satisfied that the thing is not or will not be required as evidence in any proceedings in respect of an offence under this Act, the provincial court judge shall order that the thing seized be restored to the applicant

(*a*) on the expiration of four months after the date of the seizure, if no proceedings in respect of an offence under this Act have been commenced before that time; or

(*b*) on the final conclusion of any such proceedings, in any other case.

(4) Where no application has been made for the return of any narcotic or other thing seized under section 11 within two months after the date of the seizure, or an application therefor has been made but, on the hearing of the application, no order of restoration is made, the thing seized shall be delivered to the Minister, who may make such disposition thereof as the Minister thinks fit. R.S., c. 27 (1st Supp.), s. 203.

Forfeiture on conviction — Forfeiture of conveyance on application.

16. (1) Where a person has been convicted of an offence under section 3, 4 or 5, any narcotic seized under section 11, by means of or in respect of which the offence was committed, any money so seized that was used for the purchase of that narcotic and any hypodermic needle, syringe, capping machine or other apparatus so seized that was used in any manner in connection with the offence is forfeited to Her Majesty and shall be disposed of as the Minister directs.

(2) Where a person has been convicted of an offence under section 4 or 5, the court may, on application by counsel for the Crown, order that any conveyance seized under section 11 that has been proved to have been used in any manner in connection with the offence be forfeited and, on the making

of that order, the conveyance is forfeited to Her Majesty and, except as provided in sections 17 to 19, shall, on the expiration of thirty days after the date of the forfeiture, be disposed of as the Minister directs.

Application by person claiming interest in forfeited conveyance — Date of hearing — Notice to Minister — Order by judge — Appeal.

17. (1) Where any conveyance is forfeited to Her Majesty under subsection 16(2), any person (other than a person convicted of the offence that resulted in the forfeiture or a person in whose possession the conveyance was when seized) who claims an interest therein as owner, mortgagee, lienholder or holder of any like interest may, within thirty days after the forfeiture, apply by notice in writing to a judge for an order under subsection (4).

(2) The judge to whom an application is made under subsection (1) shall fix a day not less than thirty days after the date of filing of the application for the hearing thereof.

(3) The applicant for an order under subsection (4) shall serve a notice of the application and of the hearing on the Minister at least fifteen days before the day fixed for the hearing.

(4) Where, on the hearing of an application made under subsection (1), it is made to appear to the satisfaction of the judge

(*a*) that the applicant is innocent of any complicity in the offence that resulted in the forfeiture and of any collusion in relation to that offence with the person who was convicted thereof, and

(*b*) that the applicant exercised, with respect to the person permitted to obtain possession of the conveyance, all reasonable care that the conveyance was not likely to be used in connection with the commission of an unlawful act or, in the case of a mortgagee or lienholder, that the applicant exercised, with respect to the mortgagor or lien-giver, all reasonable care in order to be so satisfied,

the applicant is entitled to an order declaring that the interest of the applicant is not affected by the forfeiture and declaring the nature and extent of the interest.

(5) The applicant or the Minister may appeal to the court of appeal from an order made under subsection (4) and the appeal shall be asserted, heard and decided according to the ordinary procedure governing appeals to the court of appeal from orders or judgments of a judge.

Definitions.

18. In section 17,

"court of appeal" means, in the province in which an order under section 17 is made, the court of appeal for that province as defined in the definition "court of appeal" in section 2 of the *Criminal Code*;

"judge" means

(*a*) in the Province of Ontario, a judge of the Ontario Court (Generel Division),
(*b*) in the Provinces of Quebec, a judge of the Superior Court for the district in which the conveyance, in respect of which an application for an order under section 17 is made, was seized,
(*c*) in the Province of Nova Scotia, a judge of the county court for the county court district in which any such conveyance was seized,
(*d*) in the Provinces of New Brunswick, Manitoba, Saskatchewan and Alberta, a judge of the Court of Queen's Bench,
(*e*) in the Province of British Columbia, the Yukon Territory and the Northwest Territories, a judge of the Supreme Court, and
(*f*) in the Provinces of Prince Edward Island and Newfoundland, a judge of the Trial Division of the Supreme Court. R.S. c. 27 (2nd Supp.), s. 10; 1990, c. 16, s. 18; 1990, c. 17, s. 36(1), (2); 1992, c. 1, s. 98.

Direction of Minister for restoration or payment.

19. The Minister shall, on application made to the Minister by any person who has obtained a final order under section 17, direct that the conveyance to which the interest of the applicant relates be returned to the applicant or that an amount equal to the value of that interest, as declared in the order, be paid to the applicant.

Proceeds of Crime

Possession of property obtained by certain offences — Punishment.

19.1 (1) No person shall possess any property or any proceeds of any property knowing that all or part of the property or of those proceeds was obtained or derived directly or indirectly as a result of
(*a*) the commission in Canada of an offence under section 4, 5 or 6; or
(*b*) an act or omission anywhere that, if it had occurred in Canada, would have constituted an offence under section 4, 5 or 6.

(2) Every person who contravenes subsection (1)
(*a*) is guilty of an indictable offence and is liable to imprisonment for a term not exceeding ten years, where the value of the subject-matter of the offence exceeds one thousand dollars; or
(*b*) is guilty
(i) of an indictable offence and is liable to imprisonment for a term not exceeding two years, or
(ii) of an offence punishable on summary conviction,
where the value of the subject-matter of the offence does not exceed one thousand dollars. R.S. 1985, c. 42 (4th Supp.), s. 12.

Laundering proceeds of certain offences — Punishment.

19.2 (1) No person shall use, transfer the possession of, send or deliver to any person or place, transport, transmit, alter, dispose of or otherwise deal with, in any manner and by any means, any property or any proceeds of any property with intent to conceal or convert that property or those proceeds and knowing that all or a part of that property or of those proceeds was obtained by or derived directly or indirectly as a result of

(*a*) the commission in Canada of an offence under section 4, 5 or 6; or

(*b*) an act or omission anywhere that, if it had occurred in Canada, would have constituted an offence under section 4, 5 or 6.

(2) Every person who contravenes subsection (1)

(*a*) is guilty of an indictable offence and is liable to imprisonment for a term not exceeding ten years; or

(*b*) is guilty of an offence punishable on summary conviction. R.S. 1985, c. 42 (4th Supp.), s. 12.

Part XII.1 and Part XII.2 of the Criminal Code applicable — *Idem*.

19.3 (1) Sections 462.3 and 462.32 to 462.5 of the *Criminal Code* apply, with such modifications as the circumstances require, in respect of proceedings for

(*a*) an offence under section 4, 5, 6, 19.1 or 19.2; or

(*b*) a conspiracy or an attempt to commit, being an accessory after the fact in relation to, or any counselling in relation to an offence referred to in paragraph (*a*).

(2) For the purposes of subsection (1),

(*a*) a reference in section 462.37 or 462.38 or subsection 462.41(2) of the *Criminal Code* to an enterprise crime offence shall be deemed to be a reference to an offence mentioned in paragraph (1)(*a*) or (*b*); and

(*b*) a reference, in relation to the manner in which forfeited property is to be disposed of, in subsection 462.37(1) or 462.38(2), paragraph 462.43(*c*) or section 462.5 of the *Criminal Code* to the Attorney General shall be deemed to be a reference to the Minister. R.S. 1985, c. 42 (4th Supp.), s. 12.

General

Regulations.

20. The Governor in Council may make regulations

(*a*) providing for the issue of licences for the importation, export, sale, manufacture, production or distribution of narcotics and for the cultivation of opium poppy or marihuana;

(*b*) prescribing the form, duration and terms and conditions of any licence described in paragraph (*a*) and the fees payable therefor, and providing for the cancellation and suspension of licences described in that paragraph;

(*c*) authorizing the sale or possession of or other dealing in narcotics and prescribing the circumstances and conditions under which, and the persons by whom, narcotics may be sold, had in possession or otherwise dealt in;
(*d*) requiring physicians, dentists, veterinarians, pharmacists and other persons who deal in narcotics as authorized by this Act or the regulations to keep records and make returns;
(*e*) authorizing the communication of any information obtained under this Act or the regulations to provincial professional licensing authorities;
(*f*) prescribing the punishment by a fine not exceeding five hundred dollars or imprisonment for a term not exceeding six months, or both, to be imposed upon summary conviction for breach of any regulation; and
(*g*) generally, for carrying out the purposes and provisions of this Act.

Designation of analyst.

21. The Minister may designate any person as an analyst for the purpose of this Act.

Amendment of schedule.

22. The Governor in Council may amend the schedule by adding thereto or deleting therefrom any substance, the inclusion or exclusion of which, as the case may be, is deemed necessary by the Governor in Council in the public interest.

PART II

[*To be proclaimed in force*]

Preventive Detention and Custody for Treatment

Sentence of preventive detention.

23. Where a person is convicted of an offence under section 4 or 5, the court shall, if that person

(*a*) has been previously convicted on at least one separate and independent occasion of an offence under section 4 or 5 of this Act or an offence under subsection 4(3) of the *Opium and Narcotic Drug Act*, chapter 201 of the Revised Statutes of Canada, 1952, or

(*b*) has been previously sentenced to preventive detention under this section,

impose a sentence of preventive detention in a penitentiary for an indeterminate period, in lieu of any other sentence that might be imposed for the offence of which that person was convicted.

Remand for observation and examination.

24. Where any person is charged with an offence under section 3, 4 or 5, the court or any judge having jurisdiction to try the offence may, on application by counsel for the Crown, or on application by the person charged with the offence or by counsel for that person, either before or after that person is committed for trial and before any sentence that might be imposed for the offence is passed, remand that person, by order in writing, to such custody as the court directs for observation and examination for a period not exceeding seven days.

Conviction after remand — Sentence to custody for treatment — Appeal — Application of Criminal Code.

25. (1) Where a person who has been remanded to custody for observation and examination pursuant to section 24 is convicted of the offence in respect of which the peson was remanded, the court shall, before passing sentence, consider the evidence arising out of the observation and examination, including the evidence of at least one duly qualified medical practitioner and such other evidence as may be adduced.

(2) Where the court is satisfied, on consideration of the evidence under subsection (1), that the convicted person is a narcotic addict, the court shall, notwithstanding anything in section 23, sentence that person to custody for treatment for an indeterminate period in lieu of any other sentence that might be imposed for the offence of which that person was convicted.

(3) A person who is sentenced to custody for treatment for an indeterminate period under this section may appeal to the court of appeal against the sentence on any ground of law or fact or mixed law and fact.

(4) The provisions of section 759 of the *Criminal Code* with respect to appeals against a sentence of detention in a penitentiary for an indeterminate period apply, with such modifications as the circumstances require, to an appeal under this section.

Confinement for treatment — Application of Parole Act — Expiration of sentence.

26. (1) Where a person is sentenced to custody for treatment for an indeterminate period, the person shall be confined for treatment in an institution maintained and operated pursuant to the *Penitentiary Act.*

(2) A person who is sentenced to custody for treatment for an indeterminate period is subject to the *Parole Act* and, for all purposes of that Act, shall be deemed during the period of confinement of that person, to be an inmate within the meaning of that Act, and on release under certificate of the Parole Board, to be a paroled inmate within the meaning of that Act.

(3) A sentence of custody for treatment for an indeterminate period, where the person so sentenced has not, at any time before the conviction resulting in the sentence, been convicted of an offence under this Act or the *Opium and Narcotic Drug Act*, chapter 201 of the Revised Statutes of Canada, 1952, expires at the end of such period, not exceeding ten years after the date of the person's release under certificate of the Parole Board, as may be fixed

by the Parole Board, unless before that time the person's parole is forfeited or revoked.

[1992, c. 20, s. 215(1)(*c*) will repeal the expression "*Parole Act*" wherever it occurs in section 26 and substitute the expression "Part II of the *Corrections and Conditional Release Act*".]

[1992, c. 20, s. 216(1)(*c*) will repeal the expression "*Penitentiary Act*" wherever it occurs in section 26 and substitute the expression "Part I of the *Corrections and Conditional Release Act*".]

Agreement with province — Idem.

27. (1) Where the legislature of a province enacts legislation that is designed to provide custody for treatment for persons who, although not charged with the offence of possession of a narcotic, are narcotic addicts, the Minister may enter into an agreement with the province, subject to the approval of the Governor in Council, for the confinement and treatment of those persons in institutions maintained and operated pursuant to the *Penitentiary Act* and for the release and supervision of those persons pursuant to the *Parole Act*.

(2) A narcotic addict who is committed to custody for treatment pursuant to an Act of the legislature of a province shall be deemed, for the purposes of the *Penitantiary Act* and the *Parole Act*, to have been sentenced to custody for treatment under this Act.

[1992, c. 20, s. 215(1)(*c*) will repeal the expression "*Parole Act*" wherever it occurs in section 27 and substitute the expression "Part II of the *Corrections and Conditional Release Act*".]

[1992, c. 20, s. 216(1)(*c*) will repeal the expression "*Penitentiary Act*" wherever it occurs in section 27 and substitute the expression "Part I of the *Corrections and Conditional Release Act*".]

Coming into force

Coming into force.

28. Part II or any provision thereof shall come into force on a day or days to be fixed by proclamation of the Governor in Council.

SCHEDULE

(*Sections 2 and 22*)

1. Opium Poppy (Papaver somniferum) its preparations, derivatives, alkaloids and salts, including:

(1) Opium,
(2) Codeine (Methylmorphine),

(3) Morphine,
(4) Thebaine,

and their preparations, derivatives and salts, including:

(5) Acetorphine,
(6) Acetyldihydrocodeine,
(7) Benzylmorphine,
(8) Codoxime,
(9) Desomorphine (dihydrodeoxymorphine).
(10) Diacetylmorphine (heroin),
(11) Dihydrocodeine,
(12) Dihydromorphine,
(13) Ethylmorphine,
(14) Etorphine,
(15) Hydrocodone (dihydrocodeinone),
(16) Hydromorphone (dihydromorphinone),
(17) Hydromorphinol (dihydro-14-hydroxymorphine),
(18) Methyldesorphine (*D*-deoxy-6-methylmorphine),
(19) Methyldihydromorphine (dihydro-6-methylmorphine),
(20) Metopon (dihydromethylmorphinone),
(21) Morphine-N-oxide (morphine-N-oxide),
(22) Myrophine (benzylmorphine Myristate),
(23) Nalorphine (N-allylnormorphine),
(24) Nicocodine (6-nicotinylcodeine),
(25) Nicomorphine (dinicotinylmorphine),
(26) Norcodeine,
(27) Normorphine,
(28) Oxycodone (dihydrohydroxycodeinone),
(29) Oxymorphone (dihydrohydroxymorphinone),
(30) Pholcodine (*B*-4-morpholinoethylmorphine), and
(31) Thebacon (acetyldihydrocodeinone),

but not including:

(32) Apomorphine,
(33) Cyprenorphine,
(34) Naloxone,
(35) Narcotine,
(36) Papaverine, and
(37) Poppy seed.

2. Coca (*Erythroxylon*), its preparations, derivatives, alkaloids and salts, including:

(1) Coca leaves,
(2) Cocaine, and
(3) Ecgonine (3-hydroxy-2-tropane carboxylic acid).

3. *Cannabis sativa*, its preparations, derivatives and similar synthetic preparations, including:

(1) Cannabis resin,
(2) Cannabis (marihuana),
(3) Cannabidiol,
(4) Cannabinol (3-n-amyl-6,6,9-trimethyl-6-dibenzopyran-1-ol),
(4.1) Nabilone ((±)-trans-(diméthylheptyl-1,1)-3 hexahydro-6, 6a, 7, 8, 10, 10a hydroxy-1 diméthyl-6,6 9H-dibenzo [b,d] pyrannone-9),
(5) Pyrahexyl (3-n-hexyl-6,6,9-trimethyl-7,8,9,10-tetrahydro-6-dibenzopyran-1-ol), and
(6) tetrahydrocannabinol.

but not including:

(7) non-viable Cannabis seed.

4. Phenylpiperidines, their preparations, intermediates, derivatives and salts, including:

(1) Allylprodine (3-allyl-1-methyl-4-phenyl-4-piperidyl propionate),
(2) Alphameprodine (α-3-ethyl-1-methyl-4-phenyl-4-piperidyl propionate),
(3) Alphaprodine (α-1-,3-dimethyl-4-phenyl-4-piperidyl propionate),
(4) Anileridine (ethyl 1-[2-p-aminophenyl) ethyl]-4-phenylpiperidine-4-carboxylate),
(5) Betameprodine (β-3-ethyl-1-methyl-4-phenyl-4-piperidyl propionate),
(6) Betaprodine (β-1, 3-dimethyl-4-phenyl-4-piperidyl propionate),
(7) Benzethidine (ethyl 1-(2-benzyloxyethyl)-4-phenylpiperidine-4-carboxylate),
(8) Diphenoxylate (ethyl 1-(3-cyano-3,3-diphenylpropyl)-4-phenylpiperidine-4-carboxylate),
(9) Etoxeridine (ethyl 1-[2-(2-hydroxyethoxy) ethyl]-4-phenylpiperidine-4-carboxylate),
(10) Furethidine (ethyl 1-(2-tetrahydrofurfuryloxethyl)-4-phenylpiperidine-4-carboxylate),
(11) Hydroxypethidine (ethyl 4-(m-hydroxyphenyl)-1-methyl-4-phenylpiperidine-3-carboxylate),
(12) Ketobemidone (1-[4-(m-hydroxyphenyl)-1-methyl-4-piperidyl]-1-propanone),
(13) Methylphenylisonipecotonitrile (4-cyano-1-methyl-4-phenylpiperidine),
(14) Morpheridine (ethyl 1-(2-morpholinoethyl)-4-phenylpiperidine-4-carboxylate),
(15) Norpethidine (ethyl 4-phenylpiperidine-4-carboxylate),
(16) Pethidine (ethyl 1-methyl-4-phenylpiperidine-4-carboxylate),

(17) Phenoperidine (ethyl 1-(3-hydroxy-3-phenylpropyl)-4-phenylpiperidine-4-carboxylate),
(18) Piminodine (ethyl 1-[3-(phenylamino) propyl]-4-phenylpiperidine-4-carboxylate),
(19) Properidine (isopropyl 1-methyl-4-phenylpiperidine-4-carboxylate), and
(20) Trimeperidine (1,2,5-trimethyl-4-phenyl-4-piperidyl propionate),

but not including:

(21) Carbamethidine (ethyl 1-(2-carbamylethyl)-4-phenylpiperidine-4-carboxyalte),
(22) Oxpheneridine (ethyl 1-(2-hydroxy-2-phenylethyl)-4-phenylpiperidine-4-carboxylate).

5. Phenazepines, their preparations, derivatives and salts, including:

(1) Proheptazie (hexahydro-1,3-dimethyl-4-phenyl-4-azepinyl propionate),

but not including:

(2) Ethoheptazine (ethyl hexahydro-1-methyl-4-penylazepine-4-carboxylate),
(3) Metetholpheptazine (ethyl hexahydro-1,3-dimethyl-4-phenylazepine-4-carboxylate), and
(4) Metheptazine (ethyl hexahydro-1,2-dimethyl-4-phenylazepine-4-carboxylate).

6. Amidones, their preparations, intermediates, derivatives and salts, including:

(1) Dimethylaminodiphenylbutanonitrile (4-cyano-2-dimethylamino-4,4-diphenyl butane),
(2) Dipipanone (4,4-diphenyl-6-piperidino-3-heptanone),
(3) Isomethadone (6-dimethyllamino-5-methyl-4,4-diphenyl-3-hexanone),
(4) Methadone (6-dimethylamino-4,4-diphenyl-3-heptanone),
(5) Normethadone (6-dimethylamino-4,4-diphenyl-3-hexanone), and
(6) Phenadoxone (6-morpholino-4,4-diphenyl-3-heptanone).

7. Methadols, their preparations, derivatives and salts, including:

(1) Acetylmethadol (6-dimethylamino-4,4-diphenyl-3-heptanyl acetate),
(2) Alphacetylmethadol (α-6-dimethylamino-4,4-diphenyl-3-heptanyl acetate),
(3) Alphamethadol (α-6-dimethylamino-4,4-diphenyl-3-heptanol),
(4) Betacetylmethadol (β-6-dimethylamino-4,4-diphenyl-3-heptanyl acetate),
(5) Betamethadol (β-6-dimethylamino, 4,4-diphenyl-3-heptanol),
(6) Dimepheptanol (6-dimethylamino-4,4-diphenyl-3-heptanol), and

(7) Noracymethadol (α-6-methylamino-4,4-diphenyl-3-heptanyl acetate),

8. Phenalkoxams, their preparations, derivatives and salts, including:

(1) Dimenoxadol (dimethylaminoethyl 1-ethoxy-1,1-diphenylacetate),

(2) Dioxaphetylbutyrate (ethyl 2,2-diphenyl-4-morpholino butyrate) and,

(3) Dextropropoxyphene ([S-(R*,S*)]-α-[2-(dimethylamino)-1-methylethyl)]-α -phenyl-benzeneethanol, propanoate ester).

9. Thiambutenes, their preparations, derivatives and salts, including:

(1) Diethylthiambutene (N,N-diethyl-1-methyl-3,3-di-2-thienylallylamine),

(2) Dimethylthiambutene (N,N,1-trimethyl-3,3-di-2-thienylallylamine), and

(3) Ethylmethylthiambutene (N-ethyl-N,1-dimethyl-3,3-di-2-thienyllallylamine).

10. Moramides, their preparations, intermediates, derivatives and salts, including:

(1) Dextromoramide (*d*-1-(3-methyl-4-morpholino-2,2-diphenylbutyryl) pyrrolidine),

(2) Diphenylmorpholinoisovaleric acid (2-methyl-3-morpholino-1,1-diphenylpropionic acid),

(3) Levomoramide (*l*-1-(3-methyl-4-morpholion-2,2-diphenylbutyryl) pyrolidine), and

(4) Racemoramide (*d,l*-1-(3-methyl-4-morpholino-2,2-diphenylbutyryl) pyrrolidine).

11. Morphinans, their preparations, derivatives and salts, including:

(1) Levomethorpham (*l*-1,2,3,9,10,10a-hexahydro-6-methoxy-11-methyl-4H-10, 4a-iminoethanophenanthrene),

(2) Levorphanol (*l*-1,2,3,9,10,10a-hexahydro-11-methyl-4H-10, 4a-iminoethenophenanthren-6-ol),

(3) Levophenacylmorphan (*l*-1,2,3,9,10,10a-hexahydro-11-phenacyl-4H-10, 4a-iminoethanophenanthren-4-ol),

(4) Norlevorphanol (*l*-1,2,3,9,10,10a-hexahydro-4H-10, 4a-iminoethanophenanthren-6-ol),

(5) Phenomorphan (*d,l*,-1,2,3,9,10,10a-hexahydro-11-phenethyl-4H-10, 4a-iminoethanophenanthren-6-ol),

(6) Racemethorphan (*d,l*-1,2,3,9,10,10a-hexahydro-6-methoxy-11-methyl-4H-10, 4a-iminoethanophenanthrene), and

(7) Racemorphan (*d,l*-1,2,3,9,10,10a-hexahydro-11-methyl-4H-10, 4a-iminoethanophenanthren-6-ol),

but not including:

(8) Dextromethorphan (*d*-1,2,3,9,10,10a-hexahydro-6-methoxy-11-methyl-4H-10, 4a-iminoethanophenanthrene),
(9) Dextrorphan (*d*-1,2,3,9,10,10a-hexahydro-11-methyl-4H-10, 4a-iminoethanophenanthren-6-ol),
(10) Levallorphan (*l*-11-allyl-1,2,3,9,10,10a-hexahydro-4H-10, 4a-iminoethanophenanthren-6-ol),
(11) Levargorphan (*l*-11-propargyl-1,2,3,9,10,10a-hexahydro-4H-10, 4a-iminoethanophenanthren-6-ol),
(12) Butorphanol and its salts, and
(13) Nalbuphine (17-(cyclobutylmethyl)-4-5α-epoxymorphinan-3,6α, 14-triol).

12. Benzazocines, their preparations, derivatives and salts, including:
(1) Phenazocine (1,2,3,4,5,6-hexahydro-6,11-dimethyl-3-phenethyl-2,6-methano-3-benzazocin-8-ol), and
(2) Metazocine (1,2,3,4,5,6-hexahydro-3,6,11-trimethyl-2,6-methano-3-benzacocin-8-ol),
(3) Pentazocine (1,2,3,4,5,6-hexahydro-6,11-dimethyl-3-(3-methyl-2-butenyl)-2 ,6-methano-3-benzazocin-8-ol),

but not including
(4) Cycloazocine (1,2,3,4,5,6-hexahydro-6,11-dimethyl-3-(cyclopropylmethyl)-2,6-methano-3-benzacocin-8-ol).

13. Ampromides, their preparations, derivatives and salts, including:
(1) Diampromide (N-[2-(methylphenethylamino)-propyl]-propionanilide), and
(2) Phenampromide (N-[2-(1-methyl-2-piperidyl)-ethyl]-propionanilide),
(3) Propiram (N-(1-methyl-2-piperidinoethyl)-N-2-pyridylpropionamide).

14. Benzimidazoles, their preparations, derivatives and salts, including:
(1) Clonitazene (2-(p-chlorobenzyl)-1-diethylaminoethyl-5-nitrobenzimidazone), and
(2) Etonitazene (2-(p-ethoxybenzyl)-1-diethylaminoethyl-5-nitrobenzimidazole).

15. Phencyclidine, its salts and derivatives.

16. Fentanyl (1-phenylethyl-4-(phenylpropionylamino)-piperidine), its salts and derivatives.

17. Sulfentanil (N-[4-methoxymethyl)-1-[2-(2-thienyl) ethyl]-4-piperidinyl]-N-phenylpropanamide), its salts and derivatives.

18. Tilidine (3-cyclohexene-1-carboxylic acid, 2-(dimethylamino)-1-phenylethyl ester, trans (±), its preparations, derivatives and salts.

19. Carfentanil (methyl 4-[(1-oxopropyl) phenylamino]-1-(2-phenylethyl)-4-piperidine-carboxylate), its salts and derivatives.

20. Alfentanil (N-[1-[2-(4-ethyl-4,5-dihydro-5-oxo-1H-tetrazol-1-yl)ethyl]-4-(methoxymethyl)-4-piperidinyl]- N-phenylpropanamide), its salts and derivatives.

YOUNG OFFENDERS ACT

TABLE OF CONCORDANCE

S.C. 1980-81-83 c. 110	R.S.C. 1985, c. Y-1
110	**Y-1**
1	1
2	2
	2.1
3	3
4	4
5	5
6	6
7	7
	7.1
	7.2
8	8
9	9
10	10
11	11
12	12
13	13
14	14
15	15
16	16
17	17
18	18
19	19
20	20
21	21
22	22
23	23
	24
24	24.1 to 24.5
25	25
26	25.1
	26
27	27
28	28
29	29
30	30
31	31
32	32
33	33
34	34
35	35
36	36
37	37
38	38
39	39
40	40
41	41
42	42
43	43
44	44
	44.1
	44.2
45	45
	45.1
	45.2
46	46
47	47
48	48
49	49
50	50
51	51
52	52
53	53
54	54
55	55
56	56
57	57
58	58
59	59
60	60
61	61
62	62
63	63
64	64
65	65
66	66
67	67
68	68
69	69

S.C. 1980-81-83 c. 110	R.S.C. 1985, c. Y-1	S.C. 1980-81-83 c. 110	R.S.C. 1985, c. Y-1
110	**Y-1**	**110**	**Y-1**
70	70	77	77
71	71	78	78
72	72	79	
73	73	80	
74	74	81	
75	75	Sch/Ann	Sch/Ann
76	76		

YOUNG OFFENDERS ACT

R.S.C. 1985, c.Y-1

As amended by R.S. 1985, c. 27 (1st Supp.), ss. 187, 203, Schedule V; c. 24 (2nd Supp.), ss. 1-44; c. 1 (3rd Supp.), Schedule; c. 1 (4th Supp.), ss. 38-45; 1991, c. 43, ss. 31-34; 1992, c. 1, s. 21; 1992, c. 11.

An Act respecting young offenders

SHORT TITLE

Short title.

1. This Act may be cited as the *Young Offenders Act.*

INTERPRETATION

Definitions — Words and expressions.

2. (1) In this Act,

"adult" means a person who is neither a young person nor a child;

"alternative measures" means measures other than judicial proceedings under this Act used to deal with a young person alleged to have committed an offence;

"child" means a person who is or, in the absence of evidence to the contrary, appears to be under the age of twelve years;

"disposition" means a disposition made under section 20 or sections 28 to 32 and includes a confirmation or a variation of a disposition;

"offence" means an offence created by an Act of Parliament or by any regulation, rule, order, by-law or ordinance made thereunder other than an ordinance of the Yukon Territory or the Northwest Territories;

"ordinary court" means the court that would, but for this Act, have jurisdiction in respect of an offence alleged to have been committed;

"parent" includes, in respect of another person, any person who is under a legal duty to provide for that other person or any person who has, in law or in fact, the custody or control of that other person, but does not include a person who has the custody or control of that other person by reason only of proceedings under this Act;

"predisposition report" means a report on the personal and family history and present environment of a young person made in accordance with section 14;

"progress report" means a report made in accordance with section 28 on the performance of a young person against whom a disposition has been made;

"provincial director" means a person, a group or class of persons or a body appointed or designated by or pursuant to an Act of the legislature of a province or by the Lieutenant Governor in Council of a province or his delegate to perform in that province, either generally or in a specific case, any of the duties or functions of a provincial director under this Act;

"review board" means a review board established or designated by a province for the purposes of section 30;

"young person" means a person who is or, in the absence of evidence to the contrary, appears to be twelve years of age or more, but under eighteen years of age and, where the context requires, includes any person who is charged under this Act with having committed an offence while he was a young person or is found guilty of an offence under this Act;

"youth court" means a court established or designated by or under an Act of the legislature of a province, or designated by the Governor in Council or the Lieutenant Governor in Council of a province, as a youth court for the purposes of this Act;

"youth court judge" means a person appointed to be a judge of a youth court;

"youth worker" means a person appointed or designated, whether by title of youth worker or probation officer or by any other title, by or pursuant to an Act of the legislature of a province or by the Lieutenant Governor in Council of a province or his delegate, to perform, either generally or in a specific case, in that province any of the duties or functions of a youth worker under this Act.

(2) Unless otherwise provided, words and expressions used in this Act have the same meaning as in the *Criminal Code*. R.S., c. 24 (2nd Supp.), s. 1.

Powers, duties and functions of provincial directors.

2.1 Any power, duty or function of a provincial director under this Act may be exercised or performed by any person authorized by the provincial director to do so and, if so exercised or performed, shall be deemed to have been exercised or performed by the provincial director. R.S., c. 24 (2nd Supp.), s. 2.

DECLARATION OF PRINCIPLE

Policy for Canada with respect to young offenders — Act to be liberally construed.

3. (1) It is hereby recognized and declared that

(*a*) while young persons should not in all instances be held accountable in the same manner or suffer the same consequences for their behaviour as adults, young persons who commit offences should nonetheless bear responsibility for their contraventions;

(*b*) society must, although it has the responsibility to take reasonable measures to prevent criminal conduct by young persons, be afforded the necessary protection from illegal behaviour;

(*c*) young persons who commit offences require supervision, discipline and control, but, because of their state of dependency and level of development and maturity, they also have special needs and require guidance and assistance;

(*d*) where it is not inconsistent with the protection of society, taking no measures or taking measures other than judicial proceedings under this Act should be considered for dealing with young persons who have committed offences;

(*e*) young persons have rights and freedoms in their own right, including those stated in the *Canadian Charter of Rights and Freedoms* or in the *Canadian Bill of Rights*, and in particular a right to be heard in the course of, and to participate in, the processes that lead to decisions that affect them, and young persons should have special guarantees of their rights and freedoms;

(*f*) in the application of this Act, the rights and freedoms of young persons include a right to the least possible interference with freedom that is consistent with the protection of society, having regard to the needs of young persons and the interests of their families;

(*g*) young persons have the right, in every instance where they have rights or freedoms that may be affected by this Act, to be informed as to what those rights and freedoms are; and

(*h*) parents have responsibility for the care and supervision of their children, and, for that reason, young persons should be removed from parental supervision either partly or entirely only when measures that provide for continuing parental supervision are inappropriate.

(2) This Act shall be liberally construed to the end that young persons will be dealt with in accordance with the principles set out in subsection (1).

ALTERNATIVE MEASURES

Alternative measures — Restriction on use — Admissions not admissible in evidence — No bar to proceedings — Laying of information, etc.

4. (1) Alternative measures may be used to deal with a young person alleged to have committed an offence instead of judicial proceedings under this Act only if

(*a*) the measures are part of a program of alternative measures authorized by the Attorney General or his delegate or authorized by a person, or a person within a class of persons, designated by the Lieutenant Governor in Council of a province;

(*b*) the person who is considering whether to use such measures is satisfied that they would be appropriate, having regard to the needs of the young person and the interests of society;

(*c*) the young person, having been informed of the alternative measures fully and freely consents to participate therein;
(*d*) the young person has, before consenting to participate in the alternative measures, been advised of his right to be represented by counsel and been given a reasonable opportunity to consult with counsel;
(*e*) the young person accepts responsibility for the act or omission that forms the basis of the offence that he is alleged to have committed;
(*f*) there is, in the opinion of the Attorney General or his agent, sufficient evidence to proceed with the prosecution of the offence; and
(*g*) the prosecution of the offence is not in any way barred at law.

(2) Alternative measures shall not be used to deal with a young person alleged to have committed an offence if the young person
(*a*) denies his participation or involvement in the commission of the offence or
(*b*) expresses his wish to have any charge against him dealt with by the youth court.

(3) No admission, confession or statement accepting responsibility for a given act or omission made by a young person alleged to have committed an offence as a condition of his being dealt with by alternative measures shall be admissible in evidence against him in any civil or criminal proceedings.

(4) The use of alternative measures in respect of a young person alleged to have committed an offence is not a bar to proceedings against him under this Act, but
(*a*) where the youth court is satisfied on a balance of probabilities that the young person has totally complied with the terms and conditions of the alternative measures, the youth court shall dismiss any charge against him and
(*b*) where the youth court is satisfied on a balance of probabilities that the young person has partially complied with the terms and conditions of the alternative measures, the youth court may dismiss any charge against him if, in the opinion of the court, the prosecution of the charge would, having regard to the circumstances, be unfair, and the youth court may consider the young person's performance with respect to the alternative measures before making a disposition under this Act.

(5) Subject to subsection (4), nothing in this section shall be construed to prevent any person from laying an information, obtaining the issue or confirmation of any process or proceeding with the prosecution of any offence in accordance with law.

JURISDICTION

Exclusive jurisdiction of youth court — Period of limitation — Proceedings continued when adult — Powers of youth court judge — Court of record.

5. (1) Notwithstanding any other Act of Parliament but subject to the *National Defence Act* and section 16, a youth court has exclusive jurisdiction in respect of any offence alleged to have been committed by a person while he was a young person and any such person shall be dealt with as provided in this Act.

(2) No proceedings in respect of an offence shall be commenced under this Act after the expiration of the time limit set out in any other Act of Parliament or any regulation made thereunder for the institution of proceedings in respect of that offence.

(3) Proceedings commenced under this Act against a young person may be continued, after he becomes an adult, in all respects as if he remained a young person.

(4) A youth court judge, for the purpose of carrying out the provisions of this Act, is a justice and a provincial court judge and has the jurisdiction and powers of a summary conviction court under the *Criminal Code*.

(5) A youth court is a court of record. R.S., c. 24 (2nd Supp.), s. 3.

Certain proceedings may be taken before justices.

6. Any proceeding that may be carried out before a justice under the *Criminal Code*, other than a plea, a trial or an adjudication, may be carried out before such justice in respect of an offence alleged to have been committed by a young person, and any process that may be issued by a justice under the *Criminal Code* may be issued by such justice in respect of an offence alleged to have been commited by a young person. R.S., c. 24 (2nd Supp.), s. 4.

DETENTION PRIOR TO DISPOSITION

Designated place of temporary detention — Exception — Detention separate from adults — Transfer by provincial director — Exception relating to temporary detention — Authorization of provincial authority for detention — Determination by provincial authority of place of detention.

7. (1) A young person who is

(*a*) arrested and detained prior to the making of a disposition in respect of the young person under section 20, or

(*b*) detained pursuant to a warrant issued under subsection 32(6)

shall, subject to subsection (4), be detained in a place of temporary detention designated as such by the Lieutenant Governor in Council of the appropriate province or his delegate or in a place within a class of such places so designated.

(1.1) A young person who is detained in a place of temporary detention pursuant to subsection (1) may, in the course of being transferred from that place to the court or from the court to that place, be held under the supervision and control of a peace officer.

(2) A young person referred to in subsection (1) shall be held separate and apart from any adult who is detained or held in custody unless a youth court judge or a justice is satisfied that

(*a*) the young person cannot, having regard to his own safety or the safety of others, be detained in a place of detention for young persons; or

(*b*) no place of detention for young persons is available within a reasonable distance.

(3) A young person who is detained in custody in accordance with subsection (1) may, during the period of detention, be transferred by the provincial director from one place of temporary detention to another.

(4) Subsections (1) and (2) do not apply in respect of any temporary restraint of a young person under the supervision and control of a peace officer after arrest, but a young person who is so restrained shall be transferred to a place of temporary detention referred to in subsection (1) as soon as is reasonably practicable, and in no case later than the first reasonable opportunity after the appearance of the young person before a youth court judge or a justice pursuant to section 503 of the *Criminal Code.*

(5) In any province for which the Lieutenant Governor in Council has designated a person or a group of persons whose authorization is required, either in all circumstances or in circumstances specified by the Lieutenant Governor in Council, before a young person who has been arrested may be detained in accordance with this section, no young person shall be so detained unless the authorization is obtained.

(6) In any province for which the Lieutenant Governor in Council has designated a person or a group of persons who may determine the place where a young person who has been arrested may be detained in accordance with this section, no young person may be so detained in a place other than the one so determined. R.S., c. 24 (2nd Supp.), s. 5.

Placement of young person in care of responsible person — Condition of placement — Removing young person from care — Order — Effect of arrest.

7.1 (1) Where a youth court judge or a justice is satisfied that

(*a*) a young person who has been arrested would, but for this subsection, be detained in custody,

(*b*) a responsible person is willing and able to take care of and exercise control over the young person, and

(*c*) the young person is willing to be placed in the care of that person, the young person may be placed in the care of that person instead of being detained in custody.

(2) A young person shall not be placed in the care of a person under subsection (1) unless

(*a*) that person undertakes in writing to take care of and to be responsible for the attendance of the young person in court when required and to comply with such other conditions as the youth court judge or justice may specify; and

(*b*) the young person undertakes in writing to comply with the arrangement and to comply with such other conditions as the youth court judge or justice may specify.

(3) Where a young person has been placed in the care of a person under subsection (1) and

(*a*) that person is no longer willing or able to take care of or exercise control over the young person, or

(*b*) it is, for any other reason, no longer appropriate that the young person be placed in the care of that person,

the young person, the person in whose care the young person has been placed or any other person may, by application in writing to a youth court judge or a justice, apply for an order under subsection (4).

(4) Where a youth court judge or a justice is satisfied that a young person should not remain in the custody of the person in whose care he was placed under subsection (1), the youth court judge or justice shall

(*a*) make an order relieving the person and the young person of the obligations undertaken pursuant to subsection (2); and

(*b*) issue a warrant for the arrest of the young person.

(5) Where a young person is arrested pursuant to a warrant issued under paragraph (4)(*b*), the young person shall be taken before a youth court judge or justice forthwith and dealt with under section 515 of the *Criminal Code*. R.S., c. 24 (2nd Supp.), s. 5.

Offence and punishment.

7.2 Any person who wilfully fails to comply with section 7, or with an undertaking entered into pursuant to subsection 7.1(2), is guilty of an offence punishable on summary conviction. R.S., c. 24 (2nd Supp.), s. 5.

Application to youth court — Notice to prosecutor — Notice to young person — Waiver of notice — Application for review under section 520 or 521 of Criminal Code — Idem — Interim release by youth court judge only — Review by court of appeal.

8. (1) [Repealed, R.S. 1985, c. 24 (2nd Supp.), s. 6.]

(2) Where an order is made under section 515 of the *Criminal Code* in respect of a young person by a justice who is not a youth court judge, an application

may, at any time after the order is made, be made to a youth court for the release from or detention in custody of the young person, as the case may be, and the youth court shall hear the matter as an original application.

(3) An application under subsection (2) for release from custody shall not be heard unless the young person has given the prosecutor at least two clear days notice in writing of the application.

(4) An application under subsection (2) for detention in custody shall not be heard unless the prosecutor has given the young person at least two clear days notice in writing of the application.

(5) The requirement for a notice under subsection (3) or (4) may be waived by the prosecutor or by the young person or his counsel, as the case may be.

(6) An application under section 520 or 521 of the *Criminal Code* for a review of an order made in respect of a young person by a youth court judge who is a judge of a superior, county or district court shall be made to a judge of the court of appeal.

(7) No application may be made under section 520 or 521 of the *Criminal Code* for a review of an order made in respect of a young person by a justice who is not a youth court judge.

(8) Where a young person against whom proceedings have been taken under this Act is charged with an offence referred to in section 522 of the *Criminal Code*, a youth court judge, but no other court, judge or justice, may release the young person from custody under that section.

(9) A decision made by a youth court judge under subsection (8) may be reviewed in accordance with section 680 of the *Criminal Code* and that section applies, with such modifications as the circumstances require, to any decision so made. R.S. 1985, c. 24 (2nd Supp.), s. 6.

NOTICES TO PARENTS

Notice to parent in case of arrest — Notice to parent in case of summons or appearance notice — Notice to relative or other adult — Notice to spouse — Notice on direction of youth court judge or justice — Contents of notice — Service of notice — Proceedings not invalid — Exception — Where a notice not served.

9. (1) Subject to subsections (3) and (4), where a young person is arrested and detained in custody pending his appearance in court, the officer in charge at the time the young person is detained shall, as soon as possible, give or cause to be given, orally or in writing, to a parent of the young person notice of the arrest stating the place of detention and the reason for the arrest.

(2) Subject to subsections (3) and (4), where a summons or an appearance notice is issued in respect of a young person, the person who issued the summons or appearance notice, or, where a young person is released on giving his promise

to appear or entering into a recognizance, the officer in charge, shall, as soon as possible, give or cause to be given, in writing, to a parent of the young person notice of the summons, appearance notice, promise to appear or recognizance.

(3) Where the whereabouts of the parents of a young person

(*a*) who is arrested and detained in custody,

(*b*) in respect of whom a summons or an appearance notice is issued, or

(*c*) who is released on giving his promise to appear or entering into a recognizance

are not known or it appears that no parent is available, a notice under this section may be given to an adult relative of the young person who is known to the young person and is likely to assist him or, if no such adult relative is available, to such other adult who is known to the young person and is likely to assist him as the person giving the notice considers appropriate.

(4) Where a young person described in paragraph (3)(*a*), (*b*) or (*c*) is married, a notice under this section may be given to the spouse of the young person instead of a parent.

(5) Where doubt exists as to the person to whom a notice under this section should be given, a youth court judge or, where a youth court judge is, having regard to the circumstances, not reasonably available, a justice may give directions as to the person to whom the notice should be given, and a notice given in accordance with those directions is sufficient notice for the purposes of this section.

(6) Any notice under this section shall, in addition to any other requirements under this section, include

(*a*) the name of the young person in respect of whom it is given;

(*b*) the charge against the young person and the time and place of appearance; and

(*c*) a statement that the young person has the right to be represented by counsel.

(7) Subject to subsections (9) and (10), a notice under this section given in writing may be served personally or may be sent by mail.

(8) Subject to subsection (9) and (10), failure to give notice in accordance with this section does not affect the validity of proceedings under this Act.

(9) Failure to give notice under subsection (2) in accordance with this section in any case renders invalid any subsequent proceedings under this Act relating to the case unless

(*a*) a parent of the young person against whom proceedings are held attends court with the young person; or

(*b*) a youth court judge or a justice before whom proceedings are held against the young person

(i) adjourns the proceedings and orders that the notice be given in such manner and to such persons as the judge or justice directs, or

(ii) dispenses with the notice where the judge or justice is of the opinion that, having regard to the circumstances, the notice may be dispensed with.

(10) Where there has been a failure to give a notice under subsection (1) in accordance with this section and none of the persons to whom such notice may be given attends court with a young person, a youth court judge or a justice before whom proceedings are held against the young person may

(*a*) adjourn the proceedings and order that the notice be given in such manner and to such person as he directs; or

(*b*) dispense with the notice where, in his opinion, having regard to the circumstances, notice may be dispensed with. R.S., c. 24 (2nd Supp.), s. 7(1); 1991, c. 43, s. 31.

(11) [Repealed, R.S. 1985, c. 24 (2nd Supp.), s. 7(2).]

Order requiring attendance of parent — Service of order — Failure to attend — Appeal — Warrant to arrest parent.

10. (1) Where a parent does not attend proceedings before a youth court in respect of a young person, the court may, if in its opinion the presence of the parent is necessary or in the best interest of the young person, by order in writing require the parent to attend at any stage of the proceedings.

(2) A copy of any order made under subsection (1) shall be served by a peace officer or by a person designated by a youth court by delivering it personally to the parent to whom it is directed, unless the youth court authorizes service by registered mail.

(3) A parent who is ordered to attend a youth court pursuant to subsection (1) and who fails without reasonable excuse, the proof of which lies on that parent, to comply with the order

(*a*) is guilty of contempt of court;

(*b*) may be dealt with summarily by the court; and

(*c*) is liable to the punishment provided for in the *Criminal Code* for a summary conviction offence.

(4) Section 10 of the *Criminal Code* applies where a person is convicted of contempt of court under subsection (3).

(5) If a parent who is ordered to attend a youth court pursuant to subsection (1) does not attend at the time and place named in the order or fails to remain in attendance as required and it is proved that a copy of the order was served on the parent, a youth court may issue a warrant to compel the attendance of the parent. R.S., c. 24 (2nd Supp.), s. 8(1).

(6) [Repealed, R.S., c. 24 (2nd Supp.), s. 8(2).]

RIGHT TO COUNSEL

Right to retain counsel — Arresting officer to advise young person of right to counsel — Justice, youth court or review board to advise young person of right to counsel — Trial, hearing or review before youth court or review board — Appointment of counsel — Release hearing before justice — Young person may be assisted by adult — Counsel independent of parents — Statement of right to counsel.

11. (1) A young person has the right to retain and instruct counsel without delay, and to exercise that right personally, at any stage of proceedings against the young person and prior to and during any consideration of whether, instead of commencing or continuing judicial proceedings against the young person under this Act, to use alternative measures to deal with the young person.

(2) Every young person who is arrested or detained shall, forthwith on his arrest or detention, be advised by the arresting officer or the officer in charge, as the case may be, of his right to be represented by counsel and shall be given an opportunity to obtain counsel.

(3) Where a young person is not represented by counsel

(*a*) at a hearing at which it will be determined whether to release the young person or detain him in custody prior to disposition of his case,

(*b*) at a hearing held pursuant to section 16,

(*c*) at his trial, or

(*c*.1) at any proceedings held pursuant to subsection 26.1(1), 26.2(1) or 26.6(1), or

(*d*) at a review of a disposition held before a youth court or a review board under this Act,

the justice before whom, or the youth court or review board before which, the hearing, trial or review is held shall advise the young person of his right to be represented by counsel and shall give the young person a reasonable opportunity to obtain counsel.

(4) Where a young person at his trial or at a hearing or review referred to in subsection (3) wishes to obtain counsel but is unable to do so, the youth court before which the hearing, trial or review is held or the review board before which the review is held

(*a*) shall, where there is a legal aid or assistance program available in the province where the hearing, trial or review is held, refer the young person to that program for the appointment of counsel; or

(*b*) where no legal aid or assistance program is available or the young person is unable to obtain counsel through such a program, may, and on the request of the young person shall, direct that the young person be represented by counsel.

(5) Where a direction is made under paragraph (4)(*b*) in respect of a young person, the Attorney General of the province in which the direction is made

shall appoint counsel, or cause counsel to be appointed, to represent the young person.

(6) Where a young person at a hearing before a justice who is not a youth court judge at which it will be determined whether to release the young person or detain him in custody prior to disposition of his case wishes to obtain counsel but is unable to do so, the justice shall

(*a*) where there is a legal aid or assistance program available in the province where the hearing is held,

(i) refer the young person to that program for the appointment of counsel, or

(ii) refer the matter to a youth court to be dealt with in accordance with paragraph 4(*a*) or (*b*); or

(*b*) where no legal aid or assistance program is available or the young person is unable to obtain counsel through such a program, refer the matter to a youth court to be dealt with in accordance with paragraph (4)(*b*).

(7) Where a young person is not represented by counsel at his trial or at a hearing or review referred to in subsection (3), the justice before whom or the youth court or review board before which the proceedings are held may, on the request of the young person, allow the young person to be assisted by an adult whom the justice, court or review board considers to be suitable.

(8) In any case where it appears to a youth court judge or a justice that the interests of a young person and his parents are in conflict or that it would be in the best interest of the young person to be represented by his own counsel, the judge or justice shall ensure that the young person is represented by counsel independent of his parents.

(9) A statement that a young person has the right to be represented by counsel shall be included in

(*a*) any appearance notice or summons issued to the young person;

(*b*) any warrant to arrest the young person;

(*c*) any promise to appear given by the young person;

(*d*) any recognizance entered into before an officer in charge by the young person;

(*e*) any notice given to the young person in relation to any proceedings held pursuant to subsection 26.1(1), 26.2(1) or 26.6(1); or

(*f*) any notice of a review of a disposition given to the young person. R.S., c. 24 (2nd Supp.), s. 9; 1992, c. 11, s. 1.

APPEARANCE

Where young person appears — Waiver — Where young person not represented by counsel — Where youth court not satisfied.

12. (1) Where a young person against whom an information is laid first appears before a youth court judge or a justice, the judge or justice shall (*a*) cause the information to be read to him; and

(*b*) where the young person is not represented by counsel, inform him of his right to be so represented.

(2) A young person may waive the requirement under paragraph (1)(*a*) where the young person is represented by counsel.

(3) Where a young person is not represented in youth court by counsel, the youth court shall, before accepting a plea,

(*a*) satisfy itself that the young person understands the charge against him; and

(*b*) explain to the young person that he may plead guilty or not guilty to the charge.

(4) Where the youth court is not satisfied that a young person understands the charge against him, as required under paragraph (3)(*a*), the court shall enter a plea of not guilty on behalf of the young person and shall proceed with the trial in accordance with subsection 19(2).

MEDICAL AND PSYCHOLOGICAL REPORTS

Medical or psychological assessment — Purpose of assessment — Custody for assessment — Presumption against custodial remand — Report of qualified person in writing — Application to vary assessment order where circumstances change — Disclosure of report — Cross-examination — Report may be withheld from young person, parents or prosecutor — Report to be withheld where disclosure unnecessary or prejudicial — Report to be withheld where disclosure dangerous to any person — Idem — Disclosure by qualified person — Definition of "qualified person".

13. (1) A youth court may, at any stage of proceedings against a young person

(*a*) with the consent of the young person and the prosecutor, or

(*b*) on its own motion or on application of the young person or the prosecutor, where the court has reasonable grounds to believe that the young person may be suffering from a physical or mental illness or disorder, a psychological disorder, an emotional disturbance, a learning disability or mental retardation and the court believes a medical, psychological or psychiatric report in respect of the young person is necessary for a purpose mentioned in paragraph (2)(*a*) or (*b*),

by order require that the young person be assessed by a qualified person and require the person who conducts the assessment to report the results thereof in writing to the court.

(2) A youth court may make an order under subsection (1) in respect of a young person for the purpose of

(*a*) considering an application under section 16; or

(*b*) making or reviewing a disposition under this Act, other than a disposition made under section 672.54 or 672.58 of the *Criminal Code*.

(3) Subject to subsections (3.1) and (3.3), for the purpose of an assessment under this section, a youth court may remand a young person to such custody as it directs for a period not exceeding thirty days.

(3.1) A young person shall not be remanded in custody pursuant to an order made by a youth court under subsection (1) unless

(*a*) the youth court is satisfied that on the evidence custody is necessary to conduct an assessment of the young person, or that on the evidence of a qualified person detention of the young person in custody is desirable to conduct the assessment of the young person and the young person consents to custody; or

(*b*) the young person is required to be detained in custody in respect of any other matter or by virtue of any provision of the *Criminal Code*.

(3.2) For the purposes of paragraph (3.1)(*a*), when the prosecutor and the young person agree, evidence of a qualified person may be received in the form of a report in writing.

(3.3) A youth court may, at any time while an order in respect of a young person made by the court under subsection (1) is in force, on cause being shown, vary the terms and conditions specified in that order in such manner as the court considers appropriate in the circumstances.

(4) Where a youth court receives a report made in respect of a young person pursuant to subsection (1),

(*a*) the court shall, subject to subsection (6), cause a copy of the report to be given to

(i) the young person,

(ii) a parent of the young person, if the parent is in attendance at the proceedings against the young person,

(iii) counsel, if any, representing the young person, and

(iv) the prosecutor; and

(*b*) the court may cause a copy of the report to be given to a parent of the young person not in attendance at the proceedings against the young person if the parent is, in the opinion of the court, taking an active interest in the proceedings.

(5) Where a report is made in respect of a young person pursuant to subsection (1), the young person, his counsel or the adult assisting him pursuant to subsection 11(7) and the prosecutor shall, subject to subsection (6), on application to the youth court, be given an opportunity to cross-examine the person who made the report.

(6) A youth court shall withhold all or part of a report made in respect of a young person pursuant to subsection (1) from a private prosecutor, where

disclosure of the report or part, in the opinion of the court, is not necessary for the prosecution of the case and might be prejudicial to the young person.

(7) A youth court shall withhold all or part of a report made in respect of a young person pursuant to subsection (1) from the young person, the young person's parents or a private prosecutor where the court is satisfied, on the basis of the report or evidence given in the absence of the young person, parents or private prosecutor by the person who made the report, that disclosure of all or part of the report would seriously impair the treatment or recovery of the young person, or would be likely to endanger the life or safety of, or result in serious psychological harm to, another person.

(8) Notwithstanding subsection (7), the youth court may release all or part of the report referred to in that subsection to the young person, the young person's parents or the private prosecutor where the interests of justice make disclosure essential in the court's opinion.

(9) A report made pursuant to subsection (1) shall form part of the record of the case in respect of which it was requested.

(10) Notwithstanding any other provision of this Act, a qualified person who is of the opinion that a young person held in detention or committed to custody is likely to endanger his own life or safety or to endanger the life of, or cause bodily harm to, another person may immediately so advise any person who has the care and custody of the young person whether or not the same information is contained in a report made pursuant to subsection (1).

(11) In this section, "qualified person" means a person duly qualified by provincial law to practice medicine or psychiatry or to carry out psychological examinations or assessments, as the circumstances require, or, where no such law exists, a person who is, in the opinion of the youth court, so qualified, and includes a person or a person within a class of persons designated by the Lieutenant Governor in Council of a province or his delegate. R.S. 1985, c. 24 (2d Supp.), s. 10; 1991, c. 43, s. 32.

(12) [Repealed, R.S. 1985, c. 24 (2nd Supp.), s. 10.]

Statements not admissible against young person — Exceptions.

13.1 (1) Subject to subsection (2), where a young person is assessed pursuant to an order made under subsection 13(1), no statement or reference to a statement made by the young person during the course and for the purposes of the assessment to the person who conducts the assessment or to anyone acting under that person's direction is admissible in evidence, without the consent of the young person, in any proceeding before a court, tribunal, body or person with jurisdiction to compel the production of evidence.

(2) A statement referred to in subsection (1) is admissible in evidence for the purposes of

(*a*) considering an application under section 16 in respect of the young person;

(*b*) determining whether the young person is unfit to stand trial;
(*c*) determining whether the balance of the mind of the young person was disturbed at the time of commission of the alleged offence, where the young person is a female person charged with an offence arising out of the death of her newly-born child;
(*d*) making or reviewing a disposition in respect of the young person;
(*e*) determining whether the young person was, at the time of the commission of an alleged offence, suffering from automatism or a mental disorder so as to be exempt from criminal responsibility by virtue of subsection 16(1) of the *Criminal Code*, if the accused puts his or her mental capacity for criminal intent into issue, or if the prosecutor raises the issue after verdict;
(*f*) challenging the credibility of a young person in any proceeding where the testimony of the young person is inconsistent in a material particular with a statement referred to in subsection (1) that the young person made previously; or
(*g*) establishing the perjury of a young person who is charged with perjury in respect of a statement made in any proceeding. 1991, c. 43, s. 33.

APPLICATION OF PART XX.1 OF THE CRIMINAL CODE (MENTAL DISORDER)

Sections of Criminal Code applicable — Notice and copies to counsel and parents — Proceedings not invalid — Exception — No hospital order assessments — Considerations of court or Review Board making a disposition — Cap applicable to young persons — Application to increase cap of unfit young person subject to transfer — Consideration of youth court for increase in cap — *Prima facie* case to be made every year — Designation of hospitals for young persons.

13.2 (1) Except to the extent that they are inconsistent with or excluded by this Act, section 16 and Part XX.1 of the *Criminal Code*, except sections 672.65 and 672.66, apply, with such modifications as the circumstances require, in respect of proceedings under this Act in relation to offences alleged to have been committed by young persons.

(2) For the purposes of subsection (1), wherever in Part XX.1 of the *Criminal Code* a reference is made to

(*a*) a copy to be sent or otherwise given to an accused or a party to the proceedings, the reference shall be read as including a reference to a copy to be sent or otherwise given to
  (i) counsel, if any, representing the young person,
  (ii) any parent of the young person who is in attendance at the proceedings against the young person, and
  (iii) any parent of the young person who is, in the opinion of the youth court or Review Board, taking an active interest in the proceedings; and
(*b*) notice to be given to an accused or a party to proceedings, the reference

shall be read as including a reference to notice to be given to counsel, if any, representing the young person and the parents of the young person.

(3) Subject to subsection (4), failure to give a notice referred to in paragraph (2)(*b*) to a parent of a young person does not affect the validity of proceedings under this Act.

(4) Failure to give a notice referred to in paragraph (2)(*b*) to a parent of a young person in any case renders invalid any subsequent proceedings under this Act relating to the case unless

(*a*) a parent of the young person attends at the court or Review Board with the young person; or

(*b*) a youth court judge or Review Board before whom proceedings are held against the young person

(i) adjourns the proceedings and orders that the notice be given in such manner and to such persons as the judge or Review Board directs, or

(ii) dispenses with the notice where the youth court or Review Board is of the opinion that, having regard to the circumstances, the notice may be dispensed with.

(5) A youth court may not make an order under subsection 672.11 of the *Criminal Code* in respect of a young person for the purpose of assisting in the determination of an issue mentioned in paragraph 672.11(*e*) of that Act.

(6) Before making or reviewing a disposition in respect of a young person under Part XX.1 of the *Criminal Code*, a youth court or Review Board shall consider the age and special needs of the young person and any representations or submissions made by the young person's parents.

(7) Subject to subsection (9), for the purpose of applying subsection 672.64(3) of the *Criminal Code* to proceedings under this Act in relation to an offence alleged to have been committed by a young person, the applicable cap shall be the maximum period during which the young person would be subject to a disposition by the youth court if found guilty of the offence.

(8) Where an application is made under section 16 to proceed against a young person in ordinary court and the young person is found unfit to stand trial, the Attorney General or the agent of the Attorney General may, before the youth court makes or refuses to make an order under that section, apply to the court to increase the cap that shall apply to the young person.

(9) The youth court, after giving the Attorney General and the counsel and parents of the young person in respect of whom an application is made under subsection (8) an opportunity to be heard, shall take into consideration

(*a*) the seriousness of the alleged offence and the circumstances in which it was allegedly committed,

(*b*) the age, maturity, character and background of the young person and any previous findings of guilty against the young person under any Act of Parliament, (*c*) the likelihood that the young person will cause significant harm to any person if released on expiration of the cap that applies to the young person pursuant to subsection (7), and

(*d*) the respective caps that would apply to the young person under this Act and under the *Criminal Code*,

and the youth court shall, where satisfied that the application under section 16 would likely succeed if the young person were fit to stand trial, apply to the young person the cap that would apply to an adult for the same offence.

(10) For the purpose of applying subsection 672.33(1) of the *Criminal Code* to proceeedings under this Act in relation to an offence alleged to have been committed by a young person, wherever in that subsection a reference is made to two years, there shall be substituted a reference to one year.

(11) A reference in Part XX.1 of the *Criminal Code* to a hospital in a province shall be construed as a reference to a hospital designated by the Minister of Health of the province for the custody, treatment or assessment of young persons. 1991, c. 43, s. 33.

PRE-DISPOSITION REPORT

Pre-disposition report — Contents of report — Oral report with leave — Report to form part of record — Copies of pre-disposition report — Cross-examination — Report may be withheld from private prosecutor — Report disclosed to other persons — Disclosure by the provincial director — Inadmissibility of statements.

14. (1) Where a youth court deems it advisable before making a disposition under section 20 in respect of a young person who is found guilty of an offence it may, and where a youth court is required under this Act to consider a pre-disposition report before making an order or a disposition in respect of a young person it shall, require the provincial director to cause to be prepared a pre-disposition report in respect of the young person and to submit the report to the court.

(2) A pre-disposition report made in respect of a young person shall, subject to subsection (3), be in writing and shall include,

(*a*) the results of an interview with the young person and, where reasonably possible, the results of an interview with the parents of the young person;

(*b*) the results of an interview with the victim in the case, where applicable and where reasonably possible; and

(*c*) such information as is applicable to the case including, where applicable,

(i) the age, maturity, character, behaviour and attitude of the young person and his willingness to make amends,

(ii) any plans put forward by the young person to change his conduct or to participate in activities or undertake measures to improve himself,

(iii) the history of previous findings of delinquency under the *Juvenile*

Delinquents Act, chapter J-3 of the Revised Statues of Canada, 1970, or previous findings of guilt under this Act or any other Act of Parliament or any regulation made thereunder or under an Act of the legislature of a province or any regulation made thereunder or a by-law or ordinance of a municipality, the history of community or other services rendered to the young person with respect to those findings and the response of the young person to previous sentences or dispositions and to services rendered to him,

(iv) the history of alternative measures used to deal with the young person and the response of the young person thereto,

(v) the availability of community services and facilities for young persons and the willingness of the young person to avail himself of those services or facilities,

(vi) the relationship between the young person and his parents and the degree of control and influence of the parents over the young person, and

(vii) the school attendance and performance record and the employment record of the young person.

(3) Where a pre-disposition report cannot reasonably be committed to writing, it may, with leave of the youth court, be submitted orally in court.

(4) A pre-disposition report shall form part of the record of the case in respect of which it was requested.

(5) Where a pre-disposition report made in respect of a young person is submitted to a youth court in writing, the court

(*a*) shall, subject to subsection (7), cause a copy of the report to be given to

(i) the young person,

(ii) a parent of the young person, if the parent is in attendance at the proceedings against the young person,

(iii) counsel, if any, representing the young person, and

(iv) the prosecutor; and

(*b*) may cause a copy of the report to be given to a parent of the young person not in attendance at the proceedings against the young person if the parent is, in the opinion of the court, taking an active interest in the proceedings.

(6) Where a pre-disposition report made in respect of a young person is submitted to a youth court, the young person, his counsel or the adult assisting him pursuant to subsection 11(7) and the prosecutor shall, subject to subsection (7), on application to the youth court, be given the opportunity to cross-examine the person who made the report.

(7) Where a pre-disposition report made in respect of a young person is submitted to a youth court, the court may, where the prosecutor is a private prosecutor and disclosure of the report or any part thereof to the prosecutor

might, in the opinion of the court, be prejudicial to the young person and is not, in the opinion of the court, necessary for the prosecution of the case against the young person,

(*a*) withhold the report or part thereof from the prosecutor, if the report is submitted in writing; or

(*b*) exclude the prosecutor from the court during the submission of the report or part thereof, if the report is submitted orally in court.

(8) Where a pre-disposition report made in respect of a young person is submitted to a youth court, the court

(*a*) shall, on request, cause a copy or a transcript of the report to be supplied to

(i) any court that is dealing with matters relating to the young person, and

(ii) any youth worker to whom the young person's case has been assigned; and

(*b*) may, on request, cause a copy or a transcript of the report, or a part thereof, to be supplied to any person not otherwise authorized under this section to receive a copy or transcript of the report if, in the opinion of the court, the person has a valid interest in the proceedings.

(9) A provincial director who submits a pre-disposition report made in respect of a young person to a youth court may make the report, or any part thereof, available to any person in whose custody or under whose supervision the young person is placed or to any other person who is directly assisting in the care or treatment of the young person.

(10) No statement made by a young person in the course of the preparation of a pre-disposition report in respect of the young person is admissible in evidence against him in any civil or criminal proceedings except in proceedings under section 16 or 20 or sections 28 to 32. R.S., c. 24 (2nd Supp.), s. 11.

DISQUALIFICATION OF JUDGE

Disqualification of judge — Exception.

15. (1) Subject to subsection (2), a youth court judge who, prior to an adjudication in respect of a young person charged with an offence, examines a pre-disposition report made in respect of the young person, or hears an application under section 16 in respect of the young person, in connection with that offence shall not in any capacity conduct or continue the trial of the young person for the offence and shall transfer the case to another judge to be dealt with according to law.

(2) A youth court judge may, in the circumstances referred to in subsection (1), with the consent of the young person and the prosecutor, conduct or continue the trial of the young person if the judge is satisfied that he has not been

predisposed by information contained in the pre-disposition report or by representation made in respect of the application under section 16.

TRANSFER TO ORDINARY COURT

Transfer to ordinary court — Order — Considerations by youth court — Pre-disposition reports — Where young person on transfer status — Court to state reasons — No further applications for transfer — Effect of order — Jurisdiction of ordinary court limited — Review of youth court decision — Extension of time to make application — Notice of application — Inadmissibility of statement.

16. (1) At any time after an information is laid against a young person alleged to have, after attaining the age of fourteen years, committed an indictable offence other than an offence referred to in section 553 of the *Criminal Code* but prior to adjudication, a youth court shall, on application of the young person or the young person's counsel or the Attorney General or the Attorney General's agent, after affording both parties and the parents of the young person an opportunity to be heard, determine, in accordance with subsection (1.1), whether the young person should be proceeded against in ordinary court.

(1.1) In making the determination referred to in subsection (1), the youth court shall consider the interest of society, which includes the objectives of affording protection to the public and rehabilitation of the young person, and determine whether those objectives can be reconciled by the youth remaining under the jurisdiction of the youth court, and if the court is of the opinion that those objectives cannot be so reconciled, protection of the public shall be paramount and the court shall order that the young person be proceeded against in ordinary court in accordance with the law ordinarily applicable to an adult charged with the offence.

(2) In considering an application under subsection (1) in respect of a young person, a youth court shall take into account

(*a*) the seriousness of the alleged offence and the circumstances in which it was allegedly committed;

(*b*) the age, maturity, character and background of the young person and any record or summary of previous findings of delinquency under the *Juvenile Delinquents Act*, chapter J-3 of the Revised Statues of Canada, 1970, or previous findings of guilt under this Act or any other Act of Parliament or any regulation made thereunder;

(*c*) the adequacy of this Act, and the adequacy of the *Criminal Code* or any other Act of Parliament that would apply in respect of the young person if an order were made under this section, to meet the circumstances of the case;

(*d*) the availability of treatment or correctional resources;

(*e*) any representations made to the court by or on behalf of the young person or by the Attorney General or his agent; and

(*f*) any other factors that the court considers relevant.

(3) In considering an application under subsection (1), a youth court shall consider a pre-disposition report.

(4) Notwithstanding subsections (1) and (3), where an application is made under subsection (1) by the Attorney General or the Attorney General's agent in respect of an offence alleged to have been committed by a young person while the young person was being proceeded against in ordinary court pursuant to an order previously made under this section or serving a sentence as a result of proceedings in ordinary court, the youth court may make a further order under this section without a hearing and without considering a pre-disposition report.

(5) Where a youth court makes an order or refuses to make an order under this section, it shall state the reasons for its decision and the reasons shall form part of the record of the proceedings in the youth court.

(6) Where a youth court refuses to make an order under this section in respect of an alleged offence, no further application may be made under this section in respect of that offence.

(7) Where an order is made under this section, proceedings under this Act shall be discontinued and the young person against whom the proceedings are taken shall be taken before the ordinary court.

(8) Where an order is made under this section that a young person be proceeded against in ordinary court in respect of an offence, that court has jurisdiction only in respect of that offence or an offence included therein.

(9) An order made in respect of a young person under this section or a refusal to make such an order shall, on application of the young person or the young person's counsel or the Attorney General or the Attorney General's agent made within thirty days after the decision of the youth court, be reviewed by the court of appeal, and that court may, in its discretion, confirm or reverse the decision of the youth court.

(10) The court of appeal may, at any time, extend the time within which an application under subsection (9) may be made.

(11) A person who proposes to apply for a review under subsection (9) shall give notice of the application in such manner and within such period of time as may be directed by rules of court.

(12) No statement made by a young person in the course of a heariong held under this section is admissible in evidence against the young person in any civil or criminal proceeding held subsequent to that hearing. 1992, c. 11, s. 2.

(13) [Repealed, 1992, c. 11, s. 2]

(14) [Repealed, R.S. 1985, c. 24 (2nd Supp.), s. 12.]

Detention pending trial — Young person under 18 — Detention pending trial — Young person over 18 — Review — Who may make application — Notice — Statement of rights — Limit — Age 20.

16.1 (1) Notwithstanding anything in this or any other Act of Parliament, where

(*a*) an order is made under section 16 that a young person who is under the age of eighteen be proceeded against in ordinary court, and

(*b*) the young person is to be in custody pending the proceedings in that court,

the young person shall be held separate and apart from any adult who is detained or held in custody unless the youth court judge is satisfied, on application at the time of the making of the order, that the young person, having regard to the best interests of the young person and the safety of others, cannot be detained in a place of detention for young persons.

(2) Notwithstanding anything in this or any other Act of Parliament, where

(*a*) an order is made under section 16 that a young person who is over the age of eighteen be proceeded against in ordinary court, and

(*b*) the young person is to be in custody pending the proceedings in that court,

the young person shall be held in a place of detention for adults unless the youth court judge is satisfied, on application at the time of making of the order, that the young person, having regard to the best interests of the young person and the safety of others, should be detained in a place of custody for young persons.

(3) On application, the youth court shall review the placement of a young person in detention pursuant to this section and, if satisfied, having regard to the best interests of the young person and the safety of others, and after having afforded the young person, the provincial director and a representative of a provincial department responsible for adult correctional facilities an opportunity to be heard, that the young person should remain in detention where the young person is or be transferred to youth or adult detention, as the case may be, the court may so order.

(4) An application referred to in this section may be made by the young person, the young person's parents, the provincial director, the Attorney General or the Attorney General's agent.

(5) Where an application referred to in this section is made, the applicant shall cause a notice of the application to be given

(*a*) where the applicant is the young person or one of the young person's parents, to the provincial director and the Attorney General;

(*b*) where the applicant is the Attorney General or the Atorney General's agent, to the young person, the young person's parents and the provincial director; and (*c*) where the applicant is the provincial director, to the young person, the parents of the young person and the Attorney General.

(6) A notice given under subsection (5) by the Attorney General or the provincial director shall include a statement that the young person has the opportunity to be heard and the right to be represented by counsel.

(7) Notwithstanding anything in this section, no young person shall remain in custody in a place of detention for young persons under this section after the young person attains the age of twenty years. 1992, c. 11, s. 2(3).

Placement on conviction by ordinary court — Factors to be taken into account — Report necessary — Review — Who may make application — Notice.

16.2 (1) Notwithstanding anything in this or in any Act of Parliament, where a young person who is proceeded against in ordinary court as the result of an order made under section 16 is convicted and sentenced to imprisonment, the court shall, after affording the young person, the parents of the young person, the Attorney General, the provincial director and representatives of the provincial and federal correctional systems an opportunity to be heard, order that the young person serve any portion of the imprisonment in

(*a*) a place of custody for young persons separate and apart from any adult who is detained or held in custody;

(*b*) a provincial correctional facility for adults; or

(*c*) where the sentence is for two years or more, a penitentiary.

(2) In making an order under subsection (1), the court shall take into account

(*a*) the safety of the young person;

(*b*) the safety of the public;

(*c*) the young person's accessibility to family;

(*d*) the safety of other young persons if the young person were to be held in custody in a place of custody for young persons;

(*e*) whether the young person would have a detrimental influence on other young persons if the young person were to be held in custody in a place of custody for young persons;

(*f*) the young person's level of maturity;

(*g*) the availability and suitability of treatment, educational and other resources that would be provided to the young person in a place of custody for young persons and in a place of custody for adults;

(*h*) the young person's prior experiences and behaviour while in detention or custody;

(*i*) the recommendations of the provincial director and representatives of the provincial and federal correctional facilities; and

(*j*) any other factor the court considers relevant.

(3) Prior to making an order under subsection (1), the court shall require that a report be prepared for the purpose of assisting the court.

(4) On application, the court shall review the placement of a young person

in detention pursuant to this section and, if satisfied that the circumstances that resulted in the initial order have changed materially, and after having afforded the young person, the provincial director and the representatives of the provincial and federal correctional systems an opportunity to be heard, the court may order that the young person be placed in

(*a*) a place of custody for young persons separate and apart from any adult who is detained or held in custody;

(*b*) a provincial correctional facility for adults, or

(*c*) where the sentence is for two years or more, a penitentiary.

(5) An application referred to in this section may be made by the young person, the young person's parents, the provincial director, a representative of the provincial and federal correctional systems and the Attorney General.

(6) Where an application referred to in this section is made, the applicant shall cause a notice of the aplication to be given

(*a*) Where the applicant is the young person or one of the young person's parents, to the provincial director, to representatives of the provincial and federal correction systems and to the Attorney General;

(*b*) where the applicant is the Attorney General or the Attorney General's agent, to the young person, the young person's parents and the provincial director and representatives of the provincial and federal correction systems; and

(*c*) where an applicant is the provincial director, to the young person, the parents of the young person, the Attorney General and representatives of the provincial and federal correction systems. 1992, c. 11, s. 2(3).

Order restricting publication of information presented at transfer hearing — Offence — Definition of "newspaper".

17. (1) Where a youth court hears an application for a transfer to ordinary court under section 16, it shall

(*a*) where the young person is not represented by counsel, or

(*b*) on application made by or on behalf of the young person or the prosecutor, where the young person is represented by counsel,

make an order directing that any information respecting the offence presented at the hearing shall not be published in any newspaper or broadcast before such time as

(*c*) an order for a transfer is refused or set aside on review and the time for all reviews against the decision has expired or all proceedings in respect of any such review have been completed; or

(*d*) the trial is ended, if the case is transferred to ordinary court.

(2) Every one who fails to comply with an order made pursuant to subsection (1) is guilty of an offence punishable on summary conviction.

(3) In this section, "newspaper" has the meaning set out in section 297 of the *Criminal Code.*

TRANSFER OF JURISDICTION

Transfer of jurisdiction.

18. Notwithstanding subsections 478(1) and (3) of the *Criminal Code*, where a young person is charged with an offence that is alleged to have been committed in one province, he may, if the Attorney General of the province where the offence is alleged to have been committed consents, appear before a youth court of any other province and,

(*a*) where the young person signifies his consent to plead guilty and pleads guilty to that offence, the court shall, if it is satisfied that the facts support the charge, find the young person guilty of the offence alleged in the information; and

(*b*) where the young person does not signify his consent to plead guilty and does not plead guilty, or where the court is not satisfied that the facts support the charge, the young person shall, if he was detained in custody prior to his appearance, be returned to custody and dealt with according to law.

ADJUDICATION

Where young person pleads guilty — Where young person pleads not guilty — Application for transfer to ordinary court.

19. (1) Where a young person pleads guilty to an offence charged against him and the youth court is satisfied that the facts support the charge, the court shall find the young person guilty of the offence.

(2) Where a young person pleads not guilty to an offence charged against him, or where a young person pleads guilty but the youth court is not satisfied that the facts support the charge, the court shall proceed with the trial and shall, after considering the matter, find the young person guilty or not guilty or make an order dismissing the charge, as the case may be.

(3) The court shall not make a finding under this section in respect of a young person in respect of whom an application may be made under section 16 for an order that the young person be proceeded against in ordinary court unless it has inquired as to whether any of the parties to the proceedings wishes to make such an application, and, if any party so wishes, has given that party an opportunity to do so. R.S., c. 24 (2nd Supp.), s. 13.

DISPOSITIONS

Dispositions that may be made — Coming into force of disposition — Duration of disposition — Combined duration of dispositions — Custody first — Conditional supervision suspended — Duration of dispositions made at different times — Disposition continues when adult — Reasons for the disposition — Limitation on punishment — Application of Part XXIII of Criminal Code — Section 787 of Criminal Code does not apply — Contents of probation order.

20. (1) Where a youth court finds a young person guilty of an offence, it shall consider any pre-disposition report required by the court, any representations made by the parties to the proceedings or their counsel or agents and by the parents of the young person and any other relevant information before the court, and the court shall then make any one of the following dispositions, othr than the disposition referred to in paragraph (*k*.1), or any number thereof that are not inconsistent with each other, and where the offence is first degree murder or second degree murder within the meaning of section 231 of the *Criminal Code*, the court shall make the disposition referred to in paragraph (*k*.1) and may make such other disposition as the court considers appropriate:

(*a*) by order direct that the young person be discharged absolutely, if the court considers it to be in the best interests of the young person and not contrary to the public interest;

(*b*) impose on the young person a fine not exceeding one thousand dollars to be paid at such time and on such terms as the court may fix;

(*c*) order the young person to pay to any other person at such time and on such terms as the court may fix an amount by way of compensation for loss of or damage to property, for loss of income or support or for special damages for personal injury arising from the commission of the offence where the value thereof is readily ascertainable, but no order shall be made for general damages;

(*d*) order the young person to make restitution to any other person of any property obtained by the young person as a result of the commission of the offence within such time as the court may fix, if the property is owned by that other person or was, at the time of the offence, in his lawful possession;

(*e*) if any property obtained as a result of the commission of the offence has been sold to an innocent purchaser, where restitution of the property to its owner or any other person has been made or ordered, order the young person to pay the purchaser, at such time and on such terms as the court may fix, an amount not exceeding the amount paid by the purchaser for the property;

(*f*) subject to section 21, order the young person to compensate any person in kind or by way of personal services at such time and on such terms as the court may fix for any loss, damage or injury suffered by that person in respect of which an order may be made under paragraph (*c*) or (*e*);

(*g*) subject to section 21, order the young person to perform a community service at such time and on such terms as the court may fix;

(*h*) make any order of prohibition, seizure or forfeiture that may be imposed under any Act of Parliament or any regulation made thereunder where an accused is found guilty or convicted of that offence;

(*i*) subject to section 22, by order direct that the young person be detained for treatment, subject to such conditions as the court considers appropriate, in a hospital or other place where treatment is available, where a report has been made in respect of the young person pursuant to subsection 13(1) that recommends that the young person undergo treatment for a condition referred in paragraph 13(1)(*e*);

(*j*) place the young person on probation in accordance with section 23 for a specified period not exceeding two years;

(*k*) subject to sections 24 to 24.5, commit the young person to custody, to be served continuously or intermittently, for a specified period not exceeding

(i) two years from the date of committal, or

(ii) where the young person is found guilty of an offence for which the punishment provided by the *Criminal Code* or any other Act of Parliament is imprisonment for life, three years from the date of committal; and

(*k*.1) order the young person to serve a disposition not to exceed five years less a day comprised of

(i) a committal to custody, to be served continuously, for a period that shall not, subject to subsection 26.1(1), exceed three years from the date of committal, and

(ii) a placement under conditional supervision to be served in the community in accordance with section 26.2; and

(*l*) impose on the young person such other reasonable and ancillary conditions as it deems advisable and in the best interest of the young person and the public.

(2) A disposition made under this section shall come into force on the date on which it is made or on such later date as the youth court specifies therein.

(3) No disposition made under this section, other than an order made under paragraph (1)(*h*), (*k*) or (*k*.1), shall continue in force for more than two years and, where the youth court makes more than one disposition at the same time in respect of the same offence, the combined duration of the dispositions, except in respect of an order made under paragraph (1)(*h*), (*k*) or (*k*.1), shall not exceed two years.

(4) Subject to subsection (4.1), where more than one disposition is made under this section in respect of a young person with respect to different offences, the continuous combined duration of those dispositions shall not exceed three

years, except where one of those offences is first degree murder or second degree murder within the meaning of section 231 of the *Criminal Code*, in which case the continuous combined duration of those dispositions shall not exceed five years less a day.

(4.1) Where a disposition is made under this section in respect of an offence committed by a young person after the commencement of, but before the completion of, any dispositions made in respect of previous offences committed by the young person,

(*a*) the duration of the disposition made in respect of the subsequent offence shall be determined in accordance with subsections (3) and (4);

(*b*) the disposition may be served consecutively to the dispositions made in respect of the previous offences; and

(*c*) the combined duration of all the dispositions may exceed three years, except where the offence is, or one of the previous offences was, first degree murder or second degree murder within the meaning of section 231 of the *Criminal Code*, in which case the continuous combined duration of the dispositions may exceed five years less a day.

(4.2) Subject to subsection (4.3), where a young person who is serving a disposition made under paragraph (1)(*k*.1) is ordered to custody in respect of an offence committed after the commencment of, but before the completion of, that disposition, the custody in respect of that subsequent offence shall be served before the young person is placed under conditional supervision.

(4.3) Where a young person referred to in subsection (4.2) is under conditional supervision at the time the young person is ordered to custody in respect of a subsequent offence, the conditional supervision shall be suspended until the young person is released from custody.

(5) Subject to section 741.1 of the *Criminal Code*, a disposition made under this section shall continue in effect in accordance with the terms thereof, after the young person against whom it is made becomes an adult.

(6) Where a youth court makes a disposition under this section, it shall state its reasons therefor in the record of the case and shall

(*a*) provide or cause to be provided a copy of the disposition, and

(*b*) on request, provide or cause to be provided a transcript or copy of the reasons for the disposition

to the young person in respect of whom the disposition was made, the young person's counsel and parents, the provincial director, where the provincial director has an interest in the disposition, the prosecutor and, in the case of a custodial disposition made under paragraph (1)(*k*) or (*k*.1), the review board, if a review board has been established or designated.

(7) No disposition shall be made in respect of a young person under this section that results in a punishment that is greater than the maximum punishment that would be applicable to an adult who has committed the same offence.

(8) Part XXIII of the *Criminal Code* does not apply in respect of proceedings under this Act except for sections 749, 750 and 751 and subsection 736(2), which provisions apply with such modifications as the circumstances require.

(9) Section 787 of the *Criminal Code* does not apply in respect of proceedings under this Act.

(10) The youth court shall specify in any probation order made under paragraph (1)(j) the period for which it is to remain in force. R.S., c. 27 (1st Supp.), s. 187, Schedule; R.S., c. 24 (2nd Supp.), s. 14; c. 1 (4th Supp.), s. 38.; 1992, c. 11, s. 3(1)-(6).

(11) [Repealed, R.S. 1985, c. 24 (2nd Supp.), s. 14(2).]

Where a fine or other payment is ordered — Fine option program — Rates, crediting and other matters — Representations respecting orders under paras. 20(1)(*c*) to (*f*) — Notice of orders under paras. 20(1)(*c*) to (*f*) — Consent of person to be compensated — Order for compensation or community service — Duration of order for service — Community service order — Application for further time to complete disposition.

21. (1) The youth court shall, in imposing a fine on a young person under paragraph 20(1)(*b*) or in making an order against a young person under paragraph 20(1)(*c*) or (*e*), have regard to the present and future means of the young person to pay.

(2) A young person against whom a fine is imposed under paragraph 20(1)(*b*) may discharge the fine in whole or in part by earning credits for work performed in a program established for that purpose

(*a*) by the Lieutenant Governor in Council of the province in which the fine was imposed; or

(*b*) by the Lieutenant Governor in Council of the province in which the young person resides, where an appropriate agreement is in effect between the government of that province and the government of the province in which the fine was imposed.

(3) A program referred to in subsection (2) shall determine the rate at which credits are earned and may provide for the manner of crediting any amounts earned against the fine and any other matters necessary for or incidental to carrying out the program.

(4) In considering whether to make an order under paragraphs 20(1)(*c*) to (*f*), the youth court may consider any representations made by the person who would be compensated or to whom restitution or payment would be made.

(5) Where the youth court makes an order under paragraphs 20(1)(*c*) to (*f*), it shall cause notice of the terms of the order to be given to the person who is to be compensated or to whom restitution or payment is to be made.

(6) No order can be made under paragraph 20(1)(*f*) unless the youth court has secured the consent of the person to be compensated.

(7) No order may be made under paragraph 20(1)(*f*) or (*g*) unless the youth court

(*a*) is satisfied that the young person against whom the order is made is a suitable candidate for such an order; and

(*b*) is satisfied that the order does not interfere with the normal hours of work or education of the young person.

(8) No order may be made under paragraph 20(1)(*f*) or (*g*) to perform personal or community services unless those services can be completed in two hundred and forty hours or less and within twelve months of the date of the order.

(9) No order may be made under paragraph 20(1)(*g*) unless

(a) the community service to be performed is part of a program that is approved by the provincial director; or

(b) the youth court is satisfied that the person or organization for whom the community service is to be performed has agreed to its performance.

(10) A youth court may, on application by or on behalf of the young person in respect of whom a disposition has been made under paragraphs 20(1)(*b*) to (*g*), allow further time for the completion of the disposition subject to any regulations made pursuant to paragraph 67(*b*) and to any rules made by the youth court pursuant to subsection 68(1). R.S., c. 24 (2nd Supp.), s. 15.

Consent for treatment order — Where consent of parent dispensed with.

22. (1) No order may be made under paragraph 20(1)(*i*) unless the youth court has secured the consent of the young person, the parents of the young person and the hospital or other place where the young person is to be detained for treatment.

(2) The youth court may dispense with the consent of a parent required under subsection (1) if it appears that the parent is not available or if the parent is not, in the opinion of the court, taking an active interest in the proceedings.

Conditions that must appear in probation orders — Conditions that may appear in probation orders — Communication of probation order to young person and parent — Copy of probation order to parent — Endorsement of order by young person — Validity of probation order — Commencement of probation order — Notice to appear — Warrant to arrest young person.

23. (1) The following conditions shall be included in a probation order made under paragraph 20(1)(*j*):

(*a*) that the young person bound by the probation order shall keep the peace and be of good behaviour; and

(*b*) that the young person appear before the youth court when required by the court to do so.

(2) A probation order made under paragraph 20(1)(*j*) may include such

of the following conditions as the youth court considers appropriate in the circumstances of the case:

(*a*) that the young person bound by the probation order report to and be under the supervision of the provincial director or a person designated by the youth court;

(*a*.1) that the young person notify the clerk of the youth court, the provincial director or the youth worker assigned to his case of any change of address or any change in his place of employment, education or training;

(*b*) that the young person remain within the territorial jurisdiction of one or more courts named in the order;

(*c*) that the young person make reasonable efforts to obtain and maintain suitable employment;

(*d*) that the young person attend school or such other place of learning, training or recreation as is appropriate, if the court is satisfied that a suitable program is available for the young person at that place;

(*e*) that the young person reside with a parent, or such other adult as the court considers appropriate, who is willing to provide for the care and maintenance of the young person;

(*f*) that the young person reside in such place as the provincial director may specify; and

(*g*) that the young person comply with such other reasonable conditions set out in the order as the court considers desirable, including conditions for securing the good conduct of the young person and for preventing the commission by the young person of other offences.

(3) Where the youth court makes a probation order under paragraph 20(1)(*j*), it shall

(*a*) cause the order to be read by or to the young person bound by the probation order;

(*b*) explain or cause to be explained to the young person the purpose and effect of the order and ascertain that the young person understands it; and

(*c*) cause a copy of the order to be given to the young person and to a parent of the young person, if the parent is in attendance at the proceedings against the young person.

(4) Where the youth court makes a probation order under paragraph 20(1)(*j*), it may cause a copy of the report to be given to a parent of the young person not in attendance at the proceedings against the young person if the parent is, in the opinion of the court, taking an active interest in the proceedings.

(5) After a probation order has been read by or to a young person and explained to him pursuant to subsection (3), the young person shall endorse the order acknowledging that he has received a copy of the order and acknowledging the fact that it has been explained to him.

(6) The failure of a young person to endorse a probation order pursuant to subsection (5) does not affect the validity of the order.

(7) A probation order made under paragraph 20(1)(*j*) comes into force

(*a*) on the date on which the order is made; or

(*b*) where the young person in respect of whom the order is made is committed to continuous custody, on the expiration of the period of custody.

(8) A young person may be given notice to appear before the youth court pursuant to paragraph (1)(*b*) orally or in writing.

(9) If a young person to whom a notice is given in writing to appear before the youth court pursuant to paragraph (1)(*b*) does not appear at the time and place named in the notice and it is proved that a copy of the notice was served on him, a youth court may issue a warrant to compel the appearance of the young person. R.S., c. 24 (2nd Supp.), s. 16; c. 1 (4th Supp.), s. 39.

Conditions of custody — Pre-disposition report — Report dispensed with.

24. (1) The youth court shall not commit a young person to custody under paragraph 20(1)(*k*) unless the court considers a committal to custody to be necessary for the protection of society having regard to the seriousness of the offence and the circumstances in which it was committed and having regard to the needs and circumstances of the young person.

(2) Subject to subsection (3), before making an order of committal to custody, the youth court shall consider a pre-disposition report.

(3) The youth court may, with the consent of the prosecutor and the young person or his counsel, dispense with the pre-disposition report required under subsection (2) if the youth court is satisfied, having regard to the circumstances, that the report is unnecessary or that it would not be in the best interests of the young person to require one. R.S., c. 24 (2nd Supp.), s. 17.

Definitions — Order to specify type of custody — Conditions for secure custody — Idem.

24.1 (1) In this section and sections 24.2, 24.3, 28 and 29,

"open custody" means custody in

(*a*) a community residential centre, group home, child care institution, or forest or wilderness camp, or

(*b*) any other like place or facility

designated by the Lieutenant Governor in Council of a province or his delegate as a place of open custody for the purposes of this Act, and includes a place or facility within a class of such places or facilities so designated;

"secure custody" means custody in a place or facility designated by the Lieutenant Governor in Council of a province for the secure containment or restraint of young persons, and includes a place or facility within a class of such places or facilities so designated.

(2) Where the youth court commits a young person to custody under paragraph 20(1)(*k*) or (*k*.1), or makes an order under subsection 26.1(1) or

paragraph 26.6(2)(*b*), it shall specify in the order whether the custody is to be open custody or secure custody.

(3) Subject to subsection (4), no young person who is found guilty of an offence shall be committed to secure custody unless the young person was, at the time the offence was committed, fourteen years of age or more and unless

(*a*) the offence is one for which an adult would be liable to imprisonment for five years or more;

(*b*) the offence is an offence under section 26 of this Act in relation to a disposition under paragraph 20(1)(j), an offence under section 144 (prison breach) or subsection 145(1) (escape or being at large without excuse) of the *Criminal Code* or an attempt to commit such offence; or

(*c*) the offence is an indictable offence and the young person was

(i) within twelve months prior to the commission of the offence, found guilty of an offence for which an adult would be liable to imprisonment for five years or more, or adjudged to have committed a delinquency under the *Juvenile Delinquents Act*, chapter J-3 of the Revised Statues of Canada, 1970, in respect of such offence, or

(ii) at any time prior to the commission of the offence committed to secure custody with respect to a previous offence, or committed to custody in a place or facility for the secure containment or restraint of a child, within the meaning of the *Juvenile Delinquents Act*, chapter J-3 of the Revised Statues of Canada, 1970, with respect to a delinquency under that Act.

(4) A young person who is found guilty of an offence and who was, at the time the offence was committed, under the age of fourteen years may be committed to secure custody if

(*a*) the offence is one for which an adult would be liable to life imprisonment;

(*b*) the offence is one for which an adult would be liable to imprisonment for five years or more and the young person was at any time prior to the commission of the offence found guilty of an offence for which an adult would be liable to imprisonment for five years or more or adjudged to have committed a delinquency under the *Juvenile Delinquents Act*, chapter J-3 of the Revised Statues of Canada, 1970, in respect of that offence; or

(*c*) the offence is an offence under section 26 of this Act in relation to a disposition under paragraph 20(1)(j), an offence under section 144 (prison breach) or subsection 145(1) (escape or being at large without excuse) of the *Criminal Code* or an attempt to commit that offence. R.S., c. 24 (2nd Supp.), s. 17; 1992, c. 11, s. 4.

(5)-(16) [Repealed, R.S. 1985, c. 24 (2nd Supp.), s. 17.]

Place of custody — Warrant of committal — Exception — Young person to be held separate from adults — Subsection 7(2) applies — Transfer — Transfer from secure to open custody — No transfer from open custody to secure custody — Exception.

24.2 (1) Subject to this section and sections 24.3 and 24.5, a young person who is committed to custody shall be placed in open custody or secure custody, as specified in the order of committal, at such place or facility as the provincial director may specify.

(2) Where a young person is committed to custody, the youth court shall issue or cause to be issued a warrant of committal.

(3) A young person who is committed to custody may, in the course of being transferred from custody to the court or from the court to custody, be held under the supervision and control of a peace officer or in such place of temporary detention referred to in subsection 7(1) as the provincial director may specify.

(4) Subject to this section and section 24.5, a young person who is committed to custody shall be held separate and apart from any adult who is detained or held in custody.

(5) Subsection 7(2) applies, with such modifications as the circumstances require, in respect of a person held in a place of temporary detention pursuant to subsection (3).

(6) A young person who is committed to custody may, during the period of custody, be transferred by the provincial director from one place or facility of open custody to another or from one place or facility of secure custody to another.

(7) No young person who is committed to secure custody may be transferred to a place or facility of open custody except in accordance with sections 28 to 31.

(8) Subject to subsection (9), no young person who is committed to open custody may be transferred to a place or facility of secure custody.

(9) The provincial director may transfer a young person from a place or facility of open custody to a place or facility of secure custody for a period not exceeding fifteen days if

(*a*) the young person escapes or attempts to escape lawful custody; or

(*b*) the transfer is, in the opinion of the provincial director, necessary for the safety of the young person or the safety of others in the place or facility of open custody. R.S., c. 24 (2nd Supp.), s. 17.

Consecutive dispositions of custody — Concurrent dispositions of custody.

24.3 (1) Where a young person is committed to open custody and secure custody, any portions of which dispositions are to be served consecutively, the disposition of secure custody shall be served first without regard to the order in which the dispositions were imposed.

(2) Where a young person is committed to open custody and secure custody, any portions of which dispositions are to be served concurrently, the concurrent portions of the dispositions shall be served in secure custody. R.S., c. 24 (2nd Supp.), s. 17.

Committal to custody deemed continuous — Availability of place of intermittent custody.

24.4 (1) A young person who is committed to custody under paragraph 20(1)(*k*) shall be deemed to be committed to continuous custody unless the youth court specifies otherwise.

(2) Before making an order of committal to intermittent custody under paragraph 20(1)(*k*), the youth court shall require the prosecutor to make available to the court for its consideration a report of the provincial director as to the availability of a place of custody in which an order of intermittent custody can be enforced and, where the report discloses that no such place of custody is available, the court shall not make the order. R.S., c. 24 (2nd Supp.), s. 17.

Transfer to adult facility — Where disposition and sentence concurrent.

24.5 (1) Where a young person is committed to custody under paragraph 20(1)(*k*) or (*k*.1), the youth court may, on application of the provincial director made at any time after the young person attains the age of eighteen years, after affording the young person an opportunity to be heard, authorize the provincial director to direct that the young person serve the disposition or the remaining portion thereof in a provincial correctional facility for adults, if the court considers it to be in the best interests of the young person or in the public interest, but in that event, the provisions of this Act shall continue to apply in respect of that person.

(2) Where a young person is committed to custody under paragraph 20(1)(*k*) or (*k*.1) and is concurrently under sentence of imprisonment imposed in ordinary court, the young person may, in the discretion of the provincial director, serve the disposition and sentence, or any portions thereof, in a place of custody for young persons, in a provincial correctional facility for adults or, where the unexpired portion of the sentence is two years or more, in a penitentiary. R.S., c. 24 (2nd Supp.), s. 17; 1992, c. 11, s. 5.

Transfer of disposition — No transfer outside province before appeal completed — Transfer to a province where person is adult.

25. (1) Where a disposition has been made under paragraphs 20(1)(*b*) to (*g*) or paragraph 20(1)(*i*), (*j*) or (*l*) in respect of a young person and the young person or a parent with whom he resides is or becomes a resident of a territorial division outside the jurisdiction of the youth court that made the disposition, whether in the same or in another province, a youth court judge in the territorial division in which the disposition was made may, on the application of the Attorney General or his agent or on the application of the young person or his parent with the consent of the Attorney General or his agent, transfer the disposition and such portion of the record of the case as is appropriate to a youth court in the other territorial division, and all subsequent proceedings relating to the case shall thereafter be carried out and enforced by that court.

(2) No disposition may be transferred from one province to another under this section until the time for an appeal against the disposition or the finding on which the disposition was based has expired or until all proceedings in respect of any such appeal have been completed.

(3) Where an application is made under subsection (1) to transfer the disposition of a young person to a province in which the young person is an adult, a youth court judge may, with the consent of the Attorney General, transfer the disposition and the record of the case to the youth court in the province to which the transfer is sought, and the youth court to which the case is transferred shall have full jurisdiction in respect of the disposition as if that court had made the disposition, and the person shall be further dealt with in accordance with this Act. R.S., c. 24 (2nd Supp.), s. 18.

Interprovincial arrangements for treatment, probation or custody — Youth court retains jurisdiction — Waiver of jurisdiction.

25.1 (1) Where a disposition has been made under paragraphs 20(1)(*i*) to (*k*.1) in respect of a young person, the disposition in one province may be dealt with in any other province pursuant to any agreement that may have been made between those provinces.

(2) Subject to subsection (3), where a disposition made in respect of a young person is dealt with pursuant to this section in a province other than that in which the disposition was made, the youth court of the province in which the disposition was made shall, for all purposes of this Act, retain exclusive jurisdiction over the young person as if the disposition were dealt with within that province, and any warrant or process issued in respect of the young person may be executed or served in any place in Canada outside the province where the disposition was made as if it were executed or served in that province.

(3) Where a disposition made in respect of a young person is dealt with pursuant to this section in a province other than that in which the disposition was made, the youth court of the province in which the disposition was made may, with the consent in writing of the Attorney General of that province or his delegate and the young person, waive its jurisdiction, for the purpose of any proceeding under this Act, to the youth court of the province in which the disposition is dealt with, in which case the youth court in the province in which the disposition is so dealt with shall have full jurisdiction in respect

of the disposition as if that court had made the disposition. R.S., c. 24 (2nd Supp.), s. 19.

Failure to comply with disposition.

26. A person who is subject to a disposition made under paragraphs 20(1)(*b*) to (*g*) or paragraph 20(1)(*j*) or (*l*) and who wilfully fails or refuses to comply with that order is guilty of an offence punishable on summary conviction. R.S., c. 24 (2nd Supp.), s. 19.

Continuation of custody — Idem — Factors — Youth court to order appearance of young person — Report — Written or oral report — Provisions apply — Notice of hearing — Statement of right to counsel — Service of notice — Where notice not given — Reasons — Review provisions apply — Where application denied.

26.1 (1) Where a young person is held in custody pursuant to a disposition made under paragraph 20(1)(*k*.1) and an application is made to the youth court by the Attorney General, or the Attorney General's agent, within a reasonable time prior to the expiration of the period of custody, the provincial director of the province in which the young person is held in custody shall cause the young person to be brought before the youth court and the youth court may, after affording both parties and the parents of the young person an oportunity to be heard and if it is satisfied that there are reasonable grounds to believe that the young person is likely to commit an offence causing the death of or serious harm to another person prior to the expiration of the disposition the young person is then serving, order that the young person remain in custody for a period not exceeding the remainder of the disposition.

(1.1) Where the hearing for an application under subsection (1) cannot be completed before the expiration of the period of custody, the court may order that the young person remain in custody pending the determination of the application if the court is satisfied that the application was made in a reasonable time, having regard to all the circumstances, and that there are compelling reasons for keeping the young person in custody.

(2) For the purpose of determining an application under subsection (1), the youth court shall take into consideration any factor that is relevant to the case of the young person including, without limiting the generality of the foregoing,

(*a*) evidence of a pattern of persistent violent behaviour and, in particular,

(i) the number of offences committed by the young person that caused physical or psychological harm to any other person,

(ii) the young person's difficulties in controlling violent impulses to the point of endangering the safety of any other person,

(iii) the use of weapons in the commission of any offence

(iv) explicit threats of violence,

(v) behaviour of a brutal nature associated with the commission of any offence, and

(vi) a substantial degree of indifference on the part of the young person as to the reasonably foreseeable consequences, to other persons, of the young person's behaviour;

(*b*) psychiatric or psychological evidence that a physical or mental illness or disorder of the young person is of such a nature that the young person is likely to commit, prior to the expiration of the disposition the young person is then serving, an offence causing the death of or serious harm to another person;

(*c*) reliable information that satisfies the youth court that the young person is planning to commit, prior to the expiration of the disposition the young person is then serving, an offence causing the death of or serious harm to another person; and

(*d*) the availability of supervision programs in the community that would offer adequate protection to the public from the risk that the young person might otherwise present until the expiration of the disposition the young person is then serving.

(3) Where a provincial director fails to cause a young person to be brought before the youth court under subsection (1), the youth court shall order the provincial director to cause the young person to be brought before the youth court forthwith.

(4) For the purpose of determining an application under subsection (1), the youth court shall require the provincial director to cause to be prepared, and to submit to the youth court, a report setting out any information of which the provincial director is aware with respect to the factors referred to in subsection (2) that may be of assistance to the court.

(5) A report referred to in subsection (4) shall be in writing unless it cannot reasonably be committed to writing, in which case it may, with leave of the youth court, be submitted orally in court.

(6) Subsections 14(4) to (10) apply, with such modifications as the circumstances require, in respect of a report referred to in subsection (4).

(7) Where an application is made under subsection (1) in respect of a young person, the Attorney General or the Attorney General's agent shall cause such notice as may be directed by rules of court applicable to the youth court or, in the absence of such direction, at least five clear days notice of the hearing to be given in writing to the young person and the young person's parents and the provincial director.

(8) Any notice given to a parent under subsection (7) shall include a statement that the young person has the right to be represented by counsel.

(9) A notice under subsection (7) may be served personally or may be sent by registered mail.

(10) Where notice under subsection (7) is not given in accordance with this section, the youth court may

(*a*) adjourn the hearing and order that the notice be given in such manner and to such person as it directs; or

(*b*) dispense with the giving of the notice where, in the opinion of the youth court, having regard to the circumstances, the giving of the notice may be dispensed with.

(11) Where a youth court makes an order under subsection (1), it shall state its reasons for the order in the record of the case and shall

(*a*) provide or cause to be provided a copy of the order, and

(*b*) on request, provide or cause to be provided a transcript or copy of the reasons for the order

to the young person in respect of whom the order was made, the counsel and parents of the young person, the Attorney General or the Attorney General's agent, the provincial director and the review board, if any has been established or designated.

(12) Subsections 16(9) to (11) apply, with such modifications as the circumstances require, in respect of an order made, or the refusal to make an order, under subsection (1).

(13) Where an application under subsection (1) is denied, the court may, with the consent of the young person, the Attorney General and the provincial director, proceed as though the young person had been brought before the court as required under subsection 26.2(1). 1992, c. 11, s. 7.

Conditional supervision — Conditions to be included in order — Other conditions — Temporary conditions — Conditions to be set at first opportunity — Report — Provisions apply — Idem.

26.2 (1) The provincial director of the province in which a young person is held in custody pursuant to a disposition made under paragraph 20(1)(*k*.1) or, where applicable, an order made under subsection 26.1(1), shall cause the young person to be brought before the youth court at least one month prior to the expiration of the period of custody and the court shall, after affording the young person an opportunity to be heard, by order, set the conditions of the young person's conditional supervision.

(2) In setting conditions for the purposes of subsection (1), the youth court shall include in the order the following conditions, namely, that the young person

(*a*) keep the peace and be of good behaviour;

(*b*) appear before the youth court when required by the court to do so;

(*c*) report to the provincial director immediately on release, and thereafter be under the supervision of the provincial director or a person designated by the youth court;

(*d*) inform the provincial director immediately on being arrested or questioned by the police;

(*e*) report to the police, or any named individual, as instructed by the provincial director;

(*f*) advise the provincial director of the young person's address of residence on release and after release report immediately to the clerk of the youth court or the provincial director any change

(i) in that address,

(ii) in the young person's normal occupation, including employment, vocational or educational training and volunteer work,

(iii) in the young person's family or financial situation, and

(iv) that may reasonably be expected to affect the young person's ability to comply with the conditions of the order;

(*g*) not own, possess or have the control of any weapon, as defined in section 2 of the *Criminal Code*, except as authorized by the order; and

(*h*) comply with such reasonable instructions as the provincial director considers necessary in respect of any condition of the conditional supervision in order to prevent a breach of that condition or to protect society.

(3) In setting conditions for the purposes of subsection (1), the youth court may include in the order the following conditions, namely, that the young person

(*a*) on release, travel directly to the young person's place of residence, or to such other place as is noted in the order;

(*b*) make reasonble efforts to obtain and maintain suitable employment;

(*c*) attend school or such other place of learning, training or recreation as is appropriate, if the court is satisfied that a suitable program is available for the young person at such a place;

(*d*) reside with a parent, or such other adult as the court considers appropriate, who is willing to provide for the care and maintenance of the young person;

(*e*) reside in such place as the provincial director may specify;

(*f*) remain within the territorial jurisdiction of one or more courts named in the order; and

(*g*) comply with such other reasonable conditions set out in the order as the court considers desirable, including conditions for securing the good conduct of the young person and for preventing the commission by the young peson of other offences.

(4) Where a provincial director is required under subsection (1) to cause a young person to be brought before the youth court but cannot do so for reasons beyond the young person's control, the provincial director shall so advise the youth court and the court shall, by order, set such temporary conditions for the young person's conditional supervision as are appropriate in the circumstances.

(5) Where an order is made under subsection (4), the provincial director shall bring the young person before the youth court as soon thereafter as the

circumstances permit and the court shall then set the conditions of the young person's conditional supervision.

(6) For the purpose of setting conditions under this section, the youth court shall require the provincial director to cause to be prepared, and to submit to the youth court, a report setting out any information that may be of assistnce to the court.

(7) Subsection 26.1(3) and (5) to (10) apply, with such modifications as the circumstances require, in respect of any proceedings held pursuant to subsection (1).

(8) Subsections 16(9) to (11) and 23(3) to (9) apply, with such modifications as the circumstances require, in respect of an order made under subsection (1). 1992, c. 11. s. 7.

Suspension of conditional supervision.

26.3 Where the provincial director has reasonable grounds to believe that a young person has breached or is about to breach a condition of an order made under subsection 26.2(1), the provincial director may, in writing,

(*a*) suspend the conditional supervision; and

(*b*) order that the young person be remanded to such place of custody as the provincial director considers appropriate until a review is conducted under section 26.5 and, if applicable, section 26.6. 1992, c. 11, s. 7.

Apprehension — Warrants — Peace officer may arrest — Requirement to bring before provincial director — Release or remand in custody.

26.4 (1) Where the conditional supervision of a young person is suspended under section 26.3, the provincial director may issue a warrant in writing, authorizing the apprehension of the young person and, until the young person is apprehended, the young person is deemed not to be continuing to serve the disposition the young person is then serving.

(2) A warrant issued under subsection (1) shall be executed by any peace officer to whom it is given at any place in Canada and has the same force and effect in all parts of Canada as if it had been originally issued or subsequently endorsed by a provincial court judge or other lawful authority having jurisdiction in the place where it is executed.

(3) Where a peace officer believes on reasonable grounds that a warrant issued under subsection (1) is in force in respect of a young person, the peace officer may arrest the young person without the warrant at any place in Canada.

(4) Where a young person is arrested pursuant to subsection (3) and detained, the peace officer making the arrest shall cause the young person to be brought before the provincial director or a person designated by the provincial director

(*a*) where the provincial director or the designated person is available within a period of twenty-four hours after the young person is arrested, without unreasonable delay and in any event within that period; and

(*b*) where the provincial director or the designated person is not available within the period referred to in paragraph (*a*), as soon as possible.

(5) Where a young person is brought, pursuant to subsection (4), before the provincial director or a person designated by the provincial director, the provincial director or the designated person,

(*a*) if not satisfied that there are reasonable grounds to believe that the young person is the young person in respect of whom the warrant referred to in subsection (1) was issued, shall release the young person; or

(*b*) if satisfied that there are reasonable grounds to believe that the young person is the young person in respect of whom the warrant referred to in subsection (1) was issued,

may remand the young person in custody to await execution of the warrant, but if no warrant for the young person's arrest is executed within a period of six days after the time the young person is remanded in such custody, the person in whose custody the young person then is shall release the young person. 1992, c. 11. s. 7.

Review by provincial director.

26.5 Forthwith after the remand to custody of a young person whose conditional supervision has been suspended under section 26.3, or forthwith after being informed of the arrest of such a young person, the provincial director shall review the case and, within forty-eight hours, cancel the suspension of the conditional supervision or refer the case to the youth court for a review under section 26.6. 1992, c. 11, s. 7.

Review by Youth Court — Order — Reasons — Provisions apply — Idem.

26.6 (1) Where the case of a young person is referred to the youth court under section 26.5, the provincial director shall, as soon as is practicable, cause the young person to be brought before the youth court, and the youth court shall, after affording the young person an opportunity to be heard,

(*a*) if the court is not satisfied on reasonable grounds that the young peson has breached or was about to breach a condition of the conditional supervision, cancel the suspension of the conditional supervision; or

(*b*) if the court is satisfied on reasonable grounds that the young person has breached or was about to breach a condition of the conditional supervision, review the decision of the provincial director to suspend the conditional supervision and make an order under subsection (2).

(2) On completion of a review under subsection (1), the youth court shall order

(*a*) the cancellation of the suspension of the conditional supervision, and where the court does so, the court may vary the conditions of the conditional supervision or impose new conditions; or

(*b*) the continuation of the suspension of the conditional supervision for such period of time, not to exceed the remainder of the disposition the young person is then serving, as the court considers appropriate, and where the court does so, the court shall order that the young person remain in custody.

(3) Where a youth court makes an order under subsection (2), it shall state its reasons for the order in the record of the case and shall

(*a*) provide or cause to be provided a copy of the order, and

(*b*) on request, provide or cause to be provided a transcript or copy of the reasons for the order

to the young person in respect of whom the order was made, the counsel and parents of the young person, the Attorney General or the Attorney General's agent, the provincial director and the review board, if any has been established or designated.

(4) Subsections 26.1(3) and (5) to (10) and 26.2(6) apply, with such modifications as the circumstances require, in respect of a review under this section.

(5) Subsections 16(9) to (11) apply, with such modifications as the circumstances require, in respect of an order made under subsection (2). 1992, c. 11, s. 7.

APPEALS

Appeals for indictable offences — Appeals for summary conviction offences — Deemed election — Where the youth court is a superior court — Where the youth court is a county or district court — Appeal to the Supreme Court of Canada — No appeal from disposition on review.

27. (1) An appeal lies under this Act in respect of an indictable offence or an offence that the Attorney General or his agent elects to proceed with as an indictable offence in accordance with Part XXI of the *Criminal Code*, which Part applies with such modifications as the circumstances require.

(1.1) An appeal lies under this Act in respect of an offence punishable on summary conviction or an offence that the Attorney General or his agent elects to proceed with as an offence punishable on summary conviction in accordance with Part XXVII of the *Criminal Code*, which Part applies with such modifications as the circumstances require.

(2) For the purpose of appeals under this Act, where no election is made in respect of an offence that may be prosecuted by indictment or proceeded with by way of summary conviction, the Attorney General or his agent shall be deemed to have elected to proceed with the offence as an offence punishable on summary conviction.

(3) In any province where the youth court is a superior court, an appeal under subsection (1.1) shall be made to the court of appeal of the province.

(4) In any province where the youth court is a county or district court, an appeal under subsection (1.1) shall be made to the superior court of the province.

(5) No appeal lies pursuant to subsection (1.1) from a judgment of the court of appeal in respect of a finding of guilt or an order dismissing an information to the Supreme Court of Canada unless leave to appeal is granted by the Supreme Court of Canada within twenty-one days after the judgment of the court of appeal is pronounced or within such extended time as the Supreme Court of Canada or a judge thereof may, for special reasons, allow.

(6) No appeal lies from a disposition under sections 28 to 32. R.S., c. 24 (2nd Supp.), s. 20.

REVIEW OF DISPOSITIONS

Automatic review of disposition involving custody — Idem — Optional review of disposition involving custody — Grounds for review under subsection (3) — No review where appeal pending — Youth court may order appearance of young person for review — Progress report — Additional information in progress report — Written or oral report — Provisions of subsections 14(4) to (10) to apply — Notice of review from provincial director — Notice of review from person requesting it — Statement of right to counsel — Service of notice — Notice may be waived — Where notice not given — Decision of the youth court after review.

28. (1) Where a young person is committed to custody pursuant to a disposition made in respect of an offence for a period exceeding one year, the provincial director of the province in which the young person is held in custody shall cause the young person to be brought before the youth court forthwith at the end of one year from the date of the most recent disposition made in respect of the offence, and the youth court shall review the disposition.

(2) Where a young person is committed to custody pursuant to dispositions made in respect of more than one offence for a total period exceeding one year, the provincial director of the province in which the young person is held in custody shall cause the young person to be brought before the youth court forthwith at the end of one year from the date of the earliest disposition made, and the youth court shall review the dispositions.

(3) Where a young person is committed to custody pursuant to a disposition made in respect of an offence, the provincial director may, on his own initiative, and shall, on the request of the young person, his parent or the Attorney General or his agent, on any of the grounds set out in subsection (4), cause the young person to be brought before the youth court at any time after six months from the date of the most recent disposition made in respect of the offence or, with leave of a youth court judge, at any earlier time, and, where the youth court

is satisfied that there are grounds for the review under subsection (4), the cour shall review the disposition.

(4) A disposition made in respect of a young person may be reviewed unde subsection (3)

(*a*) on the ground that the young person has made sufficient progress to justify a change in disposition;

(*b*) on the ground that the circumstances that led to the committal to custody have changed materially;

(*c*) on the ground that new services or programs are available that were not available at the time of the disposition; or

(*d*) on such other grounds as the youth court considers appropriate.

(5) No review of a disposition in respect of which an appeal has been taken shall be made under this section until all proceedings in respect of any such appeal have been completed.

(6) Where a provincial director is required under subsections (1) to (3) to cause a young person to be brought before the youth court and fails to do so, the youth court may, on application made by the young person, his parent or the Attorney General or his agent, or on its own motion, order the provincial director to cause the young person to be brought before the youth court.

(7) The youth court shall, before reviewing under this section a disposition made in respect of a young person, require the provincial director to cause to be prepared, and to submit to the youth court, a progress report on the performance of the young person since the disposition took effect.

(8) A person preparing a progress report in respect of a young person may include in the report such information relating to the personal and family history and present environment of the young person as he considers advisable.

(9) A progress report shall be in writing unless it cannot reasonably be committed to writing, in which case it may, with leave of the youth court be submitted orally in court.

(10) The provisions of subsections 14(4) to (10) apply, with such modifications as the circumstances require, in respect of progress reports.

(11) Where a disposition made in respect of a young person is to be reviewed under subsection (1) or (2), the provincial director shall cause such notice as may be directed by rules of court applicable to the youth court or, in the absence of such direction, at least five clear days notice of the review to be given in writing to the young person, his parents and the Attorney General or his agent

(12) Where a review of a disposition made in respect of a young person is requested under subsection (3), the person requesting the review shall cause such notice as may be directed by rules of court applicable to the youth cour or, in the absence of such direction, at least five clear days notice of the review to be given in writing to the young person, his parents and the Attorney Genera or his agent.

(13) Any notice given to a parent under subsection (11) or (12) shall include a statement that the young person whose disposition is to be reviewed has the right to be represented by counsel.

(14) A notice under subsection (11) or (12) may be served personally or may be sent by registered mail.

(15) Any of the persons entitled to notice under subsection (11) or (12) may waive the right to that notice.

(16) Where notice under subsection (11) or (12) is not given in accordance with this section, the youth court may

(*a*) adjourn the proceedings and order that the notice be given in such manner and to such person as it directs; or

(*b*) dispense with the notice where, in the opinion of the court, having regard to the circumstances, notice may be dispensed with.

(17) Where a youth court reviews under this section a disposition made in respect of a young person, it may, after affording the young person, his parents, the Attorney General or his agent and the provincial director an opportunity to be heard, having regard to the needs of the young person and the interests of society,

(*a*) confirm the disposition;

(*b*) where the young person is in secure custody, by order direct that the young person be placed in open custody; or

(*c*) release the young person from custody and place the young person on probation in accordance with section 23 for a period not exceeding the remainder of the period for which the young person was committed to custody or, where the young person is in custody pursuant to a disposition made under paragraph 20(1)(*k*.1) or an order made under paragraph 26.6(2)(*b*), place the young person under conditional supervision in accordance with paragraph 20(1)(*k*.1) for a period not exceeding the remainder of the disposition the young person is then serving. R.S., c. 24 (2nd Supp.), s. 21(1), (2); 1992, c. 11, s. 8.

(18) [Repealed, R.S. 1985, c. 24 (2nd Supp.), s. 21(3).]

Recommendation of provincial director for transfer to open custody or for probation — Contents of notice — Application to court for review of recommendation — Subsections 28(5), (7) to (10) and (12) to (17) apply — Where no application for review made under subsection (2) — Conditions in probation order — Notice where no direction made — Provincial director may request review — Where the provincial director requests a review.

29. (1) Where a young person is held in custody pursuant to a disposition, the provincial director may, if he is satisfied that the needs of the young person and the interests of society would be better served thereby, cause notice in writing to be given to the young person, his parent and the Attorney General or his agent that he recommends that the young person (*a*) be transferred from a place or facility of secure custody to a place or facility of open custody, or

(*b*) be released from custody and placed on probation or, where the young person is in custody pursuant to a disposition made under paragraph 20(1)(*k*.1), placed under conditional supervision,

and give a copy of the notice to the youth court.

(1.1) The provincial director shall include in any notice given under subsection (1) the reasons for the recommendation and,

(*a*) in the case of a recommendation that the young person be placed on probation, the conditions that the provincial director would recommend be attached to a probation order; and

(*b*) in the case of a recommendation that the young person be placed under conditional supervision, the conditions that the provincial director would recommend be set pursuant ot section 26.2.

(2) Where notice of a recommendation is made under subsection (1) with respect to a disposition made in respect of a young person, the youth court shall, if an application for review is made by the young person, his parent or the Attorney General or his agent within ten days after service of the notice, forthwith review the disposition.

(3) Subsections 28(5), (7) to (10) and (12) to (17) apply, with such modifications as the circumstances require, in respect of reviews made under this section and any notice required under subsection 28(12) shall be given to the provincial director.

(4) A youth court that receives a notice under subsection (1) shall, if no application for a review is made under subsection (2),

(*a*) in the case of a recommendation that a young person be transferred from a place or facility of secure custody to a place or facility of open custody, order that the young person be so transferred;

(*b*) in the case of a recommendation that a young person be released from custody and placed on probation, release the young person and place him on probation in accordance with section 23; or

(*b*.1) in the case of a recommendation that a young person be released from custody and placed under conditional supervision, release the young person and place the young person under conditional supervision in accordance with section 26.2, having regard to the recommendations of the provincial director; or

(*c*) where the court deems it advisable, make no direction under this subsection.

(4.1) Where the youth court places a young person on probation pursuant to paragraph (4)(*b*), the court shall include in the probation order such conditions referred to in section 23 as it considers advisable, having regard to the recommendations of the provincial director.

(4.2) Where a youth court, pursuant to paragraph (4)(*c*), makes no direction under subsection (4), it shall forthwith cause a notice of its decision to be given to the provincial director.

(4.3) Where the provincial director is given a notice under subsection (4.2), he may request a review under this section.

(5) Where the provincial director requests a review pursuant to subsection (4.3),

(*a*) the provincial director shall cause such notice as may be directed by rules of court applicable to the youth court or, in the absence of such direction, at least five clear days notice of the review to be given in writing to the young person, his parents and the Attorney General or his agent; and

(*b*) the youth court shall forthwith, after the notice required under paragraph (*a*) is given, review the disposition. R.S., c. 24 (2nd Supp.), s. 22(1)-(3); c. 1 (4th Supp.), s. 40; 1992, c. 11, s. 9.

(6) [Repealed, R.S., c. 24 (2nd Supp.), s. 22(4).]

Review board — Other duties of review board — Notice under section 29 — Notice of decision of review board — Decision of review board to take effect where no review — Decision respecting release from custody and supervision.

30. (1) Where a review board is established or designated by a province for the purposes of this section, that board shall, subject to this section, carry out in that province the duties and functions of a youth court under sections 28 and 29 other than releasing a young person from custody and placing the young person on probation or under conditional supervision.

(2) Subject to this Act, a review board may carry out any duties or functions that are assigned to it by the province that established or designated it.

(3) Where a review board is established or designated by a province for the purposes of this section, the provincial director shall at the same time as any notice is given under subsection 29(1) cause a copy of the notice to be given to the review board.

(4) A review board shall cause notice of any decision made by it in respect of a young person pursuant to section 28 or 29 to be given forthwith in writing to the young person, his parents, the Attorney General or his agent and the provincial director, and a copy of the notice to be given to the youth court.

(5) Subject to subsection (6), any decision of a review board under this section shall take effect ten days after the decision is made unless an application for review is made under section 31.

(6) Where a review board decides that a young person should be released from custody and placed on probation, it shall so recommend to the youth court and, if no application for a review of the decision is made under section 31, the youth court shall forthwith on the expiration of the ten day period referred to in subsection (5) release the young person from custody and place

him on probation in accordance with section 23, and shall include in the probation order such conditions referred to in that section as the court considers advisable having regard to the recommendations of the review board.

(7) Where a review board decides that a young person should be released from custody and placed under conditional supervision, it shall so recommend to the youth court and, if no application for a review of the decision is made under section 31, the youth court shall forthwith, on the expiration of the ten day period referred to in subsection (5), release the young person from custody and place the young person under conditional supervision in accordance with section 26.2, and shall include in the order under that section such conditions as the court considers advisable, having regard to the recommendations of the review board. R.S. 1985, c. 24 (2nd Sup.), s. 23; 1992, c. 11, s. 10.

Review by youth court — Subsections 28(5), (7) to (10) and (12) to (17) apply.

31. (1) Where the review board reviews a disposition under section 30, the youth court shall, on the application of the young person in respect of whom the review was made, his parents, the Attorney General or his agent or the provincial director, made within ten days after the decision of the review board is made, forthwith review the decision.

(2) Subsections 28(5), (7) to (10) and (12) to (17) apply, with such modifications as the circumstances require, in respect of reviews made under this section and any notice required under subsection 28(12) shall be given to the provincial director. R.S. 1985, c. 1 (4th Supp.), s. 41.

Review of dispositions not involving custody — Grounds for review — Progress report — Subsections 28(8) to (10) apply — Subsections 28(5) and (12) to (16) apply — Compelling appearance of young person — Decision of the youth court after review — New disposition not to be more onerous — Exception.

32. (1) Where a youth court has made a disposition in respect of a young person, other than or in addition to a disposition under paragraph 20(1)(*k*) and other than a disposition under paragraph 20(1)(*k*.1), the youth court shall on the application of the young person, the young person's parents, the Attorney General or the Attorney General's agent or the provincial director, made at any time after six months from the date of the disposition or, with leave of a youth court judge, at any earlier time, review the disposition if the court is satisfied that there are grounds for a review under subsection (2).

(2) A review of a disposition may be made under this section

(*a*) on the ground that the circumstances that led to the disposition have changed materially;

(*b*) on the ground that the young person in respect of whom the review is to be made is unable to comply with or is experiencing serious difficulty in complying with the terms of the disposition;

(*c*) on the ground that the terms of the disposition are adversely affecting the opportunities available to the young person to obtain services, education or employment; or

(*d*) on such other grounds as the youth court considers appropriate.

(3) The youth court may, before reviewing under this section a disposition nade in respect of a young person, require the provincial director to cause o be prepared, and to submit to the youth court, a progress report on the erformance of the young person since the disposition took effect.

(4) Subsections 28(8) to (10) apply, with such modifications as the circum-tances require, in respect of any progress report required under subsection 3).

(5) Subsections 28(5) and (12) to (16) apply, with such modifications as he circumstances require, in respect of reviews made under this section and ny notice required under subsection 28(12) shall be given to the provincial lirector.

(6) The youth court may, by summons or warrant, compel a young person n respect of whom a review is to be made under this section to appear before he youth court for the purposes of the review.

(7) Where a youth court reviews under this section a disposition made in espect of a young person, it may, after affording the young person, his parents, he Attorney General or his agent and the provincial director an opportunity o be heard,

(*a*) confirm the disposition;

(*b*) terminate the disposition and discharge the young person from any further obligation of the disposition; or

(*c*) vary the disposition or make such new disposition listed in section 20, other than a committal to custody, for such period of time, not exceeding the remainder of the period of the earlier disposition, as the court deems appropriate in the circumstances of the case.

(8) Subject to subsection (9), where a disposition made in respect of a young erson is reviewed under this section, no disposition made under subsection 7) shall, without the consent of the young person, be more onerous than the emaining portion of the disposition reviewed.

(9) A youth court may under this section extend the time within which a lisposition made under paragraphs 20(1)(*b*) to (*g*) is to be complied with by young person where the court is satisfied that the young person requires nore time to comply with the disposition, but in no case shall the extension e for a period time that expires more than twelve months after the date the lisposition would otherwise have expired. R.S., c. 24 (2nd Supp.), s. 24(1), 2); 1992, c. 11, s. 11.

(10), (11) [Repealed, R.S. 1985, c. 24 (2nd Supp.), s. 24(3).]

33. [Repealed, R.S. 1985, c. 24 (2nd Supp.), s. 25.]

Sections 20 to 26 apply to dispositions on review — Orders are dispositions.

34. (1) Subject to sections 28 to 32, subsections 20(2) to (8) and section 21 to 25.1 apply, with such modifications as the circumstances require, i respect of dispositions made under sections 28 to 32. R.S., c. 24 (2nd Supp. s. 25.

(2) Orders under subsections 26.1(1) and 26.2(1) and paragraph 26.6(2)(*b* are deemed to be dispositions for the purposes of section 28. 1992, c. 11, 12.

TEMPORARY RELEASE FROM CUSTODY

Temporary absence or day release — Limitation — Revocation of authorizatio for release — Arrest and return to custody — Prohibition.

35. (1) The provincial director of a province may, subject to any terms c conditions that he considers desirable, authorize a young person committe to custody in the province pursuant to a disposition made under this Act

(*a*) to be temporarily released for a period not exceeding fifteen days wher in his opinion, it is necessary or desirable that the young person be absen with or without escort, for medical, compassionate or humanitarian reason or for the purpose of rehabilitating the young person or re-integrating hi into the community; or

(*b*) to be released from custody on such days and during such hours a he specifies in order that the young person may

(i) attend school or any other educational or training institution,

(ii) obtain or continue employment or perform domestic or other dutie required by the young person's family, or

(iii) participate in a program specified by him that, in his opinion, wi enable the young person to better carry out his employment or improv his education or training.

(2) A young person who is released from custody pursuant to subsectio (1) shall be released only for such periods of time as are necessary to attai the purpose for which the young person is released.

(3) The provincial director of a province may, at any time, revoke a authorization made under subsection (1).

(4) Where the provincial director revokes an authorization for a youn person to be released from custody under subsection (3) or where a youn person fails to comply with any term or condition of release from custod under this section, the young person may be arrested without warrant an returned to custody.

(5) A young person who has been committed to custody under this Ac shall not be released from custody before the expiration of the period of hi custody except in accordance with subsection (1) unless the release is ordere

under sections 28 to 31 or otherwise according to law by a court of competent jurisdiction. R.S., c. 24 (2nd Supp.), s. 26; c. 1 (4th Supp.) s. 42.

EFFECT OF TERMINATION OF DISPOSITION

Effect of absolute discharge or termination of dispositions — Disqualifications removed — Applications for employment — Punishment — Finding of guilt not a previous conviction.

36. (1) Subject to section 12 of the *Canada Evidence Act*, where a young person is found guilty of an offence, and

(*a*) a youth court directs under paragraph 20(1)(*a*) that the young person be discharged absolutely, or

(*b*) all the dispositions made under this Act in respect of the offence have ceased to have effect,

the young person shall be deemed not to have been found guilty or convicted of the offence except that,

(*c*) the young person may plead *autrefois convict* in respect of any subsequent charge relating to the offence;

(*d*) a youth court may consider the finding of guilt in considering an application for a transfer to ordinary court under section 16;

(*e*) any court or justice may consider the finding of guilt in considering an application for judicial interim release or in considering what dispositions to make or sentence to impose for any offence; and

(*f*) the National Parole Board or any provincial parole board may consider the finding of guilt in considering an application for parole or pardon.

(2) For greater certainty and without restricting the generality of subsection (1), an absolute discharge under paragraph 20(1)(*a*) or the termination of all dispositions in respect of an offence for which a young person is found guilty removes any disqualification in respect of the offence to which the young person is subject pursuant to any Act of Parliament by reason of a conviction.

(3) No application form for or relating to

(*a*) employment in any department, as defined in section 2 of the *Financial Administration Act*,

(*b*) employment by any Crown corporation as defined in section 83 of the *Financial Administration Act*,

(*c*) enrolment in the Canadian Forces, or

(*d*) employment on or in connection with the operation of any work, undertaking or business that is within the legislative authority of Parliament,

shall contain any question that by its terms requires the applicant to disclose that he has been charged with or found guilty of an offence in respect of which he has, under this Act, been discharged absolutely or has completed all the dispositions.

(4) Any person who uses or authorizes the use of an application form in

contravention of subsection (3) is guilty of an offence punishable on summary conviction.

(5) A finding of guilt under this Act is not a previous conviction for the purposes of any offence under any Act of Parliament for which a greater punishment is prescribed by reason of previous convictions. R.S., c. 24 (2nd Supp.), s. 27.

YOUTH WORKERS

Duties of youth worker.

37. The duties and functions of a youth worker in respect of a young person whose case has been assigned to him by the provincial director include

(*a*) where the young person is bound by a probation order that requires him to be under supervision, supervising the young person in complying with the conditions of the probation order or in carrying out any other disposition made together with it;

(*a*.1) where the young person is placed under conditional supervision pursuant to an order made under section 26.2, supervising the young person in complying with the conditions of the order;

(*b*) where the young person is found guilty of any offence, giving such assistance to him as he considers appropriate up to the time the young person is discharged or the disposition of his case terminates;

(*c*) attending court when he considers it advisable or when required by the youth court to be present;

(*d*) preparing, at the request of the provincial director, a pre-disposition report or a progress report; and

(*e*) performing such other duties and functions as the provincial director requires. R.S., c. 24 (2nd Supp.), s. 28.

PROTECTION OF PRIVACY OF YOUNG PERSONS

Identity not to be published — Limitation — Ex parte application for leave to publish — Order ceases to have effect — Application for leave to publish — Contravention — Provincial court judge has absolute jurisdiction on indictment.

38. (1) Subject to this section, no person shall publish by any means any report

(*a*) of an offence committed or alleged to have been committed by a young person, unless an order has been made under section 16 with respect thereto, or

(*b*) of any hearing, adjudication, disposition or appeal concerning a young person who committed or is alleged to have committed an offence

in which the name of the young person, a child or a young person who is a victim of the offence or a child or a young person who appeared as a witness in connection with the offence, or in which any information serving to identify the young person or child, is disclosed.

(1.1) Subsection (1) does not apply in respect of the disclosure of information in the course of the administration of justice where it is not the purpose of the disclosure to make the information known in the community.

(1.2) A youth court judge shall, on the *ex parte* application of a peace officer, make an order permitting any person to publish a report described in subsection (1) that contains the name of a young person, or information serving to identify a young person, who has committed or is alleged to have committed an indictable offence, if the judge is satisfied that

(a) there is reason to believe that the young person is dangerous to others; and

(b) publication of the report is necessary to assist in apprehending the young person.

(1.3) An order made under subsection (1.2) shall cease to have effect two days after it is made.

(1.4) The youth court may, on the application of any person referred to in subsection (1), make an order permitting any person to publish a report in which the name of that person, or information serving to identify that person, would be disclosed, if the court is satisfied that the publication of the report would not be contrary to the best interests of that person.

(2) Every one who contravenes subsection (1)

(*a*) is guilty of an indictable offence and liable to imprisonment for a term not exceeding two years; or

(*b*) is guilty of an offence punishable on summary conviction.

(3) Where an accused is charged with an offence under paragraph (2)(*a*), a provincial court judge has absolute jurisdiction to try the case and his jurisdiction does not depend on the consent of the accused. R.S., c. 27 (1st Supp.), s. 203; R.S., c. 24 (2nd Supp.), s. 29.

Exclusion from hearing — Exception — Exclusion after adjudication or during review — Exception.

39. (1) Subject to subsection (2), where a court or justice before whom proceedings are carried out under this Act is of the opinion

(*a*) that any evidence or information presented to the court or justice would be seriously injurious or seriously prejudicial to

(i) the young person who is being dealt with in the proceedings,

(ii) a child or young person who is a witness in the proceedings,

(iii) a child or young person who is aggrieved by or the victim of the offence charged in the proceedings, or

(*b*) that it would be in the interest of public morals, the maintenance of order or the proper administration of justice to exclude any or all members of the public from the court room, the court or justice may exclude any person from all or part of the proceedings if the court or justice deems that person's presence to be unnecessary to the conduct of the proceedings.

(2) Subject to section 650 of the *Criminal Code* and except where it is necessary for the purposes of subsection 13(6) of this Act, a court or justice may not, pursuant to subsection (1), exclude from proceedings under this Act

(*a*) the prosecutor;

(*b*) the young person who is being dealt with in the proceedings, his parent, his counsel or any adult assisting him pursuant to subsection 11(7);

(*c*) the provincial director or his agent; or

(*d*) the youth worker to whom the young person's case has been assigned.

(3) The youth court, after it has found a young person guilty of an offence, or the youth court or the review board, during a review of a disposition under sections 28 to 32, may, in its discretion, exclude from the court or from a hearing of the review board, as the case may be, any person other than

(*a*) the young person or his counsel,

(*b*) the provincial director or his agent,

(*c*) the youth worker to whom the young person's case has been assigned, and

(*d*) the Attorney General or his agent,

when any information is being presented to the court or the review board the knowledge of which might, in the opinion of the court or review board, be seriously injurious or seriously prejudicial to the young person.

(4) The exception set out in paragraph (3)(*a*) is subject to subsection 13(6) of this Act and section 650 of the *Criminal Code*. R.S., c. 24 (2nd Supp.), s. 30.

MAINTENANCE AND USE OF RECORDS

Records that may be Kept

Youth court, review board and other courts — Exception.

40. (1) A youth court, review board or any court dealing with matters arising out of proceedings under this Act may keep a record of any case arising under this Act that comes before it.

(2) For greater certainty, this section does not apply in respect of proceedings held in ordinary court pursuant to an order under section 16. R.S., c. 24 (2nd Supp.), s. 31.

Records in central repository — Police force to provide record.

41. (1) A record of any offence of which a young person has been found guilty under this Act may be kept in such central repository as the Commissioner of the Royal Canadian Mounted Police may, from time to time, designate for the purpose of keeping criminal history files or records on offenders or keeping records for the identification of offenders.

(2) Where a young person is found guilty of an offence under this Act, the police force responsible for the investigation of the offence shall provide a record of the offence, including the original or a copy of any fingerprints or photographs of the young person taken by or on behalf of the police force, for inclusion in any central repository designated pursuant to subsection (1). R.S., c. 24 (2nd Supp.), s. 31.

(3) [Repealed, R.S., c. 24 (2nd Supp.), s. 31.]

Police records.

42. A record of any offence alleged to have been committed by a young person, including the original or a copy of any fingerprints or photographs of the young person, may be kept by any police force responsible for, or participating in, the investigation of the offence. R.S., c. 24 (2nd Supp.), s. 81.

(2)-(5) [Repealed, R.S., c. 24 (2nd Supp.), s. 31.]

Government records — Private records.

43. (1) A department or agency of any government in Canada may keep records containing information obtained by the department or agency

(*a*) for the purposes of an investigation of an offence alleged to have been committed by a young person;

(*b*) for use in proceedings against a young person under this Act;

(*c*) for the purpose of administering a disposition;

(*d*) for the purpose of considering whether, instead of commencing or continuing judicial proceedings under this Act against a young person, to use alternative measures to deal with the young person; or

(*e*) as a result of the use of alternative measures to deal with a young person.

(2) Any person or organization may keep records containing information obtained by the person or organization

(*a*) as a result of the use of alternative measures to deal with a young person alleged to have committed an offence; or

(*b*) for the purpose of administering or participating in the administration of a disposition.

(3), (4) [Repealed, R.S., c. 24 (2nd Supp.), s. 32.]

Fingerprints and Photographs

Identification of Criminals Act applies — Limitation.

44. (1) Subject to this section, the *Identification of Criminals Act* applies in respect of young persons.

(2) No fingerprints or photograph of a young person who is accused of committing an offence shall be taken except in the circumstances in which an adult may, under the *Identification of Criminals Act*, be subjected to the measurements, processes and operations referred to in that Act.

(3)-(5) [Repealed, R.S., c. 24 (2nd Supp.), s. 33.]

Disclosure of Records

Records made available — Exception — Introduction into evidence — Disclosures for research or statistical purposes — Record made available to victim — Disclosure of information and copies of records.

44.1 (1) Subject to subsection (2), any record that is kept pursuant to section 40 shall, and any record that is kept pursuant to sections 41 to 43 may, on request, be made available for inspection to

(*a*) the young person to whom the record relates;

(*b*) counsel acting on behalf of the young person;

(*c*) the Attorney General or his agent;

(*d*) a parent of the young person or any adult assisting the young person pursuant to subsection 11(7), during the course of any proceedings relating to the offence or alleged offence to which the record relates or during the term of any disposition made in respect of the offence;

(*e*) any judge, court or review board, for any purpose relating to proceedings relating to the young person under this Act or to proceedings in ordinary court in respect of offences committed or alleged to have been committed by the young person, whether as a young person or an adult;

(*f*) any peace officer,

(i) for the purpose of investigating any offence that the young person is suspected on reasonable grounds of having committed, or in respect of which the young person has been arrested or charged, whether as a young person or an adult, or

(ii) for any purpose related to the administration of the case to which the record relates during the course of proceedings against the young person or the term of any disposition;

(*g*) any member of a department or agency of a government in Canada, or any agent thereof, that is

(i) engaged in the administration of alternative measures in respect of the young person,

(ii) preparing a report in respect of the young person pursuant to this Act or for the purpose of assisting a court in sentencing the young person after he becomes an adult or is transferred to ordinary court pursuant to section 16,

(iii) engaged in the supervision or care of the young person, whether as a young person or an adult, or in the administration of a disposition or a sentence in respect of the young person, whether as a young person or an adult, or

(iv) considering an application for parole or pardon made by the young person after he becomes an adult;

(*h*) any person, or person within a class of persons, designated by the Governor in Council, or the Lieutenant Governor in Council of a province, for a purpose and to the extent specified by the Governor in Council or the Lieutenant Governor in Council, as the case may be;

(*i*) any person, for the purpose of determining whether to grant security clearances required by the Government of Canada or the government of a province or a municipality for purposes of employment or the performance of services;

(*j*) any employee or agent of the Government of Canada, for statistical purposes pursuant to the *Statistics Act*; and

(*k*) any other person who is deemed, or any person within a class of persons that is deemed, by a youth court judge to have a valid interest in the record, to the extent directed by the judge, if the judge is satisfied that the disclosure is

(i) desirable in the public interest for research or statistical purposes, or

(ii) desirable in the interest of the proper administration of justice.

(2) Where a youth court has withheld the whole or a part of a report from any person pursuant to subsection 13(6) or 14(7), the report or part thereof shall not be made available to that person for inspection under subsection (1).

(3) Nothing in paragraph (1)(*e*) authorizes the introduction into evidence of any part of a record that would not otherwise be admissible in evidence.

(4) Where a record is made available for inspection to any person under paragraph (1)(*j*) or subparagraph (1)(*k*)(i), that person may subsequently disclose information contained in the record, but may not disclose the information in any form that would reasonably be expected to identify the young person to whom it relates.

(5) Any record that is kept pursuant to sections 40 to 43 may, on request, be made available for inspection to the victim of the offence to which the record relates.

(6) Any person to whom a record is required or authorized to be made available for inspection under this section may be given any information contained in the record and may be given a copy of any part of the record. R.S., c. 24 (2nd Supp.), s. 34; 1992, c. 1, s. 21.

Disclosure by peace officer during investigation — Disclosure to insurance company.

44.2 (1) A peace officer may disclose to any person any information in a record kept pursuant to section 42 that it is necessary to disclose in the conduct of the investigation of an offence.

(2) A peace officer may disclose to an insurance company information in any record that is kept pursuant to section 42 for the purpose of investigating any claim arising out of an offence committed or alleged to have been committed by the young person to whom the record relates. R.S., c. 24 (2nd Supp.), s. 34.

Non-Disclosure and Destruction of Records

Non-disclosure — Record in central repository to be destroyed — Other records may be destroyed — Young person deemed not to have committed offence — Deemed election — Application to delinquency.

45. (1) Subject to sections 45.1 and 45.2, records kept pursuant to sections 40 to 43 may not be made available for inspection under section 44.1 or 44.2 in the following circumstances:

(*a*) where the young person to whom the record relates is charged with the offence to which the record relates and is acquitted otherwise than by reason of a verdict of not criminally responsible on account of mental disorder, on the expiration of two months after the expiration of the time allowed for the taking of an appeal or, where an appeal is taken on the expiration of three months after all proceedings in respect of the appeal having been completed;

(*b*) where the charge against the young person is dismissed for any reason other than acquittal or withdrawn, on the expiration of one year after the dismissal or withdrawal;

(*c*) where the charge against the young person is stayed, with no proceedings being taken against the young person for a period of one year, on the expiration of the one year;

(*d*) where alternative measures are used to deal with the young person, on the expiration of two years after the young person consents to participate in the alternative measures in accordance with paragraph 4(1)(*c*);

(*e*) where the young person is found guilty of the offence and it is a summary conviction offence, on the expiration of five years after the young person is found guilty; and

(*f*) where the young person is found guilty of the offence and it is an indictable offence, on the expiration of five years after all dispositions made in respect of that offence and all dispositions made in respect of any other indictable offence of which the young person may have been found guilty after he was found guilty of that offence but prior to the expiration of the five year period have been completed.

(2) Any record kept pursuant to section 41 shall be destroyed forthwith when the circumstances set out in subsection (1) are realized in respect of that record.

(3) Any record kept pursuant to sections 40 to 43 may, in the discretion of the person or body keeping the record, be destroyed at any time before

or after the circumstances set out in subsection (1) are realized in respect of that record.

(4) A young person shall be deemed not to have committed any offence to which a record kept pursuant to sections 40 to 43 relates when the circumstances set out in paragraphs (1)(*d*), (*e*) or (*f*) are realized in respect of that record.

(5) For the purposes of paragraphs (1)(*e*) and (*f*), where no election is made in respect of an offence that may be prosecuted by indictment or proceeded with by way of summary conviction, the Attorney General or his agent shall be deemed to have elected to proceed with the offence as an offence punishable on summary conviction.

(6) This section applies, with such modifications as the circumstances require, in respect of records relating to the offence of delinquency under the *Juvenile Delinquents Act*, chapter J-3 of the Revised Statues of Canada, 1970, as it read immediately prior to April 2, 1984. R.S., c. 24 (2nd Supp.), s. 35; 1991, c. 43, s. 34.

Where records may be made available — Notice — Use of record.

45.1 (1) A youth court judge may, on application by any person, order that any record to which subsection 45(1) applies, or any part thereof, be made available for inspection to that person or a copy of the record or part thereof be given to that person, if a youth court judge is satisfied that

(*a*) that person has a valid and substantial interest in the record or part thereof;

(*b*) it is necessary for the record, part thereof or copy thereof to be made available in the interest of the proper administration of justice; and

(*c*) disclosure of the record or part thereof or information is not prohibited under any other Act of Parliament or the legislature of a province.

(2) An application under subsection (1) in respect of a record shall not be heard unless the person who makes the application has given the young person to whom the record relates and the person or body that has possession of the record at least five days notice in writing of the application and the young person and the person or body that has possession has had a reasonable opportunity to be heard.

(3) In any order under subsection (1), the youth court judge shall set out the purposes for which the record may be used. R.S., c. 24 (2nd Supp.), s. 35.

Records in the custody, etc. of archivists.

45.2 Where records originally kept pursuant to section 40, 42 or 43 are under the custody or control of the National Archivist of Canada or the archivist for any province, that person may disclose any information contained in the record to any other person if (*a*) the Attorney General or his agent is satisfied that the disclosure is desirable in the public interest for research or statistical purposes; and

(*b*) the person to whom the information is disclosed undertakes not to disclose the information in any form that could reasonably be expected to identify the young person to whom it relates. R.S., c. 24 (2nd Supp.), s. 35; c. 1 (3rd Supp.), s. 12(5).

Prohibition against disclosure — Exception for employees — Prohibition against use — Offence and punishment — Absolute jurisdiction of provincial court judge.

46. (1) Except as authorized or required by this Act, no record kept pursuant to sections 40 to 43 may be made available for inspection, and no copy, print or negative thereof or information contained therein may be given, to any person where to do so would serve to identify the young person to whom it relates as a young person dealt with under this Act.

(2) No person who is employed in keeping or maintaining records referred to in subsection (1) is restricted from doing anything prohibited under subsection (1) with respect to any other person so employed.

(3) Subject to section 45.1, no record kept pursuant to sections 40 to 43, and no copy, print or negative thereof, may be used for any purpose that would serve to identify the young person to whom the record relates as a young person dealt with under this Act after the circumstances set out in subsection 45(1) are realized in respect of that record.

(4) Any person who fails to comply with this section or subsection 45(2)

(*a*) is guilty of an indictable offence and liable to imprisonment for a term not exceeding two years; or

(*b*) is guilty of an offence punishable on summary conviction.

(5) The jurisdiction of a provincial court judge to try an accused is absolute and does not depend on the consent of the accused where the accused is charged with an offence under paragraph (4)(*a*). R.S., c. 27 (1st Supp.), s. 203; c. 24 (2nd Supp.), s. 36.

CONTEMPT OF COURT

Contempt against youth court — Exclusive jurisdiction of youth court — Concurrent jurisdiction of youth court — Dispositions — Section 708 of Criminal Code applies in respect of adults — Appeals.

47. (1) Every youth court has the same power, jurisdiction and authority to deal with and impose punishment for contempt against the court as may be exercised by the superior court of criminal jurisdiction of the province in which the court is situated.

(2) The youth court has exclusive jurisdiction in respect of every contempt of court committed by a young person against the youth court whether or

not committed in the face of the court and every contempt of court committed by a young person against any other court otherwise than in the face of that court.

(3) The youth court has jurisdiction in respect of every contempt of court committed by a young person against any other court in the face of that court and every contempt of court committed by an adult against the youth court in the face of the youth court, but nothing in this subsection affects the power, jurisdiction or authority of any other court to deal with or impose punishment for contempt of court.

(4) Where a youth court or any other court finds a young person guilty of contempt of court, it may make any one of the dispositions set out in section 20, or any number thereof that are not inconsistent with each other, but no other disposition or sentence.

(5) Section 708 of the *Criminal Code* applies in respect of proceedings under this section in youth court against adults, with such modifications as the circumstances require.

(6) A finding of guilt under this section for contempt of court or a disposition or sentence made in respect thereof may be appealed as if the finding were a conviction or the disposition or sentence were a sentence in a prosecution by indictment in ordinary court.

FORFEITURE OF RECOGNIZANCES

Applications for forfeiture of recognizances.

48. Applications for the forfeiture of recognizances of young persons shall be made to the youth court.

Proceedings in case of default — Order for forfeiture of recognizance — Judgment debtors of the Crown — Order may be filed — Where a deposit has been made — Subsections 770(2) and (4) of Criminal Code do not apply — Sections 772 and 773 of Criminal Code apply.

49. (1) Where a recognizance binding a young person has been endorsed with a certificate pursuant to subsection 770(1) of the *Criminal Code*, a youth court judge shall,

(*a*) on the request of the Attorney General or his agent, fix a time and place for the hearing of an application for the forfeiture of the recognizance; and

(*b*) after fixing a time and place for the hearing, cause to be sent by registered mail, not less than ten days before the time so fixed, to each principal and surety named in the recognizance, directed to him at his latest known address, a notice requiring him to appear at the time and place fixed by the judge to show cause why the recognizance should not be forfeited.

(2) Where subsection (1) is complied with, the youth court judge may, after giving the parties an opportunity to be heard, in his discretion grant or refuse

the application and make any order with respect to the forfeiture of the recognizance that he considers proper.

(3) Where, pursuant to subsection (2), a youth court judge orders forfeiture of a recognizance, the principal and his sureties become judgment debtors of the Crown, each in the amount that the judge orders him to pay.

(4) An order made under subsection (2) may be filed with the clerk of the superior court or, in the province of Quebec, the prothonotary and, where an order is filed, the clerk or the prothonotary shall issue a writ of *fieri facias* in Form 34 set out in the *Criminal Code* and deliver it to the sheriff of each of the territorial divisions in which any of the principal and his sureties resides, carries on business or has property.

(5) Where a deposit has been made by a person against whom an order for forfeiture of a recognizance has been made, no writ of *fieri facias* shall issue, but the amount of the deposit shall be transferred by the person who has custody of it to the person who is entitled by law to receive it.

(6) Subsections 770(2) and (4) of the *Criminal Code* do not apply in respect of proceedings under this Act.

(7) Sections 772 and 773 of the *Criminal Code* apply in respect of writs of *fieri facias* issued pursuant to this section as if they were issued pursuant to section 771 of the *Criminal Code*.

INTERFERENCE WITH DISPOSITIONS

Inducing a young person, etc. — Absolute jurisdiction of provincial court judge.

50. (1) Every one who

(*a*) induces or assists a young person to leave unlawfully a place of custody or other place in which the young person has been placed pursuant to a disposition,

(*b*) unlawfully removes a young person from a place referred to in paragraph (*a*),

(*c*) knowingly harbours or conceals a young person who has unlawfully left a place referred to in paragraph (*a*),

(*d*) wilfully induces or assists a young person to breach or disobey a term or condition of a disposition, or

(*e*) wilfully prevents or interferes with the performance by a young person of a term or condition of a disposition

is guilty of an indictable offence and liable to imprisonment for a term not exceeding two years or is guilty of an offence punishable on summary conviction.

(2) The jurisdiction of a provincial court judge to try an adult accused of an indictable offence under this section is absolute and does not depend on

the consent of the accused. R.S., c. 27 (1st Supp.), s. 203; R.S., c. 24 (2nd Supp.), s. 37.

APPLICATION OF THE CRIMINAL CODE

Application of Criminal Code.

51. Except to the extent that they are inconsistent with or excluded by this Act, all the provisions of the *Criminal Code* apply, with such modifications as the circumstances require, in respect of offences alleged to have been committed by young persons.

PROCEDURE

Part XXVII and summary conviction trial provisions of Criminal Code to apply — Indictable offences — Attendance of young person — Limitation period — Costs.

52. (1) Subject to this section and except to the extent that they are inconsistent with this Act,

(*a*) the provisions of Part XXVII of the *Criminal Code*, and

(*b*) any other provisions of the *Criminal Code* that apply in respect of summary conviction offences and relate to trial proceedings

apply to proceedings under this Act

(*c*) in respect of a summary conviction offence, and

(*d*) in respect of an indictable offence as if it were defined in the enactment creating it as a summary conviction offence.

(2) For greater certainty and notwithstanding subsection (1) or any other provision of this Act, an indictable offence committed by a young person is, for the purposes of this or any other Act, an indictable offence.

(3) Section 650 of the *Criminal Code* applies in respect of proceedings under this Act, whether the proceedings relate to an indictable offence or an offence punishable on summary conviction.

(4) In proceedings under this Act, subsection 786(2) of the *Criminal Code* does not apply in respect of an indictable offence.

(5) Section 809 of the *Criminal Code* does not apply in respect of proceedings under this Act.

Counts charged in information.

53. Indictable offences and offences punishable on summary conviction may under this Act be charged in the same information and tried jointly.

Issue of subpoena — Service of subpoena.

54. (1) Where a person is required to attend to give evidence before a youth court, the subpoena directed to that person may be issued by a youth court judge, whether or not the person whose attendance is required is within the same province as the youth court.

(2) A subpoena issued by a youth court and directed to a person who is not within the same province as the youth court shall be served personally on the person to whom it is directed.

Warrant.

55. A warrant that is issued out of a youth court may be executed anywhere in Canada.

EVIDENCE

General law on admissibility of statements to apply — When statements are admissible — Exception in certain cases for oral statements — Waiver of right to consult — Statements given under duress are inadmissible — Parent, etc. not a person in authority.

56. (1) Subject to this section, the law relating to the admissibility of statements made by persons accused of committing offences applies in respect of young persons.

(2) No oral or written statement given by a young person to a peace officer or other person who is, in law, a person in authority is admissible against the young person unless

(*a*) the statement was voluntary;

(*b*) the person to whom the statement was given has, before the statement was made, clearly explained to the young person, in language appropriate to his age and understanding, that

(i) the young person is under no obligation to give a statement,

(ii) any statement given by him may be used as evidence in proceedings against him,

(iii) the young person has the right to consult another person in accordance with paragraph (*c*), and

(iv) any statement made by the young person is required to be made in the presence of the person consulted, unless the young person desires otherwise;

(*c*) the young person has, before the statement was made, been given a reasonable opportunity to consult with counsel or a parent, or in the absence of a parent, an adult relative, or in the absence of a parent and an adult relative, any other appropriate adult chosen by the young person; and

(*d*) where the young person consults any person pursuant to paragraph (*c*), the young person has been given a reasonable opportunity to make the statement in the presence of that person.

(3) The requirements set out in paragraphs (2)(*b*), (*c*) and (*d*) do not apply in respect of oral statements where they are made spontaneously by the young

person to a peace officer or other person in authority before that person has had a reasonable opportunity to comply with those requirements.

(4) A young person may waive his rights under paragraph (2)(*c*) or (*d*) but any such waiver shall be made in writing and shall contain a statement signed by the young person that he has been apprised of the right that he is waiving.

(5) A youth court judge may rule inadmissible in any proceedings under this Act a statement given by the young person in respect of whom the proceedings are taken if the young person satisfies the judge that the statement was given under duress imposed by any person who is not, in law, a person in authority.

(6) For the purpose of this section, an adult consulted pursuant to paragraph 56(2)(*c*) shall, in the absence of evidence to the contrary, be deemed not to be a person in authority. R.S., c. 24 (2nd Supp.), s. 38.

Testimony of a parent — Evidence of age by certificate or record — Other evidence — When age may be inferred.

57. (1) In any proceedings under this Act, the testimony of a parent as to the age of a person of whom he is a parent is admissible as evidence of the age of that person.

(2) In any proceedings under this Act,

(*a*) a birth or baptismal certificate or a copy thereof purporting to be certified under the hand of the person in whose custody those records are held is evidence of the age of the person named in the certificate or copy; and

(*b*) an entry or record of an incorporated society that has had the control or care of the person alleged to have committed the offence in respect of which the proceedings are taken at or about the time the person came to Canada is evidence of the age of that person, if the entry or record was made before the time when the offence is alleged to have been committed.

(3) In the absence, before the youth court, of any certificate, copy, entry or record mentioned in subsection (2), or in corroboration of any such certificate, copy, entry or record, the youth court may receive and act on any other information relating to age that it considers reliable.

(4) In any proceedings under this Act, the youth court may draw inferences as to the age of a person from the person's appearance or from statements made by the person in direct examination or cross-examination.

Admissions — Other party may adduce evidence.

58. (1) A party to any proceedings under this Act may admit any relevant fact or matter for the purpose of dispensing with proof thereof, including any fact or matter the admissibility of which depends on a ruling of law or of mixed law and fact.

(2) Nothing in this section precludes a party to a proceeding from adducing evidence to prove a fact or matter admitted by another party.

Material evidence.

59. Any evidence material to proceedings under this Act that would not but for this section be admissible in evidence may, with the consent of the parties to the proceedings and where the young person is represented by counsel, be given in such proceedings.

Evidence of a child or young person.

60. In any proceedings under this Act where the evidence of a child or a young person is taken, it shall be taken only after the youth court judge or the justice, as the case may be, has

(*a*) in all cases, if the witness is a child, and

(*b*) where he deems it necessary, if the witness is a young person,

instructed the child or young person as to the duty of the witness to speak the truth and the consequences of failing to do so. R.S., c. 24 (2nd Supp.), s. 39.

(2), (3) [Repealed, R.S., c. 24 (2nd Supp.), s. 39.]

61. [Repealed, R.S., c. 24 (2nd Supp.), s. 40.]

Proof of service — Proof of signature and official character unnecessary.

62. (1) For the purposes of this Act, service of any document may be proved by oral evidence given under oath by, or by the affidavit or statutory declaration of, the person claiming to have personally served it or sent it by mail.

(2) Where proof of service of any document is offered by affidavit or statutory declaration, it is not necessary to prove the signature or official character of the person making or taking the affidavit or declaration, if the official character of that person appears on the face thereof.

Seal not required.

63. It is not necessary to the validity of any information, summons, warrant, minute, disposition, conviction, order or other process or document laid, issued, filed or entered in any proceedings under this Act that any seal be attached or affixed thereto.

SUBSTITUTION OF JUDGES

Powers of substitute youth court judge — Transcript of evidence already given.

64. (1) A youth court judge who acts in the place of another youth court judge pursuant to subsection 669.2(1) of the *Criminal Code* shall,

(*a*) if an adjudication has been made, proceed with the disposition of the case or make the order that, in the circumstances, is authorized by law; or

(*b*) if no adjudication has been made, recommence the trial as if no evidence had been taken.

(2) Where a youth court judge recommences a trial under paragraph (1)(*b*), he may, if the parties consent, admit into evidence a transcript of any evidence already given in the case. R.S., c. 27 (1st Supp.), s. 187, Schedule V.

FUNCTIONS OF CLERKS OF COURTS

Powers of clerks.

65. In addition to any powers conferred on a clerk of a court by the *Criminal Code*, a clerk of the youth court may exercise such powers as are ordinarily exercised by a clerk of a court, and, in particular, may

(*a*) administer oaths or solemn affirmations in all matters relating to the business of the youth court; and

(*b*) in the absence of a youth court judge, exercise all the powers of a youth court judge relating to adjournment.

FORMS, REGULATIONS AND RULES OF COURT

Forms — Where forms not Prescribed.

66. (1) The forms set prescribed under section 67, varied to suit the case, or forms to the like effect, are valid and sufficient in the circumstances for which they are provided.

(2) In any case for which forms are not prescribed under section 67, the forms set out in Part XXVIII of the *Criminal Code*, with such modifications as the circumstances require, or other appropriate forms, may be used. 1988, R.S. 1985, c. 1(4th. Supp.), s. 43

Regulations.

67. The Governor in Council may make regulations

(*a*) prescribing forms that may be used for the purposes of this Act;

(*b*) establishing uniform rules of court for youth courts across Canada, including rules regulating the practice and procedure to be followed by youth courts; and

(*c*) generally for carrying out the purposes and provisions of this Act. R.S., c. 24 (2nd Supp.), s. 41.

Youth court may make rules — Rules of court — Publication of rules.

68. (1) Every youth court for a province may, at any time with the concurrence of a majority of the judges thereof present at a meeting held for the purpose and subject to the approval of the Lieutenant Governor in Council, establish rules of court not inconsistent with this Act or any other Act of Parliament or with any regulations made pursuant to section 67 regulating proceedings within the jurisdiction of the youth court.

(2) Rules under subsection (1) may be made

(*a*) generally to regulate the duties of the officers of the youth court and any other matter considered expedient to attain the ends of justice and carry into effect the provisions of this Act;
(*b*) subject to any regulations made under paragraph 67(*b*), to regulate the practice and procedure in the youth court; and
(*c*) to prescribe forms to be used in the youth court where not otherwise provided for by or pursuant to this Act.

(3) Rules of court that are made under the authority of this section shall be published in the appropriate provincial gazette.

YOUTH JUSTICE COMMITTEES

Youth justice committees.

69. The Attorney General of a province or such other Minister as the Lieutenant Governor in Council of the province may designate, or a delegate thereof, may establish one or more committees of citizens, to be known as youth justice committees, to assist without remuneration in any aspect of the administration of this Act or in any programs or services for young offenders and may specify the method of appointment of committee members and the functions of the committees.

AGREEMENTS WITH PROVINCES

Agreements with provinces.

70. Any Minister of the Crown may, with the approval of the Governor in Council, enter into an agreement with the government of any province providing for payments by Canada to the province in respect of costs incurred by the province or a municipality for care of and services provided to young persons dealt with under this Act. R.S., c. 24 (2nd Supp.), s. 42.

SCHEDULE

[Repealed, R.S. 1985, c. 24 (2nd Supp.), s. 43.]

INDEX

Criminal Records Act, *CRA*; Extradition Act, *EA*; Identification of Criminals Act, *ICA*; Canada Evidence Act, *CEA*; Interpretation Act, *IA*; Food and Drug Act, *FDA*; Canadian Bill of Rights, *CBR*; Narcotic Control Act, *NCA*; Young Offenders Act, *YOA*.